THE ROUND THE WORLD AIR GUIDE

Katharine Wood-de Winne was born in Edinburgh in 1960 of Belgian and English parents. She was educated there, reading Communications, then English language and literature at Edinburgh University. Following a short period as a freelance public relations consultant she entered the world of travel journalism. An eighteen-month spell touring Europe and North Africa resulted in the guidebook *Europe by Train* (published by Fontana), which she wrote in conjunction with George McDonald. As well as working on a series of guidebooks for the package market, the Fontana Holiday Guides, she is currently involved in several projects encompassing every aspect of the travel industry – from backpacking students to round-the-world first-class tours. In the course of her work she has travelled to thirty-six countries. She is married and lives in Aberfoyle, Scotland, with her husband and young son, Andrew, who frequently accompanies her on her globe-trots.

George McDonald was born in Dumfries, Galloway, in 1955 and was educated at Fettes College and Edinburgh University. Following a spell on the family farm he toured Europe and North Africa with Katie Wood to research the guidebook *Europe by Train*. He continues to travel for a living, researching for the various guidebooks he is involved in. In recent years he has travelled hundreds of thousands of miles by air, from Venezuela to the Solomon Islands, researching for this guide.

The Round the World Air Guide

KATIE WOOD AND GEORGE McDONALD

FONTANA PAPERBACKS

First published in 1987 by
Fontana Paperbacks, 8 Grafton Street,
London W1X 3LA
Second impression April 1987

Copyright © Katie Wood and George McDonald 1987

Maps drawn by Bryan Hegney
Set in Linotron Times
Made and printed in Great Britain by
William Collins Sons & Co. Ltd, Glasgow

In memory of Hamish MacIntyre,
whose warmth and open-mindedness
made him friends wherever he travelled.

CONTENTS

ACKNOWLEDGEMENTS

Our thanks are owed to very many people who helped us get this guide together in a short space of time. Firstly, to our research journalists: *Julia Welstead*, who was responsible for the Pacific and Far East; *James Matthews*, for the USA, Canada and South America; and *Peter Carroll* for Europe, the Middle East and Africa. Also a special thanks to *Devin Scobie* who put together much of Part One, and toiled into the night, interpreting timetables and charts, and putting into plain English what the glossy brochures tried to say. These four people are responsible for much of the initial groundwork of the book, and we owe them much thanks.

Also a thank you to our journalist researchers in the locations, who willingly accepted middle of the night (their time) phone calls and checked out queries right up to the last minute.

To all the tourist boards, airlines and hotel managements we would like to say a thank you. People who were particularly helpful were John Williams of the Inter-Continental Hotel Group; Roger Fennings of Hilton International; Maggie Nixon of Oberoi Hotels; Clemencia Cardozo-Wiese of Mandarin Oriental; Pauline Marsom of Penta Hotels; and Mike Prager of Sheraton.

To Steve Jones and Ann, his secretary; Primrose Courtney-Wildman, David Snelling, Tony Powell, Ken Cook, Marilyn Cox and Roy Birnam of British Airways special thanks are owed; also to Bryan Hegney for the maps; to Brian Baker of Thomas Cook Ltd; to Maria Saidy and Colin Fittle of Hogg Robinson Business Travel Section; and to Ariane Goodman, Michael Fishwick and the team at Fontana for squeezing all the deadlines up to get this on the shelves in extra fast time.

On the home front, a big thank you to my mother for looking after one very lively little boy on the occasions he did not accompany us on the globetrots, and a special thanks to Syd, for the late-night editorial criticism and the many hours of work done on our work as well as his own. The many friends who have put us up at short notice have been a tremendous help: Malcolm's flat in London has virtually become office headquarters, Chris as the Edinburgh base, and Denis in Oxford. Without you all, it's likely George would have perished by now! Also to Eva Liccardello of Lufthansa for her early enthusiasm for the whole project.

To our families our debts are many (in every sense of the word!), and we would like to thank them above all, for their never ending patience and encouragement in what we do.

In the collating of this guide an Apple Mac 512K was used. We would like to acknowledge and thank Apple Computers for loaning us this piece of excellent machinery, without which it would have been impossible to assimilate all the information in such a short space of time. This computer travelled round the world with us, producing hard copy when needed, and storing the hundreds of pieces of information we found out daily. It has to be acknowledged as the ultimate travel journalist's tool!

WHAT THIS GUIDE'S ABOUT

In the past few years a new concept in air travel has emerged and virtually overnight it has become one of the fastest growing and most exciting developments in the travel industry.

To counter the bucketshops which were stealing the valuable long-haul flight business from authorized airlines, the major airlines of the world banded together and came up with the Round the World ticket – a pass which enables you to circumnavigate the globe, using the services of several airlines, who work in conjunction offering a wide variety of routings, which allows you to do your very own world tour, stopping off as often as you like, where you like.

Price-wise these tickets are exceptionally good value, and as long as you complete your trip within six months or a year (depending on your ticket) and fly either east or west round the world (i.e. no back-tracking) the ticket is completely flexible. The success of these tickets is due to the fact that for only a couple of hundred pounds more than the cost of a normal return to Australia you can make this the trip of a lifetime, stopping off wherever you like in South East Asia, India, Europe, the US and so on. For businessmen too, it makes good sense to combine a couple of trips and take in a holiday en route. Everyone from the idle rich jetting First Class to the great cities of the world to backpacking students working their way round the world agree that this world-shrinking pass is the ultimate travel experience.

This guide is written for any traveller making a round the world trip, whether it be on a conventional round the world ticket, or a DIY trip, taking in several long-haul destinations. There is no other book on the market which combines practical, up-to-date airline and ticket information *and* acts as a guidebook to your destinations. This guide has been researched and edited by professional travel journalists and covers all that you need to know before making the investment in your ticket, and to guide you to the right places.

Part One deals with tickets, flying, routes, how to plan your trip, and gives lots of practical and invaluable advice to all long-haul travellers.

Part Two is a guidebook to the world's 50 main stop-off points, which are covered in detail. Practical information on the country is followed by an in-depth city report. Because this is a book for the airborne, we give detailed information on all the airport facilities of the world's 50 major airports, so you can find out anything from if there's a duty free shop at Peking airport to what the check-in time is for your flight from Hong Kong to Bombay.

Also featured for every city are the Sights; a comprehensive Accommodation Directory; Useful Addresses; Dining Out and Nightlife – all these are covered in detail. Side trips and excursions are also looked at, and the information is presented in a factual manner equally suitable for the business, frequent long-haul or leisure traveller. Everything that you need to plan a trip on this scale is here in one book.

This guide is recommended by British Airways, and will be an invaluable addition to every serious traveller's suitcase. We welcome your comments and invite all our readers to write to us c/o the publishers to let us know how you found the guide and if there is any information which you feel would be useful to pass on to fellow travellers.

Part One

How to travel round the world

The advantages of air travel

There is little doubt that travelling by air over long distances is the cheapest, most practical and most efficient means of so doing. In the space of a few short decades, the concept of international air travel has exploded to the point where discount air travel is within the reach of most pockets.

The technology of air travel has expanded too. Supersonic passenger flights were just a distant dream 30 years ago and long-haul air travel meant many days of noisy, short-haul journeys in order to reach far-off Australasia or southern Africa.

It has to be remembered now that overland travel is no longer a realistic rival to air travel where long distances are involved. Overland to Africa or the Far East, with all the incumbent problems of visas and accommodation on the way, remains nearly as great an adventure now as it ever has been. In the long run such a journey would probably take many weeks longer and work out more expensive than an Economy air ticket.

The biggest single advantage of air travel is the time you save reaching your destination. Travelling long-haul, or taking the Round the World ticket option in particular, there is scarcely any corner of the world which you cannot reach within 24 hours. Anyone considering a trip to Australia or New Zealand ought to think about the vast number of Round the World tickets offered by nearly all the major airlines. Not only do you stand to make a significant saving in the ticket price for your original planned journey, but you can have a magnificent holiday in several of the world's exotic destinations into the bargain.

Air travel is safe as well. Too many people never consider the potential of air travel because they feel it is dangerous when, in fact, it is over 20 times safer to travel anywhere by air than it is to make even the shortest journey in your own car. Airline disasters happen very seldom but, unfortunately, when they do the resulting tragedy tends to dominate the world's headlines for days.

Travelling by air for those who have never flown before can be an exhilarating experience. It is clean, calm, safe and efficient, offering the best of facilities to the disabled, young children and nervous passengers unsure of flying. No other means of transport allows you to see so much of the world with so little effort. It's an old cliché, but the world really is out there just waiting to be discovered.

Long-haul air travel is good value, and never before have you had as great a choice, either of airlines or destinations from which to choose. Consider carefully all the background to long-haul flying in general (and the Round the World option in particular) which we feature and you may be convinced.

The fares: what's on offer

If you've never bought an airline ticket before then you may be quickly confused by all the different types of fare on offer. This section is an analysis of all the options available to travellers.

ROUND THE WORLD

If you are already planning a long-haul flight, perhaps to visit relatives in Australia or a lengthy business trip, then you ought to consider purchasing a Round the World ticket as an alternative. Assuming you have few time restrictions, a Round the World ticket will allow you to visit not only the place you originally intended, but also several other destinations on your way out or back home. Fuller details are in the next section, but as an example of how this works, consider that you were planning to visit relatives in Sydney, Australia, for a month. The standard Economy Class return fare, from London Heathrow, would cost you anything up to £1200. For an equivalent fare, many of the airlines we feature have Round the World routings, which include Sydney along with a host of other options ranging from the Middle East to Japan and Hong Kong.

APEX/SUPER APEX

These were the airlines' traditional cheap fares before the arrival of the Round the World ticket on the market. Apex stands for Advance Purchase Excursion and still remains the airline companies' main means of official discounting. Apex and Super Apex fares normally apply only to return tickets, excluding long-haul flights to the Far East or Australasia.

Apex flights must be booked well in advance – usually at least a fortnight before you plan to fly and occasionally up to two calendar months. Minimum stay periods are generally specified and stopovers are not permitted. You stand to lose considerably if you cancel an Apex or Super Apex booking.

The difference between Apex and Super Apex is that the latter is cheaper than the former – but is only available at the very last moment.

PEX/SUPER PEX

Similar to Apex fares, these are restricted to short-haul and predominantly European flights. They are instant purchase, bargain Economy Class tickets, valid for firm short-haul reservations. Heavy cancellation fees apply and occasionally they require a Saturday night stay at your destination.

EXCURSION FARES

Precisely like a coach or train excursion ticket, these fares offer substantial reductions on scheduled routes with restrictions on the time of travel. They are specifically for round trips abroad, usually requiring a minimum stay, and of little relevance to Round the World travellers.

Excursion passengers are not normally allowed to break their journey unless specified and must travel and return on precisely the day and flight agreed. Otherwise you will be charged the full scheduled fare, and possibly have to delay your return flight for a few days until there are seats available.

SPOUSE FARES

This is a scheme operated by many larger airlines whereby one spouse pays the full scheduled fare, and the other about 50 per cent of that. They are available predominantly inside Europe (and not on Round the World tickets).

Stopovers are not permitted, and both husband and wife must travel together on both legs of the journey. This class of fare is slowly being abolished by larger carriers (including British Airways on routes where Club Class is now available) since their popularity is declining. Couples may have to prove their relationship since unmarried couples will not be allowed any discount.

ITX FARES

ITX fares are available exclusively as part of a holiday package which includes hotel accommodation. Meaning 'Independent Inclusive Tour Excursion', ITX fares are gradually becoming more widely available for flights alone, or at least those offering a minimum of accommodation. Restrictions on length of stay are complicated on all ITX fares, but normally you must spend at least five or six nights, or a weekend (including a Saturday night), at a specific destination.

ITX fares are usually offered to just one destination at a time, mostly within Europe. Here again, like spouse fares, the ITX option is becoming less widely available amongst the major airlines.

CHILDREN'S/INFANTS' FARES

All Round the World airlines offer substantial discounts for children and infants. Those under the age of either two or three (it varies from airline to airline) will be carried free of charge *provided* they do not occupy a separate seat. They are not allowed any baggage allowance other than a carrycot or collapsible buggy. Additional infants of this age will be carried at a third or a half of the adult rate, but on the most cut-price Apex and Super Apex tickets they will not be allowed any discount at all.

Children up to the age of twelve will be carried at half the adult fare. They are entitled to their own seat as well as the full baggage allowance. Some standby fares do not allow any discount for children.

STUDENT/YOUTH FARES

These are available to young people under the age of 22, or slightly older whilst still in full-time education. Youth fares normally offer a 25 per cent reduction in the normal yearly or excursion fare – more for many longer distance routes including those to the Middle East.

Student fares offer a similar reduction but are normally only valid between the student's home country and place of education. With the growth of more promotional and discount fares aimed at young people, airlines are realizing that specific student fares are uncompetitive.

STANDBY FARES

Precisely what the term implies. Standby fares are valid only at the last minute if normal, reserved, seats have not been sold out in advance. They can usually be purchased well in advance – right up to the last check-in time before the flight is scheduled to leave, but your ticket will not become valid unless there are seats still unsold which can be allocated to standby ticket holders on a first come, first served basis.

Standby tickets are considerably cheaper than scheduled fares but you have no guarantee of travelling on the flight – or even on the day – of your choice. You cannot book a return standby without risking the same pot-luck as on your outward trip.

CHARTERS

Charters won't concern the Round the World traveller unless you specifically opt for a chartered air excursion at some stage during your trip.

The charter market is almost exclusively tied up with package holiday operators, and large companies who may occasionally choose to shuttle a few dozen of their executives backwards and forwards at their own expense.

A few tour operators charter Concorde (Kuoni, for example) and this could be an exciting alternative to the normal scheduled first or last leg of your journey. Cheap charter fares exist predominantly within Europe and across the Atlantic, but scan your local press or ask your travel agent for any charters which may be relevant to your individual trip.

SCHEDULED CONSOLIDATION FARES

These are no more than travel tickets for scheduled flights which are sold off at charter prices. Airlines occasionally sell blocks of seats to various operators who, in turn, sell them to the public. Similar to ITX fares, scheduled Consolidation fares will have a minimum-stay condition.

The rather unglamorous term for this type of fare comes from the idea of consolidating passengers, without their obvious knowledge, into groups after the issue of all the tickets!

AIR PASSES

A few airlines sell air passes allowing unlimited, or heavily discounted, air travel within a specific country. Leading the field are nearly all the US airlines, which give passengers generous concessions within their domestic networks. National prices include Continental's $329 pass allowing up to four stops in the US mainland, Canada and Mexico (within 21 days of purchase) to Delta's $695 pass allowing a dozen stops in the US, Canada and Hawaii (valid within a two-month period). Note: these air fares are not available to US residents.

Of the other countries we look at in this guide, Australia, Brazil, and India all offer internal air passes with up to 45 days' validity. On average, a single air pass flight works out at the equivalent of $80.

Round the World air tickets

Round the World air flights had their conception in the late 1940s when Pan Am and TWA greatly extended their commercial contest of the air. In so doing, they were to transform the shape of the globe for the ordinary traveller. In June 1947, Juan Trippe of Pan Am had inaugurated the first Round the World service by a single airline – travelling round the world in fourteen days with a group of newspaper owners.

Competition developed in the 1950s and 1960s, with other airlines joining the increasingly lucrative long haul market. No one airline could circumnavigate the globe, and so lasting partnerships of the air were formed: Pan Am with Cathay Pacific, British Airways with Air New Zealand, and so on. But it was not until the 1970s that the cut-price Round the World ticket really appeared. Once again, Pan Am were the aerial pioneers with their new, glossy brochures hailing 'the greatest adventure of them all . . . the ultimate vacation . . . the dream of a lifetime'.

Other airlines quickly followed Pan Am's cut-price lead and, within a few short years of its introduction, virtually every major airline was offering its own Round the World ticket. Long-haul destinations had been increasing in popularity over the previous decade anyway, and although still a long way behind the most popular European resorts (Spain, Greece, Italy and so on) their popularity was a further boost to the development of Round the World tickets.

The ticket itself is no more than an elaborate Apex discounted ticket offered by the individual airline, or pair of airlines. As with an Apex ticket, you have to make a confirmed booking about three or four weeks before your departure date. You then have up to a year, depending on what airline you choose, to circle the world. The actual ticket will look much the same as any conventional air ticket – although you may need one or two more flight tickets to accommodate the numerous destinations you will be visiting.

One of the main advantages of the Round the World ticket is the absence of any qualifications to buy one. There is no mandatory age, date of travel, or financial qualification. Nor do you have to have flown a certain number of times with a particular airline, or have been a regular customer at your local travel agency before you can purchase your ticket. A high proportion of people who have never flown before, and from every conceivable background, buy these tickets: businessmen, retired people, young professionals between jobs – and even ordinary tourists wanting to go somewhere a bit exotic for a change.

HOW TO BOOK

Booking a Round the World ticket is a simple matter once you have decided which route you would like. Choosing the routing is the most important aspect of arranging your booking, since it will determine which carrier you will fly and, more importantly, which destinations you will visit.

Once you have made up your mind, you can choose to book either through a travel agent, or bucketshop, or through an airline office itself. It is always best to book in person but if you do make a firm credit card booking by telephone (and have your tickets sent by post) *always* confirm in writing afterwards. Double check, and have confirmed, your precise itinerary and airlines.

If you book in person you will be able to discuss any last minute details before committing yourself. It is always advisable to have a chat with your travel agent or airline representative before going away to finally make up your mind.

Booking conditions vary from airline to airline, and the standard regulations are listed next. You ought to be fully aware of these before you finally book. When you eventually receive your ticket, double check all destinations, airlines and – where applicable – dates as well. All potential ticket problems are a dozen times easier to sort out before you leave home.

One last piece of advice. When you do book, always insist on paying by credit card, since that way you will have some legal protection in case of any difficulty with the outlet you choose to buy your ticket from.

RULES AND REGULATIONS

All the standard rules and regulations governing the purchase and use of any other type of air ticket also apply to Round the World tickets. Tickets are not, for example, transferable between the named user at time of booking and another. They are valid strictly for the class and route agreed at the point of sale, unless upgraded or amended with the permission of the carrier during the trip.

In addition, many Round the World tickets are governed by

specific regulations. A minimum stay (in each destination) is occasionally designated. This is normally 14 days but the requirement is being phased out as the popularity of the ticket increases. There will, however, still be a maximum stay of 180 days or, more likely, a year from the date of purchase. Within the specific conditions of each ticket there will be no minimum or maximum number of stopovers.

Reservations must be made – and paid for in full – at least three weeks before departure. Changes of travel dates are normally allowed, except on the very cheapest (under £1000) tickets, with the significant exception of the first sector of your trip. Once the first sector has been firmly booked then it cannot be altered.

Travel must always be in a continuous global direction around the world, whether east- or west-bound. This is a modest restriction but it means, for example, that a traveller going from London to Hong Kong and then on to Sydney could not double-back via the Middle East.

COMBINATIONS

One of the first things you'll learn as you delve deeper into the concept of a Round the World ticket is that the possible combinations are truly endless. For a start, all Round the World trips will involve a combination of airlines. Normally at least two, and occasionally up to four, will operate any one Round the World routing.

Choosing a combination of routings can be a more complicated matter. In theory, any combination of destinations is possible, but in practice you will have to restrict yourself to the popular options offered by the major airlines. Remembering that you must fly continuously in either an east or westward direction, your combination cannot be too ambitious by including, for example, Hong Kong with Japan, Australia and New Zealand. The combinations available are explained more fully in the following two sections.

How to get the most out of your pass

All Round the World tickets follow prearranged routings in one of three patterns. Either they include only destinations in the northern hemisphere of the globe, destinations only in the southern hemisphere, or else they include a combination of both.

If you choose a northern route, from a starting point in either Great Britain or the United States, then you will have considerably less overall flying time to reach your destinations. Most airlines, in particular the majority of northern hemisphere ones, offer routes which do not cross the equator. British Airways, with United Airlines, for instance, offer an attractive Northern Hemisphere routing which takes in London, Rome, Bahrain, Bombay, Hong Kong, Tokyo, Honolulu and at least one major city in North America.

By restricting yourself to a northern routing you will be able to avoid excesses of tropical temperatures if you so wish. Even without visiting Africa or South East Asia you can still enjoy many exotic and warm destinations – including Hong Kong and Japan – without feeling too uncomfortable in a strange climate.

If you choose a southern route your choice will be considerably less but all southern routings ought to include the option of a few stops in the north. Destinations in the southern hemisphere include South America, Australasia and most of Malaysia and Singapore. If you visit Kenya you will have the opportunity to step from north to south at the imaginary equator line.

A southern routing is ideal for those keen to visit the most far-flung corners of the world, but to do so you will need to expect a lot of long-haul flying. Several southern destinations may be of particular interest to those who are travelling as far as Australia or New Zealand. If you are keen to visit other destinations south of the equator then the bulk of the necessary long-haul flying will already be behind you once you've reached Australasia.

The ideal combination of routings is, however, one which involves both northern and southern stops. That way you can experience a wide range of climates and lifestyles without suffering the extremes of either. Remember to do a little research in advance about the best times of year to visit the various destinations.

CHANGE OF ROUTINGS

When you purchase your Round the World ticket it will be valid for a specific series of destinations – in order. Different airlines will have their own policies about whether or not to charge you for changing a previously set routing before you leave. Some carriers won't allow you to change at all, but those which do may charge you up to £25 ($35) for the service.

You will experience a few more problems trying to change a date of travel. Once your ticket is bought and paid for then no change will be allowed to your departure date. If you cannot travel on that day, no matter why, you *must* cancel the ticket altogether. If this occurs within three weeks of the original departure date you can stand to lose 25 per cent of your total ticket price paid.

When you've actually left you will be allowed one change of date (and occasionally a change of route as well) without charge. First and Business Class passengers enjoy greater flexibility in terms of changing routings or dates. Economy Class passengers can expect more problems when it comes to altering firm confirmations.

If you do intend changing your routing then it is advisable to do so as soon as possible. To have a sudden last-minute change of heart at a departure airport is not a good idea. It is worth bearing in mind that the larger airlines can accommodate route changes more easily. Not only will they have more actual route options (theoretically) available, but they ought to have had more experience processing such changes.

Round the World tickets are not open tickets for you to circle the globe as and when you please. If you have really no idea where you'd like to go, or in what order, then you ought to consider a do-it-yourself ticket. By patching together your own choice of destinations, whether in advance, or as you reach each new city, then the potential problems of changing previously arranged routings will not arise.

RESERVATIONS AND PAYMENT

Making a confirmed reservation for a Round the World ticket involves much the same procedure as for any other air ticket. You will have to have a fairly clear idea where exactly you wish to visit, and which airline you wish to travel with, before making a booking. Consider carefully the various outlets open to you to make your reservation – bucketshop, travel agent, press advertisement or through a discount travel organization like WEXAS. Information about the pros and cons of each of these outlets is given later in Part One.

You ought to make your reservation *at least* 21 days before you plan to leave, and ideally a lot earlier if you can. Bear in mind which countries you may need visas for (including Australia, and the United States for British travellers) since they may take up to a month to get sorted out. This is particularly important if you need several visas during your trip. In such a situation you must know a few months in advance where exactly you plan to visit so you can complete the necessary formalities in time. Advance reservations have the additional advantage of allowing you more time to get accommodation organized, if you intend to do so, before you leave home. Round the World travellers with British Airways, for instance, can take advantage of an extensive MiniStay programme at all their worldwide destinations. Other large airlines, including Cathay Pacific, Air Canada and Singapore Airlines, offer their own good value Round the World stopover accommodation deals which can be booked at the same time as your ticket.

Payment for the ticket – and any additional accommodation arranged through your ticket retailer – must be made at the point of purchase unless you have already made credit or invoice arrangements. For obvious reasons of personal security, it's not advisable to wander into a local travel agency with your entire ticket price in cash. Make your payment instead by personal cheque, or preferably by credit card. Remember your credit limit if you do pay with plastic and try to ensure it is paid by the time you leave. Otherwise the ticket price will eat a large hole into your credit limit if you intend to use your card much abroad. If you make your reservation a few months in advance this shouldn't be a problem.

Once you've purchased your Round the World ticket it will remain valid for up to a year from the date of issue. Certain tickets are only valid for six months (or 180 days) so do make sure which time limit applies to your ticket if you intend a lengthy trip of more than six months.

If you plan to get maximum value from your Round the World trip and spend fully six months or a year abroad, depending on which ticket you purchase, then you ought to delay buying it as long as possible. Otherwise you stand to lose a few weeks' potential travelling time if there is a significant gap between the date of ticket purchase and that of your first flight.

STOPOVERS

Your Round the World routing will be made up of a number of stopovers and will most likely start and end at the same city – probably London or New York. When the Round the World ticket first appeared as a commercially successful idea, in the late 1970s, a minimum stay requirement was included automatically. This was to safeguard the interests of full-fare scheduled passengers whose interests would theoretically have been damaged had Round the World travellers been allowed an identical long-haul, short-stay trip at a reduced cost.

The minimum stay requirement is the shortest length of time which you are allowed to stay away from your original departure airport in order to ensure the ticket's return validity. In other words, if you reached your last stopover before home barely a week after leaving then you'd need to spend at least a week there before the ticket would be valid for the final leg.

The minimum stay requirement is, however, gradually dying out. Canadian Pacific has phased it out on all its routes except for its option with Cathay Pacific. Japan Airlines and American Airlines have reduced the requirement to merely eight days, whereas many other airlines, including British Airways and Singapore Airlines, have removed it altogether. No Round the World airline demands a minimum stay greater than 14 days and, since more and more carriers seem to be abolishing it altogether, check when you buy your ticket how you're affected. It's always worth knowing anyway just in case you have to return home unexpectedly.

If you intend to travel in a large country such as the US or Canada, and you wish to make several internal stop-offs, look carefully at the airline's conditions. Some will allow as many stop-offs as you want within the country (i.e. New York, Chicago, Denver, San Francisco) as long as you keep going in the one direction; others only allow one or two stop-offs within a country. It all depends on the airline and the class of your ticket.

REDUCTIONS

A few ticket holders will qualify for specific additional reductions which can reduce the cost of your trip considerably. Discount cards (including Countdown and Lift Off), whether available through a travel industry discount organization or an airline itself, can reduce ticket costs by up to a third. Larger airlines operate a 'frequent user' club similar to that offered by the large hotel chains.

Airline employees qualify for some of the best discounts. Under a reciprocal arrangement, many major airlines recognize sister companies and allow employees to travel at a greatly reduced cost. The discount for employees on their own airline is usually 90 per cent but certain restrictions apply which give normal fare-paying passengers priority for seat allocation.

EXTRAS AND ADD-ONS

In addition to the scheduled routing on your ticket it will normally be possible to purchase discounted 'extras' from particular destinations. The most popular extensions include visits to parts of South America, Africa or the Caribbean islands. If one of your host airlines is an American carrier then it will be relatively inexpensive to venture into South America. Cathay Pacific's routing with Pan Am includes optional extra trips into Argentina, Brazil, Chile, Guatemala, Mexico, Uruguay or Venezuela. Although it is possible to book any other airline's regular scheduled flight wherever you choose, specific extras available at the time of booking will work out noticeably cheaper than if purchased normally at new destinations.

British Airways offer some good value extras to their Round the World routings. For an additional £141 ($197), Economy Class travellers can visit up to three United Airlines North American mainland destinations. First Class ticket holders can have these included at no extra cost. For a further payment of about £100 ($140) (£200 ($280) if First Class) ticket holders can visit Nairobi, Harare, Johannesburg, Durban or Cape Town and travel onwards from Harare to Perth in Australia. All the major airlines offer similar add-on extras which are worth checking out before you leave.

One less attractive add-on which you will need to bear in mind is airport departure taxes. You obviously won't have any choice about whether or not to pay, and since they can frequently set you back £10–£15 ($14–21) (or the equivalent in dollars or local currency) you may need to write off up to £100 ($140) for these annoying little extras. Try and find out before you leave a country whether a departure tax will be payable or else you may find yourself having to change back money at the last minute – and being stuck with the remainder of a $50 bill in Peruvian intis or whatever!

CHILDREN'S DISCOUNTS

All airlines offer substantial discounts to children. Those under the age of two (occasionally three on some airlines) will either be carried free or at a nominal 10 per cent of the adult fare. They will not be given a seat nor allowed any baggage allowance of their own since they are expected to be held by a parent or guardian at all times.

Older children, up to about eleven or twelve, will be carried at half or two-thirds of the adult fare. They are allowed a seat to themselves and the normal baggage allowance.

In addition, most airlines operate a Youth Fare for younger people under 22. The Round the World ticket seldom qualifies for this particular discount (usually about 25 per cent off normal fare) but the discounts for younger children should be offered by all airlines.

CANCELLATION PENALTIES AND REFUNDS

In the case of voluntary cancellation more than three weeks before your first departure date, a full refund will be given. Very occasionally a minor charge of a few pounds (or dollars) will be levied for administration charges, but on the whole a full refund will be forthcoming.

If you have to cancel your trip less than three weeks before you planned to leave, you will lose about 25 per cent of the total ticket price. This lost portion cannot be kept as a credit for later use so if there is *any* reasonable doubt that you may have to cancel with less than three weeks' notice then you ought to do so. In the case of illness or death, either of the named passenger or an immediate family member, then a full refund will normally be issued regardless of how little notice has been given. Do not expect it as a right, however.

If you decide to cancel the remainder of your trip whilst en route, a 75 per cent refund of the portion of the trip not yet used will normally be given. The money will, naturally, be more readily available if you have a particularly sound reason – bereavement, illness or even destitution – rather than simply a sudden dislike of foreign food or tropical weather. In such cases, the refund you will receive (if allowed) will be 75 per cent of the difference between the ticket price and the appropriate fare to fly you back to your original departure point. Refunds are an important consideration which you ought to be clear about from your travel agent or airline office before you leave home.

CONCORDE OPTION

Flying by Concorde has fairly been called a 'total experience' which deserves to be savoured and enjoyed. Certainly it is one of life's great experiences. Concorde travels faster than a rifle bullet and at twice the height of Mount Everest. If you choose to fly a stage of your trip by Concorde, most likely across the Atlantic, you will be treated very much as a privileged passenger with special check-in facilities and First Class luxury treatment throughout.

Of the two airlines which operate a commercial Concorde service, only British Airways has Round the World tickets available. They include a Concorde option at an additional £250 ($350) for First Class passengers and an additional £600 ($840) for Club Class ticket holders. For this extra payment, you are entitled to cross the Atlantic by Concorde – a journey of three and a half hours from New York to London – in either direction, according to preference. The Concorde option is not available on any other route or any other airline.

For those wishing to experience the ultimate Round the World trip, Kuoni offer two outstanding package itineraries, travelling exclusively by Concorde and costing £13,050 ($18,270) and £15,100

($21,140). For your money you get two weeks of shameless luxury, staying in the finest international hotels, and with approximately 40 hours total flying time on board Concorde. Kuoni's choice of destinations includes Peking, Shanghai, Bangkok, Colombo, Fiji and Las Vegas. The luxury and exclusivity of this trip is reflected in the price, which falls into the 'if you have to ask the price you can't afford it' category.

QEII ATLANTIC OPTION

An interesting alternative to Concorde, or even flying at all across the Atlantic, is to travel in style on board the *Queen Elizabeth II*. As the magnificent flagship of the Cunard fleet, she maintains a regular timetable of transatlantic crossings between Southampton and New York.

Cunard offer one-way trips on the *QEII* for as little as £920 ($1288), taking five days to complete the crossing. This fare includes an Economy Class return air ticket back to the States or the UK, depending on where you started from, but this extra bonus won't necessarily concern Round the World ticket holders. Prices rise steeply to over £4000 ($5600) for luxury outside cabins, and if you travel in the middle of summer, so be warned that five days of transatlantic luxury can quickly double your overall ticket price.

Cabins are available in no less than 21 different price ranges – the lowest is a youth fare of only £365 ($511) (standby) for people under 26. Cunard also offer a *QEII*/Concorde option whereby you cross the Atlantic by Concorde and return on the *QEII* – in either direction first depending on your choice. Prices start from £1000 ($1400) depending on your date of travel, or from £1300 ($1820) if you choose to add a couple of nights in New York's famous Waldorf Astoria Hotel. At least six flights a year return to British airports outside London – including Edinburgh, Manchester and Bristol.

Which Round the World ticket to go for

Many of the world's larger international airlines now offer Round the World tickets. Altogether, there are almost 200 fare alternatives available. Obviously particular routings – and prices – change from one month to the next but this section outlines the main options open. Bear in mind that as the popularity of Round the World tickets grows, the number of airlines operating them and specific routings grow frequently.

It is also worth remembering that most major airlines will allow you to start and finish your trip at just about any one of their main destinations – and frequently offer different prices from different starting points. Cathay Pacific, for example, operate different routings from each of their four major offices in Sydney, London, Hong Kong and Bahrain.

Your choice of destination will obviously depend a lot on personal preferences and budget – to say nothing of tight time constraints if you're travelling on business. But, equally, choosing a routing to suit your lifestyle is crucial. Older travellers, for instance, who want to endure the minimum of hassle abroad should stick to the well-known 'civilized' cities. Possible routings include Sydney, Hong Kong, Singapore, Rome, Paris, London, New York, Bermuda, Auckland and so on.

For younger people, or those simply craving the unusual, then many of the world's more exotic destinations (Bangkok, Penang, Seoul, Delhi, Bombay, Taiwan or Mombasa) could form the basis of their routing.

For those keen to see a microcosm of a host of totally new foreign countries then a routing composed exclusively of capital cities will provide such an insight. Almost always you will be visiting the country's largest population centre, which will offer a diverse range of people and sights unsurpassed in that country! For a varied trip, you ought to consider a route like London–Bahrain–Singapore City–Manila (Hong Kong)–Ottawa–London. Alternatively a more adventurous southern hemisphere routing could include Mombasa or New Delhi as well.

Because of the constantly changing market in tickets it's a good idea to get hold of the *Hogg Robinson Around the World Fares Planner*. This free brochure from any Hogg Robinson travel agent lists all published Round the World tickets, as well as detailing their own constructed fares.

There now follows a basic analysis of the major airlines involved:

No.	Partnership	First Class	Bus. Class	Econ. Class	Via Nth. Pac.	Via Sth. Pac.	Min. advance booking (1st Sector only)	Stopover Restrictions	Validity	Discounts Child%	Discounts Infant%	Cancellation Fee	Additional Comments
1.	American Airlines/ Cathay Pacific	£2499	£1699	£1250	✓		14 days	Min. 3. At least 1 in Cont. U.S.A. max. 1 at any 1 point.	Min. 14 days Max. 6 months	33%	90%	25%	
2.	Qantas/TWA	£3350	£2180	£1328[1] £1488[2]		✓	21 days	Min. 3. Max. 1 at any 1 point. Max. 12 flight coupons for travel in U.S.A.	Min. 14 days Max. 1 Year	33%	90%	25%	1. Includes New Zealand provided there is no back-tracking to Australia. 2. Includes New Zealand if back-tracking to Australia is required. 3. Supplement if exit from Manchester. 4. Supplement for Transatlantic travel in Business Class TWA (Applies to y only). 5. Supplement to Caribbean.
3.	Northwest Orient/ Gulf Air	£2035	N/A	£1028	✓		14 days	Min. 3 Max. 1 at any 1 point.	Min. 14 days Max. 1 year	33%	90%	10%	
4.	Northwest Orient/ Cathay Pacific	£2035 £2499	N/A	£1028 £1150		S	14 days	Min. 3 Max. 1 at any 1 point.	Min. 14 days Max. 180 days	33%	90%	25%	The higher fares apply for issues from 01.07.86
5.	Northwest Orient/ Air India	£2035	N/A	£1028	✓		14 days	Min. 3 Max. 1 at any 1 point.	Min. 14 days Max. 1 year	33%	90%	10%	
6.	Northwest Orient/ British Caledonian Cunard	£2035	N/A	£1028	✓		14 days	Min. 3 Max. 1 at any 1 point.	Min. 14 days Max. 1 year	33%	90%	10%	Supplement for Cunard line transatlantic voyage on the QE2. B.Cal. apply 21 day lead time, Max. stay 180 days and no stopover restrictions.
7.	Northwest Orient/ South African Airways	£2188	N/A	£1459	✓		14 days	Min. 3 Max. 1 at any 1 point.	Min. 14 days Max. 1 year	33%	90%	10%	
8.	Northwest Orient/ KLM	£2035	N/A	£1028	✓		14 days	Min. 3 Max. 1 at any 1 point.	Min. 14 days Max. 1 year	33%	90%	25%	
9.	Northwest Orient/ Sabena	£2035	N/A	£1028	✓		14 days	Min. 3 of at least 48 hrs. each. Other required Stopovers need not achieve this min. duration. Max. 1 at any 1 point.	Min. 14 days Max. 1 year	33%	90%	10%	
10.	Northwest Orient/ Garuda Airways	£2035	N/A	£1028	✓		14 days	Min. 3 Max. 1 at any 1 point.	Min. 14 days Max. 1 year	33%	90%	10%	
11.	Northwest Orient/ Thai Airways	£2035	N/A	£1028	✓		14 days	Min. 3 Max. 1 at any 1 point.	Min. 14 days Max. 1 year	33%	90%	10%	

No.	Partnership	First Class	Bus. Class	Econ. Class	Via Nth. Pac.	Via Sth. Pac.	Min. advance booking (1st Sector only)	Stopover Restrictions	Validity	Discounts Child%	Discounts Infant%	Cancellation Fee	Additional Comments
12.	Northwest Orient/Malaysian Airlines	£2035	N/A	£1028	✓		14 days	Min. 3 Max. 1 at any 1 point.	Min. 14 days Max. 1 year	33%	90%	10%	
13.	Northwest Orient/Kuwait Airways	£2035	N/A	£1028	✓		14 days	Min. 3 Max. 1 at any 1 point.	Min. 14 days Max. 1 year	33%	90%	10%	
14.	British Caledonian/Korea Air/Eastern	£2035	N/A	£1028	✓		21 days	Min. 1 at any 1 point. Max. 4 flight coupons by Eastern Airlines.	Min. 14 days Max. 180 days	33%	90%	10%	
15.	British Caledonian/UTA/Eastern	£2999	N/A	£1250		✓	21 days	Max 1 at any 1 point.	Min. 14 days Max. 1 year	33%	90%	10%	Certain UTA transpacific sectors may not be available in First Class. In these circumstances First Class RTW passengers are entitled to rebates for Economy Class travel.
16.	KLM/Continental Airlines	£2499	£1978	£1499		✓	21 days	Min. 3 Max. 1 at any 1 point.	Min. 14 days Max. 1 year	33%	90%	25%	
17.	Singapore Airlines/TWA	£2035	N/A	£1028	✓		14 days	Min. 3 Max. 1 at any 1 point. travel within the USA.	Min. 14 days Max. 6 months	33%	90%	10%	Economy Class RTW allows transatlantic Business Class by TWA upon payment of additional Supplement for Caribbean.
18.	Singapore Airlines/Air Canada	£2035	£1634	£1028	✓		14 days	Min. 3 Max. 1 at any 1 point.	Min. 14 days Max. 6 months	33%	90%	25%	
19.	Pan Am/Cathay Pacific	£2499	£1699	£1199	✓	S	14 days	Min. 3 Max. 1 at any 1 point.	Min. 14 days Max. 6 months	33%	90%	25%	
20.	Pan Am/Thai Airways	£2499	£1699	£1199	✓	S	14 days	Min. 3 Max. 1 at any 1 point.	Min. 14 days Max. 1 year	33%	90%	25%	The only sectors permitted by TG are Delhi/Bangkok/Hong Kong or vice versa.
21.	Pan Am/Saudi Airlines	£2499	£1699	£1199	✓	S	14 days	Min. 3 Max. 1 at any 1 point.	Min. –14 days Max. 6 months	33%	90%	25%	
22.	Alia/Korean Airlines/American Airlines	£2035	N/A	£1028	✓		14 days	Min. 3 Max. 1 at any 1 point.	Min.–None Max. 1 year	33.3%	90%	25%	
23.	CP Air/Alitalia	£2163	£1792	£1236		S	14 days	Max. 4 within Canada	Min.–None Max. 1 year	33%	90%	10%	Specified supplements to include specified destinations in Argentina/Brazil/Chile/Peru and/or from Milan or Rome to selected European points (Excluding W. Germany).
24.	CP Air/Philippine/Airlines	£2039	£1639	£1029		S	14 days	Max. 1 at any 1 point.	Min.–None Max. 6 months	33%	90%	10%	Specified supplements to include specified destinations in Argentina/Chile/Peru.

No.	Airlines												Conditions
25.	SAS/Thai Airways/Continental	£3350	N/A	£1328	✓		21 days	Min. 4 Max. 1 at any 1 point.	Min. 14 days Max. 6 months	33%	90%	10%	Specified supplements on certain destinations.
26.	British Airways/Air New Zealand/United Airlines	£3400	£2333	£1399	✓		21 days	Min. 3 Max. 3 on UA network within USA/Canada. Only 1 Stopover or transfer allowed at Nadi.	Min. 14 days Max. 1 year	33%	90%	25%	Specified supplement: Max. of 4 flight coupons for travel within USA/Canada by UA. Payable in Economy Class only £141. Supplement for travel Ex Manchester.
27.	Alitalia/Continental Airlines	£2596	£2040	£1360	✓		21 days	No restriction except that within USA max.4 (max.3 flight coupon). 1 additional Stopover in USA permitted at extra charge.	Min.–None Max. 1 year	33%	90%	25%	Specified supplements for side trips from Milan or Rome to selected European points (Except in W. Germany).
28.	Northwest Orient/Air France	FFR 29300	N/A	FFR 16900	✓		21 days	Min. 3 Max. 1 at any 1 point.	Min. 22 days Max. 180 days	33%	90%	10%	Travel at these fares must commence in Paris.
29.	Cathay Pacific/Air New Zealand	£3350	£2180	£1328	✓		21 days	Min. 3 Only 1 Stopover or transfer allowed at Nadi.	Min. 14 days Max. 1 year	33.3%	90%	25%	
30.	CP Air/Cathay Pacific	£2035 £2499	£1634 £1699	£1150	✓	S	14 days	Min. 3 Max. 1 at any 1 point.	Min. 14 days Max. 6 months	33%	90%	10%	CP Air apply a 10 day Min. stay and no Stopover minimum. Specified supplements to include specified destinations in Argentina/Chile/Peru. The higher fares apply for issues from 01.07.86.
31.	JAL/TWA	£2035	N/A	£1028	✓		21 days	Min. 3 at least one of which must be in the Continental USA. Max. 12 flight coupons for travel within the USA. Max. 1 at any 1 point.	Min. 8 days Max. 180 days	25%	90%	25%	Economy Class RTW allows transatlantic Business Class by TWA upon payment of additional charge. Supplement for Caribbean.
32.	British Airways/United Airlines	£2599	£1699	£1150	✓	S	21 days	Min. 3 Max. of 3 within USA/Canada.	Min. 14 days Max. 1 year	33%	90%	25%	1. Supplement if transatlantic leg by Concorde. First and Business Class only. 2. Supplement for travel Ex Manchester.
33.	CP Air/South African Airways	£2499	£1999	£1599		Either Not Both	14 days	Max. 1 at any 1 point.	Min.–None Max. 1 year	33%	90%	10%	Specified supplements to include specified destinations in Argentina/Brazil/Chile/Peru.
34.	Swissair/In partner-/ship with 35 other Airlines	N/A	N/A	SFR 3850	✓	S	21 days	a. Max. 6 free of charge. b. Up to 4 additional Stopovers may be purchased. c. Within Europe Stopovers are prohibited but transfers are unrestricted.	Min. 21 days Max. 6 months	33%	90%	25%	1. It is strongly advised that full advantage is taken of the free stopover/transfer allowance at the time of the original booking is made. Failure to do so will result in the application of charges. 2. Transfer connections count as stopovers.
35.	Pan Am/Singapore Airlines	£3599	£2449	£1799	✓		14 days	Min. 3 Max. 1 at any 1 point.	Min. 14 days Max. 6 months	33%	90%	25%	1. Specified supplements to certain destinations. 2. Travel at this fare must be via Australia or New Zealand or both.
36.	Northwest Orient/Qantas	£3350	£2180	£1328	✓		14 days	Min. 3. Max. 1 at any 1 point. Max.12 flt.cpns. within N.Am.	Min. 14 days Max. 1 year	33%	90%	25%	Supplement if travel out of Glasgow or Manchester.

No.	Partnership	First Class	Bus. Class	Econ. Class	Via Nth. Pac.	Via Sth. Pac.	Min. advance booking (1st Sector only)	Stopover Restrictions	Validity	Discounts Child%	Discounts Infant%	Cancellation Fee	Additional Comments
37.	Air Canada/ Air New Zealand	£3350	£2180	£1328		✓	21 days	Min. 3 Max. 1 at any 1 point. Max. 1 Stopover or transfer allowed at Nadi.	Min. 14 days Max. 1 year	33.3%	90%	25%	Specified supplements for certain side-trips.
38.	Cathay Pacific/ Air Canada	£2499	£1599 £1699	£1099 £1150		S	14 days	Min. 3 Max. 1 at any 1 point.	Min. 14 days Max. 6 months	33%	90%	25%	The higher fares shown apply for issues from 01.07.86
39.	British Caledonian/ Malaysian Airlines/ Continental Airlines	£2999	£1950	£1250		✓	21 days	Max. 4 within the USA. Max. 1 at any 1 point.	Min. 14 days Max. 1 year	33%	90%	10%	Supplement for Cunard line transatlantic voyage on the QE2 if required.
40.	American Airlines/ JAL	£2035	N/A	£1028			21 days	Min. 3 at least 1 of which must be in the Continental USA. Max. 1 at any 1 point.	Min. 8 days Max. 180 days	25%	90%	25%	Supplement for transatlantic Business Class by American Airlines.
41.	Singapore Airlines/ Air New Zealand	£3350	£2180	£1328		✓	21 days	Min. 3 Max. 1 at any 1 point. Only 1 Stopover or transfer allowed at Nadi.	Min. 14 days Max. 1 year	33%	90%	25%	
42.	Cathay Pacific/ Continental Airlines	£3189	£1980	£1395	✓		14 days	Min. 3 Max. 1 at any 1 point.	Min. 14 days Max. 6 months	33%	90%	10%	
43.	Pan Am/KLM	£2499	£1699	£1199	✓	S	14 days	Min. 3 Max. 1 at any 1 point.	Min. 14 days Max. 6 months	33%	90%	25%	Supplements for specified destinations.
44.	Thai Airways/ Air New Zealand	£3350	£2180	£1328		✓	21 days	Min. 3 Max. 1 at any 1 point. Only 1 Stopover or transfer allowed at Nadi.	Min. 14 days Max. 1 year	33%	90%	25%	
45.	British Caledonian/ JAL/Eastern Airlines	£2035	N/A	£1028	✓		21 days	a. Min.3 one of which must be in Canada/USA/Hawaii b. Max. 1 at any 1 point. c. Max. 4 Sectors within USA/ Canada.	Min. 14 days Max. 180 days	33%	90%	25%	1. Supplements for Mexico. 2. Supplement for travel in Executive Class by B.Cal.
46.	Northwest Orient/ Saudia	£2035	N/A	£1028	✓		14 days	Min. 3 Max. 1 at any 1 point.	Min. –14 days Max. 180 days	33%	90%	10%	
47.	JAL/Air Canada	£2035	N/A	£1028	✓		21 days	a. Min. 3 at least 1 of which must be in Canada.	Min. 8 days Max. 180 days	25%	90%	25%	Supplement for transatlantic travel in Business Class by Air Canada.

No.	Airline							Min/Max	33%	90%	25%	Notes
48.	Alitalia/Singapore Airlines/Eastern Airlines	£2287	£1916	£1360	✓	14 days	a. Max. of 4 within the USA (Max. 3 flight coupons) with 1 extra such Stopover permitted subject to the payment of extra charge. b. Max. 1 Stopover at any 1 point.	Min.–None Max. 6 months	33%	90%	25%	Supplement payable for a side-trip from Milan or Rome to selected points in Europe.
49.	British Airways/Qantas/United Airlines	£3400	£2333	£1399	✓	21 days	Min. 3 Max. 3 within USA/Canada. Max. 1 at any 1 point.	Min. 14 days Max. 1 year	33%	90%	25%	1. Supplement for travel commencing and terminating in Manchester. 2. Specified supplements for certain destinations. 3. Supplement in Economy Class for up to 3 Stopovers in USA/Canada £141. 4. Supplement for transatlantic leg by Concorde (available in First/Business Classes only).
50.	Air India/Continental Airlines	$4399	N/A	$2099		21 days	Max. 1 at any 1 point.	Min.–None Max. 1 year	33.3%	90%	25%	
51.	Delta Airlines/Singapore Airlines	£2035	£1634	£1028	✓	14 days	Min. 3	Min. 14 days Max. 6 months	33%	90%	25%	
52.	Delta Airlines/Thai Airways	£2035	$2999	£1028	✓	14 days	Min. 3	Min. 14 days Max. 6 months	33%	90%	25%	
53.	Air New Zealand Aerolineas Argentinas	N/A	N/A	£1328	✓	21 days	Max. 1 at any 1 point.	Min.–None	33.3%	90%	25%	This fare has been applied for but is not yet approved and political considerations may lead to disapproval.
54.	American Airlines/Qantas	£3350	£2180	£1465	✓	21 days	Min. 3 Min. 1 within USA/Canada. Max. 12 flight coupons within USA/Canada. Max. 1 at any 1 point.	Min. 8 days Max. 1 year	33%	90%	25%	1. Supplement for travel commencing and terminating in Manchester. 2. Supplement for transatlantic Business Class by American Airlines (applies to Economy Class fare only). AA apply 14 days min. stay.
55.	Canadian Pacific/Singapore Airlines	£2999	£1980	£1350	✓	14 days	Min. 3 Max. 1 at any 1 point.	Min. 14 days Max. 1 year	33%	90%	10%	Supplement for travel to Argentina, Chile or Peru.
56.	Delta Airlines/Qantas	£3350	£2180	£1465	✓	21 days	Min.3 at least 1 of which be in the USA. Max. 1 at any 1 point.	Min. 14 days Max. 180 days	33%	90%	25%	Supplement for travel commencing and terminating in Manchester. Qantas apply 8 day min. stay.
57.	Air New Zealand KLM	£3350	£2180	£1328	✓	21 days	Min. 3 Max. 1 at any 1 point. Only 1 Stopover or transfer allowed at Nadi.	Min. 14 days Max. 1 year	33.3%	90%	25%	

N.B. S = Supplement for travel via alternative directional routing.
Cathay Pacific are applying the higher fare levels shown for Fares 4, 30 and 38 now for travel from 01 July.
Prices correct at time going to press – May 1986.

AIR CANADA

Travelling in conjunction with Cathay Pacific, Singapore Airlines, Japan Airlines or Air New Zealand, Air Canada's four combinations represent some of the best value fares available. From only a little over £1000 ($1400) you can stop over in India, Hong Kong or Seoul, together with a wide choice of North American destinations.

Numerous side trips from Canada are available; for example, you can side-trip from Montreal to Miami, Florida, for well under £200 ($280). Stopovers are unlimited whichever option you choose and there is no minimum stay.

AIR INDIA

Founded in 1948 upon India's independence, Air India has earned a poor safety reputation which it doesn't entirely deserve. Offering two classes of ticket – First and Economy – Air India's destinations, in conjunction with North-West Orient, include all the major US and South East Asian cities.

Air India make a charge for young children (under two) of 10 per cent of the adult fare. In addition they insist on an unusually lengthy 21-day minimum stay. This option is one of the least attractive available. Air India's publicity for their Round the World fares is sadly no more than a photostat sheet which doesn't even include a contact number.

AIR NEW ZEALAND

Flying the Maori 'Koru' emblem, New Zealand's national airline offers two routings with year-long validity and unlimited stopovers. Both include New Zealand and the option of visiting numerous different cities within Australasia.

Air New Zealand produce a glossy *Good Night Book* each year – available free on application to any of their offices. An impressive range of worldwide accommodation options are listed at rates specially quoted for Air New Zealand travellers. Without a doubt one of the best accommodation services offered by any airline, most rooms are available on a 'walk in' basis when you reach a new destination. Rooms are available in four categories between Budget (no frills) from £15 ($21) for a double room and Luxury, up to £100 ($140) for a double per night.

BRITISH AIRWAYS

British Airways has a range of Round the World fares providing travel on its route network and in association with the flights of partner airlines. Currently British Airways offer four fares of this type from the United Kingdom – two in partnership with United Airlines, one with Qantas and one with Air New Zealand.

With British Airways' Round the World fares, passengers can fly to a wide range of cities, including stopovers in the Far East, Australia and New Zealand, the Pacific islands, the USA and Canada. British Airways offer a large choice of destinations and the maximum number of stopovers allowed on Round the World fares is unlimited.

The market for these fares is diverse and they are particularly attractive to passengers travelling for a second time who want to visit a larger number of cities than on their first journey. Round the World fares are popular in the Gulf and Middle East, whereby an expatriate's home leave can be combined with a holiday on the way. The fares are available for travel in First Class, Super Club and Economy, thus widening further their appeal.

Each of the partner airlines has particular benefits to offer the British Airways passenger. United Airlines has a very large route network in the USA offering a choice from over 100 cities. Qantas routes in India and the Far East link up with British Airways at Bombay, Bangkok, Singapore, Manila, Tokyo, Hong Kong and Peking – a wide range of popular stopover points. Air New Zealand provide good connections to the South Pacific islands.

British Airways Round the World passengers can choose additional, separately priced options to increase the travel available using these fares. Examples of these are:

—The British Airways/Qantas and British Airways/Air New Zealand fares provide the option of travel to a further three mainland North American cities with United Airlines (this option is free of charge with First Class and Super Club fares).

40   The Round the World Air Guide

—The British Airways/United Airlines and British Airways/Qantas fares provide the unique opportunity for First Class and Super Club passengers to travel on Concorde.

—The British Airways/United Airlines (South Pacific routing) fare has an option to visit up to three United Airlines destinations in Hawaii and mainland North America. (This option is free of charge in mainland North America with First Class and Super Club Round the World fares.) This fare also enables all passengers to visit both Hong Kong and Singapore or Hong Kong and Bangkok as part of its permitted routing – the only fare to offer this combination.

—The British Airways/United Airlines (North Pacific routing) fare offers the opportunity for Economy Class passengers to include a visit to South America.

—The British Airways/Qantas fare provides an option for travel via Africa and a free option to visit New Zealand.

Although in most countries airlines are able to determine their own prices, a new situation is emerging where some governments are directing fares and rules or are creating guidelines within which approval will be given. In the UK, the Civil Aviation Authority creates guidelines in this respect. British Airways Round the World fares (as at 1 September 1986) from the UK range from £1150 ($1610) for an Economy Class routing via the North Pacific to £3870 ($5418) for a First Class South Pacific routing also including the extra options of a Concorde sector and travel via Africa.

During 1985, British Airways carried approximately 10,000 passengers on Round the World fares. On average five stopovers were made and the most popular stopover points include London, New York, Los Angeles, Singapore, Hong Kong, Sydney, Melbourne, Perth, Auckland, Amsterdam and Paris.

In addition to origination points in the UK and Europe, Round the World fares can commence from specified cities in the Middle East, Far East, Australasia and North America. Further origin points are being evaluated and new fare options are being considered for the future – for example, with Cunard for travel on the *QEII*. For hotel accommodation at stopover points, British Airways offer a range of MiniStays.

BRITISH CALEDONIAN

British Caledonian offer five Round the World fares in conjunction with selected partner airlines. Three of the fares are available for northern hemisphere travel via Japan or Korea in conjunction with any one of a number of Asian airlines.

Two other arrangements are available for southern hemisphere travel via Australasia and the south-west Pacific in conjunction with Malaysian Airlines, Continental Airlines, Eastern Airlines and UTA. Fares are available from most areas of the world.

CANADIAN PACIFIC AIRLINES

An outgrowth of the famous Canadian Pacific railroads, CPAir offer six alternatives ranging from £1029 ($1440) Economy Class with Philippine Airlines to over £3000 ($4200) First Class with Cathay Pacific.

CPAir fares seem particularly susceptible to change but their choice of routings ought to cover most popular destinations. On South Pacific fares, routing via Auckland is possible for an additional charge. Validity and length of stay limits vary between routings.

CATHAY PACIFIC

Offering a range of eight basic routings, each with at least as many individual options, Cathay Pacific allow Round the World departures from four destinations around the world. In addition to routings which include all the popular northern and southern destinations we cover in this guide, Cathay Pacific also offer a splendid safari excursion in conjunction with Kenya Airways. Two such options are available, although both are expensive. From Hong Kong it is possible to travel via Bangkok–Bombay–Dubai–Nairobi–London and back to Bangkok.

Cathay Pacific have justly earned one of the highest in-flight service reputations and this alone makes their extensive glossy publicity worthy of careful consideration.

CHINESE AIRLINES

One of the newest airlines to enter the Round the World ticket market. With three options – all under £1000 ($1400) – Chinese Airlines represent one of the cheapest Round the World choices available. Each routing includes five or six preset options (for instance, London–Tokyo–Honolulu–Los Angeles–London from £795 ($1113) low season). No routing includes any destination within China itself.

These options, flying in conjunction with British Caledonian or Korean Airlines, are the cheapest scheduled Round the World fares at the time of writing. Remember that they do restrict you to strictly prearranged destinations, but there is no minimum stay.

JAPANESE AIRLINES

Offering to fly the Pacific in idyllic comfort, aboard luxurious B747 jets, Japanese Airlines invite potential travellers to fly the world with them in conjunction with TWA, British Caledonian, Air Canada or American Airlines.

About all the world's major air routes are covered by JAL's numerous Round the World options. Many departure points around the world are available – including London, Paris and various airports in Canada and the United States. One change in itinerary is allowed without charge and the use of JAL's magnificent Nikko Hotels International Group (96 around the world) is encouraged.

KLM ROYAL DUTCH AIRLINES

KLM Royal Dutch Airlines have introduced new Apex-type fares for Round the World itineraries in association with other international airlines. One of the world's oldest airlines (founded in 1919) KLM's Round the World tickets are valid from any UK airport served by KLM and her partners.

Fares start from £1028 ($1440) for Tourist Class, rising steeply for Business and Royal (First) Class. KLM allow for unlimited stopovers, with a minimum of three, and offer a wide range of routings in association with Pan Am, United Airlines, Air New Zealand and Continental. Connecting services are available with their extensive worldwide network via Amsterdam's Schiphol Airport. KLM are one of the world's most reliable airlines – but their Round the World ticket literature doesn't include details of any destinations!

KUONI

Kuoni, Britain's leading long-haul tour operator, offers two distinct kinds of Round the World trip. In addition to the 'conventional' type of routing (which can include Australia and Fiji from about £1400 Economy) they offer two outstanding itineraries travelling exclusively by Concorde.

Unlike subsonic Round the World tickets, Kuoni's Concorde options are inclusive package holidays of 17 nights each and featuring First Class hotels throughout. Only two departure dates will be offered each in 1987 and 1988 – 20 February and 16 October – so advance booking through their Dorking offices is essential.

Kuoni: Kuoni House, Dorking, Surrey RH5 4AZ, England.

MALAYSIAN AIRLINE SYSTEM

Originally operating a primarily domestic and Australasian service (albeit extensive), MAS are fast earning a reputation for an efficient and high quality service. In addition to a pair of Round the World options, MAS offer a choice of high standard hotel accommodation at discount rates. For stays within Malaysia these are particularly competitive – and include transfers between airport and hotel.

The Malaysian Airline System ticket option offers one further bonus. The cancellation fee is only 10 per cent of the fare, whereas most airlines insist on a hefty 25 per cent if you cancel less than three weeks before you're due to leave. Definitely the airline to consider if you plan to make South East Asia a highspot of your trip.

NORTH-WEST ORIENT

Started as an air mail carrier in 1926 and still expanding. North-West's glossy brochure is one of the clearest and best presented of any airline offering Round the World tickets. They also offer the most impressive range of Round the World routings, spanning the globe in conjunction with any other of 15 possible airlines.

North-West Orient's in-flight service is exemplary – one of the most elegant and luxurious available. First Class ticket holders enjoy Royal Doulton china, wide movie screens, high quality international cuisine – and arguably the fairest First Class ticket prices available (from only £2035 ($2849)). Definitely worth checking out since their ticket prices, and range of destinations, are (at the time of writing) unbeatable.

QANTAS

Qantas offer a variety of Round the World tickets in conjunction with some of the world's major airlines – particularly British Airways from the UK and also TWA, North-West Orient, American Airways and Delta.

Competitively priced and offering multiple stopovers, Qantas also offer the advantages of the new Qantas Connections Scheme. Available for all passengers who fly more than half their journey with Qantas, the Connections card gives the bearer access to over 2000 discounts in Australia and at major stopover points. Money can be saved on accommodation, shopping, sightseeing, ground transport and hundreds of Australian-bound services.

First Class, Business and Economy tickets start from £1328 ($1859) and are valid for one year so travelling with this Australian airline will be an ideal way to visit down under and see a lot of the world on the way.

SINGAPORE AIRLINES

Named the 'Easy World Fare', the Pan Am influence on Singapore Airlines' publicity is striking. Stacks of glossy, colourful, informative brochures are available promoting not only their Round the

World fare options but also details of a whole host of side trips and stay-away accommodation packages.

Singapore have no advance payment requirement but have a minimum stay condition of 14 days. All their routings (which in summer 1986 began at an amazing £860 ($1204) for a routing which included Australia) visit Singapore. Their stopover packages represent excellent value which, combined with impressive fare options and a good customer relations reputation, make Singapore Airlines one of the best all-round possibilities.

UNITED AIRLINES

Pan Am, the originator of the popular Round the World fare, sold its transpacific routes to United Airlines in 1985. United have managed to retain an imaginative range of destinations which include Seoul, Tokyo and Australasia.

Three stopovers (minimum) are required, but there is no maximum. A wide spectrum of exotic side trips are available – most at a standard £350 ($490) extra for Economy ticket holders and £600 ($840) for First Class. These optional extensions include Brazil, Chile, Uruguay, Mexico, the Bahamas, Trinidad, St Lucia, St Kitts and the US Virgin Islands.

Do-it-yourself Round the World ticket

It is possible to make up your own Round the World ticket, using the assortment of discount long-haul tickets which are available from bucketshops and local travel agencies. It must be borne in mind, however, that it will not be possible for you to put together your own ticket any more cheaply than the lowest priced tickets already available. If you plan to follow an itinerary similar to one already on offer by a major airline then you stand to save nothing since those commercially available are the cheapest.

Where do-it-yourself Round the World tickets really come into their own is when you decide to include a few more unusual destinations in your itinerary. Then you have the option of either booking a standard Round the World ticket and adding on a few more out-of-the-way destinations (for example Moscow or Peking) or else having an entirely original itinerary made up from standard scheduled or discounted flights.

If you do decide to completely make up your own itinerary then as much advance planning as possible will be necessary. In some cases you may only need to book one or two long-haul flights to have a whole lot of potential stopover points included. Travelling by Aeroflot to Entebbe, in Uganda, for example, travellers would have stopover options at Moscow and Mombasa en route.

Working out a series of complicated onward connections before you leave home, and over a long period of time, is not always easy. It will be nigh on impossible if you try to insist on discount tickets all the time. The adventurous Round the World traveller ought to consider booking no more than the first leg of his or her trip before leaving and, provided money and time are not pressing concerns, leave the rest to chance. You may opt initially for a bustling week in Prague or Budapest and only after that decide where to move on to next.

The combinations for a do-it-yourself Round the World traveller are endless but it is in your own best interests to be well versed in the potential options available to you. Call a few big airlines many months before you plan to leave and flick through their timetables. You may then decide to 'do' something like every western capital, or all the East European centres (American travellers will need to allow plenty of time for visas!). You may prefer to concentrate on one corner of the world – perhaps spending several months going overland in China or the Far East – and then take in a few big cities on the way home.

A number of airlines offer good value cut-price travel which is ideal for DIY Round the World travellers. Wardair have very competitive seats to Canada, and further afield within their global routings. Virgin Atlantic are one of the cheapest airlines flying across the Atlantic, with one-way fares between London, New York and Miami costing as little as £99 depending on what time of year you travel.

Virgin also offer an excellent Upper Class service to New York, Miami, and the Netherlands. For considerably less than other scheduled carriers, Virgin offer luxury handling all the way with a spacious lounge, complimentary newspapers, magazines, amenity kits and a full range of audio and movie entertainment. Complimentary chauffeur and helicopter links are also available to Upper Class passengers, and for every Upper Class flight made Virgin offer a free Economy ticket voucher valid for a subsequent trip across the same route.

Doing it all yourself will be more expensive, more time-consuming and administratively a much greater hassle than the alternative of simply buying a 'standard' Round the World ticket. But you will have unlimited freedom of where to visit and how long to spend in each destination. Doing it yourself is not easy, though, so do plan *well* in advance.

Classes

You will automatically have the option of buying either a First Class or Economy Class ticket. You may in addition have the option of buying a Business Class, an intermediary grade, ticket. As a general indication you can expect the following from each class:

FIRST CLASS

How you fly will be governed by how much you can afford to pay for your ticket. To fly First Class you will need to pay almost double the Economy Class ticket price but, in return, you will receive preferential handling and attention throughout your trip.

Not only will you have a greater baggage allowance (30 kg instead of Economy's 20 kg) but you will have a special check-in desk operating much quicker than normal check-ins, and access to the airline's First Class or VIP lounge. Your luggage too will receive preferential handling.

On board you will have a much larger and more comfortable seat, partitioned off from Economy Class seating and situated to the front of the cabin. Leg-room will be almost double that in Economy and, on long-haul flights, your seat will turn into a comfortable sleeperette.

You will be treated to the highest quality catering, served by professional cabin staff, and will have unlimited drinks and snack facilities at your disposal. Wardrobe space, leading newspapers and magazines, a free gift from the airline and – above all – total flexibility of travel arrangements, in terms of bookings and cancellations, are all included.

On a Round the World ticket, travelling first class entitles one to fewer restrictions and more stop-offs, on certain airlines.

BUSINESS CLASS

Super Club Class tickets (as British Airways call them) cost approximately an Economy Class ticket plus half the difference between First and Economy. A £2000 ($2800) First Class, Round the World ticket would therefore cost around £1000 ($1400) Economy and £1500 ($2100) Club Class.

The standard of service is markedly better than Economy, and only marginally less comfortable than First Class. Increasingly now at larger airports Club Class passengers have their own check-in desk (but no extra baggage allowance) and high quality meals served on board. Free drinks and much the same in-flight entertainment (newspapers, magazines and so on) are available. Club Class passengers also travel in their own, curtained-off part of the cabin and can usually expect favourable treatment if reservations have to be altered or rescheduled altogether.

ECONOMY CLASS

Travelling Economy does not entitle you to preferential treatment, special meals and check-in facilities or any of the other bonuses First and Club Class travellers pay extra for. You can, nevertheless, expect edible meals whenever the length of flight so justifies and liberal quantities of soft drinks on board. You should be treated with at least as much courtesy as any other class of passenger (you have, after all, still paid good money for your ticket!) but don't expect the luxury treatment reserved for First Class passengers.

For your Economy Class ticket price you will have an Economy Class seat (comfortable – but cramped if you're over six feet tall), in addition to all the basic facilities to survive your flight. By far the majority of all air travellers fly Economy Class and it is every bit as safe and convenient as any other class.

How to choose an airline

When planning a Round the World trip, your choice of airline will be of particular importance. As a potential traveller, you will be swiftly bombarded by glossy airline advertising if you wander into even one or two airline or travel agency offices. Each will tell you how wonderful their own service is, most likely showing the almost mandatory photograph of a smiling couple being served in-flight meals!

Obviously it makes sense to look for unbiased information and the most sensible starting point is personal recommendation from friends and colleagues. Most people have flown at some stage in their life, so ask around. Business colleagues who have done quite a bit of long-haul travelling are particularly useful to speak to.

Few travel agents will have experienced much long-haul air travel themselves, so their advice is unlikely to prove entirely reliable. Bear in mind that many airlines pay attractive rates of commission to travel agency staff, so any good advice they may have to offer could be a little coloured by personal motives.

When you finally come to choosing your airline, it boils down to a question of your own priorities. If you intend to travel First, or even Business Class, then it scarcely makes any difference which airline you choose. All the larger international ones – British Airways, Cathay Pacific, Qantas, Singapore Airlines, Japan Airlines, Thai International and so on – offer exemplary First and (where applicable) Business Class services. Your only criterion will be choice of route and ticket price since travelling Round the World will cost you anything between £2000 ($2800) and £3500 ($4900).

Economy Class passengers will have to consider the same price and routing criteria, though the ticket price disparity between Economy options offered by the various airlines is quite small – about £300 ($420) or equivalent for scheduled prices. The routing criteria in particular should be considered carefully. If you have a strong desire to visit New Zealand together with Australia, Singapore, and perhaps somewhere in the Caribbean as well, there are a limited number of airlines which will be able to meet your exact requirements.

Alternatively, if you have only a general idea of where you'd like to visit – perhaps the United States, Malaysia and Australia – then you ought to study the extras offered by each airline which can accommodate your choice of route. British Airways, for example, include Avis car hire at discount rates and offer a unique 'Circle Australia' domestic air fare allowing you to visit up to five cities for just £100 ($140). Qantas (with TWA), on the other hand, offer cut-price stopovers in Singapore from £12 ($17) a night on Round the World routings which include Australia.

When choosing the airline which will convey you on numerous long-haul flights, you may prefer to go for the carrier with the fewest stops. Not only will this reduce the potential for jet lag but it will lessen the risk of delays on the ground. Unless you specifically plan to stop over midway during a long-haul flight then go for the airline offering fewest stops.

Again, to use Australia as an example, British Airways and Qantas offer by far the fastest flights with just one or two stops en route (themselves appealing Round the World destinations, including Malaysia and the Gulf). The numerous Asian carriers which operate to Australasia offer finer in-flight service, including outstanding meals, but their flights involve more flying hours and so more stops.

Travellers to the Far East are now regularly presented with free drinks, free headsets and gifts regardless of what class of ticket or airline they have chosen. Some passengers have also found that the South East Asian carriers (including Singapore Airlines and Cathay Pacific) are better at looking after small children during the flight. On the other hand, because of the popularity of these airlines, you will seldom have empty seats beside you.

Most of the larger carriers will tempt prospective Round the World travellers with discount car hire or accommodation. Some may offer discount excursions but your travel agent (or the airline office) can best advise on up-to-date advantages. Remember that the tighter your personal choice of destinations the tighter your choice of airlines will be. If you at least try to avoid African, Middle Eastern and South American airlines, as a very general commendation, then you will already have avoided the bulk of the world's 'inadvisable' carriers.

You should always stick to scheduled airlines since an increasing number of regular charter organizers are entering the long-haul ticket market. Not only do you stand to lose money if you have to cancel or alter a particular reservation with a charter, but there is no guaranteeing that your particular flight exists at all. Stick to the larger, scheduled airlines which you've heard of before, unless you are *very* sure about the precise nature (including the safety and legality) of an unscheduled carrier.

How to read your ticket

Airline tickets are all printed and made out in a standard format –
usually in English. Even so, they can look incredibly complicated so
the following guide should help you translate your Round the
World ticket.

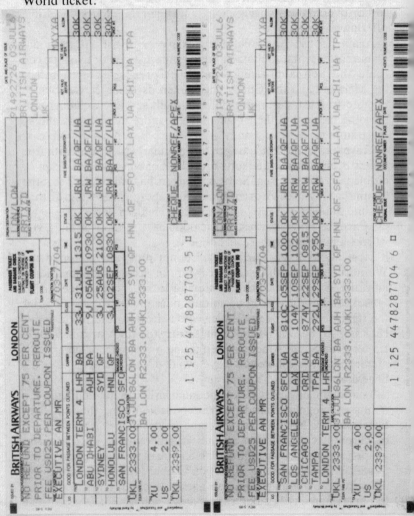

1. **Endorsements/Restrictions** – Indicates whether you have an off-peak ticket (sometimes known as a Key Fare) which disqualifies you from certain peak-time flights. Shouldn't affect Round the World travellers.
2. **Name of Passenger** – Your surname, initial and title. Should coincide with that on your passport.
3. **Coupon Not Valid After** – As it says, though this will normally be 180 days or a year.
4. **Date of Issue**
5. **Fare Calculation** – Will show the price for each additional sector but may not itemize costs for each scheduled Round the World sector. Will also detail the carrier for each sector abbreviated to two letters (e.g. BA would indicate British Airways, CX for Cathay Pacific and so on. They are not always obvious).
6. **Date and Place of Issue** – Agency or airline stamp which is essential to validate a ticket. Keep a note of this information in case you lose your ticket.
7. **Airports** – Departure and destination airports. You will probably need two or three actual tickets so keep them all safe and in order.
8. **Fare Basis** – As for 5.
9. **Baggage Allowance**
10. **Actual Baggage Weight** – Number of pieces (and weight) filled in by check-in desk.
11. **Carrier** – Airline identification code and flight number. All scheduled flights have unique numbers which should be remembered at departure airports until called.
12. **Class** – Ticket class: F – First Class; J or C – Club Class; Y – Economy; M – Special Economy or Tourist Class; R – Supersonic (Concorde).
13. **Departure Date** – The first date must be filled in, but obviously successive ones may be left to your own discretion. Don't forget to reserve onward flights when you land!
14. **Departure Flight Time**
15. **Status** – OK – confirmed seat reservation; RQ – space requested but not confirmed; NS – infant not occupying a seat; SA – subject to space being available; OPEN – reservation refused or not requested.
16. **Total Fare** – May be broken down already (at 5) into local

currencies. This box will show total fare paid in whatever currency you paid in.

17. **Ticket Number** – Keep a note of this unique number safely. It shows airline code number and ticket serial number.

Consumer protection

The greatest single risk every traveller by air takes, no matter where or when he flies, is that of being overbooked. The problem of passengers booking flights and then not claiming their seat ('no shows' as airlines refer to them) costs the airlines dearly. Many businessmen, for example, book themselves into three or four flights in order to be sure of having a guaranteed seat. As a result, airlines anticipate this potential loss of revenue by overbooking by as much as a quarter again of the total number of seats available.

On the vast majority of flights, the overbooking principle works so that all passengers with confirmed reservations can actually fly. Very occasionally there will be a problem, and you ought to bear in mind that virtually no air ticket *guarantees* you a seat – it can merely assure you of one being available and, if it isn't, too bad.

British Airways are leading in a new era of issuing firm seat guarantees, and this policy has worked well so far on their busy British domestic routes. Their publicity promises full-fare passengers a seat even supposing they need to lay on an extra flight just for you.

Present your ticket at check-in as soon as possible, to avoid being 'bumped'. Passengers who check in last are most likely to lose their seats. Rarely can you be bumped (told no seats are left) once you've been given a boarding card and been allocated a seat number.

If you travel First Class, or Business Class, then you will have priority over other passengers. First Class passengers are never completely bumped off a flight. As a last resort they will be downgraded to Business or even Economy Class and a lower class passenger bumped in their place.

No account is taken of the urgency of a particular passenger's journey. Vital business meetings, family crises and so on are largely irrelevant – unless you are prepared to make a scene in which case the airline might miraculously 'find' a spare seat in order to get rid of you! In America passengers are asked to volunteer to be bumped. Those who do are offered payment by the airline, but before this is accepted it is advisable to check precisely when the next available flight will be and whether any additional expenses (hotels, meals, telephone calls) will be paid.

Rules about claiming against airlines who bump you vary worldwide between the British and American examples. If you are bumped from a British airline then you have little grounds for complaint provided that you eventually reach your destination *within* a few hours of the original, scheduled, arrival time.

If you are delayed longer, then all passengers are entitled to a 50 per cent refund on the one-way fare for the particular route you were delayed on. At the moment, the maximum refund is £100 ($140) payable by a Miscellaneous Charges Order which can be cashed at any airline office. European rules, outside Britain, are governed by the Association of European Airlines but broadly speaking they are similar to those offered by their British counterparts.

Many Far Eastern and less developed countries do not recognize the passengers' right to denied-boarding compensation. If this happens to you then there is little which can be done other than loud protests to the appropriate airline office at the time. You could follow the matter up in writing when you return home but don't be too hopeful once even a week or two have elapsed from the departure date in question.

It is worth considering a claim against an airline if you feel you have been unfairly treated in any other way. But, if you read the regulations and conditions inside every airline ticket, you will soon realize how limited airline liability is.

No matter how much any airline's inefficiency costs you in time, hassle, lost business deals, lost hotel nights or whatever, they are *never* obliged to pay you anything. If you have a complaint then it ought to be made, first of all, on the spot. Ask for the cabin service manager if you have cause to complain on board.

If this fails to bring a satisfactory answer to your complaint then write to the Customer Relations Manager of the airline. Although not legally obliged, all major airlines will at least look into genuine complaints and possibly offer some limited compensation: a small travel voucher or token cash refund. Your letter of complaint should be brief, simple, polite and include the date, flight number, location and route of the problem flight concerned.

If this fails to satisfy you, then you ought to contact the Air Transport Users' Committee. Americans should contact the Office of Consumer Affairs, Department of Transportation, Room 10405, 400 Seventh Street, Washington DC 20590. Send them all correspondence (including copies of your own letters) which you've had with the airline and let them do the rest.

Just to close on a morbid note – if you were to have a fatal accident during your Round the World trip then your relatives could sue the carrier for every last cent. Under American laws, there is no upper limit on airline liability. There is with other national airlines.

Where to buy your ticket

Where you decide to buy your ticket depends very much on how much you are prepared to pay for it. If you are content to pay the listed, scheduled price quoted by the airline then you ought to go ahead and make your purchase through a travel agent known to you.

You may, alternatively, choose to buy direct from the airline concerned. Buying through either of these outlets, and preferably by credit card, you will stand very little chance of losing money, whether by criminal or any other means should something go wrong with your booking.

If you are looking for a bargain ticket then you ought to scan the national (and local if you live in a city) press for details of discount ticket offers. Living in London particularly, you will have the advantage of being able to scour the bucketshop capital of the world. You are guaranteed to find at least one bucketshop offering Round the World tickets at considerable discount. Try Columbus, 85 London Wall, London EC2M 7AD (tel 01-638-1101) or Rebo Travel, Commonwealth House, 15/17 New Oxford Street, London WC1A 1BH (tel 01-242-5555).

You do stand a slightly higher risk of coming across fraudulent ticket dealers if you choose either the press advertisement or bucketshop option but the money you stand to save can be quite considerable – normally up to a third off the airlines' own scheduled prices. The proportion of fraudulent bucketshop dealers is falling.

DOING YOUR OWN RESEARCH

Once you have decided what ticket you want to go for, the next decision will be which one of the three options to go for – travel agent, bucketshop or press advertisement offer.

It is sensible to consider using a good travel agent to get the benefit of expert advice but a *Holiday Which?* survey in 1980 concluded that these were thin on the ground. Seven years on the picture is no less pessimistic, except that there are so many travel agents around now that you will be able to find a reputable one provided you're prepared to visit several.

Bucketshops and press advertisements are less easy to assess since overall standards are difficult to pin down. The value of doing your own research, well in advance of committing yourself to purchasing a Round the World ticket, cannot be overstated. The following few sections will give you some basic information about all three options but, at the end of it all, the final choice remains your own. Think carefully before parting with a great sum of money on a particular Round the World ticket.

TRAVEL AGENTS

• **What they do:** Unless you are travelling as a real independent, dealing direct with airline offices, the chances are that you will come into contact with a travel agent when you book your Round the World trip. Some travel agents are small, single-owner shops; the majority are part of large nationwide networks such as, in Britain, Thomas Cook, Hogg Robinson and Lunn Poly, who have offices in most of the larger towns.

In all, there are over 6000 travel agencies in Britain representing the retail arm of the travel trade. They act as agents of the numerous tour operators and are in the business purely and simply to sell these operators' tickets and holidays. Precisely what each agency sells varies but most emphasize that they are selective and deal only with airlines and operators whom they believe offer good service. The majority of travel agents will, nevertheless, still sell a wide range of Round the World tickets.

Travel agents make their living on the commission they earn from selling all the forms of package holidays and travel tickets they can offer. For each booking they make they earn a specific commission, normally around 10 per cent on the average holiday. The larger national travel agencies – including Hogg Robinson, one of the specialists in arranging independent Round the World tickets – sell a higher proportion of tickets and so are able to forge a better bargain with the major operators. The larger agencies, in turn, are thereby able to make themselves a higher rate of commission. The commission on a scheduled airline ticket is 9 per cent, and on a Round the World ticket 8 per cent. Most types of ticket do not cost any less to the customer even if you buy them direct from the airline company.

A specific Round the World ticket, for example, will cost the same from the airline as from the agent. There might be a difference between airlines for a broadly similar choice of Round the World routings, but this difference will be standard regardless of where you eventually decide to buy your ticket and in these cases the choice comes down to a matter of personal preference between particular airlines.

As well as being able to offer sound advice about which ticket would best suit your needs, reputable travel agents should be able to offer a range of other services as well. Among other things, your agent should be able to organize the following for you: the arrangement of adequate insurance to cover your specific trip, ensuring that it is both comprehensive and competitively priced; give you advice about passports and all-important visas which are essential for many long-haul, non-European countries, including the United States and Australia for British citizens; make hotel bookings and car-hire arrangements, as well as overnight train sleeper reservations, if necessary in order for you to arrive in good time for an early morning flight; and organize foreign currency and traveller's cheques. Currency regulations are another minefield a good agent should guide you through on entering and leaving specific countries.

The range of tickets and holidays offered by each travel agent varies enormously. There is no easy way of ensuring that any one agent is offering you the best advice on long-haul or Round the World tickets, but our experience suggests that it is well worth calling on *at least* two or three travel agents before finally committing yourself.

Many airlines and travel companies have, in the past, offered impressive incentives to travel agency staff for each ticket sold. A high street store gift voucher, for example, or discounted air travel, or even a free holiday in recognition of having sold two or three dozen of a particular airline's tickets. There is quite a risk that if you restrict your choice of travel agents to simply your nearest, or one known to you locally, you might not be made aware of the full range of airlines, ticket options or potential routings available. Equally, you may well encounter a very one-sided view of the choices open. A single ten-minute chat with one inexperienced young travel agency employee, who may well be trying to sell you the particular ticket he'd like you to buy in order to pick up his fringe bonus, could paint a very different picture from the reality of options available. Check round *all* the agencies in your area before making up your mind.

• **What is ABTA?:** Most travel agents in Great Britain belong to the Association of British Travel Agents (ABTA). ABTA is the professional trade association body for all Britain's travel agents and tour operators, the vast majority of whom are members. Originally founded in 1950, ABTA was essentially designed to promote the interests of its travel membership. ABTA serves as a lobbying body to British and foreign governments alike, whilst at the same time negotiating rates and conditions with airlines, shipping companies, hotel groups, railway networks and so forth on behalf of its members.

ABTA has a code of practice for members and regulations governing standards of training and efficiency among travel agency staff. This is, in itself, quite an important consideration since travel agencies are traditionally amongst the lowest paying of all employers. Poor pay tends to discourage staff from staying and makes it equally difficult to attract well-qualified employees. Particularly outside the large multiple agency chains, like Thomas Cook, A.T. Mays and Hogg Robinson where ABTA's training standards are frequently surpassed, there is seldom much of a career structure and scarcely any chance of job advancement.

ABTA does now have a National Training Board, established five years ago in 1982, which will be able to concentrate on training young people for the travel and tourism trade once it becomes fully operational. It will be aimed at students in those colleges which offer training courses for the travel industry at the moment, although ABTA does already operate some examination courses of its own. The Certificate of Travel Agency Competence (COTAC) is one of the few travel agency qualifications now in existence, and will usually be the framed certificate frequently seen hanging by a travel agent's desk.

In many ways, the principles holding ABTA together are far from ideal. It does, after all, represent both the holiday companies and travel agents – and their own aims and principles are seldom in total harmony. The British holiday business amounts to a closed shop, since virtually all of her 6000 travel agency offices (who are members) are permitted only to sell the holidays of the tour operator members of ABTA.

From the paying customer's point of view, the position is good since membership of ABTA means that an agent agrees to abide by their tight codes of conduct, worked out in conjunction with the governmental Office of Fair Trading. Member agencies and tour operators are required to conform to the Code of Practice by way of a £5000 or £10,000 customer protection bond when they join. Companies which breach the strict ABTA codes can be cautioned, fined, or in extreme cases expelled from the Association altogether.

For the individual customer, ABTA offers financial security since, quite simply, if the travel agency goes bankrupt, or ceases trading for any reason whilst holding your money, then you are assured of receiving a refund or being offered another holiday. In really extreme cases, such as when a travel agency goes out of business whilst you are actually abroad on holiday, then your direct return trip home is guaranteed. If you buy your Round the World ticket from an ABTA member, then you can be sure that they are covered by a bond intended to provide protection to travellers should the company cease trading at any point and for any reason.

If you have bought an accommodation inclusive Round the World holiday, rather than simply the more flexible ticket on its own, then the chances are that you will be offered an alternative rather than a straight refund if your ABTA travel agency goes out of business. Such financial collapses are rare, but if you are buying an inclusive Round the World holiday from a non-ABTA agency then it is *vital* that you check what financial protection is offered.

In such cases, it is possible to arrange insurance which will cover you against the unlikely bankruptcy of your travel agency, but this additional precaution would be unnecessary if you decide to buy from an ABTA member. It is interesting to remember that in 1982, following a specific action brought by the Office of Fair Trading, the High Court in London decided that ABTA operated a restrictive practice. The practice, however, worked in the public interest, through the level of consumer protection offered to customers, and further action was not deemed necessary.

• **ASTA:** The American Society of Travel Agents has over 6500 member travel agencies representing over 8500 agency locations throughout the US and Canada. Among the membership requirements are stipulations that an applicant must have been in business, under its present ownership and control, for at least three years, and that in the year prior to ASTA admission, the applicant must have earned 50 per cent of his business income or have gross receipts of least $500,000 stemming directly from the operation of the travel agency. Such requirements indicate that ASTA members are not fly-by-night outfits. They imply that members have established successful track records with clients – reflected by their longevity of operation and amount of gross annual sales – that they get the repeat business requisite for financial stability and growth, bills are paid, and the agencies are not on the brink of financial collapse.

To be fair, not being an ASTA member is not an indication either of unprofessionalism or financial instability, just as being a member is no guarantee of competence or reliability. But ASTA is the travel industry's most important professional organization; it's likely that its membership includes most of the better travel agencies nationwide. Members can be identified by an ASTA seal affixed to an agency window, door, or some other highly visible place. The design is an oval globe with the ASTA initials on it in big bold capital letters. You can't miss it. If you don't see it, ask an agent inside if the agency belongs, but chances are it doesn't.

If you'd like to know more about the society and its members, ASTA offers two informative brochures: *What Is a Travel Agent?*

and *Answers to Questions Most Frequently Asked About ASTA*. (See page 69 for the address.)

The Institute of Certified Travel Agents is a nonprofit educational organization, not a travel trade association like ASTA. It sponsors a rigorous four-part travel management programme that usually takes two years to complete. Subjects include tourism, marketing, sales, and business management, with each course concluded by a four-hour exam. Candidates must also write an original research paper. To be eligible for certification, a person must have worked in the industry for at least five years. Upon certification a travel agent is entitled to use the monogram CTC – for Certified Travel Counselor – learn of the CTCs in your area, contact Louis Tilles, Director of Institute Relations, Institute of Certified Travel Agents, 148 Linden Street, Wellesley, MA 02181 (617 237-0280).

• **What is IATA?:** The other official looking symbol which you will frequently see inside travel agencies is that of the International Air Transport Association (IATA) to which most international airlines belong. Originally founded in 1919, IATA has survived many sweeping changes since the days when air travel was in its infancy.

Being a member of ABTA does not allow travel agencies automatically to sell IATA airline tickets. The most recent figures available, January 1986, show that only some 3094 ABTA agencies were appointed by IATA to sell tickets for its 108 active members. As with ABTA, the conditions for IATA appointment relate specifically to staff qualifications and financial stability. The requirement for agencies appointed to provide a bond is less strict and is, in any case, geared more towards the protection of the airlines than the consumer.

Traditionally not only aircraft fares are decided by IATA, but also baggage allowances, in-flight service, seat space and the all-important travel agent's commissions. IATA also sets conditions of carriage for passengers and baggage, stemming from the Warsaw Convention in 1929 which is still detailed inside the front or back cover of all airline tickets.

Until relatively recently, IATA was a powerful cartel which really worked like a closed shop against the practical interests of most travellers by fixing unnecessarily high fares and limiting in-flight service. Even into the 1970s, IATA tried to ban in-flight music headsets and movies arguing, illogically, that this could damage the interests of many airlines by encouraging competition!

Unlike ABTA, IATA offers little in the way of services or direct ticket guarantees to individual customers. It is, after all, the trade association of airlines offering scheduled services and thereby an important influence on most of the airlines offering Round the World tickets. Significantly, not every world airline has become an IATA member. Singapore Airlines and Cathay Pacific, for instance, both offer Round the World routings from London yet neither have become IATA members.

In short, you as a fare-paying customer may have little option about whether or not you buy your ticket from an IATA member. But equally, its power as a closed-shop association has been reduced markedly by de-regulation in recent years and your rights will not be affected one way or another if your eventual Round the World airline choice is a member of IATA.

BUCKETSHOPS

Buying from a bucketshop is an increasingly popular way of purchasing cheap air travel tickets. Concentrated largely in London, but increasingly in other towns like Coventry and Birmingham, bucketshops are unlicensed retail travel shops which sell discounted airline tickets bought in quantity from the airlines themselves and sold directly to individual customers. (In the US, New York, Los Angeles and San Francisco are the big cities for bucketshops, the last two being particularly good for transpacific deals.)

Although it sounds like something out of a Christmas pantomime, the term 'bucketshop' has fairly shaky origins in the Boston Stock Exchange of the late nineteenth century. Then it was used in a derogatory manner to describe those unlicensed brokers who dealt in valueless share certificates to unsuspecting rich clients by the bucketload.

Understandably, bucketshop proprietors dislike the connotations associated with the term, preferring instead to regard themselves more as discount travel agents specializing in bargain air travel. But although the bucketshop tag has firmly stuck to these popular ticket agencies, if you choose to deal with one, it is worth bearing in mind that the original pejorative meaning no longer applies.

Finding a bucketshop may present something of a problem to someone who has never dealt with one before. Traditionally, bucketshops have operated with discretion and a large number of people, including the growing number of regular business users, find their way to one through word of mouth. The business tends to be conducted in near secrecy because, by its very nature, bucketshop trading breaks established ticket trade agreements. As a result, virtually none of the 'established' bucketshops will have street-front shop premises. Do not be surprised if a given address turns out to be on the second or third floor of an office block, or a hundred yards down a gloomy passageway.

For better or for worse, it is a vital condition of lasting trade links with the airlines concerned that bucketshops maintain a low profile to avoid upsetting the established market in air ticket sales.

Most potential bucketshop customers find their way there through personal recommendation. Ask around a few friends and colleagues whom you know to be fairly regular travellers abroad.

Finding a bucketshop by accident is highly unlikely, but since traditionally they have dealt mostly with ethnic traffic the business has developed more strongly in areas with large immigrant populations. In central London, for example, there are now well over a hundred bucketshops. Equally, the business has developed well in high density immigrant areas of London like Paddington, Soho, Hounslow, Earls Court and so on, where many bucketshops became established upon the sale of cheap tickets to families returning to Pakistan and larger Commonwealth countries, like India.

If you can't find someone to give you a first-hand recommendation, then your next best course of action is either to call an airline direct or scour the press advertisements. A surprising number of airline companies will be more than willing to put you in touch with the bucketshops which they deal with. With regard to Round the World trips, this is particularly the case with Far Eastern airlines, although the larger African and most Eastern European airlines should also be able to help you find a discount outlet.

Once you've decided to contact an airline direct, try to get hold of the sales manager's office and ask to be given the name of the airline's 'consolidator'. This curious *façon de parler* is the term which the airline gives to the main agency which handles the distribution of its discounted tickets. Don't ask an airline specifically about 'bucketshops' since they probably won't acknowledge the term.

As far as British law is concerned, buying from a bucketshop is perfectly safe. Some potential bucketshop customers are put off buying discount tickets because they fear that there is something illegal about them. In fact this, technically, is the case although it *must* be stressed that it is the retailer and *not* the customer who is breaking the law. There is nothing remotely illegal, from the customer's point of view, about purchasing a Round the World (or any other kind of ticket) from a bucketshop.

Although legally safe, determining whether or not a bucketshop is reputable and financially honest is less easy. Many people are, quite rightly, initially reluctant to buy tickets from these outlets because they feel they will be sold-out or defrauded in some way. But the endless stories of bucketshop customers being stranded abroad, or told at the airport that their flight doesn't even exist, are wildly exaggerated. A Department of Trade working party looked into the question of discounted air fares and concluded that nearly all the purchasers of discounted tickets were satisfied with their bargain.

• **How do you know a bucketshop is safe?:** As with every other type of discounted bargain, it is essential to be cautious before parting with a great sum of money. Follow a few simple safety procedures before buying your ticket and you will save yourself the risk of losing out in the end.

First of all, check round a few high street (ABTA approved) travel agencies. Compare the price of the ticket you want before going to a bucketshop. That way you'll at least know how much (or possibly how little) you stand to gain by buying from a bucketshop.

Once you've found your 'discount agency' ask a lot of questions. Find out which airline (or airlines) your ticket will cover, find out which airports you'll be using and how many changes are necessary. Make notes as you go along so as you're 100 per cent clear exactly what you will be paying for. Ask if your fare has any restrictions: minimum stay requirements or a lengthy advance booking period could jeopardize your self-planned Round the World trip. Make sure that you can change or cancel your reservation once you've paid for the ticket. If not, you could lose a lot of money and sleep for no good reason.

When you eventually pay, try to insist on paying by credit card. If you do so with an Access or Visa card issued for the first time after July 1977 then your purchase will be protected by the Consumer Credit Act. Try to avoid paying all the cash in advance – suggest a 10 per cent deposit and if a bucketshop *insists* on a full payment up front then think seriously about the risk you might be about to take. Do not risk paying fully in advance before receiving your ticket.

In the US you are protected when paying by credit card because you don't have to pay the bill if you have not received the service you've paid for. This protects you against fraud by the agency as well as default (bankruptcy) by the airline – no minor matter these days.

One last tip: once you've made a firm booking with a bucketshop, and handed over your deposit, give the airline a ring themselves. There's no need to go into great details about where you bought your ticket, or how much you paid, but if the bucketshop was genuine (as most will be) then your confirmed flight reservation should be registered on the airline's central computer network, having come via the bucketshop dealer's own booking computer. If it isn't, query again, making sure the flight you've booked actually exists at a specific time and date. If the airline still hasn't heard of you, then stop your deposit cheque, contact your credit card company or kick up a fuss with the original dealer. Remember, the bigger the 'bargains', the bigger the chances are that you might be getting taken to the cleaners.

• **Why do airlines sell to bucketshops?:** The easy answer to why airlines end up selling tickets to bucketshops is because they need the money. The reason there are bucketshops at all stems from the reality that airlines agree long in advance, with their national governments, that they will not sell their tickets at rates below the official level. These rates are usually agreed, between the airlines, through IATA. Many airlines will deny that they have any dealings with discounted fares, but the reality remains that many have been *forced* to sell a percentage at discounted rates in order to fill their empty seats. In 1983, for example, there were a staggering 222 million seats left empty on scheduled flights by the world airline members of IATA. Taken together, that could have meant everyone living in Great Britain could have had, at least, a pair of free Round the World tickets taking in some of the world's most exotic locations!

• **Bucketshops: pros and cons:** Once you've found your bucketshop, in all probability you will receive an impressive price offer for the particular airline ticket you choose to buy. Without a doubt, the potential bargain you, as a customer, stand to make is the single biggest 'pro' in favour of bucketshops. (Remember that it isn't illegal either to buy, or to travel, on an illicit ticket. It's only illegal for the airline to sell it.)

Caution must be exercised, nevertheless, if you choose to deal with a bucketshop. At one level, for example, tickets may well involve changes of aircraft along the route and roughing it on a less than high quality carrier. Syrian Arab Airlines is one best avoided, even at discount prices, since delays of less than three to four hours are rare; flights are usually overbooked; and long waits at Damascus Airport are not regarded by them as a problem.

Much of dealing successfully with bucketshops is a case of knowing whether a particular airline is any good. On the whole, travel agents will give fairly sound advice about their airlines if they can offer a choice. Bucketshops seldom will but, as a thumbnail guide to which carrier you may be offered, Far East airlines are reckoned to be excellent, as are American and Australian. The European ones tend to be almost as good, the Middle East ones range from fair to terrible, and the Africans adequate to nightmare. Remember also that, whichever airline you choose, your ticket will have no validity with other airlines if you cancel.

Be careful too that your bucketshop dealer is reliable. *Don't* pay more than a deposit until you receive your ticket, and take great care that it is *exactly* what you want. There is no comeback with bucketshops, unless they're members of ABTA, so if your dealer turns out to be one of life's dangerous con-men, then you stand to lose 100 per cent. Check and double-check your ticket's validity, especially where a combination of routings are involved, and think very carefully before parting with any money.

PRESS ADVERTISEMENTS

Virtually all national newspapers and magazines, together with many local weeklies, publish large numbers of advertisements for cheap air travel. There is no easy way of finding your way around this Aladdin's Cave of discount travel, but you could start by going out and buying all the national Sunday papers one weekend. In theory, at least, you will then have several thousand discount flight options to choose from. Have a look at the *Observer*'s 'Flight Directory' section, in the 'Weekend' section of the paper, or try the wide range of long- and short-haul destinations advertised in the *Sunday Times* or *Sunday Express*. American readers should read the travel sections of the Sunday edition of the big city papers, i.e. the *New York Times*, the *CA Times*, the *Chicago Tribune*.

Daily newspapers also publish adverts for cheap air travel, although their choice tends to be less extensive than the Sunday papers. Many of the more successful bucketshops place adverts in the quality daily papers, and the classified sections of *The Times*, *Guardian*, and *Daily Telegraph* are worth checking out. Many advertisements in the quality dailies are placed by agencies who tend, on the whole, to deal with legitimate discount fares. These will include cheap charter seat fillers, semi-scheduled flights (which tend to be regular charters) and also the standard Apex discount tickets.

The tabloid papers, like the *Sun* and *Daily Mirror*, don't have much to offer. Like their news content, their advertisements don't go in for a lot of detail or facts, and so, unlike the travel adverts in the quality papers, the tabloids will almost never have long lists of cheap flights available. Even the tabloid Sunday papers, like the *Sunday People* and *News of the World*, will have far fewer air travel offers than their quality rivals.

• **Useful magazines:** As well as the daily and Sunday newspapers already mentioned, there are a wide range of magazines and other publications available which carry useful air travel advertisements. Amongst the best of those are *TNT*, *LAM* and *Exchange and Mart*. Published every Thursday, *Exchange and Mart* has an extensive travel section offering some of the best air travel deals around. Most popular magazines now have a regular travel section, including many weekly women's periodicals.

Three of the better magazines offering discount air travel advertising are *Time Out*, the news and entertainment magazine exclusively for London, *Business Traveller* and *Executive Travel*. Both the latter two are based in London and it might be worth giving them a ring if you can't get a copy of either. *Business Traveller* is based at 49 Old Bond Street (01-629 4688) and *Executive Travel* at 9 Kingsway (01-379 7995).

If you live in one of the larger towns or cities outside London, check your local weekly newspaper or freesheet for cut-price ticket offers. Even if you do live in London, these local publications can often turn up an interesting advert now and again.

In America, most national publications will regularly feature good air travel offers. There are literally hundreds to choose from, but one of the best is the New York based *European Travel and Life*. Look out for *Travelhost* in hotels and airports throughout the US.

• **Reading between the lines:** Virtually all press avertisements for cheap air travel will have the word 'lowest' or 'cheapest' in them somewhere. Failing that, 'bargain' crops up with monotonous regularity and if you see the classic sales cliché 'absolutely unbeatable' then you can just about guarantee that it won't be.

Reading between the lines is a relatively simple task – but you *must* have a fairly clear idea what sort of Round the World trip you want to book before you begin. A few press adverts will feature Round the World trips, usually with a starting price of at least a hundred pounds or so less than the lowest offered by most airlines. Start with those but beware of the little word 'from'. One specific Round the World trip offered recently, 'from £660', included scarcely the most basic of ticket guarantees and frequent aircraft changes. For a hundred or two more, however, there was no problem cutting out the frequent changeovers or issuing a few assurances about what to do if ticket details had to be changed.

As with bucketshops, follow your common sense. Look out for the few press adverts which quote an ABTA or Air Travel Organiser's Licence (ATOL) number, or say that credit card bookings are acceptable. That way you'll have some guarantee that your money is secure if the advertiser goes out of business. Ring up a lot of advertisers and negotiate details; after all, most of their sales tend to be one-off single or return tickets and a Round the World combination should give them quite a tidy profit. At all times make sure you know precisely what you are being offered – what airline you'll be using, how many changes you need to make and so on. Above all, if you're patching together your own independent Round the World ticket from offers in press advertisements, then make sure it all fits together before you leave. Double-check ticket validity by calling the airlines themselves since it is no laughing matter to suddenly realize you are stranded at Sydney Airport with nothing more than an onward ticket from Hong Kong to London!

One of the easiest things you ought to do – and this isn't obvious to everyone – is to fully read *all* the press advertisements on a particular page if you have a fairly clear idea where you want to travel to first. One recent collection of adverts in the *Observer*, for example, contained no less than a dozen bargain return fares to Los Angeles. The most striking advert was one which began 'LOWEST ROUND THE WORLD FARES WORLDWIDE' and proceeded to list a dozen destinations from Dallas to Bangkok. The return fare quoted to Los Angeles was £339 (compared with standard British Airways Economy return of £840 or £500 standby). Yet a closer study of the smaller adverts on the same page revealed no less than seven *lower* fares to Los Angeles – from £329 right down to £289.

Of course, low prices alone are no indication of the type or quality of airline you'd be flying with, but are nevertheless a reasonable indication of the importance of looking at whole pages of adverts very closely. It is vital that you shop around before finally buying a discount airline ticket. But remember also that the fares available through newspaper and magazine adverts are not necessarily cheaper than those available from an efficient high street travel agent.

Airport information

When you enter any of the world's major international airports for the first time you will feel as though you've entered a whole new city. All the larger airports, described in Part Two of this guide, have a standard range of every conceivable service and facility to make your visit there as trouble-free and enjoyable as possible. The needs of virtually every type and class of traveller, as well as the rapid daily turnaround of international airline staff and the thousands of people who flock constantly to the world's airports to meet, or say goodbye, to travellers are catered for.

Airports are the interchange points between all air services, and the point of connection between every mode of surface travel – main-line passenger train, city link bus services, taxi operators, underground trains and the inevitable package tour pick-up coaches. Airports are also businesses which must function efficiently and effectively for all those who come into contact with them. As the levels of air passenger and freight traffic have increased remarkably in the last 10 years, so too has the range of facilities and services offered by the world's major international airlines.

The following section will provide a detailed rundown on all the facilities intending air travellers can expect at any of the major airports described in this book, as well as services provided and some tips about what to do if things go wrong whilst you're actually at the airport.

AIRPORT TERMINALS

• **Information common to all airport terminals:** The larger and busier international airports will remain open 24 hours a day throughout the year. Most of these will have more than one terminal building, perhaps with one terminal serving internal (domestic) flights and another terminal serving international and intercontinental flights. Heathrow Airport in London, for example, now has four main terminal buildings after the impressive new Terminal Four was opened in April 1986. Alternatively, many airports will have separate terminals for all Departures and Arrivals, regardless of their destination or place of origin of their flight.

An important division worth remembering at airport terminals is that between the general (non-travelling) public and air travellers, whether coming or going. Try to avoid getting caught amongst anxious grannies and plane spotters when your check-in deadline draws close. The air and landward areas of a terminal are normally divided by Passport Control (for Departures) and Customs Control (for Arrivals).

All major international airport terminals display information common to them all, including flight destination boards, check-in details for passengers and baggage, and baggage claim areas.

● **Flight Destination Boards:** One of the most striking features of any international terminal will be the Flight Destination Board. This is one of the permanent facilities available to passengers and a constantly changing source of information about the comings and goings of all flights.

In many cases, a single electronically controlled flipboard in the centre of the terminal will be complemented by a number of television monitors all around. In the more advanced information systems, the monitors and flipboards will be linked to a central airport computer to ensure that all the given information is as up-to-date and accurate as possible. There is also a parallel series of monitors – generally unseen by terminal users – which display identical information through the actual working areas of the airport.

The Flight Destination Board will show all flight departure times, as well as the relevant gate numbers, cancellation information and any other immediate information essential to your trip. The lettering used on all airport boards will be scientifically researched for clarity and easy reading. In far-off international airports you may find flight departure information given in Arabic or Cyrillic letters as well as in English – the acknowledged international language of air transport.

● **Check-in details (passengers and baggage):** Printed inside your ticket, or in a few cases just mentioned to you personally when you buy your ticket, will be your first check-in time. This is the *latest* the airline will allow you to arrive at the airport in order to carry out the necessary formalities before you leave. At all major airports the check-in desk for passengers and their luggage will have the name of the airline above it. In most cases it will also have your flight number as well.

When you arrive at your airport, presenting yourself at the appropriate check-in desk is the immediate thing you ought to do.

The first page of your ticket will be torn off and you will be handed a boarding pass. It is at this stage you will be asked your preference for a smoking or non-smoking seat and, if the aeroplane isn't too full, you should be able to request a window or an aisle seat if you want.

Luggage intended to be carried in the hold will be weighed and labelled – and you will be given a tiny receipt which you *must* retain until you see your luggage again. Before you lose sight of your suitcases, check the label which has just been put on to make sure it corresponds with your first stopover destination. Remember, though, this might not necessarily mean where the aeroplane makes its first stop en route. Even if your flight does involve having to change aircraft at, for example, Bahrain, if you're travelling to Australia then your luggage *must* be labelled to Australia.

Check in early at the airport. Since scheduled passengers have much greater opportunities to alter or cancel bookings, virtually all airlines overbook flights as a matter of course. Very occasionally passengers with confirmed reservations are denied boarding – a procedure known as 'bumping'. As a result, it is latecomers who are most likely to be bumped, although a noisy passenger with a convincing case stands a good chance of being allowed to board. Advice about what to do if you are bumped is given later on in Part One when we look at Airport Blues.

• **Baggage Claim Areas:** Retrieving your luggage from the appropriate Baggage Claim Area can easily become a nightmare. But if you know what exactly you ought to be doing, then there is no need for the process to become like a massive international jumble sale rummage.

The Baggage Claim Area will be immediately obvious to you once you leave the aeroplane. If not, then follow the crowd. Eventually your luggage will appear on one huge long conveyor belt which is usually laid out in a curved shape to allow the maximum amount of space all round it. Do not expect your luggage to appear instantly once you've reached the claim area. Flights tend to arrive in bunches, and from every corner of the globe at once, so baggage-handling facilities will inevitably be stretched to their limit. To make the process as painless as possible, make your luggage look obviously different from the others. Cover it with yellow fluorescent tape strips, and that way it'll stand out when you come to retrieve it at your destination airport, and also to the baggage-handlers at both ends of your journey. If you lift the wrong suitcase, for instance one that's identical in size and colour, then you are legally bound to pay the full cost of getting it back to the owner as well as for retrieving your own.

If your luggage doesn't appear, wait until after the very last suitcase has emerged through the anonymous conveyor belt hole, then complain *at once*. Sadly, lost or mislaid luggage is neither rare nor unusual, and all airlines have a set procedure for looking into the matter. Here, again, we look at the problem of lost luggage in the Airport Blues section. Remember that patience is essential when waiting for checked baggage to reappear. In some extreme cases, the wait for luggage has taken as long as the flight itself! On the whole, you can reckon on at least 15 minutes before you'll see your luggage again after you land. Longer if it was a particularly full aircraft, or a busy time for the airport groundstaff.

CITY TERMINALS

The City Terminal, or Terminals if it is a large city requiring more than one meeting point, is usually the place at which regular bus or coach services to and from the airport set down and pick up their passengers. The City Terminal is usually sited near one of the main railway stations and/or the main bus depot of the company serving the airport. Leonardo da Vinci, Rome's international airport, for example, is served by a 24-hour bus service operating exclusively from 36 Via Giolitti, right alongside the main Stazione Termini.

In many cases, City Terminals are staffed and operated by the country's national airline. KLM, the Royal Dutch airline, provide one of several half-hourly bus services from the centre of Amsterdam to the massive Schiphol Airport, and back again to the city centre. At London's Heathrow there is no need for specific airlines to provide scheduled bus connections, since no less than ten different coach operators link the country's main airport with the city centre, Gatwick Airport, and as far afield as Bristol, South Wales, and the Midlands in single, direct connections.

Where there is no official City Terminal building, as is the case in many Far Eastern and smaller cities, transport to and from the airport normally calls at the main railway and bus stations. It may also call at a specific point in the city centre, a central plaza or national monument, and frequently at the main city hotels if there is likely to be a number of prospective air travellers staying.

Ask your travel agent before you leave about airport connections or, failing that, make it a priority *as soon as you land* at each of your Round the World destinations to find out the most efficient means of returning to the airport. Failing that, ask at your hotel or the city's information office where there should be someone who speaks enough English to understand your enquiry. In more exotic parts, allow yourself plenty of time to make your connection from City Terminal to airport. A cautious hour waited at an airport is usually more rewarding than an unscheduled extra day in a foreign country.

TRANSPORT CONNECTIONS

In theory at least, flying from country to country, even from continent to continent, will be the easiest part of your Round the World trip. What can cause a lot of unnecessary, and in many cases, unexpected, worry for air travellers is arranging transportation from the airport to the city or their onward destination, and vice versa.

The distance between a city and its airport can vary enormously. In Dubai, for example, the international airport is barely half a mile outside the capital, yet in Tokyo it is a hefty 40 miles to Narita Airport. In every case, though, the intended air traveller has a range of options how to travel the short surface journey, and in the end it is as much a matter of personal preference as anything else. As a general rule, taxis are quicker and more efficient, but equally they will cost you, on average, about five to ten times the more popular airline coach option from city centre to airport. Be warned that a Round the World trip will probably involve at least ten such connections, frequently more, so take care you do not overlook this essential expenditure when budgeting for your journey. Other than by private car, these are your four main options:

• **By air:** A few of the largest international airports have air taxi services available, by helicopter, to take you to and from the city centre. Rio de Janeiro, Paris and London Heathrow are three, for example, but this service is intended primarily for businessmen and is extremely expensive unless you are lucky enough to have an inclusive First Class ticket which covers a courtesy helicopter connection from city centre to the airport.

• **By taxi:** Certainly the quickest means of connecting city and airport, especially for individual travellers, pairs, or small groups of up to four or five people. Preset charges are normal – but by no means universal. Ensure that you hire a taxi from an authorized rank and that you can agree on at least an approximate charge *before* you set off. Make sure that you understand how much the taxi fare is worth in your own currency before agreeing to it. One American businessman who visited Britain recently paid £150 for a taxi fare into the centre of London. It was his first visit and he thought, wrongly, that the pound sterling was worth roughly the same as the French franc – which is worth approximately ten times less. The taxi driver didn't complain about his generous 'tip'!

• **By rail:** Many international airports have their own railway stations linking the airport with the city centre. Often by surface trains, but more regularly by underground trains, all are linked to the national rail network making it the most convenient mode of transport connection if you choose to continue immediate surface travel once you land. Travelling by rail is probably the cleanest, most regular and efficient means of assuring prompt arrival at the airport – or destination city centre.

• **By bus/coach:** By far the most popular method of transferring passengers, and certainly the most effective where large groups of people are involved. The *Thomas Cook Airports Guide*, published three times annually, contains detailed and up-to-date information covering virtually every regular scheduled service operating within Europe. Further afield, you will have no problem securing the necessary information at the information service desk of any of the international airports featured in this guide. In nearly every case, national and domestic airlines offer bus services connecting with the airport's scheduled flights. This mode of connection tends to be the cheapest available, and most frequent, but can quickly become overcrowded. Check well in advance, if planning to travel by bus *to* your airport from the city centre for a scheduled flight, when you ought to purchase your bus ticket. Must it be bought from the airline's office in advance (as is, for example, Olympic Airlines' policy in Greece) or can you simply board the bus and pay then?

CAR HIRE

A worthwhile option during your Round the World trip would be to hire a car for a few days at one or two of your stops. Car hiring has become a relatively simple matter, particularly since the large organizations like Avis and Hertz are able to provide both the cars and the essential back-up services in virtually every country in the world. It is worth remembering that local garages and lesser, non-international, hire companies will almost certainly be able to offer you a car at a much lower rate. But the larger organization will be able to provide *exactly* the kind of car you require and offer much more in the way of assistance and advice – especially if your hire vehicle is unfortunately involved in a collision whilst abroad, or breaks down for any reason.

International companies are able to offer a One-Way Rental which means that you can hire a car in one city, or even one country, and drive it hundreds of miles into another before leaving it. You have no obligation to return it to the hire office of origin, provided, obviously, the One-Way Rental is agreed before you leave the point where you pick up the car. This means you could arrange your Round the World trip in advance, accordingly, allowing for an overland gap in ticket scheduling between a couple of capitals – Paris and Amsterdam for example – which could be completed by hire car.

Three international organizations offer a wide range of service facilities and hire option countries. It is possible to make one, or even a series, of international car hire reservations with a single telephone call *before* leaving Great Britain. In virtually every hire agreement made, you pay in the relevant country when you pick up the car, preferably by credit card.

To reserve a hire car in any corner of the globe, contact one of the following reservation numbers before leaving Great Britain. Avis (01) 848-8733 (telex: 933936); Hertz Rent-a-Car (01) 679-1799; Godfrey Davis (01) 950-4080. In addition, Avis have the following 'local' numbers abroad should you wish to hire a car once there: in Asia, Singapore 2359142 (telex: RS50000); in the Caribbean, Puerto Rico (809) 791-5212; in Canada (1-800) 268-0303 (telex: 069-67564); in the Pacific, Sydney (2) 430488 (telex: AA71514); in the United States (800) 331-2112; in Central/South America, Mexico City (905) 578-1177 (telex: 017-077526). Anywhere in Europe, Africa or the Middle East, contact the London number given above.

Hertz are the world's largest rent-a-car company with over 5000 offices worldwide in over 120 countries and at 2000 airport locations. Wherever your travels take you, it's likely you'll be able to get hold of a Hertz car. Through their sophisticated reservations system over 60,000 reservations are made daily, and their multi-lingual staff (speaking Spanish, French, German, Italian and Japanese as well as English) can handle most requests from specific cars to baby seats. One good point is that no matter what far-flung corner of the globe you're in there's always someone at a Hertz office who speaks English.

Among the main things that Hertz have going for them are their 'programmes for leisure and foreign national travellers'. Generally what this means is that foreigners to the country they're renting in get unlimited mileage on weekly rentals, and preferential rates. They are also located at just about every airport in this book, as well as in downtown areas and in the major hotels. Their 'Computerized Driving Direction' machines can be a godsend when you arrive in a foreign land in the dead of night. They print out directions to get you to where you want to go, as well as giving out useful information on the city's sights, restaurants and so on. These machines are to be found at all major airports in Europe, Canada and the United States.

If you choose to wait until your given destination, then the two biggest international firms – Avis and Hertz – have offices at all the major airports. All will be open during the peak hours of flight arrivals, generally from 7 or 8 a.m. until around 10 p.m. at night, local time. Times will vary for individual airports, and a few will remain open 24 hours a day. If you are depending on booking a car as you arrive at the airport, then try to check in advance that the hire company's office will be open when you arrive. Alternatively, book in advance before you leave home to guarantee a vehicle will be available when you land; if you have prebooked a specific vehicle at a specific arrival time then there will be a representative of the hire company available when you land to make the necessary arrangements.

It is worth getting quotes from one or two hire companies before you leave home. Avis and Hertz are both very competitive but each is better for different types of traveller. Hertz is more popular with business travellers whereas Avis is the more popular for holiday-makers. The advantages of advance booking cannot be overstated. If you wait until you reach your destination, then you risk not getting the car of your choice, or else being landed with a big and expensive model, or even being unable to find one at all.

There are plenty of 'off-airport' car hire companies which may be able to help you should you only decide when you land to hire a car. Many offer free courtesy transport between their offices, or hire-depot, and the airport, but, obviously, the location and details about these smaller car hire companies and garages vary enormously. You may well find, though, that the rates provided by local firms may be more suitable and cheaper than the large international firms. Equally likely, they may well be higher – and they will certainly not be able to offer as comprehensive a service to include extended One-Way Rental and so on. Ask at airport information desks, on arrival, for information about local car hire companies. Most likely they will direct you initially towards the big international companies if they happen to have a desk at the airport.

AIRPORT AND TOURIST INFORMATION

All major international airports will have Information Desks providing both tourist and airport information. In some countries there will be a single desk providing both, in others the information will be handled separately. In every airport, though, the desks will offer details and advice concerning the airport and/or tourist information relevant to the city you have arrived in, together with its immediate surroundings. From this desk you can generally find out where the nearest toilet for disabled persons is, for example; whether or not the local castle is open on a Sunday morning; and where the nearest telephones might be in the massive Arrivals terminal building you've just walked into.

Airport and tourist information desks do not usually provide flight information. That can best be obtained from airline desks themselves, or the flight information indicators that will be dotted all around the terminal. In many cases, the national tourist organization of the country you are visiting will also have a desk at the airport. From here you will be able to find out information covering the whole country.

There are no clear-cut rules about the standard of service you can expect from national tourist authorities, since there are huge differences in terms of efficiency and quality of literature between countries. In Hong Kong, for instance, the tourist organization is just about the world's most efficient since you are met at the airport automatically and given masses of useful information about the city. In India, on the other hand, no one offers you anything and you must ask for every piece of information – however basic – that you want.

Transport and accommodation information is also available at a number of larger international airports. Where there is no Information Desk, or if you arrive outside its regular hours of operation (many are open 24 hours a day) then information is occasionally available from the offices of the airport operating authority, or from duty officers working at your arrival airport. If in doubt, ask someone official-looking for the relevant desk.

TRANSPORT AND ACCOMMODATION INFORMATION

All large international airports now have Information Desks for national and city transport links, as well as an accommodation finding service for the city itself.

Airport authorities allow local transport authorities to issue tickets and provide information for all passenger arrivals. These desks have the advantage of allowing passengers to purchase onward surface tickets to any part of the country without their having to make an extra stop in the city centre.

At London's Heathrow, for example, London Transport have brightly coloured information desks selling single and return underground train tickets. In common with other countries, these desks can also provide free city maps and full city transport information. National bus and rail systems (including British Rail) may have different desks within the Arrivals terminal if they are independent of city transport services.

An accommodation finding desk will normally be situated nearby, or at least in an obvious position, for newly arriving passengers. Many large hotels, particularly the international chains, will have courtesy phones at airports for intended guests to make reservations immediately on arrival. These calls are normally free of charge. Occasionally the national tourist authority will undertake to find accommodation for you. This is an excellent and reliable means of finding precisely the type of accommodation which you want in a strange city. There will be a small charge for this service, usually about one pound, in local currency.

FLIGHT ENQUIRIES

You will be able to find a Flight Enquiries Desk at all departure and transfer terminals. Larger airlines – British Airways, Qantas, TWA and so on – will each have their own desks at all the larger airports, but information about departures, arrivals and transfers on smaller airlines will only be obtainable from the Airport Information Desk.

A few airports will have specific Flight Enquiry Desks but the most reliable information about flights can be obtained from the relevant airline. In addition, transfer passengers will be able to get up-to-date information from the Transfer Passenger Desk. This will be located in the transfer waiting lounge, or nearby, and as its name implies it is specifically for the assistance of transfer passengers.

BANKS AND BUREAUX DE CHANGE

Every major international airport offers general banking services and currency exchange facilities. As a rule, the opening hours tend to be much more generous than city banks and, in many cases, they will be open 24 hours a day. This tends to be much less the case in more exotic parts of the world when frequently many non-vital airport services (including banks) become subject to local opening hours which can be erratic at the best of times.

Generally airport banking facilities will offer no more than the most basic currency exchange. Changing money *into* local currency will be no problem, but try and avoid having to change money at the last minute before you leave a country. In Eastern European and African countries it will be virtually impossible to exchange local currencies for 'hard' western dollars or pounds. If they do agree to re-exchange, then you can say goodbye to at least half its original value in 'commission'. The best way to get round this problem is to budget not to have a great deal of local money left when you reach your departure airport. Alternatively, keep *all* traveller's cheques and currency exchange receipts until you've left. That way you should at least be able to re-exchange up to the amount of local currency you can prove you have exchanged already.

Certain departure airport bureaux de change can be a little hesitant – or downright awkward – by protesting that either they've got none of the 'hard' currency you want or, more likely, can only offer you a ridiculously large denomination of banknote.

Remember that airport banks have something of a monopoly in those countries where it is illegal to export the currency. Spend what you've got left *before* you reach your departure airport if you know this to be the case, otherwise you're guaranteed to lose out when you try to change it back.

It is possible to cash traveller's cheques, or a small amount of your own currency, when you arrive at an airport. In many cases the queues are enormous, and it can save a lot of unnecessary hassle if you arranged to arrive with a modest amount of local currency on you to cover a taxi or coach fare into the city centre, or for a few drinks when you reach your hotel.

LOST PROPERTY AND LEFT LUGGAGE

Left luggage is just about a memory from the past at many international airports. The service survives at most coach and railway stations, but the increasing incidence of terrorism, and the advent of much tighter security at all the world's airports, has closed down many Left Luggage Offices. In Asia there tend to be more open, and many still have some self-operating locker facilities available.

The Lost Property Office at an airport tends to handle only items lost and found at the airport – umbrellas, briefcases, coats and so on. Items which are left or mislaid on planes, or on the courtesy transport between terminal and plane, are dealt with by the individual airlines or operating company. Occasionally lost property becomes the responsibility of the airport police or security officials. If you lose or mislay something anywhere inside the airport (but not on the plane itself) then contact the Information Desk immediately if you are unable to locate the Lost Property Office yourself.

If you lose your luggage, or if it doesn't appear on the conveyor belt, then go at once to the Lost Luggage Office. Give full descriptions and also the baggage tags which you should still have loose or stapled to your ticket. Luggage is the most common loss at airports, and if it doesn't turn up at all after a thorough search of the airport then you are entitled to claim a modest amount for basic immediate necessities – toiletries and that sort of thing. If you are given any immediate financial compensation then there is no obligation for you to return the money should your luggage eventually turn up.

DUTY FREE AND GENERAL SHOPS

Duty Free shopping has become synonymous with international air travel. Every major airport will have its Duty Free Shops selling goods such as cigarettes in large cartons of 200, spirits (usually in litre bottles), cigars, an increasingly wide range of male and female perfumery and souvenirs without the addition of local purchase taxes (including VAT). Expensive watches, calculators, sterling silver pens and even large bottles of malt Glenfiddich whisky with ornate silver tops are fast catching up on the traditional spirits and smokes as the most popular Duty Free items.

With very few exceptions, Duty Free Shops will only be found on the 'air' side of an airport terminal, after outgoing passport formalities have taken place. This is to ensure that only departing international passengers, and those in transit, have access to Duty Free goods.

The Duty Free market is big business for airports, and Heathrow for example is reckoned to take something like a third to a half of the gross takings, making Duty Free profit a high proportion of the airport's annual income. Remember, though, *not* to buy your Duty

Free spirits or tobacco as you leave Great Britain, unless you intend to use them all abroad. You will have a chance to buy more to use at home at your last departure airport (and with some airlines even on the return flight) so there is no need to weigh yourself down for your entire trip. If you do decide to buy Duty Free before you leave a country, then check what you are allowed to take into your next port of call. Middle Eastern countries, for example, are very strict about allowing you to bring in alcohol even if it is only for personal use. In Dubai, Kuwait, Saudi Arabia, Sudan and Abu Dhabi it is forbidden altogether. Only tiny Bahrain allows you up to two bottles of spirits on arrival (provided you're non-Moslem, of course).

When you return to Great Britain, bear in mind these two up-to-date lists of what you're allowed to bring back into the country Duty Free. (1) If you have come from an EEC country (Belgium, Denmark, France, West Germany, Spain, Eire, Italy, Luxembourg, the Netherlands, Greece or Portugal) and the goods were *not* bought in a Duty Free Shop or on a ship or aircraft. (2) If you have come from a country outside the EEC or if the goods *were* bought in a Duty Free Shop or on a ship or aircraft (anywhere).

	(1)	(2)
Tobacco Goods		
Cigarettes	300	200
or Cigarillos	150	100
or Cigars	75	50
or Tobacco	400 grammes	250 grammes
Alcoholic Drinks		
Over 38.8° proof (22°Gay Lussac)	1½ litres	1 litre
or not over 38.8° proof	3 litres	2 litres
or fortified wine or sparkling wine	3 litres	2 litres
and still table wine	4 litres	2 litres
Perfume	75 grammes (85.5ml)	50 grammes (57ml)
Toilet Water	⅜ litre	¼ litre
Other Goods	£163 worth	£28 worth

The above allowances for tobacco goods and alcoholic drinks are not for people under 17.

As well as Duty Free Shops, there will be a wide range of more general shops at airports which are open to anyone. All offer goods or services useful either to departing travellers or waiting visitors. News-stands and bookshops will offer material in a number of widely spoken languages, and English is one of the most easily obtainable 'foreign' languages whilst abroad. There will also be tobacconists, confectioners, gift shops, and a number of airports have their own hairdressers for both men and women. You should find shops selling camera films, occasionally chemists and frequently whole shopping arcades to really complete the 'city in miniature' reputation most international airports have developed.

Remember, though, that outside the Duty Free area you'll be paying standard shop prices. In Common Market countries, it is possible to get VAT refunded on larger purchases *provided* you fill out the necessary forms in the shop and complete the tax office formalities once you're back in Britain. Enquire at your local tax office before leaving if you foresee making a sizeable purchase abroad (for example, a car) where the saving would be considerable.

CATERING FACILITIES

The quality of airport catering facilities varies enormously around the world, yet the standard range of outlets available seldom alters. The airport authorities have basically three groups of visitors to cater for: those casual, non-travelling visitors who may or may not be at the airport to welcome or wave off relations; the mixed groups of both spectators and passengers, elderly relatives seeing their children off to distant parts or children wishing their retired parents good luck on their Round the World holiday of a lifetime; and, of course, the abundance of exclusively air travellers themselves once they've gone through the 'no-return' passport formalities into the vast and featureless departure lounges.

Most international airports should have one impressive, and quite sophisticated, restaurant. On the whole, the food will be good, and have a distinctly international flavour with perhaps a few of the country's more well-known specialities included on the menu. These smart restaurants tend to be expensive and a little impersonal. If you've got bags of time before your scheduled departure, ideally with an early evening flight, then consider having a really good last meal before you leave town.

All airports will have a proliferation of bars, even many of the Middle Eastern ones. Alcohol has the effect of dehydrating you, which will add to inevitable dehydration that occurs in flight, so if you're having one or two drinks before leaving, don't overdo it! Airlines are entitled to – and will – refuse boarding to drunk passengers. No amount of ticket-waving and moans about confirmed seat reservations will help you. In British airports, alcoholic drinks served without a meal are often available only during local licensing hours.

Quick-service snack bars and coffee bars do the most phenomenal trade at airports. In most cases their prices do not reflect this high turnover. It is advisable to eat something before you fly, if only so that you feel no compulsion to finish the airline food on board. Snack bars tend to be all you'll find on the 'air' side of the terminal so if you fancy a decent sit-down meal then have it before you clear Passport Control. Opening hours tend to vary with the time of day or time of year – most airports will have somewhere that's open 24 hours a day.

You will find an abundance of prepacked sandwiches, coffee, tea, soft (and occasionally alcoholic) drinks and usually something a little more substantial in the food line at the quick-service areas. With little else to do while waiting for a couple of hours in the departure lounge, few passengers can resist the urge to eat. It's always worth hanging on to the equivalent of a few pounds in local currency just in case you get peckish before flying out, or if your flight's delayed and you need to eat something more substantial.

If all else fails to tempt you, you may eventually succumb to the endless clatter of the airport trolley service. It will provide you with the most basic of sustenance – sandwiches, coffee, and spirit miniatures – at usually quite hefty prices. As an absolute last resort for something to eat or drink, there will be numerous vending machines dotted around all airport terminal buildings. Curiously, the 'eat' ones have a hardier rate of survival than the 'drink' ones, so you've a better chance of finding one which works, and they are a useful means of disposing of odd local coins. Usually all that's on offer are bars of chocolate, potato crisps, or some local biscuit-type monstrosity you'd think twice about giving to next door's cat. If you think these are bad, avoid the drinks machines. Invariably they either don't work at all, or if they do, you'll get a plastic cup (which'll scald your fingers) filled to overflowing with a lukewarm drainwater – with milk and about six sugars added for taste. Honestly, it's well worth waiting in the snack-bar queue if it means you can avoid using vending machines, since the prepacked, processed ingredients – for the hot drinks at any rate – will have been there for days at least and seldom produce anything worthy of human consumption!

POST OFFICE (INCLUDING TELEPHONE FACILITIES)

All international airports will have some form of postal and telephone facilities available. It goes without saying that the range of services offered will vary enormously from country to country. In some more remote locations facilities may be restricted to only a post box and stamp vending machine, together with an 'international' telephone.

Most airport Post Offices will, however, be able to provide you with the full range of postal facilities, and if you've got time to kill before your flight then that is the ideal chance to send all those postcards you'd forgotten earlier on your trip. Coin-operated stamp vending machines are another way of getting rid of excess local currency. If there is a Post Office at all, of any size, then there will also be facilities to send international telegrams. With the advent of more efficient direct telephone dialling, telegrams are slowly becoming relegated to the realms of dramatic old film sequences. They are however still the quickest means (apart from telex) of contacting home if, for any reason, it proves impossible to place an international telephone call.

Some airport Post Offices will have a specific telex office, ideal for use by business travellers, but the use of these facilities is seldom cheap. Public telephones at major airports tend, on the whole, to be efficient. As a general guide, they are usually much more plentiful on the concourse of the terminal than they are on the 'air' side once you've cleared Passport Control. At some airports, particularly those in the United States, telephones are provided in the departure lounges and at points all the way along to the embarkation gates.

Public telephones take coins more than anything else, but many countries still persist with a token system which necessitates the purchase of these metal or plastic discs in great quantities in advance of making your call (usually at a little desk near the telephones or Post Office).

In theory, this principle helps prevent telephones being broken into but, in practice, it is a nuisance. In certain countries, as well as in Britain now, you can make a call using a telephone credit card such as Phonecard. These are available in varying denominations, and allow you to make calls up to the value of a specific number of prepurchased units. It is much more convenient than coins or tokens, but an unnecessary expense if you intend to make no more than one or two brief calls. Credit cards such as Visa and Access are also accepted on specially adapted boxes. A charge is made for this service, but for international calls it is convenient.

Other countries allow you to make as long a call as you wish without the need for coins, cards, or tokens – and then charge you so much for each unit used. General Post Offices or Telecommunications HQs are the most common places to find this facility. If you use it, then keep a careful eye on the call meter which will tick over at a rate of knots during any international call. Remember that almost always this meter measures call units rather than the running cost of your call in local currency. Inevitably you can multiply the meter figure several times to get the true cost. The best idea is to decide *before* you start your call the maximum number of units you plan to spend, and how much that's going to cost. Those calls are then paid for after completion.

MEETING POINTS

Increasingly, airport terminals will have officially designated Meeting Points where incoming air passengers, and those waiting for them, can arrange to meet. As a general guide, newly arrived passengers can normally also be met at the exit from which they will appear once they have claimed their luggage and cleared incoming

Customs. This exit will be clearly marked for those arriving at an airport and is generally one of the best places, other than the specific Meeting Points, to agree to meet friends or relatives at strange airports.

Meeting Points so designated by airport authorities will usually be found in the centre of the Arrivals terminal – the most prominent and sensible place for it. It is possible for totally lost friends or relatives to be paged over the airport's public address system – although the embarrassment of hearing themselves paged usually means this option remains very much a last resort!

As well as personal Meeting Points, it is possible for messages and telegrams to be left, for incoming passengers, at an airport's central message desk. If you telephone such a message to an airport, do so through the passenger's airline company. Specify *clearly* the passenger's name, city of origin (i.e. departure point), his expected arrival time and flight number where possible. The passenger will normally be paged as he reaches the Arrivals terminal.

FACILITIES FOR BABIES/YOUNG CHILDREN/ DISABLED PEOPLE

Airport facilities for babies and young children, as well as for disabled people, are on the whole generous. Most international airports are equipped with mothers' rooms where babies can be changed and fed, and occasionally with staffed nurseries where older children can be left for short periods of time – or kept amused during long delays. All these facilities will open on demand outside normal opening hours.

London's Heathrow, for example, has a number of trained nurses on duty in a designated nursery area where children up to the age of 8 can play. The large international airport at Frankfurt usually handles up to 100 children a day. Different airlines have different policies about whether or not to allow unaccompanied children, below the age of about 6, on a flight. You should have no problems, however, taking along children of any age as long as you remain there to accompany them at all stages of the journey.

Airport authorities are becoming increasingly aware of the needs of disabled travellers and new, or improved, facilities are being added all the time to most international airports. Special features such as entrance ramps for wheelchairs, large and accessible toilets, restrooms, wide lifts, lower telephones and conveniently sited parking places are becoming commonplace at all the world's busier airports. Virtually all airports now have automatic doors and wider corridors to make the necessary ground formalities of air travel as trouble-free as possible for disabled people.

All disabled people are entitled to ask for an escort through the various terminal formalities and on to the plane itself. It is particularly recommended that blind passengers *should* exercise this option, since although they are perfectly entitled to take their guide dogs, these will almost always be carried in the aircraft's hold with other pets. Blind persons ought to remember that even guide dogs are not exempt from any country's quarantine laws – even when returning to Great Britain.

Deaf passengers are entitled to request written announcements from groundstaff so they know precisely when and where their flight will be leaving. They can also make use of this facility once aboard the aircraft so they know when to prepare for take off and landing, when to refrain from smoking and – if necessary – take emergency landing safety measures.

Both airline and airport staff will be well drilled in assisting disabled travellers, particularly those arriving in wheelchairs. Help with luggage is clearly as vital a consideration as one-to-one personal help. In most cases, the disabled Round the World traveller will be able to organize assistance at arrival airports well in advance, *provided* he or she informs the airline in good time so that the arrival groundstaff can be notified accordingly.

Most larger airlines will be able to provide special loading devices to lift disabled passengers from the runway into the aircraft. This lift will be a small enclosed compartment which will lift the passenger slowly and comfortably, whilst at the same time providing protection against the outdoor elements. Airports will be able to provide passengers with the use of a second wheelchair whilst their own is being loaded on to the aircraft. Collapsible wheelchairs will be carried free of charge by all airlines. Alternatively many international airport authorities will operate a modest shuttle service specifically for the purpose of conveying disabled passengers from the departure terminal to the aircraft.

TOILET/BATH/SHOWER FACILITIES

Wherever you go, from Abu Dhabi to Zambia, you are guaranteed to find some form of toilet facilities at the airport. Almost always, toilets are recognizable by the male and (one-legged) female symbols, and although they may vary from the primitive to the luxurious (Heathrow's Terminal Four takes some beating) their function hardly needs explanation!

Larger airports, particularly in western countries, will also offer bath and shower facilities. On the whole, they are clean and well looked after, although it is difficult to have a relaxing bath in the surrounding atmosphere of a busy international airport. Generally there will be a small charge for the basic use of bath or shower facilities, sometimes this will include soap and a clean towel but more often they are available on payment of another modest sum.

If you do decide to have a bath or shower at an airport, then obviously it isn't a good idea if you're lumbered with heavy luggage. Leave it at left luggage if that facility exists, or with a *known* travelling companion (not an obliging fellow passenger or else you may never see your luggage again). At a few airports, the bath/shower attendant will look after it for a small consideration. But the chances of relying on his (or her) goodwill are dying out as concern over airport security grows.

FIRST AID POST

All airports will have a First Aid Post, able to offer at least the most basic of First Aid facilities. This will include help with everything from tropical sunburn to routine cuts. In larger airports there will also be a doctor permanently employed, or at least on call 24 hours a day in the nearby district. Airport First Aid Posts are equipped to deal with – and expect – a relatively standard range of problems associated with air travel. This includes incidences of heart attacks, asthma, the effects of alcohol both in flight and on the ground, the early symptoms of tropical diseases and – inevitably – food poisoning.

All First Aid Posts will have at least one or two persons suitably trained in basic First Aid, and they should have a ready supply of aspirin, sticking plasters and so on if needed by any airport user. Someone will be available 24 hours a day since no one can predict when they are going to be in need of First Aid. Look for the familiar medical Cross symbol, although it almost certainly won't be red.

In more serious cases, for example after an accident or heart attack, airport First Aid Posts will contact a local hospital. Larger airports have standby air ambulance services for just such an emergency, so if you do become injured or taken ill, you will be in good hands.

IMMIGRATION OFFICE

All airports, other than small domestic airstrips, have Immigration Offices. You will almost certainly never see the inside of one and, even if you do, should have no problems continuing your trip as planned *provided* you are a bona fide air traveller and not someone who's trying to enter the foreign country illegally.

Wherever you land, you will pass through Immigration Control. Going through immigration means you show your passport, together with any relevant visa, to a uniformed and unsmiling officer. Travelling anywhere in Western Europe, you probably won't have your passport stamped and the immigration control will end with a quick glance at the photograph and expiry date in your passport. Further afield, immigration may take considerably longer. You may have to fill in landing cards, usually requiring no more than the information in your passport, and there is always a chance that you may be questioned at some length by the immigration officers before you are allowed to proceed further. If this does happen, be polite and honest. Don't offer a bribe and, above all, don't lose sight of your passport.

Younger travellers should take particular care over their personal appearance when they arrive at foreign Immigration Control. The long hair, unshaven, scruffy jeans look will almost certainly invite at least a token few questions from the immigration authorities. It is well worth taking a few minutes on the plane to smarten yourself before arrival if you are travelling rough on a limited budget.

POLICE/SECURITY SERVICES

As well as the mandatory immigration police, all large airports have a vast and extensive security presence. For the traveller, most of this won't be seen since plainclothes security officers mingle inconspicuously with all outgoing passengers and automatic security devices are usually hidden well out of sight.

Do not be put off if you see a large number of soldiers or police carrying sub-machine guns. Sadly, this is the norm at most busy internationals and the armed officers are there for your protection. Try to resist having a conversation with them, unless spoken to, or taking photographs of them on duty. In many countries, airport photography is forbidden anyway, but even when it isn't, armed security men won't thank you for capturing them on film!

Departure security procedures have now become quite a nuisance, but here again it's all essential as a precaution against mid-air terrorism which has become an increasing reality over the last decade. Your checked luggage will be X-rayed before being loaded on to the plane. You won't normally see this happening and only very rarely will the contents be queried. You should, in any case, lock *all* checked luggage.

Both you and your hand luggage will be X-rayed, and perhaps even hand-searched as well. Do not protest since the security services are perfectly within their rights to take every precaution against potential terrorists or smugglers. Airport X-ray machines will *not* do any harm to hearing aids, heart pacemakers, digital watches, cameras, or any other personal effect. The only thing they may harm will be camera film, whether exposed or not. Many X-ray machines will have notices on them stating precisely which films could be damaged. To be on the safe side, hand over all film, and your camera if you are only halfway through a film, to be hand-checked. This could save you a lot of unnecessary disappointment through losing precious memories once home, since you know you will have to pass through several such X-ray machines.

CHAPLAIN

Many large international airports will have small chapels, almost always interdenominational so that they can be of service to as many people as possible. Regular services are conducted, for the benefit of both passengers and the airport staff, and the chaplain will be available to speak to individual air travellers if you so wish. Occasionally the airport chapel will be open 24 hours a day but there won't always be a chaplain at the airport for the same length of time. Check in advance with your airline, or the airport concerned, if you think you may want to visit the chaplain.

ROOF GARDEN/SPECTATOR AREA

Even to non-travellers, airports are fascinating places where there is always something going on. A staggeringly high percentage of an airport's annual shop and catering turnover comes from non-travellers who are either waiting for or seeing off friends and relatives, or are simply passing a few interesting hours amidst the hustle and bustle of a busy airport.

As a direct result, airport authorities have designated Spectator Areas where non-travellers can go. Most of the airport will be 'public' in any case, including most of the catering and shop facilities except those on the 'air' side of Passport Control. Usually this means at least one large lounge, with hundreds of comfortable plastic chairs and magnificent wide views of the runway, will be available for visitors and travellers alike. In addition, many airports, in traditionally warmer countries, have a large roof garden for general use. The roof garden will be well signposted – and is the most spectacular way of appreciating the comings and goings of all the air traffic. Be warned, though, that roof gardens are noisy by virtue of their exposed position. Remember to keep a careful eye on the time if you're waiting on a flight since airport announcements may be difficult to hear from the roof.

PICTOGRAMS

All international airports use a wide range of simple pictograms to denote facilities and services available. The signs are generally standard around the world, with very minor variations, and we have listed all the main ones which you are likely to come across. A few of the more obvious signs, like the male and female silhouettes depicting toilets, the telephone symbol depicting international telephones, and the various knife, fork, cup and saucer symbols depicting places to eat have been omitted.

Reproduced by permission of Thomas Cook Ltd. from their 'Airports Guide–Europe' publication.

RESERVATIONS

Before you can continue your Round the World trip beyond your first destination it will be necessary to reaffirm the intention to travel on the next leg booked. The minimum time limit for reconfirmation will be printed on the ticket, but it will be 24, 48, or 72 hours before departure.

Onward reservations are best made at the airport itself or at the appropriate airline office in person. If you choose to confirm by telephone, make a note of the date, time, and name of person called in case there is a query about your reservation when you arrive at the airport.

Because your Round the World ticket offers complete flexibility about when to travel, you are unlikely to encounter any problems of missing prebooked flights unless you forget specific date reservations made before leaving home. It is best to leave onward reservations until you know precisely when you wish to travel – but don't forget the minimum time limit or else you may be heavily penalized.

When you do reconfirm, remember which class of ticket you've booked. Some airlines may allow you to travel First or Business Class for one leg of your trip (if you've got an Economy ticket) but only after paying quite a hefty supplement. The most important things to remember are your seat location – by an aisle or window, close to the toilets, or behind an exit for extra legroom, or wherever – and whether or not you wish to sit in a smoking or non-smoking area. Bear in mind that this last condition won't affect pipe or cigar smokers since they are forbidden to smoke in any area of the aircraft cabin.

SOME TIPS

Getting the best possible service from any airport ought to be a relatively simple matter provided that you know in advance what services a particular airport offers. Read the relevant section in this book before *arriving* at a new foreign airport and you'll know what to expect once you've landed. If you know, for example, that there are nurseries available for mothers with small children, or a 24-hour currency exchange facility exists, then your first memory of a new country need not be one of your child's discomfort or financial panic.

It will be equally worthwhile to have even a rough idea of the level of facilities which you might expect at your departure airport *before* you arrive at it. You can bet in advance that a large, developed, international airport like, say, Washington or Sydney, will have just about every conceivable facility, but the same cannot be said of smaller airports like Bahrain or Mombasa. So try to check in advance if the particular facility you will require is there.

Without a doubt, the most sensible tip is to arrive early at your departure airport. Not only will this allow you an uncongested check-in, but it means you stand less chance of being 'bumped' and a better chance of getting precisely the type of seat you want: by a window or aisle, smoking or non-smoking. Allow plenty of time to get yourself to the airport since they are always several miles from the city centre and you can never predict whether your taxi, train or coach will break down. If you're not used to flying, then a clear two hours or so beforehand will give you plenty of time to have a relaxing drink or meal before you are due to leave.

Try to delay passing through Customs and Passport Control as long as possible. It is always more crowded, and the facilities less extensive, on the 'air' side of any terminal though duty free shopping can occupy most of the time in this area. If your flight is delayed for any reason once you're on the air side then you'll have no option but to wait there since technically you have left the country by this time.

The world's busiest airports

All but two or three of the airports covered by this guide are busy internationals. Most are listed amongst the world's 100 busiest and you can expect to find a full range of services and facilities at each one.

Almost certainly, your Round the World trip will take you through the busiest international in the world – London's Heathrow. Over 70 airlines use Heathrow annually, with the total number of aircraft operations exceeding a quarter of a million.

Nearly 27 million passengers travelled through Heathrow last year, of which a mere 2 million were exclusively domestic users. Only two carriers operating via Heathrow transport cargo only, but even so the total amount of freight and mail handled by Heathrow annually exceeds a quarter of a million metric tonnes – making it the fifth largest freight handler in the world.

In terms of total passengers handled, Chicago's O'Hare and Atlanta Airports, in the United States, carry almost 43 million and 35 million, per annum, respectively. A staggering 70 to 80 aircraft departures per hour take place from each airport, and between them 1.25 million metric tonnes of freight and mail are carried. By far the world's largest freight handler is actually New York's John F. Kennedy Airport, which sees off 2½ times as much freight and mail, as well as almost 28 million passengers. 54 of the world's 100 busiest airports are in North America, including Los Angeles, Dallas and another 9 out of the top 12.

The five European airports listed in the book are, in fact, the five busiest in Europe. Frankfurt caters for over 17 million passengers each year, and is one of the most important transfer 'hubs' in the entire international air network. Paris has two massive internationals – Charles de Gaulle and Orly – which between them have almost 30 million passengers annually. Orly handles most of Paris's domestic air traffic, twice as much as Heathrow's 2.2 million, whereas Charles de Gaulle handles by far the bulk of France's international traffic and air freight, with over half a million tonnes yearly.

Asia's busiest airport, by a long way, is the mighty Osaka in Tokyo, with 16.4 million passengers, almost two-thirds of whom are overseas visitors to Japan. Osaka also handles a third of a million tonnes of freight and mail, and is becoming one of the most popular Round the World stopover points en route between the southern hemisphere (Australia and New Zealand) and the great land mass of China, among other destinations, further north.

Hong Kong is Asia's second largest airport, with almost 9 million passengers each year. Handling exclusively international passengers, Hong Kong has grown rapidly in wealth and importance, and as a transit destination, over the last decade. The landing lights of its massive airport stretch far out along a causeway built into the harbour and make an impressive welcome to travellers arriving at night.

Of the eleven airports included in our Pacific and Australasia section, none make it into the top 100 busiest internationals. Even Sydney's Kingsford Smith and Melbourne International handle less annual air traffic than Lisbon or, remarkably, Kuwait. Nevertheless, Australasia has an important network of domestic services making internal transportation relatively easy over long distances.

African airport facilities tend, on the whole, to be the least-developed of any around the world.

Airport blues

FLIGHT DELAYS

No airline fully *guarantees* to operate flights at the times shown in their published schedules. Accordingly, the fear of a delay at the airport haunts every traveller and there is absolutely nothing you can do to prevent it. You can make things a little easier by looking at the flight departure board *before* you check in. That way you will know if there is a delay, and if it's likely to be one of several hours you could consider postponing your flight altogether by another day.

Alternatively, if there's a similar flight on another airline you could present yourself at their check-in desk. If you have a full First Class, Business Class, or Economy ticket then you should be able to claim a refund on your original flight, depending on where you bought your ticket. Discuss this eventuality when you buy your ticket so that you know exactly where you stand in the event of any delay.

If you have checked in, and then find yourself with a few hours to kill, you are somewhat limited in terms of how to keep yourself occupied. Officially you're entitled to nothing from the airline in terms of meals or, if necessary, accommodation. In practice most couriers will give you something – a voucher for a snack and a drink for a delay up to a couple of hours, a full hot meal voucher for anything up to a few hours, and hotel accommodation if a lengthy delay occurs between 10 p.m. and 6 a.m. After a delay of even an hour, you should be allowed to send a message to your arrival airport – by telephone or telex – if someone's due to meet you. Make a nuisance of yourself until you receive something from the airline since most respectable carriers will at least ensure that you are fed and watered.

Try to avoid getting either too involved in a good book, in case you miss your eventual flight call, or the temptation to drown your sorrows at the bar since you may be refused permission to board at the end of it all. Try to keep your patience, particularly with airport groundstaff who are not responsible for your delay, but *do* certainly make your displeasure known to the airline's representatives at the airport. Don't go through Passport Control if there's likely to be a delay – if you do the time will drag even more, since the lounge will be much more crowded and facilities more limited. Technically by that stage you have left the country and under no circumstances will you be allowed back through passport and security checks. Spending hours in the no-man's land beyond Passport Control is a very lonely business!

OVERBOOKING

All airlines overbook seats. Whether because some people book on more scheduled flights than they intend to use, or because many make late cancellations or miss flights altogether, it is unfortunately a fact of life. If you are refused permission to board, despite having a confirmed seat reservation, then you will have been 'bumped' and in theory there is little you can do.

In practice, however, you ought to make your complaint as vocal as possible. To reduce your chances of this happening, check in early, particularly if you're travelling with young children or are elderly or disabled. You have no legal right to *insist* on a seat, but you can expect meal facilities, hotel accommodation for a night, and message facilities if necessary as well as a *guaranteed* seat on the next available flight. If you are bumped by a UK airline, then you are entitled to a 50 per cent refund as well, on the one-way fare of the specific flight sector concerned, provided you eventually arrive at your destination more than four hours later than planned. The same rules apply in the US.

Round the World ticket holders have the extra option of changing their destination although this will involve a slight charge. If, for example, you've been bumped from the busy London–New York flight, then why not fly to Los Angeles or Miami instead? Decide quickly after hearing you're overbooked – and then either enjoy an unexpected change of destination or else complain loudly to the airline concerned *before* leaving the airport.

LOST LUGGAGE

If you fail to find your luggage after landing, then tell the airline *at once*. Most likely it will only be mislaid, or perhaps left in the baggage handling area between the terminal and the runway, or even accidentally left in the aircraft's hold. The person you should contact will be located in the baggage area, and you should give him or her a full description of what's missing.

It is an infuriating situation, and one which you personally can do absolutely nothing about, so try to be patient. If your luggage cannot be traced at the airport, and frequently it transpires that luggage will have been misdirected on to a later flight, then you will be given a Report Form to complete. This standard formality merely asks for a description of the luggage you've lost, and a brief contents list and forwarding address should it be located. Do not surrender the small baggage check ticket, or lose your ticket, since both will be essential if you need to make a claim at a later stage.

Provided your luggage still cannot be found – and this includes a wait of several hours if, for example, you are in Rome and your luggage is at Heathrow till the next morning – then you are entitled to a small allowance for essential toiletries and so on. You must ask for this allowance, since it won't be readily offered.

To make a proper claim for compensation, you must submit full details – in writing – to the airline's airport office within 21 days of losing your luggage. If you are spending six months going round the world, then do not leave your claim until you return home or else it will be ignored. Under the Warsaw Convention of 1929, you're entitled to limited compensation but to get even that, be persistent. Make a strong complaint at the airport when it happens – without being threatening or abusive – and pester the airline after you've submitted your claim until something is done.

TARMAC TRANSFERS

Regardless of whether you're transferring to another flight, or arriving at a new destination, you will often have to make quite a lengthy transfer between the Arrivals terminal and the aircraft.

In many cases, a free courtesy bus will be laid on by the airport, but sometimes this isn't the case. You may have to make the journey of some several hundred yards on foot. If you are disabled, or travelling with a particularly elderly relative, then it would be wise to alert either the airline or the arrival airport so that they know in advance of your arrival and can arrange some means of transport.

If an expected courtesy bus doesn't appear, then you and your fellow passengers ought to complain immediately to the airport ground crew. In some airports, passengers are expected to walk up to a quarter of a mile from the aircraft and, if this is the case, you are justified in feeling this is excessive. Find out from the aircraft's cabin crew *before* you land what you ought to expect – if anything – in terms of tarmac transfers when you land.

A small point worth remembering if you're making a surface transfer outside the airport, or even simply when you're travelling to the departure airport in the first place, is that *you* are wholly responsible should you not arrive at the airport, for any reason, in time to catch your flight. If an airport coach, or underground train link, breaks down then the relevant travel company has no obligation to you if you miss your flight. It is your responsibility to allow plenty of time to reach your departure airport just in case some calamity strikes.

GETTING THROUGH THE RED TAPE

Departure and arrival red tape should cause you no problems – provided you don't break the rules. Customs and Passport Control should not hold you up for more than a few minutes if everything is in order.

If you're stopped at Customs, then you can expect little sympathy if you've broken the law. An extra litre of whisky is certainly frowned upon much less than a few grammes of an illegal drug, but even so you are still breaking the law. At best you can expect offending articles to be confiscated and little more said other than a terse warning. At worst you can expect to feel the full legal weight of the country whose laws you have just broken brought down upon you. Very occasionally genuine errors are made. People are questioned at length by either customs or immigration officers for no good reason. If this happens for any length of time, particularly if any attempt is made to detain you, *insist* on contacting your consulate or embassy. Virtually all the cities listed in this book have one, and their numbers are listed. This is your right, particularly if you are genuinely innocent, and they can at least notify friends and families of your whereabouts. If you have broken a national law, even unknowingly, then consular staff are powerless beyond being able to keep in regular contact with you.

At all times be honest and as polite as possible. Never get angry, but voicing a gently increasing anxiety about an 'onward flight' (which you can prove with your Round the World ticket, regardless of whether you've actually confirmed your next stage) can work wonders. Do not offer bribes. In some developing nations this occasionally works, but in busy international airports it'll almost certainly land you in even more trouble than you were detained for originally.

Prevention remains the best policy. Be *fully* aware of what you are and what you are not allowed to take into a country – most nations are pretty much the same in terms of obvious articles like drugs and firearms, but Moslem countries are quick to cause problems over seemingly innocuous books and alcohol. Make sure your passport and relevant visas are up to date. If you've no idea how long you'll be away, and your passport expires next month, send for a new one several weeks before you leave. You'll need a new one anyway, so get it well in advance to be on the safe side. Above all, if you do get detained for *any* reason, insist on contacting your embassy or consulate. They are there to protect your interests.

YOUR LEGAL RIGHTS

Knowing your exact legal rights when things go wrong at an airport can be a lifesaver. There are surprisingly few areas where either airlines or airport authorities can be held legally responsible so the onus is on the individual to know his position.

If you are denied permission to board a flight for any reason – if you are 'bumped' – then you have no legal grounds for complaint, even if you do have a confirmed flight time and seat reservation. Virtually all major Round the World airlines would, however, make the necessary meal and accommodation arrangements as a matter of courtesy, as well as guaranteeing you a seat on the next available flight.

If your flight is delayed and you lose money on a prepaid hotel deposit at your intended destination then the responsibility is totally your own. Airlines never guarantee specific flights at exact times, since poor weather conditions alone frequently decimate pre-arranged flight plans.

If you are injured in an air crash, or if you lose your luggage at an airport or in transit, then your legal rights *are* assured. Under the terms of the 1929 Warsaw Convention (detailed inside every airline ticket) airlines agree to accept strict liability for all accidents and losses, which means that you – as claimant – would only have to prove damage or loss and not necessarily negligence. Even though levels of compensation are set in nominal gold francs, the actual amount payable is not great. In 1986, lost luggage was worth approximately £14 per checked-in kilo.

If you have a serious complaint then do consider taking legal advice as soon as possible. Outside the somewhat dated provisions of the Warsaw Convention, there are few hard and fast rules about precisely what your legal rights are so you stand to lose little by claiming through a lawyer.

Behind the scenes

Of the world's 13,000 scheduled landing places, only about 800 qualify as international airports. Yet behind the scenes of each and every one of them a daily routine of feverish activity takes place.

The architecture of an airport can generally be traced to one of several distinct periods. There are 'first generation' airports – Moscow and Amsterdam for example – which began in the 1920s and remained primarily gigantic big buildings with little concept of

design. Then came the post-war 'extended' airports – including Los
Angeles – with massive long passenger walkways, and finally the
newer satellite structures which look like modern buildings and
have been the norm for airport construction over the past 30 years
(Gatwick and Paris Roissy are examples). Occasionally up to a
dozen such satellite hangars or terminals will ring a single,
artistically designed, main building.

Perhaps surprisingly, the internal anatomy of the workings of an
airport is relatively straightforward. There are the places where
passengers can go, and there are the places where they cannot. All
the public parts of an airport – from the toilets to the telephones –
have been outlined already. It is the prominent control tower
building which is the nerve centre of every airport. This tall, narrow
structure oversees the entire airport and, on a busy day, may control
the take off and landings of up to 2000 aircraft. In an atmosphere
that has been described as 'cool urgency', it is here that Ground
Control and Air Traffic Control keep the mechanics of every
airport's organization working smoothly.

The flight crew of your aircraft will have arrived at the departure
airport at least an hour before take off. During the time until
departure, a route will be decided, depending on other air traffic
and weather conditions, and detailed aircraft safety checks will be
carried out. Until the aircraft is airborne, it is subject to the
instructions of Ground Control who monitor all runway man-
oeuvres, taxiing and – most important of all – the strict take off
order which all aircraft must respect for safety reasons. Ground
Control give pilots permission to start their engines and perform a
vital function in preventing congestion either on the airport's
limited runway space, or in the crucial few hundred feet after take
off.

Once a plane is airborne, it becomes the responsibility of air
traffic controllers. Their basic function is keeping apart all the
dozens of aircraft that are likely to be flying in the space close to an
airport at any one time. Once a flight has been safely separated and
is climbing away on its Standard Instrument Departure (SID)
mechanism, then the air traffic controller will transfer control of the
aircraft to the first radar sector (departure) controller on its
flightpath.

This second air traffic controller will ensure further climb
clearance towards the aircraft's cruising level. This will always be

between 18,000 feet and 45,000 feet for normal subsonic jets. Private jets can fly higher, but only Concorde, flying supersonic, has a standard cruising level of around 50,000 feet. The limit of usable airspace is 75,000 feet, and then only with extreme precautions against low air pressures and oxygen deficiencies.

The authority of ground and air traffic controllers comes together when the aircraft approaches its arrival runway. Formerly, runways tended to be constructed in a triangular pattern – London Heathrow's is an excellent example. This was to ensure that at least one runway was always pointing roughly towards the wind. Modern jet aircraft are much less affected by crosswinds than their propeller predecessors and, accordingly, newer airports have a myriad of intersecting runways enabling planes to take off from one and land on the other alternately. As a rule, the hotter the country's climate, and the higher the airport is sited above sea level, then the longer the runways will have to be. If you ever reach Doha on the Persian Gulf, then the main runway there is something like three miles long! Even New York's John F. Kennedy Airport has a main runway over 500 feet shorter, which is hardly surprising when you reflect that the world's second busiest international airport has to suffer several hundred 400-ton jumbos landing, at 125 miles per hour, every day.

Flight information

Having passed through the inevitable red tape, and resisted the temptation to buy out the Duty Free Shop's entire stock, you will eventually reach your aircraft. If you've never flown before, then the first sight of a massive 400-ton jumbo jet sitting on the runway is quite something.

The following section is a detailed synopsis of all the information you'll need to know about your flight, and what to expect on board. If you read this section before you fly then you ought to be able to sit back and enjoy the experience without any unnecessary worries. Flying is, after all, what you're going to be doing rather a lot of during your Round the World trip!

CLASS DIFFERENCES

Airline carriers offer three distinct classes to passengers – First Class, Business Class and Economy Class. Some carriers may miss out either First or Business Class, but you will always have the option between travelling in comparative luxury, or more modest Economy Class comfort. Strictly speaking there is a fourth class option, Supersonic, but this is restricted exclusively to Concorde which remains the only commercial airliner in the world flying above the speed of sound. If you choose to make your Round the World trip by Concorde (Kuoni, for example, offer two superb itineraries, each costing about £14,000 for a fortnight of pampered luxury) then you can be assured of outstanding service.

Travelling First Class really does make the journey one of the highlights of your whole trip. Your ticket will cost almost exactly double the Economy Class equivalent but you will receive every luxury that air travel can provide. You will be treated with courtesy and distinction before and after the flight, as well as on board the aircraft. Together with use of the VIP lounge at your departure airport you will also be given an extra weight allowance and preferential speedy handling of your baggage. You will check in at a separate desk where queues are far smaller, and you can expect total flexibility of travel arrangements, to cancel and rebook, or to break a journey at any point.

In flight, First Class passengers can expect the highest quality catering, snacks always available, ample newspaper and magazine reading, and any number of preferential little touches like courtesy slippers, hot or cold face towels, free drinks (including limitless champagne) and a small gift from the airline.

Business Class passengers are those paying the full Economy Class fare, plus anything up to 25 per cent extra. Together with the special check-in facilities allowed to First Class passengers, Business Class travellers also have a separate compartment with more spacious seating than Economy (two to a row) and most of the facilities available to First Class passengers – except such generous allowances for drinks and snacks. As its name implies, this class is aimed very much at the business traveller.

Economy Class is what it suggests, the airline's own special fares and by far the most popular ticket option, although it can appear in any one of a wide range of names and guises. You will not be offered any of the special facilities or seats which are synonymous with the Business and First Class travellers, but with all carriers offering Round the World routings you can expect a comfortable flight and full meal services where appropriate. Although Economy remains the most used option, by many times over, Business Class travellers are increasing in number rapidly. As a result, frequent business travellers might do well to consider turning one particularly long trip into a memorable Round the World holiday.

HAND LUGGAGE

On all aircraft you will be allowed to take on board a small amount of hand luggage in addition to your main checked allowance. For safety reasons, airlines strongly recommend that you limit yourself to only one item of hand luggage when you fly, although one or two personal hand items, including a handbag or umbrella, would be allowed.

Most flights have a tight weight allowance of 20 kg (44 lb) for Economy Class passengers and 30 kg (66 lb) for First Class passengers. Strictly speaking, your hand luggage ought to be weighed as part of this limit, but most airlines won't bother provided you've got no more than one or two normal sized pieces. Hand luggage must not weigh more than 5 kg (11 lb) and its three dimensions – per piece – must not total more than 115 cm (45 inches).

In addition to a small suitcase, or similar piece of hand luggage, you are allowed certain other small items on board. A normal size lady's handbag, a coat or blanket, walking stick or umbrella, a camera, in-flight reading material, duty free goods, an infant's carrycot (provided it is collapsible and no more than 30 inches long or 16 inches wide), and either crutches or a collapsible wheelchair, provided a passenger is dependent on them, are all allowed.

Once you board your plane, it is usual for hand luggage to be stored under your seat. All newer aircraft aim to provide as much space as possible in the cabin for hand luggage. As a result, the majority of aircraft will have large overhead storage bins, capable of taking most items of hand luggage. In addition, Concorde, First and Business Class travellers will have the use of wardrobes to store jackets or suits during the flight.

In the interests of safety, hand luggage is not allowed to be kept anywhere else in the cabin – in the aisles, for example – unless it is a baby's carrycot or passenger's wheelchair. As far as possible try to avoid standing up and down repeatedly to get something from your hand luggage stored overhead. This is always a nuisance to other travellers – particularly if you are in a window seat.

In the unlikely event of an emergency evacuation of the aircraft, ignore your hand luggage. Not only will it delay your escape but it could be potentially dangerous to fellow passengers if, for example, a couple of duty free bottles were to smash at the foot of the emergency escape chute.

YOUR SEAT

To make a profit, airlines depend upon being able to carry as many passengers as possible. The less cabin space that is devoted to passenger seating, the more costly your air ticket would be. Aircraft are therefore designed to accommodate the maximum number of seats whilst also retaining as much in the way of passenger comfort as possible.

With the exception of Concorde, all the large, scheduled aircraft which you'll travel on during your Round the World trip will have a small, segregated, First Class seating area at the very front of the seating layout. These will be larger and further apart than the Economy Class seats, with contoured backrests and occasionally fitted with sleeping headrests. A more comfortable seat is one of the advantages First Class passengers pay for.

By far the majority of the aircraft's seats will be divided into two, three, or four long rows of mixed double and treble seats. The DC10, Lockheed Tristar and Boeing 747 still have a middle row of four seats, but these are amongst the more uncomfortable on any aircraft and are being gradually phased out. Unless you happen to be over six feet tall, you ought to have plenty of legroom beneath your seat. If you feel this is likely to be a problem for you, request an aisle seat or, better still, one just behind an emergency exit where there is unrestricted legroom in the interests of safety.

Above your seat, or occasionally set into the armrest, will be an individual control unit. This will enable you to call the cabin crew, operate an individual reading light and a fresh air vent, and listen through headsets to whatever variety of music is offered by the airline. One of the channels will give the film soundtrack, sometimes available in different languages. All longer flights will have some form of film entertainment, projected on to large screens on the cabin bulkhead or arranged so that they can hang down from the cabin ceiling. The film will be of as general interest as possible but obviously won't appeal to everyone. Some airlines offer a different film in another part of the aircraft, but the cabin staff will keep you informed of the options of in-flight entertainment available.

Lifejackets are usually affixed to the underside of each seat, within easy reach, and above your head will be an oxygen mask which will drop down automatically if cabin pressure falls below the safety level. Ignore both these essentials once you are aware of where and when to find them.

Tucked into the little pocket behind the seat in front of you ought to be your in-flight magazine. Provided free by the airline, this glossy publication (which you can take away with you if you want) contains many international adverts and articles of general interest, and will tell you basic information about your aircraft and airline. Occasionally the magazine will be printed in one or two different languages.

COMFORT HINTS

Ideally, if you're a particularly tall person about to embark on a long-haul trip which will involve a lot of stop-offs, you ought to consider flying First Class. Then you can be assured of getting up to double the amount of legroom provided in Economy. But even if you choose to fly Economy, as the vast majority of travellers do, there is no need to feel cramped or uncomfortable if you choose your seat properly.

Window seats tend to provide the least legroom, and aisle seats provide the most. If you're not fussy about having a decent view of the world floating past beneath you, then you could also consider trying to get a seat behind one of the emergency exits for additional legroom.

Noise levels vary little between different points on any aircraft, though clearly if you sit near the toilets or the galley then you can count on being disturbed more often. First Class seating is always located away from the engines, but occasionally Economy Class passengers sitting at the back of the aircraft may hear more noise from the rear engines. On the whole, the best seats tend to be near the front, just behind First Class, and away from the inevitable chatter of excited package holiday groups.

Sadly, the ability to sleep on a plane is something you either do or do not possess. You'll know from past experience how easy you find sleeping on a coach, train or even in a car, and this should give you some idea of the *worst* you can expect when trying to sleep in-flight.

If you're dreading a long flight, for example Cathay Pacific's 12½ hour non-stop flight from London to Hong Kong, then try going overnight. At least it'll be dark most of the way and, with a blanket from the stewardess and a bit of willpower, you will be able to induce a little slumber at least.

Most First Class seats turn into comfortable sleeperettes at night, giving you ample legroom to stretch out and snooze in comfort. Economy Class seats don't offer such relaxed luxury but most will recline if you look for the little lever under your seat, or button in your armrest. If you're by a window, pull the blind down, go to the toilet and then try to settle yourself down with the blanket on top of you. Oddly, pulling the blanket over your head can work. You may get a few odd looks, but it cuts out a lot of background light and noise. There will always be some passengers and, of course, the cabin crew who simply won't sleep.

Dehydration can be a problem on long-haul flights over four hours. It's wise to drink reasonable quantities of non-alcoholic liquids – alcohol tends to speed up the dehydration process. Avoid fizzy, carbonated drinks and stick to water or still fruit juices. On 747 and Tristar aircraft there are drinking-water fountains adjacent to the main galley and toilet areas.

You can avoid physical discomfort by rotating your neck occasionally, and similarly with your feet and ankles. Curl and relax your toes now and again but don't risk taking your shoes off unless they're a comfortable loose fitting. Feet tend to swell on long flights and you could have problems getting your footwear back on. As a rule, it is a good idea to wear loose-fitting clothes, especially round the waist, when you fly.

FOOD ON BOARD

Airline food has undoubtedly one of the worst reputations of any aspect of air travel. Just about all flights will offer you at least coffee or fruit juice and, if your flight lasts over a couple of hours, a snack or full meal as well.

On the whole, the standard of airline food is surprisingly high. It is usually prepared in vast catering centres, often leased by airlines at both ends of the routes, and loaded on to the aircraft anything up to an hour before departure. Virtually everything will be pre-cooked, with only items like prebrowned steaks being cooked on board in ovens powered from the aircraft engines.

It is worth remembering that aircraft pressurization reduces the effects of passengers' taste buds by up to 50 per cent, hence the feeling that airline food is not as tasty as an equivalent meal on the ground. Don't expect a boiling cup of coffee on board either, since pressurization also makes it impossible to properly boil water.

British Airways has one of the highest reputations for in-flight catering. A book featuring recipes from their Great Chefs Service programme, *Tables in the Sky*, went straight into the best-seller list. With all the major airlines you can expect an adequate, well-presented, meal – provided, obviously, that the length of your flight justifies one.

On their scheduled flight from Heathrow to Rio de Janeiro, for instance, British Airways Economy Class passengers were faced with a dinner menu that started with kippered salmon hors d'oeuvre. This was followed by a choice of pan-fried steaklet of veal or honey-glazed breast of chicken, both with a selection of vegetables. The meal was concluded with a Dutch apple flan dessert and either tea or coffee. First Class passengers enjoyed an outstanding, and completely different, five-course champagne supper and unlimited bar service!

All Round the World airlines should be able to provide a range of special meals at up to 48 hours' warning. Most do prefer to be notified when you book your ticket, or make a reservation for subsequent legs of your trip. Smaller airlines will have a more restricted list of special meals available, but the larger airlines ought to provide the following: Jewish (both Kosher and Kedassia), vegetarian, Asian vegetarian, infant, Muslim, diabetic, fat-free, low-calorie, salt-free, gluten-free and low-sodium meals. First Class passengers especially will have no problems getting the type of meal their diet requires, but Economy Class passengers may experience the odd niggle if they try to insist on a low-sodium, gluten-free, Asian vegetarian dish every time!

It is worth eating a snack before you leave your departure airport. Not only will this help lessen any nervous tension but you'll almost certainly enjoy your meal more there, when you can taste it better and have more room to eat it. Drink as much water and fruit juice as possible in flight, but if your service has a free bar service, try to avoid indulging it too much. If you require a special meal, order it as far in advance as possible. Even then, don't be too surprised if it doesn't appear. This is another good reason for eating something before you board your flight.

THE CREW

The crew on board every aircraft is always headed by the Captain. It is he who chooses the route, makes all the essential flight decisions, and has absolute responsibility for passengers and the aircraft. Occasionally the Captain will greet passengers as they board, but more likely he'll make at least one guest appearance in the cabin during the flight. The Captain will normally wear a black jacket, and will be recognizable by the four yellow braid bands on his jacket-cuffs.

All aircraft will also have a Co-pilot who shares flying duties with the Captain. He will be dressed identically, except for having three, rather than four, bands on his cuffs. Very occasionally there will be a First Officer on board, wearing two bands on his cuffs.

The largest passenger aircraft have a Flight Engineer to feed technical information to the pilots. He will have two yellow cuff bands, with one additional navy band between them. Once in a while there will be a Senior Flight Engineer on board instead, wearing three yellow bands with a navy strip between each.

Stewardesses seldom wear any indication of seniority other than the occasional airline or personal identification badge. The Flight Purser or senior stewardess may have an additional badge indicating her seniority.

Many airlines require their cabin staff to wear nationality badges on their uniform. These represent the national flags of the country from which they were recruited and are a good indication of what languages they will be fluent in. Flight-deck crew do not normally wear nationality badges.

TOILET AREAS

All aircraft have toilets situated towards the rear of the Economy Class seating area. Normally there will also be at least one in the First Class area, near the nose of the aircraft. Concorde is the only commercial aircraft without any toilets at the rear, having instead three at the centre of its 128 seats and another at the very front.

As a rule, aircraft toilets are tiny but start out clean. (They don't stay that way and on a long haul the best advice is to go as soon as possible!) They will generally have more facilities than an average public convenience, offering perhaps courtesy hand oil or scented facewipes. The hot water will be hot, and appear instantly as you turn on the tap. On an overnight flight you may be offered a clean, hot towel first thing in the morning.

One important safety note: *never* smoke in the toilet areas, since it is here that the highest concentration of inflammable materials are used in the aircraft furnishings. Between 1946 and 1976, over 300 accidents were caused by in-flight fires or smoke and many were proven to have started in the toilets.

SKYSCAPE

Gazing out at the clouds from an aircraft window can be one of the most outstanding sights you'll ever see. The higher your cruising height the more dramatic your view of the wispy cloud formations below will be.

The most common type of cloud is the familiar light, puffy, cumulus variety. They are formed by rising warm air, and grow much more quickly over land than sea. Cumulus clouds usually lie far below a passenger jet's cruising height of around 30,000 feet, seldom floating much above 12,000.

On a particularly windy day, you may see long, oval clouds hanging high in the sky above mountains. These are amongst the highest cloud formations, and one of the very few which occasionally drift as high as Concorde at 55,000 feet.

Dark clouds indicate stormy weather, but few pilots will deliberately fly through a storm, or even towards one. Seeing a distant thunder cloud can be a remarkable sight as its sun-drenched golden top belies its miserable interior.

Large, heavy clouds usually mean rain – especially if they're dark in colour. Elongated cumulonimbus clouds moving quickly upwards indicate an imminent thunderstorm. If you're lucky you'll see these clouds developing glorious peaks high above brilliant purple hearts.

It is possible to follow the changing landscape far below you, particularly with the aid of a pocket atlas. Predicting the weather is slightly less easy although as a general guide, remember the lighter the cloud, the lighter the weather. Long, narrow strips of cloud, normally fairly high in the sky from ground level, also indicate good weather – usually dry and quite humid. Don't be put off by seemingly fast-moving clouds – a gale at 30,000 feet above your arrival city doesn't always mean a gale on the ground.

TAKE OFF

The technology which enables a pilot to lift 400 tons of jet into the air depends entirely on the successful counter-balancing of engine power with wind forces. A Boeing 747 with its four massive Rolls-Royce engines has to exert over 200,000 pounds of thrust, and build up speed to at least 180 mph, before it can lift its massive body into the air.

The greater the total weight of aircraft, passengers and cargo, then the greater the take-off speed becomes. All aircraft have a maximum take-off weight, determined at the time of construction. Shorter runways or higher altitudes can reduce this weight considerably since neither the necessary space nor the proper air density may be available.

What exactly the pilot is doing to get airborne depends very much on whether he can ensure the aircraft reaches the vital lift-off speed along the runway. If an engine fails, or the flight-deck computer indicates a systems failure, then he can abort the take-off procedure by applying reverse thrust (depending on how fast the aircraft is going) and full brakes.

Needless to say, such occurrences are rare and, in almost all cases, the aircraft will comfortably reach the desired lift-off speed. At this precise point, the pilot will pull back on the control column in front of him in order to lift the aircraft's nose about 12 degrees into the air. The upper airflow of the oncoming airstream is forced past the aircraft's wings, causing the downward acceleration of wind speed which soon overcomes the aircraft's weight.

The aircraft climbs steeply – up to around 25 degrees – as speed is gradually built up and the cruising height channel is found. You'll probably hear a few odd clunks as all this happens in the first 10 or so minutes of flight. This is simply the landing gear and take-off wing flaps being retracted – and will be nothing to worry about.

LANDING

For the flight crew, landing is the most tense part of any journey. Each airport has its own potential complications and shortfalls, requiring total concentration from the pilot and his co-pilot. The process of landing involves the flight crew bringing to a standstill the same 400 tons of aircraft which only a few hours earlier was launched six miles high at a speed of almost 200 miles an hour.

Radio contact with the arrival airport begins long before the final approach is started. The choice of approach speed, like the speed for take off, is decided at the time of the aircraft's construction. The actual approach speed for a heavy passenger jet is around 150 mph, although really heavy aircraft will touch down faster and require a lot longer to stop.

Aircraft descend slowly, much more gradually than they take off, and you almost certainly won't notice the initial stages of landing until you're asked to put your seatbelt on again. An aircraft may circle an airport for some time before landing, in an aerial holding stack. This frequently occurs during peak times when a number of aircraft are scheduled to land at once.

Just before the final descent you may hear another loud clunk as the landing gear is lowered, and the wing flaps extended fully. The aircraft's nose will be lifted and descent speed gradually reduced by a little reverse thrust. Vital runway marks and side-lights guide the pilot to the centre as he completes his approach by gently touching the wheel brakes.

Maximum braking only occurs in an emergency since reverse throttle actually slows the aircraft more safely. You will feel a soft thud when the wheels touch down and a sophisticated anti-skid mechanism automatically takes over to prevent them from locking on a wet or frozen runway.

FLIGHT SAFETY

Flying is a safe means of transport. It is many times safer than travelling by car, boat, train, or even on foot. Yet the tiny risks in flying, however remote, remain very real. There is a well-worn adage in the aviation world that flying is not inherently dangerous – but that it is ruthlessly unforgiving of mistakes when they occur.

Aircraft design has improved markedly in recent years with regard to better flight safety. New longer and narrower passenger jets can still carry as many people as their wider-bodied predecessors, but streamlining helps reduce drag and so scientifically helps an aircraft fly further and more safely. Consider for a moment that the world's narrowest – and fastest – passenger aircraft, Concorde, has never yet crashed.

Winglets are being added to newer aircraft, so lengthening the existing wing and improving aerodynamics. Anti-misting ingredients have been developed to add to aircraft fuel and so prevent it vaporizing. Fuel vapour is the single cause of an aircraft exploding after crash landing. Carbon fibre brakes on landing gear are lighter and safer, and computer technology inside the flight deck has reduced the constant workload for pilots.

The cabin layout of your aircraft will have been designed with flight safety as a priority. Emergency lights near the floor to show the nearest emergency exit are being made compulsory on British airliners by the Civil Aviation Authority, and larger overhead lockers for hand luggage ought to reduce any danger during an emergency from luggage in the aisles.

The safest seats in an aircraft were always thought to be towards the rear, although this is increasingly less the case. The Manchester air disaster in August 1985, for example, claimed the lives of 53 passengers before the aircraft even left the ground, and the rear half of the aircraft was totally destroyed by fire. Other 'safe seats' are next to or within easy reach of an emergency exit. Even if you're sitting rows away from one, at least note their location as soon as you board so that you know instantly where to make for in the event of an emergency landing. You will also have a better chance of getting out of an aisle seat in a hurry than you will from a window seat, although it must be stressed that the chances of your ever being involved in an emergency landing are extremely remote.

WHAT TO DO/NOT TO DO IF HIJACKED

Sadly, increasing political tensions around the world mean that the risk of hijacking is as real as ever to would-be Round the World travellers. Being realistic, there is little you can do to improve your situation if you are hijacked but there are a few simple do's and don'ts that you ought to bear in mind *before* the situation ever arises.

Don't risk any heroics. There will be absolutely nothing you can do but sit and wait, making yourself as inconspicuous as possible. If you've got any reading material then read it. Even supposing you reread the in-flight magazine several times, it will help keep your mind off the situation and keep you occupied.

If you are picked on by an individual terrorist, then remain polite, speaking when spoken to, and do not offer any resistance to verbal abuse. Psychiatrists reckon that the psychological balance is a matter of survival, so try to establish some sort of rapport which you can maintain if spoken to.

Move as little as possible from your seat – and don't be surprised if you begin to feel uncomfortable, or even lose control of your bladder, during the ordeal. If the authorities storm the aircraft, and you hear gunfire, lie as low as possible on the floor. Passengers occasionally get killed when airline hijacks are ended by force as a result of their own stupidity, trying to get involved in what is going on.

A final tip before you travel, of particular relevance to Americans who frequently become the innocent victims of airline hijacks. Try and find an old, expired, passport from another nationality to keep with your own inside a jacket pocket or handbag. Hijackers looking for someone to pick on will probably not go to the bother of studying about 300 individual passports, so more likely they'll ask everyone to hold theirs up in the air. Depending on their political ideals, some passengers will be more ideologically vulnerable than others – notably those with American or Israeli passports. By holding up even an old British or Australian passport, for example, you might at least have a chance.

EMERGENCY LANDINGS

Emergency landings do occur now and again. When they do, the overriding factor for everyone's survival is the avoidance of panic. Aircraft staff are primarily on board not to serve your meals or drinks, but to prevent panic and ensure your safety in the event of a forced landing.

At the beginning of every flight you will be given a short safety briefing. The emergency evacuation procedure will be explained and the appropriate exit doors pointed out. You will also be told how to use the lifejacket, under your seat, and the oxygen masks which drop automatically when cabin pressure falls. Listen carefully to what may appear little more than an academic exercise but could, in fact, save your life.

In an emergency, survival can depend on action taken in the first 15 seconds. Almost certainly the cabin lights will go out, to prevent the danger of fire, or else the cabin may quickly fill with smoke. In any case, practise opening and closing your seatbelt a few times with your eyes closed. Children also need to be shown how to practise this as it may not be possible to help them in an emergency.

Prior to an emergency landing, you will be asked to remove all sharp objects from your clothes (including pens and pins), extinguish cigarettes and fasten your seatbelt over your thighs, rather than abdomen as normal. Immediately before landing passengers will be asked to take up the crash position using a pillow or folded blanket as a cushion for the head. Aircraft seats will fold forward sharply on impact.

After an emergency ground landing, the essential priority is to get away from the aircraft as fast as possible. Forget about your hand luggage and jump down the yellow emergency chute which will have opened automatically beneath each emergency exit. If you find the gangways blocked, then scramble over the tops of seats. Try, if possible, to breathe in long gulps and keep your mouth and nose covered by a cloth to prevent smoke inhalation.

The initial emergency landing procedure on water is precisely the same as on land – except that you *must* put your life preserver on before landing in the water. This will keep you alive for at least a few hours but there will be self-inflating life rafts for you to clamber into once free from the aircraft. They usually hold 26 people each, and contain vital food and water supplies together with a small radio transmitter.

It is *essential* that you know where at least two emergency exits are whilst flying, and how to open them. All this information is displayed on the flight safety card in the seat pocket in front of you. Do *not* open an emergency exit if there is fire outside. On large, modern passenger aircraft the escape chute will inflate automatically and extend away from the aircraft once the emergency door is opened. Do not try to rush more people than is essential to escape down the chute, otherwise there will be panic. Quickly remove your shoes and jump seat first down to the bottom.

If your aircraft has to make an emergency landing – on land or on water – move fast and forget your belongings. Above all, read the safety instructions thoroughly beforehand so that you know precisely what to do if the situation arises.

TIMETABLES

Essential to your Round the World trip will be the use of airline timetables. Luckily, virtually all the major airlines print their timetable as a standard size and with similar styles of information layout. Your timetable will normally be a long, narrow, little book crammed with schedules printed on very thin paper.

Schedules are listed alphabetically under the names of departure cities. Most timetables will have information, usually at the back, about the airline itself, and perhaps a couple of seat plans to give you some idea where you might prefer to sit. Some airlines include a glossy, pull-out map of the world showing all the destinations which they fly to.

Using a timetable is a relatively simple matter, although at first glance they can look alarmingly complicated. By doing this you can quite easily make a detailed Round the World itinerary from the comfort of your own home, although always bear in mind that one of the attractions of a Round the World ticket is that you have complete flexibility about where and when you travel.

Having found your departure city, it will be followed by a list of possible destinations. Under London Heathrow, or New York's John F. Kennedy, for example, the list in many airlines' timetable is exhausting – but the choice of where to go is yours. In order will follow the days of the week which the flight operates (either abbreviated or numbered 1–7; check the timetable key to find out whether '1' means Sunday or Monday). Then will come local departure time, local arrival time (in 24-hour clock), the flight number and a note of the number of stops en route. The class of seats available may also be listed, together with the size of aircraft. There are, for example, a couple of hundred seats more in a 747 than in a 737. So the size of aircraft may make a difference to your choice of route. Some timetables may say what meals are available in-flight, and also how long the journey should take.

SOME USEFUL HINTS

1. Make sure your timetable is up-to-date, and that it won't expire whilst you're abroad. Many airlines have winter and summer timetables, expiring around the end of March and October.
2. Find the 'how to use' key first of all – usually just inside the front cover or first few pages. Use it.
3. Remember timetables list departure cities – not destinations.
4. Check listed arrival times carefully if you plan to make an onward connection. Usually they will be local time at arrival airport.
5. Consider your total flying time. Is it worth two days cramped in Economy Class to reach Australia when you could break your journey in the Bahamas or Hawaii for a few days?

6. Double-check all the information again. Particularly times (with the airline if necessary) if an onward connection is vital. Misprints are few in airline timetables, but they do occur.
7. Check there's no 'valid only from' date beside your flight. Not all flights listed are necessarily valid within the limits of the timetable.
8. Read all the information at the back of the timetable – it may give you some useful tips about where to sit on board, or even where to stay when you land.

PUBLIC HOLIDAYS AFFECTING FLIGHTS

Public holidays around the world vary enormously. In Christian countries, the most obvious holiday periods to avoid travelling are around Christmas and Easter. From mid-December onwards, most flight services will be noticeably busy with people returning home for the festive season. Actual schedules ought not to be affected until around 24 December. On 25 and 26 December, most schedules will be cancelled altogether before another hectic spell up to the New Year.

Most flights will operate as normal on 31 December, but will be cancelled on New Year's Day itself. A limited schedule should be operating by 2 January and normal service will have resumed by the 3rd. Middle Eastern, and most African, nations are not affected by Christian holidays, but their airlines may be unable to fly scheduled services into a country which does observe the national holiday. At Heathrow, for example, services are drastically reduced on Christmas Day to around a tenth of normal. Of these, most are arrivals from long-haul departures on 24 December or operations by Middle Eastern airlines.

Airline services are also affected around Easter and, like Christmas, are liable to be busy for a day or two either side as well. Non-Christian countries tend to have rather more religious holidays which may affect their airlines' flight schedules. In Saudi Arabia, for instance, all public services within the country – including airports – are heavily restricted during the autumn month of Ramadan.

Political holidays are popular the world over, with many clustered in the month of May. Look out for Independence Days or the date when a country was either liberated many generations ago or first proclaimed a Republic. Australia and New Zealand also celebrate Anzac Day (25 April) and the Queen's birthday (early June), together with a few provincial anniversaries as a recollection of the days when they were much more closely tied, by colonial links, to Great Britain.

Many countries observe All Saints' Day on 1 November, and Japan has a remarkable number of more modern holidays stemming from economic and industrial advances since the end of World War Two. They also celebrate Children's Day (in early May) instead of a Mother's or Father's Day, and a Respect for the Aged Day in mid-September.

Public holidays affect different airlines in different ways. Individual country holidays are given in Part Two under Key Facts so if you think your journey may coincide with a major holiday find out whether or not your flight will be affected. Remember, too, that even though your flight may still be operating, public transport to take you to your departure airport may be seriously affected by a national holiday.

TIME DIFFERENCES

All the days and nights are created by the earth rotating round the sun. When it's breakfast time in London, it's early evening in Sydney since every part of the earth cannot face the sun at once. As a result, the world is neatly divided into 24 distinct time zones so that, in theory, everyone gets the sun during the day, and the moon at night.

As a rule, you will gain a few hours travelling east and lose a few travelling west. Whichever routing you choose for your Round the World trip, you will not have the option to double back (unless you pay a specific subsidy when you purchase your ticket). Travelling east tends to suit people who prefer a bit more sleep since their first day will be shortened nearer to bedtime. Travelling west has the opposite effect until you eventually gain a complete day.

Study the international time zone chart before you leave home and you may manage to avoid a few depressing 3 a.m. arrivals in a strange country.

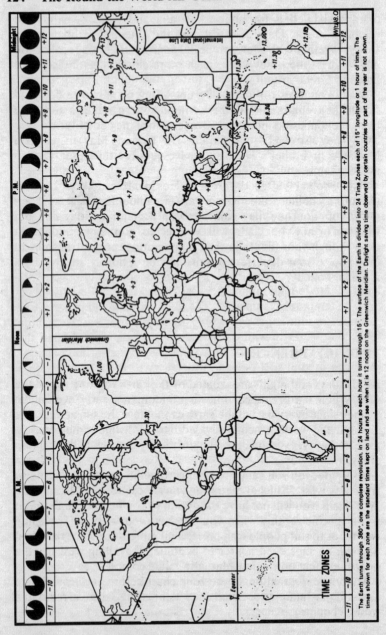

TIME ZONES

The Earth turns through 360°, one complete revolution, in 24 hours so each hour it turns through 15°. The surface of the Earth is divided into 24 Time Zones each of 15° longitude or 1 hour of time. The times shown for each zone are the standard times kept on land and sea when it is 12 noon on the Greenwich Meridian. Daylight saving time observed by certain countries for part of the year is not shown.

IN-FLIGHT BLUES

Travelling ought to be an enjoyable sensation. If you've never flown before, you will undoubtedly experience something of a thrill (for better or worse) when you feel your aircraft building up speed along the runway. Flying affects people in different ways and if you are doing a lot of long-haul flying for the first time you may well meet one or two minor problems which are perfectly natural – and generally easily overcome.

Jet lag is by far the worst problem – and even that can be easily avoided by some careful planning beforehand. Flying across different time zones in a modern jet aircraft is tiring. Your body has its own circadian rhythm, as in 'circa' meaning around and 'dies' meaning day. This tells you when to wake, sleep, feel hungry, go to the toilet and so on. It plays a crucial part in your mood and mental performance. As a result, if you fly over a few time zones your circadian rhythm will take time to catch up again.

Not only will you feel tired and hungry at all the wrong hours, but your ability to take major decisions (crucial to business travellers) may be temporarily impaired. The ideal way to avoid jet lag is to fly over as few time zones as possible in one go, or at least try to break up a long-haul trip with a few days on the way. Failing that, take things easy once you land. Resist the urge to rush around 'doing' a new city in your first day and instead try to go to bed as early as possible on the first night. Don't worry if you wake up early next morning. Waking early will pass in a couple of days as you gradually find yourself going to bed at normal times.

Both jet lag and the risk of air sickness can be helped by doing as little as possible during the 24 hours before your flight. Try to pick a flight which lets you arrive as near as possible to your normal bedtime and drink as little alcohol as possible during the flight. Wearing loose-fitting clothes and comfortable shoes helps, especially if you can also avoid the temptation to overeat during the flight. A useful little book to help you prevent or overcome jet lag is Don Kowet's *The Jet Lag Book*, published by Futura Publications in Britain.

Unlike sea or car sickness, air sickness is a rare occurrence affecting seldom more than one passenger in a thousand. It is caused by a bumpy ride, combined with anxiety and excitement. If you feel queasy – especially if you're prone to other kinds of travel sickness – keep your head as still as possible on the headrest. Avoid all fatty or fried foods as well as alcohol and cigarette smoke. If you're worried beforehand, consult your doctor at home who may prescribe something to help you.

Aircraft cabins are pressurized to a level different to that on the ground. Consequently you might encounter a little discomfort when internal gases expand, or a popping sensation in your ears when you take off and land. Here, again, the answer is to wear loose-fitting clothes and avoid carbonated, fizzy drinks. Ears popping is by far the most common in-flight blue suffered by even the seasoned traveller. It can be overcome by constant yawning or swallowing. Take a few hard sweets along with you to induce swallowing, but take care when giving them to young children, even if they do find the sensation of ear-popping unpleasant, since a sudden bump could cause them to choke.

FEAR OF FLYING

A fear of flying, for no reason whatsoever, is reckoned to affect at least a sixth of the adult population. Sensationalist headlines about air crashes twist the very minor risk of air travel out of all proportion, so why not work instead on the old saying, 'nothing is to be feared; it is only to be understood'.

According to Lloyd's, the London insurance company, you stand 25 times a greater risk of being injured travelling by car than you do by air. Even so, countless thousands of air travellers fear flying when the problem can be overcome by simply trying to relax.

In theory, a completely relaxed passenger cannot be fearful. Try relaxation exercises at home before you fly – deep breathing and mind relaxation are excellent. Think of a pleasant, peaceful place and imagine being there without a worry or a fear. Confront fears of flying as they emerge as silly and unfounded.

Try to maintain as relaxed a frame of mind as possible once you board the aircraft. If the aircraft flies through turbulence, pretend you're travelling in a car or bus over some cobbles. That situation is perfectly safe, isn't it? Consider visiting an airport to watch the comings and goings of people and aircraft. Read the first section of this book so that you know exactly what to expect when and where both at the airport and on board.

Get to your departure airport in good time. If you've never flown before, why not take a short domestic flight, perhaps from London to Edinburgh or Manchester, just to get the feel of flying?

The aircraft cabin crew can help you settle down if they know you are wary of flying. They can talk you through take off and landing, or let you have a look at the flight deck to reassure you that everything is perfectly safe. Particularly if you are travelling alone, when simple problems can often seem much worse than they really are, mention to one of the air hostesses when you board that you are worried about flying.

Once you settle into your seat, try your deep-breathing exercises again with your eyes closed. Listen out for the inevitable few clunks as the landing gear is retracted. Enjoy the impressive bird's eye views and relax with the fruit juice or coffee on offer. Get up and walk about as soon as you are allowed to remove your seatbelt. Then you'll realize how irrational a fear of flying is, and probably quite enjoy the experience.

Six months before you go

WHEN TO GO

Deciding when you ought to make your Round the World trip need not be a potential headache. Assuming you have complete flexibility about when to travel, you ought to sit down with at least six clear months before you and consider all the essential natural factors that will determine whether your holiday will be a dream or a disaster.

First of all, you will have to give a lot of thought to where you really want to go. Landing in Sydney in mid-July, with three inches of snow beneath you, can be a tremendous disappointment if you expected summer sunshine, such as you may have left back home.

Travelling Round the World you will need to accept that it won't be summer everywhere on the globe at once. But, thankfully, such is the miserable nature of the average British summer that many of the global destinations featured in this guide will have brighter and warmer winters than most British summers.

If you plan to spend most of your time in the southern hemisphere – perhaps in or around Australia or New Zealand – then the seasons will be reversed. Winter there occurs between May and September, so the ideal time to visit would be during the dismal winter months back home. This should be regarded as one of the optimum times to visit any of the subtropical destinations listed in this guide, with mid-spring or autumn as the best. Japan, for instance, lies in a temperate northern weather zone making spring and autumn the best times to visit. Large cities everywhere get extremely hot and unpleasant during the summer months.

September and October are the best months to visit either Hong Kong or Malaysia, when temperature and humidity will be at their most comfortable for western visitors. Leave it another month or so for the optimum time of year to visit South Korea, Thailand or the Philippines. Then you should at least escape the worst of the baking heat and unpredictable arrival of the monsoon season.

If you have several months to enjoy your trip not only can you afford to miss the peak summer travel months when aircraft are full, resorts bustling and the cities unbearably hot, but you will be able to delay your visit to most countries until they are at their seasonal best.

You will be able to see and enjoy little of South East Asia, for example, if you arrive during the monsoon season. Avoid travelling to India any time from mid-May until the end of June for this very reason. The six weeks or so from April until the start of the monsoon are only marginally less unpleasant in India than the rains because of baking heat which western visitors tend to find utterly unbearable.

Conditions can vary enormously for subtropical destinations, and it is always wise to try and consider destinations well in advance of when you leave. As a rough guide, however, try to avoid from April to September for most Asian and Far East destinations, and similarly for Australasia unless you don't mind the consequences of arriving mid-winter.

Temperatures vary considerably between the east and west coasts of North America – the average for the west coast never strays higher than 68°–70°F whereas Miami basks in the south east with temperatures reaching the high eighties in summer.

European temperatures follow the British pattern. Cities are warmest and busiest from June to September; coolest and least busy from January to early March. The following worldwide temperature chart will give you some indication of the temperatures you can expect at whatever time of year you choose to travel.

ROUND THE WORLD TEMPERATURE GUIDE (°F/°C)

	Jan	Feb	Mar	Apr	May	June
Amsterdam	40/4	41/5	47/8	52/11	61/16	65/18
Antigua	84/29	84/29	84/29	84/29	84/29	84/29
Auckland	73/23	73/23	71/21	67/19	62/17	58/14
Bahamas	77/25	77/25	79/26	81/27	84/29	87/30
Bahrain	68/20	70/21	75/24	84/29	92/33	97/36
Bangkok	89/32	91/32	93/34	95/35	93/34	91/33
Barbados	83/28	83/28	85/29	86/30	87/30	87/30
Bermuda	68/20	68/20	68/20	71/22	76/24	81/28
Delhi	70/21	75/24	87/30	97/36	105/41	102/39
Frankfurt	37/3	43/6	48/9	58/14	66/19	72/22
Hong Kong	64/18	63/17	67/19	75/24	82/28	85/29
Kuala Lumpur	90/32	91/33	91/33	91/33	91/33	91/33
Lima	82/28	83/28	83/28	88/31	74/23	68/20
London	43/6	44/7	50/10	55/13	62/17	68/20
Melbourne	79/26	79/26	75/24	72/20	62/17	57/14
Miami	74/23	76/24	79/26	81/27	84/29	86/30
Mombasa	87/30	77/30	90/32	89/32	85/29	83/28
New York	37/3	38/3	45/7	57/14	68/20	77/25
Penang	90/32	91/33	92/34	91/33	90/32	90/32
Rio de Janeiro	84/29	85/29	83/28	80/27	77/25	76/24
San Francisco	55/13	59/15	61/16	63/17	63/17	66/19
Singapore	86/30	88/31	88/31	88/31	89/32	88/31
Sydney	78/26	78/26	76/24	71/22	66/19	61/16
Tokyo	47/8	48/9	54/12	63/17	71/22	76/24
Vancouver	41/5	45/7	50/10	57/14	65/18	70/21

These temperatures (in °F and °C) represent the average daily maximum (in the shade) for most of the major destinations covered by this guide. Maximum temperatures normally occur from early to mid-afternoon.

ROUND THE WORLD TEMPERATURE GUIDE (°F/°C)

	Jul	Aug	Sep	Oct	Nov	Dec
Amsterdam	70/21	68/20	65/18	55/13	41/5	41/5
Antigua	84/29	84/29	84/29	84/29	84/29	84/29
Auckland	56/13	59/14	60/16	63/17	66/18	70/21
Bahamas	88/31	89/32	88/31	85/29	81/27	79/25
Bahrain	99/37	100/38	92/33	90/32	82/28	66/19
Bangkok	90/32	90/32	89/32	88/31	87/30	87/30
Barbados	86/30	87/30	87/30	86/30	85/29	83/28
Bermuda	85/29	86/30	84/29	79/26	74/23	70/21
Delhi	96/36	93/34	93/34	93/34	84/29	73/23
Frankfurt	75/24	73/23	66/19	55/13	45/7	39/4
Hong Kong	87/30	87/30	85/29	81/27	74/23	68/20
Kuala Lumpur	90/32	90/32	90/32	90/32	90/32	90/32
Lima	67/19	66/19	68/20	71/22	74/23	78/26
London	71/22	70/21	65/18	57/14	50/10	45/7
Melbourne	55/13	59/15	63/17	66/19	68/22	75/24
Miami	88/31	88/31	88/31	83/28	79/26	76/24
Mombasa	82/28	83/28	84/29	86/30	88/31	84/29
New York	82/28	80/27	79/26	69/21	51/11	41/5
Penang	90/32	89/32	88/31	89/32	88/31	88/31
Rio de Janeiro	75/24	76/24	75/24	77/25	79/26	82/28
San Francisco	65/18	65/18	70/21	68/20	63/17	57/14
Singapore	88/31	87/30	87/30	87/30	87/30	87/30
Sydney	60/16	63/17	67/19	71/22	74/23	77/25
Tokyo	83/28	86/30	79/26	69/21	60/16	52/11
Vancouver	74/23	74/23	65/18	27/14	48/9	43/6

These temperatures (in °F and °C) represent the average daily maximum (in the shade) for most of the major destinations covered by this guide. Maximum temperatures normally occur from early to mid-afternoon.

Directly related to the weather conditions of any destination is its relative altitude compared with sea level. Higher altitudes mean reduced oxygen levels and, combined with tropical temperatures, the atmosphere can prove unbearable for many visitors.

None of the 50 cities listed in this guide are at particularly high altitudes; nearly all are less than 100 feet above sea level. Hong Kong, Sydney, Singapore and Tokyo, for example, are all a mere 26 feet from sea level and island destinations tend to be as near to ground level zero as can be possible for any land mass.

South American cities are amongst the highest in the world, with the Bolivian capital climbing 12,000 feet into the sky – the cruising height of a light aircraft! The two South American destinations we feature shouldn't present any altitude problems. The Peruvian capital Lima is situated about 500 feet above sea level and Brazil's picturesque Rio de Janeiro sits squarely level with the Atlantic coastline itself.

If you have the choice when to go, then think carefully about going 'off-season' by western standards – particularly spring or autumn. It is at these times of year when most of the subtropical destinations on your route will be at their coolest, and by avoiding the peak summer travel season you ought also to avoid the bulk of the year's tourists.

Study the temperature chart closely and try to avoid the months with the heaviest rainfall. Try also to stagger your Round the World trip according to the seasonal best for the countries you plan to stay longest in, avoiding high altitudes in high temperatures.

If you are at all worried about when to see a particular country truly at its best, then give the appropriate national tourist office in London a ring well before you'd ideally like to travel and they will advise you accordingly.

DESTINATIONS

Planning your Round the World trip will be one of the most exciting parts of your holiday. Unless you are a business traveller, planning to extend a forthcoming long-haul trip with one or two more exotic locations, you will have complete flexibility about where to choose and how long to stay within the restrictions of your Round the World ticket.

By far the most popular destinations are the 50 cities listed in this guide. Round the World tickets are not, however, organized to include either obscure or dangerous destinations. They will take you to exotic and far-flung parts, but they will not intentionally take you to a country either at war or politically unstable.

Scheduled flights operate to just about every corner of the world. This even includes the likes of Ethiopia, Iran, Syria, Afghanistan, Libya and Albania, but you will have to patch together your own routing (and at your own risk) if you are keen to visit potentially dangerous countries.

Political problems have a nasty habit of blowing up out of nowhere, so wherever you take yourself, try and remain aware of the politics within the country in case a problem should arise. South Africa, for example, is a popular destination on a Round the World trip – particularly since many people still have family ties with over 800,000 British citizens living there. The political situation seems to deteriorate annually, however, and especially in the wake of the state of emergency imposed by the government last year, travellers should take extreme care now before visiting South Africa.

In recent years, a few Round the World destinations have quite definitely become 'in' places to visit. Obviously where is 'in' varies from year to year – the Côte d'Azur and California remain amongst the hardy annuals – but both China and Japan are fast becoming *the* places to visit. China is awkward to visit unless part of a group, or on a business visa, but Japan is a popular Round the World stopover point as are many other parts of the Far East.

Popular too is Mombasa in Kenya, one of Black Africa's safest countries to visit, and any of the Caribbean islands are always 'in'. Even Hong Kong as a holiday destination is becoming increasingly popular, as the years draw closer to the crucial handover date of the prosperous British colony to communist China.

ADVANCE INFORMATION

The planning of your Round the World trip should be good fun and the advantages of getting your holiday sorted out in advance are many.

Being realistic, the amount of preplanning that you will need to do before flying round the world will be many times more than you could expect before an average two-week package tour. For a start, you will almost certainly be away from home for a lot longer. A few airlines even specify a minimum of 14 days at each stopover point. You will need a lot more spending money – all of which ought to be transferred into an assortment of traveller's cheques, credit cards, current accounts and foreign currencies.

You will need plenty of time to arrange visas – particularly if you're going to more out-of-the-way destinations in the Third World, or the Far East, not covered by this guide. You may need several weeks in order to allow visas and vaccinations to take effect, and ensure the necessary certificates are authenticated in good time.

Accommodation will be one of your biggest headaches. Given several months preplanning, you (and your travel agent) ought to be able to arrange most, if not all, of your hotel bookings in advance. This can bind you to a strict schedule but is the sort of preplanning many people prefer. A few months of preplanning will allow you to ensure the safety of your home whilst you're away, too.

Getting your trip sorted out in advance also gives you time to find out more about the countries you plan to visit. Why not write to a few of the national tourist offices listed at the end of this section well before you buy your ticket? You may then consider a few far-off destinations you hadn't previously thought of visiting.

What you want to specifically see and do will be the overriding priority behind the routing you choose. Do you want to visit family in Australia, New Zealand or Canada? Do you want to head for the sun but far away from the crowded package holiday resorts? Would you like to tour the historic monuments of the world, from the Taj Mahal to the White House; or would you prefer instead to sample as many countries and cultures as possible within your own financial and time limits? Clearly if you are a business traveller then your options will be less open but you still ought to have considerable flexibility about what you would prefer to do when you reach each destination.

Depending on your age and general health, you may prefer a relaxing six weeks or so watching the world go by in a few far-flung locations. Alternatively, you may be prepared to have the most energetic and exhilarating holiday of your lifetime exploiting the potential to see as much of the world as possible within a few weeks. Only you can decide what you specifically want to see and do, so read all the glossy brochures and consult as many other guidebooks as possible before making up your mind.

Specific parts of your Round the World trip may require advance notification. If you insist on making an awkward, month-long detour across restricted countries like China or Nigeria, expect authorities to be extremely unsympathetic to your wishes. In most cases you will be refused permission outright unless you've managed to get advance clearance.

There are many countries around the world which do not allow tourists, but there is nowhere totally closed to 'business' travellers. None of the countries listed in this guide should present any problems to Round the World travellers keen to explore them away from the cities and a little more off the beaten transit tracks.

Problems arise when you wish to visit somewhere of over-whelming religious, scientific or artistic importance. In India, for example, places like Sikkim, Surat, Bhutan and Nepal usually require special advance permits. Bhutan requires advance written notification that you'd like to visit by at least two and a half months. Permits are firmly refused to mountaineers or those involved in either publicity or research (including journalists).

If you fancied an overland trek to Burma, from one of the more popular Round the World destinations in South East Asia, then you will encounter problems of requiring advance permission. Burmese visas are only granted (if at all) for up to a week. Even then you are not expected to try and visit anywhere other than Rangoon and Mandalay.

If you do feel that you wish to visit a restricted area whilst abroad, try and consult the country's embassy at home before you leave. Bear in mind that academic or scientific interest will afford you a greater chance of being granted permission to a restricted area than mere tourist's curiosity. If the country in question favoured ordinary tourists visiting then such areas wouldn't be restricted in the first place.

There are countless detailed guidebooks on the market which will give you specific, in-depth, information about each city or country you plan to visit. Start by investing a few pounds in the travel section of your local high street bookshop.

Individual countries have tourist information offices, many London-based, which will also be able to help. Be warned that their information tends to be very 'glossy' and obviously written to show their country at its best. The variety of literature you will receive from any of them will vary enormously, but in conjunction with what you receive read one or two neutral guidebooks (a few of which are listed in this section); they ought to give you an adequate introduction to the country or city concerned.

Undoubtedly the best way of finding out more, in advance of actually arriving there yourself, remains what personal information you can glean from people who have been there before you. Ask around. Business colleagues who may do quite a bit of long-haul travel are a good source, or perhaps your travel agent might put you in touch with someone who knows a city like Sydney or Mombasa well.

When finding out about a totally new place, begin with a general guide and then work your way around to more specific texts. Clearly, if you plan a Round the World trip concentrating heavily on the 'sights', as opposed to soaking up the tropical sunshine in a few far-flung corners of the globe, then you'd be better advised buying a larger text on the history of the place than a good beach guide.

Finding good maps can prove to be a greater problem than finding good background information about where you'd like to visit. General country maps can be found in any atlas but are clearly too small in terms of actual detail to be of much more use than providing basic information. Decide what scale you want. 1:50,000 (or preferably even 1:25,000) will show every last street and building as well as the tiniest natural land feature. This is the best scale to look for if you want a decent city map, though many national tourist organizations will have surprisingly good free city centre maps available. Any bookshop in your destination city ought to be able to provide you with both city and national maps in a variety of scales. The larger London bookshops stock a good supply of international maps as well.

Public reference libraries, and larger university libraries, hold stocks of international maps in many scales. If you merely wish to consult a detailed local map then try here but avoid having to take photostat copies. The copyright laws are incredibly complex relating to the copying of maps, in most cases either forbidding it altogether, or else restricting you to no more than a single A4 sheet which will seldom be adequate.

Certain large motoring organizations give away free national maps – but these are unlikely to be the scale you are looking for. Both Britain and the United States have a number of excellent map-making companies – Bartholomew and Geographia, for example – and a short telephone call to either may locate precisely the map you require should high street retailers be unable to help you.

One or two good guidebooks ought to be essential on any Round the World trip. You are, of course, reading the best guidebook at the moment for someone considering, or about to embark on, a Round the World trip! But there are other, more general, travel guides that are well worth taking a look at:

The Traveller's Handbook – edited by Melissa Shales and published by WEXAS International Ltd. By far the most comprehensive general travel guide. Meticulously researched and covering every corner of the globe. Contains plenty of useful information for Round the World air travellers.

The Complete Traveller by Joan Bakewell. Published by Hamlyn. A less comprehensive version of the above aimed more at the package traveller but with a few useful tips. Hasn't been updated since 1979, and is not widely available.

500 Inside Tips for the Long Haul Traveller by Richard Harrington. An excellent little WEXAS publication, reprinted in 1985. Basic (and occasionally very perceptive) advice on everything from visas to car rentals. Handy pocket-size, too.

A Consumer's Guide to Air Travel by Frank Barrett. Published in 1983 by the *Daily Telegraph*. Says a lot about fares and tickets, but not so much about the basics of flying, what to do once you land, or anything else.

As well as the more general guides just listed, there are countless individual country guides available. Probably the best on the market at the moment is the *Fodor* series of easily digestible country guides – ideal for the first time visitor. For visitors to Asia, the annually updated *All Asia Guide* (published by the *Far East Economic Review*) is useful, although aimed much more at the business traveller.

Whichever guidebooks you do decide to buy, remember that most will be utterly dull and tedious to read until you reach your destination. Then, if they're good, they will come alive and remain a vital lifeline, crammed with fascinating background and holiday recommendations relevant to where you're visiting, until you leave.

Of the countries we cover in this guide, **the following have national tourist offices in London:**

Antigua National Tourist Office
15 Thayer Street, London W1 (01-486 7073)

Australian Tourist Commission
4th Floor, Heathcote House, 20 Savile Row, London W1X 1AE (01-434 4371)

Bahamas Ministry of Tourism
23 Old Bond Street, London W1X 4PQ (01-629 5238)

Barbados National Tourist Office
263 Tottenham Court Road, London (01-636 9448)

Bermuda Department of Tourism
9/10 Savile Row, London W1X 2BL (01-734 8813/4)

Canadian Commercial Division
Canada House, Trafalgar Square, London SW14 5BJ (01-629 9492)

East Caribbean Tourist Association
(St Kitts & Nevis/St Lucia/St Vincent & the Grenadines)
10 Kensington Court, London (01-937 9522)

French Government Tourist Office
178 Piccadilly, London W1V 0AL (01-491 7622)

(West) **German** National Tourist Office
61 Conduit Street, London W1R 9TD (01-629 1664)

Hong Kong Tourist Association
125 Pall Mall, London SW1Y 5EA (01-930 4775)

Government of **India** Tourist Office
7 Cork Street, London W1X 2AB (01-437 3677/8)

Italian State Tourist Office
1 Princes Street, London W1R 8AY (01-408 1254)

Japan National Tour Organization
167 Regent Street, London W1R 7FD (01-734 9638)

Kenya National Tourist Office
13 New Burlington Street, London W1X 1FF (01-839 4477)

Korean National Tourism Corporation
Vogue House, 1 Hanover Square, London W1R 9RD (01-408 1591)

Malaysian Tourist Office
17 Curzon Street, London W1Y 7FE (01-499 7388)

New Zealand Tourist Office
New Zealand House, Haymarket, London SW1Y 4TQ (01-930 8422)

National Tourist Office of the **Philippines**
199 Piccadilly, London W1V 9LE (01-439 3481)

Singapore Tourist Promotion Board
33 Heddon Street, London W1R 7LB (01-437 0033)

Taiwan
c/o Free Chinese Centre
4th Floor, Dorland House, 14/16 Regent Street, London SW1Y 4PH (01-930 9553/4)

Tourist Authority of **Thailand**
9 Stafford Street, London W1X 3FE (01-499 7679)

United States Travel and Tourism Administration
22 Sackville Street, London W1X 2EA (01-439 7433)

and the following have offices in New York:

Australia
1270 Avenue of the Americas, New York, NY10020 (489 7550)

Bermuda
Rockefeller Center, 630 5th Avenue, New York, NY10111 (397 7700)

Brazil
551 5th Avenue, New York, NY10017 (682 1055)

Britain
680 5th Avenue, New York, NY10019 (581 4700)

Caribbean
20 E. 46th Street, New York, NY10017 (682 0435)

China
159 Lexington Avenue, New York (725 4950)

France
610 5th Avenue, New York, NY10020 (757 1125)

West Germany
747 3rd Avenue, New York, NY10017 (308 3300)

Hong Kong
548 5th Avenue, New York, NY10036 (947 5008)

India
30 Rockefeller Plaza, New York, NY10020 (586 4901)

Jamaica
2 Dag Hammarskjold Plaza, New York (688 7650)

Japan
45 Rockefeller Plaza, New York, NY10020 (757 5640)

Kenya
15 E. 21st Street, New York, NY10022 (486 1300)

Korea
460 Park Avenue, New York, NY10016 (688 7543)

New Zealand
630 5th Avenue, New York, NY10020 (586 0060)

Philippines
556 5th Avenue, New York, NY10036 (575 7915)

South Africa
610 5th Avenue, New York, NY10020 (245 3720)

Taiwan
Coordination Council for North American Affairs, 801 Second Avenue, New York, NY10017 (697 1250)

Thailand
5 World Trade Center, New York, NY10048 (432 043)

RED TAPE

To travel round the world British citizens will need a valid ten-year passport. For most countries outside Western Europe, a one-year Visitor's Passport will not be accepted. British citizens must apply for a passport on a special form obtainable from any Post Office or Passport Office. Allow at least four to six weeks for your new passport to be sent back from your nearest Passport Office, the address of which will be on the back of the form, although it will probably arrive much sooner.

Provided you are a British citizen, with the appropriate birth certificate or naturalization document to prove it, then there will be no problem about being issued with a passport. It is worth knowing in advance that British applicants will need to have both the two photographs required signed by a bank manager, solicitor, doctor, Church minister, police officer or Member of Parliament who has known them personally for at least two years.

When you receive your new passport it will contain surprisingly little information about you other than date and place of birth, and physical details. Even your occupation is no longer included.

US citizens – if you're applying for the first time or your current passport was issued before your eighteenth birthday or if it's more than eight years old, you'll have to go along in person to any US Post Office or Passport Agency, otherwise you can send off a DSP 82 form by mail. Along with your application you should include two recent passport-type photos, signed on the back, plus around $35. If you have to go along in person, you'll need your US birth certificate and around $42 ($28 if you're under eighteen). Passports are valid for ten years if you're over eighteen, five if you're under. If you've any problems, contact the Passport Office, Department of State, Washington, DC 20520, and ask them for their free booklet 'Your Trip Abroad'. Canadian passports are valid for five years only and can be obtained by mail from the Passport Office, Department of External Affairs, 125 Sussex Drive, Ottawa, Ontario KIA OG3. Allow six to eight weeks' processing time from March to September, and four to six weeks from October to February.

To visit certain other destinations you will also need a visa. This is simply an official permit to enter a country, granted by the government of that country, and usually rubber-stamped into your passport. Of the countries listed in this guide, British passport holders will need visas for the following countries only: United States, Australia, Thailand, the Philippines (Manila) and Taiwan. United States passport holders will need visas for the following: Australia, Japan, Singapore (for business visitors only, tourists don't need one), Taiwan, India, Bahrain, South Korea and Kenya.

Visas are obtainable in advance from the national embassy of the country you intend to visit. Most will cost you between £5 and £10 – occasionally more – and it's best to obtain them in reverse order, starting with the last visa you need first of all. Visas are obtainable either by post (write first for an application form) or in person from the appropriate embassy in your home country.

Wherever you visit, make a note in advance of the address of your own national embassy or consulate. If you lose your passport, or come into any other serious difficulty, then consular assistance will be essential. Part Two gives all the relevant addresses for the destinations included in this guide.

The traveller who may choose to hire a car abroad needs additional documentation. An international driving licence is vital (consult any national motoring organization) and, if you choose to take your own car abroad, a whole host of other documents are essential. Health and comprehensive vehicle insurance, together with an international registration disc and vehicle registration certificate, will be necessary. Depending on which countries you plan to visit, additional documents (including your birth certificate) may be required.

HEALTH

To consider embarking on a Round the World trip when you are less than fit would be very foolish. But even if you are in good health, there are a number of important precautions which you ought to observe before you leave.

British travellers ought to obtain Social Security Form E111 before they leave. It will entitle you to free, or heavily reduced, medical treatment in most European countries as well as New Zealand and Hong Kong. Travelling further afield you will also need DHSS leaflet SA35, which gives all the information you need about vaccinations and other health precautions. Both SA35 and

E111 application forms are available from any DHSS office or by post from: DHSS Leaflets Unit, Stanmore, Middlesex HA7 1AY.

Whilst on holiday, you ought to carry with you at all times vital medical information about yourself. Your blood group, allergies (especially against drugs) and diabetic or steroid treatment dosages if applicable. A doctor's letter outlining any particular problems, translated into the appropriate languages of countries you plan to visit, is also worthwhile if you're away for some time or heading for exotic locations.

Many long-haul destinations will require, or it will be strongly recommended, that you have certain vaccinations before you leave. Of the countries in this guide, the following table gives details where vaccinations are either compulsory or strongly advised. Remember that it is always sensible to have a vaccination against typhoid wherever cholera vaccination is recommended. Even transit passengers ought to consider any appropriate vaccinations.

	Cholera	Yellow Fever	Malaria	Polio and Typhoid	Infectious Hepatitis
Bahrain				Yes	
Brazil		Yes		Yes	Yes
India	Yes		Yes	Yes	Yes
Kenya	Yes	Yes	Yes	Yes	Yes
South Korea				Yes	Yes
Kuwait				Yes	
Malaysia	Some country areas		Yes	Yes	Yes
Philippines	Yes		Yes	Yes	Yes
Singapore	Some country areas			Yes	
Taiwan				Yes	

Plan your vaccinations in advance – yellow fever, polio and hepatitis cannot normally be given within three weeks of each other. If you arrange a lengthy trip, certain vaccines will need renewed. Cholera vaccine, for example, only lasts for 6 months and does not give complete protection in any case.

A few chemically unstable vaccinations will need to be given at one of the vaccination centres licensed by the government. There are also several equally capable licensed private centres in London, including one at 45 Berkeley Street (01-499 4000) run by Thomas Cook, and at the Medical Centre in Regent Street run by British Airways (01-439 9584). Both are licensed to give yellow fever vaccinations which most local doctors are not.

Remember that a vaccination without a certificate is no good – and it *must* be the approved international certificate, signed by a doctor and rubber-stamped by the local public health authority. They are all a standard size, slightly larger than a British passport.

Before you leave, try to consider the track record of any tropical or less developed country which you plan to visit. Consult your own doctor about additional health risks in a specific country, and consider spending a few hours in your local library preparing yourself for any unexpected risks.

Once you're actually there, remember a few basic precautions. Stay as cool as possible, wearing clothes light in weight and light in colour. Avoid nylon socks and underpants. Drink plenty of water. Temperatures over 26°C (80°F) mean you ought to drink at least 8 pints of liquid every 24 hours – 10 pints over 38°C (100°F). Add some extra salt to your food since your body loses vital salt reserves through sweating in a hot climate. Consider enteric coated salt tablets, on a daily basis, if you don't normally eat salt with meals. Avoid drinking tap water as well if you can – ask for purified water in your hotel room.

Take care when eating the local food abroad. In general the safest foods are fresh fruits and vegetables with unbroken skins. They can then be washed and peeled before eating, but this rules out foods like lettuce and strawberries. It is advisable to avoid milk products as well in much warmer climates unless they are boiled or used in cooking. Having said that, one of the pleasures of travelling abroad is briefly sampling another country's food, and a Round the World trip is as good a way as any to do that. Ask a local what he's eating and then try some of that. A surprising number of suspect looking foreign dishes are delicious!

Diarrhoea remains the most common travellers' disorder. Combined with jet lag, it can make you feel distinctly under the weather for days. Your stomach and intestines will need a few days to get used to new eating habits, but if diarrhoea is accompanied

144 The Round the World Air Guide

with aches and pains, fever or vomiting then see a doctor *immediately*. Likewise if it occurs after returning home see a doctor at once and tell him which countries were visited and when.

A final word of warning: immigration authorities can be very strict about vaccination requirements for their country. Find out well in advance what the current requirements are for everywhere outside Europe and North America which you plan to visit, then get the necessary vaccinations *and* keep the properly signed and authenticated certificate. If you do not, then you may find yourself being refused entry into a country, or even vaccinated at your arrival airport and kept in isolation for up to 14 days – longer if you need more than one injection.

LIKELY PROBLEMS

Travelling through different time zones, and to many countries, you are likely to encounter a great number of problems. Being aware of them in advance will go a long way to solving them.

● **Travel stress:** Crossing a large number of time zones will cause your body some disorientation. Rushing to catch the scheduled flight you've reserved for the next leg of your trip will frustrate you. Getting held up at Customs will annoy you. All will contribute to travel stress – quite different from a fear of flying.

Stress is caused by an underlying panic in some form or other. To counter this, avoid leaving reservations and airport coach bookings to the last minute. Do everything in as relaxed (and preplanned) a manner as possible. Try occasionally to stay away from the busy main streets, crowded restaurants and noisy department stores. Take your holiday easy, especially during the first 24 hours, and try to plan your arrival in a new country as near as possible to your normal bedtime. Enjoy the new surroundings and new environment as much as possible and don't constantly be worrying about money, tickets, visas, vaccinations – or even your favourite pot plant abandoned back home. For as stress-free a holiday as possible, take things easy, and ensure essentials are considered well in advance of your departure so that they won't cause you any worry whilst away.

• **Sunburn/tropical temperatures:** If you visit India or Dubai in midsummer then you can expect to feel uncomfortable as the daily temperature soars well past the 100°F mark. There is no reason, however, for you to suffer any lasting effects either from tropical temperatures in general or sunburn in particular.

If you're planning to travel extensively in hot countries train for it beforehand by spending a few sessions in a sauna bath. Curiously, this will help teach your body to perspire at lower temperatures and so generally improve your circulation in heat. Once you reach your hot destination, protect yourself with loose clothing and a hat if you're out a lot in the open, until you've built up a tan.

Take things easy in hot weather. Rest frequently, and eat and drink *before* you need to so as to replace vital body salts. Drink non-fizzy, purified water as much as possible.

If you do feel ill after being in strong sun, cool yourself with cold water sponging or ice packs. Take plenty of fluid, drink slowly, and try a couple of aspirin to reduce your headache or temperature. If the problem persists, don't hesitate to call a doctor.

• **Sexual precautions:** The simplest sexual precaution any Round the World traveller can take is to avoid sexual encounters. Sadly, venereal diseases like gonorrhoea and syphilis have been spread worldwide largely as a result of the increase in air travel. But human nature being what it is, sexually transmitted disease contracted abroad will always be a potential hazard.

Diagnosis can be difficult, especially in women, and prevention is better than cure. A sheath gives quite a bit of protection against VD, as well as being a useful contraceptive precaution. If you restrict sexual contact to a single partner then obviously your risk will be minimal. Take an ample supply of contraceptives with you if necessary since you may have difficulty obtaining them abroad. Strongly Roman Catholic countries will disown contraceptive enquiries and you may even cause offence by just asking.

If you feel you may have contracted a disease through sexual contact, seek medical advice at once. The symptoms are increasingly painful, and still occasionally fatal, but treatment after infection is always successful to a degree. Remember at all times that few countries condone obvious promiscuity and, in some cases, a seemingly innocent gesture or show of affection can get you arrested.

● **Rabies:** Rabies remains one of the world's most hideous diseases. Once contracted, there is no known cure and death is guaranteed, so understandably precautions against rabies can never be too strict.

There is a vaccine against rabies, but this is highly toxic and is only given to special risk cases – vets or those actually bitten by a rabid animal. Only *immediate* vaccination after you've been bitten will offer any hope of survival. The answer, then, is to be highly cautious of all animals when abroad.

As a rule, simply avoid animals as much as possible. Don't befriend strays, and advise children likewise. If you are bitten or scratched, by *any* animal abroad, wash the wound at once with soap or detergent and plenty of water. Try to have someone find the animal's owner and exchange addresses. Say that you must be informed if the animal becomes ill within two weeks. At least make a note of the time and place of the incident and what the animal looked like.

Above all, report to the nearest doctor or hospital *at once*. A course of vaccination may be necessary, and report the incident to your own doctor when you get back home.

All this fuss may seem totally unnecessary, and in most cases it will be, but the potential consequences of contracting rabies is the worst type of horror film illness (and death) that you could imagine.

● **Delhi belly:** Delhi belly is probably the best-known name for the particularly virulent form of diarrhoea which can affect most air travellers. Known as everything from Kathmandu Quickstep to Montezuma's Revenge, there is little precaution against it other than choosing very carefully what you eat. Advice on how best to cope with diarrhoea is listed under Health.

Travellers' diarrhoea can strike at any stage of your journey. It can occasionally be avoided by cutting down on food consumption – so reducing the risk of eating food bearing the disease-causing organisms. Try to be moderate in your eating to prevent the stomach upset that will spoil your trip. Food, and especially water, warrant the utmost care at all times when abroad. Be particularly warned that a sudden onset of profuse watery diarrhoea in an epidemic area calls for immediate attention. It may be an early sign of cholera.

• **What to do if you get ill:** Obviously this varies dramatically from country to country, and with your symptoms. If you suffer an accident, or heart attack, or another sudden serious disorder then you will receive immediate medical attention wherever you are. Get yourself to a doctor or hospital at once.

Depending on what part of the world you're in you may or may not have to pay for your treatment. Private medical insurance, taken out before you leave, is *strongly* recommended, since few countries will allow you medical care totally free of charge. If you have an E111 then let the doctor or hospital authorities know (assuming, of course, you're in a country where it is valid).

Initially you will almost certainly be required to pay for your treatment abroad. Be warned that this will be expensive so adequate insurance and a reserve of traveller's cheques really ought to be essentials. If in doubt about your medical condition then you ought to see a doctor – and worry about the cost later.

Medical care abroad will generally be adequate to good. Even in larger Third World cities (for instance, Mombasa) the standard of medical care will be perfectly acceptable. Be prepared to fill in endless forms (assuming you're not quite at death's door, and even then it's not unknown), wherever you go. Do not expect the medical practices of your home country to be reciprocated abroad. Some practitioners include routine physical examinations and expensive drugs for the simplest of problems. Multiple vitamin therapy and the occasional suppository are common practice – and can add heavily to your bill. Consider shopping around or, better still, wait until you're home for non-essential treatment.

• **Suggested medical emergency kit:**
Assorted sticking plasters
Assorted small bandages
One large bandage (big enough for a sprained wrist or ankle)
12 gauze swabs
Small pack of cotton wool
1 bar soap
Small bottle of disinfectant (Dettol or TCP)

1 pair of (blunt-ended) scissors
Safety pins
Thermometer (not a mercury one – not allowed in aircraft)
Disposable syringes (essential for diabetics and a few other medical cases – helpful to have doctor's letter as well to prevent suspicion of illegal drug use at Customs)
100 soluble aspirin
Adhesive medical tape (Menolin)
Anti-malarial tablets (if necessary)
Insect repellent
Water purification tablets
Diarrhoea prevention tablets (Diocalm excellent)
Sunburn lotion

That list, in a waterproof box and clearly labelled, contains the minimum essentials for most minor emergencies. Obviously a lot more could be added (sleeping tablets, any prescribed drugs, anti-worm tablets, insect powder and so on) but a lot will depend on where you plan to visit. Consult your doctor for sound advice before you leave.

Insurance

Insuring yourself before you travel is essential. Legally (unless you're travelling exclusively by car) there is nothing to prevent you travelling uninsured, but you would be very foolish indeed to travel without it.

Car insurance is something you ought to be aware of well before you leave if you plan to take your own car on any stage of the trip. Hire cars will be comprehensively insured beforehand by reputable firms (including all the major ones we list under Car Hire).

Most people have, in addition, life insurance before they leave home. This can be extended, or else a new policy taken out altogether, before you leave. Medical expenses abroad as a whole can be extremely expensive – and the most likely insurance claim called upon.

If your Round the World trip ranges through areas of no particular hazard, for instance exclusively major westernized cities like London, New York and Sydney, then modest cover of only a few thousand pounds (or dollars) will be sufficient. Certain trips may merit a certain type of insurance: a jungle trek in Kenya or one involving dangerous sports, for example. Particularly in areas with poor hospital resources, extra coverage in case an emergency helicopter flight is necessary should be taken out. For such trips you ought to consider coverage up to £10,000 (or equivalent in dollars) depending on the precise nature of your trip.

All medical insurance ought to include the cost of repatriation for serious, or long-term, treatment, together with that of a travelling companion. Always look for an insurance company offering total cover rather than specified maximum amounts for medication, hospital beds, or whatever.

Luggage insurance, together with coverage for contents (including money), is sensible. Companies will set a limit to each claim for such losses – otherwise you could fairly claim the earth for losses which never occurred! Specific valuables – jewellery, furs, cameras, and so on – deserve individual insurance.

Traveller's cheques normally don't need to be insured, provided you keep the receipts safely in case of loss. If you insist on carrying large sums of cash around, then this should be covered although think carefully about whether taking cash really is a good idea. The moment you discover a loss, you *must* report it to the local police to fulfil a standard insurance policy condition. Try to obtain some written proof from the police about how much you reported lost.

If you travel abroad on business, try to get your employers to pay for your travel insurance as a fringe benefit. Many employers will agree readily, and it can often be the best way of ensuring maximum coverage at no (or minimal) cost to yourself.

Most travel agents, tour operators and airlines will offer special insurance to their customers. Liability varies enormously, needless to say, and terms change regularly – the matter is best discussed with your airline or travel agent before you decide on a ticket.

Budgeting

Deciding exactly how much you are likely to spend on a Round the World trip depends entirely on your personal tastes. The first consideration ought to be how long you are planning to go for and what class of accommodation you intend to occupy since the difference between comfortable two-star and deluxe five-star hotels will easily double or treble the amount you'll need.

Staying with friends or relatives will cut your costs considerably. So too will a couple of weeks lying on a few tropical beaches as opposed to frantic sightseeing and organized excursions. Work out in advance how much the limit of your accommodation budget will be, how much you are prepared to spend on drinks, meals, presents, duty free goods, car hire and so on. Note also the hidden costs of departure taxes from airports and visas. On average they'll cost you between £5 and £10 each. This can swiftly add £100 to a six-stop Round the World trip.

As a useful pointer, bear in mind that if you plan to stay exclusively in hotels belonging to a large international chain (such as Hilton International, Sheraton or Inter-Continental) then their prices are pretty standard the world over, although the average cost of living in the country will influence your final costs. In summer 1986, for example, a double room in the New Delhi Sheraton would have cost you £65. The same double room in London or Rome would have cost you £110 per night.

What is classed as a cheap or expensive country depends, of course, on your own country of residence. As a general rule, the most expensive countries in the world to visit are the Middle Eastern Gulf States – including Bahrain, Dubai and (especially) Kuwait. Assuming that you are staying at a first-class hotel and eating in good city restaurants, the following table should give you some guidance about where is cheap and where is not:

Very Expensive:	Kuwait, Bahrain and Dubai
Expensive:	Japan, Hong Kong, Caribbean islands and USA
Moderate:	Brazil, Australia, Singapore, Great Britain, France, South Korea, Malaysia, Canada and West Germany
Inexpensive:	New Zealand, Philippines, Kenya, Peru, India, Thailand, Taiwan, Italy and Netherlands

If you are planning your Round the World trip on as limited a budget as possible, then you would be well advised not to visit the most expensive countries we've listed. Gulf States, where every other person in a country like Kuwait seems to live like a millionaire, should be avoided if possible.

You may like to consider applying for one or two discount cards before you leave, and we've listed some of the better known ones later in this section. If you cannot cut costs by staying with friends or relatives then at least avoid the large international hotels. Ask at the airport information when you land about cheaper hotels and be honest about your price limit. Occasionally it will be possible to stay as paying guests of local people at a fraction of the cost of a first-class hotel.

Drinking costs can be cut considerably by stocking up with your duty free allowance each time you land. Draining a duty free bottle of whisky in your hotel room may be less sociable than sampling the local highspots but it will certainly work out much cheaper – and more intimate.

Similarly, with your choice of eating places, there is no need to have the hotel's expensive five-course dinner every night (unless, of course, it is included in the price of your room). Find out where the best local restaurants are or, better still, ask someone who lives in the city to recommend where they would eat for an evening out. That way not only will you save yourself quite a bit of money but you may also stumble across a restaurant much more typical of the country you're visiting than an international hotel will ever be.

If you are travelling on a limited budget you'll need to appreciate well in advance that you cannot afford to buy expensive presents and souvenirs everywhere you go. Handling at least half a dozen currencies can lull you into a false sense of security about precisely how much or how little money you really have with you. If money is a major factor governing where you stay and what you eat then think very carefully every time you spend even a little.

If you are travelling whilst still a student (regardless of age) you ought to invest £3.50 for an International Student Identity Card (ISIC). This can be obtained easily from your student travel shop, or occasionally from your Students' Association offices, on production of a valid matriculation card. As well as the fee, you will need two recent passport photos signed on the back.

Your ISIC will allow you reduced (or even free) admission to many museums, galleries and historic sights. Many airlines will allow limited concessions on ticket prices to ISIC holders – sometimes by as much as a third off the normal ticket price. It is worth carrying some other proof of your status as a student in case you are challenged. Don't expect a student discount as a right but instead as a bonus wherever you go. It costs nothing to ask if a student discount is available, mind you.

Another young person's discount card is the Federation of International Youth Travel Organizations' card (FIYTO) which is available to anyone under the age of 26, regardless of whether a student or not. 125 organizations around the world (which specialize in youth travel) belong to FIYTO, and the card entitles holders to similar, but nevertheless fewer, concessions to those given to ISIC holders.

The FIYTO card costs only £2 and is issued with a comprehensive handbook listing all the concession entitlements. Young persons under 26 wishing to apply for a FIYTO discount card should write for an application form to:

Central Bureau of Educational Visits and Exchanges (CBEVE),
Seymour Mews House,
Seymour Mews (off Wigmore Street),
London W1.

Discount organizations

The largest and best known is the World Expeditionary Association (WEXAS), founded in 1970. Membership is open to anyone and currently 27,000, predominantly business travellers, have joined from almost 100 countries.

WEXAS offer a worldwide and comprehensive programme of low-cost flights, including about 40 different Round the World options. Members of WEXAS receive *The Traveller* magazine four times a year and are eligible to receive other WEXAS publications.

WEXAS call themselves 'the trendsetters in travel' and invite potential clients to shop around. Their ticket prices do represent excellent value for money – and can all be booked by credit card, thereby offering you a full guarantee that you will actually receive a valid ticket precisely as ordered.

Anyone can join WEXAS, although there is an annual membership fee of £17.58 ($25). This will almost certainly be recovered when you book your first discount flight through them. It is not worth joining WEXAS, however, exclusively in the hope of being offered a discount Round the World ticket. Comparing the airlines' own literature with WEXAS ticket prices (for summer 1986), there are no ticket reductions at all and in one case (British Caledonian with Malaysian and Continental) the WEXAS Round the World Economy price was £100 ($140) *higher* than the £1250 ($1875) offered by the airline itself.

Other discount organizations, some of which may be restricted to business travellers or available directly through your employers, will offer value for money reduced-cost tickets. On the whole, discounts will not be available for Round the World tickets since they are all heavily reduced in price by the airline in the first place. Ensure before you go ahead and join any discount organization that you will be able to get some sort of discount on a Round the World ticket and that the ticket concerned is precisely the one with the routing you want as well.

Retired people and pensioners will have more time on their hands than most. Many elderly people use their retirement years to see parts of the world they had neither the time nor the money to enjoy when they were younger. To make travel easier for them, airlines often offer special discounts for pensioners. These vary from airline to airline so ask around before you commit yourself to a particular Round the World ticket.

A few airlines, for instance, offer discounts to pensioners visiting family in Australia or New Zealand, or will alternatively have a standard 10 or 20 per cent discount to retired persons as a matter of policy.

Pensioners are also likely to benefit from further travel discounts when they reach new destinations. In France, for example, there is a specific Carte Vermeil which allows retired people of any nationality to travel by rail at reduced fares.

AIRLINE DISCOUNTS

Airline discounts vary enormously from one company to another. It is worth bearing in mind that a Round the World ticket will initially represent a considerable saving on the full scheduled return fare between the two furthest destinations on your routing.

The commonest airline discount offered is to young people. Babies and very young children under the age of about 3 will normally either be carried free, or at a nominal 10 per cent of the adult fare provided they don't occupy a seat to themselves. Babies and infants will not be allowed any baggage allowance other than their carrycot.

Slightly older children, to about 12 or 13, will usually be allowed a substantial discount of up to 50 per cent. They will be entitled to have their own seat and a baggage allowance. Above the age of 13, most airlines operate a Youth Fare facility whereby young persons are allowed about 25 per cent off any fare. Proof of age is required and the upper age limit will be around 21.

Separate student fares are occasionally offered for full-time students, over the age of 21, travelling between their home and place of education. Written proof of student status, from the appropriate college or university, is required.

Last minute organization (two weeks): what to take with you

LUGGAGE

People's needs, and personal preferences, of what type of luggage to choose vary enormously. If you are planning to do a lot of air travel, as you will be during a Round the World trip, then a sturdy but lightweight form of luggage is essential.

Leather looks good and lasts, but it costs a small fortune to buy, scratches easily and weighs a lot. A large leather suitcase empty will weigh about as much as a canvas holdall full, thereby reducing your airline free baggage allowance by a few vital kilogrammes.

Soft-sided cases, either fabric or plastic, are now becoming more fashionable. Not only do they generally look good but they are lightweight and sturdy – provided, of course, that you've bought a respectable make with strong straps and secure backing inside. Soft-sided cases are gradually taking over a larger share of the market once held by the hard-sided, moulded cases.

Lighter and more rigid than leather, moulded cases will last longer than any others. Good makes are strong and reliable companions for any air traveller which can last a generation or more. Hard-sided cases, however, offer less flexibility about how much you can pack into them than their soft-sided counterparts, but they do stand up to the rigours of baggage handling better.

Younger travellers may consider taking a rucksack instead of a bulky suitcase. The rucksack is basically a container bag, with or without a supporting frame, which lies directly on the back of the carrier supported by two shoulder straps. Rucksacks offer several advantages over more conventional suitcases.

They weigh, on average, much less at scarcely more than a kilogramme or two. They are a much more comfortable means of carrying luggage, particularly if you have a tent, than suitcases and allow you both hands free for tickets, passports and so on. Rucksacks can stand up to a lot of wear and good ones are generally cheaper than good suitcases.

It is easy to overpack a rucksack, mind you, and more often than not a full rucksack will weigh considerably over the international Economy Class baggage allowance of 20 kg. Rucksacks can be extremely antisocial objects as well, especially if you're travelling overland on a crowded bus or train once you reach your destination. A loaded rucksack will also cause your back to sweat because of the lack of air between you and your pack.

The biggest single disadvantage that rucksacks bring lies in the harsh reality that some airlines will simply refuse to carry them altogether unless they are packed in a box. They see rucksacks, with all the attendant pots, pans and stores hanging loose, as an unnecessary inconvenience to themselves and the international baggage handlers. Loaded rucksacks, after all, don't stack anything like as well as neatly constructed suitcases.

Whatever you decide to choose – suitcase or rucksack – remember your luggage allowance which will be made clear when you buy your ticket. It is usually 20 kg (44 lb) for Economy Class and 30 kg (66 lb) for First Class. Excess baggage will cost you a small fortune – 1 per cent of the full First Class fare per extra kilogramme for each leg of your trip on which your luggage is overweight.

Delsey, the French luggage manufacturer of up-market cases, have come up with a range of cases ideally suited to the long-haul air passenger. Referred to as 'cabin cases', these are small cases designed to be taken on flights as hand luggage, to hold all that you need on a long-haul trip. They are made to fit under any airline seat, and have ample room for your overnight kit, reading material, toiletries, and so on. They come in several designs and also double as a handy weekend case.

All airlines will accept unaccompanied baggage if you feel it is essential to take a great deal with you. In such circumstances, if you know in advance that your baggage will exceed weight allowances, you can arrange for it to be sent on ahead of you by cargo or freight and collect it at your next arrival airport. This will work out much cheaper than paying the cost of normal accompanied (excess) baggage rates. Consult your travel agent or airline well in advance if you foresee this problem.

For easy recognition (and in many cases insisted upon by the airline) you should put your name and address on the outside of your baggage. This ought to be your name and permanent home address, together with a destination address if known, *stuck* on to the outside of your baggage. External name tags can easily come loose, or be cut off at your first departure airport by thieves looking for empty homes to burgle. Make sure you put the same information inside all baggage as well.

PACKING

Knowing what best to pack for a lengthy Round the World trip – and how to make it all fit – can be a big problem. The overriding priority must be weight. You should, first of all, aim to leave home with suitcases no more than three-quarters full. Otherwise you will have no room left for all these precious – and heavy – souvenirs you'll inevitably bring back. If you leave your departure airport with a suitcase weighing 19.5 kilogrammes then you will have problems bringing much home unless you're prepared to pay excess baggage charges (or travel First Class and have an extra 10 kilogrammes allowed).

Realistically, the amount of clothes you take ought to be kept to a minimum, but this will obviously depend on where you plan to visit. Hot countries require few clothes – but lots of them. A busy round of international business meetings will require a few changes of formal dress. If you're going to a shopping mecca such as Hong Kong take hardly anything and stock up there.

Different guide books will give you different advice about how best to pack. In the end, it's a matter of personal choice and common sense but start with one simple rule. Once you've made your (first) choice of what to pack, spread it all out on your bed. Survey what will, almost certainly, be something like two-thirds of your total wardrobe and then half the numbers of *everything* there. Honestly, that will be enough! At the same time double the amount of money you were planning to take. At worst, you won't spend the extra, and merely have to put it back in the bank again.

When you've cut down to a minimum what to pack, start with the awkward items at the bottom of your suitcase, pairs of shoes wrapped in plastic bags, travel iron and so on. Then add clothes in layers interlaced with large sheets of tissue. Alternatively cover clothes with the large polythene bags you get back from the dry cleaners. One or two sweaters (always essential since you never know when that tropical sunshine will disappear for a week), shirts, blouses, trousers or skirts (left on their hangers), with T-shirts, underwear and so on left near the top. Last of all, something soft like a coat or dressing gown on top of everything else. Resist filling every remaining gap since you'll need *some* space for presents and so on bought abroad!

Toiletries ought best to be packed in separate units – hair, first aid, medicines, that sort of thing. What best to take is covered next under Essentials.

Surprisingly, you will need more clothes in summer than in winter and ideally you want clothes which you can mix and match with each other. Cotton jerseys are ideal for both men and women for this purpose, and cotton clothes in general are best for casual wearing in hot climates.

When you do pack, remember that to avoid the inevitable fights, couples should never share the same suitcase! If you need more than one case each, then a nylon or canvas holdall is ideal for shared extras such as fold-away raincoats, toiletries and so on.

A small point worth remembering is that every woman is allowed a handbag in addition to whatever other luggage she may have. Take a large one – big enough to hold all your make-up, jewellery, undies, travel documents, money, and a few paperbacks for the flight.

ESSENTIALS

Most essentials should be fairly obvious even to the inexperienced traveller. In addition to travel documents, check and double-check that you've got all the *articles* of clothing you will need. Make sure, for instance, that your six pairs of socks don't get left behind on the bed, and that you've included at least two changes of shoes. Otherwise theft, wear and tear, or just a good soaking will mean you wasting a couple of precious days wandering round a strange city looking for a new pair!

Pack essential toiletries into separate groups, each in its own small bag or waterproof box. Try packing one bag for medicines – including basic first aid items like aspirin, sticking plasters and any prescribed medicines – another bag for haircare, another for washing – sponges, soap, and so on. Double-check all toiletries and women should remember to take a generous supply of tampons and contraceptives if necessary. Outside developed western nations these can be difficult and expensive to obtain, and it is always best to travel as prepared as possible for the unexpected.

If you take a travel iron or electric hairdryer then remember also an adaptor for different plug fittings. These will always be 110V or 220–240V in major cities.

LUXURIES

In addition to the duty free allowances of alcohol and tobacco, listed earlier in the Airport Information section of Part One, British visitors returning home are allowed only a nominal £28 worth of 'other goods' without having to pay any duty.

You are allowed £208 worth of goods obtained duty- and tax-paid from any of the twelve EEC countries. Outside the obvious restrictions (drugs, firearms, pornographic material and so on) there is a surprisingly long list of other prohibited goods which you may have considered bringing home. Exotic foreign plants, even as seeds, and pieces of dead wood with bark still intact, for instance, are forbidden. Beware of purchasing large electrical appliances or jewellery since although they are legal, excise duty on these items can be very high. Diamond jewellery, for example, is often brought back from Amsterdam where it can be purchased at much lower prices without the Value Added Tax. The shock of having to pay 15 per cent on top of £1000 or so for an already-paid sparkling souvenir can be frightening!

If in doubt, go through the Red Customs channel – but beware that *all* luxury items are liable to excise payment on returning home. American travellers will be faced with equally tight restrictions. Check your legal allowance before you leave with your nearest Excise Office, although restrictions for Americans tend to be much the same as those for British travellers.

VALUABLES

Being sensible, your best policy with regard to valuables would be to take as few as possible with you. To take a lavish amount of jewellery on a lengthy trip, involving numerous changes of hotel and destinations, is to invite the possibility of loss, damage or theft. Sadly, obviously affluent tourists are a prime target for robbery the world over.

The best advice to travellers who wish to take valuables with them is to wear them as much as you can. That way you'll at least know where they are, but in tropical climates this will prove impractical (try swimming with a full display of bracelets and necklaces!) to say the least of looking ridiculous. Evidence of wealth should be avoided in poorer countries except, obviously, in social situations where it wouldn't look out of place. You would be very foolish indeed, for instance, to stroll the back streets of Delhi bedecked in gold and diamond jewellery.

Above all, think very carefully before taking valuables with you. Take your second best gold bracelet or leave your largest stones at home, and once abroad, hang on to them very carefully.

The second best option, other than wearing jewellery as often as is practical, is to entrust it to the safest hands available. Do *not* leave jewellery, money, passport or any other vital health or travel documents in your hotel room. You ought, of course, to be comfortably insured before you leave since explaining any loss in a foreign country, to strangers who speak a strange language, will seldom be easy.

Most larger hotels will offer safety deposit facilities. These are your best bet if you prefer not to carry valuables about with you. On the whole, they are reliable although many cheaper hotels, and those in less developed countries, have earned a poor reputation. Always ask for a written receipt of what you deposit, if one is not automatically offered (it should be) – you may not be popular in so doing but it ought to provide some safeguard against 'loss' for any reason.

TRAVEL CLOTHING/SHOES

When travelling, you ought to wear clothes which are as light and comfortable as possible. Particularly on a long-haul flight, you will be restricted to a fairly small area of space which can quickly become very uncomfortable if you choose to wear a jacket and tie, or tight clothing around the waist.

Due to air pressure, your body will swell slightly during flight. As a result, clothes which are comfortably tight on the ground will be extremely uncomfortable in the air. Shoes particularly will be a problem so avoid wearing tight, or brand new, footwear. It's not a bad idea to keep your shoes off altogether once you're safely airborne, and you might like to carry a pair of lightweight slippers with you for the occasional stroll to the toilet (many airlines supply slipperettes).

There is little purpose wearing particularly smart or dressy clothing when you are flying. Not only will you want to change anyway once you reach your destination, but clothes can get badly crumpled or creased on a long-haul flight, making them look untidy for the rest of your holiday unless you can get them ironed again.

A final consideration ought to be made about the climate of your destination. Leaving somewhere like London or New York in midwinter for Australasia or the Far East in full winter clothing will make your first few hours after arriving extremely unpleasant. Bear in mind that aircraft tend always to be very warm and if you do get chilly then you can always ask for a blanket. For comfortable travel stick to light and loose clothing, along with loose-fitting shoes.

• **Recent developments in lightweight gear:** Fashions around the world are constantly changing, but a design revolution in lightweight clothes that started in the early 1980s has particular relevance to long-haul air travellers.

Lightweight clothes are essential to really comfortable air travel. Many clothing retailers now market lightweight clothing, aimed more at the lucrative summer market, but ideal for long-haul air travel all year round.

For British travellers, one manufacturer worth looking out for is a company called Blacks Camping & Leisure, who produce this type of light travel clothing. Their garments are well designed, don't crease even after the hardiest of journeys, and both wash and dry easily.

Blacks specialize normally in camping and leisure equipment but market their popular lightweight clothing under the label *Freestyle*. As yet, though, the *Freestyle* range is not available in the United States.

MONEY

Regardless of your overall budget, money will remain one of the most important factors throughout your Round the World trip. If you budget sensibly, and are realistic about how much you are liable to spend, then money will present no problems provided you're cautious about looking after it abroad. Knowing what form to best take your holiday money in can be the biggest nuisance, but the ideal situation will be for you to take a mixture of several forms abroad.

● **Traveller's cheques:** You can buy traveller's cheques in two forms: foreign currency or sterling/dollars in the case of US readers. Foreign currency cheques will probably cost slightly more than sterling cheques on account of currency fluctuations (especially against the American dollar). Most issuers will charge commission on a percentage basis; American Express, for instance, charge 1 per cent with a minimum fee of £1 per purchase. Not only do you know precisely how much foreign currency you have left, but you will not have to pay any commission with this form of traveller's cheque *provided* you cash it wherever that currency would normally be valid (for example, Australian dollars in Australia). You will lose a noticeable commission when changing unused cheques on your return.

Sterling traveller's cheques cost approximately the same as foreign currency ones (although some building societies offer them commission-free to account holders). They tend to be a relatively safe form of carrying money abroad, particularly if you are visiting numerous countries as you will be on a Round the World trip. They will generally incur a small commission charge when you exchange the cheques abroad. American Express are, on average, the cheapest to purchase and among the most widely accepted, with offices worldwide. Their impressive new refund service, in more popular tourist destinations, is worth remembering. (Note – sterling traveller's cheques are unpopular in America.)

● **Currency:** Taking actual cash with you has certain advantages. A small amount of local currency will be essential for your taxi from the airport, or to pay for your first night's food and accommodation. Taking much more than enough for your initial needs on arrival is a bad idea, however. Not only do you stand to lose money on your surplus currency should the exchange rate fall (as it frequently does) but you have absolutely no means of reclaiming foreign currency should it be lost or stolen. Some countries restrict the amount of currency you can take in or out so if you are over the limit you may even have it confiscated if stopped when leaving.

Sterling or US dollars can be imported and exported freely from Great Britain or the United States and a small amount with you is recommended. Not only will you be able to exchange it around the world, often at more 'advantageous' rates than the official rate for traveller's cheques, but in many less developed countries, sterling or dollars can often be more readily accepted than their own currency. You will also need some additional currency from your home country for expenses at your first departure airport, and when you eventually arrive back again, for meals, connections to your home address, telephone calls, and so on.

● **Credit cards:** Credit cards are perfect for travel expenses. They are safer and more convenient than cash, and will not incur any extra commission at the point of sale (and don't be hoodwinked into being charged an extra percentage if you pay by credit card in places like India where the traders often insist they must levy this additional charge as it is 'charged to them otherwise'). In addition, you have at least a month to pay although interest charges will rise steeply if you do not pay in full within a month or so of making the plastic payment. If you are planning to spend several months abroad, credit cards are not suitable, unless, of course, you make a prior written agreement with your credit card company for payment to go in occasionally, before you leave home. For Round the World trips of up to a month they are an ideal way of spending money safely but remember to watch your overall spending limit. Write to your company, in advance, and ask if they will raise your credit limit. This will cost you nothing to arrange and may be a sensible precaution against unforeseen expenses abroad.

• **Eurocheques:** Eurocheques are another alternative for British travellers. They can work out expensive and are not accepted outside Europe or North Africa (Morocco and Tunisia). Eurocheques can be made out for precisely the amount you require but are a more expensive alternative to credit cards or traveller's cheques. They will cost you approximately £4 a year, just for owning them, plus a 1.25 per cent handling charge and an additional 30 pence *per cheque*. Eurocheques are not a sensible purchase for intended Round the World travellers because of their limited use.

• **Looking after your money:** Looking after your money ought to remain a priority at all times abroad, and the most sensible precaution you can take is not to carry lots of cash about with you. Cash traveller's cheques only when necessary and keep a firm hold of wallets and purses at all times. Remember that it is absolutely *vital* that you keep a separate note of your traveller's cheque numbers in case of loss or theft. If you don't then you will have no chance of securing a refund should you lose your cheques for any reason and your trip could be ruined.

A wise investment for any traveller is a money belt, worn around the waist beneath a shirt or blouse like a normal belt. Depending on what size you choose, a money belt should be able to hold most of your traveller's cheques, all of your currency notes, and possibly your passport as well. It is quite common for women particularly to sew extra pockets on to a money belt for other valuables including jewellery which ought never to be left in hotel rooms.

• **Financial services worldwide:** If you buy traveller's cheques from a major supplier – American Express, Thomas Cook or Visa – then you will have access to a worldwide network of company offices.

The three major issuers all offer on-the-spot refunds at tens of thousands of outlets around the world. American Express, for example, claimed 44 per cent of the market share for traveller's cheques sold in 1985 and have over 90,000 refund points, in every major country, including virtually every destination listed in this book.

In some cases it may be possible to have mail sent on to worldwide offices of your cheque issuing company. Find out if this facility exists before you leave home. Whichever company you choose ought to be able to give you a pocket-sized directory of major offices worldwide. That way you will have some idea what services are available at your destinations before you arrive.

Having money sent on to you abroad involves a lot more hassle than having pre-empted an emergency by taking a few extra 'untouchable' reserves with you. Nevertheless, emergencies can involve you having money sent on and this is best done by telephoning, sending a telex or telegram, to your bank manager at home.

You must say (briefly) why you want the money, how much you want, whether you want it urgently (by telegraph) or more slowly (by airmail) and the address of the bank where you want to collect it. The charges for British travellers may vary from bank to bank although it is about 25 pence per £100 sent with a minimum charge of between £10 and £20. American travellers should contact their bank manager with the same information and expect to pay slightly less. The Bank of America in San Francisco, for example, make a flat charge of $15 regardless of sum cabled.

• **Hard and soft currencies:** A hard currency is a strong one. One in which people have faith, and one which does not have a poor track record of being destroyed by inflation or over-issued by weak governments. Classed as hard are the stronger Western European currencies, together with the Japanese yen, the Canadian and (best of all) the American dollar. Some western currencies are stronger than others: the pound sterling, Swiss franc and West German mark are best. At the opposite end of things, the Italian lira and Greek drachma are only welcomed as hard currencies when compared with money from nearby Eastern bloc countries.

Soft currencies include virtually all Third World and Communist countries. Some are 'less soft' than others: the Yugoslavian dinar and South African rand, for instance, are more in demand than others from their respective Eastern bloc or African parts of the world.

Exchanging a soft currency into a hard one will cause you immense problems, and considerable expense, unless you are very lucky. *Never* convert more than you need from hard to soft – and keep all receipts until you leave the 'soft' country since you may be required to produce them as you leave the country.

• **Living off credit:** Living off credit can be the ideal way to enjoy a relatively short Round the World trip – your few hundred pounds or dollars worth of traveller's cheques supplemented by cautious use of a credit card. It has, however, to be organized sensibly to avoid a huge bill when you return home which you simply cannot afford to pay.

If your budget is really tight then you may be allowed the option, by your travel agent, of paying the biggest expense of all – your Round the World ticket itself – in instalments. Alert agencies will grant credit over a certain period to applicants who appear creditworthy and complete the necessary forms.

Thomas Cook offer a specific Budget Account, with a loan limit of 15 times what the account holder can afford to pay monthly. The current interest rate is 2.25 per cent monthly, and Thomas Cook say the account can be used to purchase Round the World tickets.

Many airlines and hotel chains provide credit cards to regular users (rather like high street store charge-cards). The immediate advantages are obvious and using any form of limited-period credit for a Round the World trip is an excellent idea in principle. In practice, however, you must *always* remember just how swiftly your credit can add up. Sooner or later you'll have to pay for it all and the longer you prolong the payment, the higher the interest and the less glamorous the holiday memories can become.

Last minute reminders

Once you're packed and just about ready to leave, double-check all the essentials for your trip.

Make sure you've got an adequate mix of clothes, without bringing your entire wardrobe with you. Remember to leave at least a little room in your luggage for presents and souvenirs from your trip, and once everything is packed, ensure your luggage is not too heavy to carry, since you will have to lift it around yourself quite a bit at airports.

Check you've made all the necessary arrangements for your own home whilst you are away. Cancel the milk, papers and so on. If you are away for over a month you ought to have your telephone, electricity and gas supplies cut off temporarily, and check your credit cards will be paid whilst away. Tidy up your garden as well since, particularly in summer, weeds can grow at a phenomenal rate and will make the outside of your home look very untidy. It also suggests to potential burglars that your home is unoccupied.

Most important of all, just before you leave, is to check that you have remembered every one of the various documents you will need. Make sure you have your ticket, with precisely the routing you wanted written on it. Remember your passport, and check again that it will remain valid throughout the duration of your trip, with the necessary visas attached. You may be allowed to enter some countries (outside those listed in this guide) with a tourist card issued in advance from the appropriate embassy, instead of a visa. If you need any tourist cards, make sure you remember them also.

Travelling to South America, Asia, or Africa you will probably need up-to-date vaccination certificates. Some of these (cholera, for example) remain valid for as little as 6 months, so be sure that any necessary health certificates will remain in order when you travel to the risk country – and that you keep them with your passport since they are just as important.

If you have any airline credit cards, or an International Telecommunications Credit Card, then don't leave those behind. Young people should also remember any discount cards (ISIC or FIYTO) and further proof of their student status, if applicable.

One last vital document you daren't risk forgetting is your address book. Not only will this be essential for postcards and mail home, but it is the best place for you to make a note of your embassy or consulate addresses abroad. These addresses are essential to keep a handy note of in the event of some misfortune (lost passport, stolen money, bereavement abroad and so on) befalling any member of your party. Remember, it costs you nothing to check, double-check, and check again that you've remembered *everything* from visas to toothpaste. The alternative could be a miserable or even disastrous holiday.

When you're there: first priorities after touchdown

CITY LINKS/TRANSPORT SYSTEMS

How to get to your airport has been looked at already in Part One, under Transport Connections. Much the same advice applies to connections to the city centre when you arrive in a new city.

Travelling *by train* (surface or underground) will be one of your quickest options. Most international airports have underground stations with direct connections to the city centre, and tickets are occasionally on sale inside the Arrivals terminal itself. The train is quick and clean but it can get very crowded when a high proportion of the average 300–400 people on a busy flight suddenly find themselves wanting to travel into the city centre by this means. It is not the best option either if you've got a lot of luggage, since space is limited. Travelling by train, mind you, remains not only one of the cheapest but frequently the quickest way of getting you into the city centre from most airports listed in this guide.

Transferring *by bus* allows you to take along more luggage with less hassle than on the train, and it also allows you a mini-tour of the outskirts of your destination into the bargain. But like the train, space for people can frequently be at a premium on a bus so you may find yourself cooped up for half an hour, in subtropical temperatures, having just landed from a long-haul flight in similar circumstances.

Bus connections too are cheap, and frequently offer direct links to towns other than the main city (from Heathrow, for example, you can travel on single journeys as far afield as South Wales and Bristol). But travelling by bus you have the inevitable problem of city traffic which you won't have to suffer on the train. Traffic lights and bottlenecks increase alarmingly in number as you enter any developed city!

You may prefer instead to take a *taxi*. Not only will this convey up to five people and a considerable amount of luggage, but it will also take you right to the door of your hotel. Taxis are always available at airports, but they can be expensive. Always find out (and agree upon) the fare in advance in a Third World country or else you could have a huge amount to pay.

Your final option is to *hire a car*. This can be done in advance, either before you leave home or your last departure city, or else at your arrival airport. Car hire can eat into your budget quickly – especially if you agree to pay only a reduced initial rental depending on how many miles you cover. But a hired car gives you unlimited freedom to explore a new destination and is the perfect means of transporting you backwards and forwards from the airport. Driving abroad can be a strain, particularly in strange cities, so lengthy spells of car hire shouldn't be entered into lightly. The advantages, however, can easily end up outweighing the potential problems.

TOURIST INFORMATION

National tourist authorities around the world vary enormously in terms of efficiency, literature and information available once you're actually there. You can get a rough indication of how good they will be by contacting them before leaving your home country. Ask for some general information to be sent about your destination and maybe make one or two specific enquiries about something like museum opening hours in the capital or how to visit restricted artistic sites. If you get an adequate response before arriving then you can generally expect good service abroad. Be prepared, though, for some dramatic changes in efficiency. The West German Tourist Authority, for example, is one of the best anywhere – with offices all over the country and literature available on just about every conceivable tourist highlight.

Tourist authorities will always have at least one office in the country's capital, and frequently one or two more in larger towns and cities. Clearly in countries like Australia and Great Britain you can expect an extensive network of tourist offices which you won't be able to find everywhere.

Many countries will have representatives of their tourist authorities available at your arrival airport. At Hong Kong, for example, arriving international visitors are met at the airport by someone from the Hong Kong Tourist Association.

National authorities ought to be able to provide you with as much verbal information as is available without any charge. If someone tries to charge you for just giving information then you are being conned. Refuse to pay for merely having a few questions answered.

In addition to verbal information, you should be able to obtain a wide range of free literature about your destination – usually glossy leaflets – without charge. Make sure anything you lift in a tourist office *is* free before walking off with a large handful and causing a lot of mutual embarrassment! Tourist authorities generally have a range of publications available for sale as well. If the free leaflets don't give you enough information then a general guide to the city, or the country as a whole, can be worth buying. Be sensible, though, since there's little point buying a £10 guidebook if you're planning no more than a few days by the beach. Remember, also, just how much books can weigh. Half a dozen hardback guidebooks accumulated during your trip will not only take up valuable space in your luggage but your precious airline weight allowance as well. Stick to paperback guides and, even then, consider if they're really worth the expense for a short stay.

Tourist office opening hours vary, but on the whole they tend to be longer than for other shops and offices in the country. Office and shopping hours are listed in Part Two of this guide under the individual countries, so use these as a minimum indication of when tourist offices will be open.

English is widely spoken around the world. Certainly at all the major cities we cover you can be sure of finding someone who speaks at least enough English for routine tourist enquiries to be understood. It always helps, no matter where you are, if you have mastered even a word or two of the local language. Supposing it's no more than 'thank you' or 'hello', non-native English speakers the world over will appreciate even the token effort on your part.

Getting the maximum use of tourist facilities abroad does not necessarily mean acquiring every free leaflet and guidesheet available, but it does involve getting as much useful information as possible for nothing. Try and ask specific questions rather than for general advice. Be patient with non-native speakers of English, and speak slowly and clearly yourself. Don't expect overwhelming cooperation as a right, since it won't always be forthcoming at many tourist offices (for example, in India).

Accommodation

BOOKING AHEAD

The main advantage of booking ahead is that it guarantees you somewhere to stay. You know that at certain specific dates you have a hotel room booked at precisely the hotel and destination you choose. The security and peace of mind this allows travellers often makes booking ahead worthwhile.

The disadvantages can mount up against you, however. For a start, it commits you to certain hotels on precise dates and this may prove inconvenient. If, for example, you fell in love with a particular destination on the way, then it would be awkward to stay there for another few days without cancelling, or more likely losing your deposit, for advance accommodation you had intended to take up next. If this happens, then the domino effect takes over and you lose out on further hotels booked in advance. If you're delayed for even a day, then all the rest of your bookings will quickly go out of line. Flight delays are particularly unpredictable and can swiftly produce a domino effect on any bookings made far ahead.

Many people are content simply to find somewhere when they land – and you *always* can, no matter where you are. But a sensible compromise for those staying in a large, international chain would be to book your next onward accommodation before you leave your previous stop. Very soon you will also have accumulated the necessary six or seven hotel receipts to join the chain's frequent guest club (designed originally for businessmen), and this can allow you to claim preferential treatment for future stays.

Unless you've made hotel reservations well in advance, accommodation ought to be your first priority after landing. The following section is a rundown on the type of facilities available around the world, and how much you can expect to pay. To keep it all as simple as possible, we divide this section up using the same format as the Accommodation section for individual cities (see Part Two).

It is worth remembering, once you arrive in any new destination, that tourist authorities will not automatically fix you up with hotels if you ask. Occasionally they may be able to do so free of charge but more likely they will make a small charge for the service, or else direct you to a specific accommodation finding service nearby. These services are very useful and ought to be made use of unless, of course, you decide to stick to the better known (and easily accessible) internationals – Hilton, Inter-Continental and so on – throughout your trip.

• **Airport Hotels:** Whether within the main complex, or close nearby, airport hotels are one of the most obvious options open to you. As they cannot be in the city centre, they are a realistic choice if you're staying only a few hours or a day or so. On the whole, airport hotels will be similar in price and quality to their equivalents found in city centres. One distinct advantage generally available to airport hotel guests is courtesy transport to and from the terminal itself. Airport hotels fall roughly into three categories, First Class, Business Class (which in this book we refer to as Super Club) and Economy, identical to all hotels worldwide.

• **First Class:** Very much international luxury hotels which are likely to be of interest to First and Business Class passengers. You can expect air conditioning and television in all rooms; central heating; a bathroom en suite; laundry service; international direct dial telephone; and attentive service around the clock. Meals will be of the highest international standards and you can expect a host of other extras including a complimentary daily newspaper, fresh fruit and quality toiletries in your room. Don't expect to pay less than US$100 a night for a double room (or local equivalent – frequently higher). Most of the international hotel chains we regularly mention are decidedly First Class, with special facilities for business travellers.

– *Hilton International:* With over 90 hotels in 74 countries, the Hilton group has been on the go for almost 40 years now. It started in Puerto Rico when its first international luxury hotel was opened in San Juan. Hilton say that their hotels reflect the culture of the country in which they are located, and that indigenous art materials are used in the interior design and decor.

Hilton remains probably the most famous international hotel name in the world (although their US hotels operate under the name Vista International). Hilton and Vista are world leaders in the food and beverage field, and remain the only international chain operating in major cities in Japan. A full range of business facilities exist in all Hilton hotels.

– *Holiday Inns:* The largest international hotel group, having around 1700 all over the world. With scarcely the most minor variations in decor, all their hotels are identical wherever you go from London to Auckland. A particular bonus is that virtually all Holiday Inns have swimming pools as a matter of policy.

Holiday Inns don't offer any single bedrooms, and their twin-bedded rooms tend to have double beds instead of two singles. The hotel service can arrange babysitting and positively welcome children. Those under 12 are allowed to stay in their parents' rooms free, and most extend this useful concession to young people under 19.

– *Inter-Continental:* Offering First Class luxury to leisure and business travellers, Inter-Continental have more than 80 hotels situated all over the business world. Their hotels are centrally located in the heart of each destination, and boast multi-lingual switchboards.

For the advantage of the business traveller, all Inter-Continental hotels offer secretarial services and worldwide telegram and telex facilities. Many of their hotels have full-sized health clubs available for guests.

– *Mandarin International:* A small international hotel group, only formed in 1974, with the objective of operating the best possible hotels in selected major city centres within the Pacific Basin.

With a dozen top-class hotels, and a few more planned, Mandarin manage to combine the qualities of calmness, sophistication and elegance in all their properties. A string of international travel press awards rate all Mandarin Oriental hotels amongst the best in the world.

– *Oberoi Hotels International:* Operating 22 hotels in mainly Middle and Far Eastern locations, Oberoi have yet to become a popularly recognized name in the international hotel market. They offer preferential treatment for business travellers, including VIP courtesies for frequent guests, and three telephones in each bedroom – on the desk, by the bedside and even in the bathroom!

– *Sheraton:* The world's second largest chain, with more than 600 hotels open by the end of this decade. They have a vast range of bustling downtown and convenient airport locations in all the world's major business and holiday cities.

Sheraton offer a unique hotel-within-a-hotel facility as well – the Sheraton Towers. There you'll find exclusive, personal service in a small luxury hotel atmosphere in about seven or eight of the cities we cover. Use of Sheraton Towers is more expensive, but considerably more exclusive than normal Sheraton accommodation.

– *Westin:* A primarily American-based chain with a growing number of operations in the Far East, Westin has won top international awards five times out of the past seven years. On each occasion its imposing luxury and slightly more expensive than standard accommodation was voted by *Travel/Holiday* magazine best inside and outside the United
States.

– *Business Facilities:* All the top international hotel groups offer excellent facilities for the business traveller. Each one has special discount rates for companies and, in addition, business travellers can expect access to translation and secretarial facilities. International telegram and telex services will almost always be available, and a direct dial international telephone will be standard in each bedroom.

Frequent business travellers can expect rapid check-in and check-outs together with preferential reservation handling. Hilton International offer, in addition, an exclusive – but expensive – worldwide courier service.

All the large chains have conference facilities available as well, but precisely what's on offer varies markedly from hotel to hotel.

The major groups also have special clubs for frequent business travellers and the impressive range of facilities differs surprisingly little from group to group. Hilton International have an Executive Business Service (EBS) offering special rates for business travellers through their Vista Club. Inter-Continental, through their Six Continents Business Club, together with Sheraton and Oberoi, all offer preferential handling and reservation priority to business guests who stay, on average, at least six nights a year in hotels of that group.

Business Club membership entitles guests to upgraded room accommodation, in most cases, provided the hotel isn't full. A limit in international telephone call surcharges is a useful bonus when compared with those normally charged to guests, and courtesy newspapers in English are available.

● **Business (Super Club) Class:** Very comfortable hotels, likely to be of interest to business travellers as holidaymakers as well since the facilities offered differ only marginally from the more expensive First Class hotels – but the rooms are cheaper. Service will be less attentive and the fringe benefits of courtesy newspapers, fresh fruit in the room and so on will be fewer.

Business Class hotels will all have their own private bathrooms, with bath or shower and toilet, as well as telephone, radio and probably colour television as well. Most rooms have mini-bars, and guests will have access to in-house movies, smart public bars and usually secretarial and translation services as well. Penta Hotels, with 15 hotels all over Europe (plus one each in New York and Bombay) are one of the best international groups in this class.

● **Economy Class:** Economy hotels cater for the vast majority of travellers, on a more limited budget. They offer clean and comfortable accommodation without any of the fringe benefits of First or Super Club Class hotels. The better local hotels (from about US$50 downwards for a double room) tend to fall into the upper ranges of this category and will inevitably offer a more realistic taste of living in a foreign country than any of the international chains can.

This vast Economy accommodation category includes a whole range of options from cheaper hotels and local pensions, right down to youth hostels, camping and even sleeping out in the airport itself where this is permitted.

INTERNATIONAL YOUTH HOSTEL FEDERATION (IYHF)

There is no age limit for staying at youth hostels around the world so the name itself is something of a misnomer. Youth hostel facilities are not run for profit, but to help predominantly young people travel and to promote the interaction of international culture.

Each country runs its own hostels independently under the auspices of a national Youth Hostel Association. These are, in turn, linked through the IYHF which lays down basic standards which national associations ought to observe.

Anyone can join the IYHF, regardless of age, giving them access to any of 4500 hostels in 50 countries. For a nominal nightly charge you can then hire a bed and use communal cooking facilities. The requirement to fulfil a domestic chore is all but extinct now outside youth hostels in Great Britain.

For details of membership those resident in England and Wales should apply to: YHA, Trevelyan House, 8 St Stephen's Hill, St Albans, Herts. AL1 2DV. Those resident in Scotland should apply to: 7 Glebe Crescent, Stirling FK8 2JA. American residents should apply to: American Youth Hostels Inc., National Campus, Delaplane, VA 22025.

YOUNG MEN/WOMEN'S CHRISTIAN ASSOCIATIONS

The YMCA and YWCA operate in at least 85 countries and list many thousands of addresses where semi-permanent or travelling guests may stay. There is no age limit or special qualifications needed to join. Places tend to be limited in the youth-hostel type accommodation which is available, so writing ahead is advisable. YM/WCAs can also offer spiritual and legal advice to travellers and are best contacted through their annual directory published in England. Male travellers should write, for information, to: National Council of YMCAs, 640 Forest Road, Walthamstow, London E17 3DW. Women should write to: YWCA of Great Britain, Hampden House, 2 Weymouth Street, London W1.

CAMPING

One of the cheapest accommodation options, and undoubtedly one of the most adventurous, remains camping. Weight will be your main consideration and the ideal type of tent is a lightweight, two-person model with one person carrying the poles and pegs, and the other the main canvas. The best way to carry a tent is tied on to the foot of a rucksack, thereby allowing your hands to remain free. Make sure poles and pegs are securely packed before you lose sight of a rucksack into an aircraft's hold!

Depending on your destinations, and personal preference, you may wish to take a lightweight mattress or a small stove with you as well. Once again, remember your airline weight allowance – and also that standard stove gas cylinders are not allowed to be carried on most airlines.

A number of excellent camping guidebooks are available in Britain and the United States. Two of the better ones are *Camping Complete* by P. F. Williams (published by Pelham Books) and *Camper's and Backpacker's Bible* edited by C. B. Colby (published by Stoeger Publishing Company).

PRIVATE ACCOMMODATION

Private accommodation can normally be a cheaper, and in many ways more memorable, alternative to hotels. It allows you to live in someone else's home, as a paying guest, and generally use the common facilities therein – bathroom, living area and so on.

Staying privately allows you to gain the tiniest of insights into how a typical family home operates in a foreign country. Like any home, you can expect to be disturbed by the couple arguing, the family dog barking, or an elderly relative complaining in the corner.

It does work out much cheaper – though it is essential that you agree on a price beforehand. Booking private accommodation far in advance from home isn't that easy but the local tourist office when you reach your destination should be able to fix you up with something. Try not to be fussy about exact location in a city, or special bedroom facilities. If a coffee-maker, for example, heaps of hot water and morning alarm-call are all essential to you then book a hotel instead, otherwise you may well be disappointed by living within the native atmosphere of a foreign home.

Dining out

Nothing can adequately prepare you for what you can expect dining out abroad. Local delicacies around the world vary tremendously and sampling many of those foreign dishes ought to be one of the highlights of your trip.

It would be impossible to give even a general indication of what to expect abroad. Standards of preparation and regional tastes vary from village to village, let alone from country to country but, if you want a good starting point, find a local taverna, or even a little restaurant away from the main streets, and watch what the locals are eating. If your host speaks English, find out what his most popular dish is and try that. If you're in the Far East, don't be too surprised if it sounds repulsive at first (something like octopus or boiled fish heads!).

Almost always you will be welcomed warmly by the host or waiter. Really small establishments seem to love foreign tourists, and in less well developed countries (for example, India or Kenya) the host sees it as a sort of status symbol to be entertaining far-travelled foreigners. Always respond politely to any welcome offered – and try to say how much you'd like to try some of the local delicacies.

Prices and hygiene standards obviously vary with the class of establishment you choose to eat at. The safest (but by no means immune) places to eat in are the restaurants of the big international hotels. They also tend to be among the more expensive. Wherever else you choose to eat, try and have a look at your meat before it's cooked. Meat, poultry, fish and shellfish should look and smell fresh and be thoroughly cooked at all times. As a general rule, it should be eaten whilst still hot as far as possible. Eggs, butter and hard cheeses are normally safe – soft cheeses and milk, especially, can often cause upset stomachs. In a few far-flung corners of the world, including much of Africa, you may be able to see an animal (especially poultry or fish) being killed and cooked in front of you.

However unconventional to your eyes, this is one of the best ways to ensure meat is really fresh!

You should avoid vegetables and fruit unless the skin is firmly intact. Wash them thoroughly and peel them yourself if you plan to eat them raw no matter where you are (even in London or New York). Cold foods, especially salads which can't be peeled, are a risk at *all* times.

Tipping remains largely a matter of personal preference wherever you go, but most countries now have a 'service' charge of between 5 and 15 per cent included automatically in the bill. There are very few countries where tipping remains strictly forbidden (for instance, parts of Eastern Europe) and it remains advisable to tip if service has been particularly good. Use your discretion, but 10 per cent of the final bill (including wine) is reasonable wherever you are. Don't leave enormous tips or else your bill may be artificially inflated if you eat there again. The management may recognize you as a 'wealthy tourist'!

Licensing laws, for drinking alcohol, tend to be fairly liberal around the world. Britain has tight laws, forbidding the sale or consumption of alcohol by anyone under 18 and regulating rigidly the hours when alcohol can be sold. In many other westernized countries, on the other hand, licensing laws simply don't exist. Restaurants, tavernas and pubs all open and close when they want, and serve who they want (with obvious restrictions against children). Remember in a few Middle Eastern countries alcohol is banned altogether. The national tourist office, at home or at your destination, can best advise about current licensing laws – if any.

Courtesy and caution are the best watchwords when dining out abroad. If you plan to make eating a special part of your Round the World trip rather than merely a necessity, then you should invest in a general food guide to the world. A surprising number of these 'Foods of the World' books seem to appear in bargain or discount bookshops so have a look round one or two of those before you leave. Most general guides, and all specific city guides, will give you some information about what type of food you can expect abroad.

Categories of restaurants are listed in Part Two, under each city, as in accommodation, as First, Super Club and Economy Class.

First Class establishments offer the highest quality international cuisine. There you can expect every possible service and a fine choice of wines. The finest of the country's national dishes ought to be available, together with more internationally recognized meals. In First Class restaurants meals will generally be very expensive. Up to £50 per person is not uncommon, for example, in the very finest of London's restaurants for dinner with good wines.

Super Club Class restaurants differ only marginally in quality and price from First Class. Depending on which city you are visiting, many restaurants will have a reputation for catering specifically for a high number of business visitors.

Economy Class restaurants encompass every eating place below Club and First Class establishments. From the tiniest taverna to grandest Economy hotel, this class offers by far the best opportunity for you to sample the 'average' food of your destination. If you are prepared to forgo the finest wines and silver cutlery of the best restaurants, you will usually be rewarded with a taste of the best 'real' food of the country.

Standards will vary enormously, needless to say, but if you remember the few simple health precautions you shouldn't have any problems. Don't be surprised if the waiter brings endless baskets of bread, or jugs of water (drink with caution – have wine instead!) since this is the norm in many countries. If you don't expect the earth in any Economy Class restaurant you shouldn't be disappointed.

Nightlife

It is impossible to generalize about what types of nightlife are available around the world. So much depends on personal preferences – and the company you choose to travel with (if any) can have a lot of bearing on it.

Large, westernized, cities undoubtedly have the best reputation for an active 'night scene'. The discos, clubs and bars of London, Paris, New York – and increasingly Hong Kong and Rio de Janeiro as well – are unequalled around the world. They are expensive and exhausting, but if you want to travel round the world's most exhilarating nightspots then it is perfectly feasible.

Don't waste time in the Middle East or picturesque island destinations if you want to be at the centre of the swinging cosmopolitan nightlife. Watch out, too, for what is authentic and what is not. Avoid the large touristy resorts – particularly those in Europe thick with less adventurous travellers from home. The night scene in some of the large resort complexes seldom resembles the authentic society nightlife of the country you're visiting.

What you should aim to find are the exclusive 'in' places (but not inaccessible) where local society goes for a night out. If you go along as an interested visitor, looking for a good night out, rather than as a tourist then you ought to be made most welcome. What's not authentic generally stands out a mile, but the biggest giveaway is gatherings of package holiday makers. They almost never reach the really best nightspots in any destination.

Staying in a hotel and patronizing the bar can be one of the best meeting places for single travellers. Travelling alone requires a certain degree of initiative and perseverance – and few lone travellers sit around in their rooms all night! Organized excursions, or more likely the not uncommon visit to a local hostelry afterwards, are another good means of meeting people. Noisy, intimidating, foreign discos are not the best place to meet fellow singles.

In Part Two, under each city, we list the best local nightspots for those travellers keen to sample nightlife which is a little more socially active than an intimate evening in a quiet bar somewhere.

Shopping

Shopping on new continents will be an exciting experience. Even in the international shopping meccas like London and Hong Kong, the colourful contrast to what you are used to at home will be memorable.

If you travel as far as Africa or the Far East, then visiting the side-street shopping markets is a must. Take care, though, not to get cheated since it's all too easy either to forget the exact value of your foreign money, or else get taken in by the appealing smile of a wily market trader!

To British or American travellers, haggling can be one of the worst problems since it is expected in many of the world's exotic locations. If you find yourself having to haggle then grit your teeth and avoid giving in. If you don't, not only will you be paying far more than the seller wants, but you may even offend him. Offer a third of his asking price and haggle till you reach about half or two-thirds the original price. Never pay any more, and avoid any barter deals whereby you exchange a personal item (watch, wallet, jeans and so on) for a local item. More often than not you will be getting the worst deal.

Local products tend to be the best buys abroad, and make the most original souvenirs. Hand-crafted woodwork, silver jewellery or fine cloth, for instance, can be a memorable souvenir obtainable only in specific parts of the world. As ever, though, be sensible about the size and weight of your purchases – and avoid seeds, plants and genuine antique artifacts altogether since you won't normally be allowed back into your home country with them.

Opening hours for shops, and offices, of individual countries are listed in Part Two. As a very general guide, virtually all really warm countries conduct the bulk of their shop and office business during the cooler morning hours. Be prepared for long afternoons on the beach, or strolling round the sights when all the shops may be closed. Quite often shops will open again in the evening for a few hours – a convenience many western tourists appreciate.

Sightseeing

The national tourist authorities of nearly all the countries we cover will organize a wide range of sightseeing excursions from the major cities. These are often the cheapest, and most effective, means of introduction to the highlights of a new destination. As always, consult the national tourist office once you land about the availability of organized excursions and you should be offered a wide range. Two- or three-hour 'quickie' tours around the city on a coach may be offered alongside a whole host of excursions including expensive trips lasting a few days to more remote destinations.

You also have the option of doing it all yourself, either by train, coach or ferry. Provided you can learn how best to use the various means of public transport available, sightseeing independently will give you total freedom to take your time and perhaps enjoy a picnic or meal on the way as well.

The final alternative is to hire a car or camper van for sightseeing further afield. Camper vans are particularly useful since they will solve your sightseeing and accommodation problems in one. Although camper vans are more expensive to hire than cars, they often work out much cheaper than hotels.

Getting the best value out of sightseeing can occasionally be difficult. Consider the following few tips:

1. Try visiting places early in the morning. Particularly in subtropical destinations, life starts early and by so doing you ought to avoid the worst of the day's tourists.
2. Be careful where and when you take photographs since the interiors of many national tourist sites (particularly churches and galleries) are not allowed to be photographed.
3. Consider your dress carefully when visiting religious sights. Muslim countries expect women particularly to be well covered up, and even wearing a headscarf can be an advantage.
4. Resist the temptation to take little bits of major attractions home! There are a number of people who can't resist taking a little piece of the Acropolis, Taj Mahal, Tower of London or wherever, and if everyone did this there would be no sights left. It can also land you in very serious trouble.
5. Don't drop litter. Even a small amount can quickly spoil the look of a place.

Opening hours of museums and so on are not always standard across a particular country but the well-known sights do tend to be open longer. Most countries have at least one day a week when all the state-run museums and galleries are closed. In Paris, for example, it's Tuesday.

The drawing power of some of the world's great festivals motivates many people to travel. Most of the biggest festivals are based in deep-rooted national yearnings which materialize in magnificent annual gatherings. Two of the largest are the Rio Carnival, every February in Brazil, and tulip time in Amsterdam in April. For visitors to London in August, you may like to consider coming north to visit the Edinburgh International Festival for a couple of days. This three-week-long festival of music, theatre and art has gone from small beginnings 41 years ago to become the world's biggest cultural festival.

TAKING GOOD PHOTOGRAPHS

Wherever, and however, you finally decide to see the sights of your various destinations you will probably want to take good photographs to remember it all by. Bear in mind the following few tips and you shouldn't be disappointed.

1. If this is a trip of a lifetime, and you're a keen photographer, consider taking two cameras: one good one with lenses for slides of landscapes, buildings, etc.; and a pocket instamatic for prints of people.
2. Keep your film as cool as possible – both when exposed and unexposed.
3. Take more film than you think you'll need with you (be generous). It can often be difficult to obtain abroad – and expensive.
4. Keep a note, even roughly, of where and when you used each film. The alternative is sorting through dozens of attractive but anonymous prints when you're home.
5. Don't bother processing film until you're home – provided you return within six months or so. Foreign processing techniques can be expensive and unreliable.
6. Be sensible where you take photographs and avoid obvious 'no go' areas like military installations, national borders and so on.
7. As far as possible, take your time when taking a photograph. Double-check light and distance settings (where applicable) and ensure nothing is obscuring the lens. Hold the camera as still as possible when you press the button.
8. Don't take candid snaps of people without their permission. Particularly in Far Eastern and African countries this can cause annoyance and distress.

Communications

MAIL

Keeping in touch with home is essential – if not for your own benefit then for that of friends and family who may be worrying about your travels around the world.

International air mail services are improving all the time – the surface alternative remains much slower and seldom any cheaper unless you're sending large packages or gifts. Air mail to either Great Britain or the United States from anywhere should take no more than ten days, frequently less. Be warned that postcards will take considerably longer, especially from the less developed countries we cover – India, Thailand and Kenya.

To give you a rough indication, air mail letters from Australasia to Great Britain or the United States will take about a week to arrive; from London to the United States about a week as well, and from Bahrain or Hong Kong to London about five days.

Ordinary, urgent, and letter telegrams, as well as telex, can be sent from all the countries we cover. For telegrams you are always safer sending them from the largest Post Office or Telegraph Office you can find. Telex facilities are very limited in many tropical parts of the world.

Make sure you see whatever you wish to send off actually disappear. In Third World and Asian countries especially, make sure you see stamps being franked on *all* outgoing mail (including postcards) otherwise Post Office officials may remove and resell them!

Poste Restante facilities are available around the world. This is a bonus facility offered to American Express traveller's cheque holders whereby mail can be held, pending their arrival, for a few weeks at an onward Amex office.

Alternatively you can have mail sent to the main Post Offices of towns or cities you plan to visit. Have mail addressed to you as follows: A. Traveller (first initial and surname *only*), Poste Restante, Main Post Office, (Town or City), (Country). Check when collecting mail that it hasn't been filed under the initial of your first name instead of your surname.

You may sometimes be able to have mail sent to your consulate or embassy marked 'To await collection'. Check in advance, whenever possible, that there is a consulate or embassy in the place you plan to visit and that it will hold mail for you.

TELEPHONE AND TELEGRAM

International telephones can be found in most large Post Offices, inside the big chain hotels, and occasionally at specific telephone company offices. By a process of trial and error, you may discover that just about any telephone in some countries (including Great Britain, the United States, and much of Western Europe) will allow you to make direct dial international calls. In a few countries, though, only certain phones at main Post Offices can be used.

Beware of making lengthy telephone calls from your hotel room. The undoubted convenience of direct dial (or even switchboard connected) hotel room telephones will be paid for heavily when you get your bill. The hotel sometimes surcharges the call by as much as twice the basic call charge – and this can be *very* expensive on international calls. In the United States as well, for instance, you will often be charged up to a couple of dollars for a call which doesn't even connect! Even if the number dialled just rings, you will be billed.

When you call home from abroad, you shouldn't expect cheap rate as a right. Some countries allow a cheap rate at weekends, for example, Israel and Great Britain to most countries, but most don't allow one at all. Indeed, some countries even restrict the hours you can make international calls. To dial direct to Great Britain from India, for instance, you can only do so *between* 6.30 p.m. and 6.30 a.m. GMT, and even then only from Bombay and Delhi.

As a rule, though, British Telecom advises that it is possible to dial direct to Great Britain from just about anywhere in the world. In some countries you may need to dial a few times before being connected, but as far as countries in this guide are concerned, Thailand is the only one from which you cannot dial direct. American travellers shouldn't experience many difficulties either, although international direct dialling to small towns in the States may be difficult.

Telegrams are traditionally the quickest means of sending unwordy messages home, but they can also be sent to passengers in transit via their next arrival airport. All major internationals will accept telegrams for passengers, provided they arrive bearing the following information: Passenger's name, departure and arrival city, date and scheduled arrival time of flight, and the name of the airline along with the relevant flight number. A typical telegram could be headed 'For the attention of: MR THOMAS SCOTT, passenger arriving at London Heathrow from New York. British Airways flight no. BA365 expected 16.10.'

Post Office opening hours are similar to shop and office hours, indicated in Part Two, but bear in mind opening hours for American Express offices abroad as well if you plan to have telegrams (or mail) sent on ahead for you. Amex offices at home will be able to advise on up-to-date opening hours.

Whenever you contact home from abroad, bear in mind what time it will be. Refer to the world time chart earlier in Part One before you call home, since an international phone call to friends or family in the middle of the night may worry (or at least annoy) them unnecessarily.

NEWS IN ENGLISH

Keeping in touch with the world news is always advisable to long-haul travellers. The BBC World Service provides the most comprehensive English language service and the following waveband chart will let you know where to find it wherever you are.

Africa
Central and West

kHz	6005	7105	7185	7320	9410	9580	11720	15070	15105	21470	21660	21710	25650
m		49	41		31		25	19		13			11

East

kHz	1413	6005	7185	7320	9410	9580	11750	11860	15070	15420	17885	21470	25650
m	212	49	42		31		25		19		16	13	11

North and North West

kHz	5975	7185	7320	9410	9580	11750	12095	15070	17705	21710	25650
m	49	41		31		25		19	16	13	11

Southern

kHz	6005	7185	7320	9410	11750	11820	15070	15400	17885	21660	25650
m	49	41		31	25		19		16	13	11

America
Central and Caribbean

kHz	5975	6175	6195	7325	9510	11750	11775	15070	15260	17830
m	49			40	31	25		19		16

North

kHz	5975	6120	6175	9510	9590	7325	11750	11775	15070	15260	17830	21710
m	49			31		40	25		19		16	13

South

kHz	6005	9575	9915	11750	15260
m	49	31		25	19

Asia
Indian Sub-continent

kHz	1413	6195	7135	9410	9740	11750	11955	15070	15310	17770	17790	21550	25650
m	212	49	41	31		25		19		16		13	11

South East and East

kHz	3915	6195	9570	9740	11750	11955	15280	15435	17770	17880	21550	25650
m	75	49	31		25		19		16		13	11

Europe
Central

kHz	1296	3955	6050	6195	9410	9750	12095	15070	17790	21550	21710
m	231	75	49		31		25	19	16	13	

Northern

kHz	648	1296	5975	6050	6180	7120	9410	15070	15420	17695	17790	21550	25650
m	463	231	49			41	31	19			16	13	11

South East

kHz	3955	5975	6050	6180	7185	7320	9410	12095	15070	17790	21470	21710
m	75	49			41		31	25	19	16	13	

South West

kHz	3970	5975	7185	7320	7320	9410	9580	9760	9915	12095	15070	17705	21710
m	75	49	41			31				25	19	16	13

Western

kHz	648	5975	6050	7120	7185	7320	9410	9750	12095	15070
m	463	49		41			31		25	19

Middle East

kHz	1323	693	6050	7140	9410	11760	12095	15070	15310	17770	17790	21710	25650
m	212	469	49	41	31	25		19		16		13	11

As a general rule, the lower frequencies usually give better results early in the morning and late in the evening. Likewise better results for higher frequency in the middle of the day.

English language newspapers are generally available in major cities around the world. In communist countries you may, however, experience some difficulty, and American papers will be unavailable.

Buying newspapers in English abroad will cost you considerably more than normal and, with the possible exception of those sold at large airports, they will be at least a day out of date as well. The *International Herald Tribune* will be available in most countries we cover, and if you buy a copy before leaving home, the price guide at the top of the front page will give you an indication of its cost abroad. As a rough guide, don't expect to pay any less than £1 (or about $1.50 to $2) for an English language newspaper abroad.

Special requirements

Selecting travelling companions, or deciding whether instead to travel on your own, may be a problem. The first thing to remember is that all travelling groups including couples *will* have the occasional storm. Don't pretend it won't happen to you.

Choosing your companion is a matter of personal choice – and common sense. If you choose to travel alone, then the lone male traveller can expect fewer problems than the lone female. Single men are not uncommon travelling on business. The single woman must, unfortunately, anticipate many more hassles.

Being worried by men is the single biggest hassle. You can expect many odd glances, the occasional remark and a few unoriginal advances. There is little beyond a few obvious self-defence precautions that single women travellers can prepare for. Try, however, to avoid South America, India and Moslem countries particularly – in

Middle Eastern countries lone women are regarded as fair game by local men. Being realistic, travelling as a single woman, without the protection or even moral support of a companion, is a very brave thing to consider anywhere in the world.

Professional women ought to behave as coolly as possible – avoiding, for example, one-to-one business contacts with unknown male colleagues. Venturing out alone after dark is to invite trouble. Single travellers of either sex may meet suitable companions while on the trip, but you mustn't count on this. Be prepared to be totally self-reliant and enjoy your own company.

ELDERLY AND DISABLED TRAVELLERS

A large proportion of the Round the World ticket market goes to elderly or retired travellers. One of the advantages for the retired traveller is having more time on your hands. Children have grown up and you no longer have to rush back either to family or job. But elderly travellers ought to be realistic about how much they feel they can do.

Choose your destinations carefully – avoiding warm cities in midsummer and exhausting itineraries. Try to break up your trip into small, easily manageable portions, perhaps a week in each of four destinations rather than two or three days in a host of foreign cities. Consider breaking up long-haul flights with an overnight stop. This way you will 'see' another city and be able to get a good night's sleep somewhere. Off-peak and out-of-season travel is not only good value but more sensible in the long run for elderly people looking to have a relaxing trip.

For the disabled, a Round the World trip can provide a magnificent escape from the day-to-day restrictions which you will normally have to put up with. Most airports and airlines are equipped to deal with handicapped passengers but it is important to tell either your travel agent or airline of your disability before you leave home. Remind the airline of your booking and the provisions you require a day or so before you fly.

Depending on your mobility, toilets particularly can present problems during a long flight. Limiting fluid intake and requesting a seat near the toilet can help but you ought to ask your doctor for medication if you will be completely unable to use aircraft toilets.

A series of Mobility International guides give a selection of accessible hotels in Europe, and in the USA the National Easter Seal Society, at 2023 W. Ogden Avenue, Chicago, IL 60612, publishes *Motels with Wheelchair Units* which may be a help to you. The American President's Committee on Employment for the Handicapped, Washington DC 20210, publish *A List of Guidebooks for Handicapped Travellers* covering almost a hundred cities in North America and Europe.

TRAVELLING WITH BABIES AND CHILDREN

Travelling with babies and children can cause particular problems. Babies up to 6 months are no problem on flights as more or less the normal feeding and changing routine can be adhered to. The problems increase between 6 and 12 months and can become a real nightmare between one and three years! Cabin crew will help and generally relieve the pressure from overwrought parents but bear in mind a few useful tips.

1. Time flights at children's bedtimes and consider giving them travel sickness pills to induce sleep.
2. Get a seat at the front of the cabin, with extra legroom. This is particularly important if the child has no seat of his or her own.
3. Try to change nappies on your lap. Changes in cabin loos are very difficult since there's hardly enough room for an adult to answer nature's call, let alone manipulate wipes, cream, tissues and nappies round a wriggling baby! Ask the cabin crew where the best place to change an infant is.
4. Warn the airline well in advance of any special needs for children – and take a favourite toy along if all else fails to keep him amused.
5. Travel First or Business Class where possible. Well worth it for the extra space if you're travelling with a young child without any seat.
6. Take a bottle or drinking cup for drinks when taking off and landing. Pressure can cause discomfort to a young child.
7. Keep a young baby in its papoose – and don't give up the buggy till boarding at the very last minute (it helps to carry the duty free!).

8. Remember that most people in this world, at some point, have children. Consequently they are likely to make allowances and sympathize with you more than you would think.

HOW TO FIND WORK ABROAD

Giving advice about how to find work abroad is impossible in a few brief paragraphs. But one way you can certainly not find work abroad is simply writing to the national embassy of a few countries requesting it. Many of the best working holidays, or even full-time jobs, are arranged on the spot after a preliminary search through local newspapers. University careers services at home can provide the best advice for young people interested in working abroad and, of course, there remains no substitute for personal contacts.

Several publications, updated annually, can provide sound information about finding work abroad. These include *Working Holidays* (published by the CBEVE) and *The Directory of Summer Jobs Abroad* (published by Vacation Work Publications). American readers should also look out for *Employment Abroad: Facts and Fallacies*, a pamphlet published by the US Chamber of Commerce. In addition, many holiday companies employ seasonal workers so you could do well to contact a few of those *well* in advance of when you'd like to leave.

Problems and emergencies

Problems and emergencies do occasionally occur – and it would be foolish to embark on any long trip without having some idea where to turn when they do.

POLICE

Always within easy reach (sometimes too easy). All losses must be reported, as should any serious personal injuries, accidents or information which you would normally pass on to police at home.

The police are always within easy reach by telephone; if necessary go into a hotel or office and explain whom you are trying to reach. Be patient with non-English speakers. Crowded city streets normally have at least one police officer on duty, or at least pavement-side telephones to call them. Never delay having to call the police, no matter where you are.

MEDICAL AID

If needed urgently, medical services can be contacted through any of the sources suggested for reaching the police, as well as travel agencies and airline offices. Routine medical aid is available via any large hospital but non-urgent complaints are best left until you're home again. Minor problems (for example, a sprained wrist or a small burn) ought to be able to be treated from your own travel medical kit, or else through a first aid officer which many large hotels and airports employ.

UK AND US EMBASSIES AND CONSULATES

These can be contacted through local telephone directories, or the addresses listed in this guide. Keep a note of the ones applicable to your destinations in a wallet or purse. Remember they *cannot* give legal advice, investigate a crime, trace missing persons or pay any bill for you. They can issue emergency passports, contact relatives and friends to ask for help with money and provide a list of local lawyers and doctors. All British embassies and consulates have a duty officer on call throughout the weekend and overnight.

MONEY EMERGENCIES

If all your money is stolen then you will have only minimal problems getting reimbursement on traveller's cheques *provided* you've still got a note of the cheque numbers stolen, and you get in touch with the nearest issuing office of the company at once. You must *always* report your loss to the local police, and ideally to your nearest consulate as well.

If you've lost every last penny, with no receipts, then go at once to your local consulate. As a last resort, they can make a repayable loan for repatriation but there's no law that says the Consul must do this. Before he does so he will want to be satisfied that you really are destitute and that there is absolutely no one else you know at home who can wire money to you. If there is someone, however, the Consul can advise you about how this can be done.

Part Two
Stop Off Destinations

1. AFRICA

Kenya

RED TAPE

● **Passport/Visa Requirements:** A full, valid passport is required by all visitors, and a visa by all except those from the following: Denmark, Italy, Spain, Norway, Turkey, San Marino, Uruguay, Ethiopia, Sweden, Federal Republic of Germany, Ireland, Finland, and all Commonwealth countries except Australia, Nigeria and Sri Lanka. Entry permits cost about £5 and are valid for 3 months. Applications to: Kenya High Commission, 45 Portland Place, London W1N 4AS. Applicants must have adequate funds to cover their stay, and a return or ongoing ticket. Entry is refused to whites of South Africa and Zimbabwe. As unemployment is high, work permits are difficult to obtain, and bribes may be necessary.

CUSTOMS

● **Duty Free:** Visitors are allowed to bring in 200 cigarettes or 50 cigars or 225 grammes of tobacco; 1 bottle of spirits or wine; 0.76 litre of perfume. There are special restrictions on gold, diamonds and skin or game trophies unless from the authorized Kenyan government department. Personal effects are duty free but gifts will be charged duty. Imports from South Africa and Zimbabwe prohibited.

HEALTH

1. Visitors from a smallpox-infected area should be vaccinated and certified.
2. Malaria is rare in Nairobi and the Highlands but endemic in humid areas around the coast and bush. Medical precautions against malaria should be taken.
3. Tap water is safe to drink unless indicated. The sea and swimming pools are safe to swim in, but lakes, rivers and reservoirs may be infected by bilharzia parasites, and the water should certainly not be drunk for fear of contracting dysentery or typhoid.
4. Health insurance is essential, and should include entitlement to free air transport and the services of the Flying Doctor.

CAPITAL – Nairobi. Population – 736,000.

POPULATION – 17,000,000.

LANGUAGE – Kiswahili is the national language and English the official language, with other African languages also spoken.

CURRENCY – Kenyan Shilling (Ks). Notes – 5, 10, 20, 50, 100. Coins – 1 shilling, 5, 10, and 50 cents.
£1 = 23 Ks; US$1 = 17 Ks.

BANKING HOURS – 0900–1400 Monday to Friday, and 0900–1100 the first and last Saturday of each month. Airport banks open until midnight.

POLITICAL SYSTEM – Independent republic within the British Commonwealth. Democratic system, but in fact a one-party state.

RELIGION – 50 per cent Christian, 40 per cent Animist and some Muslims and Hindus.

PUBLIC HOLIDAYS – 1 January, 1 May, 1 June, 12 October, 20 October, 12 December, 25, 26 December. Also moveable Christian and Muslim holidays, such as Good Friday, Easter Monday, Eid-el-Fitr and Eid-el-Adha.

TIME DIFFERENCE – GMT + 3.

COMMUNICATIONS

● **Telephone:** IDD service from most places, but phone from hotels and major Post Offices. The country code is 010 254 and the codes for Nairobi and Mombasa are 2 and 11 respectively.

● **Post:** Use airmail service when sending letters abroad. Prices, within African Zone: 4 Ks; to Europe: 5 Ks; to US and Australia: 7 Ks. Sending parcels can involve long delays.

ELECTRICITY – 240v AC, 50 Hz.

OFFICE/SHOPPING HOURS – Government offices: 0800–1300 and 1400–1700 Monday to Friday. Shops: 0830–1230 and 1400–1630 Monday to Saturday.

● **Best Buys:** Silver and gold, native cloth, basketwork and wood carvings, handbags, belts and other articles made from animal and reptile skins (these need export licences which are obtainable at place of purchase).

INTERNAL TRAVEL

● **Air:** Kenya Airways runs an extensive internal air service, including Mombasa, Malindi and Kisumu among other destinations. There are also several private airlines.

● **Rail:** Daily services between Nairobi and Mombasa with connections to Kisumu. There are branch lines to Nyeri, Nanyuki and through Voi to Tanzania. (For details: tel. Chief Traffic Manager, Nairobi 21211.)

● **Road:** Trunk roads are good quality, but elsewhere may deteriorate, especially in the rainy season. Taxis in tour centres may not operate meters so a fare should be negotiated. Long distance taxi firms operate between main cities. Hire cars are easily available and can be hired with the services of a chauffeur if required. To hire a car, phone Nairobi – Avis (334317), Hertz (331960); Mombasa – Avis (23048), Hertz (20741). Drivers must obtain a circulation permit from the licensing officer in Nairobi, and have their driving licences endorsed at a local police station.

MAJOR SIGHTS OF THE COUNTRY

NAIROBI, the capital, is a modern city which thanks to its altitude has an extremely pleasant climate with warm sunny days and cool evenings. It is a colourful city with many parks and gardens. The National Museum and Snake Park are well worth a visit, as are the shopping areas and city market. Only a few kilometres outside the city is the NAIROBI NATIONAL PARK which is a very convenient way to see a huge variety of wildlife in its natural habitat. The animal orphanage at the entrance to the park cares for sick animals and abandoned young. THE BOMAS OF KENYA, also just outside Nairobi, is a cultural centre designed to display the heritage and traditions of Kenya's 16 different ethnic groups.

MOMBASA, 300 miles from Nairobi, is the second largest city and chief port of Kenya. Built upon an island, this historic city has a maze of narrow alleys and medieval buildings in the Old Town, and a medieval harbour where visitors can take a dhow cruise. For further details turn to our *City Guide* to Mombasa on p. 205.

KENYA'S COASTLINE is idyllic, with wide sandy beaches, palm trees and a beautiful blue sea protected by coral reefs. There are four distinct areas: the south coast, centred around the DIANI BEACH area; the north coast, north of Mombasa; MALINDI and WATAMU; and the LAMU ARCHIPELAGO.

A visit to one or more of Kenya's National Parks and Game Reserves should be high on any visitor's itinerary. There are 37 protected wildlife areas, covering 10 per cent of the country and nearly all species of life in Africa as well as a vast range of landscape. The 6 most recommended are TSAVO, NAIROBI, AMBOSELI, MERU, SAMBURU and MUSAI MORA. If you can make it down south to the Amboseli Game Reserve, you will see possibly the most dramatic and attractive area in the whole country, with MOUNT KILIMANJARO looming majestically just over the border in Tanzania. Also worth considering is the LAKE NAKURU NATIONAL PARK, which is famous for its thousands of pink flamingoes. These almost cover the lake and form a most spectacular sight.

HOTELS

There are three types: town hotels; vacation hotels; lodges and country hotels. All are graded according to amenities. Many of Nairobi's hotels are up to international standards, some in colonial style, and can be very luxurious. There is an Inter-Continental and a Hilton in Nairobi. There are also many less expensive hotels, from about 20 Ks a night, but some are very primitive. River Round is the place to find most of this cheaper accommodation in Nairobi.

There are Youth Hostels throughout Kenya, costing about 12.50 Ks. These tend to be found in Nairobi and the resorts.

Campers are in little or no danger from wildlife but plenty from thieves – including animals stealing food! There are campsites in all the game parks and reserves, in Nairobi and at tourist centres.

NIGHTLIFE AND RESTAURANTS

Hotels offer a high standard of cuisine, and the town restaurants have a wide variety of food from many countries. Kenyan national dishes are on most hotel menus, and the beef, chicken, lamb and pork dishes are all worth looking out for, as are the tropical fruits such as paw paws, mangoes and avocados. Some of the game park lodges serve gazelle, impala and buffalo steaks. Of the local drinks, the coffee-based Mount Kenya Liqueur is one of the best. Most of the hotels have discotheques, as does the Casino in Nairobi, and there are clubs with a more African feel. The Kenyan National Theatre in Nairobi hosts dramatic, dancing and musical shows, and there are also many cinemas in the city, including several showing English films.

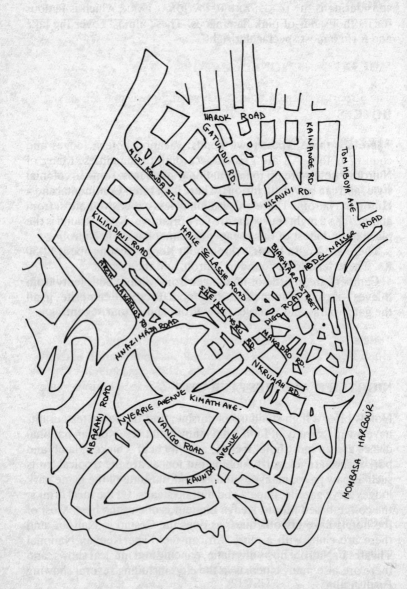

Mombasa

MOI INTERNATIONAL AIRPORT

The airport is open 24 hours a day, and there is one terminal.

AIRPORT FACILITIES

Information Desk	On the public concourse in the land side.
Restaurants	There are bars, buffets and restaurants in the airport and 2 sweet shops for the less hungry.
Banks	Banking facilities, including foreign exchange, are available whenever there is a flight.
Duty Free/Shops	There are 2 shops selling cigarettes, wines, spirits, perfume, cameras, films etc. Payment must be in an acceptable foreign currency.
Toilets	Available in all areas of airport.
Hotel Reservations	Reservation and accommodation finding service desk in public concourse.
Post	Post Office open 0745–1630 hours Monday to Friday.
Medical Centre	There is a hospital next to the airport, and a first aid centre in the terminal.
Nursery	No nursery facilities.
Car Rental	Desks in public concourse.
Taxis	Available outside the terminal.

AIRPORT INFORMATION

Check-in Times	Domestic – 30 minutes. International – 1 hour.
Airport Tax	US$ 12

Transferring Flights   Arriving passengers on international flights must clear Customs before transferring to local flights.

AIRPORT HOTELS

There are no airport hotels, but there are plenty in the town and along the beaches. Hotel coaches are available on request.

CITY LINKS

No rail links. Taxi to the city centre approximately 120 Ks; Bus 3 Ks.

TOURIST INFORMATION

The tourist information office is on Kilindini Road, next to the giant tusks (Box 80091), and is open 0800–1200 and 1400–1630 Monday to Friday, and 0800–1200 on Saturdays.

ADDRESSES

British Council – City House, Nyerere Avenue, PO Box 90590 (tel. 23076).
Thomas Cook Authorized Representative – United Touring Co. Ltd, Kilindini Road, PO Box 84782 (tel. 20741).

GETTING ABOUT

The *bus* lines, Coast Bus Services, Goldlike Ltd and Kenya Bus Services, are located on Mwembe Tayari Road, Malindi.
Taxis are on Jomo Kenyatta Avenue, and Mombasa Peugeot Services in Haile Selassie Road.

SIGHTS

The city has a long history and has been the scene of many battles. FORT JESUS, built in 1593 by the Portuguese, has been at the centre of many of these, frequently changing hands. It now houses a museum and is probably the city's most impressive historical monument. Other sights include the Hindu temple on Mirayogo Road, with its dome of pure gold, and the temple on Haile Selassie Road with an exquisitely painted door. The old harbour can be toured in a dhow, and the market and bazaar are worth walking round. The OLD TOWN is in the south-eastern part of the island, and with its alleys and museums has a character and charm which should not be missed. Other places to visit include the luxury room, just off Treasury Square, which is open from 8 a.m. to 12 noon; the Uhuru Fountain built in the shape of Africa; and the elephant tusks which span the Kilindini Road.

ACCOMMODATION

Top Kenyan hotels can be very luxurious, some still very traditional, even colonial in style. There seems, however, to be a plentiful supply of cheaper accommodation, the most economical of which is in the town itself. Many people prefer to find a hotel nearer the beach, and these tend to be lively establishments, often with bars and discotheques.

• **First Class:** (around 1500 Ks for a double)
Inter-Continental – Diani Beach (tel. 485811). Magnificently equipped luxury hotel, with fine restaurants, floodlit tennis courts, air-conditioned squash courts, and a unique deep-water pool, where you can learn how to scuba dive.

Mombasa Beach – PO Box 90414 (tel. 471861). A modern luxury hotel built on a cliff overlooking a beach, 8 km from the city centre. There are 100 rooms, a restaurant, bar, discotheque, cinema, live shows, swimming, water-sports and golf available.

Nyali Beach – PO Box 90581 (tel. 471551). On the beach front 6½ km from the city, with transport into Mombasa provided daily. As well as restaurants, bars, sports, and golf, the hotel has, most importantly, a private beach.

● **Super Club Class:** (around 1000 Ks for a double)
Oceanic Hotel – Mbuyoni Road, PO Box 90371 (tel. 311191). Overlooks the sea, 1 km from the city centre. There are 85 rooms, a restaurant, 2 bars, casino, swimming, golf and water-skiing available.

Castle Hotel – Moi Avenue, PO Box 84321 (tel. 23403). Comfortable hotel just a stroll from the Old Port.

Outrigger Hotel – Ras Liwatoni, PO Box 84231 (tel. 20822). Close to the city, but quiet and relaxing. Swimming pool faces Kilindini Harbour.

● **Economy:** (300–700 Ks for a double)
Manor Hotel – Nyerere Avenue, PO Box 84851 (tel. 21821). Top of range hotel.

Hydro Hotel – Digo Road near the market (tel. 23784). Cheap and clean. Good place to meet other travellers.

Hotel Splendid – Digo Road, again. Similar standards to Hydro. Handy for Old Town. Good restaurant.

YMCA and YWCA – Kimathi Avenue (tel. 312846). Full board, which means four meals a day.

DINING OUT

● **First Class:** (over 1000 Ks for two)
Mvita Grill – At the Nyali Beach Hotel (tel. 471551). Situated right on the beach and decorated with colourful kikois. The sauces are light and delicious. Excellent *flambés*.

Makuti – At the Diani Reef (tel. Diani 2062). Fine restaurant with interesting 'gastronomic weeks' when they feature the food of a particular country.

Ali Barbour's – Diani Beach (tel. Diani 2163). Dine under the stars in this unique cave restaurant. International cuisine, with seafood specialities.

• **Super Club Class:** (160–180 Ks for two)
Fontanella – Situated near the Manor Hotel (tel. 27356). Seafood is the speciality here.

Ndege Grill – At the Reef Hotel (tel. 471771). Features live piano music on Wednesdays and Fridays.

Le Joli Colin – Near Severin Sea Lodge (tel. 485480). The Indian food here is good, but the seafood is the speciality, featuring charcoal grilled lobster. Closes on Tuesdays.

• **Economy:**
Rooftop Restaurant – At the Hotel Splendid. Splendid seafood and Indian cuisine.

Blue Fin Fish – Tel. 21666. Serves a very good fish, chips and salad.

Central Tea Rooms – On Digo Road, does very reasonable curries.

Ashur's – On Jomo Kenyatta Avenue. Worth looking at.

NIGHTLIFE

There are several cinemas in Mombasa. The city's nightlife is centred around the KILINDINI ROAD (which is also known as Moi Avenue) where there are many bars and nightclubs, the most popular of which seems to be the SUNSHINE CLUB. Many hotels have a disco and casinos, and there are many nightclubs along the coast, some in very exotic locations such as inside natural caves.

EXCURSIONS

THE SHIMBA HILLS GAME RESERVE is the closest wildlife park to Mombasa, situated to the south, off the Mombasa–Tanga road. It is famous for its sable antelope, and also contains elephant, lion and leopard.

TSAVO NATIONAL PARK is on the Mombasa–Nairobi road, roughly halfway between the two. There is a wide variety of landscape and wildlife, with the main features being the elephant and hippo populations.

FRERETOWN was founded as a colony for freed slaves in the last century. It has one of the oldest Christian churches in East Africa. It is reached by going over the Nyali Bridge and taking the first turning left (the Malindi road); a few hundred yards further on, a track to the left leads to the church.

NYALI ESTATE, reached by going over the Nyali Bridge and straight on, has magnificent gardens. It is close to the Nyali Beach and Mombasa Beach hotels. The MAZERAS MUNICIPAL GARDENS AND NURSERIES are beautiful gardens about twelve miles from Mombasa, on the Nairobi road.

THE KAYA OF THE GIRIAMA, reached by driving along the Nairobi road to Mariakoni, lies to the north-east along a dirt track (about 30 miles away in total). The Kaya is the central tribal council house of the Nyiha tribe, and well worth a visit.

MALINDI, a town to the north of Mombasa, has a long history. It is now a fishing port, with excellent surfing and swimming. Trips can be taken in glass-bottomed boats to see the living coral, and there are deep-sea fishing trips, best from October to April, which can be very successful even for a complete novice! This can be an expensive pastime, however.

LAMU is an island to the north of Mombasa. Although a long trip, Lamu is worth the effort. It is one of the most remarkable places left in the modern world, remaining incredibly unspoilt. There are no cars or bicycles even and the lifestyle of the island is slow and dreamy. There are historical sights to see, shops to wander round without being pestered to buy, interesting walks, a beautiful empty beach, and a very restful atmosphere, and there is a first class hotel on the island, Peponi's which can be reached from Mandu airstrip by launch. James Kishman, the archaeologist, wrote of Lamu: 'It is refreshing to find one place in the world that does not pretend to believe in progress or indeed in motion at all.'

South Africa

RED TAPE

• **Passport/Visa Requirements:** In addition to a full, valid passport, visas are required by all visitors except nationals of the United Kingdom, the Republic of Ireland, Switzerland, Liechtenstein, Botswana, Lesotho, Swaziland, Transkei and West Germany, but the situation may well change, so check with South African Embassy first.

Visitors will have to satisfy Passport Control that they have enough funds for their stay in South Africa, and may be refused entry if they have ever been deported from or refused entry to South Africa, convicted of any crime in any country, or are suffering from any contagious disease.

CUSTOMS

• **Duty Free:** Visitors are allowed to import the following without incurring Customs duties: 400 cigarettes and 50 cigars and 250 grammes of tobacco; 1 litre of spirits and 1 litre of wine; 300 ml of perfume; and gifts up to the value of R200.

HEALTH

1. A yellow fever vaccination certificate is required by travellers who have visited infected countries.
2. There is a malaria risk throughout the year in the north-east and western low altitude areas.
3. Water is purified in all towns but precautions are necessary elsewhere.
4. Health insurance is required. Medical facilities are excellent.

CAPITAL – Pretoria (Administrative); Cape Town (Legislative); Bloemfontein (Judicial).

POPULATION – 23,771,970.

LANGUAGE – Afrikaans, English, Zulu, Xhosa and other African languages.

CURRENCY – Rand (= 100 cents). Notes – R20, 10, 5 and 2. Coins – R1, and cents 0.5, 1, 2, 5, 10, 20 and 50.
£1 = R3.2; US$1 = R2.13.

BANKING HOURS – 0900–1530 Monday, Tuesday, Thursday, Friday; 0900–1300 Wednesday; 0830–1100 Saturday.

POLITICAL SYSTEM – The President, and members of the Senate and House of Assembly are elected by the white minority only. Any genuinely representative black organizations are officially banned. The apartheid system is still strongly held together by an extremely efficient army and police force. The instability of the South African government and society is largely exaggerated. Most of the troubles and suffering are confined to black areas: the white community is still largely untouched. The political future of South Africa is impossible to predict, however, as outside pressure continues to grow, and it is certainly possible that sanctions against tourism to South Africa will be introduced by some countries. Although the political situation in South Africa should not cause undue fears to a white visitor's safety, it may trouble his/her conscience. A South African stamp on a passport can cause severe problems when travelling to other areas of the world.

RELIGION – Most are Christians of various denominations.

PUBLIC HOLIDAYS – 1 January, 31 May, 1st Monday in September, 10 October, 16 December, 25, 26 December, and the moveable holidays on Good Friday, Easter Monday and Ascension.

CLIMATE – South Africa has an agreeable and temperate climate. Summers are warm to hot and temperatures vary from 21°C to 28°C. The Cape coastal belt has a very Mediterranean climate, while elsewhere it is hotter and drier. You should bring light- to medium-weight clothing (depending on the season) and warmer clothes if you are intending to travel in the mountains, where it can get quite chilly at night. Remember that the South African summer corresponds to British winter.

TIME DIFFERENCE – GMT + 2.

COMMUNICATIONS

• **Telephone:** Direct trunk lines link all the major towns and direct dialling is available to many European capitals and to North America. Public telephones accept 20c, 10c and 5c coins with a minimum charge of 5c per call. The code for Cape Town is 021.

• **Post:** All mail to and from South Africa should be sent airmail, which can take up to a week.

ELECTRICITY – 380–220 volts AC/50 Hz, except Pretoria 415–240v; and Port Elizabeth 433–250v and 380–220v.

OFFICE/SHOPPING HOURS – 0830–1700 Monday to Friday; the shops also on Saturday 0830–1300.

INTERNAL TRAVEL

• **Air:** There are several flights a day linking Cape Town, Johannesburg, Durban, Port Elizabeth, East London, Kimberley and Bloemfontein on South African Airways. Other services are operated by Air Cape, Commercial Airways and Namakwaland Air Services.

• **Rail:** There are international routes to Zimbabwe, Botswana and Mozambique. Train travel between the major cities can be luxurious but a lengthy business, and fares often include sleeping reservations. There are sometimes only a few trains a week between the major cities, although local trains are more frequent.

• **Road:** An International Driving Licence will be necessary. There are *hire cars* in all the major cities, but visitors should take note of the long distances between all cities and consequent fuel costs. Avis, Hertz and Budget are nationwide. Traffic travels on the left, and speed restrictions should be observed; South Africa has one of the world's highest accident rates.

Taxi charges vary and quotations should be sought for long journeys. *Bus and coach* services run tours for sightseeing as well as intercity express links.

MAJOR SIGHTS OF THE COUNTRY

JOHANNESBURG has grown from its beginning as a gold mining camp in the 1880s to its present size as the largest city in the country, with a population of 2 million. It is the industrial and commercial centre of the country, and the most cosmopolitan and sophisticated city, with a wide range of entertainments.

PRETORIA, less than an hour's drive from Johannesburg, retains more of an old-world atmosphere. The city holds the Voortrekker Monument, preserved as a national shrine by the Afrikaner population, as well as many museums and the Union Buildings of the government.

THE KRUGER NATIONAL PARK, covering 19,500 square kilometres of the eastern Transvaal, contains hundreds of species of animals and birds.

DURBAN is known as the Holiday City, being the country's most popular resort thanks to its sub-tropical climate and beautiful coastline. Durban is a large colourful city with all the amenities associated with a major tourist and industrial centre. A string of resorts stretch along the coastline north and south of Durban; inland are the ZULULAND GAME PARKS.

BLOEMFONTEIN is the capital of the central province, the ORANGE FREE STATE, which is a gold mining and agricultural area, with the beautiful Malutis mountain range composed largely of golden cave sandstone to the east of the province.

South Africa contains a wide spectrum of climates and land-scapes. The vast distances involved make it a difficult country to explore, but spectacular and rewarding scenery is sure to be within reaching distance – no matter where a visitor is based.

HOTELS

Hotel accommodation in South Africa is of a very high standard: all hotels are registered with the Hotel Board and are graded from 1 to 5 star. There are also many self-catering holiday flats and guest houses, and motels are plentiful along motorway routes. There are rest camps in the game parks, which can be very luxurious. Camping and caravanning are also well catered for, with camps in most of the tourist towns being of high standard.

NIGHTLIFE AND RESTAURANTS

Cape Town is the cultural centre of the country, but distances being so great, the major towns and cities have evolved their own independent entertainment scenes. The country gets most American and English films and music, except for those that are censored. Some bars have restrictions prohibiting coloured people and women.

The thriving agriculture of the country produces excellent fresh fruit and vegetables and salads are always popular. South African wine is of a very high quality, and restaurants serve a large variety of both international and traditional fare. Seafood is a speciality, especially rock lobster tails.

Mild curry dishes such as *bobotie*, which is curried minced lamb, and vegetable stews, known as *bredies*, were introduced by the Malays in the Cape area. Venison is available in the winter months.

Cape Town

D.F. MALAN AIRPORT

D.F. Malan Airport is 8 miles from the city centre, served by 6 airlines, and handles about 15,000 passengers a year. It has 4 terminals.

AIRPORT FACILITIES

Some facilities are open during scheduled flights and on request only.

Information Desk	Will only give information on flights, not tourist information generally. The airport's telephone number is 9312261.
Restaurants	4, open 0600–2300. The main restaurant is in Terminal A. The restaurant in the Arrivals Terminal is open 24 hours.
Snack Bars	There is a self-service snack bar in Terminal A.
Bars	6
Banks/Foreign Exchange	The Volkskas bank in Terminal A is open 0900–1530. There is also a bank in the International Terminal open whenever there are flights.
Duty Free/Shops	There is a shop at the Arrivals Hall for Terminals A and B, open 0600–2300. The Duty Free Shop at the International Terminal is open approximately 2 hours before the departure of overseas flights, selling liquor and cigarettes. International Arrivals only has a shop selling books, magazines etc.
Hotel Reservations	Not available.
Disabled	There are wheelchairs available at the airport. There are toilets for the disabled in all terminals.
Nursery	Only in Terminal A, including cot and washing of nappies.
Car Rental	There are 4 desks: Hertz, Avis, Imperial, Budget; in the Domestic Arrivals Hall (A and B), open whenever the airport is open.
Taxis	There are taxis and buses operating whenever the airport is open.

AIRPORT INFORMATION

Check-in Times   Domestic – 30 minutes.
                        International – 1 hour.

AIRPORT HOTELS

None, but Cape Town itself has no shortage of accommodation.

CITY LINKS

● **Road:** The only link with the city is by road. Buses depart regularly for the city until well into the night (tel. 931 8000 for information).

There is a taxi rank at the airport and the trip to the city centre takes about 20 minutes. Agree on a price with the driver before you get in the cab.

TOURIST INFORMATION

The Cape Tourism Authority (Cape Town) has two offices: on the Strand Concourse (in the underground pedestrian mall in Adderley Street), PO Box 863, Cape Town 8000 (tel. 25-3320); and at Atlantic Road, Muizenberg, PO Box 60, Muizenberg 7945 (tel. 88-1898). There are multi-lingual staff who can assist with accommodation, car rentals and tour enquiries. Free maps, guides and information brochures are available.

The S.A. Tourism Board is situated at Room 330, Broadway Centre, Heerengracht. Postal address: PO Box 6187, Roggebaai 8012 (tel. 21-6274). This gives tourist information on South Africa as a whole.

ADDRESSES

British Embassy – 91 Parliament Street (tel. 227583, summer only).
British Consulate-General – 11th Floor, African Eagle Centre, 2 St George's Street, PO Box 1346 (tel. 411466/8).
US Consulate – Broadway Industries Centre, Heerengracht, Foreshore (tel. 471280).

GETTING ABOUT

There is an excellent road network around the city and Cape
Province. The main *bus* terminal is the Golden Acre bus terminal.
Tel. 45-5450 for timetables and details. There is also a *tram service*
operating around the city.

There are *taxi* ranks in the city centre at Lower Adderley Street,
opposite the Airways Terminal, Upper Adderley Street outside
Groote Kerk, Green Market Square, and in St George's Street at
the Cape Sun Hotel. It is not usual to hail passing taxis, and it is
advisable to establish a cost before engaging a taxi.

Most major *car hire* firms are available. Drivers must be 21 years
old and hold a valid driving licence. There are many *coach tours*
around the Province and an extensive *rail* network. Information on
both of these can be obtained from the South African Railways
Travel Bureau, Station Concourse, Adderley Street (tel. 218-2191).

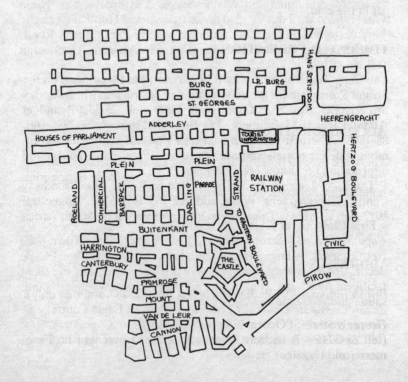

SIGHTS

Cape Town is the oldest city in South Africa, and one of the most beautiful and spectacular in the world. The city lies in the shadow of the famous TABLE MOUNTAIN, which offers panoramic views of the city and environs. The cable car ride to the top is worth doing in its own right. The city was founded in 1652, and retains many places of historical interest. The old TOWN HOUSE on Greenmarket Square houses a collection of 17th-century Dutch and Flemish paintings, and is open 1000–1730 hours. There are also art galleries at the Rust-en-Ureurg, at 78 Buitenhart Street, and the South African National Gallery off Government Avenue. There are many museums, including one in the CASTLE OF GOOD HOPE in Castle Street, which was built in 1666 and is the oldest building in South Africa. In Newlands, on the slopes of Table Mountain, are the Kirstenbosch National Botanic Gardens. There is a Flea Market in Green Market Square on Wednesdays and Saturdays. The 'Noon Gun' is fired each day at 1200 hours from Signal Hill. Children can be entertained at the Children's Recreation Park, Beach Road, Green Point, or the Peninsula Ice Rink, showgrounds, Goodwood (tel. 54-4919).

ACCOMMODATION

There are over 80 hotels in Cape Town graded 1 to 5 star, totalling over 5000 rooms. There are also many beds available in pensions, holiday flats, bungalows, cottages and caravan parks.

● **First Class:** (over SAR70 for a double)
Cape Sun Hotel – Strond Street, PO Box 4532, Cape Town 8000 (tel. 23-8844). A large, bright, modern hotel with traditional Cape decor. 364 bedrooms with yellow wood furniture, and excellent facilities, including conference arrangements, swimming pool, sauna and restaurants. Multi-racial.

Heerengracht – St George's Street, PO Box 2936, Cape Town 8000 (tel. 21-3711). A modern hotel with 210 spacious and luxurious rooms and excellent facilities.

Mount Nelson Hotel – 76 Orange Street, PO Box 2608, Cape Town 8000 (tel. 23-1000). A stylish hotel set in beautiful gardens, with an extremely impressive entrance drive. 149 rooms, excellent facilities including swimming, squash and tennis, restaurants and conference rooms. Multi-racial.

● **Super Club Class:** (SAR140 for a double)
De Waal – Mill Street Gardens, PO Box 2793 (tel. 45-1311). A 4-star hotel with 130 rooms, restaurant, steakhouse and bars. The hotel is at the foot of Table Mountain, and within easy walking distance of the city centre. Multi-racial.

Inn on the Square – Greenmarket Square, PO Box 3775, Cape Town 8000 (tel. 23-2040). A 3-star hotel. Glamorous and central. Multi-racial.

Town House Hotel – 60 Corporation Street, PO Box 5053, Cape Town 8000 (tel. 45-7050). Another international hotel with sauna, squash, swimming, restaurant and excellent facilities combined with the character, grace and the convenience of a central site. Multi-racial.

● **Economy:**
Carlton Heights Hotel – 88 Queen Victoria Street (tel. 23-1260). In a quiet attractive setting yet only an 8-minute walk from the city centre, the hotel is directly opposite the Botanic Gardens. This is a 2-star establishment with good facilities including an à la carte restaurant.

Tudor Hotel – Green Market Square, Cape Town 8000 (tel. 24-1335). This is a very good value comfortable establishment, with 40 rooms, and a restaurant.

Garden Village – Union Street Gardens, Cape Town 8001 (tel. 24-1460). A 2-star hotel with restaurant and swimming pool.

Castle – 42 Canterbury Street (tel. 22-9227). A good value hotel in a central site.

DINING OUT

● **First Class:** (SAR50 for two)
Tastevin French Restaurant – At the Cape Sun Hotel (tel. 23-8844).
Especially good for executive luncheons, it has a sophisticated
elegant atmosphere and excellent French cuisine. The fish specialities are particularly recommended. Closed Sundays.

Van Donck – At the Hotel Heerengracht (tel. 21-3711). Situated on
the 32nd floor, the restaurant has a spectacular view, elegant setting
and live classical music. Specializes in 'nouvelle cuisine'. Closed
Saturday lunch and Sundays.

Grill Room – Mount Nelson Hotel (tel. 23-1000). Specializes in
South African game during the game season. Cantertal music for
dancing. Closed Saturday lunch and Sundays.

● **Super Club Class:** (SAR30–40 for two)
Hatfield House – At 133 Hatfield Street Gardens (tel. 45-7387). An
intimate dining setting with a courtyard for outside luncheons.
Fresh local ingredients used only.

The Town House – At the Town House Hotel, 60 Corporation
Street (tel. 45-7050). An old-world ambience is created by the
traditional elegant setting. Friendly, with excellent food and
reasonable prices. Continental cuisine. Pianist.

Oriental Restaurant – At the Oriental Plaza, Sir Lowny Road (tel.
46-5858). The best oriental cuisine in town. Closes Tuesdays and
Sundays.

● **Economy:** (under SAR25)
Table Mountain Restaurant – At Table Mountain Cable Way (tel.
52-1734). The restaurant on top of Table Mountain has a cosy
atmosphere and specializes in grilled king klip and filled croissants.

Dichwich Tavern – 55 St George's Street (tel. 23-5210). Has a very
reasonable wine list. Specializes in fish dishes.

Marius Restaurant – At 31 Barnet Street (tel. 45-2096). Intimate and friendly Greek restaurant which describes itself as specializing in 'peasant food'. You can take your own wine.

Le Trianon – At 2 Radio City, Tulbugh Square (tel. 25-4965). Good atmosphere and excellent Indonesian and Dutch food. You can also bring your own wine here.

NIGHTLIFE

Cape Town is the cultural centre of South Africa, and opera, drama, ballet and classical music are well represented. The Cape Town Symphony Orchestra performs on Thursdays and Sundays in the Grand Hall of the City Hall. There are several theatres, the biggest and best known being the Nico Milan Theatre Centre on D.F. Malan Street (tel. 21-5470). There is a Shakespeare season in January on the outdoor stage at Maynardville and in April the Cape Town Festival fills the theatres, gardens and streets with sights and sounds. There are venues for pop, jazz and folk music, and the most popular clubs are the CRAZY HORSE at the Century Hotel, SEA POINT, and the VAN DONCK at the top of the Heerengracht, St George's Street.

EXCURSIONS

The coastline and beaches in the Cape area are beautiful, and many deep-sea fishing tours, boating excursions and diving expeditions are available. The climate is Mediterranean, which is ideal for fruit growing, and there is an abundance of orchards and vineyards in the area.

The WEST COAST REGION has magnificent beaches, sweeping bays and colourful fishing villages.

BLOUBERGSTRAND, 25 km from Cape Town, is a popular resort with a fine view of Table Mountain and Table Bay. DARLING, 76 km from Cape Town, is famous for its wildflowers.

LANGEBAAN LAGOON, 26 km long and 4.5 km wide, has many species of fish and is a feeding spot for a wide variety of birds. The village of LANGEBAAN, 128 km from Cape Town, is popular with swimmers, yachtsmen and aquaplaners.

Inland from Cape Town is a fertile area known as the WINELANDS, passing through the mountains which separate the coastal area from the BREEDE RIVER. The scenery hereabouts is magnificent. The JONKERSHOEK NATURE RESERVE, 61 km from Cape Town at the foot of the STELLENBOSCH MOUNTAINS, is sited in a beautiful glen with a waterfall, tall oak trees and many flowering plants.

The historic town of STELLENBOSCH, 42 km from Cape Town, is known as 'the Town of Oaks', and has many sights, museums and places of historical interest to visit. The WIESENHOF GAME PARK, 60 km from Cape Town, is a 700 acre fauna and flora reserve with spectacular views, a large variety of wildlife roaming freely, and facilities such as a restaurant, swimming pool, boating lake and picnic area. For bookings phone 0211-5181.

Beyond the mountains the BREEDE RIVER VALLEY is a fertile farming area. SWELLENDAM, 220 km from Cape Town, is a historic town founded in 1747, with museums and galleries to visit. CERES is known as 'the Switzerland of South Africa', nestling as it does among ice-capped mountains.

The coastal region south of Cape Town has a mild dry climate with an old-world atmosphere. HERMANUS is a popular holiday resort and famous angling centre with a lagoon for yachting. There are scenic drives around the town which provide panoramic views along the coast. CAPE AGULHAS is the southernmost point of the African continent. There are many hiking tracks in the Cape hinterlands which allow visitors to break away from the roads and towns, and explore the mountains, rivers and forests of the area. More information can be obtained from The National Hiking Way Board, Department of Forestry, Room 1317, Plein Park Building, Plein Street (tel. 45-1224).

2. AUSTRALASIA AND OCEANIA

Australia

RED TAPE

• **Passport/Visa Requirements:** A full, valid passport is required by all travellers to Australia. Visas are required by everyone except Australian and New Zealand passport holders. Visitors' visas may be used for up to 6 months by those who do not intend to seek employment in the country. Working Holiday visas are available for 18–25-year-olds who wish to travel in Australia for a maximum of one year and seek casual employment during that time. Applications for either type of visa should be made to the Australian Consulate in your nearest city, or to the Visa Section, Australian High Commission, Australia House, Strand, London WC2B 4LA (tel. 01-836 7161); or Australian Embassy, 1601 Massachusetts Avenue, NW, Washington DC 20036 (tel. 202 797 3000).

CUSTOMS

• **Duty Free:** Each visitor may take in the following without incurring duty: 200 cigarettes or 250 grammes tobacco or 50 cigars, plus 1 litre of wine, 1 litre of spirits and gifts worth up to A$20,000. There are very strict regulations against the import of foodstuffs and other potential sources of disease and pestilence.

HEALTH

Australia has very strict health controls on entering and leaving the country. A yellow fever certificate is required by travellers coming

from infected areas (this includes former endemic areas) and the
right is reserved to isolate any person who arrives without the
required certificates. Carriers of the disease are responsible for the
isolation expenses of all fellow travellers who have not been
vaccinated.

Insurance is recommended as health costs are high in Australia.
Water is safe to drink except in extreme outback areas.

CAPITAL – Canberra (in Australian Capital Territory). Population – 245,500.

LANGUAGE – English. Aborigines speak their own language
which includes many corrupted English words.

CURRENCY – Australian Dollar. A$1 = 100 cents. Notes – 1, 2, 5,
10, 20, 50, 100 dollars. Coins – 1, 2, 5, 10, 20, 50 cents and 1 dollar.
£1 = A$2.13; US$1 = A$1.52.

BANKING HOURS – 1000–1500 hours Monday to Thursday,
1000–1700 hours Friday (hours vary slightly throughout the
country).

POLITICAL SYSTEM – Democracy, with Federal and State
Governments.

RELIGION – Church of England with a Roman Catholic minority.

PUBLIC HOLIDAYS

January 1	New Year's Day
January (1 day)	Australia Day
March (1 day)	Labour Day (Western Australia, Tasmania, Victoria)
March (1 day)	Canberra Day (Australian Capital Territory)
March/April (3 days)	Good Friday, Easter Saturday, Easter Monday
April 25	Anzac Day

May (1 day)	May Day (Northern Territory); Labour Day (Queensland); Adelaide Cup (South Australia)
June (1 day)	Foundation Day (Western Australia); Queen's Birthday (all except Western Australia)
July (1 day)	Alice Springs, Katherine, Tennant's Creek and 'Darwin Show Days (one public holiday each)
August (1 day)	Bank Holiday (New South Wales); Picnic Day (Tasmania)
September (1 day)	Melbourne Show (Victoria)
October (1 day)	Labour Day (New South Wales, Australian Capital Territory, South Australia); Queen's Birthday (Western Australia)
November (1 day)	Melbourne Cup Day (Victoria); Recreation Day (Tasmania)
December 25, 26	Christmas and Boxing Day.

CLIMATE – Broadly speaking, there are 2 climatic zones in Australia. In the north, above the Tropic of Capricorn, there are 2 seasons – wet from November to March and dry from April to October. In the southerly, temperate regions there are 4 seasons – summer from December to February, winter from June to August and spring and autumn in between. Summer in Australia is hot everywhere (temperatures vary with regions but can reach 40°C (104°F) inland) with cooler nights in the south. Winter months tend to have warm, clear days with colder nights in the south. Snow is confined to the mountainous regions of the south-east.

TIME DIFFERENCE – North-east/south-east: GMT + 10; Central: GMT + 9.5; West: GMT + 8. All states except Northern Territory and Queensland: + 1 March–October.

COMMUNICATIONS

• **Telephone:** Australia's telephone system is similar to the UK's. Local coin operated calls are 20 cents. Many hotel rooms have IDD. International access code 0011, country code 61.

• **Post:** Post Offices in all the main towns are open 0815–1700 hours Monday to Friday. Telex facilities are available at central Post Offices in major cities. Telegrams can be sent through the telephone operator. In outback areas two-way radio communication is used.

ELECTRICITY – 240/250v, AC; 50 Hz. The Australian 3-pin power outlet is for flat, not round pins. Most leading hotels have universal outlets for 240v or 110v shavers.

OFFICE/SHOPPING HOURS – Offices: 0900–1700 hours Monday to Friday. Shops: 0900–1730 hours Monday to Friday, 0900–1200 hours Saturday.

• **Best Buys:** All the major cities of Australia have good shopping facilities: department stores, arcades, malls, boutiques, craft shops and so on. Sydney, Melbourne and Perth are especially well endowed with a wide array of shops. Australian opals are perhaps the most famous of their precious and semi-precious stones. Silver and enamelled jewellery is also a common sight in the shops. Woollen and leather goods are of a high quality in Australia, but can be quite expensive, as can fashion and sports clothes. In the art and craft business the Aboriginals' work features widely and every city has a plentiful supply of Aboriginal art shops. Souvenir stamps are always popular and sets are sold at philatelic desks in main Post Offices.

INTERNAL TRAVEL

• **Air:** The vast distances between the cities of Australia make flying the only realistic option for those with limited time. The major domestic airlines, Ansett Airlines of Australia and Trans Australia Airlines (TAA), operate regular scheduled services between state capital cities, regional centres and resort areas of the country. Regional airlines provide services from the cities to provincial areas. Advance reservations are always advisable, these are made through travel agents or the airline direct. There are a variety of discount fares and the 'Go Australia Airpass' (where you 'buy' so many thousand miles of air travel and work out your own route, within the confines of the scheduled flights) is particularly worth considering.

● **Rail:** Australia's rail network is fairly limited and mainly serves the east of the country and the south coast. From each regional capital a network of services operates to rural areas, but these tend to be slow and expensive. The famous Indian–Pacific line from Perth to Sydney takes 64 hours, crosses the Nullarbor Plain and goes through 3 states en route. This can be a wonderful experience, though the expense and the tendency for one or other of the states' railways to be on strike makes it an option to be investigated thoroughly before taking. The Austrailpass allows either First or Economy Class travel on any of the lines for a specified duration. It can also give you car rental discounts with Hertz, Avis and Budget and accommodation discounts with Flag Inns, Travelodge or Parkroyal Hotels and Zebra Motor Inns.

● **Bus:** For those with time to spare this is the best way to travel around Australia. The major coachlines, Greyhound, Ansett Pioneer and Deluxe, all have spacious, smooth-running, comfortable coaches. Their drivers tend to be both friendly and knowledgeable about the country they drive you through. Greyhound and Ansett Pioneer do 15-, 30- or 60-day bus passes which makes bus travel a well priced option. Deluxe sell a 'Platypass' which includes accommodation.

● **Car:** Renting a car (or a campervan, as many Australians do for their holidays) is another good way to see the country. An International Driving Licence is not mandatory as long as your own licence is valid. Driving is on the left hand side of the road.

NOTE – Once you leave the main highways much of Australia's roads are just dust tracks, which a little rain can reduce to a quagmire – so beware! Nationwide firms such as Hertz, Avis, Budget, Letz, and Thrifty can arrange for one-way hires which in a country this size is particularly useful.

MAJOR SIGHTS OF THE COUNTRY

The oldest and most populous state is NEW SOUTH WALES. Its landscape ranges from the sub-tropical north to the Snowy Mountains of the south. SYDNEY is the state capital and largest city in Australia. At its heart is the superb natural harbour, with the Opera House and Sydney Harbour Bridge adding to its famous beautiful skyscape. Nearby BOTANY BAY is a botanist's delight and BONDI BEACH a surfer's paradise. The south-eastern SNOWY MOUNTAIN ranges offer good skiing from June to September and WAGGA WAGGA is one of the few thriving inland cities of Australia. CANBERRA, the national capital, is set within NSW in AUSTRALIAN CAPITAL TERRITORY. It is a modern, stylish city with some fine civic architecture, though it lacks the 'heart' of Sydney or Perth.

To the south of NSW is VICTORIA. Although the second smallest landmass, this is the most densely populated and agriculturally productive of the states. MELBOURNE is a cosmopolitan city, having sizeable Greek, Italian and Chinese minority groups. Architecture here is a fascinating blend of ornate stucco and cast iron, graceful spires and modern skyscrapers.

Keep going south, across the Bass Strait, and you will hit TASMANIA. This sizeable island has a surprisingly English air with Cornish-style fishing villages along its coast. HOBART is the capital, with a beautiful, deep harbour, many Georgian buildings (mostly built by convict labour) and the majestic Mount Wellington rising up behind. LAUNCESTON, to the north of Hobart, is a quiet provincial town known for its charming gardens lined with European oaks and elms.

In direct contrast to this is the north-eastern state of QUEENSLAND, renowned for its world famous Gold Coast and Great Barrier Reef. As with the other states, there is also the beauty of the wild, barren outback to discover in Queensland. Wildlife abounds in these remote parts and the two regions of Queensland. Really worth a look if you have the time are the south-western Diamantina County and the northern Cape York Peninsula. BRISBANE is the capital here and you'll notice a big difference in the style of Queenslanders' houses. They are big and spacious, surrounded by well-planned verandahs, often held up from the ground by wooden stilts. The city of Brisbane is well spread out, making good use of the commodity this part of Australia has aplenty – space.

The NORTHERN TERRITORY landscape is dramatic. Bare red soil gives way to scrubby bush and huge rock masses such as the Olgas and the famous AYER'S ROCK. This is located near ALICE SPRINGS, and is one of Australia's most spectacular sights, if a bit touristy now. Much further north is DARWIN, a modern provincial city since its rebuilding after the destruction wrought by Cyclone Tracy in 1974. After the desert-like red-hot centre of the country it comes as a surprise to see the tropical lushness of this area.

WESTERN AUSTRALIA takes up a huge chunk of the continent, but much of it is barren land. Its coastline is very rich in flora and fauna, earning Western Australia its name of the Wildflower State. In the north KIMBERLEY is a spectacular area, with boab trees and rocky outcrops. BROOME is a pretty town which thrives on the pearl industry and makes a good resting place if you are travelling down to PERTH. The America's Cup Challenge is fast putting Perth, and especially nearby FREMANTLE, on the tourist map and doubtless the tourist facilities being built for this event (held 1987) will be put to good use in the following years as this area becomes increasingly popular for holidays. Down on the south coast, around ALBANY, is yet more striking landscape, this time of giant trees, vivid green pastures and dramatic cliffs.

SOUTH AUSTRALIA is a sparsely inhabited region of rock and desert. The picture changes around ADELAIDE, where white sandy beaches, the fertile vineyards of the BAROSSA VALLEY and the spectacular gorges and peaks of the FLINDERS RANGES are to be found.

Brisbane

BRISBANE AIRPORT INTERNATIONAL

Queensland's major airport is 4 miles from Brisbane, at Eagle Farm. There is one passenger terminal which deals with all arriving and departing passengers. As well as the numerous internal flights to and from Brisbane, there are regular international flights to and from Asia, Europe, North America, the Pacific islands, New Zealand and Papua New Guinea.

AIRPORT FACILITIES

These include: buffet; bar; Car Rental Desk; Accommodation Desk; Currency Exchange; shop; and Post Box. Duty Free shop – this stocks a full range of duty free goods and accepts major currencies and credit cards or traveller's cheques.

AIRPORT INFORMATION

Check-in Times	90–120 minutes prior to international flight departure times; 60 minutes prior to domestic flight departure times.
Airport Tax	All adults (over 12 years of age) must pay A$20 on international departure.
Flight Transfers	Transferring passengers will be ushered to the departure lounge within the same building.
Flight Information	Telephone Brisbane 268-9511.

CITY LINKS

• **Bus:** Skennar's Coach Service runs a city-to-airport, airport-to-city bus service from 0630–1830 hours daily. Bookings should be made (tel. Brisbane 832-1148).

• **Taxi:** Taxis to the city cost about 4 times the bus fare, but are still quite reasonable. They are metered and wait in a taxi rank outside the terminal building.

BRISBANE

Brisbane, Australia's third largest city and capital and chief port of Queensland, was originally a convict settlement. In 1823 Lieutenant John Oxley landed on the banks of the Brisbane River. The settlement was opened to colonists in 1842 and became state capital when Queensland was formed (named after Queen Victoria) in 1859. At this time Brisbane was still a primitive town but had some

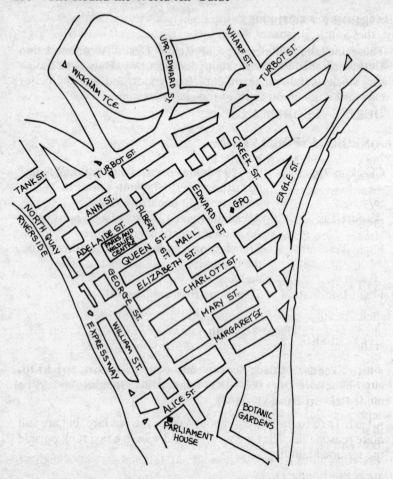

notable buildings. Unfortunately 1864 saw a huge fire destroy most of the city centre and very few of its historic buildings survived.

Today Brisbane is a thriving and growing metropolis which is fighting hard to lose its reputation as a cultureless, northern, provincial town. The broad, airy streets of the centre are planned on a grid system and named after members of the British Royal Family. The wide-banked Brisbane River winds its way through the city to the Sunshine Coast at Moreton Bay. The famous Story Bridge (designed by Dr Bradfield, who also designed Sydney Harbour

Bridge) crosses the river at Petrie Bight and Victoria Bridge crosses at the South Brisbane Reach. The city's chief industries are engineering, shipbuilding, oil refining, food processing and wool scouring. Wool and meat form the major export goods.

TOURIST INFORMATION

Brisbane Visitors and Convention Bureau – Brisbane City Hall, King George Square (tel. 221-8411).
Queensland Government Travel Centre – Corner of Adelaide and Edward Streets (tel. 31-2211).
GPO – 216 Queen Street.
Emergency Number – 000 for ambulance, fire or police services.
Brisbane Area Code Number – 07.

GETTING ABOUT

When finding your way around the city centre it is useful to remember that all the streets with queens' or princesses' names run parallel and at right angles to those of the kings' names.

• **Bus:** A regular bus service runs between 0530 hours and 2300 hours. Timetables are available from the Public Transport Information Centre at 69 Ann Street or details can be obtained by telephoning 225-4444. Buses often need to be hailed before they will stop. Discount tickets are available (from the above mentioned office) and a free 'Downtowner' bus runs from the city to its suburbs every 10 minutes from 1800 hours to 2100 hours on Friday nights (late night shopping).

• **Train:** The city rail network is fairly extensive and details can be seen at Central Station in Anne Street. Daily services operate between 0430 and 0130 hours. Co-ordinating bus services are available on some lines. For details telephone 225-1877 during office hours or 225-1244 after hours.

• **Ferry:** Travelling along or across Brisbane River is a convenient way of getting around the city. Ferries run several routes at 15-minute intervals, often with co-ordinating bus services. For details telephone 399-4768. The Golden Mile Ferry from Greek Street to Bulimba is one of the most scenic trips (details from 399–5054).

● **Taxi:** 24-hour taxi services operate in Brisbane. Major companies are the Ascot Taxi Service (tel. 221-1422); the Black and White Cab Company (tel. 229-1000); and the Yellow Cab Company and Taxis Combined Systems (tel. 391-0191). Fares are metered and uniform for all companies. Luggage and unsocial hours (1800–0600 hours) surcharges apply.

● **Car Rental:** Budget Rent-A-Car (tel. 52-0151), Manx Auto Rentals (tel. 52-7288), Letz Rent-A-Car (tel. 262-3222), Scotty Rent-A-Car (tel. 52-7400), Hertz (tel. 221-6166) and Avis (tel. 52-7111) are the main car hire firms in Brisbane.

SIGHTS

ANZAC SQUARE, Adelaide Street, is a beautiful square with the Shrine of Remembrance at its heart. It was built in 1930 in memory of the Australian soldiers who died in World War I. The unusual Queensland bottle (boab) trees can be seen in the park.

THE DEANERY, at 417 Ann Street, is one of the few remaining 19th-century buildings in Brisbane. It was built by Andrew Petrie in 1853 and was used as Queensland's Government House from 1859–62. It is in the grounds of ST JOHN'S CATHEDRAL, a beautiful, Gothic cathedral, built in the early 20th century and open for guided tours on Wednesdays and Fridays at 1100 hours.

THE TREASURY is a huge, Italian Renaissance style building, occupying the block surrounded by William, Queen, George and Elizabeth Streets. It was built between 1885 and 1928 on the site of the penal settlement's officers' quarters.

On the corner of Alice and George Streets stands PARLIAMENT HOUSE, a fine example of French Renaissance architecture built in 1865. It has recently been re-roofed with copper from Mount Isa (Western Queensland). Daily tours begin at 1030 and 1430 hours when parliament is not sitting.

CITY HALL is an impressive building on King George Square (Adelaide Street) with richly decorated rooms and grand, marble staircases. The 91.5m clock tower has a 76m observation deck (reached by lift) which shows off the city admirably. Off Alice Street are long established Botanic Gardens with many unusual tropical plants. This is also the venue for Brisbane's FREEPS (Free Recreation and Entertainment in Parks) programme. For details see Brisbane's Saturday papers.

QUEENSLAND ART GALLERY is in the celebrated Queensland Cultural Centre, a modern complex just over Victoria Bridge in South Brisbane. Australian, British and European collections are accompanied by a constant stream of exhibitions from all over the world. Open 1000–1700 hours daily and until 2100 hours on Friday. The Queensland Cultural Centre incorporates the Art Gallery, a Performing Arts Complex, the Queensland Museum and restaurants and bars. There are guided tours Monday to Saturday from 1000 hours to 1600 hours (for one hour each).

ACCOMMODATION

Brisbane is not particularly well endowed with hotels and can therefore be quite a difficult place in which to find accommodation. This is especially true during the Warana Festival held annually in September/October. International standard hotels are available and, as a rule, are very good. There are also a number of good guest houses and motels fairly near the centre.

● **First Class:** (Double A$120–180)
Sheraton Brisbane – 249 Turbot Street, Brisbane 4000 (tel. 835-3535). A luxurious place to stay with elegant surroundings and extensive facilities.

Hilton International – 190 Elizabeth Street, Brisbane (tel. 224-9740). A brand-new addition to the Hilton International Group which lives up to all the 'Hilton' standards very well. The rooms are beautifully furnished and the whole building is elegantly designed.

Brisbane Parkroyal – Corner of Alice and Albert Streets (tel. 221-3411). One of Brisbane's finest hotels which overlooks the Botanic Gardens. The interior has recently been completely upgraded and the friendliness and efficiency of the staff is commendable.

● **Super Club Class:** (Double A$80–120)
Gazebo Ramada Hotel – 345 Wickham Terrace, Brisbane (tel. 831-6177). A very good hotel in peaceful gardens within walking distance of the city centre.

Crest International Hotel – King George Square, Ann Street, Brisbane (tel. 229-9111). Excellent accommodation and facilities in a lovely part of central Brisbane.

Brisbane Gateway Hotel – 103 George Street, Brisbane (tel. 221-6044). Very comfortable accommodation and good facilities.

● **Economy:** (Double A$40–80)
Dorchester – 484 Upper Edward Street, Spring Hill, Brisbane (tel. 831-2967). Comfortable accommodation in self-contained apartments within easy reach of the city centre.

Capital Hotel – Corner of Ann and Edward Streets (tel. 32-0231). A very convenient and comfortable hotel with good service.

Marrs Town House – 391 Wickham Terrace, Brisbane (tel. 831-5388). A very reasonably priced guest house with basic but comfortable rooms.

Hotel Canberra – Corner of Ann and Edward Streets, Brisbane (tel. 32-0231). A well run, well priced hotel with breakfast included.

The Tourist Private Hotel – 555 Gregory Terrace, Brisbane (tel. 52-4171). Adequate accommodation on a main bus route (number 7) from the city centre. Prices include breakfast.

YMCA Youth Centre – 387 Lutwyche Road, Windsor (tel. 57-6482). Very low priced and good accommodation.

DINING OUT

Although Australia does not really have a native cuisine, Queensland is famous for the variety of fish, fruit and beer which it exports or serves in its restaurants. Mud crabs, king and tiger prawns, barramundi and Moreton Bay bugs are some of the better known varieties of seafood available. Many of Brisbane's restaurants have a BYO (bring your own wine or beer) system.

● **First Class:** (A$80–110 for two)
Muddies Seafood Restaurant – 5 Edward Street (tel. 31-1996). A magnificent array of seafood can be tried here, and the view over Brisbane River is lovely.

Matilda's – In Lennons Brisbane Hotel, 66–76 Queen Street (tel. 222-3222). A luxurious, intimate restaurant for lunch, dinner or late supper after the theatre.

Dennison's Rooftop Restaurant – In the Sheraton Hotel, 249 Turbot Street (tel. 835-3535). For elegance, taste and style Dennison's is the place to go.

● **Super Club Class:** (A$50–80 for two)
Sombrero's Mexican Cantina – 735 Sandgate Road, Clayfield (tel. 262-7207). Delicious Mexican food which is very filling. Live entertainment is often going on during the evening.

Baguette Licensed Restaurant – 150 Racecourse Road, Ascot (tel. 268-6168). Between the city and the airport this restaurant has a fine menu plus a tropical bar and courtyard. The Galerie Baguette beside the restaurant exhibits Queensland's top artists' works.

Benjamin's – 195 Musgrave Road, Red Hill (tel. 369-9297). A popular BYO vegetarian and seafood restaurant.

Little Tokyo – Bowen Street (off Turbot Street) (tel. 831-7751). Traditional Japanese Sukiyaki and Teppanyaki – very tasty.

● **Economy:** (under A$50 for two)
Sweet Patootie – 480 St Paul's Terrace, Valley (tel. 52-9606). Australian pasta dishes with live jazz at weekends (midday) and every night.

Jo Jo's – Corner of Queen and Albert Streets (upstairs). This is a wonderful innovation whereby tables are scattered between stalls selling Greek, French, Italian, Mexican, Chinese or Lebanese dishes. Drinks are sold at other stalls, so you can 'design' your own meal regardless of what your company wishes to eat.

Tortilla Cantina – Elizabeth Arcade. A popular Spanish/Mexican restaurant.

Arcade Bistro – Brisbane Arcade. Straightforward steaks and salad – very good value.

NIGHTLIFE

Pubs and bars featuring live music (especially jazz) is Brisbane's speciality. The MELBOURNE HOTEL has good jazz sessions and the ADVENTURER'S CLUB features jazz or folk music usually. There are some classy nightclubs such as the BRISBANE UNDERGROUND, which has good food as well as dancing, REFLECTIONS in the Sheraton Hotel and TRACKS at George Street Station.

For a more cultured evening's entertainment the BRISBANE PERFORMING ARTS COMPLEX always has something going on. Theatres in the city area include Brisbane Arts Theatre at 210 Petrie Terrace, Suncorp Theatre in Turbot Street and the Twelfth Night Theatre in Cintra Road. Details of weekly entertainment are in the weekend newspapers or *Time Off*, an entertainment paper.

EXCURSIONS

There is a lot to see and do around Brisbane, both on the famous GOLD and SUNSHINE COASTS, which are only about 1½ hours away by coach, and inland. 12 miles north of the city is the MORETON BAY area with popular fishing, sailing and picnicking beaches. SANDGATE, in this area, is an old established resort. Further north is REDCLIFFE, the original settlement in Queensland and a thriving bayside city with many good beaches nearby.

Inland, 11 miles up the Bruce Highway, is BUNY PARK WILDLIFE SANCTUARY where visitors can walk among the Australian animals and birds and have picnics or barbecues. Keep going up the Bruce Highway and you will reach the turn off to KALLANGUR, where there is a zoo, and NORTH PINE DAM (at LAKE SAMSONVALE) which is a popular water-sports area.

The Pacific Highway runs south of Brisbane to the Gold Coast, passing through the city of LOGAN. DAISY HILL FOREST PARK is just off the highway, some 18 miles out of Brisbane. This is an ideal area for bushwalking, horse riding and picnicking or barbecuing.

IPSWICH is 25 miles west of Brisbane and is the oldest provincial city in Queensland, at one time rivalling Brisbane as the capital. As a result Ipswich has a wealth of historic buildings. To the north-west is the picturesque town of ESK, surrounded by mountains, which has

LAKE SOMERSET lying to its east, a long, winding lake with plenty of water-sport facilities.

There are several islands to the east of Brisbane. Two of the larger ones, MORETON and NORTH STRADBROKE, have superb surfing beaches. Back on the mainland, the REDLANDS DISTRICT is an important vegetable and fruit growing area, especially famous for its strawberries.

Cairns

CAIRNS INTERNATIONAL AIRPORT

The Cairns airport was officially opened as an international airport in March 1984. It is only about 4 miles from Cairns city centre and its one terminal is used for both international and domestic flight passengers.

AIRPORT FACILITIES

These include: Information Desk; telephones; toilets (and baby care room); Currency Exchange; buffet; bar; shops; and Car Hire Desks. Duty Free shops – a wide range of duty free goods are sold. Major currencies and credit cards are accepted.

AIRPORT INFORMATION

Check-in Times	90 minutes prior to international flight departure times; 60 minutes prior to domestic flight departure times.
Airport Tax	A$20 is payable by all departing passengers (on international flights).

Flight Transfers	All arrivals and departures are in the same terminal building. As you enter from the aeroplane side the international section is straight ahead, the domestic terminal section for Ansett is on the left and the domestic terminal section for TAA is on the right.
Flight Information	Telephone Cairns 51-3555.

CITY LINKS – Regular *buses* travel the short distance between city and airport. They stop at either end of the terminal building. *Taxis* are also available on the road outside the terminal. *Car hire* is available within the terminal building.

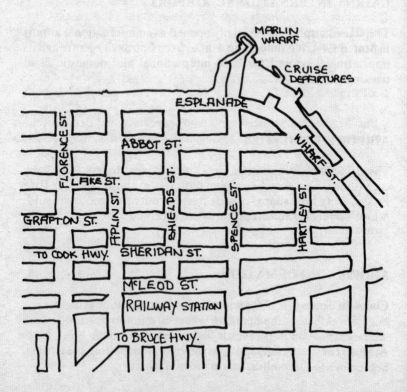

CAIRNS

Cairns is the most northerly city in Queensland, and the closest to the Great Barrier Reef. This region has a strong Aboriginal history and today the growing city of Cairns is supported by the industries of agriculture (sugar cane, tropical fruits, tobacco etc.), forestry, mining, fishing and tourism. The city centre, standing back from the waterfront, is well laid out with broad streets and decorative flowers and bushes. Mangrove swamps surround Cairns to the north and south, and to the west is a beautiful rural hinterland. The sea in front of the city is shallow and turns to mud at low tide. A wide variety of water birds can be seen here.

TOURIST INFORMATION

Queensland Government Travel Centre – 12 Shields Street, Cairns (tel. 51-4066).
Cairns Area Telephone Code – 070.

GETTING ABOUT

• **Bus:** Several bus services operate in Cairns city. For details of the northern beach bus service, which goes up to Ellis Beach, telephone Cairns 55-3079.

• **Taxi:** These are provided by one company and during peak times they can be scarce. The fare is metered and reasonable.

• **Car Rental:** There are several car hire firms with offices in the city or at the airport.

SIGHTS

CAIRNS HARBOUR is a natural harbour at Trinity Inlet which has been developed as the home for a fleet of gamefishing vessels and cruise craft. MARLIN JETTY is a famous spot where the big game is weighed in, especially during the black marlin season, from September to December.

Edged with palm trees, THE ESPLANADE makes a scenic picnic spot and viewing point for the wide variety of birdlife.

CAIRNS BOTANICAL GARDENS is a large parkland featuring 200 species of palms and thousands of other plant species. A short walk from the Botanic Gardens is MOUNT WHITFIELD, which provides panoramic views of the city.

CITY PLACE is a picturesque mall and square in the city centre.

WINDOWS ON THE REEF, a unique theatre in the Great Barrier Reef Cruise Centre on the waterfront. By sophisticated use of special effects the audience experience the impression of diving to 30 metres in the clear waters of the Great Barrier Reef. Meanwhile an audio-visual programme tells the story of the reef. Open daily with 'dive' times posted at the Wharf Street entrance (tel. 51-7800). THE WATERWORKS is another way to see pictures of the reef, this time in an exciting/terrifying 'splash-down'. Participants race through the maze of coloured water slides at great speed. Open daily in Lake Street (tel. 51-6164).

On the corner of Lake and Shields Street is the HISTORICAL MUSEUM, with a display of Aboriginal arts. Open 1000–1500 hours weekdays. The LAROC CORAL JEWELLERY FACTORY, corner of Aumuller and Comport Streets, makes an interesting visit as the factory is designed so that visitors can watch the intricate jewellery-making process. Open 0800–1700 hours weekdays and 0900–1200 weekends (tel. 51-6924).

BLUEWATER MARINE DISPLAY, Aumuller Street, Portsmith: marlin, sailfish, turtles, corals and various other sea creatures can be seen here (tel. 51-5797). CENTENARY LAKES, Greenslopes Street, Cairns North, is a beautiful parkland with two lakes which attract a great variety of bird life, and ADMIRALTY ISLAND is a tiny mangrove-sand island surrounded by clear, calm waters in Trinity Inlet.

ACCOMMODATION

Top class accommodation is limited in Cairns, but there are plenty of good quality motels, guest houses and holiday flats. For most of the year its accommodation is in great demand, so book early.

• **First Class:** (Double A$90–140)
Tradewinds Esplanade – The Esplanade, Cairns (tel. 51-5266). A

newly opened, luxury hotel ideally located on the esplanade. The facilities are extensive, the suites spacious and the service excellent.

Tuna Towers – 145 Esplanade, Cairns (tel. 51-4688). A top quality standard of accommodation overlooking the Cairns waterfront. A pool and spa are among the extensive facilities.

Tradewinds Outrigger – Corner of Lake, Florence and Abbott Streets, Cairns (tel. 51-6188). Luxurious suites in Cairns' city centre. The building is of a typical, tropical North Queensland style with spacious balconies all around.

● **Super Club Class:** (Double A\$50–90)
Bay Village Tropical Retreat – 227–9 Lake Street, Cairns (tel. 51-4622). Set in one acre of prizewinning tropical gardens, this complex has a tropical decor, a large pool and an exotic Jungles Restaurant.

Cairns Colonial Club – 18–26 Cannon Street, Cairns (tel. 53-5111). A tropical resort set in 4 acres of gardens with a huge freeform pool and a beach area. Spacious rooms and units have good amenities.

Rainforest Grove – 40 Moody Street, Cairns (tel. 53-6366). One- or two-bedroomed units nestle in tropical gardens 2 miles from the city centre. Every unit has a balcony or private patio.

Pearl Lugger Apartments – 123–5 Esplanade, Cairns (tel. 51-7666). Self-contained, spacious studio apartments, with balconies overlooking the waterfront.

● **Economy:** (Double A\$20–50)
Oasis Inn Holiday Apartments – 276 Sheridan Street, Cairns (tel. 51-8111). One- or two-bedroom apartments (with kitchen) surrounded by gardens. One mile from Cairns' centre.

Esplanade Motel – 81 Esplanade, Cairns (tel. 51-2326). A small motel on the seafront with limited self-catering facilities in rooms.

Acacia Court – 230–8 Lake Street, Cairns (tel. 51-5011). Holiday flats or rooms with kitchen facilities. Central Cairns.

Tropicana Lodge – 158C Martyn Street (tel. 51-1729). Rooms with limited kitchen facilities. Prices include breakfast.

Parkview – 174–80 Grafton Street, Cairns (tel. 51-3573). Rooms with shared facilities or holiday flats. Very good value and friendly staff.

Cairns Tropical Hostel – 123 Esplanade, Cairns (tel. 51-2323). A spacious old building with pleasant rooms and shared facilities. Very popular.

DINING OUT

For its size, Cairns is very well endowed with a wide variety of restaurants. Seafood is a favourite but you can also find all sorts of European and Eastern cuisines on offer. Most of Cairns' restaurants close quite early and many of them are BYO (bring your own alcohol).

• **First Class:** (A$60–80 for two)
Fathoms – Corner of Grove and Digger Streets (tel. 51-2305). An exciting à la carte menu specializing in seafood. Excellent, friendly service and delicious sweets. A visit to Fathoms is a real treat.

Freshwater Connection – Kamerunga Road, Freshwater (tel. 55-2222). An unusual setting for a restaurant, in a disused rail station. You can eat a delicious meal on the platform or in an intimate carriage.

Duke's Restaurant – 86 Lake Street (upstairs), Cairns (tel. 51-8333). Excellent local seafood, international cuisine and house specialities. Live entertainment and piano bar.

• **Super Club Class:** (A$40–60 for two)
Benji's Licensed Restaurant – 53 Spence Street, Cairns (tel. 51-6805). A lively, atmospheric restaurant with fresh seafood a menu speciality.

Casa Gomez – 48 Aplin Street, Cairns (tel. 51-2805). A BYO Spanish restaurant with flamenco dancers providing entertainment while you eat the excellent cuisine.

Casbah – 47 Vasey Esplanade, Trinity Beach (tel. 55-6319). Cairns' only open-air beachfront restaurant. It's a BYO and serves Mediterranean cuisine plus local seafood.

• **Economy:** (under A$40 for two)

Toko Baru – 42 Spence Street, Cairns (tel. 51-2067). Traditional Indonesian cuisine. BYO.

Thuggee Bill's – 42B Aplin Street, Cairns. Good Indian curries.

Strawbs – 74 Shields Street, Cairns. Excellent value meals in a relaxed, friendly atmosphere.

Mexican Pete's – 61 Spence Street, Cairns. Delicious Mexican dishes and interesting decor.

NIGHTLIFE

Cairns is a lively place at night. Many of the pubs have local live entertainment (listen to Radio 4 CA for details) and there are numerous nightclubs, piano bars and discos. MAGNUM'S (70 Abbott Street) is a sophisticated restaurant, nightclub and bar all rolled into one. SCANDALS (at Tradewinds Sunlodge, Lake Street) is a classy nightclub and piano bar. In the Great Northern Hotel is the yachties' and fishermen's favourite meeting place, the MARTIN BAR. OSCAR'S BISTRO BAR is in the same hotel. Every Sunday the CAIRNS FOLK AND JAZZ CLUB meets at the Theatre Shop (behind Grafton Street).

EXCURSIONS

Although there are many things to see around Cairns, the biggest attraction has to be the GREAT BARRIER REEF. The Reef (actually a multitude of coral reefs) stretches along Australia's north-east coast from Gladstone to Cape York. It can be seen by glass-bottomed boat, by snorkelling, by scuba-diving or even by air. Whichever way you decide to see the Reef the Queensland Government Travel Centre, 12 Shields Street, Cairns (tel. 51-4066) is the best place to organize trips.

Another famous area in Queensland is the ATHERTON TABLE-LAND. This is a rich volcanic plateau which lies to the west of Cairns, within a day's drive. Dense tropical forests, abundant animal, bird and plant life and fabulous scenery make this a very worthwhile area to visit.

Immediately north of Cairns is the MARLIN COAST – a strip of coast lined with palm-fringed, sheltered beaches such as Holloways Beach, Clifton Beach, Trinity Beach and Palm Cove. Off this coast is GREEN ISLAND, a true coral cay, heavily wooded and surrounded by reefs and tropical marine life. South of this is FITZROY ISLAND and to the north are the LOW ISLES, more coral cays.

PORT DOUGLAS, 40 miles north of Cairns, is a fairly quiet seaside town (although once a busy gold-rush port) where the shell jewellery trade flourishes. Further north, COOKTOWN is the historic site of Captain Cook's 1770 landing to repair the *Endeavour*.

Although rather a long way from Cairns, LIZARD ISLAND is a coral wonderland and big game fisher's paradise. It is only 50 miles away by aeroplane and has good tourist accommodation.

Melbourne

MELBOURNE AIRPORT

Melbourne Airport is situated in the semi-rural area of Tullamarine, 12 miles north-west of the city. It was commissioned as an international airport for Victoria in 1970 due to the old airport at Essendon's inability to cope with international jet airliners. The terminal is a three-storey building with a central international section flanked by two domestic sections. Of these, Ansett Airlines of Australia uses the south side and Trans-Australia Airlines the north. The airport is unusual in that it is quite a tourist attraction, having an extensive garden display and mini art gallery.

AIRPORT FACILITIES

Information Desk	In the International Terminal; open 0800–1600 hours.
Bank/Foreign Exchange	On the ground floor, International Arrivals Hall; open 0700–2000 hours or according to international flight arrival times.

Accommodation Desk	There is a hotel/motel selector board on the ground floor of the Domestic Terminals.
Insurance Facilities	International airline companies can provide insurance on behalf of insurance companies for coverage of baggage loss etc.
Bar/Buffet/Restaurant	Buffet bars and bars are on the first floor. A cocktail lounge/bar and a restaurant are on the second floor. These facilities are open for the arrival/departure of the majority of flights.
Duty Free	All the usual items are sold in the 3 duty free shops. Two are in the International departure area and concourse and the third is in the International Arrivals area. Australian, British, New Zealand and United States currencies are accepted, as are any of the major credit cards.
Post Office	On the first floor; open 0900–1700 hours Monday to Friday.
Baggage Deposit	Lockers are located on the ground floor of both Domestic and International Terminals with a charge of A$2 per day.
Shops	Newsagent, chemist and gift or souvenir shops throughout the terminals.
Medical Services	A nursing sister is on duty from 0830–1700 hours daily.
Toilets	Located in all terminals on each floor; open 24 hours. The International Terminal also has showers within the toilet area.
Car Rental	Desks for Avis, Hertz, Budget and Thrifty are on the ground floor of each terminal.

AIRPORT INFORMATION

Check-in Times	2 hours before international flight departure times or 1 hour before domestic departure times.
Departure Tax	A$20 is payable by all departing international passengers over the age of 12.
Transferring Flights	International-to-international flight passengers go straight to their ongoing flight. International-to-domestic flight passengers go through Customs and must then make their own way to the Domestic Terminal. The luggage is transferred direct.
Airport Hotel	(First Class) The Travelodge, Melbourne Airport (tel. 338-2322). Within walking distance of the terminal. Courtesy transport from hotel to airport can be arranged using a direct line telephone from the ground floor of the International Terminal.

CITY LINKS

• **Skybus:** Operates a regular service between airport and city which takes 30 minutes. The service runs from 0630–2345 hours daily.

• **Taxi:** Provides a good and not too expensive service to hotels. Taxis can be shared with up to 4 people.

MELBOURNE

The city of Melbourne was founded as the capital of Victoria State in 1835. After the 1851 gold rush it developed rapidly to become

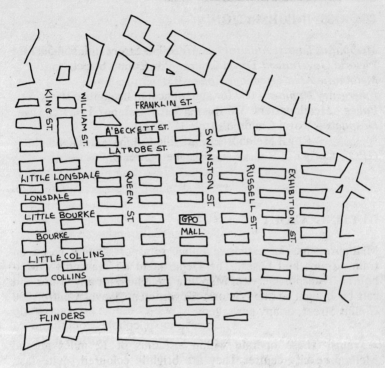

Australia's second largest city, with a population of 2,888,000, yet this city had humble beginnings, with John Batman buying the land on which it stands from the Aborigines for a few strings of beads. What seemed at the time an ideal site for a small village has turned into a major cultural, commercial and financial centre. The chief industries are heavy engineering, food processing and textile manufacture. The Yarra River (known as the upside down river because it is so muddy that its surface hardly resembles water) runs through the city to Port Melbourne 2½ miles away on the coast. The centre is a well organized grid of streets, the middle one being Bourke Street, a pedestrian shopping mall. For all Melbourne's cosmopolitan air (it is the world's third largest Greek city plus having substantial Italian, British, Yugoslav, Turkish, Dutch, Maltese and Chinese populations) it still lives up to its reputation of being somewhat conservative and prim in its attitudes.

TOURIST INFORMATION

Melbourne Tourist Authority – 247 Collins Street (tel. 654-5088).
Victoria Government Travel Centre – 230 Collins Street.
Melbourne Area Telephone Code – 03.
Emergency Number – 000 for ambulance, police or fire services.
Police – Headquarters: 376 Russell Street (tel. 667-1911).
Hospitals – Royal Children's (tel. 347-5522).
　　　　　　Royal Melbourne, Parkville (tel. 347-7111).
GPO – Corner of Bourke and Elizabeth Streets.

GETTING ABOUT

Melbourne has an extensive public transport system based on trains, trams and buses. The Department of Transport's 'Melbourne Transport Services Map' is a great help for any visitor and can be bought at the Victoria Government Travel Centre, 230 Collins Street, or any newsagent.

• **Trams:** These operate within a radius of 12 miles around Melbourne city centre. They are brightly coloured, quite fast, regular and cheap.

• **Train:** The Melbourne Underground Rail Loop is one of the most modern in the world. It is worth going on just to marvel at the architectural ingenuity, but it seems a shame to miss out on the sights of the city above ground.

• **Bus:** This is a good, regular service with an extensive network.

• **The Met:** The new Metropolitan Transport System allows one ticket to be valid on any of the above three modes of city transport. You can buy a ticket on a train, bus or tram and then swop. The Neighbourhood Ticket gives 2 hours unlimited travel, the Travel Card gives 24 hours unlimited travel and the Weekly Travel Card does the same for 1 week plus free weekend travel for a whole family.

SIGHTS

THE MUSEUM OF VICTORIA at 328 Swanston Street is a place of great interest which boasts an impressive Planetarium. Open 1000–1700 hours daily. OLD MELBOURNE GAOL in Russell Street has a set of exhibitions portraying early penal life and displaying the armour of Australia's famous bushranger, Ned Kelly. Open 1000–1700 hours daily (tel. 654-3628).

COMO HOUSE, Como Avenue, South Yarra, is an elegant colonial mansion set in 2½ acres of gardens, open 1000–1645 hours daily (tel. 241-2500).

MELBOURNE CRICKET GROUND, Yarra Park, Jolimont, the largest in the world. Tours of the facilities and sports museum are held each Wednesday at 1000 hours (tel. 63-6066).

PARLIAMENT HOUSE, in Spring Street, was built in 1856 and is used by the Victorian Legislative Council and Assembly. Guided tours (when out of season) are at 1000, 1100, 1400 and 1500 hours Monday to Friday (tel. 651-8911).

The ROYAL MELBOURNE ZOOLOGICAL GARDENS are at Elliot Avenue, Parkville and have an excellent exhibition of Australian and exotic birds and animals. Open 0900–1700 hours daily (tel. 347-1522).

For music lovers, the SYDNEY MYER MUSIC BOWL, Kings Domain, is an architecturally intriguing outdoor auditorium which holds free concerts during the summer.

A restored 1880s sailing ship, the *Polly Woodside*, now lives in the Yarra River (Phayer Street) and is used as a maritime museum. Open 1000–1600 hours Monday to Friday, 1200–1700 hours Saturday and Sunday (tel. 699-9760).

Built in honour of Australia's citizens lost during the war, the SHRINE OF REMEMBRANCE is at the corner of Domain and St Kilda Roads. Open 1000–1700 hours daily except Sunday 1400–1700 hours. Also in St Kilda Road is the VICTORIAN ARTS CENTRE, one of Melbourne's most prized possessions. This complex of buildings includes the National Gallery of Victoria, Melbourne Concert Hall and the Performing Arts Museum. Open 1100–1800 hours Monday to Saturday (closed Tuesday) and 1200–1800 hours Sunday.

QUEEN VICTORIA MARKET, at the corner of Victoria and Elizabeth Streets, is a crowded and colourful market where you can buy anything from clothing to vegetables to souvenirs. Buskers add

atmosphere and entertainment. Open Tuesday to Thursday 0600–
1400 hours, Friday 0600–1800 hours, Saturday 0600–1200 hours and
Sunday 0900–1600 hours.

ACCOMMODATION

Melbourne has a good selection of hotels and motels catering for all
standards. During late September Melbourne begins to fill up for
the Melbourne Cup, held in November, so unless you have
reservations it can be difficult to get accommodation.

● **First Class:** (Double A$100–140)
The Hotel Windsor (Oberoi Hotels) – 103 Spring Street (tel.
63-0261). Fondly known as the 'Grand Old Lady of Spring Street',
this hotel has an old-world elegance and architectural grandeur. It is
in a prime position, adjacent to Parliament House, and overlooking
Treasury Gardens. The Winston Cocktail Lounge and Cricketers
Club Bar are well known and popular, as are the Windsor's
excellent restaurants.

The Regent – 25 Collins Street (tel. 63-0321). A high-rise hotel with
unparalleled views from its upper rooms. This is an elegant, stylish
hotel with superb service and facilities.

The Hilton – 192 Wellington Parade (tel. 419-3311). The usual top
quality standards of facilities and service. The hotel overlooks
Melbourne Cricket Ground and Yarra Park. Excellent restaurants
and bars make this a good venue for nights out.

● **Super Club Class:** (Double A$70–100)
Sheraton – 13 Spring Street (tel. 63-9961). A very good standard of
accommodation set in central Melbourne opposite gardens.

Hotel Australia – 266 Collins Street (tel. 63-0401). Good facilities
and friendly service in the city centre.

Noah's Hotel Melbourne – Corner of Exhibition and Little Bourke
Streets (tel. 662-0511). A well furbished, comfortable hotel with all
the required facilities and services plus a swimming pool and
licensed restaurant.

Old Melbourne Motor Inn – 5 Flemington Road, North Melbourne (tel. 329-9344). Slightly to the north of the city centre on the way to the airport, but within easy reach of both shops and sights. Good quality accommodation.

● **Economy:** (Double A$30–70)
Crossley Lodge – 51 Little Bourke Street (tel. 662-2500). In the heart of the city. Good facilities.

The Victoria – 215 Little Collins Street (tel. 63-0441). A comfortable hotel near the Town Hall in the centre.

Travel Inn Motel – Corner of Gratton and Drummond Streets, Carlton (tel. 347-7922). A 'Flag Inn' member with good facilities. Near the University and 10 minutes out of the city.

Park Avenue Motel – 461 Royal Parade, Parkville (tel. 380-6761). Good accommodation, near the zoo, golf course and various sporting facilities.

Magnolia Court – 101 Powlett Street, East Melbourne. Rooms with kitchen facilities; a light breakfast is included in the price.

Inn-Keepers Ramada Inn – 539 Royal Parade, Parkville (tel. 380-8131). In the sporting area of Parkville with a golf course, football pitch and other games areas. Comfortable accommodation.

DINING OUT

Melbourne has a great combination with regard to food – top quality Aussie meat and plenty of skilled continental chefs. The result is a plethora of extremely good restaurants which cater for all the tastes and nationalities in the city. The homegrown Australian wines are very good and many of Melbourne's restaurants have adopted a BYO (bring your own) wine system.

● **First Class:** (A$70–100 for two)
Stephanie's – 405 Tooronga Road, East Hawthorn (tel. 20-8944). Set in a luxurious Victorian mansion, the menu and wine list make this one of the city's best restaurants.

Le Restaurant – 35th Floor, Regent Hotel, 25 Collins Street (tel. 63-0321). Formal silver service dining in one of Melbourne's top restaurants. Superb views of the city.

Telford Old Melbourne Hotel – 5–17 Flemington Road, North Melbourne (tel. 329-9344). À la carte dining in a charming old colonial setting. Entertainment is provided.

● **Super Club Class:** (A$40–70 for two)
Empress of China – 120 Little Bourke Street (tel. 663-1883). Famed for its Cantonese dishes and exquisite decor. Licensed or BYO.

Sketches – 67 Drummond Street, Carlton (tel. 663-5825). Fine food served in a lighthearted, entertaining atmosphere. Does good business lunches. Licensed or BYO.

Kenzan Japanese Restaurant – 45 Collins Street (tel. 662-2933). Traditional Japanese cuisine in a very well organized restaurant. Licensed.

The Fish Exchange Restaurant – 349 Flinders Lane (tel. 62-7808). Delicious seafood of all varieties. You can dance to the Latin American music while you are there. Licensed.

● **Economy:** (A$20–40 for two)
Yum Cha Chinese Restaurant – 150 Albert Road, South Melbourne (tel. 699-3652). A favourite venue for Melbourne's office workers. The Yum Cha is superb. Licensed or BYO.

Wholemeal Inn – 182 Collins Street (tel. 63-1596). Vegetarian and selected meat and fish dishes. Smorgasbord available.

Rajah Sahib – 23 Bank Place (tel. 67-5521). Traditional Indian cuisine and hospitality. Special business lunches. BYO.

Pasta Galore – 11 Queen Street (tel. 61-2036). Melbourne's newest and most popular pasta place. Good, filling and inexpensive.

NIGHTLIFE

As with any big city, there is always a lot going on in Melbourne after dark. Theatre restaurants are popular and entertainments vary from comedy shows to cultural dancing. Trendy discos or

sophisticated nightclubs are all over the city centre. Theatres
include the ATHENAEUM, 188 Collins Street (tel. 654-4000), and the
COMEDY THEATRE, 240 Exhibition Street (tel. 663-3211). For
performance details the weekly publication *This Week in Melbourne* is good (from newsagents). Some of the many good
nightclubs and discos are listed below. JULIANA'S – Hilton Hotel,
192 Wellington Parade, East Melbourne (tel. 419-3311): an elegant
place to dance and eat the night away. MADDISON'S – corner of
Flinders and Russell Streets (tel. 654-1122): lively until 3 a.m. YORK
BUTTER FACTORY – 62 King Street (tel. 62-0111): a trendy disco.
BILLBOARD IN CONCERT – 170 Russell Street (tel. 663-2989): the
emphasis is on rock music.

EXCURSIONS

Melbourne's surrounding area has several interesting towns, villages, parks, etc., which can be visited within a day, by car or bus.

The BLUE DANDENONG RANGES are 22 miles east of the city. The
wooded hills, lush vegetation and picturesque villages are lovely to
drive through, or you can take a ride on 'Puffing Billy', a steam train
that runs between Belgrave and Emerald Lake. SHERBROOKE
FOREST is the home of the lyrebird and OLINDA, SASSAFRAS,
MENZIES CREEK or KALLISTA make good picnic spots.

Going south, the MORNINGTON PENINSULA is a popular resort area
with beautiful bays and beaches. The west coast is densely
populated and served with a good highway, but it's worth going off
on to the rough tracks to see some of the wilder west coast. PHILIP
ISLAND is off this coast and is a penguin, seal and koala sanctuary. It
also has a variety of bird life and good beaches. The nearby islands
of Churchill and French Island are of particular historic interest.

BALLARAT, west of Melbourne, was a small rural town until its
nearby gold fields were mined. It is now an elegant city of parks and
gardens, but its gold-rush past can be seen at Sovereign Hill where
the whole era has been faithfully reconstructed. To the south-west is
GEELONG, Victoria's largest provincial city and an important wool
centre. Although there are some interesting old buildings, Geelong
is a very industrialized coastal town.

For a look at some vineyards the YARRA VALLEY makes a good
day trip. Some 40 miles along is Healesville Sanctuary for koalas,

kangaroos and other Australian birds and animals. Also to the east of Melbourne is ELTHAM, where there is an artists' colony at MONTSALVAT. Numerous pottery, art and craft shops and galleries make this an interesting place to visit.

There is a good selection of bus tours to these and other areas of Victoria. For details pick up some of the Tourist Board's leaflets at 230 Collins Street.

Perth

PERTH INTERNATIONAL AIRPORT

The airport is situated 6¼ miles east of Perth's central business district, within the Shire of Swan and the city of Belmont. It is a busy airport and at present a new, international terminal is under construction, to complement the existing passenger terminal. This should be ready for use by 1987/88 but until then both international and domestic flight passengers use the same terminal.

AIRPORT FACILITIES

Information Desk	In the Domestic Arrivals Hall; opening hours coincide with flight arrival peaks.
Bank/Foreign Exchange	In the main concourse and Transit Lounge; open 1½ hours before an international flight departure.
Accommodation Desk	In the Domestic Check-in area; open 0900–1700 hours and 2000–2200 hours.
Bar	First floor level; open 0900–midnight.
Buffet	First floor level; open 24 hours daily.
Restaurant	First floor level; open 1100–1400 hours and 1800–2200 hours.

Post Office	In the main concourse; open 0500–midnight (agency only).
Shops	Gift Shop – main concourse, open 0500–midnight. 'Purely Australian' – main concourse, open 0830–midnight. Florist – main concourse, open during domestic peaks.
Duty Free	Shops located on the first floor, International Departure Lounge and Transit Lounge. There is also one Inward Duty Free shop on the ground floor which sells only spirits, wines, tobacco and perfumes. All the others sell a wide range of the usual duty free goods. Currencies of Australia, New Zealand, the UK and the USA are accepted, as are Mastercard, Visa, American Express, Bankcard and Diners Card.
Toilets	Throughout the terminal; open 24 hours.
Car Rental Desks	Avis, Thrifty, Budget, Hertz desks all in the Domestic Arrivals Hall; open 0800–2130 hours. (After hours car keys are left with international or domestic airlines desks.)

AIRPORT INFORMATION

Check-in Times	International flight passengers may check in up to 2 hours prior to flight departure time. Domestic (and Cathay Pacific) flight passengers may check in up to 4 hours prior to flight departure time.
Airport Tax	A$20 departure tax on all international passengers over 12 years of age.

| Flight Transfers | All within the same terminal. You will be ushered to the Transit Lounge to await onward flights. |
| Airport Hotel | (Economy) – Marracoonda Motel. |

CITY LINKS

• **Skybus:** An airport-to-hotel service for about A$4 each. It leaves from in front of the Domestic Arrivals Hall and the International end of the terminal.

• **Metropolitan Transport Trust Bus:** An airport-to-city bus which costs around A$2 each and leaves from a point adjacent to the Arrivals Hall (Domestic).

• **Taxis:** From airport to city costs about A$8–10. Taxi ranks are in front of both International and Domestic ends of the terminal.

• **Chauffeur Driven Hire Cars:** Should be pre-booked before your arrival, through your travel agent.

PERTH

The 17th-century British navigator William Dampier described the western edges of the Australian continent as barren and useless for agriculture. The discovery of gold at Kalgoorlie in 1893 changed that opinion, rapidly. Western Australia is now known to be one of the world's richest mineral stores as well as being well endowed with good agricultural land. Perth was founded as the capital city in 1829 and expanded rapidly following the gold discovery. It is the commercial and cultural centre for the state, with a population of around 900,000. The ports of Fremantle and Kwinana (both to the south of the city) are growing industrial centres. Fremantle's tourist industry is currently enjoying an all-time boom due to the 1987 America's Cup yachting regatta.

The city of Perth is quite a phenomenon, set on the edge of 1 million square miles of sparsely populated country, 1,750 miles from its nearest city neighbour, Adelaide, but despite its geo-

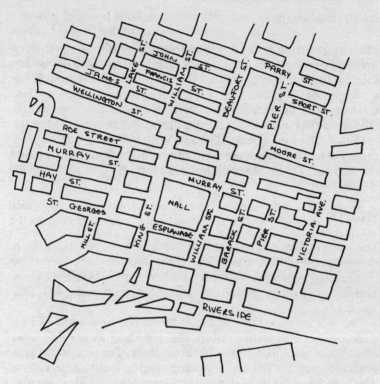

graphical isolation this is a cosmopolitan, exciting and beautiful place to visit. It is a well planned city architecturally, with plenty of character and a spacious, sunny appearance. The broad Swan River flows gracefully through the centre, with Mill Point on its south bank and the central business and shopping area to the north.

TOURIST INFORMATION

W.A. Department of Tourism – 772 Hay Street, Perth (tel. 321-2471).
Bus and Train Information – Telephone 322-3022.
British Consulate-General – Prudential Building, 95 St George's Terrace, Perth (tel. 321-5611).
Perth Area Telephone Code – 09.

GETTING ABOUT

The city is served by bus, rail and ferry services. A zonal fares structure covers all modes of transport and tickets issued on one are valid for transfer to either of the others. Local trains run from Perth to Armadale, Midland and Fremantle. In the city centre bus services from an extensive network of routes are regular and efficient. Free city buses for tourists and shoppers operate Monday to Friday. The Red, Green, Blue and Yellow 'Clipper' buses have a variety of routings which are clearly marked. On Saturday mornings the Red and Yellow buses continue the service.

SIGHTS

The ABORIGINAL ART GALLERY at 242 St George's Terrace is an extensive collection of arts and crafts such as bark paintings, boomerangs, weapons and woven baskets. Open 0900–1645 hours Monday to Friday, 1000–1200 hours Saturday and 1400–1700 Sunday.

The W.A. ART GALLERY in James Street is a new building with traditional and modern exhibits plus travelling exhibitions from other countries. Open 1000–1700 hours daily. The W.A. MUSEUM in Francis Street has displays including veteran and vintage cars, a 25m-long Blue Whale skeleton, the 11-ton Mundrabilla meteorite and an Aboriginal gallery. The Old Gaol is also part of the complex, now restored and full of interesting mementoes from Perth's early days. Open 1030–1700 hours Monday to Friday, 0930–1700 hours Saturday, and 1400–1700 hours Sunday.

PARLIAMENT HOUSE has conducted tours commencing at 1115 hours Monday to Friday and 1500 hours Monday and Friday.

Between Hay Street and St George's Terrace is LONDON COURT, a Tudor-style shopping arcade built in 1937. The decorative wood and wrought-iron work, statues of Dick Whittington and Sir Walter Raleigh, and the clock with jousting knights which appear every 15 minutes, are all worth a look.

ZOOLOGICAL GARDENS on Laboucher Road, South Perth: take the ferry from Barrack Street Jetty to South Perth, then it's a 5-minute walk to the zoo. There is a good selection of exotic animals and birds in this attractive setting. Open daily 1000–1700 hours.

PERTH CONCERT HALL was opened on Australia Day, 1973. It is a complex of performance facilities for anything from opera to folk concerts. It also contains a restaurant, tavern and cocktail lounge.

At the top of Dumes House, on the corner of King's Park Road and Havelock Street is LEGACY LOOKOUT, a good place from which to see a bird's eye view of Perth. Open 0930–1630 hours weekdays and 0930–1730 hours weekends.

The COUNCIL HOUSE is near the corner of St George's Terrace and Barrack Street. An imposing modern building opened by Queen Elizabeth II in 1963. Visitors may inspect the Council Chambers and the Lord Mayor's Suite – which has one of the finest views in Perth.

HYDE PARK is reminiscent of its famous namesake, with a lake and island sanctuary for many species of wildfowl. Buses 53, 59 or 60 from Barrack Street will take you there and numbers 18, 19 or 20 return to the city from Fitzgerald Street (walk west along Vincent Street from the north-west corner of the park).

At the southern end of Narrows Bridge, the OLD MILL is a restored flour mill dating from 1835 and housing pioneer relics. Open 1300–1700 hours Monday, Wednesday, Thursday and Sunday and 1300–1600 hours Saturday.

KING'S PARK is the pride of Perth, a parkland which shows off the multitude of Western Australia's wildflowers, provides a picturesque backdrop for the city and houses a 6-acre Botanic Gardens.

The SWAN RIVER is a busy waterway and thoroughfare through the city. Barrack Street Jetty is the place to catch the continuous service to Mends Street Jetty at South Perth. There are also Swan River cruises to Fremantle, upriver to the Swan Valley vineyards, or out to Rottnest Island.

ACCOMMODATION

Perth has a good range of hotels and, with the America's Cup Yachting Regatta being held at the nearby port of Fremantle, many are being upgraded or extended. For those who would like to get out of the city there is a 'Host Farm and Homestay' system in Western Australia whereby you can stay with Australian families on their farm properties. For details telephone 322-2999 or go to 772 Hay Street, Perth.

● **First Class:** (Double A$75–115)
Parmelia Hilton International – Mill Street, Perth (tel. 322-3622). As always with Hilton hotels, the service and facilities are superb. This hotel overlooks the Swan River, in the heart of Perth's business centre.

Sheraton Perth – 207 Adelaide Terrace, Perth (tel. 325-0501). A luxurious hotel with everything one would expect of an establishment run by the Sheraton group. The rooms have splendid views across the Swan River.

Orchard – Corner of Milligan and Wellington Streets (tel. 327-7000). An excellent hotel with lots of luxurious touches and several good restaurants to choose from.

● **Super Club Class:** (Double A$45–75)
Kings Ambassador – 517 Hay Street, Perth (tel. 325-6555). A well run and very comfortable hotel in central Perth.

Miss Maud European Hotel – 97 Murray Street, Perth (tel. 325-3900). A small but exceptionally good hotel run by Miss Maud – a very personable Scandinavian lady who also runs the excellent restaurant downstairs.

Chateau Commodore – Corner of Victoria Avenue and Hay Street (tel. 325-0461). Very good accommodation, service and facilities.

Town House – 778 Hay Street, Perth (tel. 321-9141). A fairly small, friendly hotel with good facilities including a pool.

● **Economy:** (Double A$20–45)
Pacific – 111 Harold Street, Highgate (tel. 328-5599). Reasonably central self-contained units with modern facilities, including a pool.

Adelphi Centre – 130a Mounts Bay Road, Perth (tel. 322-4666). Well equipped, self-contained rooms at the bottom of King's Park.

Greetings King's Park Lodge – 255 Thomas Street, Subiaco (tel. 381-3488). Adequate accommodation at very economic rates.

Swanview – 1 Preston Street, Como (tel. 367-5755). Comfortable rooms and good service, on the Swan River bank.

YMCA/YWCA – 119 Murray Street, Perth (tel. 325-2744). Very good accommodation and facilities right in the city centre.

City Waters Lodge – 118 Terrace Road, Perth (tel. 325-5020). Centrally located, self-contained units at very good rates.

DINING OUT

Perth has a remarkable variety of restaurants, bistros and coffee houses considering its size. Northbridge is a popular restaurant area near the city centre where good, inexpensive meals can be had. Perth also has some excellent food centres where tables are set up around counters serving every imaginable sort of international cuisine. The great advantage is that you do not have to eat from the same menu as your companions. Top class seafood restaurants are another of Perth's specialities.

• **First Class:** (A$50–70 for two)
The Oyster Beds – 26 Riverside Road, East Fremantle (tel. 339-1611). Built over the Swan River, this restaurant serves up memorable seafood dishes. Try the famous rock lobster (or cray fish) – 'lobster thermidor' is delicious.

Haskins Garden Restaurant – 82 Outram Street, West Perth (tel. 322-5106). An exciting continental menu is matched by the elegant setting – both in and out of doors. Bring your own wine, port or whatever and don't be surprised to see a famous film star or two in the restaurant.

Luis – 6 The Esplanade (tel. 325-2476). A long-established, elegant French restaurant. It is expensive but very well worth the cost.

• **Super Club Class:** (A$30–50 for two)
Miss Maud – Corner of Pier and Murray Streets (tel. 325-3900). A popular, friendly restaurant run by the Scandinavian Miss Maud. Being open from 0700 to midnight, this is a very popular break-fasting venue – and the choice of breakfast dishes is remarkable.

Lee Gardens – 18 Plain Street (tel. 325-8906). Good Cantonese food is served here, the Sang Chow Bow being the house speciality.

Masons Brasserie – 64 South Terrace, Fremantle (tel. 335-1334). Elegant Australian-style dining and old colonial decor. The building (Freemasons Hotel) is a supreme example of restored Victorian architecture.

● **Economy:** (under A$30 for two)
Papa Luigi's – 33 South Terrace, Fremantle (tel. 336-1599). A wonderful Italian restaurant where everything is delicious from the gelati and the cappucino to the full, wholesome Italian meal. This is a favourite meeting spot with the locals and is always full of people and friendliness.

Himalayas – 963 Hay Street (tel. 322-2554). Good Indian food. The vegetarian and tandoori dishes are notable.

Cheong On – 477 Hay Street (tel. 325-5187). One of Perth's most popular, inexpensive Chinese restaurants.

Zorba the Buddha – 6 Collie Street, Fremantle (tel. 335-7035). An excellent and popular vegetarian restaurant.

NIGHTLIFE

In the past few years Perth has changed its nightlife image tremendously and it is now one of Australia's liveliest cities. The ENTERTAINMENT CENTRE in Wellington Street has facilities which attract the world's larger theatre companies and productions. The CONCERT HALL in St George's Terrace provides a venue for the Western Australia Symphony Orchestra and other symphony concert orchestras. Theatres include HIS MAJESTY'S THEATRE on Hay Street, the PLAYHOUSE THEATRE in Pier Street and the HOLE-IN-THE-WALL THEATRE in Hamersley Road, Subiaco suburb. A major attraction is the newly completed BURSWOOD ISLAND CASINO, over the causeway from the city centre. As well as gambling you can see cabaret, play golf or look around the exhibition centre.

Theatre restaurants have become popular in Perth. The CIVIC THEATRE RESTAURANT in Beaufort Street is one of the best. DIRTY DICKS in Cambridge Street, Wembley is bawdy but good fun. Discos are numerous. HANNIBAL'S in Lake Street, Northbridge, GOBBLES in Wellington Street or BEETHOVEN'S in Murray Street are popular with the younger set. JULIANA'S in the Parmelia Hilton Hotel, is more sophisticated.

Pubs are everywhere in Perth, many with live jazz or folk music. For details of these or any night entertainment see the *Daily News* or *Weekend News* papers.

EXCURSIONS

Perth's surrounding hills and coastline are both picturesque and full of interesting places to visit. Popular beaches within easy reach by car or bus include COTTESLOE, CITY BEACH and SCARBOROUGH. The coastal port of FREMANTLE is 12 miles south-west of Perth. Here you will find excellent shops, outdoor cafés (the coffee and ice-cream served up at Papa Luigi's is the best ever), an open market and, of course, the harbour and marinas. The America's Cup yachting event in 1987 has caused a great upsurge in building and renovating throughout Fremantle, but it should keep its old-colonial port atmosphere.

Going inland, the DARLING RANGES are 12½ miles east of Perth and make an ideal area to spend a day in the Australian bushland – seeing valleys, orchards and small towns. The wildflowers in springtime are a fabulous sight. Further east (62 miles) is the Avon Valley, a rich agricultural land with the historic towns of Northam, York and Toodyay in its midst.

On the coast to the north of Perth are two noteworthy NATIONAL PARKS, at Yanchep and Nambung. The former boasts native animals, limestone caves, wildflowers, black swans and a koala colony. Nearby is Atlantis Marine Park with its oceanarium, dolphins and seals. The latter, Nambung, has a special feature in the curious Pinnacles, a petrified forest.

Out to sea is ROTTNEST ISLAND, 12 miles from Fremantle. This is best known for its resident marsupial, the quokka, which resembles a tiny and energetic kangaroo. Island resort areas are dotted round the coastal beaches and provide facilities for snorkelling, surfing, scuba-diving, boating or cycling.

Going inland again, GUILDFORD is 6 miles north-east of Perth. It is an old river port from the bygone colonial era and has some fine examples of buildings from those days.

Just over 16 miles south of the city is a working re-creation of Perth as it was over 100 years ago. The Pioneer Village is at ARMADALE and exhibits, trades and crafts people can be seen at work from 1000–1700 hours Monday to Friday and Sunday, and 1200–1700 hours Saturday.

Sydney

KINGSFORD-SMITH INTERNATIONAL AIRPORT

Situated on the north shore of Botany Bay, some 5 miles from Sydney, this is Australia's busiest air terminal. There are 3 passenger terminals: 1 international and 2 domestic. The airport is named as a tribute to the famous Australian airman, Sir Charles Kingsford-Smith, who achieved a pioneer flight across the Pacific Ocean from San Francisco to Australia in 1928. All the terminals are accessible during non jet curfew hours, i.e. 0600–2300 hours daily.

AIRPORT FACILITIES

Information Desk	Each airline supplies their own enquiry desk.
Banks/Foreign Exchange	In the International Terminal.
Accommodation Information	Supplied by Travellers' Information Services.
Insurance Facilities	Supplied by Travellers' Information Services.
Bars, Buffet and Restaurants	In all terminals.
Post Office	In all terminals.
Baggage Deposit	In the International Terminal.
Nursery	Mothers' rooms available in the International Terminal.
Shops	In all terminals.

Duty Free	There are duty free shops in the city centre as well as in the International Terminal. All the usual tobaccos, spirits, perfumes, watches etc. are on sale and a variety of currencies plus major master cards are accepted.
Medical Centre	Nurses on call with each airline.
Toilets	In all terminals.
Car Rental	Desks in all terminals.

AIRPORT INFORMATION

Check-in Times	30 minutes prior to departure of domestic flights; 60–90 minutes prior to departure of international flights.
Airport Tax	A$20 payable on departure, in Australian currency. Children aged under 12 years are exempt if they produce proof of their age.
Airport Hotel	(First Class) Hilton Airport, 20 Levey Street, Arncliffe 2205 (tel. 597-0122). Very convenient for the airport, excellent facilities and adjacent golf course.
Airport Enquiries	Sydney (02) 667-9111.
Transferring Flights	International-to-international flight passengers are transferred within the same terminal. International-to-domestic (or vice versa) flight passengers can use the 'Airport Express' buses which run a 20–30 minute service for a small fare. The distance between terminals is 3 miles by road.

CITY LINKS

• **Bus:** The 'Airport Express' bus service also operates between the airport and the city. Buses depart from the International Terminal every 20 minutes from 0625–2215 hours daily, stopping at the Domestic Terminal on the way to the city. City-to-airport start at Jetty 2, Circular Quay (near city centre) with central city, Eddy Avenue and Central Station pick ups. Fares are around A$2 and transfer time is 40 minutes. The Kingsford-Smith Airport Service (KSA) operates a bus service between airport, city and Kings Cross area which synchronizes with international and major domestic flights. For a KSA city-to-airport transfer phone 1 hour beforehand for pick up times and locations (usually at the hotel) tel. 667-3221 or 667-0663. Fares are slightly higher on these buses, but they do take you directly to your hotel. Generally they'll operate from 0600–2000. Fare around $3.

• **Taxis:** Fast (30–45 mins), convenient and readily available at the airport. Fares are around the A$12 mark and groups of 3–4 people can share taxis. (Make sure the driver knows that *you* know what the fare should be.)

• **Chauffeur Cars:** Limousine services from the airport to the city cost about A$20. Contact: Hughes Chauffeured Limousines (tel. 669-3111), VIP Limousines Pty Ltd (tel. 357-1193) or Legion Chauffeured Limousines (tel. 211-2844).

SYDNEY

Captain James Cook sighted Australia's east coast on 20 April 1770 from his ship, the *Endeavour*. Not until 1787 was anything done about this sighting. It took till then for Captain Phillip to set sail from England with 736 convicts – destined to become the first white settlers in Australia. During the years of convict transportation (1787–1868) some 160,000 felons were moved from Britain to Australia, forming about one-ninth of the total population. Sydney Cove was the site of the first settlement – now the Circular Quay area in the heart of the city. Surrounding bushland was converted to productive farm land, the native Aborigines were pushed inland –

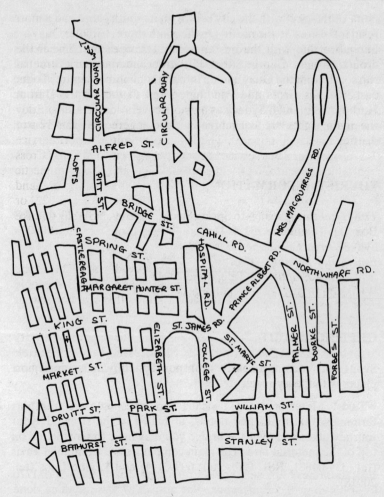

by force if necessary – and the new colony began to prosper on its
wool and gold industry.

Today Sydney is one of the east coast's major seaports, serving a
large hinterland rich in minerals and agriculture. It is also an
important communications base and leading financial centre for
Australia. Sydney's beauty, sophistication and cultural wealth puts
it among the world's top cities. The harbour is very much the focal

point of the city, with the city centre on its south shore and a more residential area on the north. On the south shore, Circular Quay is a hubbub of life with the bus and ferry terminals and The Rocks around its piers. George Street, Pitt Street and Macquarie Street all run south from the Quay and up into the commercial centre. To the east is Kings Cross and Paddington and to the west is Darling Harbour. Although Sydney as a whole covers a huge area of land, the main sights are conveniently close together in this central district.

TOURIST INFORMATION

Travel Centre of NSW – 16 Spring Street, Sydney, NSW 2000 (GPO Box 11), Telephone 231-4444.
Sydney Area Telephone Code – 02.
Emergency Number – 000.
Rail Travel Enquiries – Telephone 20942.
What's on in Sydney – Telephone 11586.

GETTING ABOUT

Sydney has a comprehensive transport system which brings most places within easy reach.

● **Taxis:** Meter-operated taxicabs can be sought at transport terminals, taxi ranks and hotels, or hailed in the street. If your journey takes you over the bridge you may have to pay the toll on top of the metered fare. The main companies are Combined Taxis (tel. 339-0488), RSL Cabs (tel. 699-0144) and Legion Cabs (tel. 20918).

● **Buses:** These are quick, efficient and cheap. They can be hailed from stops marked by yellow posts. During peak hours you buy your ticket from a conductor while waiting at the stop. Buses run from 0400–2330 hours. A free city bus (No. 777) runs every 10 minutes Monday to Friday from 0930–1530 hours, circling the downtown area. The 'Sydney Explorer' (red) bus takes a 10½ mile circular route round 20 of the major sights. A day ticket allows you to alight and rejoin the service at any point in the route.

• **Train:** Suburban trains operate through a city subway system from 0430–2400 hours. The main downtown stations are Wynyard, Town Hall, Circular Quay, St James and Museum for most suburban lines, and Martin Place for the eastern suburbs. Central Railway Station serves country, interstate and suburban travellers.

• **Ferry:** Urban Transit Authority ferries (blue and white) serve all the harbourside suburbs, departing from Circular Quay. Scheduled ferries run from 0600–2300 hours going to Balmain, Long Nose Point, Hunter's Hill, Greenwich, Kirribilli, Neutral Bay, Cremorne Point, Mosman, Taronga Zoo or Manly. Hydrofoils also serve Manly. 'Explorer' cruises depart from jetties 4, 5 and 6 and allow passengers to alight and reboard at each port of call.

• **Special Fares:** Tickets for 1 or 7 days allow travel within Sydney on trains, buses and ferries. Buy them at rail stations, bus depots or Circular Quay.

• **Car Rental:** This is a reasonably inexpensive way of getting about in Australia. Driving is on the left and most overseas driver's licences are acceptable.

• **Bicycle:** For hire all over Sydney. This is both energetic (Sydney is quite hilly) and brave in the city centre where traffic is heavy. It is, however, a super way of seeing the sights and catching the atmosphere.

SIGHTS

The ART GALLERY OF NSW, in Art Gallery Road, has regular temporary exhibitions plus permanent Australian and 19th-century art. Open 1000–1700 Monday to Saturday, 1200–1700 Sunday. Free. (Tel. 221-2100.)

AUSTRALIAN MUSEUM, 6 College Street, has a large natural history section with Aboriginal artefacts, films and special exhibits. Open 1000–1700 Tuesday to Saturday, 1200–1700 Sunday and Monday, and is also free. (Tel. 339-8111.)

Between Pitt and Castlereagh Streets is SYDNEY TOWER, 325m above sea level with shops, restaurants and superb views over the city. Open 0930–2130 Monday to Saturday, 1030–1830 Sunday. Entrance charge (tel. 231-6222). The MINT MUSEUM in Queen's

Square has displays of stamps, coins and decorative arts in what used to be the notorious 'RUM HOSPITAL' in 1817. Open 1000–1700 daily except Wednesday 1200–1700. (Tel. 217-0111.)

CHINATOWN is a fascinating mixture of shops, markets and restaurants. Dixon Street is its focal point. HYDE PARK BARRACKS are in Queen's Square. The restored building displays early colonial historic features. Open 1000–1700 daily except Tuesday 1200–1700 (tel. 217-0111).

The ROYAL BOTANIC GARDENS in Macquarie Street are beautiful and spacious gardens with Australian flora, exotic trees and hothouses with ferns and orchids. Guided tours take place on Wednesday and Friday at 1000 from the Visitors' Centre. Gardens open 0800–sunset (tel. 231-8111).

SYDNEY OPERA HOUSE is not to be missed. At Bennelong Point, it is an architectural phenomenon built on the harbour front in 1973. It is a comprehensive performing arts centre. Guided tours take place daily between 0900–1600 from the Exhibition Hall foyer. (Tel. 20588 ext. 250 or ext. 589 for performance bookings.) There is an admission charge.

SYDNEY HARBOUR BRIDGE was completed in 1932. The bridge is 134m high with a single span of 503m. A pylon lookout provides good city views on the south-east side of the bridge. Open 0930–1700 Saturday, Sunday and Monday (tel. 218-6325). There is a small admission charge.

At Circular Quay West are THE ROCKS, an area full of historic buildings from Australia's first white settlement, plus art and craft shops, pubs, galleries and waterfront restaurants. The Rocks Visitor Centre, 104 George Street, is open from 0830 daily (tel. 27-4972).

TARONGA ZOO PARK, at Mosman, is reached by ferry from Jetty 5, Circular Quay. A zoo on the water's edge with animals and birds from all countries but especially Australia. Open 0930–1700 daily (tel. 969-2777). Admission charge.

ACCOMMODATION

Sydney boasts a host of excellent hotels and motels with a wide price range. There are plenty of top class, luxury hotels and hundreds of B & B or self-catering establishments for the more budget minded.

Booking in advance is advisable, especially over holiday periods (Christmas and Easter).

● **First Class:** (Double A$100–140)
Intercontinental – 117 Macquarie Street (tel. 230-0200). Opened in 1985 on the edge of the Botanic Gardens. Excellent service and luxurious facilities. One of this group's finest hotels.

The Regent – 199 George Street (tel. 238-0000). Positioned so that, from its city centre location, you can see right over the harbour. Top class, modern facilities.

Hilton – 259 Pitt Street (tel. 266-0610). All the usual top quality Hilton-style facilities and service, situated in the heart of the city.

● **Super Club Class:** (Double A$70–100)
Southern Cross Hotel – Corner of Elizabeth and Goulburn Streets (tel. 20-987). A small, intimate hotel run by some very hospitable Australians. On the roof garden is a heated pool and a sauna and inside the rooms are very comfortable.

The Park Apartments – 16–32 Oxford Street (tel. 331-7728). Suites with separate lounge and dining areas, fully equipped kitchens and a laundry. Central location at the southern end of Hyde Park.

Wynyard Travelodge – 7–9 York Street (tel. 20-254). Good facilities and reliable service. Close to Wynyard Station.

Manly Pacific International Hotel – 55 North Steyne, Manly (tel. 977-7666). A modern hotel on the beachfront of Sydney's best-known northern beach. Extensive facilities.

● **Economy:** (Double A$30–70)
The Jackson Hotel – 94 Victoria Street, Potts Point (tel. 358-5144). A small, private hotel in a restored classic Victorian building. Prices include a light breakfast.

Plainsman Motor Inn – 40 Bayswater Road, Kings Cross (tel. 356-3511). Modern, stylish and close to the Kings Cross centre. Suites have kitchenettes and comfortable furnishings.

Breakers Motel, Bondi – 164 Campbell Promenade, Bondi Beach (tel. 309-3300). Right on the beach and about 5 miles from Sydney city centre. Suites include separate bedroom, lounge, full kitchen and balcony. Good facilities.

New Crest Hotel – 111 Darlinghurst Road, Kings Cross (tel. 358-2755). A large, modern hotel with adequate facilities, set in the heart of Kings Cross.

Manhattan Hotel – 8 Greenknowe Avenue, Potts Point (tel. 358-1288). Adequate facilities in a reasonably convenient situation.

Grantham Lodge Holiday Apartments – 1 Grantham Street, Potts Point (tel. 357-2377). Studio-type rooms with well equipped kitchens and most with balconies.

DINING OUT

Australians are dedicated gourmets, as is reflected in the number and standard of Sydney's restaurants. The main local speciality is seafood: Sydney rock oysters, Balmain bugs (odd looking but tasty crustaceans), Blue Swimmer crabs, John Dory and barramundi are just some examples of the dishes on offer. To combine this with prime Aussie beef try a 'carpet-bag' steak stuffed with oysters. Sydney's selection of ethnic restaurants are to be found in specific districts. French cuisine is best sought in Crow's Nest or Bondi. Northbridge is 'Tokyo-town' with some excellent Japanese restaurants, while Chinatown is obviously the location for Chinese cuisine. For Italian food go to Leichhardt; for Lebanese food try Campsie; and for Vietnamese delicacies, Punchbowl is the place. The list could go on, but suffice it to say that Sydney is one of the world's best and most cosmopolitan cities for eating out.

● **First Class:** (A$70–100 for two)
San Francisco Grill – Hilton Hotel (tel. 266-0610). Tables here are very much in demand, the food and surroundings are of such high quality, so book in advance.

Kables – Regent Hotel (tel. 238-0000). Again, an excellent restaurant with haute cuisine, an international clientele and first class service.

D'Arcy's – 92 Hargrave Street, Paddington (tel. 32-3706). An expensive but extremely good eastern suburb restaurant.

• **Super Club Class:** (A$40–70 for two)
New Hellas – 287 Elizabeth Street (tel. 264-1668). Good, modestly priced, Greek food on the third floor so you can enjoy the city view.

Beppi's – Corner of Stanley and Yunong Streets, East Sydney (tel. 357-4558). A favourite with the Italian community.

La Potiniere – 178 George Street (tel. 922-6437). Very high quality French cuisine.

Malaya – 787 George Street (tel. 211-0946). Specializes in Chinese, Indonesian and Malayan dishes.

• **Economy:** (A$20–40 for two)
Ceylon Tea Centre – 64 Castlereagh Street. Open for lunches only, but worth going for its great curries.

Dixon – 51 Dixon Street. One of the best Chinese restaurants in Chinatown.

Nagoya Sukiyaki House – 188 Victoria Road, Kings Cross. Authentic Japanese and very good.

Stuyvesant's House – 45 Alexander Street, Crow's Nest. Quite far from the city centre, but good Dutch food.

NIGHTLIFE

Sydney is always a lively place to be, but at night it's just non-stop action. There are top class discos like JULIANA'S at the Hilton; Greek nightclubs; pubs with live bands playing nightly or theatres like the NIMROD, ENSEMBLE or BELVOIR STREET Theatre. Jazz is extremely popular. Two of the best places must be the DON BURROWS JAZZ CLUB at the Regent Hotel and the SOUP PLUS RESTAURANT at 282 George Street, but many pubs and clubs have excellent live jazz bands. SYDNEY OPERA HOUSE always has some form of entertainment on, whether it be ballet, chamber music, opera or big production shows like *Cats*. Two areas of Sydney which are always lively at night are THE ROCKS and KINGS CROSS. The latter is renowned for its bohemian atmosphere, sleazy nightspots, strip shows and other off-beat activities.

EXCURSIONS

The Sydney area is surrounded by beaches, mountains, national parks and other towns. There are numerous organized trips which will take you around these, and the city centre sights. The Travel Centre at 16 Spring Street will give detailed information of bus tours. Some of the sights within a day's drive of Sydney are listed below.

OLD SYDNEY TOWN – 45 miles north, at Somersby, is this re-creation of Sydney Cove as it was in the 1800s. The whole Gosford area is very picturesque. ERIC WORRELL'S AUSTRALIAN REPTILE PARK is at Gosford, 52 miles north. Snakes, crocodiles and kangaroos are on show here. RIVER BOAT POSTMAN CRUISE – the only remaining postal service by water, and now mainly kept going for the tourists. Departure is from Brooklyn Wharf at 0930 hours Monday to Friday (connecting trains leave Sydney just after 0800 hours). The journey includes most of the inhabited islands in the Hawkesbury River. PITT TOWN, 6 miles from Windsor, is a historic town of mid-19th-century homes.

WARRAGAMBA DAM is 40 miles from Sydney via Parramatta, a beautiful spot and incorporating a safari with lions, tigers, bears, dolphins and sea-lions. FEATHERDALE is another wildlife park, this time with kangaroos, koalas, wallabies, wombats and possums. It is on the Kildare Road at Doonside, 26 miles west of Sydney.

KATOOMBA, a town in the heart of the famous Blue Mountains, is within easy reach of the Three Sisters, Giant Stairway and Minehaha Falls. It is 66 miles west of Sydney.

One of Australia's major wine producing regions, the HUNTER VALLEY, is 120 miles north of Sydney. CAMDEN is a district full of historic interest where the famous strain of merino sheep was developed by John MacArthur. This is still big sheep country and has a thriving wool industry.

Finally, the SNOWY MOUNTAINS: although more than a day's trip away, this area has to be mentioned as part of Australia's largest national park, and the only place where you will see snow in the country. Cooma, 265 miles south of Sydney, is the main town.

The Cook Islands

RED TAPE

• **Passport/Visa Requirements:** A full, valid passport is required by all except New Zealanders, who only require personal identification (birth certificate, permanent residence certificate or certificate of identity are accepted). Entry permits are not required by bona fide visitors (those entering the Cook Islands for a holiday, not employment) provided they possess onward passage (booked and paid for) and intend to stay less than 31 days. A stay of up to 4 months is allowable with a permit (applied for in Rarotonga) which is issued on a monthly basis provided the visitor has adequate finances.

CUSTOMS

• **Duty Free:** Each visitor may bring in 200 cigarettes or ½ lb tobacco or 50 cigars, and 2 litres of spirits or wine or 4½ litres beer. Duty free alcohol is available to arriving passengers at the airport. All plants, fruits and animals brought into the country must be declared for inspection.

HEALTH

Vaccinations are not necessary unless you are arriving from any infected area.

CAPITAL – Avarua, Rarotonga.

POPULATION – 21,000.

LANGUAGE – Cook Islands Maori is the local language and English is also spoken by almost everyone.

CURRENCY – The New Zealand Dollar: £1 = NZ$2.72; US$1 = NZ$1.94. Coinage is minted for local use only (NZ$1 = 100 cents) and is not usable outside the islands.

BANKING HOURS – The National Bank of New Zealand in Avarua (Rarotonga) is open 0900–1500 hours, Monday to Friday.

POLITICAL SYSTEM – Independent democracy.

RELIGION – Cook Islands Christian Church – a kind of amalgam of the sects.

PUBLIC HOLIDAYS

January 1	New Year's Day
March/April	Good Friday, Easter Monday
April 25	Anzac Day
June	Queen's Birthday
August 4	Constitution Day
October 26	Gospel Day
December 25, 26	Christmas Day, Boxing Day

CLIMATE – The coolest months of May–October have a temperature range of 65–80°F (18–27°C). November–April sees temperatures of 70–85°F (22–30°C) and infrequent tropical storms. Humidities of 75–80 per cent are experienced and the average annual rainfall is 80 inches.

TIME DIFFERENCE – GMT–10.

COMMUNICATIONS

● **Newspapers:** A small, daily newspaper containing mainly local news is published Monday–Saturday.

● **Radio:** Two local radio stations operate from 0600–2300 hours daily with several overseas newscasts each day.

● **Phone and Postal:** International mail, telephone, telegram and telex services are available through the Post Office and Cable and

Wireless Service (Avarua). Internal telephones are available at all hotels and most motels in Rarotonga.

ELECTRICITY – 230/240v; 50 Hz. Some hotels have provision for 110v AC electric shavers. Most power sockets are designed for 3 pin, flat plugs.

OFFICE/SHOPPING HOURS – Offices: 0730–1530 Monday to Friday; 0730–1130 Saturday. Shops: 0800–1600 Monday to Friday; 0800–1130 Saturday. Some village stores and shops near entertainment centres are open in the evening.

• **Best Buys:** The Cook Islands are not a shopper's paradise. There are no big department stores, shopping centres or souvenir arcades. The island's economy is primarily agricultural and on market days you will be able to buy some of their produce, but professional shoppers may be disappointed. Secondary industries include clothing and local artefact production. The Women's Federation Handicraft Shop in Avarua sells wooden bowls, shell jewellery, woven straw hats, 'tivaevae' cloth spreads and Tangarva-god handcarved statues. Curio houses offer a wide range of fine examples of weaving. The Philatelic Bureau issues distinctive Cook Island stamps and the Numismatic Bureau offers a fine range of Cook Island coins in mint finish. The dollar coin bearing the symbol of the god Tangarva is popular with coin collectors.

INTERNAL TRAVEL

• **Air:** Cook Islandair provide an air service from Rarotonga to the nearby islands of Aitutaki, Atiu, Mitiaro and Mauke. Once or twice a week is the usual frequency of these flights (flights to Aitutaki are more frequent) so beware of getting stuck somewhere without accommodation. Air Rarotonga operate the Beechcraft Commuter Liner to Aitutaki, Atiu, Mauke and Mangaia. Scenic flights over Rarotonga are also available and chartered flights to all airports in the Cook Islands possible.

• **Sea:** An inter-island shipping service is operated by a local shipping company, taking cargo and visitors to other islands. Trips to the southern islands are more frequent than trips to those in the north and, in either case, details are often not firm until a few days before departure. Information is from the shipping company in Rarotonga.

• **Driving:** Drivers of any vehicle need a Cook Islands Driver's Licence – instantly available from the Avarua Police Station for NZ$1. Driving is on the left hand side of the road. A number of companies hire out cars or motorcycles; the latter are very popular for touring the islands so it's worth booking in advance.

• **Bicycle:** Available for hire from several shops and hotels. This is a wonderful and relaxing way of seeing round these tiny islands (Rarotonga, the largest, is only 32 miles round!).

• **Taxi:** Services are run by a number of local companies and fares are government controlled and displayed in each car.

THE ISLANDS

The 15 islands which make up the Cook Islands group extend over 850,000 square miles of ocean with Penrhyn 9° south of the equator and Mangaia just north of the Tropic of Capricorn. The islands fall naturally into two groups, the northern flat coral atolls and the southern volcanic islands. Those in the north are Palmerston, Nassau, Pukapuka, Suwarrow, Rakahanga, Manihiki and Penrhyn. South of these lie Aitutaki, Munuae (actually a coral atoll), Takutea, Mitiaro, Atiu, Mauke, Rarotonga and Mangaia. The most visited islands are the fertile, volcanic ones around Rarotonga. Aitutaki is renowned for its magnificent lagoon, white, sandy, palm beaches and incredibly friendly locals. The main town is smaller than any of Rarotonga's villages and the bank manager only comes across once a month – the pace of life is very slow! It is one hour's flight north-east of Rarotonga and accommodation can be sought at the Aitutaki Resort Hotel (tel. 20-234 Rarotonga; double around NZ$70), the Rapae Cottage Hotel (tel. 77 Aitutaki; double around NZ$50) or the Aitutaki Guest House (tel. 25-511 Rarotonga; double around NZ$40). Atiu, Mauke, Mangaia and Mitiaro all have recently completed airstrips which bring them into the air network. Local accommodation will be simple but comfortable (details from the Cook Islands Tourist Authority in Avarua). These islands are for those who really want to 'get away from it all' and, as such, are tropical paradises (but don't expect any organized entertainment). Fishing, snorkelling, scuba-diving or just walking, swimming and sunbathing are all perfect pastimes on any of these islands surrounded by protective and beautiful coral reefs.

Rarotonga

RAROTONGA INTERNATIONAL AIRPORT

The Cook Islands' only international airport is about 3 miles from Avarua on Rarotonga. It is a small airport, serving only a few airlines, and the facilities are limited.

AIRPORT INFORMATION

Check-in Times	60 minutes before any flight departure time.
Airport Tax	On departure adults must pay NZ$20, children (2–12) NZ$10; infants are exempt.
Flight Transfers	Everything is within the same terminal building. Transferring passengers will be ushered to the departure lounge area. Transfers to international flights have 45-minute connecting times. Transfers to domestic flights have 60-minute connecting times.

AIRPORT HOTELS

● **Economy:**
Matareka Heights – PO Box 587. Three self-contained units close to the airport and the coast.

Tiare Village Motel – PO Box 489. Three self-contained units, also close to both airport and the coast.

CITY LINKS

The airport is about 3 miles along the coast from Avarua. Many of the hotels and lodges will send staff to meet incoming flights and bedeck their guests with flowers. The hourly bus service drives past the airport on its way round the island. Travel agents in Avarua will organize transport to and from the airport if need be.

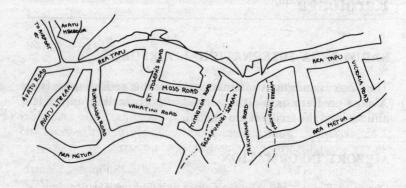

RAROTONGA

Largest of the 15 Cook Islands, Rarotonga lies at the southern end of the group and is one of the great beauty spots of the Pacific. Although the group was named in honour of the great explorer, Captain James Cook, the main island of Rarotonga was sighted during the 7th- and 8th-century migratory voyages of the Polynesian people. Cook diligently charted 5 of the islands in the 1770s and traditional island tales claim that the *Bounty* mutineers anchored off the Rarotonga coast in 1789 to barter with the natives. In 1823 the London Missionary Society established schools and churches on the islands and created a highly moralistic Protestant theocracy. 1888 saw the Cooks become a British protectorate and at the turn of the century they were annexed under the British crown. Today the Cook Islands is a self-governing democracy with its major industry in fruit farming. Rarotonga is an island of green valleys, sharp, steep ridges and spiky peaks of over 2000 ft. Like most of the islands, it is protected from the Pacific Ocean by a coral reef which encircles a lagoon and many sandy-beached bays.

TOURIST INFORMATION

Cook Islands Tourist Authority – PO Box 14, Rarotonga, Cook Islands (tel. 29435).
Medical Services – Available 24 hours every day in Avarua. There is a modern, well equipped hospital 3 miles from Avarua and a mile from the airport.

GETTING ABOUT

With a circumference of 32 miles, getting about on Rarotonga is not really a problem. In the main town of Avarua walking is probably the best way to explore the streets, although taxis are available. Cars, motorcycles and bicycles are all available for hire in shops and hotels around Rarotonga. Some firms to note are:

Rental Cars (CI) Ltd, PO Box 326, Avarua Shopping Centre, Rarotonga (tel. 24442 or 24441 after business hours).
Budget Rent-A-Car (Polynesian Rentals Ltd), PO Box 607, Rarotonga (tel. 20888).
Stars Travel Rarotonga Ltd, PO Box 75, Rarotonga (tel. 23683 or 23669). For car and scooter rental or sightseeing tours.
Union Travel, PO Box 54, Rarotonga (tel. 21780). For car, bike and scooter rental or organized tours.
Buses – A local bus company operates an hourly bus service around Rarotonga from 0700–1600 hours Monday to Friday and 0700–1200 hours Saturday. Buses are also available from some hotels to take visitors into town.

SIGHTS

The capital and centre of manufacturing, AVARUA has the slow-paced atmosphere of a 19th-century South Sea Island trading post.

Outrigger canoes are moored on the beach under old ironwood trees, from where the island traders depart for their day's work. The main port is Avatiu Harbour, with a small boat harbour at Avarua. The LIBRARY in Avarua provides extensive reading matter on the history of the islands and the MUSEUM OF THE COOK ISLANDS is not to be missed.

MURI BEACH is home to the Rarotongan Sailing Club and also the venue for a tradition of bareback horseracing – in which everyone is welcome to participate!

MOUNT IKURANGI is a Rarotongan sacred mountain whose name means 'tail of the sky'. Being less than 500m high it makes a pleasant early morning climb and from the top you can see the encircling reef and the bright colours of tomato patches and citrus plantations. In the VILLAGES clusters of neat, trim houses (ares) sit amongst the trees and are surrounded by flowers, groves of palms and banana, pineapple and citrus plants. By law no building may be higher than its surrounding palm trees – a law which has so far kept the big names in mass tourism away. Most villages are near the coast, idyllically nestling in the tropical-green valleys.

ARA METUA is an ancient inner road which also runs right round the island (the coastal road is the one commonly used). It is said to be the oldest in Polynesia, with foundation coral blocks laid almost 1000 years ago. Ruins of old temples can be found along the way.

On Sundays nearly everything in the Cook Islands, except the CHURCHES, is closed. Given that, why not spend the Sabbath touring a few of Rarotonga's churches, for they are of particular interest. Most were built in the mid 1800s from slabs of coral taken from the reef. The church at Titikaveka, the oldest on the island, has a service in Maori at dawn and again at 5 p.m. and one in English at 10 a.m. The choral singing to be heard during these services is likely to be one of your most lasting memories of your time here.

ACCOMMODATION

All the accommodation on Rarotonga is attractive, comfortable and informal. Big resort hotel chains haven't reached here yet (thankfully) so all the hotels and lodges are quite simple, small and quiet, though not lacking in facilities.

● **First Class:** (Double NZ$65–80)
Rarotongan Resort Hotel – PO Box 103, Arva, Arorangi, Rarotonga (tel. 25800). On its own beach, about 20 minutes' drive from
town. Facilities include a fresh-water pool and poolside bar, 3
restaurants, tennis and volleyball courts and windsurfers or snorkel
gear for hire. Conference facilities make this an idyllic business
setting.

The Tamure Resort – PO Box 17, Rarotonga (tel. 22415). Just over a
mile from Avarua and set in beautiful tropical gardens on the
ocean's edge. Excellent facilities and service. Club Pacific is based
here and offers very good inclusive packages for 7 or 15 days of
organized sightseeing (it's not too organized and takes you to some
of the best island spots).

The Beach Motel – PO Box 700, Rarotonga (tel. 27652). On the
beach in Arorangi village – about 10 minutes' drive from Avarua.
There are 20 self-contained beach or garden villas, all exceptionally
well equipped and furbished. The lagoon beach is wonderful for
swimming, snorkelling or reef-walking.

● **Super Club Class:** (Double NZ$40–50)
Muri Beachcomber Motel – PO Box 379, Rarotonga (tel. 21022). In
a gorgeous venue, facing Muri Lagoon and surrounded by palm
trees. Very comfortable and good value.

Puaikura Reef Lodges – PO Box 397, Rarotonga (tel. 23537).
Comfortable, fully self-contained lodges just across the road from
the beach.

Lagoon Lodges – PO Box 45, Rarotonga (tel. 22020). Next door to
the Rarotongan Resort Hotel, with good, family-sized lodges.

Palm Grove Lodges – PO Box 23, Rarotonga (tel. 20002). Four very
pretty lodges set opposite their own, private swimming beach. Well
furnished.

● **Economy:** (Double NZ$20–40)
The Kii Kii – PO Box 68, Rarotonga (tel. 21937). A larger complex
of self-contained units (20 of them) set in gardens on the water's
edge. About one mile from Avarua.

Are Renga Motel – PO Box 223, Rarotonga (tel. 20050). Single or
twin rooms in Arorangi village with cooking facilities in all units.

Orange Grove Lodge – PO Box 553, Rarotonga (tel. 20192). Two spacious units set in a citrus and banana plantation near the Palm Grove Lodges. The grounds and flowers are lovely and fruit in season is free for the picking.

Dive Rarotonga Hostel – PO Box 38, Rarotonga (tel. 21873). The first hostel in Rarotonga, and it has very good facilities. Kitchen, lounge, showers etc. are communal to the 9 rooms. Reliable diving equipment is hired out and the best dive sites shown. Rates are around NZ$13 each per night or NZ$110 (double) per week.

DINING OUT

In such a small place it's surprising to find restaurants ranging from Chinese and Mexican to Italian and Polynesian. The hotel restaurants serve good, if not especially exciting food, which nearly always includes fresh New Zealand lamb and local fish. Three notable restaurants are:

Brandi's – Upstairs at the Rarotongan Resort Hotel. The most extensive menu and wine list in the Cook Islands. The Chardonnays in the New Zealand wine range are very good.

Outrigger – Over the road from the Beach Motel is this superb little restaurant. Dinner plus wine for two costs around NZ$30.

Vaima – Further along the road from the Rarotongan and comparable to the Outrigger in quality but a few dollars more expensive.

Cook Islanders will not accept tips – they are actually offended by them – so remember *not* to leave any change on your table.

NIGHTLIFE

The locals excel at dancing, singing and drumming and their performances are quite fantastic. Floor shows are put on during regular dance nights in the hotels and local dance spots around the island will often feature exuberant half-hour shows between disco bouts. *The* place to go is the BANANA COURT BAR in the centre of Avarua. Quite simply, everyone goes there – so there's no fear of the action being somewhere else! As the Banana Bar closes, at around midnight, the HAPPY VALLEY disco starts up – the locals have a very diplomatic and uncompetitive approach to business!

EXCURSIONS

The locals are very good at showing people around – tourism is still small enough for them to take a genuine pride in welcoming and looking after their foreign visitors. Consequently the organized tours all tend to be well run and good value. For those who dislike formal organization, it's easy just to hire a vehicle and head off round the island – you can't really get lost!

Exham Tours – Rarotonga. Exham Wichman takes you through Arorangi village and plantations. His personality and local knowledge make this an exceptional insight into the Maori life. Afternoon tea at Exham's home, prepared by his wife, ends the tour.

Tipani Tours – PO Box 4, Rarotonga (tel. 22792). Tours around Rarotonga or day trips and overnight excursions to Aitutaki and other islands. They are also agents for Air Rarotonga and Cook Islands Airways.

Stars Travel – PO Box 75, Rarotonga (tel. 23683 or 23669). Next to the Tourist Authority in Avarua. Circle Island tours, scenic flights, deep-sea fishing, scuba-diving and special interest tours are organized here. They also rent out vehicles.

Union Travel – PO Box 54, Rarotonga (tel. 21780). All sorts of island tours plus fishing, diving and 'Island-style Meet-the-People' evenings. Day tours to Aitutaki island by air.

Dive Rarotonga – PO Box 38, Rarotonga (tel. 21873). Barry and Shirley Hill will provide you with reliable diving equipment and point out the best sites. Great underwater cities of coral and tropical fish, in visibilities of 100 ft plus, make this a divers' paradise. Most of it is no deeper than 12 ft so snorkellers can see just about as much. Individual and club rates are very reasonable.

Fiji Islands

RED TAPE

• **Passport/Visa Requirements:** A full, valid passport is required by all except British protected persons holding a certificate of identity. A British Visitor's Passport is acceptable. Visas are required by all except citizens of Commonwealth countries, most of Europe and the USA. Tourist visas are valid for up to 30 days and can be extended, once in Fiji, for up to 6 months.

CUSTOMS

• **Duty Free:** Each visitor may bring in 200 cigarettes or ½ lb tobacco and 1 litre of spirits or 2 litres of wine or beer. Up to 4 oz of perfume and goods to the value of F$30 may also be brought in. Visitors may not bring fruit or plant materials into the country.

HEALTH

No vaccination certificates are essential but precautions against typhoid and polio are recommended.

CAPITAL – Suva on Viti Levu.

POPULATION – 634,000.

LANGUAGE – English, Fijian, Hindi and Cantonese.

CURRENCY – Fijian Dollar = 100 Cents. Notes are in denominations of 1, 2, 5, 10 and 20 dollars. Coins are in denominations of 1, 2, 5, 10, 20 and 50 cents.
£1 = F$1.62; US$1 = F$1.16.

BANKING HOURS – 0800–1630 hours Monday to Friday.

POLITICAL SYSTEM – Democracy.

RELIGION – Methodist and Hindu with Muslim and Roman Catholic minorities.

PUBLIC HOLIDAYS

January 1	New Year's Day
March/April (3 days)	Easter
June 18	Queen's Birthday
August (1 day)	Bank Holiday
October 8	Fiji Day
October 24	Diwali Festival
November 14	Prince of Wales' Birthday
December 7	Prophet Mohammed's Birthday
December 25	Christmas Day

CLIMATE – The Fiji Islands enjoy a tropical climate with a dry season from May to October and a rainy season from November to April. Maximum temperatures can reach 91°F (33°C) in December to February. Minimum temperatures of around 63°F (17°C) occur between June and August.

TIME DIFFERENCE – GMT + 12.

COMMUNICATIONS

• **Telephone:** The internal telephone system is fairly good. There is no IDD (international direct dialling) so international calls must be put through the operator.

• **Post:** Airmail takes up to 10 days to reach Europe. Postal services and international telecommunications are available in most tourist centres. Telex facilities are available in Suva.

ELECTRICITY – 240v AC

OFFICE/SHOPPING HOURS – Office: 0800–1630 hours Monday to Friday; 0900–1200 hours Saturday. Shops: 0800–1630 hours Monday to Friday (half-day closing by some shops on Wednesday); 0800–1300 hours Saturday.

• **Best Buys:** Duty free shopping is a popular tourist occupation in Suva, Lautoka and Nadi but 'duty' free items have 10 per cent fiscal tax added to their price and are not such good bargains as many believe them to be. Better buys are to be found in the native arts and crafts of Fiji. Filigree jewellery, wood carvings, kava bowls, polished coconut shells, woven materials, tapa cloth and ornamental sea shells are just some of Fiji's many locally made items. Bargaining is not the rule in Fiji but some shopkeepers will give discounts with large purchases.

INTERNAL TRAVEL

• **Air:** Air Pacific and Fiji Air provide regular inter-island services. Air Pacific also operates a shuttle service between Nadi International Airport and Nausori Airport on the other side of Viti Levu. Turtle Airways operates flights to tourist island resorts and also does flight-seeing tours. Pacific Crown Aviation operates helicopter tours.

• **Sea:** Passenger services link the outer islands to Nadi and Suva. Passenger facilities on these services are basic. Yachts and cruise boats are available for charter.

• **Bus:** Bus services operate on all Fiji's major islands. On Viti Levu the most important routes are between Lautoka and Suva either on the King's Road (9 hours by local bus) or on the Queen's Road (8 hours by local bus). There are express buses which are more expensive and not so good from the sightseeing point of view. Vanua Levu and Taveuni also have good bus services between their major towns.

• **Car Rental:** Car rental rates are high in Fiji and road maintenance is poor so driving yourself around can be more trouble than it is worth. Driving is on the left hand side and most countries' drivers' licences are acceptable.

MAJOR SIGHTS OF THE COUNTRY

The Fiji Islands are scattered over a large area of the South Pacific Ocean in a horseshoe-shaped archipelago enclosing the shallow Koro Sea. Although there are over 300 islands, only about 105 are inhabited. Of these, the bulk of the population live on Viti Levu and Vanua Levu, the two largest islands. Most of the islands are the volcanic peaks of a continent now lying below sea level. Their surrounding coral reefs are among the largest and most colourful in the world.

Viti Levu is Fiji's main island and holds some 74 per cent of the total population. A central divide separates the dry, leeward side of the island, where Nadi and Lautoka are the main towns, from the wetter, windward side where the capital Suva is situated. The vast majority of Fiji's tourists spend their time on this, the largest of the islands. Of the other islands Vanua Levu and Taveuni are the most accessible to tourists. Vanua Levu's land is taken up by coconut plantations, tropical vegetation and white, sandy beaches. The two main towns of Labasa and Savusau are small and sleepy. Taveuni Island is still smaller and quieter with tiny villages and copra plantations dotted around the lowlands of a central volcanic mountain. Waiyevo, the main village, only has one hotel and very few tourists go there.

Nadi

NADI INTERNATIONAL AIRPORT

Fiji's international airport is situated 5 miles north of Nadi and 15 miles south of Lautoka. The Domestic and International Terminals are housed in the same building. The airport and all its facilities and services operate on a 24-hour, round-the-clock basis, except where otherwise stated below.

AIRPORT FACILITIES

Information Desk	In the Arrivals Concourse.
Bank and Currency Exchange	Next to the Transit Lounge.
Hotel Reservations Desk	In the Arrivals Concourse.
Insurance Facilities	Through individual airlines.
Bar	Within the Transit Lounge, available to all internationally departing passengers.
Buffet/Snacks	Available at the Airport Cafeteria.
Post Office	Open 0800–1600 hours Monday to Friday and 0800–1030 hours Saturday. There are post boxes within the Transit Lounge.
Duty Free	Shops sell a full range of duty-free items and accept any foreign currencies that have no fiscal restrictions.
Baggage Deposit	Baggage lockers are available.
Toilets	Throughout the terminal.
Nursery/Mothers' Room	Within the Transit Lounge.

Shops	Within the Transit Lounge, for all internationally departing passengers.
Medical Centre	Next to the Baggage Claim area.
Car Rental Desk	In the Arrivals Concourse (8 companies are represented).

AIRPORT INFORMATION

Check-in Times	60 minutes before international flight departure times; 30 minutes before domestic flight departure times.
Airport Tax	F$10 is payable on departure by all except those less than 16 years old.
Flight Transfers	Transferring passengers remain in the same building and await their onward flight in the Transit Lounge.

AIRPORT HOTELS

• **First Class:**
Tanoa – PO Box 9211, Nadi Airport. Top class facilities and excellent service. Courtesy transport to the airport.

• **Super Club Class:**
Castaway Gateway – Nadi Airport. Ideally situated near the airport and recently renovated to provide very good accommodation.

CITY LINKS

Many of the hotels around Nadi provide courtesy transport to and from the airport. There are also regular public buses which run between the airport terminal and Nadi or Lautoka. Taxis available from the terminal are metered and not too expensive.

NADI

Nadi, the nearest town to Fiji's international airport, lies on the west coast of Fiji's main island, Viti Levu. The town itself is small and not particularly interesting, but Viti Levu and the other islands of Fiji are both historically and geographically fascinating. Research indicates that the islands must have been first settled by Polynesians around 1500 BC, followed by Melanesians and Tongans much later. Fijian customs were barbarous – people were buried alive as foundations for houses, war canoes were launched over rows of young girls and cannibalism was common practice. Tasman, a Dutchman, was the first European to discover these savage islands in 1643. He did not land and the next European visitor was Captain Cook in 1779. During the 19th century the search for sandalwood brought many European ships and tribal warfare, helped along by the sailors, was widespread. In 1874 Fiji was ceded to Britain and it became independent within the British Commonwealth in 1970.

The Fiji Islands are chiefly agricultural, the main cash crop being sugar cane. Viti Levu has some gold mines and the main exports from here are sugar, copra, coconut oil and gold. Tourism is a fast developing industry on the two main islands. The town of Nadi is 5 miles south of the airport on Nadi Bay. Apart from the hotels and a long street of duty free tourist shops, the town has very little to offer. There is, however, a surprisingly interesting market in the centre which is very lively on Saturday mornings.

TOURIST INFORMATION

Fiji Visitors' Bureau – At Nadi Airport.

GETTING ABOUT

• **Bus:** Buses serve the whole island and are inexpensive. The bus station is right in the centre of Nadi.

• **Taxi:** Town taxis are metered and not too expensive. For longer distances a fare table should be evident within the cab.

• **Car Rental:** This is expensive and road maintenance is poor on the island. The cheapest cars can be hired from Khans Rental Cars (tel. 71 009) at the garage opposite Nadi Motel.

SIGHTS

Within Nadi there is very little worth seeing. Nadi Bay and Wailoaloa Beach are quite pleasant to walk around and the town market is colourful and lively, especially on Saturday mornings. Duty free shops line most of Nadi's streets and shopping here is a popular tourist pastime. Apart from this Nadi should really be used as a base while looking around the rest of the island.

ACCOMMODATION

Fiji has a good number of luxury hotels on its main island of Viti Levu and some exotic island resorts off the coast of Viti Levu and Vanua Levu. There are also many small, inexpensive hotels, motels, lodges and dormitory-type accommodation on the main islands. A group called the South Pacific Budgetels offer cheap but clean and comfortable rooms with the use of a bar, restaurant and swimming pool.

• **First Class:** (Double F$70–140)
The Regent of Fiji – PO Box 441, Narewa Road, Nadi Bay, Viti Levu (tel. 70700). A luxurious South Pacific resort with all the beach space and facilities one could possibly want.

Nadi Travelodge – Votualevu Road (tel. 72277)
All the luxury expected of one of the Travelodge group of hotels. Located at the airport.

Fiji Mocambo – Namaka (tel. 72000/72479)
A top class yet reasonably priced hotel on the road between the airport and Nadi.

• **Super Club Class:** (Double F$40–70)
Seashell Cove – Momi Bay (tel. 50309)
This is actually about 11 miles out of Nadi, set on a beautiful bit of

coast with lots of sports facilities. Apart from the hotel rooms there are dormitory rooms and campers are welcomed.

Dominion International – (tel. 72255)
A comfortable hotel at the airport, with good facilities which include swimming pools and a pitch and putt golf course.

Westgate – (tel. 72444)
A well run and moderately priced hotel with all the amenities required for a comfortable stay.

The Melanesian – Nadi Airport (tel. 72438)
The hotel rooms here are very comfortable and the rates reasonable. There is also dormitory accommodation available.

• **Economy:** (Double less than F$40)
Sunseekers Hotel – Narewa Road, Nadi (tel. 70400)
A lively, friendly hotel (it can be noisy at night) on the edge of Nadi. Continental breakfast is included.

Fong Hing Hotel – Vunavou Road (tel. 71011)
A traditionally run Chinese hotel in Nadi's downtown area.

Coconut Inn – Queen's Road, Nadi, Viti Levu (tel. 72553). A good, cheap place to stay which is convenient for both the airport and Nadi.

Nadi Hotel – (tel. 70000)
Basic but cheap accommodation in central Nadi. Each room has a fridge and private bath.

Sandalwood Inn – Queen's Road (tel. 72553)
Also in downtown Nadi, this may be slightly more expensive but it is good value. Some rooms share facilities.

Nadi Youth Hostel –
An official YHA hostel which is of reasonable standard.

DINING OUT

Fiji has many good, inexpensive restaurants and bars serving food. Chinese and Indian cuisine is popular, the latter being of the native Fijian Indian variety. Native dishes include duruka (an asparagus-like vegetable), kakoda (marinated local fish steamed in coconut cream and lime), raurau (taro leaves with various fillings) and kassaua (tapioca cooked in coconut cream with sugar and banana). The major hotels have the most extensive menus which tend to include European dishes and, at the other end of the scale, a real taste of Fiji can be obtained by buying lunch at the local market.

● **First Class** (over $40)
Ocean View Restaurant, The Regent of Fiji, Narewa Road (tel. 70700).

Steak House, same location as above.

Gardenview Restaurant, same as above.
All these restaurants offer top class service and excellent cuisine in the luxury hotel of the island.

● **Super Club Class** (over $20)

Blue Orchid Restaurant, Castaway Gateway Hotel, Nadi Airport (tel. 72444). Good food and a varied menu catering to the international jet set.

Makosoi Room, Tanoa Hotel (near Queen's and Votualevu Roads), Namaka (tel. 72300). Traditional dishes and a good atmosphere.

Club Room, Nadi International Airport (tel. 73027). Informal location to have anything from a pre-flight snack to a full dinner.

● **Economy** ($10–20)

Curry Restaurant, Clay Street (tel. 70960). Delicious authentic Indian dishes.

Poon's Restaurant, Main Street (tel. 70896). Good Chinese and European food at reasonable prices.

Fong Hing Restaurant, Vunavou Road (tel. 71011). Good, very cheap Chinese dishes in the Fong Hing Hotel.

Mama's Pizza Inn, 498 Main Street, Queen's Road (tel. 70221). Good Italian varieties of pizzas at low prices.

NIGHTLIFE

Although most of the major hotels and resorts have their own evening entertainment laid on and many have nightclubs, most of Fiji's socialites frequent private clubs. Visitors can obtain temporary membership through their hotel. Mokeo, the Fijian traditional form of entertainment, is performed in hotels which work on a rotational basis so there is something on somewhere every night. Cinemas show films in English and Indian. If there are any feasts on offer during your stay do try to go as they usually have excellent food and dancing.

The *Bamboo Palace Night Club* at the Nadi Hotel has a live band from 10 p.m.–1 a.m. on Fridays and Saturdays, while near to Poon's Restaurant, the Farmer's Club is where to meet the locals (great after a rugby match: held on Saturdays 12 noon from February–November).

EXCURSIONS

Nadi makes a good base from which to explore Viti Levu. On the west coast, north of Nadi, is LAUTOKA. This is Fiji's second city and the centre of the sugar industry. There are plenty of things to see here: a good market, the sugar mill, the Mosque and the Sikh Temple to name but a few. The tourist centre is beside the sugar mill and can arrange tours. Lautoka is an important departure point for many cruise boats to the outer islands and island resorts. BEACHCOMBER ISLAND is one of the most popular with beautiful beaches and decent accommodation. Boats to the YASAWA ISLANDS, which also leave from Lautoka, have very reasonable fares.

Between Lautoka and Nadi is the village of VISEISEI. This is a pretty town with fine views over Nadi Bay. Going down to the south coast, the SINGATOKA area is known as the Coral Coast and has many tourist resorts extending right along to SUVA. Halfway along the south coast is NAVUA from where boats leave for MBENGGA ISLAND, home of the Fijian firewalkers. Suva is the capital of the Fiji Islands and is worth a visit. The airport at NAUSORI, just north of Suva, is the main domestic terminal.

New Zealand

RED TAPE

• **Passport/Visa Requirements:** A full, valid passport is required by all visitors except travellers arriving direct from Australia who are Australian citizens, or citizens of other Commonwealth countries or the Republic of Ireland who have been granted indefinite Australian residence. (Australian citizens require a passport to re-enter Australia.) Bona fide visitors must intend a short, holiday stay only and have onward tickets and sufficient funds to maintain themselves whilst in New Zealand. Visas are required and can be obtained at the point of arrival for those in the following categories:

(a) Visits not exceeding 6 months: citizens of the UK, Ireland, Canada, Belgium, Denmark, Liechtenstein, Luxembourg, Monaco, Netherlands, Norway, Sweden, Switzerland and France.
(b) Visits not exceeding 3 months: citizens of the German Federal Republic, Finland, Iceland, Malta.
(c) Visits not exceeding 30 days: citizens of the USA (excluding American Samoans), Japan.

For all visitors others than those mentioned prior application is required to the Chief Migration Officer, New Zealand High Commission, New Zealand House, 80 Haymarket, London SW1Y 4TQ, or New Zealand Embassy, 37 Observatory Circle, Washington DC 2008, telephone (202) 328 4800.

CUSTOMS

• **Duty Free:** Each visitor may bring in 200 cigarettes or 50 cigars or 250g tobacco, and 4.5 litres wine plus a 1125 ml or 40 oz bottle of spirits. You are advised not to take fruits or plants in with you.

HEALTH

No vaccination certificates are needed to enter New Zealand. Health insurance is advisable. The water is purified and drinkable.

CAPITAL – Wellington (population 343,200).

POPULATION – 3,100,000.

LANGUAGE – English and Maori (spoken by the Maori people).

CURRENCY – New Zealand Dollar divided into 100 Cents. Notes – 1, 2, 5, 10, 20, 50, 100. Coins – 1c, 2c, 5c, 10c, 20c, 50c. £1 = NZ$2.72; US$ = NZ$1.94.

BANKING HOURS – 1000–1600 hours Monday to Friday.

POLITICAL SYSTEM – Constitutional monarchy.

RELIGION – Church of England, Presbyterian, Roman Catholic, Methodist, Baptist.

PUBLIC HOLIDAYS

January 1	New Year's Day
February 6	Waitangi Day
March/April	Good Friday, Easter Monday
April 25	Anzac Day
June	Queen's Birthday
October	Labour Day
December 25, 26	Christmas Day, Boxing Day

CLIMATE – The north of New Zealand is sub-tropical, the south temperate. Long hours of sunshine are enjoyed throughout the country. Winter (June–August) is mild with temperatures ranging from 15°C (60°F) to 8°C (46°F). October to April is warm with temperatures of 25°C (77°F) to 18°C (65°F). Rainfall is variable but there is usually more in the winter.

TIME DIFFERENCE – GMT + 12 (+1 October to March).

COMMUNICATIONS

• **Telephone:** In public booths local calls can be made for 10c. Trunk or international calls must go through the operator. Most hotel rooms have telephones. International direct dialling is available on hotel or private telephones.

• **Post:** Post Offices open 0900–1700 hours Monday to Friday, where postal, cable, telegram, telex and telephone services are available. Airmail to the UK takes 4–5 days.

• **Newspapers:** The *New Zealand Herald*, the *Dominion*, the *Press* and the *Evening Post* are printed daily and provide international and national news.

ELECTRICITY – 230v AC, 50 Hz. Most hotels and motels provide 110v AC sockets for electric razors. Most power sockets accept 3 pin flat plugs.

OFFICE/SHOPPING HOURS – Offices: 0900–1700 hours Monday to Friday. Shops: 0900–1730 hours Monday to Thursday/Friday, 0900–2100 hours Friday (or Thursday in the suburbs). 0900–1200 hours Saturday.

• **Best Buys:** New Zealand's specialities are based on the natural gemstones found here and the Maori style of arts and crafts. Jewellery made from New Zealand greenstone (a type of jade) or iridescent paua shell is widely available. Wood carvings inlaid with paua shell and carved greenstone Tikis (Maori charms) are found in Maori craft shops. Other good buys include New Zealand woollen goods (travel rugs, jumpers, floor rugs and leather and skin products), pottery and New Zealand wine. Native New Zealand timber is made into many products such as bowls, toys, plates and wine goblets.

INTERNAL TRAVEL

New Zealand has a comprehensive network of road, rail, sea and air transportation services.

• **Air:** Air New Zealand is the primary domestic airline, whose network links 24 major towns and cities on the North and South

Islands. 14- or 21-day air passes are available to non-residents (they must be purchased outside New Zealand).

Mount Cook Airlines caters mainly for city-to-resort journeys. It also operates Britten–Norman Islander provincial airline routes on South Island. A Mount Cook Airline Kiwi Pass is valid for one month and must also be purchased outside New Zealand.

● **Rail:** The mainline rail services are fast, efficient and comfortable, and pass through some of the most spectacular of New Zealand's scenery. The New Zealand Rail Tourist Pass gives unlimited rail, ferry and coach travel over specified periods. These must be bought outside New Zealand.

● **Coach:** Scheduled services operate throughout the country, on a connecting network. It is advisable to book in advance and reserve seats. A Kiwi Coach Pass can be purchased outside New Zealand for 7 or 10 days' travel.

● **Ferry:** Regular passenger/car ferry services link the North and South Islands, between Wellington and Picton. The crossing takes 3 hours 20 minutes and the ferry has snack and bar facilities. Another ferry service links South and Stewart Islands, between Bluff and Oban. Places should be reserved, especially during Christmas and Easter periods.

● **Car:** New Zealand's highways are of a high standard and driving is on the left hand side. An International Driving Licence is necessary except for those whose licences conform to the 1949 International Road Traffic Convention. A wide range of rental cars is available throughout New Zealand.

● **Taxi:** Available in all towns and cities and for city–airport transfer, taxis are metered and may be hailed in the street or telephoned for.

MAJOR SIGHTS OF THE COUNTRY

AUCKLAND is New Zealand's largest city and is built around many extinct or dormant volcanic cones, between Waitemata and Manukau harbours. This is also New Zealand's fastest growing city: its streets teem with department stores, boutiques, nightclubs, restaurants and Maori craft centres. An exciting and lively place to visit, it also makes a good base for sightseeing in the North Island.

BAY OF ISLANDS is Northland's major resort area with a sub-tropical climate and access to many tranquil beaches, bays and rain forests. Historically, Waitangi was the venue for the 1840 ceding of New Zealand to Queen Victoria by the Maori chiefs. South-east of Auckland is the BAY OF PLENTY, a big resort area where long golden beaches and exciting deep-sea fishing facilities are the major attractions. The east coast, in contrast, is an 'off the beaten track' area although it also has fine beaches and coastal scenery.

For an incredible sight of huge geysers, boiling mud, springs of hot mineral water and hissing fumaroles head for ROTORUA. There are all sorts of other things to see and do here, and the villages of OHINEMUTU and WHAKAREWAREWA are fascinating places to experience first hand Maori culture.

TONGARIRO NATIONAL PARK is a great place for winter or summer sports, located beside 3 active volcanic peaks – Mounts Ruapehu (2976m), Ngauruhoe (2290m) and Tongariro (1968m).

New Zealand's capital, WELLINGTON, has many interesting sights including the Houses of Parliament, government buildings, Art Gallery and War Memorial Museum. The city lies on the shores of a magnificent harbour with Mount Victoria in the background. Ferries run from Wellington to PICTON from where cruises can be taken through the beautiful labyrinth of the MARLBOROUGH SOUNDS.

South Island's main city is CHRISTCHURCH, known as the 'Garden City of New Zealand' for its expanses of well kept parks and gardens. Further south, the most stunning glaciers can be seen in the WESTLAND NATIONAL PARK. The FOX and FRANZ JOSEF GLACIERS have their source 2500m up in the Southern Alps and terminate among native forests some 2320m below. In the centre of the alpine region is MOUNT COOK (3763m) and the nearby TASMAN GLACIER, where ski-equipped aircraft make spectacular landings.

DUNEDIN is aptly named the 'Edinburgh of the South'. Steeped in history of the Scottish settlers, the buildings, bagpipes, statues and parks impart a Caledonian atmosphere to the harbourside city. New Zealand's southernmost city, INVERCARGILL, also maintains its Scottish atmosphere while being the administrative centre of the Southland Province and the gateway to STEWART ISLAND. Hills, forests, sandy bays and a refuge for a wide variety of birds and animals make this island popular with hikers and naturalists.

Auckland

AUCKLAND INTERNATIONAL AIRPORT

North Island's major airport is 14 miles south of Auckland at Mangere. There are two passenger terminals; the International Terminal deals with flight arrivals on the ground floor and departures on the first floor; the Domestic Terminal deals with arrivals and departures on the ground floor.

AIRPORT FACILITIES

• International Terminal:

Information Desk	Ground floor.
Bank/Foreign Exchange	Ground floor.
Hotel Reservations	Ground floor.
Baggage Lockers	Ground floor.
Insurance Facilities	Ground floor.
Car Rental Desks	Avis and Hertz, ground floor.
Shops	Ground and first floor.
Post Office	First floor.
Buffet	First floor.
Nursery	First floor.
First Aid Station	First floor.
Bar and Restaurant	Second floor.
Observation Deck	Second floor.
Duty Free Shop	Sells cigarettes, lighters, tobacco, wines, spirits, liqueurs, cameras, watches, radios, jewellery. All convertible currencies plus American Express, Visa and Diners Club cards are accepted.

• **Domestic Terminal:**

Post Office	Ground floor.
Shops	Ground floor.
Car Rental Desks	Avis and Hertz, ground floor.
Snack Bar	Mezzanine floor.

AIRPORT INFORMATION

Check-in Times	60 minutes prior to international flight departure times; 20 minutes prior to domestic flight departure times.
Airport Tax	Departing international flight passengers must pay NZ$2 in cash.
Flight Transfers	An inter-terminal bus runs every 30 minutes. International-to-international flight connections have at least 55 minutes' wait and international-to-domestic flight connections have at least 90 minutes' wait.

AIRPORT HOTELS

• **Super Club Class:**
Auckland Gateway Lodge – Kirkbride Road, Mangere (tel. 275 4079). Situated less than 2 miles from the airport, with courtesy transport available.

CITY LINKS

• **Bus:** The Johnson Coachline runs every half hour from 0600–2100, stopping at Airport Travelodge, Sheraton, Hyatt Kingsgate and South Pacific Hotels, before reaching the downtown terminal. Approximately NZ$5.

● **Taxi:** These will be waiting outside the terminals and are not too expensive (roughly 4 times the bus fare). Some hotels have courtesy coaches to and from the airport. The trip to town takes 45–60 minutes and should cost about NZ$22.

● **Private Limousine:** Hire to town approximately NZ$50.

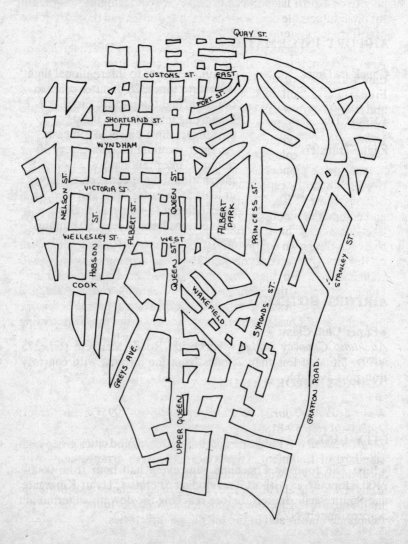

AUCKLAND

60,000 years ago the Auckland isthmus was dramatically shaped by the eruptions of over 60 volcanoes in a concentrated area. In AD 900 a Polynesian explorer, Kupe, landed and established the Maori people on North Island. The prized Auckland isthmus was fought for on innumerable occasions over the centuries and the scars of the Maori trench systems can still be seen today.

The first European to sight New Zealand was a Dutch navigator, Abel Tasman, in 1642, who left the land alone after a troublesome time with the natives. In 1769 Captain Cook and De Surville (a Frenchman) simultaneously landed on opposite sides of the islands and from 1790 onwards Europeans commenced lumber, flax, whale and seal trading from lonely settlements. After 50 years of lawlessness, bloodbaths and untreated disease the British made New Zealand a colony and set about 'civilizing' the country.

Auckland's pioneer history since 1840 is preserved in its distinctive architecture, especially that of the churches built by Bishop Selwyn in the 1850s. Today it is New Zealand's largest industrial and commercial centre and also the world's largest Polynesian city. The Polynesians have retained their culture and customs and tend to live in their own communities. Karangahape Road, to the north of the city, has a concentrated Polynesian community who will welcome you into their brightly coloured bars and restaurants. Queen Street is the main street of Auckland, running along a narrow valley with side streets rising off it. Most of the big hotels are on or close to Queen Street, as are many of the most interesting shops.

TOURIST INFORMATION

New Zealand Tourist & Publicity Offices – 99 Queen Street, Auckland (tel. 79-8180).
Medical Services – Public hospitals in all towns and cities give a high standard of treatment. Hotels normally have arrangements with local doctors who will visit in emergency cases.
Emergency – Dial 111 for fire, police or ambulance authorities in major centres. Elsewhere full details will be found inside the telephone booths and in the telephone directories.

GETTING ABOUT

● **Taxis:** Metered taxis operate throughout the city. You can telephone for one, take one from taxi stands or hail them in the street.

● **Buses:** Buses operate on timetabled routes throughout the city with fares based on the distance or number of 'sections' travelled.

● **Car Rental:** A wide selection of car hire firms have offices in Auckland. Rates of hire vary very little between firms. Driving is on the left hand side and an International Driving Licence is required by all except those whose licence conforms to the 1949 International Road Traffic Convention. As a rule, the hirer must be at least 21 years old.

SIGHTS

The presence of New Zealand's unique bird, the kiwi, makes a visit to Auckland's otherwise not very outstanding zoo worthwhile. The AUCKLAND DOMAIN is a large parkland whose attractions are sports fields, the Winter Gardens and the Auckland Museum. The museum's extensive collection of Maori and South Pacific artefacts is particularly worth visiting.

Opposite Orakei Wharf, close to the city is KELLY TARLTON'S UNDERWATER WORLD, an aquarium with a difference, one where you are taken on an 8-minute trip through an underwater tunnel lined with windows while sharks, stingrays and many other fish swim round you (not for the claustrophobic or hydrophobic, but a tremendous journey for anyone else!).

MOUNT EDEN is one of the many extinct volcanic cones around the city, with a road spiralling up to the summit (643 ft). The panoramic view from the top of city, oceans and other craters is worth the climb.

PARNELL ROSE GARDEN is a beautiful place to visit in November, when the famous roses are in bloom. ONE TREE HILL used to be the site of a fortified Maori village and is now the site of the Auckland observatory, a 70 ft obelisk in honour of 'the father of Auckland', Sir John Logan Campbell, and a single tree.

Although the MUSEUM OF TRANSPORT AND TECHNOLOGY sounds rather tedious, it is actually a fascinating museum with displays of many obsolete machines. Aircraft, trams, vintage cars and carriages are among the collection.

ACCOMMODATION

Like any big city, Auckland has plenty of hotels and motels of all standards. Many of the motels have cooking facilities in the units and some serve breakfast. During the holiday seasons, Christmas and Easter, it is advisable to make advance reservations. Neither a service charge nor tipping is usual.

● **First Class:** (Double NZ$120–190)
Sheraton Auckland – 85 Symonds Street (tel. 795-132). The usual Sheraton high standards and luxurious accommodation. Centrally located, with excellent sports facilities and conference rooms.

Hyatt Kingsgate Auckland – Corner of Princes Street and Waterloo Quadrant (tel. 797-220). A top quality hotel less than 1 mile from the city centre. Extensive facilities include restaurants, bars, jacuzzis and a jogging track.

The Regent of Auckland – Albert Street, Auckland 1 (tel. 398-882). Superbly located in the centre of the business district with high standards of service and a wide range of facilities. It is ideal for conferences and businessmen or as a base for Auckland sightseers.

● **Super Club Class:** (Double NZ$70–120)
South-Pacific Hotel – Corner of Queen and Customs Streets (tel. 778-920). In a mid-city location, comfortable and well furbished.

White Heron Regency – 138 St Stephens Avenue, Parnell (tel. 796-860). A good location, in Parnell village and next to the Rose Gardens. A good medium-grade hotel.

Townhouse Auckland – 150 Anzac Avenue (tel. 798-509). Near the city centre and the railway station. Good, comfortable accommodation.

Takapuna Beach Motel – The Promenade, Takapuna Beach (tel. 497-126). On the east coast of Auckland. The accommodation consists of studios with kitchen facilities plus restaurants and bars.

• **Economy:** (Double NZ$30–70)
Mon Desir Hotel – 144 Hurstmere Road, Takapuna (tel. 495-139).
On the north shore of Takapuna Beach. A small, well priced hotel with restaurant, bar, pool and sauna. 6 miles from the city centre.

Royal Hotel – Victoria Street West (tel. 31-359). In the city centre with adequate facilities, a restaurant and bars.

Railton Travel Hotel – 411 Queen Street (tel. 796-487). On the main street of the city is this reasonably priced hotel, with breakfast included in the bill.

YMCA Hostel – Corner of Pitt Street and Grays Avenue (tel. 32-068). For the really budget conscious this is very good value. Dinner and breakfast included in the bill.

DINING OUT

The dining rooms of Auckland reflect New Zealand's reputation as a leading producer of meat and dairy produce. New Zealand pork and beef dishes are on every menu, as well as the famous lamb. Fish is also a popular dish for the New Zealanders – snapper, grouper and John Dory being three of the many varieties. The country's traditional dessert is Pavlova – a type of meringue topped with fresh fruit (often kiwi fruit). Whatever you choose to eat you can be sure of a generous helping – New Zealanders are big eaters! Auckland also has a plentiful supply of Eastern and European restaurants plus 'fast food' chains and 'take-aways'. Some of the new restaurants along Ponsonby Road are very good value.

• **First Class:** (NZ$60–90 for two)
Number Five – 5 City Road. French nouvelle cuisine of superb quality.

Fisherman's Wharf – Northcote. As the name suggests, seafood is the speciality here.

Yamato – 183 Karangahape Road. Japanese food and surrounds.

• **Super Club Class:** (NZ$40–60 for two)
Antoine's – 333 Parnell Road. Delicious French cuisine served in a French colonial atmosphere.

The Genghis Khan – 126 Vincent Street (tel. 397-624). A very good Mongolian barbecue restaurant. The food is cooked on a log fire.

Orsinis – 50 Ponsonby Road. A fine menu and very elegant surroundings.

• **Economy:** (under NZ$40 for two)
Harleys – 25 Anzac Avenue. Great New Zealand fare and one of the most popular BYO restaurants with the locals.

NIGHTLIFE

Late night entertainment is not one of New Zealand's strong points, but if you're going to find any, it will be in Wellington or Auckland. Auckland is trying to brighten up her evening image and several nightclubs and trendy bars are appearing. There are, of course, plenty of pubs to choose from, many with beer gardens so that you can take in the evening air. The BIRD CAGE, on the corner of Victoria Street and Franklin Road (tel. 789-104), is an 'Old English Pub' with garden bar. Bistro-style meals are available and on Saturdays a jazz band and barbecue are laid on.

CHEERS, 12 Wyndham Street (tel. 398-779), is a cocktail bar, café and Sunday brunch venue, often with live evening entertainment. STEPS, 15 O'Connell Street (tel. 799-599), is a sophisticated and elegant nightclub at which you can dance until 3.30 a.m., and SPATZ, 17 Albert Street (tel. 770-304), calls itself a 'Cocktail Piano Bar' and the pianist plays the night away on a revolving grand piano.

EXCURSIONS

From Auckland it is possible to take one- or two-day trips into Northland or the region to the south of the city. One of the most beautiful and exciting trips is along the beach bus route of Ninety Mile Beach to Cape Reinga at the top of Northland. The whole peninsula is 273 miles long so it can comfortably be done in two days. KAITAIA is a thriving commercial town and being in the centre of the North, it is a popular place to stay for a night or two. From here a trip to the BAY OF ISLANDS, with its beautiful beaches and 144 islands, is a short hop. Coming further south, the KAIPARA HAR-

BOUR is one of the longest in the world and has a magnificent 62-mile beach.

On the east coast of Northland is WHANGAREI, a city famous for the spectacular Whangarei Falls. Further south OREWA lies between WAIWERA, home of some thermal pools, and the pretty peninsula of WHANGAPARAOA.

HELENSVILLE is a prosperous dairying district north of Auckland with hot mineral pools at Aquatic Park. Much closer to Auckland is WAITEMATA HARBOUR, spanned by the Auckland Harbour Bridge, with RANGITOTO ISLAND in the background. Beyond this is the HAURAKI GULF where sailing excursions can be made round the many islands. Beaches within easy driving distance of the city are MARAETAI to the south and PIHA and MURIWAI to the west. The western WAITAKERE RANGES offer scenic walks and drives in the spectacular native bush. Trans Tours-Grayline and Scenic Tours run half- or full-day tours of the Auckland area. Harbour cruises are also available and leave regularly from the Ferry Building at the foot of Queen Street.

The HENDERSON area, to the north of Auckland, is renowned for its vineyards and produces many of New Zealand's finest wines. Tours of the vineyards and wine tasting sessions at each make for a good day out.

An exciting alternative to driving or touring on buses is aerial sightseeing. This can be arranged through travel agents or airline companies in Auckland.

Christchurch

CHRISTCHURCH INTERNATIONAL AIRPORT

The only international airport on South Island is at Christchurch, making it the main point of arrival for travellers from the North Island or direct from Australia. It is not a large airport, by international standards, but the two passenger terminals (one international, one domestic) both have good facilities.

AIRPORT FACILITIES

Information Desk	In concourse. Open 0800–2000 hours daily.
Bank/Foreign Exchange	In concourse. Open 1000–1600 hours daily and on arrival of international flights.
Bar	On the first floor. Open 1000–2200 hours daily.
Cafeteria	Ground floor. Open 0700–2030 hours daily.
Restaurant	First floor. Open 1100–2000 hours daily.
Post Office	In the concourse. Open 0900–1700 hours daily.
Baggage Deposit	Ground floor. Open 0630–2030 hours daily.
Nursery	In the concourse. Open 24 hours.
Shops	In the concourse. Open 0800–2000 hours daily and 2 hours before each international flight departure.
Duty Free Shops	Sell an extensive range of products. Accept New Zealand, Australia and United States dollars plus major credit cards.
Toilets	Throughout terminal. Open 24 hours.
Car Rental	Desks in concourse centre.
Hairdresser	In concourse.
Florist	In concourse.

AIRPORT INFORMATION

Check-in Times	30 minutes before an international flight departure; 15 minutes before a domestic flight departure.
Airport Tax	NZ$2.
Transferring Flights	On your arrival you will be told which gate to go to for your onward flight.

AIRPORT HOTELS

● **First/Super Club Class:**
White Heron Travelodge – Memorial Avenue, Christchurch (tel. 583-139). Good conference facilities and a complimentary car service to and from the airport.

● **Economy:**
Airport Lodge Motel, 105 Roydvale Avenue (tel. 585-119). Motel flats 1½ miles from the airport with a complimentary car/bus service.

CITY LINKS

Christchurch International Airport is 7½ miles from the city. All transport to and from the airport stops immediately outside the main terminal entrance.

● **Taxi:** Metered taxis will take you to the city centre, or to your hotel. Rates are quite expensive (about 8 times that of the buses).

● **Bus:** A regular service is provided by the Christchurch Transport Board. The bus route takes in Worcester Street, Cashel Street, Riccarton Avenue, Riccarton Road, Ilam Road and Memorial Avenue.

CHRISTCHURCH

This is South Island's largest city, with a population of 300,000. Nicknamed the 'Garden City', it is spread out across the Canterbury Plains, the largest area of flat land in New Zealand. In the 1850s John Robert Godley arrived in one of the first ships to land at Christchurch and the city was named after the Oxford college which he had attended. The city clings strongly to the trappings of its heritage and is said to be the most English city outside England. With its neat parks and gardens, cricket grounds, rowing and tennis

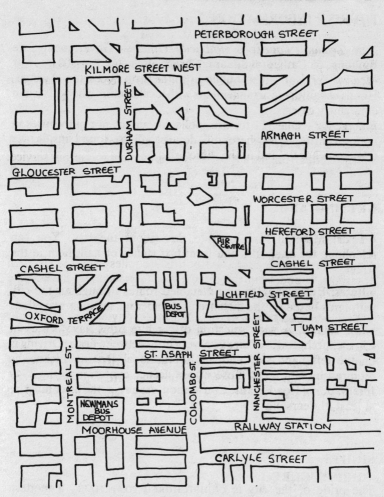

clubs and dignified, charming atmosphere it certainly lives up to its image. The Avon River meanders gracefully through the centre of the city with Oxford and Cambridge Terraces running parallel, to the north and south. Behind the city, the Southern Alps form a majestic backdrop and provide climbing and skiing venues while the city's surrounding bays and beaches are superb for water-sports fanatics.

TOURIST INFORMATION

New Zealand Tourist & Publicity Office – Government Life Building, 65 Cathedral Square, Christchurch (tel. 794-900).
Medical Services – The public hospital is on Riccarton Avenue. Hotels usually have arrangements with local doctors who will visit in emergency cases.
Emergency – Dial 111 for fire, police or ambulance authorities in major centres. Elsewhere full details will be found inside the telephone booths and in the directories.

GETTING ABOUT

● **Taxis:** Metered taxis operate throughout the city. You can telephone for one, take one from taxi stands or hail them in the street.

● **Buses:** Buses operate on timetabled routes throughout the city with fares based on the distance or number of 'sections' travelled.

● **Car Rental:** A wide selection of car hire firms have offices in Christchurch. Rates of hire vary very little between firms. Driving is on the left hand side and an International Driving Licence is required by all except those whose licence conforms to the 1949 International Road Traffic Convention. As a rule, the hirer must be at least 21 years old.

SIGHTS

The pride of the city is CHRISTCHURCH TOWN HALL, a modern cultural complex opened in 1972. It contains a theatre, concert hall, banquet room and restaurant.

QUEEN ELIZABETH II PARK STADIUM was built for the 1974 Commonwealth Games, and is really rather impressive. CATHEDRAL SQUARE is in the heart of the city with all the central streets leading to it. It has recently been made into a pedestrian area and is a popular lunch-time meeting place. The square is presided over by the impressive neo-Gothic cathedral.

CANTERBURY MUSEUM STREET is a street full of 1850s nostalgia, from the shop fronts to the period cottages, and to the horse-drawn cab. There is an interesting ornithological section, too. In the Canterbury Museum Street the HALL OF ANTARCTIC DISCOVERY contains equipment used by successive Antarctic parties and graphic displays telling the history of Antarctic exploration.

FERRYMEAD HISTORIC PARK AND TRANSPORT MUSEUM is a newly developed museum showing off the obsolete transport systems of the past, and McDOUGALL ART GALLERY exhibits classic paintings of the Maori people by Lindauer and Goldie.

The PROVINCIAL COUNCIL BUILDINGS are probably the finest complex of Gothic buildings in the country; and the SIGN OF THE TAKAHE is an English baronial hall of the Tudor period in style. It was actually built by Henry George Ell, a visionary whho died in 1934 having only completed this much of his plan to build a string of rest houses along the Summit Road.

Like all the parks and gardens of the city, the BOTANICAL GAR-DENS are beautifully kept and full of native flowers. Begonia House has a wide range of tropical plants and the Succulent House displays cacti. The gardens are within Hagley Park, one of the most notable of Christchurch's parks.

At ORANA WILDLIFE PARK lions, tigers, camels and other animals from different environments roam freely within its 10 acres. WILLOWBANK WILDLIFE RESERVE contains a huge variety of animals and birds, from Scottish Highland cattle to mountain lions and primitive sheep. Old farming implements are also on display.

ACCOMMODATION

Christchurch lacks the big names in hotels but has a good selection of reasonably priced, reliable hotels and motels.

• **First Class:** (Double NZ$80–120)
Chateau Regency – 187–9 Deans Avenue (tel. 488-999). Excellent accommodation and service in a peaceful location 2½ miles from the city centre.

Noah's Hotel – Corner of Worcester Street and Oxford Terrace (tel. 794-700). Over the road from the tranquil Avon River with top quality restaurants, bars and other facilities.

Kingsgate – Colombo Street (tel. 795-880). On one of the main streets leading to Cathedral Square. The facilities and accommodation are excellent.

● **Super Club Class:** (Double NZ$60–80)
Park Hotel – 50 Park Terrace (tel. 794-560). By the river bank in the city's central area. All facilities are good.

Clarendon Hotel – 78 Worcester Street (tel. 798-440). In the city centre with views over the river. A good, licensed restaurant and comfortable accommodation.

Canterbury Inn – 110 Mandeville Street, Riccarton (tel. 485-049). About one mile from the city centre. Comfortable accommodation.

Coker's Hotel – 52 Manchester Street (tel. 798-580). In the city centre with licensed restaurant and bars.

● **Economy:** (Double NZ$30–60)
Shirley Lodge Motor Hotel – 112 Marshland Road (tel. 853 034). A fair way out of the city, but courtesy transport is available. Licenced restaurant and adequate facilities including a pool.

Gainsborough Motor Lodge – 263 Bealey Avenue (tel. 798-660). Quite close to the city centre with comfortable rooms.

Australasia Motor Inn – 252 Barbados Street (tel. 790-540). Central location. Motel-type flats (with kitchen facilities) for up to 4 people.

Admiral Lodge Motor Hotel – 51 Pages Road (tel. 899-014). About 3 miles out of town. Adequate facilities.

DINING OUT

Christchurch is not one of the most sophisticated or cosmopolitan places in which to eat out. Many of the most popular, and best, restaurants serve homely fare – meat and two veg. Most of the restaurants serve very good food, and there is always plenty of it. There are, of course, a variety of international restaurants to be found: Italian, French, Chinese and Japanese to name but a few.

● **First Class:** (NZ$50–70 for two)
Michael's – 178 High Street. Excellent French/Mediterranean food.

Sign of the Takahe – Dyers Pass Road, Cashmere Hills. An elegant atmosphere and top quality European food. The restaurant is well out of the city, but worth the journey.

The Civic Regency – 198 Manchester Street. A very good Chinese/continental restaurant in Christchurch's elegant old civic chambers.

● **Super Club Class:** (NZ$30–50 for two)
Coachman Inn Restaurant – 144 Gloucester Street (tel. 793-476). An attractive, old-fashioned inn specializing in steaks of all varieties – which taste superb.

Samuels – 115 Armagh Street. An intimate restaurant with some good spaghetti dishes on the menu.

Kurasaki – Colombo Street. Traditional Japanese dishes, served in the traditional manner.

● **Economy:** (under NZ$30 for two)
Shades Tavern – Upstairs at the Shades Shopping Precinct, Cashel Street (tel. 50-859). An extensive, good and inexpensive menu and very friendly and helpful staff.

Cobb & Company Restaurant – The Bush Inn, corner of Waimairi and Riccarton Roads (tel. 487-175). A family-style restaurant which serves very good value meals.

The Coffee Pot Restaurant – 16 New Regent Street (tel. 790-087). Good square meals served by a charming couple who run the restaurant.

Town Hall – Kilmore Street. Excellent smorgasbord lunches and equally good à la carte dinners.

NIGHTLIFE

Christchurch is not the liveliest of places after dark and what entertainment there is tends to be found in the local pubs where live music and dancing goes on nightly. In the Arts Centre there is a JAZZ CENTRE (BYO – bring your own wine) which is lively on Saturday nights. The COACHMAN INN COCKTAIL LOUNGE (144 Gloucester Street) has live bands playing on Wednesday to Sunday evenings. Greek music and dancing can be found at the MYKONOS

TAVERNA on Friday and Saturday nights. For details of cinema/ theatre programmes and any other events see the 'Tourist Times' section of the newspaper *Scenic South*.

EXCURSIONS

CHRISTCHURCH makes a good base for sightseeing on South Island as it is about as central as you can get. LYTTLETON is the port of Christchurch, with the historic Timeball Station. BANKS PENINSULA, south-east of Christchurch, is an area steeped in Maori history and scenic beauty. On its point is AKAROA, a charming French settlement, and down the coast is LAKE ELLESMERE, home to thousands of waterfowl and a popular duck shooting spot.

North of Christchurch the KAIKOURA COAST is a constantly changing seascape with limestone caves and seal colonies, and the Kaikoura Ranges behind.

The road through AMBERLEY takes you up to LEWIS PASS which eventually reaches the west coast. A collection of Maori rock drawings can be seen near WAIKARI and a short detour leads to the health resort of HANMER SPRINGS where all sorts of sporting activities are available.

Another beautiful mountain pass, named Arthur's Pass, begins just south of Christchurch and takes you to ARTHUR'S PASS VILLAGE and NATIONAL PARK. There are numerous skifields in the Canter-bury region, the nearest being at METHVEN. This is also a good place for salmon and trout fishing, horse riding and tramping. The PEEL FOREST and STAVELY areas are other special places to enjoy outdoor pursuits.

Further south the town of TEMUKA boasts the famous Temuka pottery and tours of the factory are available. TIMARU is the main port of the South Canterbury district. Places of interest here include CAROLINE BAY, PLEASANT POINT RAILWAY MUSEUM, HADLOW GAME PARK and the Cave and Craigmore Maori rock drawings.

The Christchurch Transport Board runs afternoon bus tours of the city and surrounds. Personal Guiding Services will lead you (on foot or in your own car) round the city's main attractions. There is quite a good choice of more extensive, full-day bus tours and flight-seeing trips can be organized from here as well. Contact the New Zealand Tourist Office on Cathedral Square for more details on tours.

Tahiti/The Society Islands

RED TAPE

• **Passport/Visa Requirements:** A full, valid passport is required by all visitors to the Society Islands. French citizens do not require a visa for any length of stay. Citizens of Common Market (EEC) countries are allowed a 3-month visa-free stay. Citizens of most other countries are allowed a 30-day visa-free stay and a stay of up to 3 months with a visa. Extensions of stay are possible, for up to 6 months, once you arrive. Visitors must have onward travel tickets.

•

CUSTOMS

• **Duty Free:** Each visitor may bring in 400 cigarettes or 50 cigars or 500g tobacco and 1 litre of spirits or 2 litres of wine or beer. Up to 50g of perfume or 0.25 litres of eau de cologne may also be brought in.

HEALTH

No vaccination certificates are required except if arriving from an infected country.

CAPITAL – Papeete, on Tahiti.

POPULATION – 167,000.

LANGUAGE – Offically French but Tahitian is usually spoken by the Polynesians. Staff in shops and hotels can often speak English.

CURRENCY – The French Pacific Franc (or Cour de Franc Pacifique – CFP) is used by the Eastern Polynesian and New Caledonian Islands.
£1 = CFP170; US$1 = CFP121.43.

BANKING HOURS – 0800–1530 hours Monday to Friday.

POLITICAL SYSTEM – Territory of the French Republic.

RELIGION – Protestant/Catholic.

PUBLIC HOLIDAYS

January 1	New Year's Day
March 5	Anniversary of Missionary Arrival
March/April (3 days)	Easter
May 1	Labour Day
May/June (3 days)	Ascension Day, Whit Sunday and Monday
July 14	Bastille Day/National Day
November 1	All Saints Day
November 11	Armistice Day
December 25	Christmas Day

CLIMATE – The Society Islands' climate is tropical – warm and wet from November to April, cooler and dry from May to October. The hottest months, January to March, see temperatures of up to 88°F (32°C). The coolest months, June to August, see temperatures averaging 78°F (26°C). Tropical winds get quite strong between April and August.

TIME DIFFERENCE – GMT − 10.

COMMUNICATIONS

• **Telephone:** The internal system is straightforward and quite good. Long distance or international calls must be placed at the main Post Office in Papeete.

• **Post:** Postal and telecommunications services are available from the main Post Office in Papeete.

ELECTRICITY – 220v 50Hz; 110v outlets for razors only. Older hotels may still have 110v outlets throughout.

OFFICE/SHOPPING HOURS – Office: 0800–1700 hours Monday to Friday; 0800–1600 hours Saturday. Shops: 0730–1130 hours and 1400–1730 hours Monday to Friday; 0800–1130 hours Saturday.

● **Best Buys:** Papeete has developed several shopping centres which sell Parisian-style merchandise – at Parisian prices! The better bargains, and more authentic souvenirs, are to be found in shops selling local products: wood carvings, shell jewellery, Tahitian perfumes and the 'pareu' fabrics which make the traditional, brightly coloured garments, 'pareo'. Away from the shopping centres, the public downtown market in Papeete has some interesting stores including many excellent Chinese ones. For the best selection of hand-painted fabrics and dresses the island next to Tahiti, Moorea, is the place to go.

INTERNAL TRAVEL

● **Air:** The domestic airline Air Polynesie operates between Tahiti and all the neighbouring islands – Moorea, Huahine, Raiatea, Bora Bora and Maupiti. This airline also serves the Gambier Islands, Austral Islands and Marquesas Islands. Air Tahiti operates a frequent service between Tahiti and Moorea.

● **Sea:** Daily boats go between Papeete and Moorea and a twice-weekly car ferry serves Papeete, Huahine, Raiatea and Bora Bora. The Austral Islands can be reached on the *Tuhaa Pae II* cargo ship and the *Aranui* operates cruises to the Marquesas Islands. Many of the islands are served by copra boats and schooners which will take passengers.

● **Road:** Hiring a car on the main islands of Tahiti, Moorea and Bora Bora is quite easy and a good way to get around. Huahine and Raiatea have only a few hire cars available. Papeete has branches of Hertz, Avis and Budget Rent-A-Car plus local agents Robert, André and Pacificar.

Public transport on each island is by bus ('Le Truck') or taxi. Taxis are expensive, especially between 2300 and 0500 hours. Buses are cheap and entertaining – they have no timetables and operate according to the passengers' needs and the drivers' whims.

MAJOR SIGHTS OF THE ISLANDS

The Society Islands are a part of Eastern Polynesia in the South Pacific Ocean. They are sub-divided into the Windwards, or Iles du Vent (Tahiti, Moorea, etc.), and the Leewards, or Iles Sous Le Vent (Raiatea, Maupiti, Bora Bora, Huahine, etc.). Tahiti is both the largest and best known of the islands. It is an hour-glass shaped land, its shape being dictated by 2 volcanoes joined by a low isthmus which forms the island. Its main attractions for tourists are its BEACHES with their fine brown volcanic sand.

MOOREA, 10 miles north-west of Tahiti, is a much older island with a dramatic curve of peaks – the remnants of an ancient volcano. Fine white beaches are found on the north-west tip of Moorea, an area of concentrated tourism.

Further north is RAIATEA, the second largest of the islands and the ancient religious, cultural and political centre. This is a lovely island to visit, with UTUROA remaining a traditional old Polynesian town, unspoiled by tourism. The drawback is the lack of places to stay. BORA BORA has more in the way of accommodation and is also a spectacularly beautiful island. An idyllic lagoon is surrounded by a coral reef and many tiny motus (islands), and edged with soft white sands.

Several of the other Society Islands are good to visit for their peaceful tranquillity, calm seas and beautiful beaches. The nearby TUAMOTU ISLANDS are also quite spectacular, Manihi and Rangiroa being among the best.

Papeete

FAAA INTERNATIONAL AIRPORT

The Society Islands' international airport lies 4 miles west of Papeete on the island of Tahiti. It deals with both international and inter-island flights, all departures and arrivals being from the same terminal.

AIRPORT FACILITIES

Information Desk	Open for the arrival of all international flights.
Bank/Currency Exchange	Open for the arrival and departure of all international flights.
Baggage	There are baggage lockers in the terminal and there is also a baggage storage counter open 0700–1700 hours and prior to all international flight departures.
Duty Free Shop	This sells a wide range of duty free goods and accepts major credit cards and currencies.
Toilets	Throughout the terminal and open 24 hours.
Car Rental Desks	Avis and Hertz have desks at the terminal.

AIRPORT INFORMATION

Check-in Times	60 minutes prior to international flight departure time; 30 minutes prior to domestic flight departure time.
Airport Tax	CFP400.
Flight Transfers	Passengers remain in the same terminal. Connection times are a minimum of 45 minutes for international-to-international flights and a minimum of 60 minutes for international-to-domestic flights.
Baggage Fumigation	Passengers arriving from Fiji or Samoa must have their baggage fumigated. This takes about 2 hours.
Airport Flight Enquiries	Telephone Papeete 28081.

CITY LINKS

Coaches provide transport between the airport and Papeete city centre – a 10-minute journey. Two hours before every international flight departure a coach will leave the UTA office on the Quai du Commerce in the city centre. Taxis also operate between city and airport – make sure the taxi you choose has a rate card visible or you may end up being overcharged. 'Le Truck' (Papeete's buses) also have regular services between city and airport.

PAPEETE

Papeete is the capital of French Polynesia and the seat of the central government of the French Establishment of Oceania. It lies on the north-west coast of Tahiti, the largest of the Society Islands. Tahiti was settled by the Polynesians in the 14th century and first visited by Europeans in 1767 when Captain Wallis landed, hoisted the Union Jack and named the island 'King George III'. A year later Bougainville landed and, unaware of Wallis' discovery, raised the French flag over Tahiti. In 1788 HMS *Bounty* visited Tahiti and 3 years later the *Bounty* mutineers were found and captured by the crew of the *Pandora*. Just before the turn of the century the London Missionary Society Christianized the island by helping the Pomare family to power. In 1836 French Catholic missionaries arrived and, with the help of a couple of French gunboats, gained entry to Tahiti. After further struggles Tahiti became a French protectorate in 1840 and Queen Pomare fled to Raiatea. Later in the century Eastern Polynesia became a full French colony, which it remains to this day.

Tahiti's industry includes copra, sugar cane, vanilla and coffee growing plus the increasingly important tourism. French nuclear testing programmes were transferred from Algeria to Polynesia in the early 1960s amidst much controversy. Papeete itself is surprisingly cosmopolitan, with some 35,000 European, Chinese and Tahitian inhabitants. The focal point is the harbour – a busy port and yacht marina. Boulevard Pomare runs along the harbour front and Avenue Bruat, one of the main streets running inland from the harbour, connects the front with one of Papeete's busiest streets, Rue Dumont D'Urville.

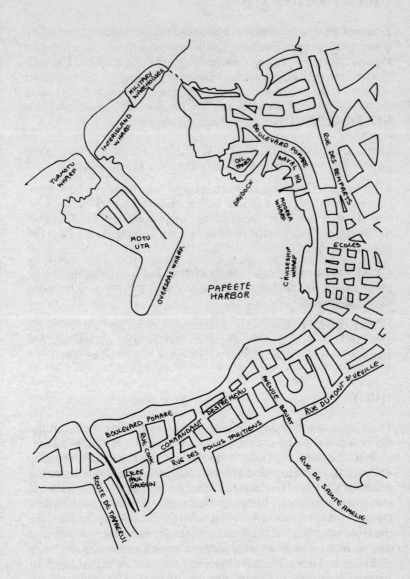

MILITARY WAREHOUSES

INTERISLAND WHARF

TUAMOTU WHARF

MOTU UTA

OVERSEAS WHARF

OIL TANKS

DRYDOCK

BOULEVARD POMARE

NAVAL HQ

NOOREA WHARF

RUE DES REMPARTS

ECOLES

CRUISESHIP WHARF

PAPEETE HARBOR

RUE DUMONT D'URVILLE

BOULEVARD POMARE

RD COOK

COMMANDANT

DESTREMEAU

AVENUE BRUAT

RUE DES POILUS TAHITIENS

LYCEE PAUL GAUGUIN

ROUTE DE TIPAERUI

RUE DE SAINTE AMELIE

TOURIST INFORMATION

Tourist Office – Boulevard Pomare, Papeete. Open 0800–1700 hours daily except Sunday.
Visitors Bureau – Vaima Centre, Papeete. Open 0730–1130 and 1330–1700 hours weekdays and half-day Saturday.

GETTING ABOUT

Tahiti has roughly 125 miles of serviceable roads. The two main forms of transport around the island are 'Le Truck' and taxis.

● **'Le Truck':** These are converted cargo vehicles which now carry passengers all over the island. Eastbound trucks park on the east side of Papeete market, those going along the western road park on the west side. Trucks also go to the airport and the Beach Hotel at Faaa very regularly.

● **Taxi:** Papeete is well endowed with taxis but it is advisable only to use the ones which display rate cards. Fares are doubled between 2200 and 0600 hours.

● **Car Rental:** The cheapest rental cars are at Robert's (tel. 29720) and André's (tel. 29404). International or foreign licences are accepted. Motorcycles and bicycles cannot be rented on Tahiti.

SIGHTS

There are not very many sights to be seen in Papeete itself, but the city makes a good base from which to explore the rest of the island. Within the city the new TERRITORIAL ASSEMBLY (Assemblée Territoriale) is surrounded by beautiful gardens and adjacent to the governor's house. The Catholic cathedral and the old Town Hall are also worth looking at. Just over 2 miles out of town, up the Fautua Gorge road is PIERRE LOTI'S POOL where one can swim and admire the sculptured bust of the famous poet. Down on the waterfront it can be very pleasant to walk along at sunset and watch the boats gliding in and out of the busy harbour. Another attractive aspect of Papeete is the early Sunday morning market. Sights around the island of Tahiti are mentioned in the *Excursions* section.

ACCOMMODATION

Hotels in Tahiti are expensive and many add a surcharge for one-night bookings. Most of the international standard hotels are in or near Papeete or have built resorts around a lagoon or beach on the coast of the island. While most of the accommodation on Tahiti is of the conventional type, many of the outer islands have rooms in over-water bamboo huts with large verandahs. A homestay organization operates throughout the islands whereby you can stay with a Tahitian family. The tourist office has lists of the families in this organization. All these hotels are close to Papeete.

● **First Class:** (Double CFP14,400–19,200)
Tahiti Beachcomber –(tel. 4125110)
Just over 4 miles from Papeete on the west coast of Tahiti, this is an idyllic setting for one of the best hotel resorts in the Society Islands. Accommodation is either in over-water bungalows or suites overlooking the sea between Tahiti and Moorea. Sports facilities are extensive and there is a small white sandy beach for hotel guests.

Tahara'a – PO Box 1015, Papeete (tel. 481122). A hotel built in terrace style on the side of 'One Tree Hill', 5 miles north-east of Papeete. The facilities are excellent and the view across to Moorea is quite breathtaking. A volcanic sand beach is available to hotel guests and is at the bottom of the hill.

Sofitel Maeva Beach Hotel – PO Box 6008, Papeete. Built on the edge of a lagoon 5 miles out of Papeete and quite close to the airport, this is a luxurious hotel with all the amenities one could wish for.

● **Super Club Class:** (Double CFP9600–14,400)
Royal Tahitien – (tel. 428113)
A good hotel 2½ miles east of Papeete on a long volcanic sand beach with tropical gardens surrounding the building.

Hotel Ibis Papeete – (tel. 423277)
Centrally located on the waterfront in Papeete with comfortable rooms and good service.

Hotel de Puunui – (tel. 571920)
Rather a long way round the island from the airport, this hotel is nevertheless a superb place to stay. Perched high on the hillside above the white sand beach and marina, the accommodation is in 2-room, self-contained bungalows.

Princesse Heiata – (tel. 428105)
This is a lively hotel on the east coast of Tahiti, 2½ miles from Papeete and within walking distance of a volcanic sand beach. At weekends the dancing and entertainments go on into the small hours, so this is not for the early-to-bedders.

● **Economy:** (CFP4800–9600)
Kon Tiki – (tel. 437282)
A modern hotel on Papeete harbour front. Each room has a balcony facing the harbour or the mountains.

Mahina Tea – Rue Sainte-Amelie, Papeete. Rooms with private bathroom facilities or studio-style accommodation in central Papeete.

Chez Nicole Sorgniard – A comfortable and friendly hotel along the street from the Mahina Tea. Breakfast is included in the moderate prices.

Chez Fineau-Tautu – 14 Rue du Pont Neuf, Papeete (tel. 37499). Cheap accommodation in an old house of great character with basic kitchen facilities. This is a good place to meet an interesting collection of travellers.

Hotel Tahiti – (tel. 429550)
Slightly more expensive accommodation than the above, but worth the extra money for the lagoon setting and old South Pacific Island atmosphere.

Chez Solange – On the coast south of Punaauia (tel. 82107). One of the few inexpensive places on the beach, this has rooms with cooking facilities and breakfast included in the price.

DINING OUT

The multi-cultural population of Tahiti has caused the emergence of a wide range of cuisines and speciality restaurants. French food is the most popular, with Chinese coming a close second. Tahitian food is actually quite hard to come by in restaurants as it is usually considered the everyday food which is only eaten in Tahitian homes. Many hotels offer regular Tahitian feasts or tamaaraas where the native cuisine can be sampled. For cheap eats the popular place to go is the waterfront where 'Les Roulottes', or lunch wagons, park and serve up steaks, chicken, fish and 'shish-kabobs' (veal) barbecued and surrounded by French fries.

● **First Class:** (CFP6400–9600 for two)
La Petite Auberge – Rue Générale de Gaulle, Papeete. An intimate French restaurant which serves superb food and has an excellent wine list.

Acajou – On the waterfront in Papeete. A continental menu which is very popular with all the tourists, especially those who like seafood. The service is friendly and an evening spent here is usually great fun.

Lagoonarium – In Punaauia, near the Beachcomber and Maeva hotels. Set over the water on the beach, this serves superb seafood and often has a floor show on during the evening.

● **Super Club Class:** (CFP3200–6400 for two)
Mandarin – Rue Fres-de-Ploërmel, Papeete. An elegant restaurant which serves traditional Mandarin cuisine. The first floor of the building offers more comfort and a nice view on to the street below.

Gauguin Restaurant – In Papeari (close to the Paul Gauguin Museum) is this popular continental and Polynesian restaurant where some delicious dishes are served up.

Le Belvedere – In the mountains behind Papeete. An evening here includes the wonderful drive up and down the mountain road from any of Papeete's hotels, good continental cuisine and wine and use of the pool.

• **Economy:** (under CFP3200 for two)
La Pizzeria – Central Papeete (on the waterfront). Pizzas prepared in a brick oven which taste delicious.

Chez Melie – Beside Compel Pacific in Papeete (quite difficult to find but all the locals will know it). A chance to sample some real Tahitian home cooking.

Waikiki Restaurant – Near the market in Papeete. A popular Chinese restaurant.

Big Burger – Just off the Place Tarahoi, Papeete. Not fast food at all but good value, filling food is often on offer on the 'plat du jour'.

NIGHTLIFE

Papeete really livens up after dark as the locals indulge in one of their favourite pastimes – dancing. Discos such as the CLUB 106 on the waterfront or the PIANO BAR and the BOUNTY CLUB on Rue des Ecoles are hives of energy and excitement until quite late. LA CAVE at the Hotel Royal and LE PUB on Avenue Bruat are slightly more relaxing venues. The HOTEL TAHITI has all-night dances every Saturday. For traditional Tahitian shows and dancing the larger hotels are the place to go. Most have performances on several times a week.

EXCURSIONS

Doing a circuit of the island, on the coastal roads, will take you to many of the historical sites worth seeing. On the north coast is the tomb of Pomare V, the last king who died in 1891. This is at ARUE, one of Tahiti's larger towns. At Pointe Venus, on the north-east tip of the island, is the site of a fort built by Captain Cook and nearby is the Museum of Discovery. Going east round the coast from here the ARAHOHO BLOWHOLE is the next interesting sight and the FAARUMAI WATERFALLS are just a bit further on down a road to the right.

Several towns and villages are passed through to reach TARAVAO on the edge of the island's central isthmus. A French fort dating from 1842 is still in use here. On the south coast of the northern bulge of Tahiti lies the PAPEARI DISTRICT where the Gauguin Museum is the main attraction. There are also some Botanical Gardens here and a giant stone-carved 'Tiki' image stands in the museum gardens, steeped in historical myth which is still firmly believed by Tahitians. A track from near here leads inland to Tahiti's only large body of fresh water, LAKE VAIHIRIA.

PAEA, back round the coast towardS Papeete, is the site of the Maraa Fern Grotto and nearby is the Marae de Arahurahu or Temple of Ashes, a mysterious relic of Tahiti's pagan past. Up the coast is the town of PUNAAUIA where the new Museum of Tahiti and the Islands has been established. On the road to this is an old French fort up on the hill to the left which was used for defence against the Tahitians. The remaining route back to Papeete takes you past several beaches and resorts.

3. ASIA

China, People's Republic of

RED TAPE

• **Passport/Visa Requirements:** All visitors to China need a full, valid passport and a visa. Tourist, business or transit visas are obtainable and valid for a negotiable length of stay. Business visas can only be obtained by those who have received an official invitation from a ministry, corporation or official Chinese organization. The vast majority of visits to China are organized through the official state travel agency, Luxingshe, and evidence of payment of funds for the trip must be presented to Luxingshe officials on arrival in China.

CUSTOMS

• **Duty Free:** Visitors staying less than 6 months may bring in 400 cigarettes, 2 bottles of wine or spirits of not more than 0.75 litre each and one camera per family. Visitors staying more than 6 months may import 600 cigarettes, 4 bottles of wine or spirits of not more than 0.75 litre each and one camera per family. Baggage declaration forms, noting all valuables (jewellery, cameras, watches etc.) must be filled out on arrival and a copy kept to give to Customs officials on departure.

HEALTH

Yellow fever vaccination certificates are required by all travellers over one year old arriving from infected or endemic areas. A malaria risk exists throughout the country below 1500m. Resistance to chloroquine has been reported. Water is unsuitable for drinking and precautions are essential. Medical costs are low and the hospital system is excellent but many medicines common to western countries are unavailable here.

CAPITAL – Beijing (Peking).

POPULATION – 1,031,000,000.

LANGUAGE – Modern Standard Chinese is now the official language, based on the dialect of North Chinese. Mandarin is the most widely used of the local dialects and large groups also speak Cantonese, Wu, Fukenese, Amoy, Hsiang, Kam and Hakka. English is spoken by many guides.

CURRENCY

Ren Min Bi (Yuan) = 10 Chiao or 1000 Fen. FEC (Foreign Exchange Certificates) = 100 Fen. Denominations of notes are 1, 2, 5, 10 and 50 RMB and 1, 2, and 5 Chiao. Coins are in denominations of 1, 2, and 5 Fen.

There are two types of currency in China: the traditional Ren Min Bi (RMB) which is often called the 'People's Currency', and the more recently introduced Foreign Exchange Certificates (FEC). FEC is accepted everywhere in China for payment and looks very much like in RMB except that it is illustrated with tourist sites, not energetic workers. In large tourist establishments you get change in FEC, while in the smaller non-tourist spots you get change in RMB.

RMB is not traded outside China and is only available in exchange for traveller's cheques in Hong Kong or China. RMB cannot be used to pay for hotel bills and meals in tourist restaurants, or in Friendship stores; FEC must be used instead. The only bank is the People's Bank, which has branches throughout China. Imported luxury items can only be bought by visitors with Foreign Exchange Certificates – these are obtained in exchange for Western currencies. Major credit cards (Visa, Master Charge, Diner and American Express) are accepted in major towns. Don't try and pay

a hotel bill with a credit card outside of regular business hours – or you'll be told you have to pay cash.
£1 = 5.34 RMB; US$1 = 3.80 RMB.

BANKING HOURS – 0930–1200 and 1400–1700 hours Monday to Friday; 0900–1700 hours Saturday.

POLITICAL SYSTEM – Communist.

RELIGION – Buddhism, Taoism and Confucianism with Muslim and Roman Catholic minorities.

PUBLIC HOLIDAYS

January 1	New Year's Day
February (3 days)	Chinese New Year
March 8	Working Women's Day
May 1	Labour Day
May 4	Youth Day
June 1	Children's Day
July 1	Communist Party Anniversary
August 1	Army Day
October (2 days)	Chinese National Days

CLIMATE – China's enormous size means that different regions have very different weather patterns. The north-east has hot, dry summers and bitterly cold winters. In the central regions hot summers and cold winters both have quite high rainfall levels. The south-east has semi-tropical summers and cool winters. Temperatures in the Beijing area range from 101°F (38°C) to 56°F (13°C) between May and August and from 53°F (12°C) to 5°F (−15°C) between December and February. Most of the rainfall is in July and August and the winter months are dry with low humidity levels.

TIME DIFFERENCE – GMT + 8 hours throughout the country.

COMMUNICATIONS

• **Telephone:** China's internal telephone system is positively anti-quated and can be very frustrating to deal with. There is no IDD service so all international calls must be put through the operator. Public telephones are found in hotels and shops where a telephone unit sign is displayed.

• **Post:** Airmail to western countries takes up to one week. Telex/telegram facilities are available at main and branch Post Offices in larger towns and cities. Hotels may offer incoming telex facilities.

ELECTRICITY – 220v AC.

OFFICE/SHOPPING HOURS – Offices: 0800–1200 and 1400–1800 hours Monday to Saturday. Shops: 0900–1900 hours daily.

• **Best Buys:** Handicraft arts in China are unique for their intricate, traditional styles and quality. Carvings, embroidery, lacquerware, fine ceramics, cloisonné, carpet making, calligraphy, clay sculpture and plaiting are just a few branches of China's art industry. Chinese porcelains enjoy high prestige in world markets, as do their carpets of traditional regional design. Patterns produced in Yixing, Shiwan and Boshan are all world famous.

Chinese silks were world famous as long ago as 100 BC and they remain of luxurious quality to this day. Tea is another good commodity found in China and the variety of flowers and types from different regions is endless. Chinese wines are also very good and popular with western as well as Chinese palates. The most precious fur of China is the pelt of marten, of which violet marten is the highest in quality.

All consumer prices are regulated by the government and bargaining is not allowed except at the free market booths you'll see in market areas and near major tourist sites. Several items, such as cigarettes and silks, may be rationed and are able to be bought only with ration coupons which are not available to tourists. The 'Friendship Stores' for tourists should not have rationing. Antiques over 100 years old are marked by the authorities with a red wax seal and require an export Customs certificate. If you have an interpreter it is worth going to the normal shops which sell souvenirs, clothes, books and posters at low prices. For the best shopping go to local factories, shops and hotels which sell handicrafts. Finally, if you see something you like, buy it; you can't count on seeing it again in the next town.

If you plan to travel on to Taiwan, remember that their Customs will refuse entry of any items bought in the People's Republic of China.

INTERNAL TRAVEL

• **Air:** Long-distance travelling within China is usually by air. The Civil Aviation Administration of China (CAAC) links Beijing to over 80 cities. There is no direct air connection with Seoul or Tapei.

• **Train:** China's railways now reach all the provinces and autonomous regions except Tibet (Xizang). The types of fare are hard-seat (crowded, uncomfortable and cheap), soft-seat (less crowded), hard-sleeper (very comfortable and popular) and soft-sleeper (luxury, but not much cheaper than flying). On all fares tourists will pay 75 per cent more than the locals, but train travel is still cheap by western standards. Another quirk is that children under 1 metre tall travel free!

• **Bus:** China's bus services are fairly good and run between the main cities. Prices compare to those of a hard-seat fare on the train. However the badly maintained roads and overcrowded state of the buses can make journeys quite uncomfortable.

• **Ferry:** China has many rivers and on all the major ones ferries operate. Coastal ferries also operate between Dalien, Tientsin, Qingdao and Shanghai.

MAJOR SIGHTS OF THE COUNTRY

BEIJING (Peking), capital of China, is really one great historical museum with the Forbidden City at its centre. In the north-eastern provinces around the city are several places of interest. BEIDAIHE is a small coastal resort which is Beijing's most popular holiday area. CHENGDE, a former retreat of the Qing Dynasty emperors, is still a popular mountain escape from the summer heat of the lowlands. Further inland the capital of the Inner Mongolia Autonomous Region, and one of China's most colourful cities, is HOHHOT.

In the eastern provinces SHANGHAI is one of the world's largest cities and is more cosmopolitan than Beijing in many ways. SUZHOU has many beautiful gardens and is likened to Heaven's Paradise in an old Chinese proverb. JINAN is a city of springs on the south bank of the legendary HUANGHE River (Yellow River). Many Buddhist relics are to be found here. QINGDAO is a popular coastal resort, surrounded by water on three of its sides and by beautiful countryside on the fourth. On the lower reaches of the CHANGJIANG River (Yangtze River) is NANJING, one of the five ancient Chinese capitals which abounds with historic relics.

Southern China's main city is GUANGZHOU (Canton). This sub-tropical metropolis is the most important foreign trade port in China. It is also an attractive city, with many interesting aspects. GUILIN is the part of China now made so familiar to western eyes by the many paintings and wall-hangings inspired by its massive, steep mountains, meandering rivers and reflective paddy fields.

Spanning the inland reaches of the Yangtze River is the city of WUHAN which, despite being heavily industrial, has some splendid sights. One of these is the intriguing lifestyle which revolves around the bridges. Also in the central provinces is XI'AN, the largest and most populous city in north-west China. This was China's capital for 11 dynasties and has been left with an amazing collection of relics and ruins.

Along the upper reaches of the Yellow River, LANZHOU is an oasis in the old trade route known as the Silk Road. Also on this route is DUNHUANG, an ancient town on the edge of the desert famous for its Magao caves – the oldest Buddhist shrines in China.

Bordering on India is the autonomous region of TIBET. This has only been open to visitors since 1980 and is still an area remote from modern cultures. LHASA is a mountain city (12,000 ft) which is horrendously cold and bleak in the winter but sunny and fascinating in the summer months.

Beijing

CAPITAL INTERNATIONAL AIRPORT

Beijing's international airport lies 18 miles north-east of the city. In design it is modelled on Paris' Orly Airport, with all flight arrivals on the ground floor and departures on the first floor.

AIRPORT FACILITIES

Information Desk	First floor.
Meeting Point	Ground floor.
Snack Bar	First floor.
Restaurant	First floor.
Bank/Currency Exchange	First floor.
Post Office	First floor.
Shops	First floor.
Duty Free Shop	This sells cigarettes, cigars and spirits. Most major convertible currencies are accepted.

AIRPORT INFORMATION

Check-in Times	60 minutes before all flight departure times.
Airport Tax	Each adult must pay 15RMB on departure.
Flight Transfers	Domestic and international arrival/departure areas are in the same building. Flight connection times are 90 minutes for international or domestic flights.
Flight Enquiries	Telephone Beijing 55-3245.

CITY LINKS

• **Bus:** The China Travel Service, Luxingshe, organizes coaches to and from the city for most parties of visitors. CAAC (Civil Aviation Administration of China) also run a bus from the airport to their city office which runs according to flight arrival/departure times.

• **Taxi:** Taxis to the city are reasonably priced by western standards and may be shared with other tourists. They leave from outside the terminal.

BEIJING

Also known as Peking or Pei-ching, this is China's capital city in every sense. From here the huge country and population is controlled by its communist leaders. The area, in Hopei Province to the north-east of the country, has a long history. There is evidence of cave dwellers from nearly half a million years ago and official records of habitation date back to 1000 BC. Known as Ta-Tu, the city first became the capital (of North China) in 1272 during the Yuan Dynasty. When the capital moved to Nanjing Ta-Tu became known as Pei-p'ing (meaning northern peace). Under the third Ming emperor Beijing once more became capital, in AD 1420, and remained so until 1928 when the Nationalist (Kuomintang) government moved the capital back to Nanjing. From 1937 to 1945 Beijing was under Japanese occupation. It became capital of the People's Republic of China which Mao established in 1949 after the overthrow of Chiang Kai-shek, who fled to Taiwan to establish the Republic of China.

Much of Beijing's old architecture was flattened in the 1950s to make room for buildings which would supposedly accommodate the population crisis. Mao's regime suffered in 1966 and the Cultural Revolution accounted for the injury or death of possibly 100 million people. By 1980 China was recovering and Beijing was reconstructed with high-rise buildings to cope with 10 million inhabitants. Limits on both population and industrial construction now keep the growth of Beijing under control.

The capital is at the north edge of the North China Plain with the vast Inner Mongolian Plateau not far to its north-west and the Bohai Sea 62 miles east. It has been symmetrically built as 3 rectangles

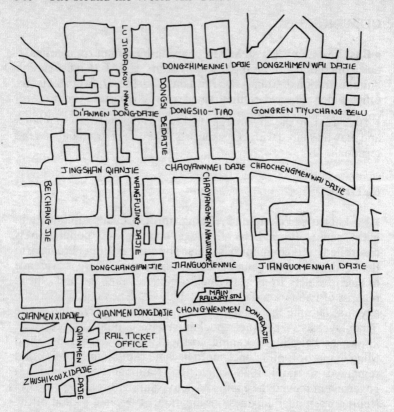

within each other. The old Imperial City lies within the inner city and at its centre the moated 'Forbidden City' contains the Imperial Palaces (now museums). The outer rectangle is the old outer city with markets and old residential areas.

TOURIST INFORMATION

China International Travel Service (CITSJ) – 6 East Chang'an Avenue, Beijing (tel. 55-1031).
International Post Office – 121 Yongan Lu, Beijing.
Overseas Operator – tel. 33-7431.
Medical Services – Capital Hospital, between Wangfujing and Dongdan, Beijing (tel. 55-3731 ext. 274 or 222 for home visits).

GETTING ABOUT

• **Bus:** Beijing's bus system is very hard for a visitor to negotiate – destinations are written in Mandarin, stops are few and far between and the buses are hopelessly crowded. A bus map from the Tourist Office helps though, and the Chinese people are always helpful and courteous. Suburban line buses have numbers in the 300s, trolley buses in the 100s and central buses under 100.

• **Subway:** This offers a limited but much better service. Platform signs are in English and the trains are less crowded. The circle line is useful for sightseeing.

• **Taxi:** These are inexpensive and plentiful (in contrast to Shanghai). Taxis can be hired for the day, in which case the driver expects to be fed as well as paid! Write down your destinations in Mandarin before you set out and show them to the driver (get your hotel staff to help).

• **Bicycle:** Beijing is very flat – ideal for cycling – and as most of its inhabitants cycle to work or to the shops you certainly won't feel out of place. The Chongwenmen intersection has a cycle hire store on its north-east side at number 94. There is also a blue shed opposite the Friendship store which hires out bicycles. Along the streets are cycle parking spots for which there is a nominal fee (do pay, because bicycles are towed away otherwise). Don't forget there are NO signs in English.

• **Car Rental:** This is available but not really advisable within the city, where the traffic is fraught. Scooters are much better for getting around the city and can be hired from the main station.

SIGHTS

Mao's magnificent creation, TIANANMEN SQUARE, occupies the city centre and is surrounded by monuments to Chinese history. The Gate of Heavenly Peace, built in the 15th century, is one of the most spectacular. THE FORBIDDEN CITY is a city within the city, which one enters through the Tiananmen Gate (Gate of Heavenly Peace). This served as the imperial court for the Ming and Qing dynasties and dates back to AD 1406. The palace buildings are now museums and must be among the best preserved relics in China. Open daily from 0830–1630 hours. The HALL OF SUPREME HARMONY (Taihedian) was the throne hall in which the emperor used to hold imperial ceremonies. It is one of the three Great Halls in the centre of the Forbidden City. The other two halls, Zhonghedian (Hall of Middle Harmony) and Baohedian (Hall of Preserving Harmony) were of lesser importance and used for banquets or imperial examinations. Other halls in the palace each had specific functions.

The IMPERIAL GARDEN is a classical Chinese garden at the northern end of the Forbidden City. The WESTERN PALACES were the homes of the empresses and concubines. The buildings have been maintained in a perfect condition and Changchunggong (Palace of Eternal Spring) is decorated with mural scenes from a Ming novel.

In the western suburbs, the SUMMER PALACE grounds are breathtakingly beautiful and the lake and pavilions blend in harmoniously to make the whole area a very peaceful place to visit.

XU BEIHONG MUSEUM is a gallery full of traditional Chinese art – paintings and sketches. Reproductions of the works are on sale. 53 Xinjiejou Beidajie, Xicheng District, open 0900–1700 hours, daily except Monday. The CHINA ART GALLERY is near the Dongsi intersection, and is an exhibition and sale of modern Chinese art works. Open 0900–1700 hours daily except Monday.

The BEIJING NATIONAL LIBRARY has a huge collection of books and periodicals, many in foreign languages and some very rare. It is south of Beihai Park and open 0800–2000 hours daily except Saturday.

North-west of the Forbidden City, BEIHAI PARK was the emperors' playground. A lake takes up half the 170 acres and the rest is landscaped gardens, pavilions and temples. The TEMPLE OF HEAVEN (Tiantan) is one of Beijing's most famous temples, set in a 668-acre parkland. Four gates mark the compass points around it and its colour, shape and sound all have religious significance. Within the temple, the Round Altar and the Hall of Prayer for Good Harvests are of particular interest.

A good guidebook is essential (for sale in hotel shops) because there are virtually NO signs in English.

ACCOMMODATION

The rapid increase in visitors to China in the 1980s has put pressure on the limited hotel capacity of the cities, especially Beijing. Major renovation and reconstruction on existing buildings, plus the building of new hotels, has helped to ease this problem, but accommodation in Beijing can still be hard to come by. Booking in advance is really essential, but if you do arrive without a hotel booking go to one of the Beijing Hotels Introduction Centres adjacent to the main railway station (tel. 55-0402), or the Yongding-men station (tel. 33-4875). The standard of accommodation is also changing – for the better. One cautionary note – the extensive new use of synthetic deep pile carpeting in Beijing's top hotels has created the nasty side-effect of static electricity build-up, so beware of touching the lift buttons!

● **First Class:** (Double 200–300 RMB)
The Great Wall Sheraton Hotel – North Donghuan Road, Beijing (tel. 50-5566). The Sheraton was built here in 1983 and immediately set itself apart as one of the most flamboyantly modern hotels in Beijing. It is luxurious and elegant, with excellent service.

The Beijing – East Chang'an Avenue, Beijing (tel. 55-8331). One of Beijing's oldest hotels and still one of its most prestigious. Everything about it is of high standard and its location is one of the most convenient.

Xiang Shan Hotel – Xiang Shan (Fragrant Hill) Park, Beijing (tel. 28-5491). This stately hotel is noted for its striking architecture and interior decor, and fantastic formal gardens. Unfortunately it is 40 minutes' drive from the city centre, but the countryside around is beautiful.

● **Super Club Class:** (Double 100–200 RMB)
Friendship Hotel – Baishigiao Road, Haidian District (tel. 89-0621). Excellent facilities include an Olympic-size pool, theatre, restaurants and tennis courts. The location is about 25 minutes from the city centre.

Jinglun (Beijing–Toronto Hotel) – Jianguomenwai Dajie, Beijing (tel. 50-2266). A modern, western-style hotel which is very efficiently managed and well located in the city centre.

Minzu (Nationalities Hotel) – Fuxingmen Avenue, Beijing (tel. 66-8541). This centrally positioned hotel has recently re-opened after a complete overhaul. Accommodation is very comfortable and the restaurants serve excellent food.

Huadu Hotel – 8 Xinyuan Xi Road, Beijing (tel. 50-1166). A large, new Chinese hotel about 4 miles north-east of the city centre. A lot of tour groups are booked in here. The accommodation and facilities are of good quality.

• **Economy:** (Double under 100 RMB)
Heping (Peace) Hotel – 4 Jinya Hutong, Dong Cheng District (tel. 55-8841). A clean, modern hotel which is used by many business travellers.

Nationalities Cultural Palace Hotel – Fuxingmen Avenue, Beijing (tel. 66-8761 ext. 230). The rooms are from the 3rd floor up in the Cultural Palace. They are very comfortable and fresh and the location could not be better.

Tiantan Tiyu Binguan (Temple of Heaven Sportsmen's Inn) – 10 Tiyuguan Road, Beijing (tel. 75-2831). A comfortable guest house in Temple of Heaven Park (2 miles from the Forbidden City) which caters well for sports enthusiasts.

Xingiao (New Citizen) Hotel – Dongjiaomin Lane, Beijing (tel. 55-7731). Superb location, low rates and comfortable rooms make this a very popular hotel. Its 2 restaurants are both excellent.

Zhu Yuan (Bamboo Gardens) Hotel – 24 Xiaoshigiao, Jo'ugulou Street, Beijing (tel.44-4661). Small, simply furnished rooms with peaceful bamboo gardens all around the complex of guest houses. They are just north-east of the Drum Tower (Gu Lou).

Guanghua Hotel – 38 Donghuan Bei Road, Beijing (tel. 59-2931). Recently refurbished rooms at very reasonable prices.

DINING OUT

The full range of Chinese cuisine is represented in Beijing's restaurants. Chinese cooking is considered an art and, having been practised for centuries, it is an exquisite and accomplished one. The

8 major provincial cuisines are Shandong, Sichuan, Jiangsu, Zhejiang, Guangdong, Hunan, Fujian and Anhui. The cookery within Beijing (famed for its roast duck) can be further divided into over 20 local branches as can that of Shanghai. Overall, the types of Chinese cuisine are endless, but they all seem to be delicious. Many new restaurants are being opened in Beijing, as the number of tourists increases annually, but there is still a shortage so book early for your evening meal. Most Beijing restaurants have a habit of closing at around 7 p.m. so you may have to get used to an earlier eating time. The hotel restaurants are generally very good, have English speaking staff, and remain open later in the evening.

● **First Class:** (120–200 RMB for two)
Fengzeyuan – West Zhushikou Street (tel. 33-2828). This serves the finest Shandong cuisine in Beijing. Although expensive, it is definitely worth the treat.

Donglaishun Fanzhuang – 16 Jinyu Hutong, Beijing (tel. 55-0069). The Muslim cuisine served here is absolutely delicious, one of the specialities being Mongolian 'hot pot'. It tends to be very hot and spicy so may not suit all palates.

Fang Shan Restaurant – Beihai Park, Beijing (tel. 44-2573). The food here is a re-creation of that eaten at emperors' banquets and is extremely good. It concentrates on the cuisine of northern regions and is very popular, so book a table as soon as you arrive.

● **Super Club Class:** (50–120 RMB for two)
Cuihualou Restaurant – 60 Wangfujing, Beijing (tel. 55-2594). Delicate northern cuisine or Shanghai-style dishes are both offered here. The unusual house dessert is delicious and refreshing to end the meal with.

Hongbing Iou – West Chang'an Avenue, Beijing (tel. 33-0967). Mongolian food is the speciality but the Beijing duck is also very good.

Huaiyang Restaurant – 217 North Xidan Street, Beijing (tel. 66-0521). Authentic Shanghai and Jiangsu cooking with a speciality in seafood dishes.

Kangle – Andingmennei Road, Beijing (tel. 44-3884). Delicious Yunnan food such as steamed chicken in herbs or duck with walnuts.

• **Economy:** (under 50 RMB for two)

Emei Restaurant – Lishi Road and North Yuetan Street intersection (tel. 86-3068). An old Sichuan eating house in which you mix with the locals and the waitresses are very good at sign language and very helpful.

Duyichu Shaomai Restaurant – 36 Qianmen Road, Beijing. Juicy pork dumplings (shaomai) are the best things to order here.

Youyi (Friendship) Restaurant – Haidian Road, Beijing (tel. 89-0621 ext. 3180). Low priced and good western or Chinese food.

Qingfeng Baozi Restaurant – 122 West Chang'an Avenue, Beijing. A good, filling meal can be had for a modest price here. Baoi – steamed, meat stuffed dough – is the house speciality.

NIGHTLIFE

Beijing's night entertainment is limited and stops early (most things have closed or finished by 9.30 p.m.). Cinemas and theatres are numerous and the cultural dance, opera and theatre of the Chinese is very spectacular. The main THEATRES are Ergi (Fuxingmenwai Dajie), Capital (22 Wangfujing), the Tiangiao (near the Temple of Heaven) and Guanghe (the oldest in Beijing, at 24–6 Qianmen Lu). Performances tend to start at 7 p.m.

Acrobatics is another Chinese accomplishment which is well worth seeing. The ACROBAT REHEARSAL HALL on Daohalan has nightly performances.

Discos and nightclubs tend to be located in the hotels, but they are neither the standard nor the late-night affairs that most Westerners are used to. The rooftop cafés at the Beijing and Friendship hotels are the most 'in' places you will find.

EXCURSIONS

Beijing's suburbs and surrounding areas are full of historical sites, old markets and touches of the rural, traditional China which is so different in every aspect to its capital city. The country is so vast that day trips out of Beijing will only give you a very small part of the overall picture, but several places are worth seeing. The GREAT WALL is best seen at BADALING, 44 miles north-west of Beijing. As one of the most incredible creations in the world, it is included in most tours of China along with the Ming tombs. From Badaling the JUYONG PASS is about 6 miles south-east. This is a garrison town from the Mongol period. The most fascinating sight here is of Cloud Terrace, a solid stone and marble archway built in 1345. In the vault of the archway are bas-reliefs of the 4 Celestial Guardians and the walls bear incantations in 6 of China's languages.

The MING TOMBS lie 31 miles to the north-west of Beijing, near CHANGPING. 13 Ming emperors chose to be buried here. Only two of the tombs have been excavated but you can also see replicas of the tomb contents in the museum.

Hong Kong

RED TAPE

● **Passport/Visa Requirements:** A full, valid passport is essential (a British visitor's passport is not acceptable). British citizens are allowed a 6-month no-visa stay, while all the dependent territories of Britain and all the Commonwealth countries can have a 3-month visa-free stay. Citizens of the USA, South America and some Western European countries are allowed a visit of up to 1 month without a visa.

Once travelling within Hong Kong visitors should carry some form of identification, with a photograph, particularly when in the New Territories or on the islands.

CUSTOMS

● **Duty Free:** The duty free allowance is a one litre bottle of alcohol plus 200 cigarettes or 50 cigars or 250g of tobacco. Perfume (60 ml) and toilet water (250 ml) is also allowed.

HEALTH

The requirements at the moment are certificates of vaccination against yellow fever, typhoid, polio and cholera only if you have been in an infected or endemic area within 14 days prior to entering Hong Kong. Do check with your travel agent when you organize your holiday, as these requirements tend to change. Health insurance is strongly recommended. The western medicine practised is first class, as is the dental care. Most hotels will have a list of government-accredited doctors.

CAPITAL – Victoria (the administrative centre, on Hong Kong Island).

POPULATION – 5,397,500 (approximately 1.2 million on Hong Kong Island, 2.5 million on the Kowloon Peninsula and the remainder in the New Territories and outlying islands).

LANGUAGE – Cantonese. In restaurants and shops most people will speak some English and hotel staff are normally fluent. Policemen who speak English wear a red flash under their shoulder number.

CURRENCY – The Hong Kong dollar. One HK$ = 100 cents. Coins are in 10, 20 and 50 cent and 1, 2 and 5 dollar denominations. Notes are in 10, 50, 100, 500 and 1000 dollar denominations. Current exchange rates are £1 = HK$10.9; US$1 = HK$7.81.

EXCHANGE – Foreign currency can be changed in banks, hotels, shops or at money-changers. Use banks preferably as they charge no commission. International credit cards and traveller's cheques are accepted everywhere. There are no restrictions on currency import or export. The rate of exchange is not fixed, so shop around before changing a large amount of money. Although all money-changers claim not to charge commission, they actually do.

BANKING HOURS – 1000–1500 hours, Monday–Friday; 0930–1200 hours Saturday.

POLITICAL SYSTEM – Hong Kong is run by a British Governor with a government-appointed executive council and a partially elected, partially government-appointed legislative council.

RELIGION – Buddhist, with Confucian, Taoist and Christian minorities.

PUBLIC HOLIDAYS

January 1	New Year's Day
February (3 days, according to moon cycle)	Chinese New Year
March/April	Easter: Good Friday to Easter Monday
April 5	Ching Ming Festival
June (1 day)	Dragon Boat Festival or 'Tuen Ng'
June 8–10	Queen's Official Birthday
August	Last Monday (Liberation Day) plus Saturday preceding
September (1 day)	Mid-autumn Festival
October (1 day)	Chung Yeung Festival
December 25, 26	Christmas

CLIMATE – Hong Kong is sub-tropical, being just south of the Tropic of Cancer. Summer temperatures stay in the 30–32°C region with humidities of 90 per cent plus and a rainy season running from June to August. Spring (March to May) and autumn (October to December) are milder and less humid with occasional rain or fog and cooler evenings. Winter can be relatively cold but most days are mild and humidity levels are low. July to September is the typhoon season, but as there is an efficient early warning system, just stay indoors when the signals go up and you should be in no danger. Flights may be delayed or diverted due to typhoons.

TIME DIFFERENCE – GMT + 8 hours.

COMMUNICATIONS

• **Telephone:** An efficient internal telephone system gives free local calls on private phones (some hotels make a small charge). Public phone booths cost HK$1 for local calls. Dial 5 before Hong Kong

Island numbers, 3 before Kowloon ones and 0 before New Territories ones (if outside the particular district).

International Direct Dialling (IDD) is available from most hotels: international access code 106 and country code 852.

Public telex facilities are available at the Cable and Wireless Office on Hong Kong Island (Mercury House, 3 Connaught Road, Central) and at larger hotels.

All emergency calls are free on 999.

• **Post:** Regular postal services get airmail to the UK in 3–5 days. There are plenty of Post Offices open 0800–1800 hours, Monday to Saturday, the main one being in Central, just behind the Connaught Centre and next to the Star Ferry pier. For further postal information call 5-231071 or 3-884111 in office hours.

• **Newspapers:** The *South China Morning Post*, the *Hong Kong Standard*, the *Asian Wall Street Journal* and the *International Herald Tribune* are the English language newspapers printed in Hong Kong (at about HK$2 each).

• **Television:** Two channels broadcast in English (mid-afternoon to late evening) with British, American and Australian items plus some local programmes.

• **Radio:** Radio 3 (567 kHz), Radio 4 (91 and 100 mHz) and Commerical Radio (1044 kHz) broadcast in English. The BBC World Service (96 and 105 mHz FM) is on the air from 0600–0645 hours and from 1500–0230 hours.

ELECTRICITY – 200v; 50 Hz. Most hotels have shaver adaptors but American and Australian plugs need special adaptors.

SHOPPING HOURS – Hong Kong Island (Central) 0900–1800 hours; 1000–2000 hours along Queen's Road.
Hong Kong Island (Causeway Bay) 1000–2200 hours.
Kowloon 1000–2200 hours.
Many shops are open on Sundays.

• **Best Buys:** Shopping must be one of the major attractions of a visit to Hong Kong. The best buys of this amazing shoppers' paradise are almost too numerous to mention, ranging from custom tailoring to cuddly toys! Hong Kong has the advantage of being a duty free port, so the only imported goods to incur duty are alcohol, tobacco, perfumes, cosmetics, cars and some petroleum goods and even on these it is low. The keen competition prompted by a free enterprise trading policy also helps to keep prices low and many bargains are to be found.

The main shopping areas are Central, Causeway Bay, Taikoo Shing and Tsim Sha Tsui. Central is expensive but classy. The Landmark is one of the many sophisticated shopping malls in this area, housing retail outlets of names such as Lanvin, Gucci, Dior and Cacharel, as well as many boutiques. Department stores sell every conceivable product and smaller shops and arcades sell more specialized goods along Queen's Road, Des Veoux Road and their side lanes.

Causeway Bay is best known for its Japanese department stores with their eye-catching displays; it also sports numerous shopping arcades and high fashion boutiques. Taikoo Shing (easily reached by MTR or buses) is where the increasingly popular Cityplaza shopping complex sells its vast range of goods. Noted for its dedication to convenience shopping, both ordinary necessities and special items can be found under one roof. A discount card available at the information centre gets you 10 per cent off in about 40 of the shops (you must show your passport).

Tsim Sha Tsui, in Kowloon, is the largest shopping area, comprising three enormous blocks – Ocean Terminal, Harbour City and Ocean Centre – plus several smaller ones. Ocean Terminal's information desk has a computer programmed to provide lists of shops by type or location with accompanying maps. Ocean Centre is the electronics haven – hi-fi, video and camera equipment abounds and the choice of makes and prices is vast, so do shop around. On the way from Ocean Centre to Harbour City are some of the best Asian craft outlets and the largest sports shop in the territory is in Harbour City itself. Shopping centres like the Silvercord Centre (Canton Road) and New World (joined to the Regent Hotel) offer attractive, up-market environments in which to shop. Their surrounding areas are good for camera, jewellery and antique shops.

As far as where-to-go-for-what is concerned, it is fair to say that all the shopping areas have shops which cater for a wide range of goods but there are certain areas which are best for certain items.

Jewellery and watch shops are concentrated in Tsim Sha Tsui and Central. Jade buyers must go to the Jade Market in Canton Road, Kowloon from about 1000–1200 hours daily. All the major stores will stock the full range of perfumes and cosmetics but for bargains try streets around Carnarvon Road, Kowloon (beware of old stock being sold off). For top of the range furs the Siberian Fur Store and the Alaskan Fur Factory, both in Tsim Sha Tsui, and the Blue Angel at Landmark in Central are some suggestions, but for the best and widest range of furs and leathers, still at reasonable prices, the famous Jindo Fur Salon at 3rd Floor, World Finance Centre, Harbour City, Canton Road, Kowloon, and at Shop B101, 1st Basement, Kowloon Hotel, Tsim Sha Tsui, should be your first stops. They are the world's largest manufacturer of quality furs and their Hong Kong prices (two and three times less than you'll pay in New York or London) are the reasons behind many visitors coming to Hong Kong.

Furs can be tailor-made, as can any garment in Hong Kong. Good tailors do tend to be found in the more central, expensive parts of the city and not, as some visitors fondly imagine, to their cost, in the back streets. There are bound to be exceptions to this rule and you may well be lucky enough to find a top-class tailor at 'back street' prices but if you want to play safe choose one of the many to be found in the main shopping areas. Custom-made suits are still a wonderful Hong Kong souvenir but they are no longer the cheap, made in 24 hours, articles they used to be. Expect to wait quite a few days and attend at least two fittings before you receive the finished garment.

Hong Kong is one of the leading garment exporters in the world and, as such, is a real fashion buyers' haven. There are a host of exclusive stores and boutiques in the Central and Tsim Sha Tsui areas including the Chanel boutique in the Peninsula Hotel and the Dior boutique next to the Landmark. Kowloon accommodates some of Hong Kong's best silk factories which have sales outlets from where you can find some very reasonably priced silk garments. Pick up the *Off Beat Shopping – Garment Factory Outlet* leaflet from any Hong Kong Tourist Authority (HKTA) centre to guide you round the many outlets. Factory outlets were originally created to cope with the leftovers of the export trade but they have now expanded into an industry in their own right. No elaborate displays are evident so you have to be prepared to search through unsorted racks of clothes but it can be well worth it. Hung Hom is the original, and still one of the best factory outlet venues. An uninspiring industrial area, it can be reached by one of the Star Ferries from Central or by taxi from Tsim Sha Tsui. Most of the outlets here are located in or around the Kaiser Estate complex in Man Yue Street (notably 'Four Seasons Garments'). Fashion bargains can also be picked up in Stanley, on the far side of Hong Kong Island, where world-famous brand name garments are sold off at a fraction of their usual cost.

Stanley Market is the best source of casual clothing, and some rattan furniture and pottery. Local furniture shops are abundant in Wanchai (Queen's Road East) and Tsim Sha Tsui (Canton Road) while the Hollywood Road/Lok Ku Road area above Central is noted for its art, craft and antique shops. For camera equipment the Stanley Street stores (Central) are excellent or, if you know what you want, the shops on Sai Yeung Choi Street South (a block away from Nathan Road and along Argyle Street) offer rock bottom prices. Videos and other electronic equipment are on sale in large department stores in all the main areas and these are the best places to shop for them. Craig's Ltd, in Ice House Street, Central (with stores in Ocean Centre, Ocean Terminal and Causeway Bay) is the place to go for tableware alongside Grenley's in Swire House, Hunter's in the Peninsula Hotel and Art Universe in the Royal Garden Hotel. Finally optical goods, from contact lenses to binoculars, are very good value in Hong Kong and local opticians are highly rated.

When doing any form of shopping in Hong Kong the golden rule is to shop around for both price and quality and, where possible, use the HKTA's distinctive red junk logo as a guide – most reputable establishments will display it. The HKTA shopping guide pamphlet is very useful and for those who really don't want to trail around searching for places, or haven't the time to do so, there are agencies which specialize in shopping services. For an hourly fee a guide will take you to where he or she thinks what you are looking for is to be found. Alternatively you can hand in a list of things you want and they will handle everything else, including gift wrapping, posting or shipping. The Hong Kong Shopping Service and Riggs Shoppers are the two companies which deal with this (ask at HKTA centres for details).

INTERNAL TRAVEL

For its small overall area, Hong Kong has a plentiful supply of a wide variety of transport systems – which is just as well considering the phenomenal number of people who use public transport.

• **Buses:** These are abundant and fares range from 70c to HK$3.50 for the longest rides from Hong Kong Island to the New Territories. Most services stop at midnight but the 121 runs through the harbour tunnel every 15 minutes from 0045 to 0500 hours. For a more comfortable but more expensive ride choose a bus numbered 200 or above.

• **Minibuses and Maxicabs:** The former are small red and cream buses which run fairly irregular routes but which you may get on or off virtually anywhere. They can be much faster, although more expensive, than the regular buses, but you have to know your way around pretty well to use them. The latter, maxicabs, are very similar but green and cream, run regular routes and are slightly cheaper.

• **Trams:** These have only one route, which runs from west to east along the north side of Hong Kong Island (with a small detour around Happy Valley for some). Very good value (60c maximum) and picturesque into the bargain, trams can even be hired for an evening, or you can join a tram-tour.

• **Rail:** The Mass Transit Railway (MTR) or subway runs from Central across the harbour to the Kowloon Peninsula. Fares are HK$2.50–4.00 or an MTR Tourist Ticket will give you HK$15 worth of travel – not a money saver but definitely more convenient. Tickets can be bought from the HKTA Information Centre (Kowloon side of the Star Ferry, or 35th floor, Connaught Centre, Central) or from big hotels or MTR station booking offices. Have your passport with you for ticket purchases.

The Kowloon to Canton overland railway (KCR) runs an express train, thrice daily, through to the China border at Lo Wu while also running a local shopping service which is good for sightseeing. Fares are very reasonable and this is another good way of reaching the New Territories.

• **Taxis:** Red with red flags or roof signs, lit up when for hire, taxis are usually in good supply (when it rains they are quickly snapped up!). Those with no roof sign will also have no meter so agree on the fare in advance. Prices start at HK$5 and after 2 km it is 70c for each additional 250m. Baggage incurs an additional charge of HK$1 per item and a journey through the harbour tunnel will add on HK$20. Sometimes they are hard to find round 4 p.m. when the shifts change, and on race days in season.

• **Ferries:** Star Ferry services provide a cheap and memorable journey across the harbour which takes all of 8 minutes. From Central they go to Tsim Sha Tsui or to Hung Hom (where the KCR railway terminus is). The former route is extremely regular (every 3 minutes at peak times) and only stops between 0200 and 0600 hours, when walla wallas (sampans) can be rented to cross the harbour. Other harbour ferries take various interesting, although longer, routes across the harbour.

  Island ferries depart from the Outlying Districts Services Pier (west of the Star Ferry pier) and take routes to all the islands. Journeys are up to an hour each way and cost about HK$14. It is advisable to buy a return ticket, which saves time, and make your excursion during the week – weekends are extremely busy and more expensive. The HKTA Information Centre will have up-to-date ferry schedules.

• **Rickshaws:** This traditional way to travel within the city has now all but died out, but remains as a tourist attraction. Even as such they are more suited to photo sessions than journeys – the rickshaw 'boys' are all getting on in years now! Photo sessions can cost between HK$5 and 20 and most rickshaws are to be found around the Star Ferry pier area.

• **Bicycles:** Cycling is not recommended in Central or Kowloon, the behaviour of Hong Kong traffic making the roads decidedly hazardous, but it is a wonderful way of seeing the more rural areas. Cycles can be hired in Hong Kong and taken through to China if you feel adventurous.

• **Feet:** Hong Kong Central is compact enough to explore on foot and the HKTA publishes several route/sightseeing guides which are freely available.

MAJOR SIGHTS OF THE COLONY

Hong Kong is not merely the land of skyscrapers, bustling streets and international business transactions which its world image shows us. The colony actually comprises 1034 square kilometres of an amazing diversity of rural and urban land. Quite apart from the densely populated areas of Hong Kong Island and Kowloon, the territory includes 235 tranquil and picturesque islands, many largely uninhabited.

HONG KONG ISLAND will no doubt be the first place which you explore. The north side of the island contains the central hub of the city, of which more will be said in the *City* section. On the other side of the island the fishing town of STANLEY has several good beaches plus a wonderful local market which sells a huge variety of local wares. To the west of this is OCEAN PARK, one of the largest marine parks in the world. ABERDEEN HARBOUR is well worth a visit if only to sample the sumptuous array of fresh seafoods while relaxing on one of the floating restaurants. A large marina here houses everything from junks to exclusive pleasure cruisers and forms a base for the water-sport enthusiasts. REPULSE BAY is a breathtakingly beautiful spot with the vivid blue South China Sea breaking on to a long stretch of golden sands. For a truly remarkable panoramic view of Hong Kong and its harbour, Kowloon and the outlying islands, the Peak Tram journey up to VICTORIA PEAK (400m) is a must.

By taking the unforgettable ferry ride across the Fragrant Harbour you will reach the mainland at KOWLOON. Here the urban area of TSIM SHA TSUI is a mass of first-class hotels, nightclubs, shops and offices. Two places to note here are the MUSEUM OF HISTORY and the SPACE MUSEUM – a prominent, egg-shaped structure on the waterfront which boasts one of the world's best planetariums. In north Kowloon, at LAI CHI KOK, is a modern re-creation of a Sung Dynasty (AD 960–1279) village which you can tour round. Another interesting village is LEI YUE MUN, a thriving fishing community with some of its buildings resting on stilts in the water.

Going further north one reaches the rural areas of the NEW TERRITORIES and, eventually, the Chinese border. The variety of Asian and Chinese origins of the rural population makes for an interesting diversity of customs and traditions within a relatively small area. There are many sights to be seen in the New Territories, not least of which is the overall view of traditional, rural Chinese life. A few notable places include the town of YUEN LONG and the nearby walled village of KAM TIN, said to date back to the 16th century. Buses will take you through the market town of TAIPO, the Chinese University and SHATIN, where you can climb to the Temple of 10,000 Buddhas, the Shatin Pagoda or the Amah Rock (all rather arduous climbs!). Also at Shatin is one of the finest racecourses in the world: go for an evening visit if the racing season is in progress.

The best 'get-away-from-it-all' part of the mainland is probably the SAI KUNG PENINSULA. Sai Kung is a fishing port from where one can take a junk to ROCKY HARBOUR or HIGH ISLAND, or walk up into the wooded hills and look down on coastal islands. Many of the coastal villages are only accessible by sea, and junks or boats can be taken from Tai Po Kau in Tolo Harbour. At CASTLE PEAK (on the way to Un Long) and TSUEN WAN there are some noteworthy temples to be seen, while LAU FAU SHAN on Deep Bay is an oyster lover's haven.

Of the ISLANDS, LANTAU is the largest yet one of the most sparsely populated, with some almost untouched areas. SILVERMINE BAY (Mui Wo) is the main town and ferry arrival point on the east coast. CHUNG HAU beach is a beautiful spot and the local Trappist Monastery makes an interesting visit. On the NGONG PING PLATEAU (750m) are some tea gardens where many varieties of tea are grown and bungalows can be rented, with horse-riding available. Also on the island is a residential and resort project called SEA RANCH which offers sports facilities, restaurants, conference facilities, etc. The many other islands are all worth visiting for their own reasons. This is obviously impossible within one holiday but a few of the more interesting islands include CHEUNG CHAU, PENG CHAU, LAMMA and DOUBLE HAVEN.

The colony of Hong Kong is small and compact enough to allow one to sample its great diversity of sights, lifestyles and atmospheres in a relatively short space of time. These are just a few suggestions of what to see and do; the choice is endless.

Hong Kong

KAI TAK AIRPORT

Hong Kong's international airport, known as Kai Tak, is both one of the busiest and one of the most efficiently run in the world. Its convenient site, 5 miles north-east of Kowloon, is advantageous to business travellers or holidaymakers on short stopovers, with Hong Kong Central only a 15-minute drive away. The Passenger Terminal Building operates on a two-level system, with arriving passengers using the ground floor and those departing using the first floor.

AIRPORT FACILITIES

• **Arrivals Floor:** The Arrivals Hall is well signposted for Immigration, the Baggage Claim area and Customs. Baggage carousels are marked with arriving flight numbers and the Baggage Enquiry Counter is next to the carousels. A supply of free baggage trolleys can be found along the right-hand wall of the Arrivals Hall. Public telephones, a 'messages' desk and toilets are also in the Arrivals Hall. Through Customs is the 'buffer' area, which is also well signposted. The Information Desk lies to your left, just beyond the left exits. Along the centre of the buffer area are desks for taxi and car hire, the Tourist Association, Left Baggage, Hotel Transport, a travel agency and a currency exchange. Rates of exchange will be poor here so try to have some Hong Kong dollars with you which will tide you over until you reach the city. There is also a Hong Kong Hotel Association desk where you should check for room availability if you have not already made accommodation arrangements. Each exit leads to different facilities. To the left is the new Airport Transportation Terminus, plus the public greeting area and a snack bar. Straight ahead is the private or hotel transport area where taxis, hire cars or hotel limousines will be waiting. To the right is the group exit, for the congregation and transportation of parties of travellers.

• **Departures Floor:** Your transport to the airport (taxi, coach or whatever) will drop you outside the check-in area, from where porters will trolley luggage to any of the 4 'islands' of check-in counters for a small fee. The counters are clearly divided according to airline company. Facilities in the check-in area are listed below:

International Call Office	To the left of the area, open 0830–2200 hours daily.
Post Office	To the right of the departure gates, open 0800–2000 hours daily.
Currency Exchange	Several desks, situated around the check-in counters and in the shopping mall to their right. Open 0700–midnight daily.
Coffee Shop/Bar and Restaurant	To the right of the Post Office, open 0700–midnight daily.
Duty Free Shops	A shopping mall lies to the right of the check-in counters and more shops can be found to the left of the departure gates. On purchasing duty free items you will be given a receipt and can pick up your goods in the Departures Hall (once through Immigration).

A flight insurance sales desk, a nursery and a chapel are other facilities available in the check-in area. Steps to the left, beyond the check-in counters, lead up to a rooftop viewing gallery.

Once through to the restricted area of the Departures Hall facilities include shops, restaurants, a currency exchange, a coffee shop and a bar.

AIRPORT INFORMATION

Check-in Time	90 minutes prior to the departure of your flight.
Airport Tax	Adults HK$120; children (2–12 years) HK$60. This is collected by personnel at the check-in counters.

Departure Times	Visual display boards give all the boarding and departure times of the flights but there are no verbal announcements so keep an eye on your watch and the boards.
Duty Free Shopping	Kai Tak Airport cannot boast the best of duty free bargains as it is actually quite expensive. Alcohol, cigarettes, perfumes, cosmetics, leather accessories, jewellery, toys and gift items are the main things sold here. Most shops will take convertible currencies, traveller's cheques and any of the well-known credit cards.
Transferring Flights	Your baggage will have been checked through to your final destination at the beginning of your travels, unless you requested otherwise. Once in Hong Kong report to the Transfer Desk (which will be signposted in the Arrivals Hall) to pick up your new boarding pass. From here you can proceed to the Departures Hall for your ongoing flight.
Security Checks	On departure all luggage is either X-rayed or hand searched. The X-ray machines here will wipe out camera film so be sure to keep your films with you and not in your main luggage.

AIRPORT HOTEL – The Regal Meridian Airport Hotel (Super Club category), San Po Road, Kowloon City, Kowloon (tel. 3-7180333). Being only a short walk from the Arrivals Hall of the airport, this is a convenient hotel for those on a very short visit or for those with an early or late flight. Extensive facilities include 'day-use' guest rooms, a health centre and sauna, conference rooms, restaurants and bars.

CITY LINKS

Kai Tak Airport is 4 miles north-east of Kowloon with its runway jutting out into the harbour. Most first-class hotels provide transport (though often not free), but if this is not available there are various ways of travelling between airport and city:

● **Taxi:** Fares will be about HK$20 plus baggage charges to the Star Ferry, or about HK$40 to Hong Kong Island. Fares to hotels and many places in the Tsim Sha Tsui area are listed by the taxi pick-up point in the airport. A HK$20 toll for the harbour tunnel is levied.

● **Airport Buses:** These link the airport with most major hotels. Number 201 runs from the airport to the bus park at Kowloon Star Ferry Terminal while number 200 goes on through the tunnel to Hong Kong Central. Buses leave the terminal every 15–20 minutes from 0730–2315 hours. The cost is around HK$2.50 to Kowloon and HK$4 to Hong Kong and en route there is a helpful recorded announcement indicating when you reach various hotels. Allow plenty of time, as numerous stops are made.

● **Airport Hire Car Service:** This can be arranged at the car hire counter in the buffer area of the Arrivals Floor.

● **Public Bus Services:** Numbers 5 and 9 run from outside the airport to the Kowloon Star Ferry. The 5 goes via Chatham Street and the 9 goes along Nathan Road – where most of the hotels are situated.

HONG KONG

On any Round the World trip add Hong Kong to your itinerary. Apart from the fact that it is a natural stopping-off location on most routings, it is also one of the most exciting and interesting places in the world. Strategically positioned on the south-east side of China, the islands and territories of Hong Kong have had an eventful history. Europeans have traded with China for over 400 years but, as the balance of trade turned more and more in favour of China, the Europeans (especially the British) started to compensate by pumping China with opium. Beginning to tire of what they termed 'foreign mud', the Chinese attempted to keep the British at bay (literally!). War ensued and at the end of the First Opium War

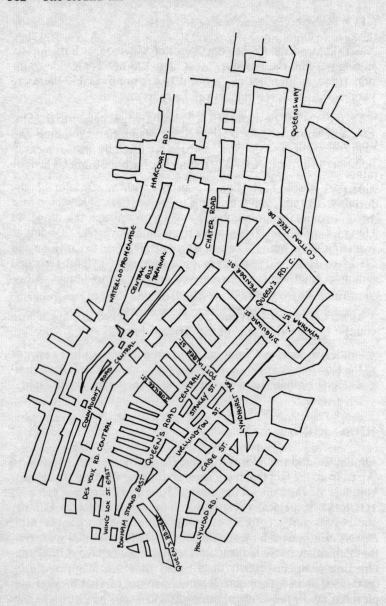

(1842) Hong Kong Island was ceded to Britain. In 1860, following the Second Opium War, Kowloon Peninsula was added to Britain's possessions and finally, in 1898, a 99-year lease was granted on the New Territories. Apart from the Japanese occupation during World War II, Hong Kong has remained British ever since. December 1984 saw China and Britain sign an agreement on the 'handing back' of Hong Kong in 1997 but subsequent negotiations continue to keep this thriving capitalistic port in existence on the edge of the largest Communist country on earth.

A capitalist's haven, with a maximum tax rate of 18 per cent and rather loose controls into the bargain, Hong Kong oozes energy in a wide variety of industries. Since the Shanghai immigrants arrived during World War II the textile and clothing industry has leapt to the fore, now accounting for over half Hong Kong's exports. Electronics, plastics and some heavy industries such as ship building and iron and steel manufacture, plus the prolific banking and insurance industries of Hong Kong Central, make up the other main activities of the colony. Agricultural land is scarce, but most plentiful in the New Territories and reclamation of land from the sea has long been important in the colony's history, as its population boomed.

Geographically the 'city' of Hong Kong (or Victoria, as the administrative centre is officially called) is on the north side of Hong Kong Island. It is separated from the mainland, on which lies Kowloon, by the Fragrant Harbour (so named because of the smells which drifted across from an incense factory on the south side of the island). Des Voeux Road is the main street of the city with Chinatown to the west and Wanchai, then Causeway Bay to the east. Victoria Peak is inland, to the south of Central, while running parallel and to the north of Des Voeux Road is the harbour.

TOURIST INFORMATION

Hong Kong Tourist Association (HKTA) – The headquarters are on the 35th floor of the Connaught Centre, Central (tel. 5-244191). Opening hours are 0800–1800 hours Monday to Friday and 0800–1300 hours Saturday. The Kowloon office (near the Star Ferry pier) has the same opening hours plus 0800–1300 hours on Sunday and 0800–1800 hours on public holidays. A new office is situated in

Tsim Sha Tsui East Side at the Empire Centre, 68 Mondy Road, open 0900–1800 hours daily. There are also HKTA desks at the airport and in the GPO (open 0800–2230 hours daily). The HKTA service is truly excellent – one of the world's best – so do use it while here.

General Post Office – In Central it is just behind the Connaught Centre, next to the Star Ferry pier. In Kowloon it is at 405 Nathan Road (between the Jordan and Yau Ma Tei MTR stations). Both open from 0800–1800 hours Monday to Saturday. All Post Offices close on Sundays and public holidays.

Medical Help – Queen Mary Hospital, Pokfulam Road, Hong Kong Island (tel. 5-8192111).

Princess Margaret Hospital, Lai King Hill Road, Laichikok (tel. 3-742111).

GETTING ABOUT

Due to the small overall size of the colony, city and 'country' transport is almost synonymous therefore all modes of city transport have been discussed in the *Internal Travel* section on page 354. The best introduction to the city is a tram ride along Des Voeux Road and a ferry ride across the harbour. Taxis, buses, minibuses, maxicabs and the subway are all efficient modes of travel but for a real city centre exploration walking is the best method.

SIGHTS

Known as THE LANES, Li Yuen Street West and Li Yuen Street East run from Queen's Road Central down to Des Voeux Road Central. Here just about every kind of garment or accessory can be bought at low and bargainable prices. In the same area, Pottinger Street specializes in haberdashery of every conceivable form, from bows to braces!

LADDER STREET is a steep street of stone steps, where one can find Chinese antiques and knick-knacks. Antiques are also in abundance in Hollywood Road and Lok Ku Road, where porcelain, silver, rosewood and blackwood furniture, paintings and Ching Dynasty clothes are among the finds.

At the junction of Ladder Street and Hollywood Road is the MAN MO TEMPLE, the oldest temple in Hong Kong, dating back to 1847.

AW BOON HAW GARDENS – also known as the Tiger Balm Gardens, because Aw Boon Haw invented the famous ointment – are 2 hectares worth of plaster statues which depict scenes of Chinese mythology. Admission is free, the gardens are open from 0900–1600 hours daily and a number 11 bus will get you there (just off Tai Hang Road) from Central. There is also a jade collection here which you can arrange to see by telephoning 5-616211 before your visit.

Steeply rising to 400m, VICTORIA PEAK gives a superb view and is the site of several places of interest. Peak Tower is a modern, elliptically structured building which houses a coffee shop, restaurant, supermarket and other shops. Peak Tower Village has traditional Chinese arts and crafts on sale. The tram stops at this area but a walk up Mount Austin Road to the gardens of Mountain Lodge (which used to be the Governor's summer residence but was demolished in 1946) is well worth it. Harlech and Lugard Roads encircle the mountain and make a scenic walk of about 40 minutes.

The ZOOLOGICAL AND BOTANICAL GARDENS are on Robinson Road, just behind the Hilton Hotel and above Government House. Birds are a speciality, with 300 species represented. The best time to visit is between 0600 and 0800 hours, when the locals will be there warming up for the day with their traditional tai chi chuan or shadow boxing.

WANCHAI is the nightclub and topless-bar venue which has been on the decline since the end of the Vietnam era. Many of the old haunts are being replaced by uninspiring office blocks in this area, which lies to the east of Central. Continue east from Wanchai and you will enter CAUSEWAY BAY, a concentration of hotels, restaurants, department stores and small shops. The Noon Day Gun, which is fired every day at noon and on New Year's Eve at midnight, is by the waterfront across from the Excelsior Hotel (New Hoi Pong Road). YAN YUEN SHEK – translated as Lover's Rock – is a 9m tall rock which leans over a 30m drop down to Wanchai. Its legend gives it magical properties to bestow love and marriage on those who worship there. On the 6th, 16th and 26th days of the lunar cycle fortune-tellers, soothsayers and incense sellers appear on Bowen Road to sell their wares and wisdoms to the lovesick worshippers.

Three notable museums are the HONG KONG MUSEUM OF ART in the City Hall (closed on Thursdays), the FLAGSTAFF HOUSE MUSEUM

OF TEA WARE on Cotton Tree Drive (closed on Wednesdays) and the FUNG PING SHAN MUSEUM in Hong Kong University (closed on Sundays). All have free entry.

Every evening the MACAU FERRY TERMINAL car park transforms into an open-air market of stalls and vendors, the Poor Man's Nightclub. A great place to get really cheap clothes and electronic goods, it is also full of action, noise, and good, cheap food such as cockles, prawns and noodle soup.

ACCOMMODATION

Hong Kong has an excellent selection of hotels but visitors are advised to book well in advance of their intended stay. During the peak periods of April/May and October/November this is especially important. Prices here are higher than in most other Asian cities.

● **First Class:** (Double HK$850–1300)
The Hilton – 2A Queen's Road, Central (tel. 5-233111). In the heart of Central with truly first-class facilities including a health club, outdoor pool and many fine bars and restaurants. This is one of the colony's most comfortable hotels, with very high standards of service. Lots of nice 'extra' little touches, including the *Wan Fu* brigantine which sails twice daily for Hilton guests. Good business facilities.

The Mandarin – 5 Connaught Road, Central (tel. 5-220111). Excellent location with a lovely view over the harbour. Luxurious accommodation and impeccable service put this hotel among the top ten in the world. Facilities for business executives are particularly noteworthy.

The Peninsula – Salisbury Road, Kowloon (tel. 3-666251). All the luxury facilities that one would expect from this world-famous name. A delight to stay in, with every detail attended to. The Gaddi Restaurant (French cuisine) is particularly good.

● **Super Club Class:** (Double HK$700–1000)
Furama Inter-Continental – 1 Connaught Road, Central (tel. 5-255111). A top-class harbour-front hotel with all the expected facilities, notably the excellent La Ronda revolving restaurant. For

its standard this is a very well priced hotel and one of Hong Kong's best.

Excelsior – New Hoi Pong Road, Causeway Bay (tel. 5-767365). Overlooking the harbour, with very comfortable accommodation and facilities which include such things as a theatre and a videodata service in rooms.

Hyatt Regency – 67 Nathan Road, Kowloon (tel. 3-662321). Central location and very good accommodation. A rooftop nightclub provides entertainment.

Shangri-La – 64 Mody Road, Tsim Sha Tsui, Kowloon (tel. 3-7212111). On the Kowloon waterfront, near the business, shopping and entertainment centre of Kowloon, and 15 minutes from the airport. A very comfortable hotel with 8 restaurants, a health club, indoor pool and extensive executive facilities.

● **Economy:** (Double HK$100–400)
Marco Polo – Harbour City, Canton Road, Kowloon (tel. 3-7215111). Well located and reasonably priced for its quality.

New World – New World Centre, 22 Salisbury Road, Kowloon (tel. 3-694111). On the waterfront near the Space Museum. Provides a babysitting facility.

Park – 61–5 Chatham Road, Kowloon (tel. 3-661371). In the centre of Tsim Sha Tsui, so not quite so close to the harbour but very close to the shops. Good facilities.

Ambassador – 4 Middle Road, Kowloon (tel. 3-666321). Traditional-style hotel in a convenient spot for both shops and harbour.

First Hotel – 206 Portland Street, Kowloon (tel. 3-3052117). Good base for economy travellers or families. Well priced.

YMCA – Salisbury Road, Kowloon (tel. 3-692211). Lots of facilities and low prices.

YWCA – Headquarter Hostel, 1 Macdonnell Road, Hong Kong Island (tel. 5-223101). Well placed and comfortable.

Caritas Bianchi Lodge – 4 Cliff Road, Yau Ma Tei, Kowloon (tel. 3-881111). Good basic accommodation which is well sited and low priced.

DINING OUT

The huge number of restaurants in Hong Kong is matched by the Chinese people's enthusiasm for eating out. Breakfast, lunch and dinner times see most of the restaurants absolutely packed out with gourmets (or gourmands!) and a quiet venue is hard to come by. As far as choice goes the list is endless. Quite apart from about six varieties of Chinese cuisine, one can choose to eat the food of Malaysia, Thailand, Korea, Israel, Japan, Vietnam, Lebanon, France or the inevitable America (Big Macs are popular here too) to name but a few. Being essentially Cantonese, Hong Kong boasts the finest Cantonese restaurants in the world, which really are worth a visit. At the other end of the scale are the dai pai dong, or street restaurants, where the food is usually good and cheap even if the surroundings lack elegance. The Poor Man's Nightclub or the Yau Ma Tei Night Market are recommendable for their street restaurants.

Dim sum dishes are a tradition of the Cantonese which may be eaten at any time between early morning and mid-afternoon. Part of the yum cha, or 'drink tea' meals, these tasty morsels are offered around by waitresses with trolleys or trays laden with a vast choice of the dim sum. Most are a mixture of meat, seafood and vegetables wrapped in thin pastry or dough. Tea is drunk with this meal: heung pin is a light, fragrant tea while bo lay is stronger and black. Some dim sum places to note are the Luk Yu Teahouse, 26 Stanley Street, Central; the Blue Heaven, 38 Queen's Road, Central; the Gold Wheel, 172 Nathan Road, Kowloon and the Oceania, Shop 281, Ocean Terminal, Kowloon.

• **First Class:** (HK$180–300 for two)
Rainbow Room – Top Floor, Lee Gardens Hotel, Hysan Avenue, Causeway Bay (tel. 5-767211). As popular with the locals as with this impressive hotel's guests, the cuisine is of an exceptionally high standard (Cantonese).

Fook Lam Moon (Kowloon) Restaurant – 31 Mody Road, Shop A, Tsim Sha Tsui, Kowloon (tel. 3-688755). Wonderful Cantonese food. So good you should reserve well ahead.

Sun Tung Lok Shark's Fin Restaurant – G/F, Harbour City, Phase III, Tsim Sha Tsui, Kowloon (tel. 3-7220288). A truly first-class Chinese restaurant. For the discerning gourmet, the delicate flavours of its dishes will come as a delight. Again Cantonese, as are most top-grade restaurants in the colony.

● **Super Club Class:** (HK$80–120 for two)
The Jumbo Floating Restaurant – Aberdeen Harbour (tel. 5-539111). An experience not to be missed when in Hong Kong. The atmosphere is certainly what makes this restaurant different and the fresh seafood is a speciality. With its unique setting and opulent Oriental decor, it is a great place for a 'farewell to Hong Kong' dinner.

Pep 'n' Chilli – 12–22 Blue Pool Road, Shop F, G/F, Happy Valley (tel. 5-768046). Szechuan cuisine at its finest.

Peking Garden Restaurant – 3/F, Star House, Tsim Sha Tsui (tel. 3-698211). Good Peking cuisine in an ever-popular restaurant.

● **Economy:** (HK$40–90)
Yung Kee Restaurant – 36–40 Wellington Street, Central (tel. 5-232343). Try the roast goose here for a culinary treat.

Riverside Restaurant – Food Street, Causeway Bay (tel. 5-779733). Very good Cantonese food at comparatively low prices.

Wishful Cottage Vegetarian Restaurant – 336 Lockhart Road, G/F, Wanchai (tel. 5-734194). Good, imaginative veggie meals at reasonable cost.

Ziyang Szechuan Restaurant – 45D Chatham Road, Tsim Sha Tsui (tel. 3-687177). For a real splurge, treat yourself here. The food is exceptionally good and prices lower than in other Szechuan restaurants.

If you are on a really tight budget make use of the many un-named little eating stalls and restaurants in the alleys off the main streets. These occur all over Hong Kong and for around HK$20 you can eat like a king with the locals. Don't expect menus or plush surroundings, but you can expect some hitherto untasted flavours, the vast majority of which will come as a pleasant surprise.

NIGHTLIFE

Hong Kong's nightlife scene includes everything from romantic cruises around the harbour to 'Canto-pop' discos in the dazzling downtown. On all its forms of entertainment the city imposes an Oriental quality which adds zest and sparkle. Much of the nightlife is centred around the hotels where nightclubs, lounges and restaurants will have live bands playing classical, blues, jazz or whatever. Chinese theatre-restaurants stage traditional shows while feeding you very well. British, Australian or Japanese-style pubs and bars seem to be popular and, of course, the infamous topless or 'girlie' bars are still there for those who don't mind paying more for their beer. Alternatively, cinemas, concert halls or cruise boats provide a good evening's entertainment. For up-to-date information read the daily or weekly press available at HKTA information centres. The vibrancy of this exciting city makes just walking through the neon-lit streets, with shops open until 10 or 11 p.m., a good way to see 'night life' completely free of charge.

Recommended NIGHTCLUBS are The Eagle's Nest at the Hilton Hotel, 2 Queen's Road, Central (tel. 5-233111). Dance through to the early hours while overlooking Hong Kong from this rooftop nightclub; the Ocean Palace Restaurant and Nightclub at 4/F Ocean Centre, 5 Canton Road, Kowloon (tel. 3-677111). An experience not to be missed while in Hong Kong. Music, dinner and a most impressive venue; and the Golden Crown Restaurant and Nightclub, 66–70 Nathan Road, Tsim Sha Tsui (tel. 3-666291). A good place to combine supper with dancing.

EXCURSIONS

With so much to see and do in this diverse area, an organized tour can be an effective way of using your time. Of the many on offer there is almost bound to be one which suits you. HKTA-run tours are better value and better organized, by a long way, than those run by private operators. Hotel tour desks or the HKTA will have all the details but here is an idea of what is on offer.

HONG KONG ISLAND TOUR is an HKTA-run tour which lasts 3–4 hours and includes visits to the Tiger Balm Gardens, Repulse Bay, Aberdeen, Wanchai, Causeway Bay, Pokfulam (University of

Hong Kong site), Western District and Victoria Peak. Routes vary and optional visits to Stanley, Shek O and the Man Mo Temple may be included.

KOWLOON AND THE NEW TERRITORIES is an HKTA-run tour now called 'The Land Between' which runs Monday to Friday. In 3–4 hours one can see a completely different side of Hong Kong – the urban, industrial and rural areas of the mainland. Resettlement estates, new towns, Chinese farms and villages are passed through to reach the border at Lok Ma Chau and look across to China. This is a very interesting and well run tour about which the HKTA has written a separate pamphlet.

The HKTA runs a LANTAU ISLETS 'Hopping' Tour which, in about 8½ hours, visits Peng Chau, Lantau and Cheung Chau islands. Lunch and drinks are provided on the ferry. Alternatively, go via Green Island and Peng Chau to Lantau where a vegetarian or European meal will be served. This tour lasts approximately 6½ hours and includes a bus journey round Lantau's sites.

Morning or afternoon trips are organized to OCEAN PARK, an oceanarium on the south side of Hong Kong Island. Once there cable car and escalator-runs show off the sites admirably while dolphins and whales go through their paces. Public transport will get you there if you don't want to be tied to a tour.

A 2–3 hour trip is run daily by the HKTA to the SUNG DYNASTY VILLAGE. Although rather overdone, this reproduction of an AD 960–1279 village is well worth a visit (and wonderful for the photo album!). A temple, a wax museum, herbalist shops and a tea pavilion are among the things to see, and a meal is served on this excursion.

FRAGRANT HARBOUR TRIPS: there is a plethora of these and how long and at what time of day you make your trip is really up to you, the choice is so immense. Again, the HKTA-run tours are the best value but check that your hotel doesn't lay on a complimentary trip round the harbour (as does the Hilton) before you book anything else. A night trip is very spectacular, with the millions of city lights reflected on the water.

Usually incorporating both harbour and city, NIGHT TOURS can be very good value and exciting, or can be a rip-off (as is the 'Invitation' nightly tram tour). By sticking to the HKTA-run or approved tours you should be all right.

THE TRAM TOUR: for those who dislike organized tours this is a wonderful (and cheap) way to see Hong Kong. The HKTA factsheet will explain both the history of the tram and the various places it passes through.

Tours OVER THE BORDER vary from a one-day trip to nearby Canton to up to 18 days visiting various Chinese sights and cities. For these trips it does seem best to take an organized group tour, even if you are normally a go-it-alone type. The well known travel agencies or companies are the best ones to book through. Thomas Cook (9th floor, Bank of America Tower, Harcourt Road, tel. 5-235151), Silkway Travel (Suite 1227A, Star House, Tsim Sha Tsui, tel. 3-7243322) and Swire Travel's China Division (Room 511, Silvercord Tower 2, 30 Canton Road, Tsim Sha Tsui, tel. 3-7212033) are some of the reputable agencies. The two Chinese state-owned travel agencies are also very good: China Travel Service (77 Queen's Road, Central, tel. 5-259121) and China International Travel Service (75 Mody Road, Tsim Sha Tsui East, tel. 3-7215317). Before buying your ticket, check the extent to which meals and accommodation are included in the price as this can vary considerably. Those who want to go independently must obtain a visa for China, either through a travel agent or from the China Travel Service Office, 77 Queen's Road, Central.

MACAU, the Portuguese territory some 40 miles south-west of Hong Kong across the mouth of the Pearl River, may be visited as a day trip or for an overnight stay. Either way, the HKTA will have information on recommended tours, or further information can be obtained from Macau Tourist Information Bureau, 1729 Star House, Kowloon, tel. 3-677747.

Despite the many organized tours on offer, do-it-yourself excursions are becoming increasingly popular and much simpler to arrange as public transportation systems within Hong Kong improve. The HKTA office is always happy to give lots of advice and information.

India

RED TAPE

• **Passport/Visa Requirements:** In addition to a full, valid passport, visas are required by all except nationals of Australia, Bulgaria, Canada, Denmark, Iceland, Finland, Norway, Sweden, and Yugoslavia, for stays not exceeding 90 days. All citizens of Commonwealth countries, including Great Britain, now require visas. There are three types of visa: tourist, business and transit.

CUSTOMS

• **Duty Free:** The following goods may be brought into India without incurring Customs duty: 200 cigarettes or 50 cigars or 250 grammes of tobacco; 1 bottle (0.95 litre) alcoholic beverage; 2 oz perfume and 0.25 litre of toilet water; two still cameras with 25 rolls of film; goods to the value of 500 Rupees.

HEALTH

1. Yellow fever – if travelling from an area where a case of yellow fever has been reported, a certificate from the World Health Organization (WHO) is required, or the person will be detained in isolation for 6 days.
2. Malaria – malaria risk exists throughout the year in all regions except some parts of the mountainous north. Resistance to chloroquine must be reported.
3. Cholera – travellers proceeding to countries that impose restrictions for arrivals from India or from an area in India infected with cholera require a certificate. Immunization advised.
4. Visitors are advised to avoid tap water and drink bottled water instead. Peel fruit and vegetables. Bring own specific medicines.

CAPITAL – New Delhi. Population – 6,870,000 (including Old Delhi).

POPULATION – c.750,000,000.

LANGUAGE – Hindi officially. 14 others, with English widely spoken throughout.

CURRENCY – Rupee, divided into 100 Paise. Notes – 1, 2, 5, 10, 20, 50, and 100. Coins – 5, 10, 20, 25, and 50 Paise, 1 and 2 Rupees. Travellers should be on the alert for torn notes.
£1 = R18; US$1 = R13.

BANKING HOURS – 1000–1400 Monday to Friday and 1000–1230 Saturday.

POLITICAL SYSTEM – Parliamentary democracy.

RELIGION – Mainly Hindu. Also Moslem, Sikh, Christian and Buddhist.

PUBLIC HOLIDAYS

January 1	New Year's Day
January 26	Republic Day
March/April	Good Friday
August 15	Independence Day
October 2	Mahatma Gandhi's Birthday
November – first week	Divali
December 25	Christmas Day

In addition to these there are many festivals and fairs throughout the country which are sometimes declared full public holidays.

CLIMATE

It is very difficult to generalize about a country nearly the size of Europe, whose seasons vary from north to south. However, most of the country is at its best in winter (November to March) with cool fresh mornings, and dry sunny days. April to June can be uncomfortably hot on the plains, and the monsoons break in

Bombay and Calcutta around June, and reach Delhi around the middle of July.

Southern India – hot tropical climate all year round, with monsoon rains between late April and July (from October to December in Tamil Nadu). It is hot and humid, so visitors should take lightweight tropical clothing, although warmer clothes may be needed for winter evenings and trips to the hills.

Central Plains – very hot and dry during the summer months, although the state of Madya Pradesh escapes the worst of the heat. The monsoons are very heavy from June until September. Temperatures can fall at night in the winter, especially in the north, so visitors should supplement their summer lightweight clothing with warmer garments during this period.

Northern Hills – pleasantly cool in the summer and an ideal respite from the very hot temperatures elsewhere in India. Winters, however, can be cold and damp, with the higher resorts under several feet of snow, making trekking, for example, almost impossible. Lightweight to medium clothing is advisable from March to October, but as the weather can change rapidly in the mountains, it is essential that travellers go suitably equipped with warmer clothes (a must during winter) and waterproofs.

TIME DIFFERENCE – GMT + 5 hours 30 minutes.

PROHIBITION – In the states of Gujarat, Bihar, and Tamil Nadu, the possession and consumption of alcohol is illegal. A Special All India Liquor Permit can be obtained by foreign tourists from the Government of India Tourist Office on production of a passport.

COMMUNICATIONS

• **Telephone:** IDD service from a number of cities, with international calls needing to be placed through the operator elsewhere.

• **Post:** Internal postal services and poste restantes are efficient. Stamps can often be bought at hotels. Airmail service to UK takes up to a week.

ELECTRICITY – 220v AC.

OFFICE/SHOPPING HOURS – Offices open 0930–1700 Monday to Friday and 0930–1300 Saturday. Some government offices open on alternate Saturdays. Shops: 0930–1800 Monday to Saturday in most large stores.

• **Best Buys:** As India's major industry is still textiles, all manner of cloths and coverings can be found with an infinite array of styles and techniques on display everywhere. The best carpets are to be found in Kashmir, which also specializes in papier-mâché works. Leather goods are good buys in the north too, while Rajasthan offers attractive pottery and jewellery. In the south, bronze figures of the gods are popular, as are wood carvings of gods and animals. Items of copper and brass can be found throughout India. Clothes are cheap, with leather shoes representing excellent value for money, but check the quality of garments on offer in the markets. The silks of Varanasi are among the best in the world.

Generally, don't be rushed into buying anything (particularly by the commission merchants whose fee will be added to the prices you pay) and be prepared to haggle!

INTERNAL TRAVEL

• **Air:** Services operated by Indian Airlines and its subsidiary Vayudoot connect over 70 cities. The 4 major international airports are Bombay, Calcutta, Delhi, and Madras. There is a special 21-day 'Discover India' air fare within India for US$375. This allows unlimited air travel within the country. Indian Airlines' fares are among the lowest in the world.

• **Rail:** The internal railway network is vast (second largest in the world) and relatively inexpensive. Express services link all the main cities. Tourists should travel first class as trains are often uncomfortably crowded. You should also consider one of the Indrail passes which allow unlimited travel nationwide within the period of validity.

• **Road:** Extensive network covering the whole country including areas where trains do not run. Many coach tours available.

Taxis and auto-rickshaws are available in large cities and fares are charged, in theory, on a kilometre basis. Drivers should display the latest chart of fares, but in practice they rarely do and unless you agree a price first, or insist they use their meters (which they rarely do) you will end up paying 4 to 5 times the cost, because you are a Westerner. Always haggle over prices and never accept their quote first time round. After 11 p.m. the cost rises by 25 per cent, not 50 per cent after 7 p.m., as is often tried. Unmetered tourist cars are also available at a far higher cost, generally chauffeur driven.

Self-drive cars are generally not available, which is probably just as well, considering the hazardous nature of driving in the major cities. A Carnet de Passage with full insurance and Green Card are required, and an International Driving Licence is recommended. Traffic travels on the left.

MAJOR SIGHTS OF THE COUNTRY

More a continent than a country, India is a land of incredible variety. From the deserts of Rajasthan to the tea gardens of Assam; from the hot and bustling cities to the serene majesty of the mountains of Kashmir; each contributes to that 'spiritual experience' which all the guidebooks assure you is India.

Not only is DELHI a historic city in its own right, uniquely combining the splendours of ancient culture with the elegance of Lutyens' new capital, but it also stands at the apex of the fabled region known as THE GOLDEN TRIANGLE (see p. 394 for details of Delhi).

First stop from Delhi will doubtless be AGRA, 125 miles to the south, and the site of the Taj Mahal. When you have seen the Taj close up you will understand why it is 'the' sight of India. The scale, fine work and sheer beauty of this monument are as overwhelming as India itself. So much attention has been lavished on the awesome Taj at Agra, however, that it is easy to forget that Delhi itself has many attractions which are worthy of your consideration. The magnificent Red Fort of Akbar, the Mogul emperor, is chief among these, with Akbar's Palace, the Jahangir Mahal, and the Jama Masjid, built by Shah Jahan in honour of his daughter, Jahanara, being some of the other main sights. For the latter were used the new building techniques of the day, which were later perfected on the Taj Mahal.

24 miles to the west of Agra lies the ghost city of Fatehpur Sikri, built in 1570 on a whim by Akbar. The third corner of the Golden Triangle is JAIPUR, the exotic 'pink city' of Rajasthan. Totally enclosed by 18th-century walls, the historic capital is dominated by the hugely impressive City Palace, and you should also not miss the Hawa Mahal (Palace of Winds), nor the weird and wonderful Jantar Mantar Observatory. South-west of Jaipur lies UDAIPUR, the 'City of Sunrise', where there are many ancient ruins.

BOMBAY is the major centre on the west coast, a busy port combining eastern bazaars with western modern industry. Its best-known landmark is the Gateway of India, situated on its attractive waterfront. Nearby are broad, sandy beaches, and 7 miles out into the Indian Ocean lies Elephanta Island, noted for the huge rock carvings which adorn its temples (details on p. 390 under Bombay section). Further south is the 70-mile stretch of coastline of GOA, which contains some of the finest beaches in the world. The area was held by the Portuguese till as recently as 1961, and consequently has a strong Mediterranean influence, with many fine churches to be visited. Further south still is the popular resort of Kovalem.

On the east, north of the fabled coast of Coromandel, lies CALCUTTA, the largest city in India, and hub of the east. Luxury hotels and fine restaurants abound, and much of the country's intellectual and creative activity is centred here. 300 miles to the north-west is the ancient city of Bodhgaya, the most sacred place for both Hindus and Buddhists. MADRAS, further south, is the centre of the Hindu tradition of Bharata Natyam (classical dancing), and also the home of the art of temple sculpture. With its excellent communications, it is a good centre from which to plan a tour of the south.

KASHMIR is the large, mountainous area in the north of India, and many tourists go to the famous Kashmir valley each year to escape the heat of the Indian summer and enjoy the splendid scenery. JAMMU is the modern capital of the region with many attractions of its own, but often tourists prefer to visit the ancient capital,

SRINAGAR, with its magnificent pleasure gardens. Sports facilities are excellent, and indeed the sporting-minded visitor can sample the delights of the highest golf course in the world, at Gulmarg. The more adventurous should head further north, to the remote land of LADAKH, with its awesome peaks and fascinating monasteries.

HOTELS

Hotels are reasonably priced in India, though in the large cities where businessmen stay on expense accounts, around R1000 a night is the norm in a first class hotel. The hotels are classified on the internationally accepted star system, with 5- and 4-star hotels offering all luxury amenities and full air-conditioning, which can be a godsend if you are in India at the torrid height of summer.

Good hotel chains in India include Oberoi, Inter-Continental, Taj, Sheraton, Ashok (government owned), and Hyatt. Prices quoted do not include board and a 10 per cent service charge is normally added, as well as the obligatory 15 per cent luxury tax.

At many tourist centres there are Travellers Lodges/Tourist Bungalows which are run by the India Tourism Development Corporation and the Forestry Department, and offer comfortable lodging and meals at more moderate prices.

In Kashmir, travellers should take the opportunity to stay on one of the splendid houseboats which are moored to the banks of the river Jhelum, and Dal and Nagin lakes, by Srinagar.

Youth hostels in India provide a cheap and convenient base for organized tours, trekking, hiking or mountaineering. There are 16 hostels spread evenly between the regions, and the YMCA also runs many campsites throughout the land.

NIGHTLIFE AND RESTAURANTS

All four major cities of India offer good nightlife and there are plenty of things to see and do. Although there are no nightclubs as such, many of the better hotels have bars, dancefloors and cabaret shows. Delhi attracts the finest performers of Indian music and dance. Calcutta and Bombay are also major centres, with the latter acting as the centre of the world's largest film industry. Theatres and cinemas are widespread, with many performances in English.

There is a spectacular range of Indian cuisine, and visitors should take every opportunity to sample the many delicious dishes on offer. It is a cuisine based on a massive array of herbs and spices, some fragrant, some ferociously hot. Meat dishes are more common in the north, with rogan josh (curried lamb) and biriyani (chicken or lamb in orange-flavoured rice, sprinkled with sugar and rose water) being notable examples. Tandooris (meat marinaded in herbs and baked in a clay oven) are ever popular. In the south, dishes are mainly vegetarian and inclined to be hotter! On the west coast there is a wide choice of fish and shellfish, with Bombay duck being the most popular Bengali speciality. Dhal (mashed lentils with various vegetables) is found everywhere, as is dhai, the yoghurt 'cooler' which often accompanies a curry.

For those with more catholic tastes, there is a wide variety of international cuisine available in the major cities, including Chinese, American, French, and Japanese. It has been said that there are more Indian restaurants in the UK than in India, but the main international hotels have anything up to four restaurants, all offering a diverse range of foods. A two-course Indian meal for two should not cost more than R200 each in a decent hotel. This price also includes a large bottle of the local – and drinkable – beer. If you want to cut expenses, though, do without alcohol as the prices in India are high.

For desserts there are countless sweet concoctions of which the Indians are most enamoured, although Westerners may prefer to stick to the wide range of fruit on offer. Fruit should be peeled prior to consumption. Tea is the national drink, usually prepared with milk and sugar, and sometimes with spices. Nimbu soda (soda and lime juice) is probably preferable to nimbu pani, which contains water and is therefore best avoided.

Alcohol is difficult to get hold of, and can be very expensive (£2.50 for a scotch; £2 for an imported beer). Watch out for local prohibition laws, and if purchasing alcohol for private consumption, make sure it's the real thing!

Bombay

BOMBAY INTERNATIONAL AIRPORT

Bombay's airport lies 18 miles to the north of the city. It is the largest airport in India and is consequently served by all the major airlines. Number of terminals: 2. Terminal 1 handles domestic flights only and is some distance away (20 minutes on bus) from Terminal 2 which handles international flights.

AIRPORT FACILITIES

• **Terminal 2:** Facilities open 24 hours per day.

Information Desk	The Tourist Information Counter is situated in front of Customs (green channel) in Arrivals Hall.
Flight Information	Telephone 535491.
Restaurant	First floor. Always open.
Snack Bar	First floor. Always open.
Foreign Exchange	There are banks on either side of the left-hand exit of the Arrivals Hall.
Duty Free	This sells cigarettes, cigars and spirits
Lost Goods	Telephone Airport Police.
Toilets	First floor. Always open.
Car Rental	Through Tourist Counter (no self-drive).
Taxis	24 hours. Turn right from Arrivals for taxi stands.

AIRPORT INFORMATION

Check-in Times	International: 2 hours. Domestic: 1 hour.
Airport Tax	There is a departure tax of R100.

Transferring Flights   There is an International Transfers
                           system in Arrivals, but if you are
                           transferring and flying British Airways,
                           you would be well advised to use their
                           'India Gateway' service, which smooths
                           the bureaucratic maze for you.

AIRPORT HOTELS

Recommended hotels located at or close to Bombay International:

● **First Class:** (around R900 double)
Leela Penta – On the main road to Bombay city and half a mile from
the airport (tel. 6300713). New and well equipped.
Centaur – 5-star hotel located right outside Arrivals (tel. 6126660).

● **Super Club Class:** (R350–650 double)
Hotel Airport Plaza – At 70C Nehru Road, Vile Parle East,
Bombay (tel. 6123390-102-3).
Hotel Transit – Just off the Nehru Road, Vile Parle East, Bombay
(tel. 6129325-6/6120661/6121087).

● **Economy:** (less than R250 double)
Hotel Lovely – Nehru Road (tel. 6124370).
Hotel Galaxy – Behind Electric House in Santa Cruz East (tel.
6125315).

CITY LINKS

Bombay International Airport is 18 miles north of Bombay.

● **Rail:** There are no rail links with Bombay as such, although the
stations of Kurla and Andheri are relatively near the airport.

● **Bus:** Buses connect Terminals 1 (Domestic) and 2 (International)
with each other and the Air India/Indian Airlines headquarters at
Nariman Point. Buses leave Terminal 2 at 3 a.m., 5 a.m., and then
every hour on the hour until 11 p.m. From Nariman Point, buses
depart at 4 a.m., 6.30 a.m., 8 a.m., and then every hour on the hour
until midnight, with an additional last bus at 1.30 a.m. The journey

from Nariman Point to Terminal 1 takes about 40 minutes and costs around R20. Terminal 2 is about an hour from Nariman Point and the fare is around R25.

● **Taxi:** Expect to pay at least R100 to get to the airport by taxi – and considerably more than that if you travel during the rush hour, when few drivers are prepared to use their meters. From the airport you can pay a set fare for a cab at the police operated booth, although this will be double the price of the metered fare. If you're up to a spot of haggling, however, it is possible to arrange a cheaper price with one of the drivers at the end of the queue, who may well take you for a lower fare rather than wait to get to the front of the line.

● **Car Hire:** Although there are no self-drive facilities, it is possible to hire chauffeur-driven cars through the Tourist Information Counter.

TOURIST INFORMATION

Tourist Office – Government of India Tourist Office, 123 Maharashi Karve Road, Churchgate (tel. 293144). Situated opposite Churchgate Station. Open 0830–1730 weekdays and every other Saturday, and 0830–1230 every second Saturday and on public holidays. Closed Sundays. There are also two branches at the airport and at the Taj Inter-Continental Hotel at Colaba. Good leaflets from the main office. Tours can be organized through the Maharashtra Tourism Development Office at CDO Hutments, Madame Cama Road (tel. 269421). There is a fortnightly 'what's on' guide entitled simply *Bombay*.

ADDRESSES

British Airways – Vulcan's Building, Veer Nariman Road (tel. 220888).
GPO – Nagar Chowk, near the Victoria Terminus Station.
UK Consulate – 2nd floor, Mercantile Bank Building, Mahatma Gandhi Road (tel. 259981).

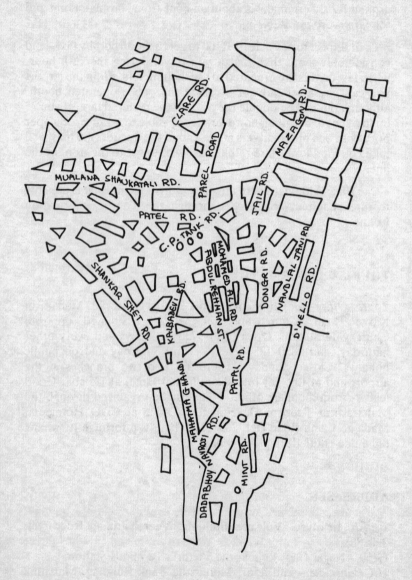

US Consulate – Lincoln House, Bhulabhai Desai Road (tel. 363611).

Taj Mahal Hotel – Apollo Bunder, Colaba (tel. 2023366). Has Tourist Information office, Air India/Indian Airlines office, plus good pharmacy and bookshop.

GETTING ABOUT

It is probably easier to get around in Bombay than in any other major Indian city due to its well developed public transport networks. *Buses* are run by BEST (Bombay Electric Supply and Transport), and they certainly live up to their acronym in that they are the most efficient in India. They are cheap too, with fares starting at around R0.50. Naturally, they can get exceptionally crowded, especially during the rush hour, and hold on to your valuables, as the dexterity of Bombay's pick-pockets is notorious.

The *rail* network is also good and worth using to get around the city at any time except the rush hour. Trains connect Bombay Central with the more convenient Churchgate every 10 to 15 minutes and the first class fare is R10.

Taxis are plentiful, but do try and insist on the meters being set, even though this will doubtless prove impossible during the rush hour and late at night. The meters will generally be out-of-date, so you will have to pay according to a revised set of charges. If these are displayed, note what they are and don't pay over the odds if you think you are being overcharged.

Auto-rickshaws are cheap and a good bet for getting across the city during the rush hour.

SIGHTS

The industrial centre of India, Bombay is India's wealthiest city. Yet it also has its history and its sights, and its position – together with its relatively good communications – ensures that it remains the gateway to India for most western businessmen and tourists alike.

Colaba is the southern promontory of Bombay and the district where most of the hotels and restaurants are located. It is also where

two of the most famous landmarks of the city are to be found: the
GATEWAY OF INDIA, a massive Arch of Triumph conceived in the
Moslem style and completed in 1924; and right behind it, the
majestic TAJ HOTEL, where you can partake of refreshment in
relaxed, period splendour. There's plenty of diverse activity on
CHOWPATTI BEACH, while a more relaxing afternoon can be spent
wandering round the PRINCE OF WALES MUSEUM, or the modern
JAHANGIR ART GALLERY. The HANGING GARDENS are most pleasant
and offer a good view of all Bombay except the mysterious TOWERS
OF SILENCE nearby, which are carefully shielded from the gaze of
sightseers, as bodies of the Parsee sect are laid out within the towers
to be picked clean by vultures. Up on plush Malabar Hill there is the
temple of WALKESWAR, an important Hindu pilgrimage site, and
further down around the coast is the oldest temple in Bombay, the
MAHALAXMI TEMPLE, which is, appropriately for this centre of
business, dedicated to the goddess of wealth. After you've prayed
to the goddess, you can go and spend it all at the nearby MAHALAXMI
RACECOURSE which is the finest in India, or at one of Bombay's
many markets, such as the teeming Chor Bazaar off Grant Road,
with its enormous range of tourist bric-à-brac.

Tours of the city are operated by the National Tourist Board
(ITDC) and the Maharashtra Development Council. Tours leave
from the Tourist Office and from the Taj Hotel and are relatively
expensive.

ACCOMMODATION

As Bombay is the business capital of India it is not surprising that it
possesses many top-class hotels. Nor is it surprising, given the
number of people who enter India through Bombay Airport, that
hotel accommodation is both expensive and hard to come by. In the
high season (November–March), accommodation, even at the
bottom end of the market where standards can be quite low, is at a
premium and you may end up having to pay more for a room than
you originally intended. If you can, book in advance, or be prepared
to hunt for rooms at the crack of dawn! Prices quoted for the better
hotels do not include board, service at 10 per cent or luxury tax at 15
per cent.

• **First Class:** (around R900 double)
The Taj Mahal Hotel – Apollo Bunder (tel. 2023366). Classy, period elegance and reputedly the finest hotel in India. Fine position near the Gateway of India, plus a wealth of facilities ranging from its own tourist office and excellent shops, to the Tanjore, one of the best restaurants in Bombay, and rooftop bars with panoramic views across the city.

Hotel Oberoi Towers – Nariman Point (tel. 2024343). 5-star hotel of great sophistication and luxury, and the tallest building in India. Choice of 6 international restaurants, with the Outrigger Restaurant specializing in Polynesian delicacies. Other facilities include a huge swimming pool, a landscaped garden on the 7th floor, and a fully equipped health club.

Welcomgroup Searock – Land's End, Bandra (tel. 535421). Another classy modern hotel offering a combination of superb location together with all mod cons.

• **Super Club Class:** (R350–650 double)
Ambassador Hotel – Veer Nariman Road (tel. 291131-20). Stylish hotel, conveniently located for business and shopping near Churchgate.

Sea Green South – Marine Drive (tel. 221613/221662/2211765/ 2211787). Right on Bombay's main promenade and the price includes taxes, meals and air-conditioning.

Sea Palace – Ramchandani Marg (tel. 241828). Large hotel on Strand Road near the Gateway of India. Restaurant. Reasonable rates, and sea views.

Sun-'n-Sand Hotel – 54 Juhu Beach (tel. 571481). One of many well equipped hotels at Juhu Beach, 11 miles to the north of Bombay. Rooms here have a full view of the sea and represent good value for money. There is a swimming pool and although the sea is badly polluted, weekend beach-life is lively.

• **Economy:** (under R250 double)
Rex and *Stiffles* – Both at 8 Ormiston Road. The Rex (tel. 231518) is on floors 3 and 4, while the Stiffles (tel. 230960) takes up floors 1 and 2. Very popular, if a little cramped. Some of the rooms have air-conditioning and all are secure. Friendly and cheap.

Shelley's – Ramchandani Marg (tel. 240229). Situated in the popular district of Colaba, this hotel offers reasonable air-conditioned accommodation with sea views to boot.

Whalley's Guest House – Mereweather Road. Communal bathrooms, but plenty of character and breakfast included in the price.

Lawrence Hotel – Ashok Kumar Lane (signposted Rope Walk Lane) round the back of the Prince of Wales Museum (tel. 243618). Very small and very popular, this hotel is inexpensive and some of the rooms have balconies.

Hotel Manama – 221/5 P. D'Mello Road (tel. 264149). Situated close to the impressive Victoria Terminus Station this hotel has recently been modernized and is the best of three in the immediate vicinity.

YWCA International Guest House – 18 Madame Cama Road (tel. 230445). Admits both men and women, but be warned as it is almost invariably booked solid 3 months in advance.

DINING OUT

Some of the best restaurants in India are to be found in Bombay and generally the prices are pretty reasonable, so that even those on a relatively tight budget can afford to eat out in style.

• **First Class:** (R300 for two)
Tanjore Restaurant at the world-famous Taj Mahal Hotel. Probably the best place for traditional Indian food, accompanied by sitar music and classical Indian dancing. Try the excellent thali, a selection of vegetable dishes served together with rice.

The Café Royal – Oberoi Towers. Reputed for its French cuisine and vintage wines served in a sophisticated setting with live music. The Oberoi also offers Indian cuisine to the accompaniment of traditional music and dance in the Moghal Room, and South Sea Island dishes and cocktails in the Outrigger Restaurant.

The Khyber Restaurant – K. Dubash Marg. A wide selection of dishes, with particularly good tandooris and kebabs.

• **Super Club Class:** (R100–200 for two)
The Nanking – Shivaji Marg, Colaba. Reputedly one of the finest Chinese restaurants in all India. Try anything, it's all good!

The Kabab Corner – Hotel Natraj, Marine Drive (tel. 294161). Serves tasty dishes, and there's live sitar music.

The Delhi Durbar – Shahid Bhaghat Singh Road. Menu similar to The Khyber's only not so expensive. Good shakes and ice creams. There is another Delhi Durbar at Falkland Street which specializes in curries.

• **Economy:** (less than R100)
The Samarkhand – in the Oberoi, overlooking Marine Drive. Offers meals and snacks and has the advantage of being open round the clock.

The Ananda Punjabi – Colaba Causeway. Tasty vegetarian food.

The Leopold Café and Stores – 6, Colaba Causeway (tel. 202 0131). Popular and a good place to relax and watch the world go by. Old, but clean and cheap.

The Sahyadi – 117 Maharashi Karve Road. Another vegetarian specialist. Good and cheap.

There are also numerous take-away stalls in Bombay, many of which sell delicious local specialities at rock-bottom prices. Try bhelpuri – a snack made from noodles and spiced vegetables – from one of the stalls along Chowpatti Beach. You can even buy good old fish and chips from some of these stalls, should you be pining for a taste of proper British nosh.

NIGHTLIFE

While there are no nightclubs as such in India, many hotels and restaurants have dancefloors, and also put on floor shows with both Indian and western dancing. You will find these facilities at all of Bombay's major hotels and restaurants (Taj, Oberoi etc.).

You can listen to top singers, or visit the theatre and see performances of classical Indian dance to soak in the local culture.

You also ought perhaps to go to the cinema, as the world's largest film industry is currently based in Bombay. You can even arrange a trip round the studios. Bombay's notorious red light district, known as 'the cages' because the girls stand behind barred doors, is centred around Falkland Street.

EXCURSIONS

Under the Gateway of India you can get a boat to ferry you the 6 miles to ELEPHANTA ISLAND, which is now Bombay's most popular tourist attraction due to the stunning rock-cut temples on the island. It's worth obtaining the services of a guide, and avoiding the weekend rush by going midweek.

Further afield, the temples of the caves of ELLORA are considered to be even more impressive, in particular the splendid Kailasa Temple. They can be visited easily from nearby AURANGABAD, 250 miles north-east of Bombay. There are more impressive caves nearby at AJANTA, whose walls are adorned with magnificent Buddhist paintings and sculptures.

For those who want merely to get away from the heat and bustle of the city, there are some excellent hill-stations to the south-east, such as MATHERAN or MAHABALESHWAR. Part of the 100-mile journey to Matheran can be made on the picturesque toy train.

PUNE, or Poona, 120 miles south-east of Bombay, has pleasant gardens and palaces, but it is to GOA that most tourists will probably want to go. This is the beautiful stretch of coastline 500 miles south of Bombay which was a Portuguese enclave until 1961. The area still betrays a strong Portuguese influence, particularly the capital PANAJI, with its whitewashed churches, winding, narrow streets and overhanging balconies. The main sights are at OLD GOA, rich in heritage and the former capital, which is 5 miles from Panaji. The other main reason for visiting Goa is that some of the best beaches in the world are to be found here. And there are nearly 70 miles of them. The only problem is which one to pick. Colva and Chapora remain beautiful and relatively unspoilt, while Anjuna is famed for its wild midnight beach parties.

Delhi

DELHI INTERNATIONAL AIRPORT

Delhi's airport lies 9 miles to the south-west of the city, and is served by 19 airlines. Nearly 5 million passengers use the airport annually, and a second main terminal was opened in 1986 to cope with increased international passenger traffic. Number of terminals: 2.

Terminal 1 is the old terminal which handles all domestic departures. Terminal 2 is the new International terminal which handles only international flights.

AIRPORT FACILITIES

Because flights arrive and depart throughout the night, all facilities are open 24 hours per day. The new terminal has everything one needs, but the facilities are basic.

● **Terminal 2:**

Information Desk	In Arrivals Hall
Flight Information	Telephone 393481 ext. 238.
Tourist Information Desk (ITDC)	In Arrivals Hall
Restaurant	First Floor
Snack Bar	First Floor
Foreign Exchange	Located on left hand of main exit of Arrivals Hall.
Bank Counters	In Departures Hall for payment of departure tax.
Duty Free	Sells cigarettes, cigars and spirits
Maurya Lounge	For First Class passengers.
Lost Goods	Telephone Airport Police on 392015.
Toilets	First floor
Car Rental	Through ITDC counter (no self-drive).
Taxis	24 hours. Taxi stands are by Arrivals Hall (see City Links section).

AIRPORT INFORMATION

Check-in Times	International: 120 minutes (60 minutes Super Club/First Class). Domestic: 60 minutes.
Airport Tax	There is a departure tax of R100.
Transferring Flights	There is an International Transfers system in Arrivals, but if you are transferring and flying British Airways, you would be well advised to use their 'India Gateway' service, which smooths the bureaucratic maze for you.

AIRPORT HOTELS

Recommended hotels located at or close to Delhi International:

• **Super Club Class:** *Centaur Hotel*, Gurgaon Road (tel. 391411). R700 for double room.

• **Economy:** At Terminal 1 (Domestic) there are a limited number of beds available. Known as 'Airport Retiring Rooms', they need booking in advance (through the Airport Manager, Delhi Airport, tel. 391351) and are allocated on a first-come, first-served basis. Economy prices.

CITY LINKS

Delhi International is 10 miles south-west of Delhi.

• **Rail:** There are no rail links with Delhi. Delhi Railway Station is 10 miles distant.

• **Bus:** Ex-Servicemen's Air Link Transport Service. Departs from the airport according to aircraft arrivals, calling at most major hotels en route to their office in Connaught Place. Buses leave for the airport opposite the underground bazaar at the following times: 4.40, 5.15, 5.45, 7.00, 7.45, 10.00 and 11.30 a.m., and 2.30, 3.30, 5.00, 6.45, 8.30, 9.30, 10.30, and 11.30 p.m. The fare is around R13.

There is a public bus service to the airport (no. 780) but it can get very crowded.

● **Taxi:** To Connaught Place. Most international flights to Delhi arrive and depart at horrendous hours of the morning, so the chances are you will have to get a taxi to the city. Drivers rarely use their meters, so do *not* pay more than R70 for a service which should officially cost much less. If you are leaving Delhi in the early hours of the morning, book a taxi the afternoon before. The yellow and black cabs are not air-conditioned and cost an extra 10 per cent after 2200. Each bag costs R1.

● **Car Hire:** Chauffeur-driven cars are available through the ITDC counter. No self-drive facilities. A limo to the centre arranged through Ashok costs around R150 a day.

TOURIST INFORMATION

Tourist Office – Government of India Tourist Office, 88 Janpath (tel. 43005-8). Open 0900–1800 all year round. They hand out maps, leaflets, accommodation lists and generally give advice, but ask for everything you need as nothing is offered voluntarily.

Excursions are organized through the Ashok Hotel office at 50B Chanakyapuri.

Accommodation and excursions can be booked through ITDC, L Block, Connaught Place, and DTDC, Bombay Life Building, N Block, Connaught Place. Ask to buy the excellent *Genesis City Guide*.

The airport desk will also help.

ADDRESSES

British Airways – 1 Connaught Place.
GPO – Junction of Baba Kharak Singh Marg and Ashoka Road.
UK Embassy – Shantipath Chanakyapuri (tel. 601371).
US Embassy – Shantipath Chanakyapuri (tel. 600651).
Medical Help – The best hospital in Delhi is the All India Medical Institute.

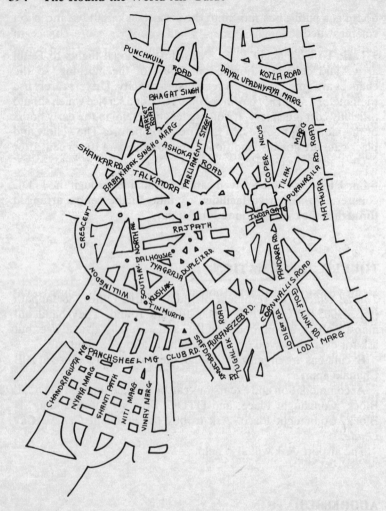

GETTING ABOUT

Getting around in Delhi can be hectic. *Buses* are run by the Delhi
Transport Corporation (DTC) and you can get a cheap route guide
from their office in Scindia House. It is best to avoid buses during
the rush hour, when they become hopelessly overcrowded. Try to

board at a starting or finishing point – such as the Regal and Plaza cinemas in Connaught Place – when you have more chance of getting a seat and less chance of being trampled upon. There is now also a deluxe bus service which offers the same routes at twice the price.

Taxi drivers are all supposed to use their meters but in practice few of them do. Try to insist on the meter being set, but don't be surprised if you get short shrift from the driver in the rush hour or in the middle of the night. As the meters are invariably out-of-date, you will have to pay according to a scale of revised charges. Note what these are – if they're displayed, that is – and only pay what *you* think is the right price.

Auto-rickshaws are cheap and widely available, and a good bet for getting across Delhi in the rush hour.

SIGHTS

Delhi's history is chequered and ancient. Its site has changed on at least seven occasions, and the ruins are still there for everyone to see. There are today two Delhis – the old city of the Moguls built by Shah Jahan, the man who built the Taj, and the new city built by the British in 1931, featuring wide boulevards and parks, and mansions designed by Lutyens. Famous sights of the city include the gracious RED FORT, the JAMA MASJID – the largest mosque in the world – and the QUTAB MINAR COMPLEX, complete with its soaring tower. The market-places are full of interesting yet inexpensive products, and the crowds are often entertained by magicians and dancing bears. The ancient narrow lanes of CHANDNI CHOUK are where to find quality jewellery, silks and perfumes.

ACCOMMODATION

Delhi has at least six international hotels, all of which provide luxury accommodation and air-conditioning. Prices are generally reasonable, although full board is not included, and a 10 per cent service charge is normally added, in addition to the obligatory 15 per cent luxury tax. From October to March, hotels can be heavily booked, and it is best to reserve accommodation in advance.

• **First Class:** (around R900 for a double room)

The Oberoi – Dr Zakir Hussain Road, New Delhi 110 003 (tel. 699571). A 5-star hotel of great sophistication and luxury, situated in central Delhi's diplomatic quarter. The hotel is the epitome of cool, quiet luxury, with excellent facilities, good restaurants, and little extras such as a free butler service, health club, and extensive business services. Choice of 4 good restaurants, including a Chinese one of international renown.

The Taj Mahal – 1 Mansingh Road, New Delhi 110 011 (tel. 386162). Established city centre hotel with all the comforts one would expect from such a famous name.

Maurya Sheraton – Diplomatic Enclave, New Delhi 110 021 (tel. 3010101). Prices for the Tower Service reflect the superior standards, which include breakfast in a private lounge with newspapers, TV, and views over south Delhi. There is an extensive range of facilities, including even a yoga centre.

• **Super Club Class:** (R450–650 for a double room)

Oberoi Maidens – 7 Sham Nath Marg (tel. 2525464). Excellent position in Old Delhi and a very good hotel.

Hotel Kanishka – 19 Ashok Road (tel. 343400). Good middle-of-the-road hotel.

Rajdoot Hotel – Mathura Road (tel. 699583). Reasonable hotel in every way. Clean and comfortable.

Claridges Hotel – 12 Aurangzeb Road (tel. 3010211). Popular with the British, comfortable and well run.

• **Economy:** (R50–250 for a double room)

Janpath Guest House – 82 Janpath (tel. 321935-7). Basic, clean and central.

YMCA Tourist Hotel – Jai Singh Road (tel. 311915). Very good value, centrally situated and cheap. Membership can be taken out for a month.

YWCA International Guest House – 10 Parliament Street (tel. 311561). Again, basic, cheap and OK for a few nights.

Tourist Camping Park – Jawaharlal Nehru Marg (opposite J.P. Narayana Hospital) (tel. 278929). Very basic, very cheap; a good place to meet western travellers. Run by ex-Indian Army officers.

Jukasso Inn – 50 Sundar Nagar (tel. 690308). More expensive, but all the better for it.

Hotel Palace Heights – D Block, Connaught Place (tel. 351369). Air-conditioned rooms if wanted. Very central and good value.

DINING OUT

The Indians don't tend to dine out as a rule, and decent eating establishments can be difficult to find, even in a city the size of Delhi. However, the larger hotels offer an excellent standard of cuisine, including Chinese, French, American, and Japanese. A good place to eat is Connaught Circus, in the heart of Delhi, where there are many good eating establishments.

● **First Class:** (R300 for two)
The Oberoi – Dr Zakir Hussain Road (tel. 699571). The Taipan Chinese restaurant on the top floor of this hotel is well worth a visit. The Szechuan cuisine is reputedly the best in Delhi.

Taj Palace – 2 Sardar Patel Road, Chanakyapuri (tel. 301 0404). This has the 'Orient Express', which serves excellent European food in an affected mock-up of a Pullman car, should the native dishes prove too hot and spicy for the western palate.

The Hyatt – Bhikaji Cama Place, Ring Road (tel. 699516). A bit off the beaten track, but well worth the distance to appreciate the excellent service. It has even opened Delhi's first Italian restaurant, complete with imported chef!

● **Super Club Class:** (R100–200 for two)
The United Coffee House – Connaught Place. Good food in cool, relaxing atmosphere.

Hotel President (Tandoor) – Asaf Ali Road (tel. 273000/277836). Tandoori of very high quality, with atmosphere enhanced by live sitar music.

Metropolis Restaurant – near New Delhi Station in the Paharganj area. Western and Chinese food of high standards.

• **Economy:** (R20–70)
Taj Mahal Hotel, House of Ming Restaurant – 1 Mansingh Road (tel. 386162). Very good Chinese food at reasonable prices.

Sona Rupa – Janpath. Tasty vegetarian Indian food at low prices. The eat-all-you-can lunch buffet is especially good value.

Nirula's – Connaught Place. Indian fast food – Western style. Full of Westerners eating everything from dhal to muttonburgers! Milkshakes, ice-cream sodas . . . the lot. Reasonable.

Kalpana's Tourist Restaurant – 84A Tolstoy Lane. Just behind the Tourist Office. Good, clean, with nothing over the R22 mark. Good place for breakfast.

NIGHTLIFE

While there aren't exactly any nightclubs in India, many hotels and restaurants have dancefloors for those who can stomach it after a vindaloo! However, don't expect the action to compare with London or New York. All the following have bars which feature regular floor shows, with classical Indian dancing as well as western style: THE OBEROI HOTEL, tel. 699571; THE ASHOKA HOTEL, 50B Chanakyapuri, New Delhi, tel. 600121; THE AKBAR HOTEL, Chanakyapuri, New Delhi, tel. 6044513; and THE CLARIDGES HOTEL, 12 Aurangzeb Road, New Delhi, tel. 3010211.

Visitors may well decide to take in some of the local culture and go to the theatre or classical dancing instead. Alternatively they could listen to some of the top singers in India, or visit the cinema, where both English and American films can be seen.

EXCURSIONS

From Delhi, you must make the 125-mile journey south to AGRA to see the TAJ MAHAL: possibly the most beautiful building in the world. Also at Agra is the huge and truly magnificent FORT, where Jahan was imprisoned by his son, in sight of the masterpiece he created, until the day he died. It took the combined efforts of four emperors to complete the Fort, and there are splendid examples of both Hindu and Muslim architecture within its walls, such as the MOTI MASJID, the largest marble mosque in the world. Agra is around 3 hours from Delhi by road or rail, and only half an hour by plane. Air-conditioned chauffeur-driven cars and coaches are available for day trips, and an air-conditioned train, the Taj Express, leaves Delhi daily at 7.05 a.m. returning late at 10.15 p.m. (around R80 first class, return). Good food is served on the trains but be sure to book your tickets in advance, and remember that first class is the only serious option on the generally crowded and stifling Indian trains. If you hire a taxi for a day to take you round the sights (R50–60), make it clear that you do not want to be dragged around all the carpet and marble shops, where the drivers just happen to get 15 per cent commission!

Visitors can choose to return via FATEHPUR SIKRI, the Imperial Capital, built by Emperor Akbar in 1570 – apparently on a whim. The project was eventually abandoned, probably due to a lack of water. The glorious Mogul courtyards and palaces are now totally deserted . . . except for the tourists.

The 'pink city' of JAIPUR is an hour's flight from Delhi, or 191 miles by train. Within the 18th-century walls are exquisite palaces and spacious and colourful markets.

UDAIPUR and CHITTORGARH are both redolent of the glamour and chivalry of ancient Rajasthan. The former is the famous 'lake city' of island palaces and parks, while the latter possesses many ruined forts and the notable Victory Tower. Romantics may care to explore the temples of nearby Khajurao with their erotic carvings.

Travellers with a few days to spare should definitely make the 400-mile trip up to Kashmir which offers unparalleled scenery and quiet respite from the rigours of the hot Indian summer. Srinagar, with its magnificent pleasure parks and luxurious lakeside house-boats, is a must. The sports facilities, ranging from skiing to the highest golf course in the world at Gulmarg, are excellent, and there is abundant wildlife for both nature-lovers and hunters alike.

Indonesia

RED TAPE

• **Passport/Visa Requirements:** Visitors now only need a valid passport to stay in Indonesia for a 2-month period. The catch is you have to enter and depart the country at one of several 'no visa' entry and departure points. These are:

Airports: Halim (Jakarta), Polonia (Medan–North Sumatra); Simpang Tiga (Pakanbaru–Sumatra); Taling (Padang–West Sumatra); Patu Besar (Batam Island–Riau Archipelago); Mokmir (Biak); Sam Ratu Langi (Manado–North Sulawesi); Patimura (Ambon); Ngurah Rai (Denpasar–Bali).

Seaports: Tanjung Priok (Jakarta); Tanjung Perak (Surabaya); Benoa (Bali); Padang Bai (Bali); Ambon (Ambon); Bitung (North Sulawesi); Belawai (Medan–North Sumatra); Batam (Batam Island–Riau Archipelago).

However, you can still leave from a 'no visa' point provided you obtain a visa *before* you arrive in Indonesia.

It can be quite difficult to extend your visa and there's lots to see in Indonesia, so if you think you're going to be spending more than 2 months in the country, apply for a Temporary Residence Permit which is valid for 3 months. Apply to: The Indonesian Embassy, 38 Grosvenor Square, London W1X 9AD. Allow plenty of time, as numerous documents will be required. The visa costs around £12.00.

In the US, the Indonesian Embassy is at 2020 Massachusetts Avenue, Washington DC 20036.

CUSTOMS

• **Duty Free:** The following may be imported into Indonesia without incurring Customs duty: 200 cigarettes or 50 cigars or 100 grammes tobacco; 2 litres spirits. Cameras and jewellery must be declared on arrival. Do not try to bring arms/ammunition, non-prescribed drugs or pornography into the country.

HEALTH

1. A yellow fever vaccination certificate is required by all visitors coming from an area where a case has been reported.
2. Malaria risk exists throughout the year everywhere except Jakarta and Surabaya. Vaccination advised.
3. There are also risks from cholera and typhoid/polio. Immunization advised.
4. Boil all water before drinking, or buy bottled water.

CAPITAL – Jakarta. Population – 6.5 million.

POPULATION – Around 160 million.

LANGUAGE – Bahasa Indonesia, a variant of Malay, with over 200 different ethnic languages and dialects also spoken. Some English is spoken and many of the older generation still speak Dutch as a second language.

CURRENCY – Rupiah (Rp) = 100 Sen. Coins are in denominations of Rp 5, 10, 25, 50 and 100. Notes – Rp 100, 500, 1000, 5000 and 10,000.
£1 = Rp2075; US$1 = c.Rp1482.

BANKING HOURS – 0800–1400 (Monday–Thursday), 0800–1100 (Friday), 0800–1300 (Saturday).

POLITICAL SYSTEM – Basically a 'guided democracy' under General Suharto.

RELIGION – Muslim majority with Christian, Hindu (mainly in Bali) and Buddhist minorities. Animist beliefs in remote and outlying areas.

PUBLIC HOLIDAYS

January 1	New Year's Day
March 4	Nyepi
March/April	Easter
April/May	Ramadan
May 1	Waicak Day

May/June (1 day)	Eid el-Fitr
August 17	Independence Day
August (1 day)	Eid el-Adha
October 9	Hijara
December 25, 26	Christmas

Ramadan lasts for a month and during this period the visitor may experience difficulty travelling around and finding restaurants open during daylight hours. Alcohol may be prohibited in many places.

CLIMATE – Basically, Indonesia has a tropical climate, which means it is hot (average temperature 27°C, 82°F) and wet all year round. However the climate does vary from region to region. The wet season generally starts later the further south-east you go. In Sumatra it is wet (very wet) from September to March; in Java from October to April; and in Bali and the south, from November to May. Avoid these times of the year, or take an umbrella! The Molucca Islands' wet season is from the beginning of April to the end of August, when the rest of Indonesia experiences its dry season.

You should take lightweight clothes made of natural fibres, such as cotton, which allow the skin to 'breathe'. It can get quite chilly in the mountains, so come suitably prepared if you intend visiting any mountainous regions. Remember to take an umbrella or light-weight raincoat if you're going to be in Indonesia during the rainy season.

TIME DIFFERENCE – Indonesia spans 3 time zones: Java, Sumatra, Bali: GMT + 7 hours; Kalimantan, Sulawesi, Timor: GMT + 8 hours; Molucca Islands, Irian Java: GMT + 9 hours.

COMMUNICATIONS

• **Telephone:** There is IDD service, but phone from the main Post Offices and hotels. The IDD code is 62. The code for Jakarta is (62) 21; the code for Denpasar (Bali) is (62) 361.

• **Post:** The post is slow and airmail letters to the UK take at least 10 days.

ELECTRICITY – 220v AC (110 in some areas), 50 cycles.

OFFICE/SHOPPING HOURS – Government offices: 0800–1500 (Monday–Thursday), 0800–1130 (Friday) and 0800–1400 (Saturday). Offices: 0900–1700 (Monday–Friday). The lunch break is between 1300 and 1400 and some offices are open on Saturday mornings. Shops are open 0830–2000 generally, though smaller ones keep irregular hours.

• **Best Buys:** Many superb batik prints, with best, though most expensive, choices in Jakarta. Other cloths worth purchasing include Sumba wall cloths, and 'ship's cloths' and gold embroidered cloths from Sumatra. Bali has excellent stone and wood carvings, sarongs, modern cloths, masks, paintings and leather, embroidered and woven ware. Shadow puppets from central Java are a popular choice, as are puppets from Bandung. Antique Chinese porcelain can still be picked up reasonably cheaply (beware of imitations) and quality contemporary Indonesian art can be purchased by contacting the Taman Ismail Marzuki in Jakarta or the School of Fine Arts in Yogyakarta. Generally, save your money for Yogyakarta, as prices here are far more reasonable than in Jakarta.

INTERNAL TRAVEL

• **Air:** Indonesia has a good internal air system linking most of the larger towns to Jakarta. Flights are operated by Garuda Indonesian Airlines, the country's major airline, which has now taken over Merpati, which used to run services to the more out-of-the-way areas of Indonesia. There is a third airline, Zamrud, based in Denpasar, Bali, which has a lot of character but severe financial problems. Fares are quite cheap, with Garuda the most expensive. It often pays to buy your ticket in advance, and do make sure that domestic airport tax is included in the price.

● **Rail:** There is a good network on Java, with connections to Bali and a more limited network on Sumatra. Trains vary, with many being hot and uncomfortable. However, the air-conditioned overnight sleepers 'Bima' (Jakarta, Yogyakarta, Surabaya) and 'Mutiara' (Jakarta, Cirebon, Semarang, Surabaya) are comfortable and have restaurant cars. The age and diverse origins of many of the islands trains have made Java into a trainspotter's paradise.

● **Sea:** As an island nation, ships are obviously important in Indonesia. Pelni go nearly everywhere, but conditions aboard ship can often be rather unpleasant. However it is possible to make some highly unusual and exciting sea-trips.

● **Road:** Java has an extensive road network and it is certainly worth taking a bus/coach for shorter journeys. Bus travel on Sumatra can be especially slow and uncomfortable, while other islands often have very poor roads which are usually impassable in the rainy reason. Taxis are easy to find in the cities, though are metered only in Jakarta. Taxis cost Rp400 for the first kilometre and Rp190 for each subsequent km. There is also an intriguing array of mini-buses, mini-cars (bajajs) and cycle-rickshaws (becaks), which all offer inexpensive city transport, although, as on buses, do be wary of thieves. Both cars and bikes can be hired in the main cities from local agents. An International Driving Licence is required, and traffic travels on the left.

MAJOR SIGHTS OF THE COUNTRY

Many of the main sights of Indonesia's 13,677 islands are concentrated in Java and Bali, the two most important islands.

JAVA: Most people enter Indonesia at its capital, JAKARTA, which is a much improved city (for further details consult our *City Guide* to Jakarta on p. 409). Jakarta is situated on the north-west coast of Java, and there are some good beaches along the nearby western coast. 35 miles south of the capital, BOGOR still has well preserved colonial architecture and the Botanic Gardens here are justifiably world-famous. South of Bogor there are one or two popular resorts such as the picturesque PUNCAK HILL STATION, where (rich) Jakartans go for weekend breaks, and, on the south coast, the resort of PELABUHAN RATU, with its beautiful beach but treacherous waters.

A hundred miles south-east of Jakarta, BANDUNG has a pleasant climate due to its situation at altitude. The city, the third largest in Indonesia, is host to a variety of cultural events. It is also a good place to buy walang golek puppets and masks, and a convenient base from which to visit the volcano of TANGKUBAN PERAHU, although the crater has now become very commercialized. From Bandung, roads lead to CIREBON on the north coast, which is a colourful port with a pair of interesting palaces (kratons), and PANGANDARAN, one of the few resorts on the south coast where it is safe to swim. The DIENG PLATEAU in central Java has beautiful scenery and many interesting temples and walks, but can get very cold at nights.

Continuing east, YOGYAKARTA is many people's favourite town. Economical to stay in, the city offers culture, the best shopping in Indonesia, and also makes a fine base from which to visit some of the finest temples in Indonesia. The PRAMBANAN is the biggest Hindu temple complex in Indonesia, while BOROBUDUR is a huge Buddhist construction covering a whole hill, decorated with hundreds of images of Buddha. SOLO (Surakarta) is a quieter version of Yogyakarta and has palaces, museums and excellent batiks and handicrafts.

In eastern Java, the two sights of greatest interest are the remains of the ancient Majapahut Kingdom, scattered around Trowulan, 35 miles from SURABAYA, the second largest city in Indonesia, and still impressive despite their shattered condition, and the stunning MORAT BROMO, which should be high on any visitor's list of sights to see. This is a live volcano 50 miles south of Surabaya and the time to see it is at dawn, when the sun rises ethereally over its two craters. While you're waiting for the sun, you can peer into the vast, brooding inner crater, lit by red-hot, sputtering lava.

BALI: For all its attractions, many people bypass Java altogether and head straight for the fabled island of Bali, and it is not hard to see why. The island is not only staggeringly beautiful but populated by a friendly people who have evolved a unique and fascinating culture. From shadow puppet plays, to gamelan orchestras, to the numerous religious dances, the diverse forms of culture centre around religion, but in a joyous and celebratory manner.

Bali has so many temples that it is known as 'the island of a thousand temples', although many officials would put the figure nearer 10,000. The most important is the BURA BESAKIH TEMPLE, the oldest and most sacred on the island, situated on the slopes of Mount Agung. Other interesting shrines are the picturesque and touristy TANAH LOT TEMPLE; the strange Elephant Cave, and the temple of PURA ULU WATU, perched high on a cliff in southern Bali. DENPASAR, the island's capital, is a small and frantic town, featuring very little of the 'real' Bali. However, nearby are popular tourist resorts such as KUTA and the more up-market SANUR, though Kuta is now very crowded all season.

In the hills north of Denpasar is UBUD, the serene cultural centre of Bali. There are many artists here and the galleries are of high quality. Ubud also has far more sights than Kuta and the town's officials are making a real effort to preserve the 'real Bali' here. North of Ubud the scenery around LAKE BADUR and MOUNT BATUR is some of the most spectacular on the island, while right on the north coast SINGARAJA has some fine, black beaches, full of people trying to get away from the hordes at Kuta.

OTHER ISLANDS OF INDONESIA: SUMATRA is a large island where travelling around can often be rather difficult. It features prime jungle, penetrated by numerous rivers, and its chief attractions are the wonderfully scenic LAKE TOBA in the north-west, and the mountain town of BUKITTINGGI, which is situated near quite a few places of interest. If you can face travelling all the way to the fiercely independent state of BANDA ATJEH, there is a splendid mosque and a good museum, with good beaches close by and friendly inhabitants. Off the west coast of Sumatra, the island of NIAS is interesting for its traditional villages, unique customs and fine beaches.

SULAWESI is another large island. There are attractive markets at UJUNG PANDANG (formerly Makassar) and fine beaches at MENADO in the north, which also possesses some of the finest coral reefs in the world. Up in the mountains there are at least a dozen places of interest within 10 miles of RANTEPAO, where there is also a tremendous festival during the months of July or August. LOMBOK, only 20 minutes flying time from Bali, is now gaining in popularity due to its superb beaches, temples and pleasure gardens, while the more adventurous can travel further out to KOMODO, which is famed for its dragons. KALIMANTAN, the Indonesian portion of Borneo, is

an anthropologist's dream, while KRAKATAU draws flocks of
botanists, eager to find out how life started again on the island after
the volcano erupted in 1888 killing all forms of life there.

HOTELS

Accommodation in Indonesia can be quite expensive unless you
decide to stay in a 'losmen', which is a type of boarding house.
International hotels are found only in major towns and suburban
areas and all hotels are graded according to facilities. A service
charge of 10 per cent is added to every bill and there is also a
government tax of 10 per cent. Prices are not helped by Indonesia's
unstable currency.

NIGHTLIFE AND RESTAURANTS

Jakarta has clubs (open till 0400 at weekends) featuring international singers and bands. There are also casinos, cinemas and
theatres. In Bali you can see all forms of diverse cultural entertainment, particularly puppet theatre, and dances accompanied by
the unique gamelan orchestras. Festivals are often lively affairs and
a festival calendar can be obtained on arrival.

Most forms of international cuisine are available in Jakarta, but if
you want quality you have to pay for it. The national dish is nasi
goreng – fried rice, occasionally served with an egg on top. The
Dutch 'rice table' is still popular from colonial days and the
Sumatran padang cuisine, which consists of rice served with various
hot and spicy side dishes, has become popular of late. Other
Indonesian specialities include satay, which are tiny kebabs served
with a spicy peanut dip, and gado gado, fresh salad with prawn
crackers and another peanut sauce. Indonesian cuisine can be
extremely hot and if you spot tiny red and green peppers floating
about in your food take suitable measures. However, *do not* quench
your raging thrist with gallons of iced water. The water may be
boiled, but what about the ice? Remember that many travellers
contract nasty stomach bugs from the food in Indonesia, so take
special care when choosing a restaurant or stall. European-style
food will be very expensive everywhere.

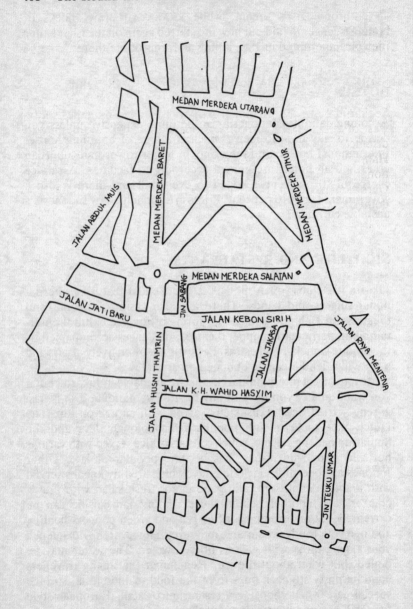

Jakarta

SOEKARNO HATTA INTERNATIONAL AIRPORT

Soekarno Hatta International Airport is situated 25 miles south-west of Jakarta. The airport was opened in 1985, and despite its distance from the city centre it is a great improvement on the old Halim Airport. There are 3 terminals. Terminal A is the international terminal; Terminal B handles domestic flights operated by Garuda, the national carrier; and Terminal C handles non-Garuda domestic traffic.

CITY TRANSPORT

Jakarta now has a very extensive *road* network, yet still has terrible traffic problems. It is the only city in Indonesia to operate an established conventional bus service of any size. Regular city double-deckers charge a fixed Rp150 and the express Patas buses, which are usually less crowded, charge Rp250. The central terminal is the new Penar Sever station to the east of Merdeka Square. There are also a number of other suburban bus stations. The regular bus service is supplemented by orange mini-buses which cost Rp150, and in some areas blue microlet buses, which cost Rp200.

Because of its sprawling nature, Jakarta also has a number of city *train* stations. The most convenient are Gambir, next to the bus station, and Kota, in the Old Town. This is where to go if you want to take the air-conditioned night trains to Surabaya and Bali.

Taxis are easy to find but make sure the meters aren't 'broken' before you get in and check that drivers switch them on. The fare is Rp400 for the first kilometre and Rp190 for each subsequent km. Make sure that this is what you pay. *Bajajs* are Indian auto-rickshaws and you can get to most places for Rp400–800. *Becaks* are bicycle rickshaws, and are even cheaper, but they aren't allowed into the city centre until after 2200.

Hiring a car is relatively straightforward, although driving in Jakarta most certainly is not. You can hire cars at hotels or through agents. If you can afford it, you would be better hiring a chauffeur as well.

TOURIST INFORMATION

The Directorate General of Tourism (the national tourist organization of Indonesia) is at Jalan Kramat Raya 81, and there is a very helpful Visitors' Information Centre on Jalan M.H. Thamrin opposite the Sarinah department store. They have a good free map of the city and a number of excellent information leaflets. The office is open 0830–1500 (Monday–Thursday), 0830–1300 (Saturday) and 0830–1100 (Friday). The Pelni shipping ticket office (tel. 358395) is at Jalan Pintu Air number 1 behind the Istiqlal Mosque, but go in the mornings as it closes at 1400. Merdeka Square is a useful landmark for orientation purposes.

ADDRESSES

UK Embassy – Jalan M.H. Thamrin 75.
US Embassy – Merdeka Selatan 5.
Emergency – The telephone numbers are 110 (Police) and 118 (Ambulance) but it is wiser to seek action through a major hotel.

SIGHTS

A good place to start is the imposing landmark of MERDEKA SQUARE. Here you can take a lift up the National Monument for Rp1250, and the views of the sprawling city from the top are tremendous. To the north of the square lies the Presidential Palace, and to the north-east is the massive ISTIQLAL MOSQUE, the largest mosque in South East Asia. The Jakarta Fair is held at the square from early June to mid-July and there are puppet theatre performances on alternate Saturday nights. Over on the west side of the square, the INDONESIAN NATIONAL MUSEUM is one of the best museums in South East Asia. There are excellent displays of pottery and porcelain and the treasure room can be viewed on Sundays. Other museums worth visiting include the Textile Museum, which is housed in an old Dutch colonial house on Jalan Satsuit Tubun, to the west of the National Museum, where there is a large collection of fabrics and looms; the Museum Jakarta, near Jalan Fatahillah in the Old Town, which has a rich collection of antiques and Dutch colonial paraphernalia; and the Museum Wayang, nearby on Jalan Pintu Besar Utara, which possesses an extremely interesting collection of various Indonesian puppets. The museums tend to close quite early in the afternoons, so go in the morning.

The OLD TOWN, also known as Kota, which lies to the north of the modern centre of Jakarta, still retains a Dutch feel with its canals and colonial architecture, and restoration continues apace. Proceeding still further north, you come to one of the best sights of the city; the magnificent old Dutch PORT. There are still some marvellous sailing ships to be glimpsed here, and a visit to the nearby fish market should also be high on any sightseer's itinerary. Near the old Halim Airport to the south-east of Jakarta lies TAMAN MINI-INDONESIA, which re-creates the sights of the whole country in one park. It takes about an hour and a half to get there from the city, but is good value for money. There is a huge amusement complex, called Taman Impian Jaya Ancol ('Dreamland'), which has several attractions including a fantastic swimming pool complex, an art gallery and numerous shops and cafés, but it can get very crowded at weekends. Half-day bus tours can be booked from most of the big hotels, with pick-up points around the town.

ACCOMMODATION

There is plenty of first class accommodation, but a distinct lack of cheaper hotels. What cheap accommodation there is centres around Jalan Jaksa, a small street centrally located in the newer part of Jakarta. Rooms are expensive by Asian standards. Due to the fluctuating nature of the Indonesian rupiah it is very difficult to issue price guidelines, and the prices quoted may well become rapidly out of date.

• **First Class:** (Rp150,000 and above for a double)
Borobudur Inter-Continental – Jalan Lep, Banteng Selatan (tel. 370108). Superb modern hotel with excellent business suites. Fine

landscaped grounds, with large pools, health club, and six tennis courts. Near shopping and commercial centre. Excellent restaurants.

Jakarta Hilton – Jalan Jend, Gatot Subroto, Senayan (tel. 583051/ 588011). Another supremely luxurious establishment 45 minutes' drive from Soekarno Hatta Airport and minutes from downtown Jakarta. Seven restaurants including a lakeside Japanese restaurant, live entertainment and unrivalled sports facilities. Features an Indonesian bazaar, including shops and an open-air theatre.

Mandarin Hotel – Jalan M.H. Thamrin, PO Box 3392 (tel. 321307). Situated in the heart of the business district, with superior standards of service and facilities. Good business amenities, restaurants, and interesting swimming pool set on a 3rd floor podium.

• **Super Club Class:** (Rp60,000–120,000 for a double)
Indonesia Jakarta – Jalan M.H. Thamrin (tel. 320008/322008). Central location in main business and entertainment district, large pool, good restaurant, and shopping arcade.

Orchid Palace – Jalan Letjen S. Parman, Slipi, PO Box 2791 (tel. 596911/593115). Delightful out-of-town garden setting, with pool, 2 restaurants and conference facilities.

Sabang Metropolitan – Jalan K.H. Agus Salim 11, PO Box 2725 (tel. 354031). Convenient location near to many places of interest. Comfortable rooms and good facilities.

• **Economy:** (under Rp50,000 for a double)
Monas Hotel – Jalan Merdeka Barat (tel. 375208). Top of range hotel in convenient central location.

Wisma Tengger – Jalan Kramat VI 28 (tel. 349519). Similar prices to above.

Hotel Karya – 32–4 Jalan Jaksa. Good hotel with rooms from around half the price of the Monas.

Wisma Delima – 5 Jalan Jaksa. King of the cheapies. Very well known hotel in the centre of the city. Friendly, and if the hotel is full (as it invariably is) the owners will give you details of other similar accommodation.

DINING OUT

You can eat very well in Jakarta – provided you're prepared to pay for it. There is a wide range of international cuisines available, but western food is shockingly expensive. You can eat quite cheaply at food stalls, but be warned that some of them pay scant attention to hygiene.

● **First Class:** (over Rp70,000 for two)
The Nelayan – At the Inter-Continental (tel. 370108). This serves steaming baskets of seafood with a wide variety of delicious sauces. Also at the Inter-Continental, the Toba Rotisserie serves fine grills.

The Oasis – Jalan Raden Saleh 47 (tel. 327818). Mixed European and Indonesian menu. Sumptuous surroundings in a Dutch colonial mansion with the charming songs of the Toba Batak singers adding to the atmosphere. Decidedly expensive.

The Hilton – (tel. 583051/588011). The hotel has a number of very distinguished restaurants and you can take your pick from Indonesian, French, Italian and Japanese cuisines. All are excellent.

● **Super Club Class:** (Rp20,000–50,000 for two)
Vic's Viking Restaurant – On Jalan M.H. Thamrin (tel. 322452). Speciality here is the 80-dish smorgasbord.

Kikugawa – On Jalan Kebon Binatang III (tel. 331804). This serves possibly the finest Japanese food in town, at very reasonable prices.

Mira Sari – On Jalan Patiunus I (tel. 712603). In the quiet residential suburb of Kebayoran Barin, the decor of this restaurant may not be outstanding but the quality of the Indonesian food most certainly is.

● **Economy:** (under Rp20,000 for two)
Jun Njam – At 69 Jalan Batu Ceper. Delicious seafood specialities at the top of this price range.

Tjahaja Kota – On Jalan Wahid Hasjim. One of the best Chinese restaurants in town.

Natrabu Restaurant – On Jalan Hagi Agus Salim. Hot and spicy Padang specialities.

Senayen Satay House – At 31A Jalan Kebon Sirih. Very reasonable Indonesian food. As you would expect, the satay is very good here.

Although one or two of the food stalls leave a lot to be desired you can eat well at the Art Market and in Jalan Tenku Umar, north of the main Post Office. The night market at Pecengongan serves tasty Chinese food and seafood.

NIGHTLIFE

There are now clubs that stay open well into the early hours at weekends, and it is fair to say that nightlife in once dull Jakarta has perked up quite a lot. However the quality of the floorshows does vary though prices are uniformly high. Good floorshows are at the TROPICANA in Jalan Manila and the BLUE OCEAN in Hajam Wurak. There are one or two good discos: the GUNSA RAMA in the Hotel Indonesia and the ORIENTAL in the Hilton. There is a huge leisure complex to the north-east of the city centre, the TAMAN IMPIAN ANCOL, where there is a theatre as well as a casino and disco. You can see traditional Indonesian dancing at places like the INDONE-SIAN BAZAAR, at the Hilton, or an English language film in one of the city's 40 or so cinemas. Cultural events take place at the TAMAN ISMAIL MARZUKI, the cultural centre of Jakarta – dance, poetry, gamelan, films, they all happen here. Events are listed in its monthly programme and in the daily *Jakarta Post*.

EXCURSIONS

Dotted around in the Bay of Jakarta are the PULAU SERIBU ISLANDS which are also known as the Thousand Islands. It's 4 hours sail from Pasar Ikan Harbour to PULAU PANGANG, and the other islands can be reached from here. Many of the islands have fine beaches and at Pulau Pangang you can choose whether to visit a deserted or crowded island. The PULAU PUTRI ISLANDS, 45 miles out, are known as Jakarta's 'tropical paradise' resort and you can get more information on the islands from their office in the Jakarta Theatre Building on Jalan Wahid Hasjim. If you don't fancy an Indonesian boat trip, but do wish to laze on a tropical beach, there are some good resorts on the west and south coasts of Java, within easy reach of Jakarta. CARITA BEACH, 3 hours west of the capital, is a good place to spend a few days doing nothing much in particular, and from here you can visit the volcanic island of Krakatau, situated 35 miles out in the Sunda Strait. Alternatively, PELABUHAN RATU, on the south coast, is a popular beach resort whose rocky cliffs, caves and gorges make for interesting walks. The beach is good too, but under no circumstances should you swim in the sea, which is extremely dangerous.

Inland, many Jakartans like to take weekend breaks at the PUNCAK HILL STATION, situated at the Puncak Pass. The climate is most agreeable here, and the views across the mountains are spectacular.

35 miles south of Jakarta, BOGOR has the huge Kebun Raya Botanical Gardens, with well over 15,000 varieties of flora and a good zoological museum. 65 miles further, on the same road, the university town of BANDUNG has a pleasant climate and is a good place to sample Indonesian culture. It also makes a good base to visit the volcano of TANGKUBAN PERAHU, 18 miles to the north. The volcano is best seen at dawn, but wrap up as it can get very chilly up at the crater. Excessive tourist development has spoiled the volcano for many people.

Japan

RED TAPE

• **Passport/Visa Requirements:** A full, valid passport is required by all except nationals of Japan or residents of Hong Kong issued with certificates of identity by Japanese consulates abroad. Passports of Chinese residents of Taiwan or of residents of South Korea are not recognized by Japanese authorities without the accompaniment of official Japanese travel documents. Tourists without financial means of support and onward travel tickets may be refused entry. Nationals of the German Federal Republic, the UK, Ireland, Austria, Mexico, Switzerland and Malaysia may visit Japan for up to 180 days without a visa. Nationals of Argentina, Bahrain,

Bangladesh, Belgium, Canada, Chile, Colombia, Costa Rica, Cyprus, Denmark, Dominican Rep., El Salvador, Finland, France, Guatemala, Greece, Honduras, Iceland, Iran, Israel, Italy, Lesotho, Luxembourg, Liechtenstein, Malta, Mauritius, the Netherlands, Norway, Pakistan, Peru, Portugal, San Marino, Singapore, Spain, Surinam, Sweden, Tunisia, Turkey, Uruguay and Yugoslavia may visit Japan for up to 90 days without a visa. Nationals of New Zealand may visit Japan for up to 30 days without a visa. Nationals of all other countries require a visa to visit Japan.

CUSTOMS

• **Duty Free:** Each visitor may bring in 400 cigarettes or 100 cigars or 500g tobacco and 3 bottles of spirits (760 ml each), 2 oz perfume, 2 watches valued at Y30,000 or less and gifts to the value of Y100,000. An oral declaration is necessary on arrival at Customs.

HEALTH

No certificates of vaccination are required to enter Japan. Protection against typhoid and polio is recommended. The water is safe to drink and medical treatment in Japan is of a very high standard.

CAPITAL – Tokyo.

POPULATION – 120,000,000.

LANGUAGE – Japanese. Some English is spoken.

CURRENCY – Japanese Yen (Y). Notes are in denominations of Y 500, 1000, 5000 and 10,000. Coins are in denominations of Y 1, 5, 10, 50, 100 and 500.
£1 = Y229; US$1 = Y163.

BANKING HOURS – 0900–1500 hours, Monday to Friday, 0900–1200 hours Saturday.

POLITICAL SYSTEM – Democracy.

RELIGION – Shinto and Buddhism.

PUBLIC HOLIDAYS

January 1	New Year's Day
January 15	Coming-of-Age Day
February 11	National Foundation Day
March (1 day)	Vernal Equinox Day
April 29	Emperor's Birthday
May 3	Constitution Memorial Day
May 5	Children's Day
September 15	Respect-for-the-Aged Day
September (1 day)	Autumn Equinox Day
October 10	Health and Sport Day
November 3	Culture Day
November 23	Labour Thanksgiving Day

CLIMATE – Japan's climate is temperate with 4 distinct seasons. Winter (December to March) is cool and sunny in the south and cold and dry in the north. Tokyo has the occasional snowfall and in the extreme north, Hokkaido is usually snow-bound for a couple of months. Spring and autumn tend to be mild and fairly dry all over Japan while summer is hot and wet. Temperatures can reach 92°F (33°C) between July and September in the Tokyo area. Typhoons, which are only likely to occur in September or October, are usually over within 24 hours.

TIME DIFFERENCE – GMT + 9 hours.

COMMUNICATIONS

• **Telephone:** Japan's internal telephone system is very efficient. Public telephones take 10- or 100-yen coins (using 10-yen coins enables you to receive change at the end of your call). Card telephones are green and will take coins or pre-paid for cards which are sold at telephone offices. For internal telephone information telephone Tokyo (03) 201 1010 during business hours.

A full IDD (International Direct Dialling) service is available in all major centres.

• **Post:** Airmail to Europe takes 4–6 days. The Central Post Office in Tokyo Station provides English-speaking personnel. Telex booths are available at main Post Offices and telegrams can be sent from Post Offices and major hotels.

ELECTRICITY – 100v AC.

OFFICE/SHOPPING HOURS – Office: 0900–1700 hours Monday to Friday, 0900–1200 hours Saturday. Shops: 0900–2100 hours Monday to Friday.

• **Best Buys:** Shopping in Japan can be rather an expensive exercise. Electrical goods are surprisingly pricey and the unusual voltage in Japan means most goods will need to be adapted for use in any other country. Cameras can be a good buy – try Tokyo's Shinjuku area for a wide choice and the best prices. Servicing of cameras in Japan is fast and efficient so this is a good place to have cameras repaired. Specifically Japanese goods which make interesting souvenirs include kimonos, mingei (local crafts such as kites and toys), lacquerware, cloisonné, damascene, porcelain, Kyoto silk and religious artefacts. Antiques should be looked over warily as the fake antique business in Japan is booming. Also beware of sales tax, which can be as high as 35 per cent, being added to the displayed price. There are some tax-free shopping areas in the major cities but prices here can be inflated anyway, so shopping around before buying is the best policy.

INTERNAL TRAVEL

• **Air:** Internal flight services are run by Japan Airlines (JAL), All Nippon Airways (ANA) and Toa Domestic Airlines (TDA). JAL links the major cities while ANA and TDA serve the more regional routes plus some major routes. Two other airlines, SWAL and

NKA, operate local flights for Hokkaido and the islands around Okinawa. JAL and ANA usually have English-speaking hostesses and ground staff. Tokyo's domestic airport is at Haneda and a rail service runs from here to Hamamatsu-cho.

• **Rail:** Japan has one of the world's most efficient railways with frequent services on all the main routes. The famous 'bullet' trains (Shinkansen) are the fastest and most comfortable. Their two routes are from Tokyo to Kyoto, Osaka and Hiroshima then up to Hakata, and from Tokyo to Morioka in the north. Fares on these are almost as much as an air fare, but the speed and efficiency of the trains make the journeys very enjoyable. Express trains have supplements added to their fares. The 'limited express', or tokkyu, trains are fast and only stop at major cities while the 'ordinary express', or kyuko, trains make more stops. The slowest and cheapest of the JNR (Japan National Railways) trains are the futsu, which stop at every station. Reservations must be made for travel in the 'Green' or first-class cars of principal trains.

An economical Japan Rail Pass is sold by the JNR to foreign tourists. It entitles you to free use of the JNR rail, bus and ferry services for anything up to 21 days. The passes are half-price for 6- to 11-year-olds.

• **Sea:** An extensive ferry system serves Japan's numerous islands and provides an inexpensive and scenic way to travel. On longer routes the ferries have bar and restaurant facilities.

• **Road:** Japan's roads are narrow and crowded with slow traffic. With the added problem of Japanese road signs, driving yourself around can be quite difficult. For those who do want to hire a car, an International Driver's Licence is required and driving is on the left.

• **Bus:** Again, because of the congested roads, buses are not used very much for inter-city travel. There is a 'highway' bus which runs between Tokyo, Nagoya, Kyoto and Osaka which is comfortable and inexpensive. Overnight buses are very popular so book well in advance (at any JTB office or JNR Green Windows).

MAJOR SIGHTS OF THE COUNTRY

TOKYO, the capital since 1868 and the nation's political and financial centre, is a vital stopping-off place on any tour of Japan. It is a lively, exciting metropolis and one of the major cities of the world. With the added advantage of being very central and on all the main air and rail routes, Tokyo makes an excellent starting point from which to discover the rest of the country. Going down the coast from the capital, KAMAKURA was the seat of a Shogunate government from 1192 to 1333 and has some interesting buildings and a colossal bronze Buddha image, the Diabutsu. Further along the same coast is TOBA, a city famed for its cultured pearl nurseries. At nearby ISE the Ise Grand Shrine is very impressive.

KYOTO and NARA are two inland cities which are well worth a visit. The former was the capital for more than 10 centuries before Tokyo took over. Rich in the nation's cultural heritage and legacies, Kyoto is a colourful and fascinating city. The latter, Nara, has an even older history than Kyoto as it was the nation's first permanent capital and the birthplace of Japan's Buddhist culture. Close to Kyoto is OSAKA, an important commercial centre. Osaka's ancient buildings and monuments were all destroyed during the war but the famous Osaka Castle (a 1931 reproduction of the ancient castle) makes a visit worthwhile. Further west are several places of interest including HIROSHIMA and NAGASAKI. There are many hot springs in this area, some of the best being at BEPPU and EBINO PLATEAU.

North of Tokyo SENDAI is a former castle town which holds the popular Tanabata Star Festival every August. MATSUSHIMA is one of Japan's prettiest spots with a beautiful bay, and HIRAIZUMI is full of historical buildings, Chusonji and Motsuji temples being of particular interest. At the north end of the main island of Honshu is the city of HIROSAKI whose castle is surrounded by fantastic gardens and grounds. From here it is not too far to Japan's most northerly large island, Hokkaido. The ferry takes you to HAKODATE, a city with a charm which most Japanese cities lack. It may not be the most attractive of places when first viewed from the port, but there are some interesting areas to wander through. The capital of Hokkaido, SAPPORO, is a thoroughly modern city with no such charm but the best nightlife north of Tokyo. It has got some places of interest, the Botanical Gardens being especially notable, but it is not the best example of a Japanese city.

Osaka

OSAKA INTERNATIONAL ITAMI AIRPORT

Itami, the location of Osaka's international airport, is just over 9 miles from the city centre. The airport is served by many major airlines who usually land in Tokyo and go on to Osaka at no extra charge. This is also a major domestic airport served by Japan Airlines (JAL), All Nippon Airways (ANA) and Toa Domestic Airlines (TDA).

AIRPORT FACILITIES

Information Desk	In the Arrivals lobby.
Bank and Currency Exchange	In the Arrivals lobby.
Duty Free Shops	Around the Departure lounge.
Restaurants	Open 0700–2130 hours daily.
Toilets	Throughout the terminal.

AIRPORT INFORMATION

Check-in Times	60 minutes before international flight departure time; 20 minutes before domestic flight departure time.
Airport Tax	Nil.

AIRPORT HOTELS

• **Super Club Class:**
The Airport Hotel – Hanshin, 3–30, Umeda 2-chome, Kita-ku, Osaka (tel. 344-1661). Comfortable rooms and excellent conference rooms.

CITY LINKS

• **Coach:** The coach service runs every 20 minutes from 0620–2120 hours from the airport to the city, stopping at the city coach terminal. On its return to the airport it stops at several of the major hotels.

• **Train:** This service runs every 15 minutes from 0430–2350 hours. It is both cheaper and quicker (20 minutes) than the coach.

• **Bus:** Buses run every 20 minutes from 0612–2130 hours. They charge the same as the coaches but do not make stops at any hotels.

• **Taxi:** These are quite expensive, especially at night when their rates increase considerably. Taxi ranks are immediately outside the terminal exit.

All forms of transport can also be taken to Kobe or Kyoto, both of which are fairly close to the airport.

OSAKA

Although Osaka is the commercial and industrial centre of western Japan it no longer possesses the political power it once enjoyed. Being a major port with which Korea and China did business, Osaka became a gateway for the art, science and philosophy which flowed into Japan during the 4th and 5th centuries. Several emperors based their courts here between the 5th and 8th centuries and in the late 16th century the powerful Hideyoshi Toyotomi chose Osaka as his capital. The prosperity and growth which followed can still be detected in the city's historical remains and relics although many of these were bombed during World War II. After Toyotomi's death Tokugawa moved the capital to Tokyo and Osaka lost its influence but continued to thrive as a major commercial centre.

Osaka may not be the most interesting of cities to visit in itself, but, as an international port of entry with the cities of Kobe, Kyoto and Nara within easy reach, it makes a great base from which to explore western Japan.

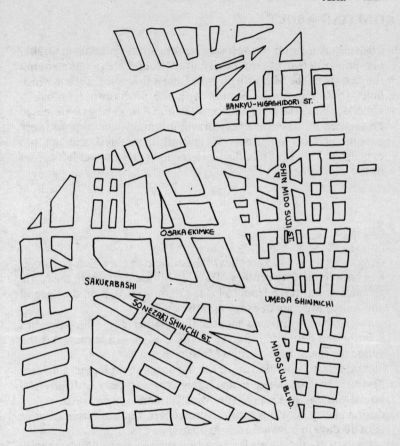

TOURIST INFORMATION

Osaka Tourist Association – No. 2 Semba Centre Building (tel. 261-3948).
Osaka City Tourist Information Office – JNR Osaka Station (tel. 345-2189).
Emergency – Dial 110 for police or 119 for fire or ambulance services.
Osaka Area Telephone Code – 06.

GETTING ABOUT

The subway is by far the best way for tourists to get about in Osaka. Six subway networks lace the city and JNR operates a route around the outskirts. The Midosuji Subway Line is the major city line which links JNR Shin-Osaka Station with the downtown terminals – Umeda, Shinsaibashi, Namba and Tennoji. Osaka's bus system is to be avoided by all but the very brave: it is highly complex and very easy to get lost on. Taxis are plentiful, metered and not too expensive. Those for hire display a red light in the lower left corner of the windscreen.

SIGHTS

OSAKA CASTLE is a 1931 replica of the ancient castle which Toyotomi had built in the 16th century. The City Museum stands in the castle grounds and is open from 0915–1645 hours (closed on the second and fourth Monday of every month).

TEMMANGU SHRINE was supposedly founded in AD 949. Sugawara is enshrined here and is known as the God of Academics. It is the venue for the famous 'Tenjin Matsuri' Festival.

THE MINT was founded in 1871 as the only mint in Japan. The Mint Museum exhibits Japanese and foreign coins and is open 0900–1600 hours Monday to Friday. The Mint Garden is open to the public during cherry blossom season. Inspection requires application at least 10 days in advance (tel. 351-5361).

OHATSU TENJIN SHRINE is a beautiful shrine which is unfortunately almost completely hidden away by the Sonezaki amusement district. It is worth seeking out and has some good little restaurants and pubs around it.

The MUSEUM OF ORIENTAL CERAMICS is full of priceless antique Korean and Chinese ceramics, open 0930–1630 hours daily except Mondays. The building is set on Nakanoshima Island, the administrative centre of Osaka, in Osaka's oldest park. The island has some other interesting buildings including the Library, the Bank of Japan and the Public Hall. The displays and exhibits at the NATIONAL MUSEUM OF ETHNOLOGY show various aspects of the Japanese lifestyle through the ages. Nearby is a traditional Japanese Garden.

KITA is Osaka's modern district, with large underground shopping areas and orderly, somewhat westernized streets and buildings. In contrast to Kita, MINAMI has retained the atmosphere of old Osaka and has many narrow streets lined with intriguing little shops, pubs and restaurants. Osaka's most concentrated shopping district is SHINSAIBASHI, with a long, covered shopping arcade lined with specialist shops.

DOTOMBORI is the liveliest night-time venue in the city, where pubs, nightclubs, cinemas and restaurants line the streets and alleys.

ACCOMMODATION

As with Tokyo, there is a wide range of styles of accommodation in Osaka. As well as plenty of international standard western-style hotels there are the Japanese-style ryokans and minshukus (inns and guest houses) which usually offer very good accommodation and friendly service at reasonable rates.

● **First Class:** (Double Y20,000–30,000)
Hilton International – 3, Umeda 1-chome, Kita-ku, Osaka 530 (tel. 344-4511). The Hilton Group's high standards have been amply maintained in the building and furbishing of this brand-new hotel. The decor is especially tasteful with some pleasing Japanese touches.

ANA Sheraton Hotel – 1-3-1, Dojimahama, Kita-ku 530 (tel. 347-1112). All the 'Sheraton' style luxuries you would expect with the added touch of Japanese hospitality. Good business facilities.

Holiday Inn Nankai – 28-1, Kyuznenom-cho, Minami-ku (tel. 213-8281). Located in the centre of the Midosuji shopping district, half an hour from the airport, this is a comfortable and well-equipped luxury hotel, complete with rooftop pool.

● **Super Club Class:** (Double Y10,000–20,000)
The Royal Hotel – 5-3-68, Nakanoshima, Kita-ku, Osaka 530 (tel. 448-1121). A good quality hotel with all the comforts and facilities one could want.

Osaka Dai-ichi Hotel – 1-9-20, Umeda, Kita-ku, Osaka 530 (tel. 341-4411). Another excellent value hotel with good facilities and friendly staff.

Hotel Nikko Osaka – 7, Nishinocho, Daihojicho, Minami-ku, Osaka 542 (tel. 244-1111). A pleasant hotel in the older district of Osaka, within easy reach of the bright lights.

Hotel New Hankyu – 1-1-35, Shibata, Kita-ku, Osaka 530 (tel. 372-5101). Right in the midst of Osaka's most modern district, this comfortable hotel could not be more conveniently placed for shopping.

• **Economy:** (Double Y5000–10,000)
Osaka Onoya – 1-16, Shimamachi, Higashi-ku, Osaka 540 (tel. 942-3745). A traditional ryokan with very high standards of accommodation and service.

Hotel Osaka Castle – 2-35-7, Kyobashi, Higashi-ku, Osaka 540 (tel. 942-1401). Clean, comfortable accommodation within easy travelling distance of the centre.

Osaka Riverside Hotel – 5-10-160, Nakanocho, Miyakojima-ku, Osaka 534 (tel. 928-3251). Adequate and reasonably priced accommodation.

Osaka YWCA Hotel – Tosabori 1-chome, Nishi-ku, Osaka (tel. 441-0892). A good standard of accommodation and services.

Osaka-Shititsu Nagai Youth Hostel – 450, Higashi-nagai-cho, Higashisumiyoshi-ku, Osaka 546 (tel. 699-5631). Japanese youth hostels tend to be of a very high standard and this one is no exception. It is 20 minutes by subway from Osaka Station.

Hattori Ryokuchi Youth Hostel – 1-3, Hattori-ryokuchi, Toyonaka 560 (tel. 862-0600). 5 minutes by bus from Sone Station which is on the main line into the city. Clean, basic rooms and facilities.

DINING OUT

Osakans are famous in Japan for their love of fine food and their city has thousands of superb restaurants. Whether large or tiny, the restaurants all tend to be friendly and relaxed in atmosphere and

most are moderately priced. Osaka's culinary specialities include
Osaka-sushi (vinegared fish or boiled eel pressed on top of rice),
fugu (globe fish dishes) and takoyaki (wheat flour dumplings with
chopped octopus and vegetables).

● **First Class:** (Y14,000–22,000 for two)
Kitamura – 46, Higashi-Shimizucho, Minami-ku (tel. 245-4129).
One of Osaka's best restaurants for Japanese fare, especially
sukiyaki and steak dishes.

Bistro Vingt-Cinq – 25, Taihoji-cho Nishino-cho, Minami-ku (tel.
245-6223). Top quality French cuisine is on offer here.

Genji – The Hilton Hotel (tel. 344-4511). A fabulous Japanese
restaurant set in the elegant surroundings of the new Hilton.

● **Super Club Class:** (Y8000–14,000 for two)
Dojima Suehiro – 2F, 1-5-17, Dojima, Kita-ku (tel. 345-1212). One
of a chain of Suehiro restaurants which are well known for their
sukiyaki and steak dishes.

Mandarin Palace – 13F, 3-2-18, Nakanoshima, Kita-ku (tel. 444-
0800). Tasty Peking cuisine, the speciality being roast duck.

Sushiman – Daimaru Department Store, 1-118, Shinsaibashisuji,
Minami-ku (tel. 252-2873). A Japanese sushi specialist restaurant.

● **Economy:** (less than Y8000 for two)
Moti – 3F, 1-6-15, Dotombori, Minami-ku (tel. 211-6878). A good
place to go for either a quick curry or a full tandoori meal.

Botan-en Bekkan – 10th Floor, Hansin Department Store, Umeda
(tel. 344-3601). Another restaurant with a wide range of dishes so
you can have a very cheap meal or splash out on the more expensive
choices on the menu.

Tenkin – 2-13, Fushimicho, Higashi-ku (tel. 231-2529). Reasonably
priced Japanese cuisine with tempura as the speciality.

Hollyhock – 5-14-12, Fukushima, Fukushima-ku (tel. 453-4530).
An interesting menu of home-made Italian dishes.

NIGHTLIFE

Kita and Minami are the two main entertainment districts of Osaka. KITA is ultra modern and full of trendy nightclubs, discos, bars and restaurants. MINAMI is equally lively but has a more traditional atmosphere and tends to be more casual and less sophisticated than Kita. The DOTOMBORI and SHINSAIBASHI districts have lots of inexpensive pubs and some less expensive nightclubs and discos. For more classical entertainment the places to go are ASAHIZA THEATRE near Nihonbashi subway, where the Bunraku Puppet Theatre performs, and at SHIN-KABUKI-ZA THEATRE near Namba Station, where Kabuki is performed. Information about the current entertainments in Osaka can be found in the daily newspapers, at the Tourist Information Centre or by asking at your hotel desk.

EXCURSIONS

The obvious places to visit from Osaka are its neighbouring cities of Nara, Kyoto and Kobe. KOBE is Japan's foremost trading port, 21 miles west of Osaka on the other side of Osaka Bay. With the Rokko Mountains as a backdrop Kobe is an attractive city, having Suma, Maiko and Akashi beaches nearby. From here it is quite easy to get to AWAJI ISLAND, the largest island in the inland sea between Honshu and Shikoku. About 35 miles west of Kobe is Himeji Castle, one of the best Japanese feudal strongholds still in existence.

NARA is an ancient city less than one hour from Osaka by train. It was the country's capital during the 8th century and was also the birthplace of Japanese arts, crafts and literature. Some of the many palaces, temples and mansions from this era still remain intact. KYOTO took over from Nara as capital in 794 and remained Japan's political centre until 1868, when Tokyo superseded it. The remnants of Kyoto's days of power can be seen in the many shrines, temples, palaces, villas and gardens. Kyoto is also known for its long history of local arts and crafts and the shops here are filled with silks, brocades, lacquerware and the like. OTSU is a town 10 minutes from Kyoto by train, on the edge of Biwa-ko Lake where fishing, swimming, boating and camping are popular pastimes.

Tokyo

NEW TOKYO INTERNATIONAL AIRPORT (NARITA)

Tokyo's new international airport was opened in 1978 amidst much controversy. The site was, and remains, one of the main problems: Narita is 40 miles out of Tokyo city and the roads to it are horrendously congested. When trying to get there from the city allow at least double the time you would expect to need for a 40-mile journey. The alternative is to book with an airline which still uses Tokyo Haneda International Airport (China Airlines is one of the few who do) which is much closer to Tokyo (12 miles out) and also handles most of Tokyo's domestic flights. To its credit though, it must be said that Narita Airport is very efficiently run and has superb facilities, so once there everything goes very smoothly for most passengers.

AIRPORT FACILITIES

All arrivals enter on the first floor of the terminal building and departures leave from the fourth floor. Immigration, Customs, quarantine, duty free shops, waiting lobbies and restaurants are on the second and third floors. The whole airport operates on a 24-hour basis.

Information Counter	On 1st and 4th floors.
Currency Exchange	On 1st and 4th floors.
Post Office	On basement level and 4th floor.
Shops	On basement level and 3rd, 4th and 5th floors.
Duty Free Shops	On 3rd floor. Sell all usual items, and accept major currencies and credit cards.
Restaurants	On 1st, 2nd, 4th and 5th floors.
Toilets	On all floors.
Telephone Office	On 1st floor.
Clinic	On the basement level.

City Bus Counters	1st floor.
Hotel Reservation Counter	1st floor.
Car Rental Desk	1st floor.

AIRPORT INFORMATION

Check-in Times	60 minutes prior to international flight departure times; 45 minutes prior to domestic flight departure times.
Departure Tax	Y2000 is payable by all departing adults (Y1000 children).
Medical Services	The clinic on the basement level provides emergency care and is very helpful and efficient.
Transferring Flights	International-to-international flight transfers are within the same terminal building. Some domestic flights go from Narita but most go from Haneda. There is a direct limousine bus service between the 2 airports (an 80-minute journey).

AIRPORT HOTELS

● **Super Club Class:**
Narita Prince Hotel – 560, Tokko Narita-shi, Chiba-ken (tel. 0476-33-1111).
Narita View Hotel – 700, Kosuge Narita-shi, Chiba-ken (tel. 0476-32-1111).

CITY LINKS

Travelling between Tokyo and the new international airport 40 miles away can be both expensive and very time-consuming. There are several ways of accomplishing the journey, each with its advantages and drawbacks. A recent trip into Tokyo took nearly three hours on the airport limousine bus, so allow plenty of time.

• **Airport Limousine Bus:** This is a non-stop service between the airport and the Tokyo City Air Terminal (TCAT). From TCAT there is a choice of hiring a cab or taking the subway to your hotel area. The subway station is a 7-minute walk from TCAT. Some of the limousine buses are scheduled to go via various hotels – check the schedule at the ticket counter in the Arrivals lobby of the airport.

• **Airport Express Bus:** Not as plush as the limousine bus and the fares are identical, but if your flight arrival time does not match the limousine's schedule then this is a good alternative. The express bus ticket counter is also in the Arrival lobby.

• **Keisei Train:** This is an inexpensive yet not too arduous way of getting into the city. Trains leave Keisei Airport Station (a 5-minute bus journey from the airport) regularly from 0630–1958 and take you to Keisei Ueno Station in downtown Tokyo (60–75 mins). This is only a short distance from Ueno JNR and subway stations. Total fare for the train/bus is Y980–1650.

• **JNR Train:** The JNR Narita Station is a 25-minute bus ride from the airport and trains from here go to JNR Tokyo Station. These trains are slightly more expensive than the Keisei trains but a Japan Rail Pass can be used on both them and on the JNR shuttle buses from airport to station.

• **Taxi:** Taxis are expensive and most have rather limited luggage space but they definitely provide the easiest way to accomplish a rather exhausting journey. For those with a lot of luggage there is a luggage delivery service (ABC Co. Ltd, who have a counter in the Arrival lobby) which will deliver to any hotel in Tokyo. It will cost you around Y20,000 for the 1½ hour trip. No tip expected.

TOKYO

With a population of over 11 million, Tokyo is one of the largest cities in the world and spreads itself over 2 counties and 7 islands. There is evidence of the site being inhabited as early as the Stone Age era and the village of Edo was founded in the 12th century. By the 17th century Edo had grown to become a city of political and cultural importance and, as Tokyo, it replaced Kyoto as the

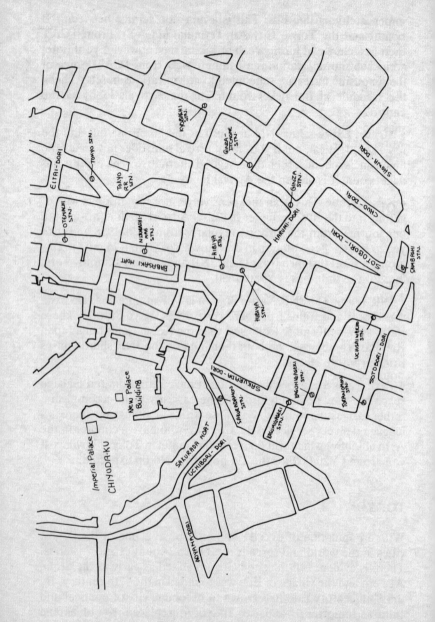

imperial city in 1868. An earthquake in 1923 and World War II bombing badly damaged the city but the industrial growth since then has been phenomenal. The inevitable side effects of this are serious atmospheric pollution and traffic congestion. However Tokyo is still an exciting city to visit with a host of things to do and see. Greater Tokyo engulfs the port at Yokohama and the industrial centre of Kawasaki and boasts over 100 universities including the massive University of Tokyo. Luckily this huge city has one of the world's most efficient and extensive public transport networks, so getting about to see the sights is not too much of a problem.

TOURIST INFORMATION

Tourist Information Centres – The main office is: Tokyo Office, 1, Yuraku-cho, Chiyodaku (tel. 502-1461). Open 0900–1700 hours Monday to Friday, 0900–1200 hours Saturday. There is also a TIC at Narita Airport.
Medical Services – St Luke's International Hospital (Seiroka Byoin), 10, Akashicho 1-chome, Chuo-ku, Tokyo (tel. 541-5151 between 0845 and 1100 hours daily).
   International Clinic, 9-5, Azabudai 1-chome, Minato-ku, Tokyo (tel. 582-2646 between 0900 and 1200 hours and 1500 and 1700 hours).
Teletourist Service – An around-the-clock information service of current events in Tokyo: tel. 503-2911 for the English version.
Emergency – Dial 110 for the police or 119 for fire or ambulance services.
Tokyo Area Telephone Code – 03.

GETTING ABOUT

Tokyo's public transport systems are rather complex to the uninitiated and a JNTO (Japan National Tourist Office) Tourist Map of Tokyo will be of great help. It has small maps of the railway and subway networks as well as a good street map.

• **Train and Subway:** 10 subways, 4 JNR commuter train lines and numerous private suburban rail lines connect Tokyo's sub-centres.

All of these operate trains every 2 to 10 minutes from early morning (about 0500 hours) to about midnight. Tickets are purchased at automatic, coin-operated vending machines in the stations, except long-distance JNR tickets which must be bought at the ticket counter or window. Tickets are collected at the exit wickets, so hang on to them.

• **Bus:** The bus system in Tokyo is complicated even to the Japanese so travelling by bus is not recommended to visitors unless they can read Japanese signs or have an interpreter with them.

• **Taxi:** Taxis are plentiful and easy to distinguish by their green licence plates. Fares are metered and increase between 2300 and 0500 hours. Tipping the driver is not customary practice. Two warnings: the back left-hand door is operated by remote control from the driver's seat, so stand back to avoid its path, and do not be surprised if the driver stops to ask the way – as many taxi drivers have come to Tokyo to search for work and are not as familiar with the street names as one would expect.

• **Car Rental:** Congested streets, Japanese signs and expensive hire car firms make driving yourself around hardly worthwhile. For those who do wish to hire a car, an international licence is required and driving is on the left.

SIGHTS

THE IMPERIAL PALACE is only actually open to the public on January 2 and April 29 – the Emperor's birthday – but the East Gardens can be walked through and the feudal gate and bridges admired. THE AKASAKA DETACHED PALACE was the residence of the Emperor Meiji in the 1800s, and this impressive building is now used for official government purposes. Dedicated to the Emperor Meiji and surrounded by acres of trees donated by the Japanese people in 1920, the MEIJI SHRINE is among the finest shrines in Japan. The grounds (180 acres) make a peaceful refuge from the bustle of the city and the Outer Gardens contain the Memorial Picture Gallery and the National Stadium (the venue of the 1964 Olympic Games).

The National Garden at SHINJUKU GYOEN has been turned into a huge recreation area (open 0900–1600 hours daily with an admission charge). Shinjuku is an important shopping and entertainment area popular with the young. A superb view over the city can be had from the top of the 52-storey Sumitomo Building to the west of Shinjuku Station.

TOSHOGU SHRINE is a 17th-century shrine which commemorates Ieyasu, the Tokugawa Shogunate founder. A 5-storey pagoda in front of the shrine dates back to 1639. And the ASAKUSA KANNON TEMPLE is a post-war concrete construction dedicated to the Goddess of Mercy. Although not really worthy of a visit in itself, the temple and its pagoda mark the centre of a lively area of the city for night-time amusements and are also the venue for the annual May Sanja Festival.

Exhibitions of modern art are interspersed with showings of specific groups of historical Japanese art works at the NATIONAL MUSEUM OF MODERN ART. Open daily (except Monday) 1000–1700 hours. Also, the METROPOLITAN FINE ART GALLERY holds exhibitions throughout the year, the most notable in the autumn. Open daily 0900–1700 hours, in Ueno Park.

GINZA is Tokyo's most concentrated area of shops, restaurants, nightclubs, theatres, etc. This is where a lot of the after-dark action is for businessmen and for company entertainment.

The CENTRAL WHOLESALE MARKET is a colourful, noisy and aromatic food market which, being on the harbourfront, is especially busy in the early morning when the fishing trawlers have returned with their catch.

TAMA ZOOLOGICAL PARK is a 106-acre zoo, much of which is 'open plan' – the animals kept captive in large areas edged by deep moats or sheer cliffs rather than fences or cages. The Lion Bus takes you through the Africa Garden, where families of lions have made their home.

In the massive UENO PARK (210 acres) many fine temples and shrines can be found as well as the National Science Museum, the Tokyo National Museum, the Tokyo University of Arts and the Metropolitan Fine Art Gallery and Festival Hall.

ACCOMMODATION

Tokyo has an amazing range of accommodation which is bound to cater for the needs of the vast majority of visitors. There are plenty of top-quality western-style hotels to choose from and there are also the Japanese-style ryokans. These are usually very comfortable and offer commendable service at reasonable prices. The differences include sleeping on a futon, or mattress, laid out on the floor of a tatami straw matted room and having access to a Japanese bath (often the communal sort) in which you can soak away the aches and strains of a hard day's sightseeing. Ryokans which have National Ryokan Association membership are guaranteed to be of good quality. Minshuku are the Japanese equivalent of guest houses which offer inexpensive, homely accommodation.

● **First Class:** (Y20,000–26,000 for a double)
Tokyo Hilton International – 6-2, Nishi-Shinjuku 6-chome, Shinjuku-ku, Tokyo 160 (tel. 344-5111). In a prime position overlooking the city's fashionable Shinjuku district, this Hilton lives up to the Hilton Group's usual high standards and is a pleasure to stay in.

Tokyo Prince Hotel – 3-1, Shibakoen 3-chome, Minato-ku, Tokyo 105 (tel. 432-1111). A huge, beautifully appointed hotel next to the Shiba Park gardens. The rooms are luxurious and the choice of cuisine in the numerous restaurants is vast.

Keio Plaza Inter-Continental Hotel – 2-2-1, Nishi-Shinjuku, Shinjuku-ku, Tokyo 160 (tel. 344-0111). One of the very best hotels in Tokyo, very luxurious with excellent facilities, and many fine restaurants serving Japanese and western cuisine.

● **Super Club Class:** (Y10,000–20,000 for a double)
Takanawa Prince Hotel – 3-13-1, Takanawa, Minato-ku, Tokyo 108 (tel. 447-1111). A very good hotel with all the comforts and services one could want to make one's stay enjoyable.

Ginza Dai-ichi Hotel – 8-13-1, Ginza, Chuo-ku, Tokyo 104 (tel. 542-5311). A fine hotel with extensive amenities and an excellent location in the busy Ginza area.

Ginza Tokyo Hotel – 5-15-9, Ginza, Chuo-ku, Tokyo 104 (tel. 541-2411). Good quality accommodation and service, also in the lively centre of the city.

The Century Hyatt – 2-7-2, Nishi-Shinjuku, Shinjuku-ku, Tokyo 160 (tel. 349-0111). An exceptionally luxurious hotel for its prices. A unique 'penthouse' swimming pool on the 28th floor offers superb views over the city.

● **Economy:** (Y5000–10,000 for a double)
Hotel Daiei – 1-15-8, Koishikawa, Bunkyo-ku, Tokyo 112 (tel. 813-6271). A clean, comfortable hotel in one of Tokyo's many suburbs.

Tokyo Hotel Urashima – 2-5-23, Harumi, Chuo-ku, Tokyo 104 (tel. 533-3111). Good accommodation in a central location.

Tokyo Kanko Hotel – 4-10-8, Takanawa, Minato-ku, Tokyo 108 (tel. 443-1211). Limited facilities but adequate accommodation and service.

Ryokan Namiju – Near Asakusa Station (tel. 841-9126). A moderately priced, good quality ryokan which will provide you with a real flavour of the Japanese lifestyle.

Ryokan Sasuiso – Near Gotanda Station (tel. 441-7475). Another very Japanese household where the staff are friendly and courteous and the rooms are very comfortable.

Yashima Ryokan – Near Okubo Station (tel. 364-2534). As with the other ryokans, this is comfortable, inexpensive and a real Japanese experience.

Minshuku Chojuso – Near Shinjuku Station (tel. 378-3810). A Japanese-style guest house in a conveniently central spot.

Tokyo Kokusai Youth Hostel – Near Iidabashi Station (tel. 235-1107). A showpiece youth hostel which would put most European ones to shame. On the 18th and 19th floors of a high-rise building, the rooms have great views over central Tokyo.

DINING OUT

Wherever you are in Tokyo, you will never be far from a restaurant. As they are popular social centres for the Japanese there are plenty of them and many serve breakfasts and lunches as well as the evening meal. Within the range of Japanese cuisine available are such dishes as sushi, tempura, tonkatsu and sukiyaki. There are many specialist restaurants which will only serve one variety of

Japanese food while others serve a wide selection of both Japanese and Japanized western food. Lunching out is popular and most restaurants serve excellent set meals called 'teishoku' at very reasonable prices. Breakfast buffets at major hotels are also good value but better value are the 'morning service' breakfasts served in coffee shops all over Tokyo. For a really good evening of eating out it is quite fun to have a different course in each of several specialist restaurants, with a pleasant walk through the streets of the city in between.

● **First Class:** (Y14,000–20,000 for two)
Chenonceaux – The Century Hyatt Hotel, 27th Floor (tel. 349-0111). French haute cuisine served in the finest surroundings and with the greatest of care and attention to your every wish.

Minokichi – B1, Roi Roppongi Building (tel. 404-0767). A Japanese restaurant serving traditional Kyoto cuisine as its speciality.

Imperial Hotel Restaurant – 1-1-1, Uchisaiwaicho Chiyoda-ku (tel. 504-1111). A world-renowned top-class restaurant where Japanese food can be tasted at its best. Booking is essential.

● **Super Club Class:** (Y6000–14,000 for two)
Ginza Suehiro – 7-108, Ginza, Chuo-ku (tel. 571-7565). A popular Japanese beef restaurant – the shabu-shabu is delicious.

Totenko – Toho Twin Tower Building, 3rd Floor, 2-1, Yuraku-cho, Chiyoda-ku. A good selection of Chinese dishes served in Chinese-style surroundings.

Ketel's – 5, 5-chome, Ginza, Chuo-ku. Good, solid German food which would satisfy even the hungriest tourist.

● **Economy:** (under Y6000 for two)
Bangawan Solo – 7-18-13, Roppongi, Minato-ku. Excellent Indonesian cuisine at very reasonable prices.

Steak-Corner Koma – Toho Twin Tower Building, 2nd Basement, 2-1, Yuraku-cho, Chiyoda-ku. One of Tokyo's many steak houses which serves top-quality steaks in a variety of ways.

Edogin – 4-5-1, Tsukiji, Chuo-ku. A sushi specialist Japanese restaurant.

Antonio's – 1-20, 3-chome Nishi Azabu, Minato-ku. A tasty Italian menu is on offer here at reasonable prices.

Many of Japan's pubs serve good pub-style meals and snacks in the evenings or at lunchtime. These are usually very good value and satisfying, especially when swilled down with Japanese beer.

NIGHTLIFE

Like any large city, Tokyo has plenty of after-dark entertainment on offer. Apart from the usual range of pubs, nightclubs, theatres and cinemas there is a distinctly Japanese type of entertainment to be found in the classic NOH PLAYS and the more lively KABUKI performances. The latter is performed daily at the Kabukisa Theatre while the former is performed in various venues around Tokyo. The National Theatre puts on several performances of BUNRAKU PUPPET THEATRE each year. Then there are the GEISHA HOUSES with their wonderful hostesses who provide fascinating evenings of folklore – contrary to popular belief they are not 'women of the night' but very gracious hostesses well versed in the arts of the Tea Ceremony and Flower Arrangement.

Japanese-style pubs (aka-chochin) are inexpensive and a good place to meet the locals. They serve beer, whisky and sake – the national drink – as well as food. Wine bars are becoming more common, especially in the Ginza and Roppongi areas. Some of Tokyo's more popular NIGHTCLUBS include the Copacabana (4-6, 3-chome, Akasaka, Minato-ku, tel. 585-5811), and the New Latin Quarter (13-8, 2-chome, Nagata-cho, Chiyoda-ku, tel. 581-1326). The Japanese are also keen pachinko (Japanese pinball) players and pachinko parlours can be found all over the city. Newspapers or the Tokyo Tourist Information Centre board will have up-to-date information on night entertainment.

EXCURSIONS

Short trips from Tokyo will show you some interesting places including some of the country's major attractions. MOUNT FUJI is a spectacular mountain and is recognized as the symbol of Japan.

Climbing it takes about 5 hours and many people set off at midnight, to reach the summit by daybreak. GOTEMBA, 50 miles south-west of Tokyo, is one of the nearest cities to Mount Fuji. Going more directly south of Tokyo, KAMAKURA is an ancient city, having been the leading city of Japan in the 13th century, full of historic remains. Its most famous sight is the Daibutsu, a huge bronze figure of Buddha. West of Kamakura is the famous beach resort of ENOSHIMA which has an aquarium and marine centre as well as good beaches. Back towards Tokyo is YOKOHAMA, the port city for Tokyo and the second largest city in Japan. KAWASAKI is the nearby industrial city which has little to interest tourists.

Off the coast of Tokyo, but within its administrative bounds, are several small islands known as IZU SHICHI-TO (Seven Islands), two of which have live volcanoes at their centre. Historically places of exile, the islands have now become popular holiday resorts.

Turning inland, the city of NARITA, near the New International Airport, is famed for its Shinsho-ji temple, built in AD 940. The park behind the temple is a pleasant place to wander around and is a good example of a well kept, traditional Japanese garden. Further north is the KASUMIGAURA LAKE area which is very scenic and over to the west is the historically interesting city of KAWAGOE. Near the latter is the huge CHICHIBU-TAMA NATIONAL PARK, made up of the two parallel valleys named Chichibu and Okutama. Trailing, hiking and nature walking are popular pastimes here.

Korea, Republic of South

RED TAPE

• **Passport/Visa Requirements:** A full, valid passport is required by everyone wishing to enter Korea. Visitors with confirmed onward tickets may stay for up to 15 days without visas. For longer visits a visa must be obtained prior to arrival in Korea, with the following exceptions: for a stay not exceeding 3 months citizens of Greece, Liechtenstein and Mexico do not need visas; for a stay not exceeding 90 days citizens of Austria, Bangladesh, Chile, Colombia, Costa Rica, Dominican Republic, Liberia, Malaysia, Peru, Singapore and Thailand do not need visas; for a stay not exceeding 60 days citizens of Belgium, Denmark, Finland, Iceland, Italy, Lesotho, Luxembourg, the Netherlands, Norway, Portugal, Spain, Sweden, Turkey and the UK do not need visas; for a stay not exceeding 30 days citizens of France and Tunisia do not need visas.

CUSTOMS

• **Duty Free:** Each visitor may bring in 400 cigarettes, 50 cigars, 250g pipe tobacco and 100g other tobacco; the total quantity not to exceed 500g. They may also bring in 2 bottles of wine or spirits, plus 2 ounces of perfume and gifts up to the value of W100,000. Duty must be paid on video tape recorders, video cameras, movie cameras and projectors. Export of Korean antiques or valuable cultural items requires approval from the Ministry of Culture and Information (tel. 725-3053 or 662-0106). Export limits of ginseng are as follows: red ginseng or white ginseng 1200 grammes, red ginseng tablets 900.

HEALTH

No vaccinations are currently required for entry to Korea, except from travellers arriving direct from a cholera-infected country. It is advisable to boil water if outside the main centres. Medical insurance is recommended. Hotels will recommend good local doctors. It is unwise to eat uncooked vegetables in Korea.

CAPITAL – Seoul.

POPULATION – 37,440,000.

LANGUAGE – Korean and English.

CURRENCY – Won = 100 Jeon. Notes are in denominations of 500, 1000, 5000 and 10,000 Won. Coins are in denominations of 1, 5, 10, 50, 100 and 500 Won.
£1 = 1100Won; US$1 = 785Won.

BANKING HOURS – 1000–1700 hours Monday to Friday, 1000–1400 hours Saturday.

POLITICAL SYSTEM – Republic.

RELIGION – Buddhist with Christian minority.

PUBLIC HOLIDAYS

January 1, 2, 3	New Year
March 1	Independence Day
April 5	Labour Day
May 5	Children's Day
May (1 day)	Buddha's Birthday
June 6	Memorial Day
July 17	Constitution Day
August 15	Liberation Day
September 10	Thanksgiving Day
September (1 day)	Chusok
October 1	Armed Forces Day
October 3	National Foundation Day
October 9	Korean Alphabet Day (Hangul)
December 25	Christmas

CLIMATE – Korea has a moderate climate with four seasons. During the hottest part of the year, from June to August, temperatures of 95°F (35°C) can be reached. This is also the rainy season and tends to be very humid. December and January are the coldest months, with temperatures of between 54°F (12°C) and −2°F (−19°C). Spring and autumn are mild and mainly dry.

TIME DIFFERENCE – GMT + 9 hours.

COMMUNICATIONS

• **Telephone:** Local calls may be made from booths in most buildings and along the streets. Two W10 coins are needed to make a call.

There is not a full IDD service so call 1030 in Seoul or 117 in Pusan to make an international call. Cables can be sent by dialling 115. The dialling code for Seoul is 02 and for Pusan 051.

● **Post:** Post Office hours are 0900–1800 Monday to Saturday. Airmail to the UK takes up to 10 days. Telex/telegrams can be sent from all main Post Offices.

ELECTRICITY – 100 and 220v AC.

OFFICE/SHOPPING HOURS – Offices: 0900–1800 hours Monday to Friday, 0900–1300 hours Saturday. Department stores: 1030–1930 hours daily. Smaller shops, markets and small businesses keep their own hours.

● **Best Buys:** Korea is rapidly becoming a famous place for shopping. Seoul, in particular, offers an endless range of goods at very reasonable prices which bargaining can bring down even further. Being host to the 1988 Olympics has caused much improvement and expansion of Seoul's shopping facilities. Antiques, embroidery, brassware, bambooware, ceramics and lacquerware are of high quality and among the best bargains in Korea. Insa-dong, or Mary's Alley, is the best-known district in Seoul for antique and art goods. Just outside Seoul are Yoju and Ich'on where you can see potters producing their wares and can often buy goods at prices lower than in the city. Similarly, the old Shilla capital city of Kyongju has great antique and traditional handicraft items.

Ginseng is probably the most popular buy in Korea. This ancient herb is considered a 'cure-all' with excellent rejuvenating powers. The root takes about 6 years to reach maturity and be harvested, but ginseng has been discovered that is over 100 years old. Red ginseng, the superior of the two types, is government controlled to ensure purity and quality. White ginseng is privately cultivated. Both are sold in root, powdered, liquid or pill form. Export of ginseng is limited (see 'Customs' section on p. 441).

Jewellery is another popular item on sale due to Korea's plentiful natural resources of the semi-precious stones amethyst and smoky topaz. Jade is also a common sight in jewellery shops here. Clothing can be bought for remarkably good prices, silk, leather and fur goods being the best value. Korea's skilled tailors and dressmakers are well worth a visit for anyone who wants a new outfit. Korea is home to the world's fur industry, and the headquarters of the largest fur company – Jindo Furs. Though their bargain luxury furs in Hong Kong are incentive enough to make thousands of people travel there just to buy them, the deals you can get in Korea pay for your airfare! Their showroom at the Yu Yeong Shopping Arcade, Itaewon Main Street, Seoul, shows a range of exclusive furs at prices ranging from US$100 to $5000. Of all the fur companies in Seoul this one has the best reputation and is the one to visit first.

Shopping areas in Seoul are all quite easily reached by buses, taxis or the new subway system. Tongdaemun Market on Chongno Street is the largest, most colourful market-place in Korea, where you can find everything from silks to buttons, fish to running shoes. Namdaemun Market is a smaller, open-air market near the downtown and first-class hotel area. Again, you will find a vast range of goods for sale but also vast numbers of people jostling along the rows of stalls – if you are a crowd hater this is not the place to go. Antique markets at Changan-dong and Tapshimni-dong, in the eastern suburbs, are the next best place to go for antiques after Insa-dong. The fashion capital of Seoul is Myong-dong, where shoe shops, silk stores and boutiques abound. This is also a popular nightspot for Korea's office workers, with fashionable restaurants, clubs, pubs and discos. For the real bargain hunters, It'aevon is the place to go. It is a long street lined with shops and entertainment spots on the south side of Mount Namsan (a few minutes' drive from downtown Seoul). Tailor-made clothes, sportswear, silks and high fashion outfits are the speciality of this area. In central, downtown Seoul are many big department stores and shopping arcades and the subway has become a warren of shopping tunnels.

Bargaining is expected in many stores and all markets but in the big department stores and high fashion boutiques prices tend to be fixed.

INTERNAL TRAVEL

• **Air:** Korean Airlines (KAL) is Korea's only domestic airline and has a good network of routes connecting major cities and tourist areas. Fares are reasonable and reservations can be made through travel agents or directly through KAL offices – Seoul 756-2000 or Pusan 44-0131. Have your passport to hand when boarding domestic flights. Officially, loaded cameras are not allowed on board.

● **Train:** Korean National Railroads maintains an extensive and efficient network of railways. There are 4 choices of train – the fast, air-conditioned Saemaul ho, the limited-stop Mugung hwa, the similar but not air-conditioned Tongil ho, and the local trains known as Wanheng. Train timetables are in Korean and very few of the ticket clerks speak English. If you are stuck, contact Seoul 392-7788 ext. 2178 for train information for tourists.

● **Bus:** Major cities are linked by high-speed, air-conditioned 'Kosok' buses. The 'Chikheng' buses serve local areas and make scheduled stops in towns, but will usually drop you off wherever you want. 'Wanheng' buses are even more local and will pick up or drop off anywhere. Fares are very reasonable on all buses.

● **Car Rental:** An International Driver's Licence is required to drive in Korea. Hertz Korean Rent-A-Car have offices in most major cities. For details call Seoul 585-0801 or Pusan 44-8888. Chauffeur-driven cars are also available.

MAJOR SIGHTS OF THE COUNTRY

SEOUL is the capital, and heart, of the Republic of Korea and contains nearly one quarter of its population. It makes a good base from which to travel to some of Korea's other cities and rural areas. The scenic Yongdong Expressway connects Seoul with KANGNUNG on the east coast. Sandy beaches and surf fishing make this a popular tourist area. Further north are several interesting towns including SOKCH'O, a fishing centre and gateway to MOUNT SORAK-

SAN NATIONAL PARK – a major attraction in the region. Just south of this is MOUNT ODAESAN, which is noted for its ski resorts and is also home to the famous Woljongsci Temple and Pagoda. Nearby, the coastal town of YONGDOK is famous for its delicious crab dishes.

Korea's central region consists of Ch'ungch'ong-buk-do, Chi'ungch'ongnam-do, and Kyong-sangbuk-do Provinces. TAEJON is the capital of Ch'ungch'ongnam-do Province and is a major city full of interesting sights. Nearby is the Yuoong resort area with hot springs. KYERYONGSAN mountain is popular for climbing and notable for its superb autumn foliage. North-east of Taejon is MOUNT SONGNISAN NATIONAL PARK, home of Popchusa Temple (which dates from AD 553). To the south of this is another famous Buddhist temple, CHICKCHISA. In Kyong-sangbuk-do Province is the city of ANDONG, an extremely interesting area where the Confucian traditions are strongly upheld. Yangban houses, preserved from the Yi Dynasty, can be seen both here and in the nearby village of HAHOE.

South-eastern Korea is rich in historical buildings and artefacts. PUSAN, on the south-eastern tip of the peninsula, is the primary port for connections with Japan. Inland is TAEGU, home to many colleges and universities and also a market town, being in the heart of Korea's agricultural country.

The west coast of Korea is often called the 'rice bin', especially in the HONAM area, as it is rich in rice paddies. Inland, the PAEKCHE region has many historical remains from when it was one of the original three kingdoms of ancient times. ONYANG is a hot spring area west of Seoul renowned for the medicinal qualities of its water and also a popular honeymoon spot. Further south on the west coast is TAECH'ON beach resort which is a popular holiday spot for families. KWANGJU, capital of Chouanam-do Province, is a fast developing city whose National Museum houses Chinese porcelains found on the ocean bottom in 1976 after 600 years of submersion.

HALLYO WATERWAY is a stretch of water running from HANSANDO ISLAND, south of Pusan, to YOSU in the west. The area encompasses 400 islands, many of which are uninhabited and have curious rock formations and caves. CHEJU-DO ISLAND, further out off the south-western coast, is said to be Korea's Hawaii. It is certainly an extremely popular tourist destination with semi-tropical weather, beaches and a central volcanic mountain whose winter snow provides good skiing.

Seoul

KIMPO INTERNATIONAL AIRPORT

Seoul's international airport is 20 miles west of the city. Its one passenger terminal deals with all international and domestic arrivals and departures.

AIRPORT FACILITIES

Information Desks
Bank with Currency Exchange
Post Office
Restaurant
Bar
Duty Free Shops
Hotel Reservation Counter
Car Rental Desk – Avis

AIRPORT INFORMATION

Check-in Times	60 minutes before international flight departure times; 30 minutes before domestic flight departure times.
Airport Tax	Each departing passenger (on international flights only) must pay Won3700 in cash.
Flight Transfers	Passengers transferring will be ushered to the departure lounge. Connections take 90 minutes for international-to-international flight transfers and 60 minutes for international-to-domestic flight transfers.

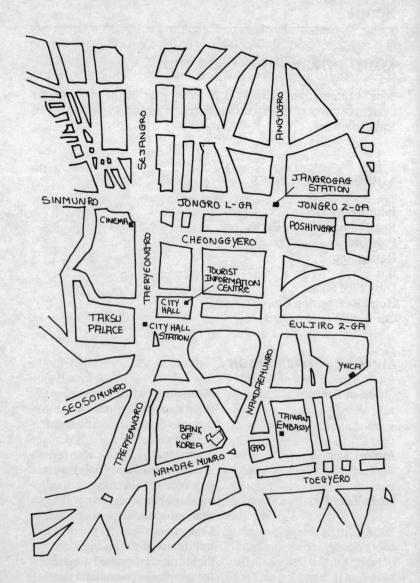

CITY LINKS

• **Bus:** Two airport bus lines connect Kim Po Airport with the city and major hotels. Number 601 goes to the Sheraton Hotel via the Plaza and Seoul Garden Hotels. Number 600 goes via Chamshil to the Palace Hotel, Express Bus Terminal, Riverside Hotel, Korea Exhibition Centre and Sports Complex. Buses depart from the airport every 15 minutes from 0600 to 2150. Bus fares are cheap (500Won).

• **Taxi:** There is a taxi rank of yellow and green cabs outside the airport terminal, or taxis can be called on Seoul 414-0150/9. The fare is about 7 times as much as the bus, and the journey takes 35–45 mins. If the driver helps with luggage, a tip is required. The city's brown taxis can be called for at the airport, though these cost more – about Won5000 to the centre.

SEOUL

The establishment of the Yi Dynasty, in 1392, resulted in the establishment of Seoul as the capital city. This dynasty lasted until 1910 and kept Korea very 'closed' to the world. It was during this time that the shrines, palaces and fortresses which can be seen today were constructed. The city served as the centre of Japanese-occupied Korea from 1910–1945 and then suffered considerable damage in the Korean War (1950–53). Since then Seoul has rapidly developed into a leading industrial, commercial, administrative and business centre, with the remaining ancient buildings jostling for space among high-rise office blocks and hotels.

Seoul is situated on the River Han near the north-west coast of South Korea. Many bridges span the river, connecting north and south Seoul, subway lines also cross the river.

Note: On the 15th of each month, the city closes down (sometime between 11 a.m.–2 p.m.) for about 30 minutes for a civil defence drill. If possible avoid being in transit at that time.

TOURIST INFORMATION

Seoul Tourist Information Centre – 311-ka, T'aep'yngno Chung-gu
(behind the City Hall), tel. 731-6337.
Medical Services – Paik Foundation Hospital, tel. 265-6121.
   Seoul National University Hospital, tel. 7610-0114.
Emergencies – Police tel. 112.
   Ambulance/Fire Brigade tel. 119.

GETTING ABOUT

● **Taxi:** Regular taxis (yellow or green) can be hailed in the street or
found at taxi ranks and are cheaper than 'call' taxis (beige) which
can be ordered by telephone (Seoul 414-0150/9). Hotel taxis are
available from major hotels.

● **Subway:** A fast, efficient and expanding system of underground
travel. Fares are distance-linked and very reasonable.

● **Bus:** Plentiful but still overcrowded, buses are cheap and usually
reliable. No English signs or timetables are available so orientation
on the bus service network can be a problem. The KNTC (tourist
organization) has launched a 'goodwill guide' campaign whereby
Korean citizens who can speak English, French, Japanese, Spanish
or German wear badges and are happy to help tourists around the
city.

SIGHTS

TOKSUGUNG-SEJONGNO-KYONGBOKHUNG (City Hall), was constructed during the Japanese occupation and stands in the main
downtown plaza of the city centre.

   TOKSUGUNG PALACE was a royal villa used as the palace during the
first 2 decades of this century. Renaissance stone buildings in the
palace grounds now house the Museum of Modern Art. Open
0900–1700 daily (November–March) and 0900–1800 daily (April–
October).

SEJONGNO BOULEVARD is an attractive street and an interesting contrast of old and new architecture. The Anglican Church, a red brick edifice dating from 1926, is in the vicinity. The SEJONG CULTURAL CENTRE complex houses auditoria for concerts, pageants and conferences of all kinds. At the head of Sejongno, the KWANGHWAMUN GATE used to guard the Kyongbokkung Palace but is now mainly decorative, the palace having another entrance. The KYONGBOKKUNG PALACE itself was originally burnt down in the 1592 Japanese invasions, and rebuilt in 1867. The main branch of the National Museum is within the palace.

The CH'ANGDOKKUNG PALACE was also burned in 1592 but restored in 1611. Its best known feature is its 'Secret Garden' (Piwon) – 78 acres of superbly landscaped gardens with pavilions, ponds and woods. Tours in English are available at 1130, 1330 and 1530 daily, April–October, and at 1000 and 1300 daily, November–March.

The CH'ANGGYONGGUNG PALACE is another royal residence from the Yi Dynasty whose grounds were used as zoological and botanical gardens. The palace and grounds are currently undergoing renovation.

PAGODA PARK is a parkland lying to the south-west of the city, on Chongno Street, renowned for its 10-storeyed Koryo Pagoda.

POSHINGAK, a famous city landmark, houses the huge bell, cast in 1468, which once tolled the closing of the city gates at dusk. Now it is only rung on special occasions. The original was actually cracked during the Korean War and is now in a museum. In August 1985 it was replaced by a new bell.

MOUNT NAMSAN is a large granite mountain in the heart of the city. Namsan Tower gives the best views over Seoul.

Finally, YOUIDO, one of the newest additions to Seoul's ever-growing metropolitan area, is on a small island in the Han-gang River.

ACCOMMODATION

Over the past few years Korea, and especially Seoul, has put a lot of time and money towards building and upgrading hotels. In preparation for the Asian Games in 1986 and the Olympics in 1988, more and more hotels are appearing. A cheap alternative to the conventional type of accommodation is the homely, Korean-style yogwans which provide basic Korean bedding (a 'yo' or mattress and an 'ibul' or quilt) with 'ondol' floor heating in the winter.

• **First Class:** (Double over W10,000 per person)
Hilton International – 395, 5-ka, Namdaemunno, Chung-gu, Seoul (tel. 753-3788/7788). The usual top-quality standards and additional luxuries. Situated on 4 acres of garden in the heart of the city's business district.

Sheraton Walker Hill – San 21, Kwangjong-dong, Songdong-gu, Seoul (tel. 453-0121). Situated amidst 139 acres of landscaped garden, this is one of Seoul's most luxurious hotels with fantastic facilities.

Westin Chosun – 87, Sogong-dong, Chung-gu, Seoul (tel. 77105). An exceptional hotel near City Hall in the very heart of Seoul. The Westin's service and hospitality makes it a lovely place to stay.

• **Super Club Class:** (Double W7500–10,000 per person)
Hotel Poong Jun – 73-1, 2-ga, Inhyon-dong, Chung-gu, Seoul (tel. 266-2151). A very comfortable hotel in downtown Seoul with extensive facilities.

Seoulin Hotel – 149 Son'n-dong, Chongno-gu, Seoul (tel. 732-0181). A business-class hotel in the city centre.

Seokyo Hotel – 354-5, Sogyo-dong, Map'o-gu, Seoul (tel. 393-7771). Located to the west of Seoul, nearer the airport. Very good sports facilities and nightclub.

Tower Hotel – San 5-5, 2-ga, Changch'ung-dong, Chung-gu, Seoul (tel. 253-9181/9). A modern, good quality hotel set in 18 acres of garden at the foot of Mount Namsan, in the city centre.

• **Economy:** (Double W5000–8000 per person)
Hotel Green Park – San 14, Ui-dong, Tobong-gu, Seoul (tel. 993-2171/8). A comfortable hotel on the slope of Mount Pukhansan in the northern suburbs of Seoul.

Central Hotel – 227-1, Changsa-dong, Chongno-gu, Seoul (tel. 265-4121/9). Good facilities in downtown Seoul.

Yoido Tourist Hotel – 10-3, Youido-dong, Yongdungp'o-gu, Seoul (tel. 782-0121/5). Limited facilities but comfortable accommodation near the National Assembly Building.

New Oriental Hotel – 10, 3-ga, Hoehyon-dong, Chung-gu, Seoul (tel. 753-0701/6). Basic but comfortable and located at the foot of Mount Namsan.

YMCA Tourist Hotel – 9, 2-ga, Chongno, Chongno-gu, Seoul (tel. 732-8291/8). A good standard of accommodation, in the downtown area, at low prices.

Boolim Tourist Hotel – 620 27, Chonnong 2-dong, Tongdaemun-gu, Seoul (tel. 962-0021/5). Adequate facilities, including a nightclub, and comfortable accommodation.

DINING OUT

Korean food tends to be highly spiced with red peppers and garlic but can be toned down on request. Rice, fish, chicken, beef and vegetables are common ingredients of a Korean dish, the most famous being kimchi (fermented, pickled vegetables) and pulgogi (marinated, charcoal grilled beef). For those who prefer more western-style food there are a variety of French, Italian and Swiss restaurants. There are also some excellent Japanese and Chinese places.

● **First Class:** (above W5000 per person)
The Seasons – Hilton Hotel (tel. 753-3788). Famed for its continental haute cuisine and elegant surroundings.

Hotel Lotte Korean Restaurant – Hotel Lotte (tel. 771-10). One of the best places in Korea to try out some excellent Korean dishes.

Arisan – Namsan (tel. 793-7396). Expensive but delicious Chinese fare.

● **Super Club Class:** (above W7500 for two)
Korea House – P'il dong (tel. 267-8752). A banquet of Korean food with a traditional Korean show going on in the background.

Chalet Swiss – It'aewon (tel. 792-1723). Excellent Swiss/continental cuisine in pleasant surroundings.

Misooun – Sogong-dong (tel. 778-1131). Japanese food and style of restaurant. Well priced.

• **Economy:** (above W3000 for two)
Taewongak – Songbuk-dong (tel. 762-0161). Good Korean food at low prices.

Banjul – Chongno (tel. 733-1800). A steak house, in true western fashion.

Heeraedung – Namsan (tel. 792-6633). Good value Chinese food.

Namgang – Sogong-dong 8 (tel. 778-1141). An interesting selection of Japanese dishes.

NIGHTLIFE

Most of Seoul's major hotels have nightclubs with music and dancing to local or western bands. This is not Korean nightlife at its best, however. Good Korean nightclubs are found in Myongdong, Chongno, It'aewon and Hannamdong areas. Suljips are Korean drinking establishments which are cheaper than the nightclubs and full of atmosphere. Gambling is strictly controlled by the government and in Seoul the only place where a variety of games can be found is in the Sheraton Walker Hill Hotel's Casino (tel. 444-9111). Seoul has a number of theatres where Korean or western plays, concerts and films are shown.

EXCURSIONS

There are many places of interest in the Seoul vicinity which are easily accessible by bus, train or car. INCH'ON, Seoul's principal port, is at the end of one of the city's subway lines. This is an active area of beaches, nightclubs and restaurants. South of the city, SUWON has interesting walled fortress architecture from the Yi Dynasty and is close to the Korean FOLK VILLAGE – a living museum in which the Yi Dynasty lifestyle has been re-created. Also nearby is YONGIN FAMILY LAND which encompasses the Hoam Museum – a fine private Korean art collection – and a fantastic children's amusement park. In the southern suburb of KWACH'ON is Seoul GRAND PARK, zoological and botanical gardens set at the foot of Mount Ch'onggyesan.

West of Seoul lies KANGHWAOO ISLANDS, where the Koryo court sought refuge from the Mongols in the 13th century and fought western nations in the 19th. The island is peaceful and picturesque, and there are temples and shrines to visit and local products to buy.

P'ANMUNJOM lies to the north of Seoul and is the site of many discussions about the North–South Korean division which persists despite the armistice of 1953. Several ROYAL TOMB CLUSTERS lie to the north-east and north-west of Seoul. These are grassy mounds which cover the graves of Korea's royalty. Remains of old mountain fortresses which used to defend the city can also be seen around this area. Further to the north-east is CH'UNCH'ON, capital of Kangwon-do Province and one of Korea's most pleasant cities.

Malaysia

RED TAPE

• **Passport/Visa Requirements:** Most travellers need only a valid passport to stay in Malaysia for 3 months. Visas are not required. If you are a male with long hair and generally look 'undesirable', you will probably be required to show an onward air ticket, a visa for your next destination and sufficient funds for your stay, before being allowed in.

CUSTOMS

• **Duty Free:** The following may be brought into Malaysia without incurring Customs duty by returning residents who have left the country for more than 72 hours and foreign visitors intending to stay more than 72 hours: 200 cigarettes or 225 grammes tobacco, 1 litre wine or spirits; souvenirs up to the value of M$200; food preparations up to the value of M$75.

Restrictions exist on the export of antiquities, so if in doubt over purchases you have made, contact the Director of the Museum Negara in Kuala Lumpur.

HEALTH

Vaccinations are necessary for smallpox, cholera and yellow fever, only if arriving from an infected country, but it is best to be on the safe side. Precautions are also advised against malaria. Make sure you have adequate health insurance, and stick to bottled water away from hotels and cities.

CAPITAL – Kuala Lumpur. Population – 1 million.

POPULATION – 15 million.

LANGUAGE – Malay (Bahasa Malaysia). Various Indian and Chinese dialects. English widely spoken.

CURRENCY – Ringgit (Malaysian Dollar), divided into 100 cents. Notes – M$ 1, 5, 10, 20, 50, 100, 500, 1000. Coins – 1, 5, 10, 20, 50 cents, 1$.
£1 = M$3.65; US$1 = M$3.
Bank rates do tend to vary.

BANKING HOURS – 1000–1500 (Monday–Friday), 0930–1130 (Saturday).

POLITICAL SYSTEM – Parliamentary democracy.

RELIGION – Islam is the official religion.

PUBLIC HOLIDAYS

• **National:**

February	Chinese New Year
May 1	Labour Day
May 23	Wesak Day
June 4	Yang di Pertuan Agong's Birthday

June	Hari Raya Puasa
August	Hari Raya Haji
August 31	National Day
September	Awal Muharram
November	Deepavali
November 14	Birthday of Prophet Muhammad
December 25	Christmas Day

• **State:** In addition to these, there are some 30 other public holidays which vary from region to region.

CLIMATE – Basically it is hot and wet all year round in Malaysia, though it does not experience the extreme temperatures to be found elsewhere in the tropics. Days are sunny (around 80°F, 25°C) and often humid, while the nights can get quite cool, especially in the hills. The monsoon brings heavy rain to the eastern part of peninsular Malaysia between November and February, while December is wettest on the west coast. The western coast is fine for visiting all year round, while you should avoid the east coast during the rainy season. In East Malaysia (along the north coast of Borneo), Sabah has heavy rains from October to April, and Sarawak from October to February. You should take lightweight tropical clothes, preferably made from natural materials such as cotton which allow the skin to breathe. A light raincoat or umbrella is also worth taking. If you intend visiting any of the hill station resorts, take warmer clothing. Women should dress modestly when entering religious temples and also in rural areas, if travelling alone, to ward off unsolicited attention.

TIME DIFFERENCE – GMT + 8 hours.

COMMUNICATIONS

• **Telephone:** There is IDD from most cities, but you are better off phoning long distance from your hotel.

• **Post:** There are regulations governing the transmission of certain dutiable items. Postal rates vary from 20–55 cents.

ELECTRICITY – 220v AC. Many hotels supply adaptors.

OFFICE/SHOPPING HOURS – Government offices are open from 0800–1245 and 1400–1615, Monday–Friday (from 1430 on Friday afternoon) and from 0800–1245 Saturday. Shops are open 0930–1900 Monday–Saturday, and supermarkets from 1000–2200. Note that in Kedah, Perlis, Kelantan and Terangganu, offices and banks are not open on Fridays.

● **Best Buys:** Handicrafts, batiks, cloths, porcelain (Selangor pewter), antique furniture. Prints in Penang. In the east, wicker-work, woodwork, kites, folk weaving and pottery, silver jewellery. MARA, the Malaysian Government board, has a string of outlets offering good batiks and other handiwork. Spectacle frames are available at far lower prices than in Europe. However, serious shoppers should bear in mind that for real bargains, tax-free Singapore is only just along the coast.

INTERNAL TRAVEL

● **Air:** Malaysian Airlines runs an extensive network connecting all the major destinations, and service is courteous and efficient. On the peninsular mainland, distances aren't all that vast and you are probably better off travelling by rail or road. However, if you want to visit Sarawak or Sabah, you will almost certainly have to fly. You can make considerable savings on these routes by flying at night.

● **Rail:** The trains, run by Malayan Railways, are comfortable and many have air-conditioning and dining cars. Fares are quite reasonable, and a 'travel anywhere' Rail Pass (M$150 for 14 days, M$75 for 10) is seriously worth considering. There are no lines in Sarawak, though a fast train does connect Kota Kinabalu with Beaufort in Sabah.

● **Road:** Malaysia's roads are among the best in South East Asia, and long distance express coaches cover most of the country.

Taxis and bicycle-rickshaws (trishaws) are available in all the cities and though fares are cheap, you will nevertheless have to press your haggling skills into service to avoid paying over the odds.

Taxi fares are slightly higher for air-conditioned vehicles, and at night. If you want to travel long distance, you can make use of Malaysia's excellent shared-taxi system whereby you pay a flat rate for a seat in a car. A seat in a full cab from Butterworth (opposite Penang) to Kuala Lumpur costs about M$30 – the price of a second-class rail ticket.

Malaysia is a good place to explore in a hired car and prices are cheaper than in neighbouring Singapore. The rate is from around M$50 per day plus mileage and petrol, and there are cheaper weekly unlimited mileage rates. You will need an International Driving Licence and traffic travels on the left.

MAJOR SIGHTS OF THE COUNTRY

PENANG is one of the most underestimated destinations in South East Asia. It is actually an island off the north-east coast of Malaysia and is treated in more detail in our *City Guide* section (see p. 469). Also off the east coast are the almost deserted LANGKAWI ISLANDS, which are ideal for those who truly want to get away from it all; and the more accessible island of PANGKOR, which has fine beaches.

The capital, KUALA LUMPUR, is a busy, modern city 200 miles south of Penang. The old, red and white Masjid Jame Mosque is worth a visit and there are some fine buildings in the Moorish style, notably the palatial Railway Station. Chinatown, just south of the Masjid Jame, is a lively place to shop or eat, while for a more relaxing experience, you could visit the National Museum and Lake Gardens.

Near the capital are the impressive BATU CAVES, including the massive and aptly named Cathedral Cave. Between Penang and Kuala Lumpur are many hill stations where you can go on cool jungle walks. The most popular of these is CAMERON HIGHLANDS, near the lively town of IPOH, which can get rather crowded during the April, August and December holiday seasons.

A hundred miles south of Kuala Lampur lies the historic city of MALACCA. The Portuguese took the city in 1511 as a port for their spice trade and the main relics of their stay are the Porto de Santiago and the now ruined St Paul's Church. The Dutch took over and built the distinctive, salmon-pink coloured Stadthuys (town hall).

The east coast of the mainland has the better beaches, and also a number of idyllic tropical islands, such as romantic TIOMAN, which was used as a setting for the Hollywood musical *South Pacific*. The resorts start at KUANTAN, which is where the eastern highway from Kuala Lumpur terminates, and extend virtually up the whole of the eastern coast. RANTAU ABANG is the prime beach for giant turtle watching, while KUALA TRENGGANU has a lovely market. 50 miles west of here marks the beginning of TAMAN NEGARA, Malaysia's huge National Park. The scenery is wonderful, the climate mild and, if you are lucky, you should spot several species of wildlife.

The main attractions of SARAWAK and SABAH are their beautiful, rugged scenery and incredible diversity of tribes. KUCHING, the capital of Sarawak, is a green spacious city with numerous temples, and a splendid museum which is definitely worth a visit. Near the capital, the BAKO NATIONAL PARK features fine beaches and unspoilt equatorial rain forest. Further along the coast the NIAH CAVES are archaeologically important and provide many of the birds' nests for the famous Chinese delicacy. You can venture inland, up the mighty Rajang, into the dense tropical jungle and stay in a longhouse with the friendly Dyaks. Sabah's main attraction is the KINABULA NATIONAL PARK, featuring Mount Kinabula, the highest mountain in South East Asia at nearly 14,000 ft. The ascent (a steep walk) takes two days, but the views are fabulous.

HOTELS

Tourist development in Malaysia is proceeding apace and there are now many hotels of international standard, although most of the big chains have yet to move in. There is plenty of good, cheap accommodation, usually in Chinese hotels or government Rest Houses, for the budget traveller. Accommodation is more expensive in the hill stations and Kuala Lumpur, and savings of up to 25 per cent can be made by staying in the smaller, outlying resorts. A 10 per cent government tax and a 10 per cent service charge are added to hotel (and restaurant) bills.

NIGHTLIFE AND RESTAURANTS

Away from the big cities, there isn't all that much to do at night. However, do take the opportunity to soak in a little of the local culture. There are numerous festivals you can attend, and the influence of Chinese and Indian cultures is strong. Malaysia's variety of racial groups, all with their own distinctive cuisines, means that it is possible to eat very well indeed. There are a number of inexpensive Chinese restaurants, and several establishments offering quality Indian dishes. While there aren't that many Malay restaurants around, there are plenty of food stalls, with the best ones being in the night markets in Kuala Lumpur. Malay food is quite spicy and you'll find that each state in the country has its own distinctive flavour. Those who prefer to stick to European food will be struggling outside the main cities, but KL, as the capital is referred to, has a surprising variety of western restaurants. Make sure you sample some of the amazing tropical fruits to be found throughout the whole of the country.

Kuala Lumpur

SUBANG INTERNATIONAL AIRPORT

Kuala Lumpur's international airport is 14 miles west of the city. There are two passenger terminals: Terminal 1 deals with international flight arrivals and Terminal 2 with international flight departures plus domestic flight arrivals and departures. Both are within the same building, which has the following facilities.

AIRPORT FACILITIES

Information Desk
Bar
Buffet   All these facilities are available
                              in either the Arrivals or
                              Departure lounges.

Restaurant
Bank with Currency Exchange
Post Office
Baggage Deposit

Car Rental Desks	Avis, Sintat and National.
Duty Free Shops	These sell cigarettes, cigars, tobacco, wines, aperitifs, spirits, lighters. UK and USA currencies are accepted, plus major credit cards.

AIRPORT INFORMATION

Check-in Times	90 minutes prior to international flight departure times; 45 minutes prior to domestic flight departure times.
Airport Tax	For domestic flights each departing passenger must pay M$2, for flights to Brunei or Singapore M$4 and for international flights M$7.
Airport Flight Enquiries	Telephone Kuala Lumpur 767-550.

CITY LINKS

• **Bus:** Of the public bus services, a number 47 goes from the Toshiba terminal on Jalan Sultan Mohamed to the airport and back every hour. Airport coaches go from the Klang bus station to the airport and back regularly. They are slightly more expensive than the public buses.

• **Taxi:** There is a coupon system in operation at the airport – the airport taxi counter takes your fare and you give the driver a receipt. This stops inflated taxi fares from airport to city, but beware of taxi touts in the airport who try to dodge the system.

KUALA LUMPUR

It was the presence of tin that caused the tiny mining settlement of Ampang to develop into the major city of Kuala Lumpur (which means 'muddy river mouth'). Two Malay chieftains named Abdullah and Juma'at arrived at the site in 1857 with about 80 hired Chinese miners and found tin. By 1880 the business was flourishing so much that the Sultan of Selangor decided to move to Kuala Lumpur and make it his state capital in preference to Klang. British colonial rule took over for the ensuing years until the Japanese occupation. In 1957 national independence was achieved and in 1963 Malaysia was founded.

Today Kuala Lumpur is a major commercial centre serving an important tin-mining and rubber-growing area. It is a busy and cosmopolitan city. The river junction between Kelang and Gombek Rivers, which gave the city its name, is in the heart of the city with Chinatown immediately to the south. The central green area, the Padang, is intersected by two of Kuala Lumpur's major roads – Jalan Tun Perak and Jalan Tuanku Abdul Rahman.

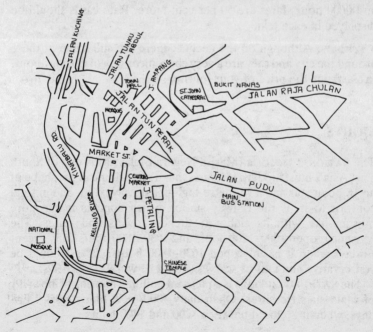

TOURIST INFORMATION

Kuala Lumpur Tourist Association – K.L. Railway Station (tel. 81-832).
Tourist Information Centre – In the TDC Duty Free Shop, Bukit Nanas Complex, Jalan Raja Chulan (tel. 206-742).
Emergency Number – Dial 999 for ambulance, fire or police.
Kuala Lumpur Area Code – 03.

GETTING ABOUT

• **Bus:** There are 2 bus systems in Kuala Lumpur – the cheaper, slower fare stage buses and the faster, fixed fare, mini-buses. The main bus terminals are the Pudu Raya terminal on Jalan Pudu and the Toshiba terminal on Jalan Sultan Mohamed.

• **Taxis:** These are plentiful and fares are reasonable. A small charge is added for anything over 2 passengers and between 0100 and 0600 hours fares are 50 per cent more. Rate cards should be displayed in each taxi.

• **Trishaw:** Although on the decline, there are still some of these around the city and they are a very convenient way of getting about. Pre-arrange the price of your journey.

SIGHTS

The NATIONAL MOSQUE (Masjid Negara Malaysia) is one of South East Asia's most modern mosques, has a main dome in the shape of an 18-point star and a 73-metre-high minaret. Next to, and in total contrast to it, is the railway station which appears much more mosque-like with its elaborate arches, towers and spires. The Mosque is open 1000–1200 hours and 1630–1800 hours daily except Fridays when it is only open 1630–1800 hours. Dress should be conservative and hats or scarves should be worn.

The NATIONAL MUSEUM is a pleasant building housing a fine array of Malaysia's treasures. Open daily 1000–1830 hours except Fridays, when it is closed between 1200 and 1400 hours.

PARLIAMENT HOUSE is a large, architecturally interesting mix of eastern- and western-style buildings. Tidy lawns and gardens surround the house and give it a spacious, peaceful atmosphere. Visitors may attend parliament sessions by obtaining a gallery pass.

As well as having a collection of Malaysian works of art the NATIONAL ART GALLERY also houses international exhibitions of contemporary art. Open 1000–1830 hours daily except Fridays when it is closed from 1200 to 1400 hours.

Masjid Jame is a beautiful old red and white mosque which marks the junction of the two rivers. It is lit up at night and looks especially spectacular.

The LAKE GARDENS consist of twin lakes surrounded by land-scaped gardens in which stand Parliament House, the National Museum, the bronze National Monument and other prominent buildings.

ACCOMMODATION

Many of Kuala Lumpur's hotels are of top international class and have excellent restaurants. It is necessary to book in advance, especially during Easter, midsummer and Christmas. The city's more basic accommodation may have kolams (a sort of water trough) instead of baths or showers. Hotel bills have 10 per cent government tax and 10 per cent service charge automatically added to them.

• **First Class:** (Double M$150–200)
The Oriental – Jalan Bukit Bintang, 55100 Kuala Lumpur (tel. 230-3000). A newly opened and very superior hotel which lives up to the Mandarin Oriental Hotel Group's excellent standards. The recreation facilities are especially good.

The Regent – Jalan Sultan Ismail, 50250 Kuala Lumpur (tel. 242-5588). This elegant hotel offers fantastic facilities for tourists or business travellers. The service and hospitality here is highly commendable.

The Hilton International – Jalan Sultan Ismail, 50250 Kuala Lumpur (tel. 242-2222). One of Kuala Lumpur's finest hotels with all the expected top-class facilities. Being on a slight hill, the Hilton's guest rooms have superb views over the city.

• **Super Club Class:** (Double M$90–150)
Ming Court – Jalan Ampang, Kuala Lumpur (tel. 248-2566). A centrally located and very well appointed hotel with good service.

Merlin – Jalan Sultan Ismail, Kuala Lumpur (tel. 248-0033). Close to the city centre with excellent facilities including a health club and pool, a bowling centre and good restaurants.

Shangri-La Hotel – 11 Jalan Sultan Ismail, Kuala Lumpur (tel. 232-2388). Extremely good accommodation and extensive facilities in the city centre.

Holiday Inn On The Park – Jalan Pinang, Kuala Lumpur (tel. 248-1066). A well furbished hotel set in tropical gardens near the city centre.

• **Economy:** (Double M$30–90)
South East Asia Hotel – Jalan Haji Hussein, off Jalan Tuanku Abdul Rahman (tel. 92-6077). Adequate accommodation with the added attraction to students that the Student Travel Office is located here.

Kuala Lumpur Mandarin – 2–8 Jalan Sultan (tel. 20-4533). Comfortable accommodation in a good area.

Hotel Emerald – 166–8 Jalan Pudu (tel. 42-9233). A clean, comfortable hotel with adequate facilities.

Shiraz Hotel – Corner of Jalan Tuanku and Jalan Medan (tel. 92-0159). Adequate facilities and rooms reasonably near to the centre.

Fortuna Hotel – 87 Jalan Berangan (tel. 41-1448). Pleasant rooms and service and a good Chinese restaurant.

The Kowloon – 142 Jalan Tuanku. Clean although basic accommodation in a rather noisy neighbourhood. Very low prices.

DINING OUT

Kuala Lumpur has restaurants serving a wide variety of European and Asian food. Indian food is popular and many restaurants offer good vegetarian dishes. Chinese, Taiwanese, Korean, Thai and Japanese cuisine are other favourites with the Malaysians. Malay food itself can be spicy and is often flavoured with ginger or coconut milk and peanuts. 'Sambals', or side-dishes of spicy sauces, accompany the main dish. To really experience Malay-style eating you should find the street-side stalls at Jalan Brickfields or Jalan Benteng near the Lang River, or at the Saturday Night Market in Kampong Bharu. Satay is the most famous and delicious of Malay dishes served here – skewered, charcoal-grilled meats and rice cakes.

- **First Class:** (M$70–110 for two)
The Paddock – Hilton Hotel (tel. 242-2222). An elegant, rooftop restaurant which serves the finest Malay and European specialities and has cultural shows and musicians.

Lotus Court – Mandarin Oriental Hotel (tel. 241-2846). The restaurant takes on the style of a classical Chinese pavilion and matches this with excellent Szechuan cuisine – the best in the city.

Le Coq d'Or – 121 Jalan Ampang. Delicious French cuisine is served in elegant surroundings with true French panache.

- **Super Club Class:** (M$40–70 for two)
Dragon Court – Merlin Hotel (tel. 48-0033). Excellent European à la carte or Chinese meals are served here.

Akhbar – Jalan Tuanku Abdul Rahman. Some of the best of Indian cuisine is to be had in this charming restaurant.

Jaq's Restaurant – Mara Building, Jalan Tuanku Abdul Rahman. Fine Malaysian dishes.

- **Economy:** (less than M$40 for two)
Fook Woh Yuen – Jalan Petaling, Chinatown. Chinese vegetarian food which is very popular (arrive early to avoid the crowds).

Bangles – 60A Jalan Tuanku Abdul Rahman. An upstairs restaurant serving good Indian food.

Coliseum Hotel Restaurant – Jalan Tuanku Abdul Rahman. Sizzling steaks are served up with fresh salad at very reasonable prices.

New Yorker – Jalan Bukit Bintang. Excellent steaks and good plonk to wash them down.

NIGHTLIFE

Much of Kuala Lumpur's nightlife is concentrated in the big hotels with western-style discos and nightclubs. The TIN MINE at the Hilton is reputed the best. Hotel Merlin's TOMORROW is also a popular nightclub and disco. Most nightclubs within hotels close between 0100 and 0200 hours; others may close earlier and a very few stay open later. For more cultural, Malay dance shows try THE HUT at Shah's Hotel, Petaling Jaya. This is also a great place to eat. Similarly the Hotel Merlin's HARLEQUIN has Chinese dancing performances while you eat Chinese cuisine.

Kuala Lumpur is well endowed with cinemas, some western (English-spoken), some Indian and some Chinese. The Cathay on Jalan Bukit Bintang and the Odeon on Jalan Campbell are both English-spoken.

The 'real' nightlife in Kuala Lumpur is in the open-air NIGHT MARKETS such as the Pasar Minggu or Sunday Market, which is actually held on Saturday nights at Kampong Bharu.

EXCURSIONS

Anyone wishing to explore Kuala Lumpur's surrounding areas will find a wealth of fascinating sights within an easy day's drive of the city. 8 miles to the north of Kuala Lumpur stand the BATU CAVES – vast limestone caverns hiding amongst thick jungle. A Hindu shrine stands at the entrance to the caves and can be reached via 270-odd steps. Also 8 miles from Kuala Lumpur, on the way to Ulu Kelang, is the NATIONAL ZOO. Malaysian reptiles, birds and animals are on view and rides are available on elephants, camels or ponies. Open 0900–1800 hours Tuesday to Sunday.

TEMPLER PARK lies about 15 miles north of Kuala Lumpur on the way to Ipoh. This is a popular spot for jungle walks, swimming, picnics and filming (it is the site of several celluloid jungle scenes).

11 miles along the road to the Genting Highlands is MIMALAND – 30 acres of forested hills with a lake fed by mountain streams. The area is full of recreational facilities such as fishing, boating, swimming and jungle trekking and children's amusement parks. The GENTING HIGHLAND area is 21 miles further on and has a golf course, a sightseeing helicopter service, a cable car to the mountain

top and, its most popular feature, the only government-approved casino in Malaysia.

All around Kuala Lumpur there are tin mines and rubber plantations. About 5 miles along the road to the zoo is a rubber plantation where you may watch the tappers tap trees for latex all morning. There is a tin mine opposite this where you may watch the tin dredging operations which release the tin from the rich soil. Visits to either of these can be arranged through local tour operators.

The historic town of MELAKA is 90 miles south of Kuala Lumpur on the west coast. The narrow streets and old buildings give the town a medieval atmosphere and there are some fine examples of Dutch and Portuguese architecture.

Penang

BAYAN LEPAS INTERNATIONAL AIRPORT

Penang's airport lies 11 miles south of Georgetown, the main town on the island. It has one terminal, newly built and designed to cope with increasing passenger traffic.

AIRPORT FACILITIES

Information Desk	The service is provided by the Tourist Development Corporation (TDC) personnel at the counter on the right-hand side of Arrivals, open 0830–1645 (Monday–Friday) and 0830–1300 (Saturday). Tour reps will also be on hand to give advice. For information, tel. 04-830501.
Restaurant/Bar	The restaurant by Kilau Utara is open 0600–2300 daily. The bar, also on the Passenger level, is open 0600–2300 daily.

Foreign Exchange/Banks	There are full banking facilities in the basement, and also by Bank Bumi Putra on the Passenger level. In addition to this there are money-changing facilities in the International Departure Hall. You should be able to exchange money whenever there are flights.
Duty Free/Shops	There are 3 duty-free shops offering a wide selection of goods, including pewter and electrical goods. There are also three handicraft shops selling a wide range of local craftwork.
Lost Goods	Get in touch with your airline and the airport authorities.
Left Luggage	Passenger level, 0600–2300.
Toilets	All areas.
Hotel Reservation	2 counters in Arrivals on Passenger level. One takes bookings for the Rasa Sayang, Golden Sands, and Palm Beach hotels (tel. 83 9402); the other accepts bookings for the Indrochitra (tel. 83 5450/83 5352).
Post	The Post Office is situated on the Passenger level and open 0800–1800.
Medical	There are medical centres on the Passenger level and in the basement.
Nursery	In the basement, tel. 83 4411, ext. 144.
Car Rental	Avis desk in Arrivals.
Taxi Hire	Outside Arrivals on the left.

AIRPORT INFORMATION

Check-in Times	International – 60 minutes before flight; domestic – 45 minutes.
Airport Tax	International – M$15. Singapore and Brunei – M$5. Domestic – M$3.

Transferring Flights   The airport operates a Minimum
                               Connection Transfer system which is
                               quite smooth. You should be able to
                               get connections quite quickly.

AIRPORT HOTELS – There are no airport hotels.

CITY LINKS

Bayan Lepas International Airport is 11 miles south of
Georgetown.

• **Taxi:** A voucher system operates between the airport and the
main parts of the island. The fares are M$16 to Georgetown, and
M$23 to Batu Ferringhi. The fares should be the same going back,
but in practice rarely are. Haggle for all you're worth.

• **Bus:** From the terminus outside the terminal. It will cost you from
M$1.05 to M$1.50 to get to Georgetown harbour. The yellow no. 66
bus takes you to the airport for M$1.50.

• **Car Hire:** From the Avis desk in Arrivals.

TOURIST INFORMATION

The Tourist Development Corporation (TDC) has an information
centre at the airport which is open 0830–1645 (Monday–Friday) and
0830–1300 (Saturday), tel. 04-830501. There is also a regional TDC
office at 10 Jalan Tun Syed Sheikh Barakbah (tel. 04-20066/
369067). This office has a good brochure called *Penang for the
Visitor*, which costs 50c. Remember that Penang is the island and
Georgetown the main town.

ADDRESSES

British High Commission – Wisma Damansara, 5 Jalan Semantan,
Kuala Lumpur.

US High Commission – 376 Jalan Pekeliling, Kuala Lumpur.
Emergency – Dial 999, or ask for the operator, who will speak
English.

GETTING ABOUT

• **Taxis:** Taxis are quite cheap in Penang, although you will almost
certainly have to bargain with the drivers as they are loath to use
their meters. Taxis officially cost 70c for the first mile and 30c for
each additional half-mile, but you'll be lucky to find a driver
prepared to take you at these rates. From 0100 to 0600 fares rise by
50 per cent. Trishaws, or bicycle-rickshaws, are good value, costing
just over M$1 for each half-mile. If you want to cycle yourself you
can hire bicycles for as little as M$5 in Georgetown (more in Batu
Ferringhi), and if you're lazier, a motorbike can be hired from
around M$30 per day.

• **Bus:** The bus network is extensive and cheap. Georgetown's buses
(MPPP Buses) all depart from the terminal at Leboh Victoria,
which is directly in front of the ferry terminal. City fares range from
25–55c. From Pengkalen Road, on the waterfront, you can take Sri
Negara buses around Georgetown. The other main stand is at Jalan
Maxwell, from where the island buses depart. Green buses run to
Ayer Itam, at the foot of Penang Hill. Blue buses run to the
northern beaches, although a change of bus is required at Tanjong
Bungha. Yellow buses run to the south and west of the island and all
the way up to Telok Bahang.

• **Car Hire:** Hire cars are available from around M$125 for
unlimited mileage, but do watch out for local signs and learn the
system of indicating, which local drivers have developed 'for their
own safety'. Remember to wear your seat belt or you could face six
weeks in prison. Not a pleasant prospect.

SIGHTS

In Georgetown, FORT CORNWALLIS dates back to the 18th century,
and round the corner from Light Street there is a small but
interesting museum, with an art gallery next door. There are

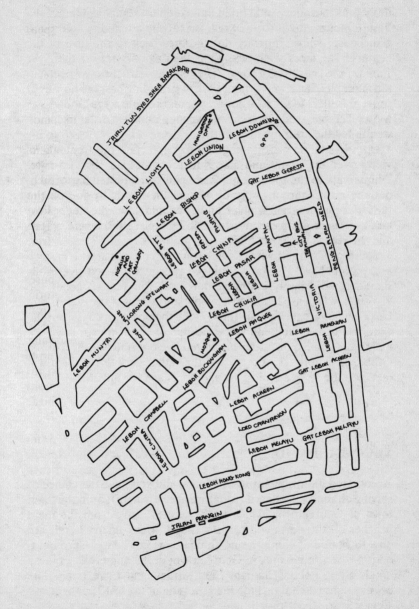

numerous mosques, and Hindu and Buddhist temples. One of the best 'temples', the KHOO KONGSI, isn't really a temple at all, but a clan house, whose intricate design dates back to the turn of the century. The most ornate temple is the KEK LOK SI, near the Ayer Itam on the outskirts of town. The temple's structure is spectacularly complex, and it is certainly worth struggling past the hordes of souvenir sellers to see it. Another popular temple is the Goddess of Mercy Temple, where you can burn paper money in order to ensure wealth for the afterlife.

PENANG HILL is worth ascending to appreciate the tremendous views over the island and across to the mainland. It's a 5-mile, 2-hour walk to the top or a quick zoom up on a rented motorbike, but the most charming way of making the trip is to hop on the funicular railway train which trundles up and down the steep slope all day. There are pleasant gardens, 2 temples, and a café on top and the return trip costs M$3.

South of Georgetown (bus 66) you can visit the SNAKE TEMPLE and pay to have a suitably drugged specimen draped over your shoulders, or simply continue out until you reach one of the BEACHES, which are relatively unspoilt at this end of the island. The best beaches are technically those along the northern coast, but the water isn't that clean and there has been a lot of tourist development. You can go on a tour organized by your hotel or the Tourist Office, or simply take the 66 and the rather elusive 76 which will take you the 45 or so miles around the island for only M$4.

ACCOMMODATION

Accommodation is plentiful in Penang and you have the choice of staying either by the beach (usually Batu Ferringhi), or in the main town of Georgetown, which is 30 minutes' drive from the main beaches on the north coast of the island. Many luxury hotels are now to be found along the north coast, while cheaper accommodation is centred mainly in Georgetown, in the numerous Chinese hotels along Leboh Chuliah, Leith Street, and Love Lane. The prices quoted do not include the government tax of 10 per cent and service, also 10 per cent.

● **First Class:** (over M$200 for a double)
The Eastern and Oriental – 10 Farquhar Street, Georgetown (tel. 04-375322). Superb old colonial hotel with spacious rooms. Excellent service, and nice swimming pool right by the sea.

Rasa Sayang Hotel – 11100 Batu Ferringhi Beach (tel. 04-811811/ 966). Modern luxury beach hotel with exceptional recreational facilities, including boating, waterskiing, golf and tennis. Lively disco.

Hotel Merlin – 25A Farquhar Street (tel. 04-23301/23423). Across the road from the E. and O., this hotel has all the facilities of its neighbour at a slightly lower cost. The Edinburgh restaurant is excellent, and there is a disco with a live band.

● **Super Club Class:** (M$100–150 for a double)
Hotel Ming Court – 202A Macalister Road, Georgetown (tel. 04-26131). Good facilities including health club and fine Chinese restaurant. Bar with friendly atmosphere and 2 cocktail lounges.

Casuarina Beach Hotel – 11100 Batu Ferringhi (tel. 04-811311). Well equipped beach hotel ideal for families. Nursery centre and indoor games centre for young children helps ease the pressures of a family holiday.

Bellevue Hotel – Penang Hill (tel. 892256/7). Fine views over the island from this hotel which is really more of a hill station resort. Pleasant climate, and a great place to relax and get away from it all.

● **Economy:** (M$25–90 for a double)
Lone Pine Hotel – 11100 Batu Ferringhi 97 (tel. 811511/2). Old-fashioned hotel with a distinctly British flavour. Restaurant even serves good fish and chips and the price includes breakfast and morning tea.

Cathay Hotel – 15 Leith Street (tel. 26271-3). Nice-looking building and a very reasonable town hotel.

Paramount – 48F Northam Road (tel. 63772). Another older-style hotel located in the residential area between town and beach. Air-conditioned and cheap.

New China Hotel – 22 Leith Street (tel. 21852). Very cheap but clean. Restaurant serves western-style food. One of many inexpensive Chinese hotels in the area.

DINING OUT

Penang has some good, cheap restaurants with a variety of cuisine on offer to tempt you. The north coast has some fine seafood restaurants and you should try one of the two types of fish soup particularly associated with Penang known as 'laksa'. Generally, however, Georgetown has a wider variety of places to eat.

● **First Class:** (M$60–100 for two)
Eastern and Oriental Hotel – (tel. 375322). There are 2 excellent restaurants at the hotel, both in sumptuous settings. One serves French cuisine, the other delicious Malay specialities. Both are recommended.

Ming Palace – At the Ming Court Hotel (tel. 26131). One of the best Cantonese restaurants on the island.

Edinburgh Restaurant – At the Hotel Merlin (tel. 23301/23423). Excellent traditional western grill.

● **Super Club Class:** (M$40–60 for two)
Town House Hotel – 70 Penang Road (tel. 368722/621/923). You can choose either Hokkien or Hylam specialities. Both are delicious.

Wing Lok – 300 Penang Road (tel. 25684). Quality Chinese restaurant offering the novelty of a steamboat for four at M$20.

Tai Tung Restaurant – 51 Cintra Street (tel. 615869). Tasty Teochew cuisine.

● **Economy:** (M$20–40 for two)
Dragon King – On the corner of Bishop Street and Pitt Street. Rare chance to sample Nonya cuisine. Take it.

Taj Mahal – On the corner of Penang Road and Chulia Street. One of many fine Indian restaurants in town. Try 'murtabak', a thin pastry stuffed with egg, vegetables and meat.

Poshni's – On the corner of Light Street and Penang Street. Splendid selection of traditional Malay food at competitive prices. One of the few 'real' Malay restaurants in town.

Hong Kong – Cintra Street. Cheap and varied menu. One of an enormous range of Chinese restaurants in Georgetown. Chicken fried rice is a popular speciality.

Night Markets – One of the best ways to sample Penang's local specialities is to pop into the selection of street stalls at places like Gurney Drive, or especially along the Esplanade.

NIGHTLIFE

There isn't that much in the way of cultural entertainment, unless you're a fan of classical dancing. However, things certainly liven up during the local festivals. The CHINESE NEW YEAR in February is always a lively and colourful occasion, and the DRAGON BOAT FESTIVAL is most spectacular in June. Other than this you'll probably have to restrict yourself to hotel discos and the cinema.

EXCURSIONS

For unspoilt beaches and tranquil, tropical beauty visit one of the 99 LANGKAWI ISLANDS, which are 8 hours by boat from Georgetown or 2 hours from KUALA PERLIS, 50 miles to the north of Penang. The main town is KUAH and the beaches are quite a distance away, but definitely worth it if you really want to get away from it all. Rather more accessible, the island of PANGKOR, just off the coast 100 miles south of Penang, has excellent beaches too and a fine round-the-island walking path. Also 100 miles from Penang, CAMERON HIGHLANDS is one of the best of Malaysia's numerous hill stations. At 5000 ft, the climate is pleasantly cool and there are some great jungle walks in this area.

If this is too far to travel, you can go instead to the BUKIT LARUT hill station at TAIPING, 45 miles from Penang. Taiping also has lovely Lake Gardens and a good museum. Other places of interest on the road to Cameron Highlands (and eventually Kuala Lumpur) include KUALA KANGSAR with its fine Royal Mosque and Coronation Hall, and IPOH, with striking Chinese rock temples and a good selection of restaurants.

The Philippines

RED TAPE

• **Passport/Visa Requirements:** A valid passport is required by all except holders of a Hong Kong ID card. Visas are not required by bona fide tourists, provided they stay no longer than 21 days. A visa is necessary for stays exceeding 21 days. Visas cost around £10 and you should apply to the Philippines Consulate, 1 Cumberland House, Kensington High Street, London W8. Visas are valid for 59 days after entry. Holders of South African passports will be refused entry.

CUSTOMS

• **Duty Free:** The following items may be brought into the country without incurring duty: 200 cigarettes or 50 cigars or 250 grammes tobacco; 1 bottle of spirits and 1 quart of wine; 0.25 litre of toilet water and a small quantity of perfume. Firearms, ammunition, non-prescribed drugs and pornography are strictly prohibited.

HEALTH

1. Yellow fever – a certificate is required if travellers have visited an infected country within the previous 6 days.
2. Malaria risk exists in most low-lying rural areas. Immunization advised.
3. Immunization is advised against cholera, typhoid and polio. Risk exists all year round.

4. Tap water is safe to drink in Manila and environs, but precautions are advised elsewhere.

Health care in the Philippines is excellent and Manila has some of the best hospitals in Asia.

CAPITAL – Manila. Population – in excess of 4 million.

POPULATION – 52 million.

LANGUAGE – Filipino, English, Spanish and local dialects.

CURRENCY – Peso (PP) = 100 Centavos. Notes – 2, 5, 10, 20, 50 and 100 pesos. Coins – 1, 5, 10, 25, 50 and 100 centavos (1 peso). £1 = PP27.25; US$1 = PP19.46.

BANKING HOURS – 0930–1600, Monday–Friday.

POLITICAL SYSTEM – Democratic republic (now that Marcos has gone).

RELIGION – 85 per cent Roman Catholic. The rest are Buddhist, Muslim, Taoist, and other non-Christian sects.

PUBLIC HOLIDAYS

January 1	New Year's Day
March/April	Easter – Holy Thursday, Good Friday
May 1	Labour Day
May 6	Day of Valour
June 12	Philippine Independence Day
September 21	Thanksgiving
November 1	All Saints' Day
November 30	National Heroes Day

CLIMATE – The Philippines has a typical tropical climate: hot and humid all year round, though tempered by constant sea breezes. There are 3 distinct seasons: rainy (July–October); cool and dry (November–February); and hot and mainly dry (March–June). Typhoons can occur between July and October, and it is generally cooler in the evenings. It is best to avoid the rainy season when planning a trip to the Philippines, and the most pleasant months are January–March. You should take lightweight clothes which allow the skin to breathe, such as cotton, although warmer clothes may be necessary for evenings and certainly for trips to the hills.

TIME DIFFERENCE – GMT + 8 hours.

COMMUNICATIONS

• **Telephone:** Full IDD service. Long distance calls need to be placed from a hotel or Post Office. The access code is 00, and the country code is 48.

• **Post:** Airmail letters cost 80 cents and take around 4 days to reach the UK.

ELECTRICITY – 220v AC, 60 cycles. 110v available in most hotels.

OFFICE/SHOPPING HOURS – Offices: 0800–1700 or 0900–1700 Monday–Friday. Shops are open 0900–1900 daily.

• **Best Buys:** The best buys are works of art and handicrafts. Choose from woodcarvings; handwoven fabrics (the barong tagalong, an embroidered long-sleeved shirt for men, is world-famous); abaca placemats, rugs and bags; bamboo and rattan furniture; shellcrafts; brasswork, especially the distinctive Moslem brassware; inlaid brass and bronzeware; Ifugao carvings from Baguio; leathergoods; and 'primitive' artworks. Other good buys include the world-famous cigars; corals and shells; jewellery; and dolls. Outside the smart stores, haggle.

INTERNAL TRAVEL

• **Air:** PAL (Philippine Airlines) runs a frequent and economical service to most parts of the country from Manila. Security is quite strict and expect to be thoroughly frisked and charged security tax each time you fly. If you have flown to the Philippines with PAL you are entitled to a 50 per cent discount on all internal flights but you must present your international ticket and coupon and buy all your subsequent tickets at one go (they are open dated and refundable in any case).

• **Sea:** Unlike Indonesia, the islands of the Philippines are relatively close to each other, and sea travel is generally cheap, comfortable and reliable. There are one or two uncomfortable services, however, and local boats can get seriously overcrowded. Cebu is the hub of shipping services, and most destinations can be reached from here.

• **Rail:** There are only three lines in the whole country: one connects Iloilo and Roxas on the island of Panay, while the other two run north and south from Manila. Trains are comfortable (as long as you don't travel third class), but often painfully slow.

• **Road:** There is an extensive bus network and fares are usually very reasonable. Departures are frequent, and buses sometimes leave early if they're full. The main companies include Pantranco and Philippine Rabbit.

Taxis abound in Manila and the fare is PP3.50 for the first 250 metres and 60 cents for every subsequent 250 metres. All taxis in Manila are metered, but as the Philippines suffers from bad inflation, these figures are likely to become swiftly out of date. However the declining value of the peso should continue to offset inflation, and fares should remain among the cheapest in the world. Also available for city transport are the even cheaper tricycles, and colourful jeepneys, which are customized ex-US jeeps which officially can carry 12, but in practice anything up to double that amount.

Car rentals are easily available in the major cities, although the minimum age limit is 25. An International Driving Licence is required and traffic travels on the left.

MAJOR SIGHTS OF THE COUNTRY

LUZON is the biggest and most important island of the Philippines. MANILA, the capital, is on the island and this is where most people enter the country. Much of historic Manila was destroyed during World War II, though it does have plenty of other attractions. It is also a good base for some interesting local excursions and for further details, turn to our *City Guide* to Manila on p. 000. North of the capital and on the west coast of the island are some fine beaches, notably at HUNDRED ISLANDS, a scattering of tiny islands off Lucap, 5 hours from Manila.

BAGUIO, Luzon's summer capital, is 150 miles north of Manila, and has a much nicer climate due to its being over 5000 ft above sea level. It is an easy-going place and you can wander around many parks and an interesting market. Nearby, LA TRINIDAD features the well preserved KABAYAN MUMMIES. North of Baguio, the terrain becomes increasingly mountainous and difficult, but it really is worth making the trek up to BANAUE to see the spectacular rice terraces, which were carved out of the sides of the mountains by the Ifugao tribe over 2000 years ago. The terraces are still as perfect today as they were then, and have been referred to as the 'eighth wonder of the world'.

Back on the west coast, historic VIGAN carries many reminders of the days when it was second in importance only to Manila during the period of Spanish colonization. The town is 4 hours by bus from San Fernando, which marks the terminus of the northern railway line.

PAGSANJAN is situated 40 miles south-east of Manila and is an exciting place to shoot the rapids on the fast-flowing Laguna, though it does get terribly crowded at weekends. The final scenes of *Apocalypse Now* were shot here. Also less than 50 miles from the capital, the volcanic lake of TAAL makes for a pleasant day-trip, with tremendous views from TAGAYTAY RIDGE. Near here you can walk the 7 lakes of SAN PABLO and visit some of the historic towns and villages in the area. The south-east peninsula contains the sublime MAYON VOLCANO, which is said to be the world's most perfect volcanic cone. It's a 2-day climb to the summit, but those not wishing to go to such lengths can get an excellent view of the volcano from the ruins of Cagsawa church nearby. Further south, TIWI has some interesting ruins and famous hot springs, though these have been commercialized rather badly. Off the east coast, the island of CATANDUANES has fine beaches and waterfalls and is relatively free from tourists.

There are 7000 other islands left to explore, though only 300 are inhabited. South of Luzon, MINDORO's lovely northern coast is becoming popular with tourists, especially PUERTA GALERA. Continuing south-east, PANAY has numerous old forts and churches, and its capital, ILOILO, contains some interesting relics of Spanish colonization. There are popular beach resorts along the island's south coast, and mention should be made of the island of BORACAY, situated between Panay and Mindoro, which is a tiny, though delightful, tropical paradise. East of Panay, CEBU is an important island, steeped in history. Its capital, Cebu City, is the oldest city in the Philippines and makes a fine base from which to start island-hopping, one of the most popular tourist activities. A short boat trip from Cebu City, BOHOL has the oldest stone church in the Philippines at BACLAYON, an interesting cave lake at DAUIS, and its most famous landmark, the curiously shaped 'CHOCOLATE HILLS'. To the south, MINDANAO has two very popular resorts, but also an ongoing guerrilla war being waged inland by Moslem separatists. On the south-western tip of the island, and over 440 miles from Manila, ZAMBOANGA has a Spanish fort of Pilar, with a good view of Rio Hondo, a Muslim village on stilts further down the coast. There is also the fine hill park of PASONANCA with a famous tree house, and a good barter trade market. On the south coast, the cosmopolitan resort of DAVAO is the fastest-growing city in the Philippines after Manila. It has a large Buddhist temple, good beaches and is near to the highest mountain in the country. MOUNT APO. It's a 4-day trek to the summit, but it's not an arduous climb; the scenery is great and the Tourist Office can fix you up with a guide if necessary.

HOTELS

There are no accommodation problems in the Philippines. In Manila alone there are some 10,000 first class hotel rooms. Prices are often quoted in US$ as well as PP and you may well obtain a favourable rate if you can pay in US$. Hotels are graded on a system of stars, from 1 to 5, according to facilities. In Manila, pensions have become popular due to their personalized service and good facilities, and there is an extensive network of Youth Hostels. A complete directory of hotels is available from the Tourist Office. Hotel rates are subject to a 15 per cent luxury tax and the usual 10 per cent service charge.

NIGHTLIFE AND RESTAURANTS

Manila's nightlife is one of the liveliest in Asia, and Filipino artists are renowned for their high quality performances. There are numerous clubs, including jazz and Spanish clubs, and plenty of bars and casinos. The performing arts are also well represented in the capital. Elsewhere, the nightlife isn't so hectic, but places like Cebu City can be equally enjoyable and interesting. Visitors should note that the months of April and May are prime festival time, and there is usually plenty happening up and down the country.

The Filipino palate is very cosmopolitan and there are many restaurants in Manila, serving food of all kinds at all prices. There are numerous Chinese restaurants and fast food has taken off in a big way. Filipino cooking is a blend of Chinese, Malay and Spanish cuisine, and is presented in a similar way to its hotter Indonesian cousin, nasi padang. Rice is the staple substance of the Filipino cuisine, but the main national dish is adobo, a dark and spicy stew made with chicken and pork. At festivals, a whole pig is often roasted, and the lechon, as it is known, is served with a delicious liver sauce. Seafood is extremely popular, and best consumed raw in a vinaigrette, or marinated in coconut-milk. The more adventurous may like to sample balut, a boiled duck's egg containing partially formed embryo. This is actually considered a great delicacy by many. Those with a sweet tooth can try a large variety of sweets and cakes, including the delicious rice-based bibingka, and you are strongly advised to take advantage of the wonderful array of tropical fruits on offer. The locally brewed San Miguel beer is very good (and very cheap) and it's certainly worth risking a glass or three of palm wine (tuba).

Manila

MANILA INTERNATIONAL AIRPORT

Manila International Airport is situated 7.5 miles south-east of Manila. The new International Terminal was completed in 1982 to worldwide acclaim, and the airport now services over 30 airlines from all over the world. There is one terminal.

The ground floor contains the breakdown and make-up areas and aprons for aircraft. Arrivals is on the first floor (level 2) as are transit facilities. Departures is on level 3 and there is an observation deck on level 4.

AIRPORT FACILITIES

Most facilities are open 24 hours.

Information Desk	There are 2 desks in the Arrivals Lobby. One is run by the Ministry of Tourism and has a good selection of leaflets.
Restaurants/Bars	3 good restaurants, 2 in Departures and the luxury Hari Raya restaurant. The main bar is in Departures. Snacks available in Arrivals.
Foreign Exchange/Banks	Exchange facilities are available 24 hours from the banks past the Customs area.
Duty Free/Shops	There is a duty free shopping arcade (open 24 hours) in Departures, and also one in Arrivals, just before Immigration. Other shops in Departures.
First Class Lounge	The Mabuhay Lounge is open to passengers flying Philippine Airlines. Other airlines also have First Class lounges.

Toilets	On all floors.
Hotel Reservation	From the desk in Arrivals. Unlike many airports, you can book a room in a cheap hotel or pension here.
Medical	There are transit desk health stations and quarantine stations on level 2 (Arrivals), together with a health centre open 24 hours.
Meeting Point	In Arrivals Lobby.
Conference Rooms	Available.
Car Rental	From Avis, Qualitran offices in Arrivals.
Taxi Hire	From ranks outside.

AIRPORT INFORMATION

Check-in Times	International – 120 minutes; Domestic – 60 minutes.
Airport Tax	International departure tax – PP200; domestic – PP10.
Transferring Flights	The procedure is simple though security is strict. You will have to go through Immigration, but not Customs. The in-transit Baggage Areas are situated on either side of the Baggage Claim Area and the Transit Lounge is on the next floor up. The facilities are good here and include showers etc. You will have to pay departure tax whether your flight is international or domestic. You should be able to get an international connection in 60 minutes and a domestic one in 75 minutes.

AIRPORT HOTELS

• **First Class:** (over PP2000 for a double)
The Philippine Village Hotel – At Nayong Pilipino, behind the

airport (tel. 831701). Complete hotel services. Casino. Free airport transfers.

CITY LINKS

Manila International Airport is 7.5 miles south of the city centre.

● **Bus:** A shuttle service operates between the airport and all the main hotels and guest houses in Manila, departing every 15–30 minutes. The fare is PP26, and the journey takes around half an hour. An even cheaper alternative is to take the yellow bus (no. 704) bearing the sign 'Santa Cruz, Monumento' to the centre of the city. The fare is a measly PP2 and the stop is situated 100 yards to the left of the terminal. The journey takes about 50 minutes, and buses go every 5 or 10 minutes. You can get a bus to the airport from the railway station, and from Recto Street.

● **Taxi:** Taxis in Manila are metered, but you may end up having to pay 50 per cent more than is shown on the meter. As taxi fares in Manila are among the lowest in the world, this is no great hardship. However, do be wary of rip-off merchants posing as tourist officials who will attempt to lure you into a pirate cab. Unsuspecting passengers have been charged as much as US$50 by these rapacious drivers, so take care.

TOURIST INFORMATION

The huge Ministry of Tourism office (tel. 502384/501703) is in the popular tourist area of Ermita, inside the National Museum, close to the junction of Rizal Park and Taft Avenue. They also have offices at the airport and in the Nayong Pilipino. Leaflets are good, especially from the office at the airport, although they can be a little difficult to come by at the vast and often chaotic head office. The student travel and information service, Ystaphil, are also helpful and their office is in the Unland Condominium, at 1656 Taft Avenue. Also worth trying for general info is the Kangaroo Club at 476 United Nations Avenue, in Ermita. There is a good tourist office next door too.

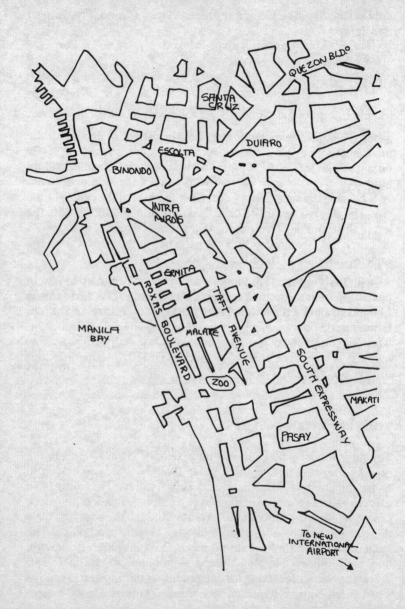

ADDRESSES

UK Embassy – Legaspi Village, Makati.
US Embassy – Roxas Boulevard.
Emergencies – Police (all of whom understand English): 599011;
  Fire Brigade: 561176;
  Ambulance: Philippine General Hospital: 596061
              North General: 471081
              Manila Medical Centre: 591661.

GETTING ABOUT

• **Bus:** There are quite a few bus companies, with many of them operating similar services, but from different stops. For areas around Manila buses depart from the station across Taft Avenue from the City Hall. The blue buses of the Metromanila company are the most modern. Fares start at PP1, or PP8 for one of the air-conditioned 'Love Buses'. It can be difficult to find your way round Manila by bus until you possess some idea of the city's geography.

• **Taxis:** Taxis are plentiful, but do make sure that the meter is on, and remember that the figure refers to pesos not dollars! You will probably have to pay a little more than is shown on the meter as the rates become rapidly out of date due to the high rate of inflation in the Philippines. Cheaper than taxis are the colourful jeepneys and bicycle-rickshaws.

• **Car Hire:** Hiring a car is easily done through a hotel or agent such as Hertz or Avis. Self-drive rates are from about PP500 per day and you will need to be over 25 and be in possession of an International Driving Licence. Chauffeur-driven cars are also available.

SIGHTS

The sprawling capital of the Philippines was formed by merging 17 towns and districts into Metro Manila. Unfortunately much of historic Manila was blitzed towards the end of World War II and only a little survives. The centre is Rizal Park, better known as the LUNETA, which is also the city's most important meeting place. There are gardens and fountains and a planetarium here. To the north is INTRAMUROS, the old Spanish walled city, although the walls are just about all that remains today. The MONASTERY OF ST AUGUSTINE, dating from the end of the 16th century, is one of the few surviving buildings from early Spanish colonial days. Its museum is open daily 0800–1700. The Roman Catholic church is also still there, though it has been destroyed and rebuilt around half a dozen times at the last count, and the ruins of FORT SANTIAGO, the city's former stronghold, where thousands were slaughtered in World War II, are also worth a visit.

Manila has several museums and a good place to start is the NATIONAL MUSEUM, in the Executive Building, next to the Luneta. The AYALA, in Makati Avenue and open until 1800, is a good bet for learning about the history of the Philippines, while other good and self-explanatory museums include the Carfel Museum of Seashells in Mabini, and the Museum of Philippine Costumes and Dolls at the top of Taft Avenue. The 'whole country in miniature' permanent exhibition, with its good handicraft shops, is out at NAYONG PILIPINO by the airport, and worth a visit, as are Malacanang Palace and Gardens, former home of the deposed Marcoses, situated on the banks of the Pasig River. Not far north of these rich hauls of corruption are some of the worst slums in the world. You can wander around the lively Chinatown region to the north of the city centre, or around the 'tourist belt' (male-orientated) areas of Ermita and Malate. Trips around the city can be arranged at hotels or through agents and a pleasant city excursion is the boat trip around Manila Bay, which is available from Gate A, South Boulevard, Rizal Park.

ACCOMMODATION

Accommodation in Manila should not present a problem. There are hundreds of hotels ranging from the outlets of the major international luxury chains to small and homely pensions. The peak season as far as prices is concerned is from March to May.

• **First Class:** (PP2500 and above for a double)
The Manila Hotel – Katigbak Drive (tel. 470011). The oldest and most famous hotel in Manila. There are luxurious suites; 4 speciality restaurants, including a barbecue patio with delightful views over Manila Bay; sumptuous bars; and excellent sports facilities including tennis courts and golf course.

The Inter-Continental – Makati Avenue (tel. 890011). Large, modern and luxurious, the Inter-Continental offers just about every conceivable luxury in its 14-storey complex. Fine restaurants, and good business and sports facilities.

The Manila Mandarin – Makati Avenue (tel. 8163601). Another fine modern hotel with impeccable standards of service and efficiency. L'Hirondelle is a very good restaurant and the health and beauty facilities are excellent.

• **Super Club Class:** (PP1000–2000 for a double)
The Admiral – 2138 Roxas Boulevard (tel. 572081). Lavish rooms and suites. Period elegance with marvellous service.

Manila Royale – 627 Echague Street (tel. 488521). All the facilities of the top hotels but at cheaper prices. Heliport; shopping centre; and cocktail lounge, coffee shop, supper club, and revolving restaurant all positioned near the top of the hotel with tremendous views of Manila and its suburbs.

El Grande – Paranaque (tel. 8271011). Sportsman's dream hotel. Apart from the pool, there are 8 pelota courts, 3 tennis courts, an 18-hole golf course, a health club, and a man-made lagoon for boating and fishing. Luxury accommodation.

• **Economy:** (PP200–800 for a double)
Grande Hotel – 88C Palanca Street, Quiapo. Situated near Chinatown, this hotel has good, air-conditioned rooms and an excellent restaurant.

Merchants Hotel – 711 San Bernardo, corner of Soler (tel. 401071). In the heart of downtown Manila. All rooms have bathrooms en suite and there is a restaurant, a hairdresser and a bank.

Kangaroo Club – 476 United Nations Avenue (tel. 599201). Right in the heart of Ermita, this Australian-run hotel has good, clean air-conditioned rooms and acts as a friendly information and meeting point.

Ryokan Pension House – 1250 J. Bocobo Street (tel. 598956). Typical pension. Large beds, clean rooms and cheap rates.

DINING OUT

● **First Class:** (over PP1500 for two)
Manila – At the Manila Hotel (tel. 470011). Elegant setting and fine food.

Via Mare – Legaspi Village, Makati (tel. 852306). Near the British Embassy and renowned for its superb seafood.

L'Hirondelle – At the Mandarin (tel. 8163601). Succulent continental cuisine, skilfully prepared and courteously served.

● **Super Club Class:** (PP750–1400 for two)
Moulin Rouge – 5347 Gen. Luna, Makati (tel. 85038). Fine reputation as possibly the best French restaurant in Manila.

Pulupandan – 7829 Makati Avenue (tel. 892536). Traditional Filipino cuisine with nightly cultural shows.

The Grove – Makati Avenue (tel. 898383). Excellent variety of native dishes from all over the Philippines.

● **Economy:** (under PP750 for two)
India House – 1718 M. Adriatico Street (tel. 572560). Fine curries.

Barrio Fiesta – 110 J. Bocobo Street. Quality Filipino specialities such as kari-kari and crispy pata.

Ambassador – Roxas Boulevard (tel. 709123). Good value Filipino restaurant open 24 hours per day. Fish specialities.

Fast Food Centres – There are 3 of them: in Makati, San Juan and Cabao. They all serve a variety of fast food from many different countries. Clean, cheap and quick.

NIGHTLIFE

Manila has a thriving night-time scene. Most of the big hotels have clubs and the most exclusive spots are centred in Roxas Boulevard. One of the most popular is the BAYSIDE, while the HILTON sports an intimate club in its basement. Nearby, there are all sorts of clubs and bars in the tourist district of Ermita. NINA'S PAPAGAYO on A. Mabini is an intimate Mexican supper club, while the HOBBIT CLUB, also in Mabini, has the dubious attraction of dwarves as waiters. Many of the clubs in this area supply 'hostesses' whose function is primarily to 'dance' with clients for the evening. Unaccompanied women are not admitted to these places. There are plenty of bars where you can have a pleasant drink; the KANGAROO CLUB in United Nations Avenue is a friendly Aussie hostelry, while the OLD ENGLISH PUB in Padre Faura serves real draught bitter. You can listen to all sorts of music in Manila's clubs. Jazz is increasing in popularity, and clubs like GUERNICA'S and EL BODEGON, both in M.H. del Pilar, have strolling Spanish guitarists and great atmospheres. Most of the big discos are in hotel complexes, such as at the TOWER in Mabini Street.

Various events take place at the CULTURAL CENTRE OF THE PHILIPPINES (CCP) in Roxas Boulevard. Details of what's on are posted on the billboards outside, and the Ministry of Tourism publishes programmes. Other theatres include the Metropolitan, the Rajah Suayman, and the Philippine Folk Arts Theatre. Folk dancing is well catered for with many restaurants putting on performances to entertain you during your meal. There is Polynesian dancing at the ZAMBOANGA RESTAURANTS in Makati Avenue and Adriatico Street, and Fiesta Pilipino at the SULO RESTAURANT in the Makati Commercial Centre. Films are advertised in the daily press and there are cinemas in Rizal Avenue, Santa Cruz, and in Adriatico Street, Ermita.

EXCURSIONS

There are quite a few places within day-trip distance of Manila. Out in the bay, the island of CORREGIDOR was supposed to have been impregnable, but eventually fell to the Japanese. 'The Rock' as it's known, is now a war museum and can be easily reached by hovercraft (50 minutes but expensive) or boat (tel. Arpan Tourist Industries on 501532/501571). To the north of Manila there are some average beaches, and most of the places of interest are to the south. At PAGSANJAN, 40 miles south-east of the capital, there is good swimming and you can have a go at shooting the rapids in a hired boat. The best time to go, when the water levels are at their highest, is August–September. Go early to avoid the crowds.

Also less than 50 miles from Manila is the volcanic LAKE TAAL. In the middle of the lake the Taal volcano rises up and there is another lake inside its crater. There are plenty of boats to the volcano and there are incredible views from TAGAYTAY RIDGE. On the way here, there is a small church at LAS PINAS which has an ancient organ with pipes made from bamboo. Further east, you can wander round the seven lakes of SAN PABLO. Some, such as the tiny crater-lake SAMPALOK, can be walked around in less than an hour. There are good beaches near to LUCENA and also the MAINIT HOT SPRINGS. The QUEZON NATIONAL PARK, one of the biggest on Luzon, is good for walks and spotting wildlife.

There are a couple of sights worth making a special effort to see. One is the perfect volcano of MAYON in south Luzon, the other is the stunning rice terraces in the mountains around BANAUE. It can take the best part of a day to reach these places from Manila, but the effort will certainly be well rewarded. Beach lovers should seriously consider spending a few idyllic days at HUNDRED ISLANDS in the north, or PUERTO GALERA on MINDORO to the south.

Singapore

RED TAPE

• **Passport/Visa Requirements:** All visitors require a full passport, and residents of the following countries need to apply for visas: Taiwan, Albania, Bulgaria, China, Czechoslovakia, East Germany, Hungary, North Korea, Vietnam, Kampuchea, Laos, Poland, Romania, USSR, Yugoslavia, and South Africa. UK citizens do not need a visa to work in Singapore, while US citizens intending to work and live in Singapore do.

CUSTOMS

• **Duty Free:** The following goods may be brought into Singapore without incurring Customs duty: 200 cigarettes and 50 cigars or 250 grammes of tobacco. Wine, beer or spirits not exceeding 1 litre each. It is prohibited to import firearms, non-prescribed drugs, and material of a pornographic nature (including even *Playboy*). Goods can be bought on arrival.

HEALTH

1. Yellow fever – certificate of vaccination required if person has visited an area within the previous 6 days where a case of yellow fever has been reported.
2. Malaria – no risk.
3. Typhoid/polio – risk exists throughout year and vaccinations advised but not compulsory.
4. Cholera – risk exists throughout year and vaccinations advised but not compulsory.
5. Water is purified although visitors might be advised to take precautions.
6. Health insurance is recommended. Health care extremely good. Singapore General deals with emergencies.

CAPITAL – Singapore. Population 2.5 million.

POPULATION – 2.5 million.

LANGUAGE – Chinese (Mandarin), English, Malay and Tamil. English is used for business and administration.

CURRENCY – Singapore Dollar. S$1.00 = 100 cents. Notes are in denominations of S$1, 5, 10, 20, 25, 50, 100, 500, 1000, and 10,000. £1 = S$3.07; US$ = S$2.19.

BANKING HOURS – 1000–1500 (Monday–Friday), and 0930–1130 (Saturday). The bank at Changi Airport is open 24 hours per day.

POLITICAL SYSTEM – Parliamentary democracy with compulsory voting.

RELIGION – Confucian, Taoist, Buddhist, Christian and Muslim.

PUBLIC HOLIDAYS

January 1	New Year's Day
February (middle)	Chinese New Year
March/April	Good Friday
May 1	Labour Day
May 14	Vesak Day
June/July	Hari Raya Puasa
August 9	National Day
August/September	Hari Raya Haji
September 21	Moon Cake Festival
November (1st week)	Deepavali (Festival of Lights)
December 25	Christmas Day

CLIMATE – Equatorial. Hot and humid all year round. Average temperatures range from 24°C (75°F) to 31°C (89°F). It rains all year round, but between November and January the north-east monsoon brings heavy yet refreshing bursts of rain. Early mornings and evenings are pleasantly cooler. Visitors should wear lightweight clothes, preferably made from natural fibres which allow the skin to breathe, such as cotton. An umbrella or light raincoat is advisable, and a pullover may well be required indoors to combat Singapore's fierce air-conditioning!

TIME DIFFERENCE – GMT + 8 hours.

COMMUNICATIONS

• **Telephone:** Full IDD service available. International access code 005, country code 65.

• **Post:** Post Offices are open from 0900 to 1700. Airmail to UK takes up to a week.

ELECTRICITY – 230v AC, 50 cycles. Some hotels have 110v outlets.

OFFICE/SHOPPING HOURS – Government offices: 0830–1630 hours. Commercial offices: 0900–1700 hours, closing at 1300 Saturdays. Shops: 1000–1800 (Monday–Saturday). Many stay open till 2200 and some are open on Sunday.

• **Best Buys:** Still a duty-free port, Singapore is excellent for shopping, with numerous shopping centres. Best buys are jewellery, especially 24-carat gold; electronic goods; Chinese rugs; and clothes. Shoppies should head for Central Point where almost any luxury good can be purchased. Serangoon Road – popularly known as 'Little India' – sells all things Indian, while Arab Street is renowned for inexpensive fabrics, jewellery and basketware. Robinson's department store is on a par with Selfridges and Harrods.

TIPPING – Hotels and restaurants add a 10 per cent service charge and the government actually discourages tipping.

INTERNAL TRAVEL

• **Air:** As Singapore is only 224 square miles an internal air network is not required.

• **Rail:** Only one international line, which connects the island with Malaysia.

• **Road:** A comprehensive network exists making it easy to get around. Buses go everywhere on the island, but whilst they are cheap, apart from special sightseeing coaches, they are not air-conditioned and can get uncomfortably crowded during the rush hour.

   Taxis are reasonably priced for a big city, and with 10,000 of them on the streets, you're always sure of getting one. There is a surcharge of S$3 per taxi for passengers wishing to travel to Changi Airport, and there is also a surcharge of S$2 per taxi – S$5 for private cars – for entering the Central Business District. Cars carrying more than 4 people do not have to pay. All taxis are metered and most are air-conditioned.

Trishaws – bicycles fitted with sidecars – offer a novel way of seeing the sights and most travel agents will arrange trishaw tours.

A list of hire car companies can be found in the Singapore Yellow Pages. Drivers need to purchase special parking coupons, and also a Daily Area Licence if they wish to enter the Central Business District. An International Driving Licence is required and traffic travels on the left.

MAJOR SIGHTS OF THE COUNTRY

Many sights are to be found in the city of Singapore itself (see *City Guide* to Singapore on p. 506) but the island has many other attractions worthy of the visitor's attention. Five miles west of the city lies HAW PAR VILLA, the legacy of Chinese millionaire Aw Boon Haw. Acres of the hillside have been carved into grottoes to house a bizarre and at times gruesome collection of statues depicting Chinese myths and legends.

Both fauna and flora thrive in Singapore's tropical climate, and the enthusiast is well catered for. Those who would rather see animals in their natural habitats should head for the BUKIT TIMAH NATURE RESERVE, a forest reserve 10 miles north-west of the city. Ornithologists can continue further west to the JURONG BIRD PARK which is a sanctuary featuring the world's tallest man-made waterfall, together with an aviary containing over 350 species of bird. Surprisingly, perhaps, for such an industrial town, JURONG also provides the location for both the Chinese and Japanese Gardens. These have been based on classical models, and are ideal spots in which to relax after a hard morning's business or sightseeing. There are also gardens and wildlife parks at MANDAI LAKE, around 15 miles to the north of the city.

A few hundred yards off the south coast and connected to the harbour by cable car and ferry lies SENTOSA, Singapore's leisure island. An idyllic tropical retreat, the island's attractions also include a coralarium, maritime museum and art centre.

HOTELS

Some of the best hotels in the world are to be found in Singapore, although there is accommodation to suit all tastes and budgets. It is better to make hotel reservations in advance, but should you arrive in Singapore without having done so, there are 2 counters in Arrivals at Changi Airport which provide a complimentary service from 0700 to 2300 hours daily, although only for luxury hotels. Given Singapore's importance as both a major business and tourist centre, many prestigious hotel chains are represented on the island, with the visitor being able to choose from Hyatt, Hilton, Mandarin, Oberoi, Westin or Sheraton. Expect to pay in excess of S$300 per night for a double room in one of these high-class establishments.

NIGHTLIFE AND RESTAURANTS

The nightlife in Singapore is excellent. There are plenty of good nightclubs on the island, ranging from pulsating discos with live pop bands to more sophisticated cocktail lounges. Most of the top hotels run nightclubs and you can combine the pleasures of dining out with exotic entertainment at one of the island's many nightclub/restaurants and theatre/restaurants. Numerous international stars, orchestras and ballet companies perform frequently in the city and there is a wide range of multi-cultural entertainment in the form of Chinese operas, concerts and Indian and Malay dancing. Finally, the 30 or so cinemas, showing films from all over the world, should be enough to keep even the most ardent of film buffs happy.

Singapore's multi-racial heritage has led to an impressive array of over 30 ethnic cuisines with which to tempt the discerning gourmet. Local specialities tend to be Chinese (the most widely available cuisine) or Malay, although the Singaporeans have gradually evolved their own cuisine, known as Nonya, by combining elements from the two. Also widespread are Indonesian, Sumatran (nasi padang) and Indian restaurants, although it is easy to find food from nearly any country. The island's seafood restaurants have built up an enviable reputation, although these tend to be situated half an hour's taxi drive east of the city. A meal in a first-class restaurant can easily cost S$200 for dinner for two. Many visitors prefer to adopt the charming local custom of street eating, and not without reason, for the food to be found in these hawker stalls or food centres – as these open-air restaurants are called – is often every bit as tasty as the fare in the top restaurants and decidedly cheaper.

All well known international wines and spirits are available in Singapore, and beer drinkers can sample the local brands, Tiger and Anchor, which aren't at all bad.

CHANGI INTERNATIONAL AIRPORT

Changi Airport lies 12 miles east of the city, and is served by 43 airlines, with direct links to 82 cities in 50 countries. The airport was purpose-built in 1981 to cope with Singapore's ever-increasing number of visitors, and has quickly established itself as one of the most comfortable and uncongested airports in the world. There is one terminal.

AIRPORT FACILITIES

Most important facilities are open round the clock, although a few are only open from 0700 to 2300 hours.

Information Desk	There are 4 Information Desks in Arrivals (open 0730–2300 hours) and also counters in Departures which are open whenever there are flights. Flight information can be obtained by ringing Changi International Airport Services (CIAS) on 542-1234. Airport leaflets excellent.
Restaurants	In Arrivals and in Viewing Gallery (open 0730–2300 hours).

Snack Bars	3 in Viewing Gallery (open 24 hours); 1 in Departures (open 24 hours); 1 in Arrivals (open 0700–2300).
Foreign Exchange	10 counters in Arrivals and Departures, all open whenever there are flights.
Banks	Located on south-east and south-west Finger Piers. Open 1000–1500 weekdays, and 0930–1130 Saturdays.
Duty Free/Shops	3 duty free shops, including one in Arrivals, where a limited range of goods can be purchased. There are a total of 46 shops at Changi. In the Departure/Transit Hall there is an excellent shopping complex, where a wide range of goods can be bought. There is also a hairdressing salon here. All major currencies and credit cards accepted.
Five Continents Restaurant and Bar Lounge	Exclusive facilities for First Class travellers at the Viewing Gallery.
Lost Goods	Office on 3rd storey of Passenger Terminal opposite Meeting Point (tel. 541-2107/ 541-2108). For baggage lost on planes, contact: 1. Airline concerned, 2. Airline's ground handling agents, which are: Singapore Airport Terminal Services (SATS) tel. 541-8554/5, or Changi International Airport Services (CIAS) tel. 541-3103/4.
Toilets	All levels of Passenger Terminal.

Hotel Reservation	Arrival Hall East and West (0700-2300 hours).
Post	Basement 2 (0800–2000); Departures (24 hours).
Medical Centre	Departure/Transit Hall, and 4th storey of Passenger Terminal (both open 24 hours).
Meeting Point	Arrivals, between Baggage Claim areas.
Supermarket	Basement 2 (0845–2130 hours).
Business Centre	Special facilities for the business traveller. In the Departure/ Transit Hall (0830–2200 hours).
Theatrette	Featuring the 'Singapore Experience' Audio-Visual Show. Departure/Transit Hall. The film (45 minutes) is shown every hour from 0800–2100 hours.
Left Luggage	In Arrivals East (0800–2200 hours) and Departures East (24 hours).
Nursery	Departure/Transit Hall (24 hours).
Day Rooms	Departure/Transit Hall (24 hours) including shower facilities.
Car Rental	Arrivals East and West, last counters along (0700–2300 hours).
Taxi Hire	From the taxi rank just outside Arrivals in Arrival Crescent. Please queue.

AIRPORT INFORMATION

Check-in Times	Domestic – 45 minutes; international – 90 minutes.

| Airport Tax | There is a departure tax of S$12 for international flights and S$5 for flights to Malaysia and Brunei. |
| Transferring Flights | Proceed to the Departure/Transit Hall where the Transfer and Information counters are located. Transferees should reconfirm their onward flights at the Transfer counter immediately, unless you have been checked through to your final destination at your place of boarding. You do not need to bother with Immigration or Customs, and your luggage will be transferred automatically. |

AIRPORT HOTELS

There are no hotels in the immediate vicinity. The nearest is 9 miles away. However, there are 13 retiring rooms at the airport run by the Sea View Hotel, and these are to be found in the Departure/Transit Hall. Prices range from S$15 to S$25 for 6 hours. Shower facilities are also available for S$7.50.

CITY LINKS

Changi Airport is 12 miles east of the city and linked to it via the East Coast Parkway. The Pan-Island Expressway links the airport with the rest of the island. There are no rail links. Four public bus services run by Singapore Bus Services Ltd (SBS) link the airport with the rest of the island. The fare to the city is S$0.80 and buses depart from Basement 2 of the Passenger Terminal, where further information about the buses can be obtained.

The taxi rank is located just outside Arrivals in Arrival Crescent. The fare to the city is around S$15, including the S$3 surcharge levied on every trip from the airport. There is no surcharge on taxis to the airport, but there is a variable flag-down rate starting at S$1.60 to add to the metered fare. In addition to this there is a S$1 surcharge for all luggage placed in the boot, and an additional surcharge of 50 per cent of the metered fare for journeys taking place between the hours of midnight and 6 a.m. Additional passengers also incur surcharges as does each piece of luggage other than hand luggage.

TOURIST INFORMATION

The Singapore Tourist Promotion Board office on Tanglin Street is open from 0800 to 1700 hours (Monday to Saturday) and has a useful range of leaflets and brochures. There are also offices at the airport. Buy a copy of the *Singapore Weekly Guide* to find out what's on. It also has a helpful map.

ADDRESSES

British Consulate – Tanglin Road, tel. 63-9333.
US Consulate – 30 Hill Street, tel. 338-0251.
GPO – Raffles Quay.
Emergency – Phone 999 for the police. In case of accidents, dial 995. Most top hotels usually have a doctor on 24-hour call.

GETTING ABOUT

Singapore has an excellent road network, making it comparatively easy to reach one's destination.

Buses are cheap and run just about everywhere. You can buy a local bus guide at bookshops and news-stands for 70 cents, or telephone the Singapore Bus Service Public Relations Office on 284-8866 (0800–1630 weekdays, 0800–1230 Saturdays) for information about how to get to a certain point. Fares range from 40 cents up to a maximum of 80 cents. There are plenty of taxis in the city, all metered and most with air-conditioning. Fares are relatively cheap but there are an awful lot of surcharges (see above in *City Links* section for the main ones). Remember that access to the Central

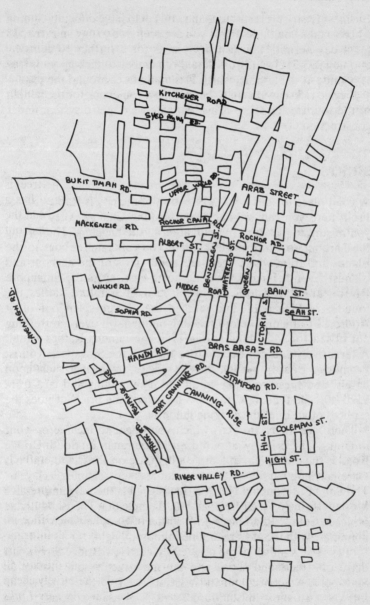

Business District is restricted, and you could have difficulty finding a taxi to take you there unless you are prepared to pay an extra S$5 for a day permit. You can book taxis for a further 40 cents by phoning 293-3111, and you should remember to pick up your free taxi guide at the airport, which lists many fares around the city.

Bicycle rickshaws seem to be making a comeback for the benefit of the tourist, and there is also an extensive metro system under construction.

SIGHTS

A good place to start a WALKING TOUR of the city is Raffles Place. From here you can wander down bustling Change Alley, where you're sure to pick up a bargain after a little haggling. Then along the harbour to Clifford Pier, where you can catch a boat to the islands and from where there are good views of the harbour and islands beyond. Finally, heading north-east, cross the Singapore River near to the historic landing place of Sir Stamford Raffles, the founder of Singapore, and take in the Gothic splendour of St Andrew's Cathedral before relaxing on the lawn over a refreshing pot of tea (or something stronger) at the famous Raffles Hotel. Alternatively you can book a tour through the Singapore Tourist Promotion Board, through travel agencies, or through most good hotels, and these will take in all the major sights and cost from S$20–40. The tours last from 3–5 hours and the price includes the services of an English-speaking guide.

There are many TEMPLES which you ought to include on your itinerary. The brightly coloured Sri Mariamman on South Bridge Road is the oldest Hindu temple still in use on the island, and has extremely popular fire-walking ceremonies several times each year. The Sultan Mosque on North Bridge Road is the most impressive Moslem shrine on the island, and the Temple of a Thousand Lights on Race Course Road has a 15 ft statue of Buddha which you can illuminate with the aforementioned thousand lights for a small fee.

CHINATOWN, north of the centre as far as New Bridge Street, is a maze of streets and shops and the most picturesque district in Singapore. A riot of colour and noise, it is well worth a visit, as is the NATIONAL MUSEUM in Stamford Road, a pleasant contrast to the bustle of Chinatown.

The nature lover is well catered for in Singapore. In addition to the outlying parks and reserves mentioned in the *Country* section for Singapore (see p. 498), there are numerous parks and gardens within the city which make for pleasant strolls. For a bird's-eye view of Singapore, take a trip up MOUNT FABER. It's less than 400 ft to the top and there's a restaurant once you get there. The BOTANIC GARDENS, near Tanglin Road, contain many exotic species of flora, while those more interested in fauna can go to the zoo or to one of the excellent outlying reserves, or even to the Singapore Turf Club, said to be one of the finest courses in the world.

ACCOMMODATION

There are a number of fine hotels in Singapore and, whether old or new, the keynote is always luxury together with all mod cons. A large number of these superior hotels are situated along Orchard Road at the heart of the city's business and shopping area, while many cheaper hotels are to be found in the north-east of the city past Bras Basah Road. Coming from the airport, the Queen Street bus terminus is convenient for most of the Bencoolen Street and Beach Road hotels. You can generally find a room without too many problems, although the island does get very crowded for the Chinese New Year in February, and hoteliers raise their prices accordingly. Many of Singapore's cheaper hotels are being upgraded or redeveloped as the island goes steadily up-market, although those on very tight budgets can still get rock-bottom accommodation in the so-called 'crash pads' which have suddenly sprung up north-east of Bras Basah Road.

● **First Class:** (over S$300 for a double)
The Hilton International – 581 Orchard Road (tel. 737-2233). Superb facilities and outstanding service. On the 22nd floor there are 12 suites which have been individually designed and decorated by the French couturier Hubert de Givenchy. On the roof is the city's highest swimming pool, with fully equipped health club below. Splendid business facilities, 4 international restaurants and lovely garden café are among the other attractions.

The Mandarin Oriental – 4 Shenton Way (tel. 225-2633). Brand-new and right on the waterfront in the Central Business District, overlooking Marina Bay. Focal point of the hotel is the uniquely designed Atrium Lounge, which sits on a slender podium 3 storeys high. First-class facilities include 2 fine restaurants, health centre, pool and own travel and tour centre.

The Oberoi Imperial – 1 Jalan Rumbia (tel. 737-1666). Another excellent hotel, with panoramic views of the city and harbour thanks to its position at the crest of Oxley Rise. Again, all the facilities you would expect from a 5-star hotel, which even extend to the elegant continental restaurant at Changi Airport. At the hotel there are 3 good restaurants, with a poolside barbecue at weekends.

● **Super Club Class:** (S$200–300 for a double)
Westin Stamford and Plaza – 2 Stamford Road (tel. 338-8585). Two luxury hotels on the same site in the heart of Singapore. The Stamford is enormous: over 1200 rooms and currently the tallest hotel in the world. There is a choice of 17 restaurants and sports facilities are excellent. Large convention centre can cater for up to 6000.

Century Park Sheraton – Nassim Hill (tel. 732-1222). Exclusive position in embassy district. Elegant lobby and rooms, with extensive choice of suites. Two restaurants, with the Unkai considered to serve the best Japanese food in town.

The Raffles Hotel – 1/3 Beach Road (tel. 337-8041). Period splendour and a welcome change from the many more modern yet anodyne establishments which are going up all around at a furious rate. Now even more luxurious than it was in Kipling's day, and certainly worth a visit for high tea or a drink in the Writers' Bar if you're staying elsewhere.

● **Economy:** (S$30–200 for a double)
The Plaza – 7500A Beach Road (tel. 298-0011). Top of range hotel with all the facilities you would expect from a first-class hotel at a much lower price. Own nightclub.

The Waterloo Hotel – Waterloo Street. Good value for the type of hotel. Comfortable and air-conditioned. Quiet position.

The South-East Asia Hotel – 190 Waterloo Street (tel. 338-2394). Modern hotel with air-conditioning. Slightly cheaper than the nearby Waterloo.

The Majestic – 31 Bukit Pasoh Road, near Chinatown. One of the few hotels in this area and close to the New Bridge bus terminal. Immaculate and quiet. Some rooms have balconies.

The Sun Sun Hotel – 260/2 Middle Road (tel. 338-4911). Very clean. Own bar and restaurant.

The Tai Loke – 151 Middle Road (tel. 337-6209). Good-sized rooms with fine old furniture. Cheap.

YMCA – Bras Basah Road, opposite Cathay Cinema. Big, new and central.

DINING OUT

● **First Class:** (around S$200 for two)
The Harbour Grill – At the Hilton International (tel. 737-2233). Emphasis on creative French cuisine using the best and freshest of natural ingredients. Superb wine list. The Hilton's Inn of Happiness, in the style of an old Chinese inn and courtyard, also has a good reputation for Cantonese cuisine.

The Unkai – At the Century Park Sheraton (tel. 732-1222). Apart from the main restaurant, there are private tatami rooms, a sushi counter, and four teppanyaki grills. Good food, traditional decor and views over parkland.

The Belvedere – At the Mandarin Singapore Hotel, Orchard Road (tel. 737-4411). The more established of the two Mandarin hotels, with an excellent reputation for French haute cuisine in sophisticated and relaxed surroundings.

● **Super Club Class:** (S$50–150 for two)
The Omar Khayyam – 55 Hill Street, opposite the American Embassy (tel. 336-1505). Kashmiri specialists, and probably the best Indian food in town. Their tandooris are simply delicious.

The Rendezvous – 4/5 Bras Basah Road, at the junction with Prinsep Street (tel. 337-6619). If you like the hot and spicy nasi padang cuisine from western Sumatra, then this is the place to go.

The Pavilion Steak House – Orchard Road. Can't abide foreign food? Then relax over a sizzling steak in the splendid colonial surroundings of The Pavilion.

• **Economy:** (less than S$50 for two)
Kheng Luck – At 50B Upper Coast Road (tel. 24-0291). Most of the seafood specialists are some distance from the city centre and most of them are worth the half-hour journey. This is a crowded (always a good sign) open-air restaurant whose speciality is chilli crab, although both the prawns in black bean sauce and the sweet and sour fish are equally good.

Apollo Banana Leaf Restaurant – Just off Serangoon Road, in the Indian quarter. Rice and curried vegetables are placed on your banana leaf 'plate', followed by one of their pungent specialities such as sweet lamb curry or spicy fish-head curry. One of many good Indian restaurants in the area.

Food Stalls – Street eating is a way of life in Singapore and you can eat better and certainly cheaper at these food centres or hawkers' stalls than at many top-notch restaurants. Often run by only one person, the system is to sit at a table outside the stall and wait for the menu (in English). The choice of food is enormous and the stalls are clean and convenient. It's how the Singaporeans themselves eat out so give it a go. Three or four dishes and a large bottle of beer should cost no more than S$15 for two, and the following are recommended:

Telok Ayer – Situated in the Central Business District in the lovely old octagonal Telok Ayer Market between Robinson Road and Shenton Way. Deservedly busy at lunch, but quiet in the evenings.

Newton Circus – A large establishment at the end of Scotts Road. Very busy at night, as it stays open late. Good duck and cuttlefish.

Rasa Singapura – On Tanglin Road next door to the Singapore Tourist Promotion Board. Heavily promoted for tourists, and therefore slightly more expensive. Tasty oyster omelette.

The Satay Club – Satay food consists of tiny pieces of spiced meat threaded on to slim bamboo skewers and served with a delicious peanut and coconut sauce. As its name suggests, this stall, on the waterfront at the foot of Stamford Road, specializes in satay with steamboats as an added attraction.

NIGHTLIFE

There's plenty to do at night, though eating out appears to be a favourite occupation. You can combine live entertainment with your meal at one of Singapore's numerous NIGHTCLUB/RESTAU-RANTS, generally to be found in the top hotels, or THEATRE/RESTAU-RANTS such as the Neptune Theatre Restaurant at Collyer Quay, or the Tropicana Theatre Restaurant in Scotts Road. There are plenty of places to dance, such as the Black Velvet and Gold Disco in the Century Park Sheraton, where they claim the atmosphere is 'pure alchemy'. Major cultural events take place at venues like the VICTORIA THEATRE, the SINGAPORE CONFERENCE CENTRE (both central) and the CULTURAL THEATRE, a couple of miles north-west of the centre. These receive visiting international stars, orchestras and ballet groups and details can be found in the easily obtainable *Singapore Weekly Guide*. There is much multi-ethnic activity, particularly during festivals when the streets resound to the colourful sound of Chinese street operas. Indian and Malay dancing are popular forms of entertainment, with the latter taking place every night at the Raffles Hotel. Films are extremely popular and the 30 or so cinemas should cater for most tastes. Finally, the highly active red-light district stretches from Jalan Besar to Serangoon Road, parallel to Desker Road.

EXCURSIONS

Unless you are planning to use Singapore as your base for an extensive tour of the Far East, there aren't really many excursions for you to choose from. You should definitely make the short journey across the water to SENTOSA, the most developed of Singapore's 50-odd islands, which has good beaches, a swimming lagoon, coralarium, maritime museum and art centre. The round trip is from S$3–6 depending on what time you go. Other islands are nowhere near as developed as Sentosa (yet). ST JOHNS and the KUSU ISLANDS have ferry connections with the city, and are good places for a quiet swim, except at weekends when many of the islands become very crowded. It's worth hiring a boat to explore the islands, or just merely to meander up and down the Singapore River.

Malaysia, Indonesia, Thailand, the Philippines and Hong Kong are relatively near by plane and there are sections on these places elsewhere in the book.

Taiwan

RED TAPE

• **Passport/Visa Requirements:** A full, valid passport is required. Carriers of passports issued by the People's Republic of China will be refused entry. Visas are required by all. A Tourist A visa allows a stay of 30 days in Taiwan; Tourist B visas allow a stay of 60 days; and Transit visas allow a stay of 14 days.

CUSTOMS

• **Duty Free:** Each visitor to Taiwan may take in 200 cigarettes or 25 cigars or 1 lb tobacco and 1 litre of spirits. A reasonable quantity of perfume and goods up to the value of NT$6000 may also be taken in without incurring duty. Prohibited items include all products of the Chinese People's Republic, narcotics, gambling articles and toy pistols. All baggage must be declared in writing.

HEALTH

There are no vaccinations necessary for entry to Taiwan but the risk of malaria, cholera, typhoid and polio makes precautions against these advisable. Water precautions should be taken everywhere in Taiwan. Emergency healthcare is available from the Mackey Memorial Hospital in Taipei.

CAPITAL – Taipei.

POPULATION – 18,457,923.

LANGUAGE – Chinese (Mandarin/Amoy dialects). English and Japanese are widely spoken.

CURRENCY – New Taiwan Dollar (NT$) = 100 cents. Notes are in denominations of NT$ 1000, 500, 100, 50, 10, 5, 1. Coins are in denominations of NT$ 10, 5, 1 and 10 and 5 cents.
£1 = NT$50; US$1 = NT$36.

BANKING HOURS – 0900–1530 hours Monday to Friday; 0900–1200 hours Saturday.

POLITICAL SYSTEM – Republic.

RELIGION – Buddhism, Taoism, Christianity and Islam.

PUBLIC HOLIDAYS

January 1	Founding Day
February (3 days)	Chinese New Year
February/March (1 day)	Lantern Festival
March 12	Labour Day
March 29	Youth Day
April 5	Ching Ming Festival
May (1 day)	Buddha Bathing Festival
June (1 day)	Dragon Boat Festival
August	The Month of the Ghosts (biggest celebration falls on the first day)
September (2 days)	Mid-Autumn Festival and Confucius' Birthday
October 10	Double Tenth National Day
October 25	Taiwan Restoration Day
October 31	Birthday of the late President Chiang Kai-shek (1877–1975)

November 12   Dr Sun Yat-sen's Birthday
December 25   Constitution Day and Christmas Day

CLIMATE – Taiwan has a sub-tropical climate with moderate temperatures in the north, where there is a winter season. Summer (June to August) sees temperatures of between 96°F (36°C) and 67°F (19°C) with fairly high humidities and a higher rainfall than in the winter months. Winter is only slightly cooler usually, but temperatures can drop to about 44°F (7°C) in January and February. Southern areas enjoy sunshine every day and temperatures are slightly higher than in the north throughout the year.

TIME DIFFERENCE – GMT + 8 hours.

COMMUNICATIONS

• Telephone: Taiwan has an extensive telephone system and IDD is widely available in city areas. Local calls from public booths cost NT$1. Most hotels have English- and Japanese-speaking switchboard operators. Taipei city code is 02.

• Post: Airmail to the UK takes up to 2 weeks. Telex is available at major hotels or at the ITA main office, 28 Hangchow South Road, Sec. 1, Taipei or one of the 4 branch offices. Telegrams can be sent from any of these offices.

ELECTRICITY – 110v AC; 60 Hz.

OFFICE/SHOPPING HOURS – Office: 0900–1730 hours with lunch 1200–1300 hours Monday to Friday; 0900–1200 hours Saturday. Shops: same but small shops often stay open late.

• Best Buys: Taiwan is not one of the world's most exciting places for shopping. The best buys are among the wide selections of oriental works of art in jade, coral, lacquer, porcelain or wood. One of the best places to shop is actually at Chiang Kai-shek Airport where some of the best quality goods can be found at competitive prices. Central Taipei also has some good shopping malls, the main area being Shiminding in Chung Hwa Road, and plenty of small handicraft shops. Taipei's night markets are well worth a visit, for the atmosphere more than the merchandise. The most frequented are at Yuan Huan (Circle), Lungshan Temple, Huahou Street, Nanchang Street, Tungmeo, Changchuan Road, Tunhua Street, Sungshan and Shihlin. They open from 6 p.m. to midnight daily.

INTERNAL TRAVEL

• **Air:** China Airlines (CAL) and Far Eastern Airlines Transport (FAT) run services to major cities from Sung Shan Airport, Taipei (40 minutes' drive from Chiang Kai-shek International Airport and 15 minutes from Taipei city). CAL also flies to Hong Kong. Island services are by Taiwan Airlines and Yong Hsin Airlines. Flights are cheap and standbys are usually available.

• **Train:** The Taiwan Railway Administration provides services along west- and east-coast routes. Air-conditioned electric trains run at least hourly from Taipei to Kaohsiung. Express train fares are only marginally more than bus fares. Tickets should be bought in advance and seats reserved as the trains are very popular.

• **Bus:** Both local and long-distance bus services are excellent – cheap and efficient. There is an extensive network of bus routes which serves the entire country.

• **Car Rental:** Car hire firms are available in major towns. An International Driving Licence is required. Street signs are not in English. For any form of public transport it is essential to know your destination name in Mandarin. The best idea is to write it in Chinese figures (or get the hotel staff to do so) so that you can show it to the driver or ticket clerk. Transport in Taiwan is a real treat – fast, efficient and cheap – so it is worth making good use of during your stay.

MAJOR SIGHTS OF THE COUNTRY

TAIPEI, Taiwan's capital and major city, makes a good base for seeing the rest of the country although it is not in itself the most interesting of places. Northern Taiwan is flanked from east to west by the Taiwan Strait, the East China Sea and the Pacific Ocean. To the north-east of Taipei is KEELUNG, one of the island's 3 major seaports. TAICHUNG is the principal economic, cultural and communications centre of central Taiwan and makes a good stopping place en route to the south. Close by is PULI, known as the island's 'butterfly' centre as more than 400 species have been sighted there. From April to August are the best times to butterfly-watch. Right in the centre of the island is SUN MOON LAKE, a stretch of water 2500 ft above sea level and surrounded by forest. The historic lakeshore temples and peacock garden add a Taiwanese flavour to the landscape.

Further east the biggest city is HUALIEN, an important seaport. Just to the north, at the beginning of the east-west Cross-Island Highway, is KAROKO GORGE, a ravine lined with towering marble covered cliffs. This spectacular stretch of road is said to be one of the most travelled in Taiwan, and has 38 tunnels en route.

Off the south-eastern coast are 2 islands – Lutan or GREEN ISLAND and Lanyu or ORCHARD ISLAND. the former is covered with low, lush green hills and most of its population lives on the coast, engaged in fishing. The latter is home to the Yami, the most primitive of Taiwan's native tribes.

Back on the mainland, the major southern city is KAOHSIUNG, the island's largest international seaport. Tainan, to the north of Kaohsiung, is the old capital of the island and noted for its historical relics. Also in the south, ALISHAN is one of Taiwan's oldest mountain resorts, with 18 peaks of over 7000 ft and a highland village at 7465 ft. The temples, forests, spectacular sunrises and cloud formations of the area draw many tourists every year.

A windswept archipelago of low flat islands lies off the central west coast of Taiwan. Collectively called PENGHU, the 4 main islands are linked by causeways and daily flights link the main town of Makung to Taipei.

Taipei

CHIANG KAI-SHEK INTERNATIONAL AIRPORT

Taiwan's international airport is located at Tayuan town in Tayuan County, about 25 miles from Taipei. It opened to international flights in 1979 and is one of the most modern airports in Asia. The Passenger Terminal is the main building in the airport, covering a huge area and having 5 storeys. Departure and arrival areas are kept separate. Departing passengers use the eastern concourse and baggage is checked in on the first floor. Arriving passengers enter on the second level and then proceed to the ground level baggage claim area, eventually leaving by the west exit of the airport.

AIRPORT FACILITIES

Information Desks	In the Departure Lounges for outbound passengers. Tourist service centres are in the Arrivals area.
Bank/Foreign Exchange	Counters in both Arrival and Departure Lounges.
Hotel Reservation Service	To the right of the Arrivals Hall.
Postal Service	There are 3 offices in the terminal building, open 0900–1700 hours Monday to Friday and 0900–1200 hours Saturday.
Telephone/Telegram	Telephone booths are positioned throughout the terminal building and an international telegram service is provided in both Departure and Arrival Lounges.
Lost Property	Phone 83-2326 for baggage lost in restricted areas or 83-2538 for baggage lost outside the restricted areas.

Restaurants	One is located on the third floor and another in the basement.
Coffee Shop	In the Departure Lobby on the second floor.
Snack Bar	In the Arrivals Lobby on the first floor.
Duty Free	The shops in the airport offer some of the best goods in Taiwan so they are definitely worth a look if you have time. Apart from all the usual duty free items there are many handicraft, jewellery and art shops to browse around. There are also several foodstores in the terminal. Major currencies and credit cards are accepted.
Shops	On the second floor of the Departure Lounge and in the Departure concourses.
Medical Services	A medical centre is located to the right of the first floor, near the Departure area. 24-hour general and emergency medical care is provided here for staff and passengers.
Toilets	Throughout the terminal; open 24 hours.

AIRPORT INFORMATION

Check-in Times	90 minutes before international flight departure time.
Departure Tax	NT$200 must be paid by all passengers departing Taiwan who are over 2 years of age. Transit passengers are exempt.

Flight Transfers

International-to-international flight transfer passengers remain in the same terminal and are ushered from the Arrivals Hall to the Departure Lounge. International-to-domestic (or vice versa) flight passengers must make their way to the relevant terminal. Sung Shan Airport, which deals with domestic flights, is 40 minutes by bus from the international terminal. There is a bus every 15 minutes from 0630 to 2230 running between the airports.

AIRPORT HOTELS

● **Super Club Class:**
CKS Airport Hotel, 66 CKS International Airport, Taoyvan (tel. 033 833666). One mile from the airport, this provides 511 rooms and good sports facilities. This is a standard businessman's hotel, where it is advisable to pre-book.

CITY LINKS

● **Road:** Taiwan Motor Transport Company operates buses from the airport to the city centre. Leading hotels in Taipei run bus services and have representatives stationed in the Arrival Lounge for arriving international passengers. Taxis are a lot more expensive than the buses and a 50 per cent surcharge is added to the fare shown on the taxi meter for journeys from CKS Airport. These taxi drivers are not renowned for their helpfulness and any problems with them should be reported to the police on 83-2242. Transport to the airport stops outside the east gates and transport to the city leaves from outside the west gates.

TAIPEI

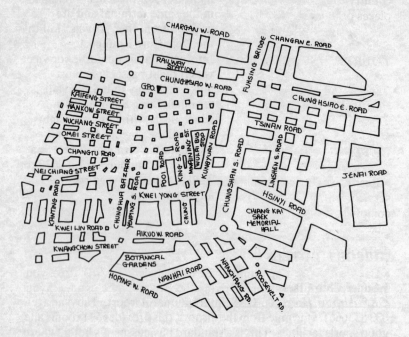

Taipei was founded as capital of Taiwan in the 18th century and from 1895 to 1945 it, along with the rest of the country, was under Japanese occupation. In 1949 Chiang Kai-shek fled from mainland China, where he had been defeated in a civil war, and established the Republic of China in Taiwan (formerly Formosa). Taipei became the seat of the Nationalist government, which now continues under the rule of Chiang Kai-shek's son, Jiang Jing Guo (or Chiang Ching-kuo). It is now an important industrial centre, especially for textiles, food processing and machinery, and is also the Republic of China's cultural centre. The city's population of well over 2 million is expanding rapidly and Taipei is one of Asia's fastest growing areas.

Geographically, Taipei is on the northern tip of Taiwan (the name means this in Chinese). It is a large, sprawling city and certainly not one of the world's most attractive. Prices in the city are vastly inflated when compared with those of the surrounding country, but it is worth staying in Taipei for a few days to see its places of interest.

TOURIST INFORMATION

Taiwan Tourist Information Bureau – 9th Floor, 280 Chung Hsiao East Road, Section 4 (tel. 721-8541 or 751-8445).

GETTING ABOUT

● **Bus:** A number of urban bus companies provide an extensive bus service within Taipei. Their routes and numbering are very complicated but the Tourist Bureau has a leaflet which helps.

● **Taxi:** City taxis are metered and quite inexpensive. Your destination must be written in Mandarin Chinese for the driver.

● **Car Rental:** Car hire firms are found all over Taipei. To drive you must have an International Driving Licence and it helps a lot if you can decipher the street signs, which are all in Mandarin.

SIGHTS

The PRESIDENTIAL BUILDING is a 12-storey red-brick building which was the Japanese governor's office during their 50-year reign. It has now been renovated as the Presidential Offices and has an impressive square in front of it. The CHIANG KAI-SHEK MEMORIAL HALL is a very tall (70m) hall which houses a bronze statue of the late President. There are also exhibition rooms with historical documents and personal articles. The CONFUCIUS TEMPLE, dedicated to Confucius, the ancient Chinese sage (551 BC–479 BC), also honours other ancient scholars such as Yentze, Tsengtze, Mencius and Confucius' disciples.

The NATIONAL PALACE MUSEUM has to be Taipei's showpiece. Sited in the wooded hills of Waishuang-hsi suburb, the museum houses the world's richest collection of Chinese art. Some of its treasures date back 4000 years and the whole exhibition gives an incredible view of Chinese culture over the centuries. Photography is not permitted here but the museum shop sells good reproductions of some of the masterpieces.

Located in Jenai Road, Section 4 and open daily from 0900–1700, the SUN YAT-SEN MEMORIAL HALL is used for free performances of Chinese opera every Saturday and Sunday afternoon. Reservations need to be made in advance (tel. 702-24110 ext. 36). There is also a library here.

HSINGTIEN PALACE is a beautiful Taoist temple in the city centre which honours Kuan Yu – the most respected god of merchants – and General Yueh Fei – an all time Chinese hero. Taoist believers occupy the temple continuously, waiting to be blessed. LUNGSHAN TEMPLE is an elaborate Buddhist temple on Kwang Chow Street which was built in 1738. Services are held at 8 p.m. and chanting can be heard at 6.30 a.m. and 5 p.m.

The NATIONAL MUSEUM OF HISTORY houses an extensive collection of Chinese arts and artefacts, some dating back to 2000 BC. It is at 49 Nanhai Road, and is open from 0900–1700 daily.

YANGMINGSHAN PARK is a beautiful classical Chinese garden with pavilions, fountains, cherry trees and azaleas. It is a 30-minute drive from the city centre, but well worth the journey. On the way to Yangmingshan Park is an area covered in Taiwan orchids, cattleya, cymbidum and phalaenopsis, WHITE CLOUD ORCHIDS. The gardens are open 0800–1800.

PEITOU, an old-fashioned town, has been enveloped by the spreading city but has retained its quaint features. A central park has a hot spring running through it and lots of flowers and greenery.

ACCOMMODATION

Taipei has a wide range of hotels, many of them of international standard. There are also lots of cheap, basic forms of accommodation – boarding houses, hostels and motels – usually reasonably close to the city centre. Whatever standard of accommodation you choose, it is best to book in advance, especially during festivals and holidays.

● **First Class:** (Double NT$3600–4200)

Lai Lai Sheraton Hotel – 12 Chung Hsiao East Road, Section 1, Taipei (tel. 321-5511). This is a place of sheer luxury with everything you could possibly wish for laid on. The sports facilities are exceptionally good and the Lai Lai Restaurant is a feast of extravagance.

Hilton International – 38 Chung Hsiao West Road, Section 1, Taipei (tel. 311-5151). Another of the Hilton chain's top-quality hotels with luxurious facilities and impeccable service. The new Roof Garden with jacuzzi is a wonderful place to relax in peace after a day in the bustling city.

The Mandarin – 166 Tunhwa North Road, Taipei (tel. 712-1201). A beautiful hotel with extensive, high-quality facilities. Good convention and banquet halls, making this an excellent place for conferences.

● **Super Club Class:** (Double NT$2800–3600)

Ambassador Hotel – 63 Chungshan North Road, Section 2, Taipei (tel. 551-1111). A central hotel with super facilities including restaurants famed for their Szechuan and Cantonese dishes.

Imperial Hotel – 600 Lin Sen North Road, Taipei (tel. 596-5111). A newly refurbished hotel with extensive facilities and good service.

Gwn'a Hotel – 369 Lin Sen North Road, Taipei (tel. 581-8111). Conveniently located in central Taipei, with a good range of facilities including good business facilities.

Century Plaza Hotel – 132 Omei Street, Taipei (tel. 311-3131). On the banks of the Tamsui River in the main Hsimenting shopping district, this is a well appointed and very well priced hotel.

● **Economy:** (Double NT$1000–2800)

Gala Hotel – 186 Sung Chiang Road, Taipei (tel. 541-5511). Very comfortable accommodation but slightly out of town. Hotel transport is available.

Hotel China – 14 Kuan Chien Road, Taipei (tel. 331-9512). Comfortable guest rooms in the central business district.

Hotel Orient – 85 Hankow Street, Section 1, Taipei (tel. 331-7211). An attractive, modern hotel in the central shopping area, with very hospitable staff.

The Leojou – 168 Chang Chun Road, Taipei (tel. 581-3111). Adequate accommodation and a very good Cantonese restaurant on the 11th floor.

Santos – 439 Chengteh Road, Taipei (tel. 596-3111). Good accommodation, about 25 minutes out of the city but in the right direction for the airport.

Golden China – 306 Sung Chiang Road, Taipei (tel. 521-5151). Adequate facilities and comfortable rooms out of the city centre.

DINING OUT

Eating in Taipei is either quite expensive or extraordinarily cheap but in either extreme the food tends to be extremely good. The ancient art of Chinese cooking, whether it be in the style of Canton, Peking, Szechuan, Shanghai, Hunan, Mongolia or Taiwan, has been perfected by the chefs of Taipei. Cantonese food tends to be more subtle and colourful than that of the other regions. Peking cooking is mild and usually barbecued or roasted, duck being the speciality. Szechuan food, with liberal use of garlic and red chilli pepper, is hot and spicy. The food of Shanghai tends to concentrate on seafood dishes with rich sauces. Hunan dishes are spicy and most often steamed, ham and honey sauce being a favourite. 'Firepot' (meat dipped in a hot sauce and barbecued) and meat and vegetables are the 2 basic Mongolian dishes. Taiwanese cookery relies on thick garlic or soy sauces covering seafoods. For those who prefer western cooking there are a variety of restaurants, although they tend not to come up to the standards of the Chinese restaurants. There are also numerous European, American or Australian-run pubs many of which serve pub food. Language barriers are easily overcome as food is generally displayed on a grill and you just point to what you fancy. (N.B. Avoid the chillies, left gratis on the tables, unless you have an asbestos gullet!)

• **First Class:** (NT$1500–2800 for two)
Rong Shing – 45 Chilin Road (tel. 521-5341). Wonderful Szechuan food. Booking advisable.

Hsin Tung – 2 Lane 49, Chung Hsiao East Road (tel. 771-5065). Cantonese cuisine at its best.

Green Leaf – 1 Lane 105, Chung Shan North Road (tel. 551-7957). Authentic Taiwanese food – delicious and still reasonably priced.

• **Super Club Class:** (NT$750–1500)
Peng Yuan – 380 Lin Sen North Road (tel. 551-9157). Hunanese cuisine – well presented and beautifully cooked.

Hsin Tung Lo – 26 Chang Chun Road (tel. 551-2888). Cantonese cuisine worth tasting whilst in town.

Mei Toe – 1 Lane 107, Lin Sen North Road (tel. 521-3200). Taiwanese food.

San Ho Lou – 2 Lane 460, Tun Hua South Road (tel. 731-5296). Popular Shanghai restaurant. Book early as becoming very well frequented by travelling businessmen.

• **Economy:** Restaurants are all over town and need no special directions. The chances are you'll stumble across them in whatever area you are located in.

NIGHTLIFE

Most of Taipei's top hotels have nightclubs which serve dinner before the show or dancing begins. Small entertainment spots can be found in bars and pubs. The streets of Taipei are always busy at night as Taiwanese opera is performed in any available open space. The Sun Yat-sen Memorial Hall and the City Hall have regular CHINESE OPERA and BALLET performances. Chinese opera can also be seen nightly at the Chinese Armed Forces Culture and Activity Centre at 64 Chung Hua Road.

EXCURSIONS

All the beauty spots in northern Taiwan are within easy reach of the city centre. KEELUNG, the north's major port, has an imposing hilltop statue of the Goddess of Mercy, Kuan Yin. The coastal road from here north is spectacular, passing the foothills of the Central Mountain Range and going through many small traditional villages. YEHLIU, a coastal town near Keelung, is noted for its remarkable rock formations and delicious seafood restaurants. Inland, WULAI is the nearest aboriginal village to Taipei. The Tayal tribe make and sell a variety of artefacts and also give lively song and dance performances. To the south of TACHI, in Tayuan County, is TZUHU. This is the temporary resting place of the late President Chiang Kai-shek who died in 1975. The site was named by him in memory of his mother.

There are many tour operators in Taiwan, the good ones being licensed by the Tourism Bureau. Agencies always ready to arrange special tours are:

China Express Transportation Co. – 68 Chung Shan North Road, Section 2, Taipei (tel. 541-6466).
Taiwan Coach Tours – 6/F, 27 Chung Shan North Road, Section 3, Taipei (tel. 595-5321).
Pinho Travel Service Co. – 3/Frj, 142-1 Chilin Road, Taipei (tel. 551-4136).
Cathay Express Co. – 306-5B, Kuangyu South Road, Taipei (tel. 731-2355).

Daily bus tours from Taipei go round the north coast, visiting the places of interest and often stopping at CHINSAN BEACH – the best beach close to Taipei.

Thailand

RED TAPE

• **Passport/Visa Requirements:** A full, valid passport plus a visa is required by everyone. For a maximum stay of 15 days you may arrive without a visa and will be granted a transit visa, provided you have an onward ticket. No visa extension is possible with this. A tourist visa for a 60-day stay, or a non-immigrant visa for a 90-day stay can be obtained from the Royal Thai Embassy, 29–30 Queen's Gate, London SW7 (tel. 01 589-0173) or often more easily and cheaply in Singapore, Penang, Kota Bharu, Khatmandu or other prior destinations. In the US, the Royal Thai Embassy is at 2300 Kalorama Road, NW Washington DC 20008 (tel. (202) 667-1446). Visa extensions are possible (although difficult at the moment) and obtainable from the Immigration Department, Soi Suan Plu, Bangkok or Soi Yod Sak in Pattaya.

CUSTOMS

• **Duty Free:** The allowance is 200 cigarettes or 50 cigars or 250g tobacco and 1 litre each of wines and spirits. No limit on perfume for personal use. There are export restrictions on some antiques and all Buddha images – check before purchasing.

HEALTH

A yellow fever vaccination certificate is required from travellers coming from infected areas. Malaria risk exists throughout the year in rural, especially forested and hilly, areas of the country. Resistance to chloroquine has been reported. Typhoid, polio and cholera are also a risk in Thailand. Certificates of vaccination against these diseases are required if coming from an infected area. Water should be boiled or otherwise treated and health insurance is strongly recommended. Medical facilities are good in Bangkok and main centres and all the major hotels have doctors on call.

CAPITAL – Bangkok; population 5 million.

POPULATION – 47,900,000.

LANGUAGE – Thai. English is widely used in Bangkok.

CURRENCY – The baht (B), divided into 100 stang. 25 and 50 stang and 1B and 5B coins are the most commonly used. The 25 stang coin may be referred to as a saleng. A variety of paper denominations exists – it may be difficult to change anything larger than 100B in rural areas.
£1 = 34.5B; US$1 = 24.64B.

BANKING HOURS – 0830–1530 hours Monday–Friday.

POLITICAL SYSTEM – Under military rule.

RELIGION – Hinayana Buddhism.

PUBLIC HOLIDAYS

December 31, January 1	New Year
February (3 days)	Chinese New Year
March (1 day)	Makha Bucha (Buddhist holy day)
April 6	Chakri Day (commemoration of King Rama I)
April 13	Songkran (Thai New Year)
May 1	National Labour Day
May 5	Coronation Day
June (1 day)	Wisakha Bucha
July (2 days)	Asanha Bucha then Buddhist Lent begins
August 12	Queen's birthday
October 23	Chulalongkorn Day (tribute to King Chulalongkorn)
December 5	Present King's birthday
December 10	Constitution Day

CLIMATE – November to February is the 'cool' dry season with temperatures of 62–84°F (17–28°C). March to May is intensely hot and May to October is humid with temperatures of 76–95°F (25–34°C). July to October is the rainy season.

TIME DIFFERENCE – GMT + 7 hours.

COMMUNICATIONS

• **Post:** Airmail to the UK takes about one week. The GPO is in New Road, Bangkok. Public telex facilities are here and telegrams may be sent from here or any telegraph office.

• **Telephone:** IDD code 66 (Bangkok 66-2 and Cheing Mai 66-53).

ELECTRICITY – 220v AC; 50 Hz.

OFFICE/SHOPPING HOURS – Offices: 0830–1200 and 1300–1630 hours Monday to Friday; 0900–1200 hours Saturday (POs only). Shops: 0830–1800 hours Monday to Saturday (major shops only).

• **Best Buys:** Bangkok is a great place for shopping, with many Thai specialities to tempt you and the exhilaration of bargaining as added excitement. Don't try to avoid bargaining in the small shops and markets – the seller enjoys it as much as you will! The larger stores have fixed prices.

Thai specialities include their exotic silks, nielloware (silver inlaid with black enamel), porcelain and antique jewellery. Temple rubbings in charcoal on rice paper or coloured on cotton are a popular buy (Wat Po is a good spot to find these), or metal Buddha heads, temple 'spirit' bells and wood carvings all make good presents. Clothes can be bought, off-the-peg or made-to-measure, at very attractive prices and the Thais have a great flair for style. Antiques of all sorts are available but as some of the best fakes come from Bangkok, beware if you want something 'real'.

Silom Road and New Road (Charoen Krung Road) are both good shopping areas. 'Design Thai' (304 Silom Road) offers an enormous range of silk lengths and made-up clothes as does 'Shinnawatra' (Sukhumvit Road, Soi 23). The silk retail shop of Jim Thomson in Suriwongse Road and other shops on Silom Road are also worth visiting. Locally made crafts and jewellery can be found at 'AA Co. Ltd' in Siam Centre Plaza or at the Thai Hill Crafts Foundation, Scapathum Palace, Ploenchit Road (behind the Siam Centre). For gemstones and jewellery 'Valentine Gems', 35 Ratchwithi Road, is good.

Markets are great places to wander around and try out your bargaining powers. Thieves Market (the Nakorn Kasem area) has endless Thai and Chinese stalls while the Weekend Market (near the Northern Bus Terminal) is the place to look for oddities and curios. In Bangkok shopping guides or touts will approach you and offer to show you to the best bargain shops – don't follow them.

INTERNAL TRAVEL

● **Air:** Thai Airways operate an internal network covering Chiang Rai, Mae Hong Song, Chiang Mai, Phitsanulok, Udon Thani, Khon Kaen, Ubon Ratchathani, Surat Thani, Phuket, Hat Yai and Penang (across the Malay border).

● **Rail:** Thai trains are slow, but comfortable, cheap and frequent. Being comparable in price to buses, but much safer, they are a preferable method of transport. On board the food is also amazingly good. Four main lines and a few side routes make up the network. The northern line goes to Chiang Mai; the north-eastern to Nong Kai; the eastern to Ubon Ratchathani and the southern to Hat Yai. It is advisable to book in advance: you can book on to any route at the Hualamphong Station in Bangkok. Railway timetables are available here, in English, and trains are punctual so be at the station in good time.

● **Bus:** A very fast (too fast!) service with a choice of 'normal' or air-conditioned buses on major routes. Service on the air-conditioned buses is extremely good: blankets (the air-con. can be a bit over-efficient!) pillows, free drinks, meals and even movies on some routes. Both public and private buses run.

● **Boat:** Travel by river or sea in Thailand is the most common form of transport. Traditional 'long-tail' boats carry passengers along waterways or out to the many offshore islands.

● **Locally:** Town transport includes taxis, samlors (cycle rickshaws or motorized tuk-tuks), songthaews (minibuses) and regular buses. With taxis and samlors bargain your fare before you commence on the journey.

MAJOR SIGHTS OF THE COUNTRY

The northern Thai capital, CHIANG MAI, makes an interesting visit (although it's now a bit touristy) and a good temporary base from which to visit the attractive, northern area. It used to be an independent kingdom which suffered many battles against Burma, Laos and Sukhothai and the remains of a moat and city wall from that era (1296 onwards) can still be seen in today's city. Treks run from here through the land of the colourful hill tribes and the Golden Triangle region, where Thailand, Laos and Burma meet and opium grows.

SUKHOTHAI, founded as Siam's first capital in 1257, was rapidly superseded by AYUTHAYA in 1379. Despite this its ruins and archives give evidence of great achievements in art, literature and economic prosperity. Other cities of the kingdom with very visible ruins are KAMPHAENG PHET and SI SATCHANALAI.

Thailand's highest peak, DOI INTHANON (2595m) has some impressive waterfalls and views, and can be visited from Chiang Mai within a day. On the way, CHOM THONG is worth a stop to see its beautiful temple (Burmese-style) called Wat Phra That Si Chom Thong. Right up in the north, near the Laos border, is CHIANG SAEN. Numerous ruins of temples, chedis, wats and other Chiang Saen period remains make this small town very interesting to visit.

In the east of Thailand, the famous Khmer ruins of Phimai can be seen in NAKHON RATCHASIMA (Khorat) but this major town also has other worthwhile sights. In the north-east, on the banks of the Mekong, lies THAT PHANOM with its famous Wat That Phanom and several buildings of Chinese-French architecture with Laotian influences.

Southern Thailand is the area to find spectacular scenery, gorgeous beaches and a clear sea in which to swim and snorkel. PATTAYA, on the Gulf of Thailand, is the biggest seaside resort in the region – for a suntan and good nightlife look no further. PHUKET, an island on the west side of the southern peninsula, has crystal-clear waters and miles of sandy beach – largely devoid of the human masses one encounters at Pattaya. The peace is mainly due to the high prices incurred in getting there by plane or the arduous bus journey involved. Club Med are about to open a holiday village on the island so this will be one option of getting here without too many problems. Off the east coast lies another beautiful island –

KOH SAMUI – which is even harder to get to (with no airport or bridge to the mainland as Phuket has). Even better beaches and more spectacular waterfalls make the boat ride worthwhile.

Bangkok

DON MUANG INTERNATIONAL AIRPORT

About 15 miles north-east of Bangkok is Don Muang International Airport. This large, busy airport is a major gateway for air transport into and within South East Asia. By 1987 the expansion and development it has been undergoing for the past years should have been completed and many new facilities will exist. There are 3 terminals: the International one serves scheduled flights for up to 40 airlines; the Domestic serves scheduled flights for 3 airlines; and the Cargo Terminal serves flights for 7 airlines.

AIRPORT FACILITIES

Information Desk	In the Departure halls; open 24 hours.
Bank	In the north end of the International Terminal: open 0800– 1530 hours.
Foreign Exchange	In both Arrival and Departure halls of the International Terminal; open 24 hours.
Accommodation Desk	In the Arrival hall; open 24 hours.
Insurance Facilities	In the Departure hall; open 0700– 2200 hours.
Bar	In the Departure hall and lounge; open 24 hours.
Restaurant	In the International Terminal (4th floor), open 24 hours; in the Domestic Terminal, open 0600– 2200 hours.

Post Office	In the Departure hall and lounge; open 24 hours.
Baggage Deposit	In the Meeting Area of the Arrival hall; open 24 hours.
Shops	In the Departure hall and lounge; open 24 hours.
Duty Free	As well as those in the Departure hall and lounge of the International Terminal, there is a Thai Airways International Duty Free Shop in town, on Silom Road. Items on sale include the usual tobaccos and spirits plus watches, radios, perfumes, jewellery, Thai silk and native products. The currencies of USA, Australia, Hong Kong, Singapore, UK, France, Germany, Japan, Malaysia, Denmark and Norway are accepted, as are American Express, Visa, Diners and Master.
Medical Centre	In the Departure hall; open 24 hours.
Toilets	In the Departure, Transit and Arrival halls; open 24 hours.
Meeting Point	Outside Arrival hall exit doors.
Barber	In the Departure hall; open 0800–1800 hours.
Beauty Salon	Next to the barber shop; open 0800–1800 hours.

AIRPORT INFORMATION

Check-in Times	90 minutes prior to flight departure time for international and domestic flights.
Airport Tax	150B for international flights; 20B for domestic flights. It is collected at the check-in counters of the Departure halls.

| Transferring Flights | International-to-international flight passengers are transferred within the terminal or by buses in the case of remote parking stands. International-to-domestic (or vice versa) flight passengers can be provided with transport by shuttle buses (about 80B per person). |
| Airport Flight Enquiries | Bangkok 286-0090 or 286-0190, ext. 153/370. |

AIRPORT HOTEL

• **Super Club Class:**
The Airport Hotel – operated by Thai Airways Ltd. Located opposite the airport, about 600 yards' walk. Courtesy minibuses are available to passengers.

CITY LINKS

There are a variety of ways of covering the 15 miles between Don Muang Airport and the city.

• **Taxi:** Drivers won't use their meters so bargain your fare before the journey starts. 200B should be the upper limit and with effort you can bargain them down to 150B or less. By flagging down taxis on the highway, just outside the airport, you can get an even cheaper ride to town.

• **Train:** Scheduled trains pass through the station some 300 yards from the airport and the fare into town is 5B.

• **Bus:** Between 0500 and 2300 hours a regular service passes in front of the airport, price 2B. Air-conditioned buses also pass, costing 5–15B according to your destination. The number 4 goes down Mitthaphap Road to Ratachaprarop/Ratachadamri Road, across Phetburi, Rama I, Ploenchit and Rama IV Roads, then down Salom, left along Charoen Krung and over the river to Thon Buri.

Number 13 goes from Pahaholyothin Road to Victory Monument to Ratchaprarop then Ploenchit and out to Sukhumvit and eventually Bang Na.

● **Thai International Minibus:** This goes to most major hotels (and others if it's a friendly driver) for 100B.

● **Limousines:** Thai International Ltd organize this glorified taxi service costing 300B.

BANGKOK

Founded in 1782 and established as the capital of Siam by King Rama I after the Burmese destroyed Ayudhaya (the capital for 400 years), Bangkok is a large and thriving city. Its 5 million people are

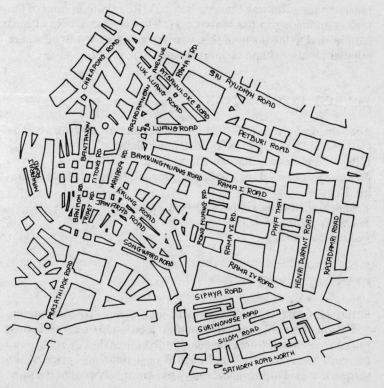

friendly and hospitable, many speaking good English. After centuries of complicated changes of kingdoms, kings and cultures, Siam underwent a peaceful coup, became a constitutional monarchy and in 1939 changed its name to Thailand (meaning 'land of the free'). After several more forced alterations the military seem, at present, to be in firm command.

Thailand's produce of rice, maize, tapioca, tin, copra and rubber provides a prosperous source of national income. Bangkok (or Krung Thep as the locals call it) has grown into one of the leading commercial centres of the eastern world. Thai, Chinese, Indian and European businesses thrive alongside each other. The main city is divided from Thon Buri by the Chao Phraya River. The older part of the city and Chinatown are nestled in a curve in the river with the main railway line virtually enclosing the area. Beyond the railway line is the modern city, with most of the hotels and the Sri Hualamphong Railway Station. Rama IV Road runs in front of the station and along to the Malaysia Hotel area. Rama I Road runs parallel and to the north of this, becoming Sukhumvit Road where popular nightspots and restaurants are to be found.

TOURIST INFORMATION

Tourism Authority of Thailand – 4 Ratchadamnoen Nok Avenue (tel. 282-1143/7). Open 0900–1630 hours daily.
GPO – New Road (Charoen Krung Road).
Medical Services – Bangkok Sanitarium and Hospital, 430 Pitsanulok Road.
  Bangkok Nursing Home, Convent Road.
Emergency Number – 191.
Police – 597-1370/9.

GETTING ABOUT

● **Bus:** Hot and crowded, frequent and cheap. To sort out the confusion of numbers and destinations a bus map from the Tourist Office is essential. Some air-conditioned buses do city routes and are cool and uncrowded although 3 or 4 times the price of the standard ones. During peak hours a bus-truck service runs the same service as the public buses – mildly illegal but ignored as it is so necessary. Bus number 17 does a circuit of the main attractions.

• **Taxi:** Plentiful and not too expensive if you first negotiate the price.

• **Samlor:** Three-wheeled tricycles (tuk-tuks are the motorized version) which will bump you around the city for a fairly low rate. As the drivers seldom understand English and don't seem to know their way around Bangkok anyway, you may end up doing a few 'scenic' routes to your destination. It's all part of the oriental charm!

• **Boat:** Water buses provide a cheap, more peaceful, fast transport service. Regular services go along the Chao Phya River and connecting klongs (canals). The Chao Phya Express is one of the best to use, stopping at several landing stages along the river.

• **Hotel Limousines:** Most first-class hotels provide these, at fixed prices, to various places in the city.

Wherever you want to go transport of some sort is usually preferable – it is far too hot and humid, as a rule, to walk any more than is absolutely necessary.

SIGHTS

THE GRAND PALACE is a walled town covering over a square mile and encompassing many architectural wonders. The typically oriental, multi-tiered roofs, spires and spectacular golden chedis (pagodas) can all be seen here. Thai palaces include the Chakri Maha Prasard, Dusit Maha Prasard and Phratinang Amanrindra Vinichai. Open 0900–1640 hours Tuesdays and Thursdays and 0900–1200 hours on other weekdays. Men must wear ties and jackets and women dresses or skirts. Cine-cameras are prohibited.

In the Grand Palace precincts, within the Royal Chapel, is the TEMPLE OF THE EMERALD BUDDHA (Wat Phra Keo), a fantastic carving dating from 1457, which is constructed from one solid piece of translucent jasper and rests on a golden throne. The chapel itself is rich and elaborate and adjoins the Golden Pagoda and the Galleries. Opening hours are the same as for the Grand Palace plus Sundays or Buddhist holidays, when admission is free.

On the other bank of the river, at Thon Buri, is the TEMPLE OF DAWN (Wat Arun), one of the most impressive edifices in Bangkok. Its central tower is 240 ft high and each spire glitters with tiny pieces of porcelain and coloured glass. A fine view can be had from the centre tower (you only need climb halfway!).

The TEMPLE OF THE SACRED FIGTREE (Wat Phra Jetubon or even Wat Po), is renowned for its gigantic statue of the reclining Lord Buddha – 49 ft high and 150 ft long. Also look at the four western towers (stupas) in green, white, yellow and blue which represent the first four kings of the present dynasty. Open 0800–1700 hours daily. The MARBLE TEMPLE (Wat Benchamaboptir) was built by King Chulalongkorn and is a fine example of modern Thai architecture. Buddha images form a unique collection in the Convocation Hall, especially the two famous walking Buddhas.

Until 1953 the statue at WAT TRIMITR was thought to be a 5½-ton bronze Buddha covered in plaster. While moving it the surface cracked revealing solid gold. Needless to say, this magnificent sight is now regarded as one of the most rare and priceless treasures of Thailand.

The NATIONAL MUSEUM is full of fascinating exhibits, notably a model war elephant. Open daily (except Monday). Free tours of the museum on Tuesday (Thai culture), Wednesday (Buddhism) and Thursday (Thai art) are well worth attending.

The SNAKE FARM was established by Queen Saovapha and is run by the Pasteur Institute. Every day at 11 a.m. the snakes are fed and have their venom extracted (for antitoxin production). Closed at weekends. The LUMPINI PARK has beautiful gardens and is a favourite with locals. The DUSIT ZOO KHAO DIN are the zoological gardens opposite the King's Palace, with many species of plants, animals and birds. Open 0800–1830 hours weekdays and 0800–1900 hours weekends.

On Soi Kasem San 2, Rama I Road, JIM THOMSON'S THAI HOUSE was built from parts of several Thai houses and contains a superb collection of Thai art and furnishings. Jim was an American Thai silk entrepreneur who mysteriously disappeared in 1967. Open 0900–1530 hours Monday to Friday; all donations go to the Bangkok School for the Blind.

The FLOATING MARKETS should not be missed. An early morning trip down the river and canals will show you the fruit, meat and fish marketers floating around while they sell their wares to housewives.

Tours of this leave from the Oriental Hotel's pier (or a group of you can hire your own boat). It is quite expensive but a typically Thai sight which really ought to be seen.

ACCOMMODATION

Bangkok is full of excellent hotels, several of them only recently opened. Thai hospitality is such that the service is usually impeccable in hotels, with lots of little extra touches to make your stay more comfortable. During the peak tourist season, between November and February, advance reservation is advisable. It is worth noting that Bangkok accommodation prices are subject to 10 per cent service charge and 11 per cent government tax.

• **First Class:** (Double 2200–3300B)
The Oriental – 48 Oriental Avenue, Bangkok 10500 (tel. 234-8621-9). This rates as one of the top hotels in the world, with impressive service, highly sophisticated surroundings and an inspiring location on the banks of the River of Kings.

Hilton International – 2 Wireless Road, Bangkok 10500 (tel. 251-7111). Another very highly rated hotel with excellent and extensive facilities surrounded by 8 acres of peaceful, tropical gardens in the centre of the bustling city.

Royal Orchid Sheraton – 2 Captain Bush Lane, Siphya Road, Bangkok 10500 (tel. 234-5599). A spacious elegance radiates from every aspect of the Bangkok Sheraton. Set on the banks of the river, it has everything you could ask of a top-class hotel.

• **Super Club Class:** (Double 1500–2200B)
Siam Inter-Continental – Srapatum Palace Property, 967 Rama I Road, Bangkok 10500 (tel. 252-9040-79). Excellent facilities and the usual Thai impeccable service and hospitality.

Indra Regent – Rajprarob Road, Bangkok (tel. 251-1111). In the heart of the business area is this stylish hotel surrounded by tropical gardens and a beautiful open-air pool. The Thai Supper Club is one of the selection of good restaurants within the hotel.

540   The Round the World Air Guide

Ambassador – Sukhumvit Road, Soi 11, Bangkok (tel. 251-0404). The biggest and most entertaining hotel in Bangkok. Speciality restaurants and a fine collection of bars and nightspots make this one of the liveliest places to be.

Narai – 222 Silom Road, Bangkok (tel. 233-3350). A recently renovated hotel in a very convenient location for shopping and sightseeing. It boasts the only revolving restaurant in the city, on the 15th storey, which gives magnificent views of the city.

• **Economy:** (Double 300–1500B)
Bangkok Palace – 1091/336 New Petchburi Road, Bangkok 10400 (tel. 252-5700). A recently opened hotel which is extremely good value. The facilities are exceptional for a hotel in this price bracket.

Manohra – 412 Surawongse Road, Bangkok 10500 (tel. 234-5070). Centrally located and comfortable. Good amenities.

Ra-Jah – 18 Sukhumvit Road, Soi 4, Bangkok (tel. 252-5102). A few blocks away from the city centre but good, comfortable accommodation.

New Amarin – 477 Sriayudhya Road, Bangkok (tel. 245-2661-7). Adequate accommodation within easy reach of the city centre.

Victory – 322 Silom Road, Bangkok (tel. 233-9060). On the main shopping street, good facilities and friendly service.

Viengtai – 42 Tanee Road, Banglamphu, Bangkok 10200 (tel. 282-8672-4). Opposite the Thai Student Travel Office and the hotel itself acts as the Student Travel Australia HQ and gives student discounts.

Royal – 2 Ratchadamnoen Avenue, Banglamphu, Bangkok 10200 (tel. 222-9111). also a student discount hotel which is cheaper than the Viengtai and in the same, central area.

The Boston Inn – Soi Si Bamphen, Rama IV Road, Soi Ngam Duphli area. Well kept rooms and friendly staff. Very low prices.

DINING OUT

Thai food is spicy and delicious but may prove too hot for European tastes. Some of Bangkok's restaurants have 'toned down' their flavouring to cater for this. Thai specialities consist of soups, fish, prawns, curried meats and noodle dishes. An alternative dessert to the lush fresh fruits of Thailand is ta ko, a delicious mixture of tapioca flour, coconut milk and sugar. Tea, the staple Thai beverage, is often drunk with or after meals and is generally green and mild. Many restaurants in Bangkok also serve European, American, Indian, Korean, Chinese, and Japanese food.

● **First Class:** (1200–1600B for two)
Aoyama – 960/1 Rama IV Road. An expensive but wonderful Japanese evening – not only is the food delicious , but a Japanese bath beforehand and a walk in the beautiful gardens after your meal make the whole evening a real treat.

Sala Thai – At the Indra Regent Hotel. A rooftop restaurant with 13th-century Thai replica decor. The menu is relatively unspiced, to suit European tastes. A dance and music show goes on every night.

Chitr Pochana – 62 Sukhumvit Road, Soi 20. The finest Thai curries are served here. Once you have eaten, take a look at the beautiful gardens.

● **Super Club Class:** (900–1200B for two)
Bankeo Ruenkwan – 212 Sukhumvit Road. Reasonably priced, very flavourful Thai food. Their speciality is seafood.

Toll Gate – 245 Sukhumvit Road, Soi 31. Traditional Thai food. The set, 6-course menu is excellent value. Closed on Sundays.

Royal Kitchen – 42/4 Sukhumvit Road, Soi 21. Set in the style of Royal banquets of the past. First-class food and immaculate surroundings.

● **Economy:** (300–900B for two)
Sorn Daeng – Rajadamnoen Avenue. An excellent and cheap pavement-side café which serves Thai and Chinese food.

Korea House – 510 Ploenchit Court. Standard Korean dishes of 'stamina' and 'hormone' barbecue (they taste better than they sound!).

Himali Cha Cha – 1229/11 New Road. Superb North Indian food in a small restaurant.

Happy Restaurant – Siam Square. Hunan food of central China which tends to be spicy. The chicken and fish dishes are especially good.

NIGHTLIFE

CLASSICAL THAI DRAMA/DANCING is something which all visitors to Thailand should see. Modelled on ancient Sanskrit drama, many of the epic tales stem from the ancient Hindu mythology of Ramakien. The dancers are graceful and very skilled, and the costumes elaborate. The National Theatre puts on performances all the year round and from November to May the Silpakorn Theatre also gives regular performances. Thai classical dances are also performed at many restaurants, including the Baan, the Thai, the Piman and at the Oriental Hotel. Several nightclubs provide dinner and dancing, catering for the international set, and the Café de Paris and the Sani Chateau offer classy, nightly shows. Some of the more popular nightspots are:

Ambassador Club – Erawan Hotel (tel. 252-9100). A dignified atmosphere.
Tropicana Disco – Rama Tower Hotel, Silom Road (tel. 234-1010). Noisy and packed out every night.
Bamboo Bar – Oriental Hotel (tel. 234-9920). Sophisticated in every way.
Casablanca – Montein Hotel (tel. 234-8060). Very lively.

There is also Diana's at the Oriental Hotel, Bubbles at the Dusit Thani Hotel, Cat's Eye Nightclub at the President Hotel and a host of other discos. After dark Patpong Road is the place to go to experience the famous (or infamous) side of Bangkok's nightlife. Soi Cowboy, Sukhumvit Road, Soi 21 is similar, with over 30 'Go-Go' bars.

EXCURSIONS

There are plenty of attractive and interesting places to visit within easy reach of Bangkok. The ROSE GARDEN is a riverside tropical park some 20 miles west of the city which has an 18-hole golf course and a traditional (but now touristy) Thai Village. 15 miles further on is NAKHON PATHOM where the world's tallest Buddhist monument, the Phra Pathom Chedi, marks the spot where the religion was introduced to the Siamese about 2300 years ago. Each November a famous fair is held at this orange-tiled chedi surrounded by galleries and cloisters.

Thailand's most vibrant floating market is at DAMNOEN SADUAK, 50 miles south-west of Bangkok. Each morning produce-laden boats congregate to sell vegetables, fruits, spices, fish and poultry. A boat trip is necessary to reach the market and the sights to be seen on the journey are as captivating as those of the market itself.

Just over 12 miles to the north of Bangkok is WAT PHAILOM, on the east bank of the Chao Phraya river in Pathumthani province. This a sanctuary for the open-bill stork and between December and June thousands of storks nest in the temple area. Further north alongside the same river is what used to be the summer residence of the early Chakri kings, BANG PA-IN PALACE, an architectural conglomeration of Thai, Chinese, Italianate and Victorian styles. Also upstream from Bangkok is the sleepy, riverine island town of AYUTTHAYA, once the Siamese capital. It was invaded by the Burmese in 1767: an event which has left magnificent ruins of palaces, temples and fortresses to provide proof of the former capital's splendour.

To the south-east of Bangkok, on the way to Pattaya, is the ANCIENT CITY, one of the world's largest outdoor museums. On display are valuable Asian pieces of art and reconstructed temples and cultural buildings from Thai history. The whole thing is laid out in the shape of Thailand and took 10 years to build. Bus tours to the City take about 4 or 5 hours altogether. For information on this, and other bus tours, go to the tourist office or to your hotel's tour desk.

4. EUROPE

France

RED TAPE

• **Passport/Visa Requirements:** In addition to a valid passport, visas are required by all, except for visits up to 3 months by citizens of the following countries: Algeria, Australia, Austria, Belgium, Benin, Canada, Central African Republic, Congo, Cyprus, Denmark, Finland, German Federal Republic, Greece, Iceland, Israel, Italy, Japan, Liechtenstein, Luxembourg, Malta, Mauritania, Monaco, Morocco, Netherlands, New Zealand, Niger, Norway, Portugal, San Marino, Senegal, Spain, Sweden, Switzerland, Togo, Tunisia, USA, UK, Upper Volta, Yugoslavia.

Other nationals require a visa. Transit visas are valid for up to 48 hours; short-stay visas for up to 3 months. Apply to local French consulate.

CUSTOMS

• **Duty Free:** Visitors from an EEC country are allowed to bring in 300 cigarettes or 75 cigars or 400g of tobacco; 1.5 litres spirits over 22 per cent or sparkling wine to 22 per cent, and 4 litres of non-sparkling wine; 75g of perfume and 37.5 cl of toilet water; plus goods to the value of 2400 FF.

Visitors arriving from non-EEC countries but normally residing within Europe: 200 cigarettes or 50 cigars or 250g tobacco; 1 litre spirits over 22 per cent or 2 litres spirits or sparkling wine up to 22 per cent; 2 litres still wines; 50g perfume and 25 cl toilet water; plus goods for personal use originating from outside the EEC up to 300 FF per person.

Passengers arriving from non-EEC countries residing outside Europe: 400 cigarettes, 100 cigars or 500g tobacco; the same alcohol, perfume and money allowances as for non-EEC residents.

CAPITAL – Paris. Population – 2,050,000 (city); 8,550,000 (conurbation).

POPULATION – 53,500,000.

LANGUAGE – French.

CURRENCY – Monetary unit is French Franc (FF), divided into 100 centimes. Notes – 10, 20, 50, 100, 200 and 500 francs. Coins – 5, 10, 20, 50 centimes, and 1, 2, 5, and 10 francs.
£1 = 9.23 FF; US$1 = 6.59 FF.

BANKING HOURS – 0900–1200 and 1400–1600 Monday–Friday. Closed either Saturdays (in large towns) or Mondays. Banks close 1200 the day before a bank holiday.

POLITICAL SYSTEM – Republic.

RELIGION – Predominantly Roman Catholic.

PUBLIC HOLIDAYS

January 1	New Year's Day
March/April	Easter Monday
May	Ascension Day, Whit Monday
July 14	Bastille Day
August 15	Assumption of the Virgin
November 1	All Saints' Day
November 11	Remembrance Day
December 25	Christmas Day

CLIMATE – Temperate in the north and Mediterranean in the south. Cooler in the mountains with heavy snowfall in winter.

TIME DIFFERENCE – Winter: GMT + 1 hour. Summer: GMT + 2 hours.

COMMUNICATIONS

• **Telephone:** Full International Direct Dialling service from call boxes. Cheap rate operates 2100–0800, Monday–Friday and all day Saturday, Sunday and bank holidays. Telephone credit cards may be used from Post Offices.

IDD code for France is 33. International access code from France is 19. Jetons for local calls from old phone boxes can be bought from cafés or Post Offices.

Reverse charge calls not accepted.

• **Post:** Stamps can be purchased at Post Offices and tabacs. Letter boxes are painted yellow. Post Offices open 0800–1900 weekdays, 0800–1200 Saturdays.

ELECTRICITY – 220/240v AC. Occasionally 120v in older hotels.

OFFICE/SHOPPING HOURS – Offices: 0900–1800 Monday–Friday, with two-hour lunch break. Food shops: 0730–1830, other shops 0900–1830 Monday–Saturday. Many hypermarkets open until 2100 or 2200; some shops close Monday mornings and in smaller towns the shops close 1200–1400 for a lunch break.

• **Best Buys:** Haute couture clothing, foodstuffs, wines, perfumery and objets d'art.

INTERNAL TRAVEL

• **Air:** Air Inter, the associate company of the national airline, Air France, operates many internal flights, mostly radiating from Paris. On the busiest routes the A300 Airbuses operate, linking all the major cities of France. Several other smaller domestic airlines are also in operation (i.e., Air Jet, Air Vendée, Air Littoral, Air Limousin, TAJ, and Brit Air which together combine to provide a very comprehensive internal flight network). See any French travel agent for details.

• **Rail:** SNCF are widely acknowledged as one of the world's leading railways with high-speed ultra-modern trains and an efficient and comprehensive national rail grid. TGV trains and Trains Corail are the top of their rolling stock and provide fast transport between all the major centres. Trans Europ Express trains are first-class only and a supplement is payable. Sleepers are operated by the Wagons-Lit Company, and on all but local country trains there will be a buffet service. Train tickets bought in France must be date-stamped before boarding the train. Failure to do so results in a fine.

• **Road:** The Europabus system links all the major centres of France en route to neighbouring countries, and the SNCF motor coach tours offer trips to the most scenic areas of France. The cities all have local buses, and in rural areas they are still a popular form of transport.

Taxis operate in all towns and cities and may be hailed in the street or phoned for.

The motorway system links the major cities and tolls are payable (roads marked 'A' are motorways). Car hire is widely available, with all the international companies represented.

MAJOR SIGHTS OF THE COUNTRY

One of the world's most beautiful cities, Paris, will be your obvious first stop, but despite the many pleasures of this metropolis, Paris is not France, any more than London is England. The diversity of this country is remarkable, from the snow-capped Alps to the sun-soaked Riviera, and from the sleepy rural villages of the Dordogne to the grand châteaux of the Loire. Every kind of scenery exists in France, and each region has its own particular beauty. As a rough guide to the highlights of the country:

NORMANDY and BRITTANY offer historic buildings, a rich folk culture, vast uncluttered beaches and open plains scenery. The LOIRE VALLEY is France's pastoral region containing many of its most impressive buildings. Most of the châteaux lie between Angers and Blois – a distance of about 80 miles easily negotiated by train. This is the regal France of centuries past: splendid castles, bishop's palaces and elegant old districts which date back to the 17th century and before. From Paris it is easy to spend a few days in the Loire valley, and several packages are available through travel agents for those wishing to do this.

ALSACE and LORRAINE show the influence of neighbouring Germany, while the ALPS offer some of Europe's most spectacular scenery. Mont Blanc pierces the sky at 15,781 feet, and this region is considered by many to combine all that is best of Europe: spectacular scenery, a healthy alpine climate, good food and wines, and a rich historical and cultural heritage. Places such as CHAMONIX offer not just excellent winter skiing, but are equally dramatic in summertime. A trip into any part of this region is guaranteed to be one of the highlights of your world tour.

BURGUNDY, apart from being a wine drinker's paradise, also possesses some of the finest abbeys in France, the most spectacular being at Vezelay, and the city of DIJON is the regional capital.

The CÔTE D'AZUR has that certain magic that no amount of commercialism can taint. The blue sea, warm sun, scented flowers, smart hotels and jet set who holiday here all exist just like you'd expect them to, but there's more. Elegant Monte Carlo, where the rich gamble their nights away; cosmopolitan Nice with its Mediterranean ambience, and the smart resorts of Juan-les-Pins, Cannes, Antibes, Menton . . . all have that certain elegance which only the Riviera can provide. Every ingredient for a perfect beach holiday is here, and after the hectic pace of Paris a few days in the south make a wonderful break.

PROVENCE will appeal to the historically minded traveller. Renowned for its perfectly cloudless skies and Roman remains, this rich countryside has attracted artists and travellers for centuries. The July and August Arts Festivals in AIX-EN-PROVENCE and AVIGNON bring life to the towns, and make pre-booking a bed essential! ARLES and NÎMES are other names to look out for if well preserved Roman buildings interest you.

The medieval gem of France is CARCASSONNE, in the Languedoc region. This is arguably Europe's best preserved relic of the Middle Ages, and certainly it is France's most impressive walled city. Walking through its narrow streets gives one a clear impression of life in medieval Europe, and it is situated in one of this country's most out-of-the-way and interesting regions.

The city of BORDEAUX is quintessentially French, in the same way that Paris is quintessentially Parisian and un-French. Renowned for its wines, culture, and gourmet restaurants, Bordeaux is reached easily from Paris by air, rail or coach. It is a good base from which to make excursions into the Lot and Dordogne regions where sleepy little villages, remote windswept castles and incredible prehistoric remains will show you the other side of this remarkably diverse country.

HOTELS

France has a wide range of hotels, from the grand luxe to cheap pensions for a few francs a night. Hotels are expensive (similar prices to the UK), with 800 FF a double being the norm for a first class hotel and even a moderately priced hotel room will cost around 400 FF for two, often without breakfast. By law there are 5 categories and French hoteliers must post their prices on the wall. They cannot charge more than the prices shown, except in deluxe hotels where the government exercise no control over them. Check that the prices posted have 'TCC' – toutes taxes comprises – otherwise you will have supplements to pay which can add up to 25 per cent to your final bill.

Starting at the top end of the market there is a chain of châteaux, manor houses and historical inns who market themselves under the title 'Relais et Châteaux'. Each of the 150 members has something unique to offer and one can be assured of the very finest cuisine and the highest standards possible in any of these establishments. For a full list write to Relais et Châteaux, 10 Place de la Concorde, 75008, Paris, or contact the French Tourist Board in your own country.

On a more moderate note the Fédération Nationale des Logis de France consists of smaller, cheaper hotels which offer regional cuisine and comfortable rooms. Their prices and details are all listed under regions and further information can be obtained from their Head Office at 25 rue Jean Mermoz, 75008, Paris.

If rural France is your destination and you require only simple accommodation the Fédération Nationale des Gites Ruraux de France will help you out on lets, which can be for anything from a week to the whole summer. These are particularly popular with British families holidaying in France so write with plenty of time to spare to 34 rue Godot de Mauroy, 75009, Paris, stating the region/s you are contemplating.

Tourist Offices will help out in finding hotel beds if you plan only a short stay or do not wish to write ahead.

At the budget end of the market there are pensions, campsites, hostels and foyers (student dorm accommodation) all over France. Paris is more expensive than the rest of the country, and the month of August can present problems in the south of France when the cities empty on to the autoroutes and all France seems to head for the south.

NIGHTLIFE AND RESTAURANTS

French cuisine is world famous and just about every meal you will eat in France, whether in a smart Parisian restaurant or a simple country inn, will be a gastronomic experience. The French have a way with food and the style to present it. They take eating and drinking very seriously and turn their evening meal into the social event of the day. Aside from eating out there are many other forms of nightlife, particularly in Paris, with theatres, opera and ballet all flourishing in France today. Every town has its 'boite' (nightclub) where you can listen to live music and drink till dawn, but perhaps healthier and more enjoyable is the Mediterranean pastime of sitting at a pavement café with a coffee or glass of wine, watching the world go by.

Paris

PARIS ROISSY-CHARLES DE GAULLE AIRPORT

(Also Paris Orly Airport which handles mainly charter flights, and Paris Le Bourget which handles domestic traffic.)

Paris' main airport has 2 terminals. The circular No. 1 handles mainly foreign airlines, and the other, No. 2, mainly Air France and Air Inter.

Most Air France flights operate from Terminal 2, 2B is for European and French domestic services of Air France/Air Inter, 2A is exclusively for Air France long-haul flights.

Over 30 airlines use Roissy, which is situated some 15 miles north of Paris.

AIRPORT FACILITIES

Most facilities listed are available 24 hours.

Tourist Information	Upstairs from the air terminal. Closed weekends and public holidays.
Telephones	
Post Office	
Rest Rooms	
Showers	
Nursery	
Medical Services	
Vaccination Centre	
Duty Free Shops	Several, though not rated as one of the best value locations for buying duty free. Located immediately inside Passport Control. Wide selection of gifts and perfumery, but prices hold no advantage over those in UK regular shops.
Chemist	
Currency Exchange	
Cafeterias	
Restaurants	
Shops	The following are sold: alcohol, tobacco, food, jewellery, fashion, leather, photographic goods, perfume, toys, books and souvenirs.

AIRPORT INFORMATION

Departure Information	Telephone 43 20 1355.
Airport Tax	Nil.
Minimum flight connection time between Roissy and Orly	35 minutes.
Inter-terminal Transfer	A shuttle connects Roissy Terminals 1 and 2 every 10 minutes from 0700–2300, and every 20 minutes from 0600–0700 and 2300–2400.

INTER-AIRPORT TRANSFER

Connecting Roissy with Orly West and South are Air France coaches which leave every 20 minutes from 0600–2300, taking 75 minutes and costing 55 FF. For passengers going on to connecting flights this service is free of charge, and a voucher must be picked up at the 'connecting flights' desk.

AIRPORT HOTELS

● **First Class:**
Holiday Inn – 54 rue de Paris, 95500, Gonesse, Paris (tel. 1/985 6111).
Ramada Paris Velizy – 22 Avenue de l'Europe, 78140, Velizy, Paris (tel. 1/946 9698).

CITY LINKS

● **Railways:** There is a railway service connecting Cité, Universi-taire, Denfert Rochereau, Port Royal, Luxembourg, Chatelet and Gare du Nord with Charles de Gaulle Airport: departures every 15 minutes from 0500 to 2330. Price 22 FF (24.60 FF with urban section).

• **Road:** Buses (RATP) from the city are: no. 350 – Gare de l'Est/Gare du Nord to Le Bourget Airport and Charles de Gaulle Airport; and no. 351 – Nation to Charles de Gaulle Airport.

Air France coaches run from Charles de Gaulle Airport – Terminal 1, gates 34 and 36, and Terminal 2, gates A5 and B6 – to Maillot terminal (2nd basement of the Palais des Congrès), Place de la Porte Maillot (central Paris) at 12-minute intervals, and from Paris to Charles de Gaulle buses leave here every 12 minutes from 0545–2300. The journey takes 20 minutes and costs 31 FF.

• **Air:** Heli-France run services between their heliport in the city centre and the airports (and will connect the airports for you). Go to Room 12, Terminal 1 (non-bonded area: 'hors-douane'). They run hourly flights from 0800–2000. The trip to the city centre takes 14 minutes and costs 350 FF. The connection to Orly takes 22 minutes and costs 450 FF.

Heli-France's Paris office is at 4 Avenue de la Porte de Sèvres, 75015, Paris (tel. 45 54 9511). Reservations on 45 57 5367.

PARIS

Everyone has his or her own impressions and expectations of Paris – so much has been said and written about it, and it all seems a cliché, yet Paris is everything you've probably ever heard, and more.

Paris has 20 'arrondissements' (districts) with the Louvre as No. 1. The city is divided into the Left Bank (Rive Gauche) and Right Bank (Rive Droite), with the River Seine dividing them. Generally speaking, the Left Bank is the trendy, studenty and less expensive area, and the Right Bank is where the smart restaurants and boutiques are.

TOURIST INFORMATION

The main office of 'Accueil de France' is at 127 Avenue des Champs Elysées (tel. 723 6172) (métro to Etoile). Open Monday–Saturday, 0900–2200, Sunday 0900–2000. They'll give you information on Paris and the rest of France. They also run an accommodation-finding service on a commission basis.

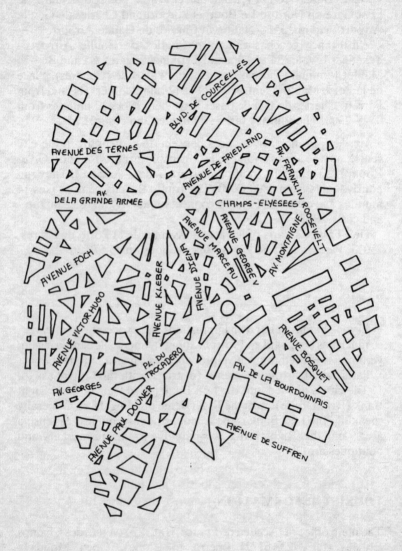

ADDRESSES

All-night Post Office and Poste Restante – 52 rue du Louvre (tel. 233 7160).
Amex – 11 rue Scribe, Monday-Friday 0900–1700, Saturdays 0900–1200 (tel. 073 4290).
UK Embassy – 35 rue du Faubourg St-Honoré, 8e (tel. 266 9955).
US Embassy – 2 Avenue Gabriel, 8e, Monday–Friday, 0900–1600 (métro Concorde) (tel. 296 1202).
Canadian Embassy – 35 Avenue Montaigne, 8e (tel. 723 0101).
Australian Embassy – 4 rue Jean-Rey, 15e (tel. 575 6200).
24-hour Chemist – Pharmacie Dhéry, 84 Avenue des Champs Elysées (métro George V).

GETTING ABOUT

• **Métro:** Public transport in Paris is very good. The famous métro is fast, cheap and efficient, and from the visitor's point of view this is your easiest way of getting from 'A' to 'B', without risking the hazards of French driving! Every métro station has a large map showing the whole métro system, and on the one ticket you can transfer as often as you like to get to your final destination. Except for the morning and evening rush hours you may use either first- or second-class carriages. The same RER métro tickets you buy also entitle you to use the network of buses which link all of Paris. Generally speaking a booklet, a carnet, of 10 tickets is your best bet, but if you're in Paris for a while ask Tourist Info for the different tickets and passes available. The 'Paris Sesame' ticket, valid for 2, 4, or 7 consecutive days, entitles you to unlimited travel on the métro, RER (express trains to the suburbs) and all RATP buses in Paris and environs. For the visitor planning on doing a lot of travelling round Paris this is probably your best bet.

• **Road:** Taxis are widely available, and car hire from all the major international companies can be easily arranged. The Tourist Office or your hotel desk will help.

SIGHTS

The ÉTOILE is the great circle at the western end of the CHAMPS
ÉLYSÉES with 12 avenues radiating out from it, literally a 'star'. In
its centre is the massive ARC DE TRIOMPHE, Napoleon's thank-you to
his army; note the sculpture of 'the Marseillaise' by Rude. At the
other end of the long and elegant Champs Elysées is the PLACE DE
LA CONCORDE, regarded as the most beautiful square in the world.
This is where Louis XVI, Marie-Antoinette and some 1300 others
met their death in the French Revolution.

On the LEFT BANK, ST GERMAIN-DES-PRÉS, the oldest church in
Paris, is surrounded by open-air restaurants and cafés and quiet
little streets like PLACE FÜRSTEMBERG which make a pleasant stroll.

BOULEVARD ST-MICHEL, the centre of Bohemian student life of
the 1960s, still makes an interesting excursion. Sitting in one of the
cafés along the 'Boul' Mich' in the Latin Quarter (so called because
the Sorbonne students were lectured to in Latin in the Middle Ages)
you're bound to make new friends. The tallest building in Europe,
TOUR MAINE-MONTPARNASSE (690 feet), gives you a great view over
the city. (The lift up is supposed to be the fastest one in Europe.)

Also on the Rive Gauche is the beautiful church of LES INVALIDES
with its golden dome and the mortal remains of Napoleon. A good
view of NOTRE DAME CATHEDRAL can be seen from SQUARE RENÉ
VIVIANI.

Opposite the LOUVRE on the RIGHT BANK is Richelieu's PALAIS
ROYAL where the Comédie Française is based, and not far from
here is the oldest square in Paris – PLACE DES VOSGES – the beautiful
Renaissance square built by Henry IV early in the 17th century;
VICTOR HUGO'S HOUSE at No. 6 is now a museum. The GEORGES
POMPIDOU CENTRE (known as the Beaubourg) is a good place to
meet trendy young Parisians and see interesting exhibitions. Closed
Tuesdays, it's open till 10 p.m. at weekends.

The SACRÉ-COEUR is the white dome that dominates all of Paris,
built on the hill at MONTMARTRE, the artists' quarter that flourished
in the late 19th century when many of the Impressionist painters
lived and worked there. A climb to the dome of the Sacré-Coeur
gives you a 30-mile view over Paris.

The tiny island where Paris began in pre-Roman times is the ÎLE
DE LA CITÉ. The oldest bridge in Paris, the PONT NEUF, leads you to
the statue of Henry IV and on to the PALAIS DE JUSTICE (law courts).

The SAINTE CHAPELLE is the gothic church which houses many holy relics and dates from 1248.

NOTRE DAME is only a short walk from here; this 13th-century cathedral is the first church of Paris, where Napoleon was crowned and all nationial celebrations are staged.

The other main sights are the OPÉRA (1875) and, of course, the EIFFEL TOWER, which looks its best floodlit at night. If you want to tour the famous PARIS SEWERS, call in at 93 Quai d'Orsay.

There are various city tours: Parisvision buses with prerecorded commentary, and Cityrama tours, or the famous bateaux-mouches which sail down the Seine (go for the evening one when the illuminations are on). Shop about, as they vary from reasonably priced to extortionate. Still, if you've only a day or two, the 3-hour Parisvision tour gives you a pretty comprehensive idea of the city.

All state-owned museums in Paris are shut on Tuesdays and those owned by the city close on Mondays. The Louvre and the Pompidou Centre are free on Sundays (and packed). There are over 100 interesting museums in the city; pick up a leaflet on them from Tourist Information. We list the few it would be a shame to miss.

THE LOUVRE: Porte Denon, Place du Carrousel (in the Tuileries Gardens). Treasures include the Venus de Milo and the Mona Lisa. Open 0945–2000 (though many departments close at 1700 or 1750).

MUSÉE DE CLUNY: 6 Place Paul-Painlevé (corner of Boulevard St Michel and Boulevard St Germain). Open 0945–1230 and 1400–1700. Medieval art housed in a 15th-century mansion next to the Roman baths of Paris.

MUSÉE DE L'HOMME: Palais de Chaillot, Place du Trocadéro. Open 1000–1800 (1700 in winter). Very good anthropological museum – documentary films are shown daily.

There is no shortage of attractive PARKS and gardens in Paris, and they make good picnic venues.

The BOIS DE BOULOGNE is the wood at the western edge of the city with 7 lakes, a waterfall, various sports facilities and a campsite. The BOIS DE VINCENNES is the wood on the south-eastern edge which tends to be a better bet to sleep rough in, but is a bit rougher (not recommended for girls alone). There's a zoo, a racetrack and a couple of museums out here too. The two most central picnic parks are the JARDIN DES TUILERIES and the JARDIN DES CHAMPS ÉLYSÉES; the LUXEMBOURG, off Boulevard St Michel, is a very picturesque, formally laid-out garden in French style.

ACCOMMODATION

Everything from the luxury of the super-luxe hotels such as the Ritz and George V to youth hostels can be found in Paris. Whatever your price range you should be able to get fixed up, and even in the height of summer there should always be a bed (in fact in August Paris is bereft of Parisians for they are all 'en vacances' at the coast, so a bed is no problem!).

The Tourist Office is not too helpful if you're looking for accommodation they consider to be 'downmarket', but you should come up with something from the suggestions here. The super-luxe and first-class hotels are all sufficiently popular to require some notice, so reserve ahead. The Tourist Board publishes a guide to hotels in Paris and Ile de France, available free of charge.

● **First Class:** (Double over 900 FF)
Meurice – 228 rue de Rivoli, 1e (tel. 260 3860). The 'hotel of kings', facing the Tuileries Gardens, in the heart of Paris. This wonderful old hotel is an institution and considered one of the world's best. Exceptionally good speciality restaurant and fashionable cocktail bar.

Hilton International Paris – 18 Avenue de Suffren, 15e (tel. 273 9200). Close to the Eiffel Tower, overlooking the Trocadéro and Palais de Chaillot, this is a particularly comfortable hotel noted for its rooftop restaurant.

Inter-Continental Paris – 3 rue de Castiglione, 1e (tel. 260 3780). Just off Place Vendôme, at the corner of rue de Castiglione and rue de Rivoli, this central hotel truly deserves its placing in the de luxe category. It offers every comfort, excellent restaurants and grill rooms, and has lots of surprise little touches that go to make it among the world's best hotels.

● **Super Club Class:** (Double around 400 FF)
Abbaye Saint-Germain – 10 rue Cassette, 6e (tel. 544 3811). Distinguished and atmospheric, this hotel was once a monastery but today offers comfortable rooms, all with bath or shower.

The Madison – 143 blvd St Germain, 6e (tel. 329 7250). Lovely position, just set back from this famous street, with the front-facing rooms receiving a most pleasant view of the church.

Hotel Burgundy – 8 rue Duphot, 1e (tel. 260 3412). The position of this hotel is a big plus – just off Place de la Madeleine. Comfortable and all rooms with bath.

Hotel Napoléon – 40 Avenue de Friedland, 8e (tel. 766 0202). An old hotel with a lot of character and a pretty impressive restaurant. In the area near to the Champs Elysées.

• **Economy:** (Double around 200 FF)
Avenir – 52 rue Gay-Lussac, 5e (tel. 354 7660). Basic but comfortable, and in the fashionable Latin Quarter.

Sorbonne – 6 rue Victor-Cousin, 5e (tel. 354 5808). Another economy base in the student quarter of Paris.

Hotel de Flandres – 16 rue Cujas, 5e (tel. 354 6730). Basic but passable, very low prices.

Centre International de Sejour de Paris – 6 Avenue Maurice-Ravel (tel. 343 1901). One for the students on a tight budget. Must be about the best value in Paris for basic accommodation. Unfortunately one has to be able to prove student identity.

Hotel Regent – 61 rue Dauphine, 6e (tel. 326 7645). OK for a couple of nights if finances are tight.

Hotel Henri IV – 9 rue St Jacques, 5e (tel. 354 5143). Very cheap, pretty spartan, but passable, and in the university area.

DINING OUT

Eating out in Paris is one of life's great joys, and there are restaurants serving excellent food and wine to suit every budget. From the gastronomic shrines of this world capital of haute cuisine to back street bistros serving set menus for 30–40 francs, Paris has literally thousands of restaurants, and if you're going to enjoy a meal anywhere on your travels, it's likely to be here. Like French hotels, all restaurants, except those classed de luxe, must by law have a priced menu displayed outside. Many of the best close at weekends, to allow the chefs (who have God-like status and salaries) to unwind on their country estates (!), and if they are open pre-booking is essential. Friday nights are extremely busy, so make a reservation as soon as you arrive in the city for your Friday dinner. The main exception to this rule is hotel restaurants. These do not close and it is usually possible to fit you in at short notice, especially if you are a guest at the hotel.

● **First Class:** (over 400 FF per person)
Taillevent – 15 rue Lamennais, 8e (tel. 536 3994). One of the world's best restaurants, and a mecca for gourmets of French cuisine. Excellent food, an endless wine list, a sumptuous château-like interior, and first-class service combine to make this one of the most difficult places in Paris to reserve a table. Write ahead (up to 2 months ahead!) to stand a chance.

Maxim's – 3 rue Royale, 8e (tel. 265 2794). World-renowned for its Parisian 'chic' and turn of the century decor, this is a restaurant where one goes to be seen as much as to eat. The food is classical French haute cuisine and the wine list impressive. Booking ahead necessary. Closed Sundays.

l'Archestrate – 84 rue de Varenne, 7e (tel. 551 4733). The home of Paris' most famous chef, Alain Senderens, and one of the best places in France to sample nouvelle cuisine. Many imaginative touches and interesting dishes. Intimate atmosphere (and invariably very busy). Closed weekends, August and all public holidays.

● **Super Club Class:** (150–350 FF per person)
Le Mange-Tout – 30 rue Lacépède, 6e (tel. 535 5393). The food is what brings one here, not the decor, but it is Auvergne specialities which make this restaurant one worth seeking out. Imaginative dishes and good French cuisine at reasonable prices. Situated in the Latin Quarter.

Restaurant Lipp – 151 blvd St Germain, 6e (tel. 548 5391). Good home cooking in the French peasant mould (plenty of garlic, baguette and house wine). Lots of atmosphere and a haunt of French politicians, 'intellectuals' and arty types. Well priced.

La Bucherie – 41 rue de la Bucherie, 5e (tel. 54 7806). Wonderfully relaxing atmosphere: open fires, classical music, intimate dining room, etc. Good nouvelle cuisine too, but pricier than the other two recommendations in this category.

• **Economy:** (40–150 FF per person)

Prix fixe menus from about 35 francs up can be found at bistros and cafés dotted all over Paris. It's a bit of a lucky dip, but if you stick to the family-run establishments you won't go far wrong. There is no point phoning to reserve in these places, just turn up and queue.

Le Petit Saint-Benoit – rue St Benoit, 6e. A wonderful old Parisian institution. Cheap, homely and full of character, the food's not half bad either! In the St Germain-des-Prés area.

Chartier's – 7 rue du Faubourg Montmartre, 9e. Communal eating in this 19th-century workers' eating hall, complete with vast mirrors, wood panelling etc. Good food and a very Gallic experience!

L'Assiette au Boeuf – 9 blvd des Italiens, 2e. One of a chain of inexpensive restaurants found all over Paris, offering basic steak, chips and salad, washed down with wine, and followed by a delicious variety of desserts. Excellent value and good food.

Chez Paul – 15 Place Dauphine, 1e. Very Parisian little bistro situated behind the law courts. Lively at lunchtime and specializing in good basic French cooking. ·

NIGHTLIFE

Nightlife in Paris can be anything you want, as long as you have the money to pay for it. Everything from cinema, theatre, opera, and ballet to striptease and wildly expensive discos are here. Many of the expensive nightclubs won't let you in unless you're accompanied by regular French customers, or are a celebrity. The publication *Pariscope* lists what's on.

Some notable clubs are:

Regine's International – 49 rue de Ponthieu, 8e. This famous name offers a luxurious setting for wining, dining and dancing. It's not the easiest place to get into, and it *is* expensive, but it's still one of *the* places in Paris.

The Folies-Bergere – 32 rue Richer, 9e. Showy, expensive, touristy and very 'glam', this is all that you'd expect in the way of a floorshow extravaganza. Another on the same lines is the *Lido*, at 116 bis, Avenue des Champs Elysées, 8e.

Crazy Horse Saloon – 12 Avenue Georges V, 8e. The most prestigious of the strip shows in Paris (if that isn't a contradiction in terms). Expensive, raunchy and highly rated by most tourists.

EXCURSIONS

VERSAILLES, the elaborate palace of Louis XIV, is the main attraction near to Paris. Take a train from Montparnasse or Invalides out to it. The palace is open Tuesday–Sunday, 1000–1700. Also within striking distance is the palace of FONTAINEBLEAU with its beautiful park-forest. Take the train from Gare de Lyon. Open 1000–1230, 1400–1800, except Tuesdays. CHANTILLY is an attractive small château, reached by train from Gare du Nord, but it's open only on Sundays and holidays. CHARTRES, home of the world's most famous gothic cathedral, is an hour away from Gare Montparnasse, and RHEIMS at the heart of Champagne country makes an interesting trip; it's 2 hours from Gare de l'Est. Don't miss the cathedral here or the free samples of bubbly from 'Mumm', 34 rue du Champ de Mars. If you really want to make a day of it, take the short train ride to Epernay where Moët et Chandon, on Avenue de Champagne, play hosts for another enjoyable tour with free samples.

Great Britain

RED TAPE

• **Passport/Visa Requirements:** Additional to a full valid passport, visas are required by nationals of all countries, *except* British Commonwealth countries and South American countries (other than Cuba), Algeria, Andorra, Austria, Bahrain, Denmark, Finland, France, West Germany, Greece, Iceland, Iran, Republic of Ireland, Israel, Italy, Ivory Coast, Japan, South Korea, Kuwait, Liechtenstein, Luxembourg, Monaco, Morocco, Netherlands, Niger, Norway, Pakistan, Portugal, Qatar, San Marino, Spain,

South Africa, Sweden, Switzerland, Tunisia, Turkey, USA, Yugoslavia – for a stay to be decided by the Immigration Officers.

All other nationals require a visa. Normally these are provided for a 3-month period.

CUSTOMS

• **Duty Free:** Visitors from an EEC country are allowed to bring in: 300 cigarettes or 75 cigars or 400g of tobacco; 1.5 litres of spirits and 3 litres of wine; 75g of perfume and 37.5 cl of toilet water. Other goods to the value of £120.

Visitors from non-EEC countries within Europe: 200 cigarettes or 50 cigars or 250g tobacco; 1 litre of spirits or 2 litres of wine; 50g of perfume and 25 cl of toilet water. Other goods to the value of £28.

Visitors from outside Europe: 400 cigarettes or 100 cigars or 500g of tobacco; 1 litre of spirits and 2 litres of wine; 50g of perfume and 25 cl toilet water. Other goods to the value of £28.

All personal effects are duty free, as are samples of no commercial value.

Liable to duty: samples of commercial value. These may be imported under an ATA Carnet.

HEALTH

If travelling from an area where smallpox is prevalent an international certificate of vaccination is required before entry is permitted.

CAPITAL – London. Population – 7,300,000.

POPULATION – 55,820,000.

LANGUAGE – English. Some Gaelic in parts of Scotland and Northern Ireland, and Welsh in western Wales.

CURRENCY – Pound Sterling (£) divided into 100 pence. Notes – 5, 10, 20, 50. Coins – 1, 2, 5, 10, 20 and 50 pence, £1.
£1 = US$1.48.

BANKING HOURS – 0930–1530 Monday–Friday; some banks in Scotland open until 1715.

POLITICAL SYSTEM – Constitutional monarchy.

RELIGION – Protestant.

PUBLIC HOLIDAYS

January 1 (and 2 in Scotland)	New Year
March/April	Good Friday, Easter Monday*
May, first Monday	May Day
August (1 day)	Spring Bank Holiday
December 25, 26	Christmas
* not in Scotland	

CLIMATE – Cooler in the north and Scotland. Rain common and rarely over 70°F/21°C.

TIME DIFFERENCE – GMT (+1 hour March–October).

COMMUNICATIONS

• **Telephone:** The internal telephone system is one of the world's most advanced and direct dialling is available from any call box to Western Europe. Cheap times for phoning are between 1800 and 0800, and coin boxes accept 10p and 50p pieces. Also card phones operate. For international calls many main Post Offices have boxes for which you pay after the call, and Post Offices also sell phone cards.

The dialling code for London is 01; for Birmingham 021, Edinburgh 031, Glasgow 041, Manchester 061.

• **Post:** Letters to the Continent of Europe are automatically sent by airmail without additional charge. Other destinations should specify if they want airmail. Internal mail has 2 classes: second is cheaper but takes 2–4 days longer. In London the Post Office on William IV Street (just north of Trafalgar Square) is open 24 hours.

ELECTRICITY – 220/240v AC; 50 Hz.

OFFICE/SHOPPING HOURS – Government offices open to the public 0930–1630 Monday–Friday. Shops open 0900–1730 Monday–Saturday. Some Sunday opening in Scotland.

• **Best Buys:** High-quality traditional clothing, such as cashmeres, classical coats and skirts, and woollen goods of all kinds are all particularly well priced and of good quality in Britain. Indeed, it is really only in Britain that one can buy the clothing that goes to make up the truly British look, so favoured by many nationalities in recent years.

Look out for the names McGeorge, Barrie and Pringle for the very highest quality cashmere and lambswool goods. These well known makes offer a wide range of styles and their prices are lower in the UK than elsewhere.

Apart from cashmeres and fine woollen goods, Harris tweed is synonymous with the well dressed British gentleman, and not surprisingly Harris jackets are a better buy in Britain (and particularly Scotland) than elsewhere. They can be found in many quality clothing shops, at prices ranging from around £55. To be sure of the real thing (which is still hand-woven by the Harris Islanders using only manual looms, and lasts a lifetime) check for the Harris tweed orb trademark on the label in the jacket.

High-quality gentlemen's and ladies' footwear is also a good buy in Britain. The traditional 'brogue' shoes and classical ladies' court shoes can be found in many of the older, smaller shoe shops, but one high street name worth looking out for, and found all over the UK, is K Shoe Shops. Try them for the classical British designs at more moderate prices.

Finally on the clothing front, sheepskin jackets are a particularly good buy in Britain. There are many makes and designs, but from our research, asking round all the specialist shops, 'Sherwood Lambskins' by K & M Sheepskins are generally considered to be the best British maker of quality sheepskin jackets and coats. Their garments can be found in specialist sheepskin and leather shops from Perth to Brighton, with the exception of the capital. It's worth noting however that for all cold-weather clothing (sheepskins, cashmeres, lambswool, kilted skirts, etc.) the further north you travel, the greater the range (and the greater the need for this type of wear!). Scotland's many specialist woollen and sheepskin shops will produce the greatest range and most competitive prices. Foreign visitors to the UK, especially those from Japan and West Germany, will find sheepskins, etc., at around half the price they'd pay at home.

Other good buys are antiques, silverware, books (try Charing Cross Road in London), fine art and jewellery. Every town will have a few antique shops worth looking around, but for really high-quality fine art you will have to head for the West End and London auction houses, such as Sotheby's and Christie's.

Records and cassettes are well priced in Britain. Look out for HMV record shops: they're a good reliable chain who offer all different types of recordings in their shops at reasonable prices. They are particularly strong in folk and contemporary music, and whilst in Britain it's worth listening to the different regional music (the Scots and Irish are noted for their folk songs and fiddle music).

Some of the markets worth checking out in London are Camden Passage (Wednesdays and Saturdays), Covent Garden (Mondays) and Portobello Road (Saturdays).

Good replicas of some of Britain's national art treasures are found in the museum and gallery shops. Most of the major ones (notably the British Museum in London) sell well priced, beautifully made facsimiles of their most popular pieces, so look in, see the priceless original, then buy a copy at a price you can afford.

Toiletries and cosmetics are always a good buy in Britain. The large department chain store, Boots the Chemist, found all over the UK, is the best place to head for to find a large selection of well priced brand names and own-make toiletries.

Whilst in London, stores such as Fortnum & Mason and Harrods are well worth a visit, to pick up those wonderfully British souvenirs of fine teas, preserves, chutneys, breakfast marmalades and the like. Apart from the hampers full of traditional goodies, which they can send on, there are plenty of small, lightweight delicacies which can be fitted into your suitcase as a reminder of Britain when you're home.

Sports equipment is considerably better value in the UK than in many other countries. Golf, tennis and squash products are particularly good, as is a lot of the hillwalking and mountaineering gear. For golf clubs, tennis and squash rackets, look out for the names Dunlop and Slazenger. Their products are particularly good value in Britain, and for the Japanese, golf clubs are virtually half-price. They do a wide selection of sports equipment, in all price ranges. Mountaineering equipment is well priced in Blacks Camping & Leisure Stores, and Millets Stores.

Hide-upholstered furniture (classics such as a chesterfield couch and club chair) are cheap in Great Britain. They're made here and have had their roots in the gentlemen's clubs and ancestral English country houses for centuries, so it's hardly surprising the market in the UK is so well developed. Even taking into account the cost of shipping and exporting, for Americans and the Japanese in particular, it still represents a good bargain. *Centurion* is about the best company in terms of price and range for hide suites. Their suites can be bought in many outlets throughout the UK, and at under £1500 for a full hide suite, this represents a tremendous saving to overseas visitors.

Musical instruments are another good buy, particularly guitars. The Japanese and Scandinavians will find in particular that high-quality instruments such as Martin guitars are about a third cheaper in the UK than in their home countries.

INTERNAL TRAVEL

● **Air:** British Airways, British Caledonian and British Midland are the country's major domestic airlines, operating services between London and Aberdeen, Belfast, Birmingham, Edinburgh, Glasgow, Guernsey, Inverness, the Isle of Man, Jersey, Leeds/ Bradford, Manchester, Newcastle and Plymouth. Also a shuttle operates between Heathrow and Gatwick Airports with 10 flights daily.

● **Rail:** British Railways connect all the major cities. The Inter-City trains are fast and efficient. The London Underground offers an extensive railway system covering all of London and environs.

● **Road:** Long-distance express coaches link the main cities. They start in London at the Victoria Coach Terminal, Buckingham Palace Road, London SW1. Rural areas are well covered by buses throughout Britain.

Taxis operate in all towns. All taxis and minicabs have fitted meters, and may be hailed in the street or phoned for.

The motorway system covers all densely populated areas of Britain, particularly the south-east of England. Hire cars are available in all towns. An International Driving Licence is required and traffic travels on the left-hand side of the road.

MAJOR SIGHTS OF THE COUNTRY

London as the capital, and former heart of one of the world's greatest empires, is a city worth getting to know. It is also a good base from which to see some of England's most attractive towns. OXFORD, home of Britain's (many think the world's) most prestigious university, dating back over 700 years, is less than an hour away. The historic buildings of the university colleges are the sort of sights which overseas visitors dream of when thinking of 'Olde England', and as an excursion from the capital Oxford offers a unique insight into the rich legacy of historical monuments which Britain has to offer.

CAMBRIDGE, Oxford's great rival, is an equally attractive market town and boasts a university dating back to the 13th century where men such as Darwin, Byron and Newton studied. Again within easy reach of London, Cambridge is the town of 'dreaming spires' and a sight not to be missed while in Britain.

STRATFORD-UPON-AVON is about two and a half hours from the capital. This is the birthplace of William Shakespeare and here you can visit the house where he was born, his wife's house, and listen to one of his works in the theatre where the Royal Shakespeare Company are based. The Elizabethan town is most attractive and, being on the same railway line, can be combined easily with a visit to Oxford.

BATH, the Georgian gem of England, is one and a quarter hours away from London. The architectural legacy left by the 18th-century aristocracy who came here to take the waters contrasts with the Roman remains left many centuries earlier, and the combination is a town with a very special charm and atmosphere. This is one of *the* sights of Britain, and should not be missed.

Down in the attractive rolling countryside of Buckinghamshire, not far from Windsor Castle, is one of the grandest English stately homes in the country, which because it has now been turned into a de luxe hotel allows a rare opportunity to sample the gracious living of a bygone era. CLIVEDEN is steeped in history: former home of 3 dukes, the Prince of Wales, and later the famous Astor family, this great country house will be of particular interest to American visitors. Here it was that Nancy Astor hosted grand dinner parties early this century, and where heads of state and key political figures stayed for long country-house weekends. The hotel has been impeccably restored, and though it decidedly falls into the 'de luxe' category, a stay here is the sort of experience that will be one of the highlights of your trip, and it *is* unique to Great Britain. Book well ahead. Write to Cliveden, Taplow, Buckinghamshire SL6 0IB (tel. 06286 64246).

For those prepared to go a bit further afield the city of YORK will be another high spot in your British wanderings. There are impressive Roman remains to be seen, a beautifully preserved medieval city, and Britain's finest gothic cathedral. York gives its name to the surrounding region, Yorkshire, which is totally different in its history, customs and people, to those in the south of England and London. Rural Yorkshire is particularly charming and of great appeal for a few relaxing days after the hustle of London and international travel.

For people with true romance in their blood though you have to make it up to Scotland while in the UK. Only 5 hours from London by train (or an hour's flying time) is EDINBURGH, capital of Scotland. A beautiful and dramatic city, built on extinct volcanoes, it has a fairytale castle dominating the scene and the hills and sea all around. The New Town, dating from the Georgian era, even surpasses Bath's Georgian buildings, and the medieval Old Town, with its castle, Palace of Holyrood and numerous interesting museums and houses, transports you back to the days when Scotland was an independent nation and bloody battles with the English were fought in the cobbled streets here.

The HIGHLANDS, the mountainous region 80 miles or so north-west of Edinburgh, are magnificent in their unspoilt beauty. (From London fly to Inverness and travel west to the Western Highlands.)

Gleneagles Hotel, in the heart of the rolling Perthshire country-side, makes a wonderful sidetrip after the bustle of London. Only an hour's shuttle, and an hour's drive away from the capital, a weekend here can show you all the best of Scotland, encapsulated

into one place. Scene of many major world conferences and one of
the country's most prestigious hotels, Gleneagles offers, beside
excellent accommodation and cuisine, the chance of a round of golf
on one of the best courses in Scotland, many outdoor pursuits, and
an ideal touring base to see some of the many attractions close by.
With Gleneagles' reputation stretching worldwide booking ahead is
essential. Tel. 07646 2231.

Services between Heathrow and Edinburgh or Glasgow (for the
West Highlands) are extremely good. British Airways and British
Caledonian run several services daily, but another smaller airline
worth checking out for these internal trips is British Midland. They
have 7 daily flights to each destination, and their prices are more
competitive than their rivals. The service, in terms of little extras, is
Business Class, with hot breakfasts, lunches and dinners on board;
free breakfast newspapers, and a complimentary bar service. These
services at no extra charge do give them the edge over the other two
airlines. Their Super Key return, which requires 2 weeks' prior
booking, is actually cheaper than the standard train journey to
Scotland, and standby flights are an attractive option, however late
in the day you decide to travel.

In theory it is possible to spend just one day in Edinburgh, and
make a day trip of it. A 7 o'clock-ish flight will get you into town by
the time the shops open (selling lovely woollens, cashmeres and
tweeds) and a 6 or 7 p.m. return flight will see you back in London
city centre by 8 p.m. Day returns are available (and on British
Midland these are valid for 3 days), and if it's a shopping trip for
quality woollens and classic clothing the price of your flight can
easily be saved on the shopping price differential.

If you're in London on a Qantas/American Airlines Round the
World ticket why not take advantage of the Guernsey Airlines
routings and visit the Channel Islands? JERSEY and GUERNSEY are
both self-governing states who rightly enjoy the reputation of being
the holiday islands of Great Britain, for they agreeably combine the
best qualities of their two neighbours – France and England – and
along with superb unspoilt scenery, no VAT and excellent cuisine
they enjoy the best sunshine record in the British Isles.

For a truly luxurious weekend in historic mansion-house setting
try either the Longueville Manor, St Saviour's, Jersey (tel. 0534
25501) or the Hotel Bella Luce, St Martin's, Guernsey (tel. 0481
38764).

Even a small amount of time will show you some of the great diversity of the United Kingdom, from the remote and beautiful Highlands, through the historical industrial north of England where the empire's money was made, to Yorkshire, Oxfordshire, East Anglia and the beautiful West Country – just some of the counties where in the rural areas life ambles on, and the unique things that Britain can offer can be glimpsed. These are some of the picture-book areas of Britain to seek out on a quick trip.

HOTELS

Hotel accommodation in Britain is expensive. £75 a night in a first class hotel is the norm, with even a 'C' grade (economy) costing an average of £20 per person. In the de luxe grade standards are very high and there are many historical houses now opening their doors as hotels and offering exceptionally fine service.

Large hotel chains in Britain include Sheraton, Hilton, Holiday Inn, Trust House Forte, Crest Hotels.

Away from hotels, for the economy traveller, the great British institution of 'Bed & Breakfast' exists. Here you stay in someone's home as a paying guest for the night (or longer). Pricewise B&Bs cost around £10 per person per night and it is one of the best ways of getting to meet the British in their own environment. The breakfast is usually a full British breakfast consisting of eggs, bacon, sausage, tomato etc., and is sufficient to set one up for the day!

Both Youth and Young Men/Women's Christian Association hostels operate in Britain, and offer basic accommodation in main centres for very little cost. Youth Hostels require membership, which can be taken out on the spot, and they can be found both in the cities and in rural areas. An average hostel price is £4 a night.

Camping is well catered for in Britain, and there are many official sites offering good facilities. The only thing that is against camping is the erratic weather.

NIGHTLIFE AND RESTAURANTS

London is the centre of the entertainment business in Britain. The West End is the heart of the film, theatre and music world, and there is no shortage of things to see or do. Theatres play to full houses all year round and the standards are high. Cinema houses can be found all over the country, but generally new films are shown first in the West End of London. Dancing of every kind can be found here. Discos and progressive music are at their best in London, and there are numerous exclusive nightclubs where live music, dancing and a meal can be enjoyed.

London is also home to several opera and ballet companies (the Royal Opera Company, Sadler's Wells, English National Opera), as well as to many world-acclaimed orchestras. The Barbican Centre, Albert Hall, Royal Festival Hall and the South Bank Complex are venues for top-class performances of music and ballet. (Full details of events can be had from the Tourist Information Offices.)

Outside London all the major British cities have organized nightlife along these lines. Cinemas can be found in even the smallest towns, but the trend for cinema-going is declining. Discos are also found all over the country, as are pubs – public houses – where the locals meet and chat, playing games such as draughts, cards and darts, and any type of alcoholic or soft drink can be bought. The British are proud of their beers and a wide variety will be found in any pub. Bitter is a dark rich beer, sold on tap; stout is sweet and rich; light ale is lighter and more akin to lager; lager is lager; and real ale is the naturally fermented brew that enthusiasts will walk miles to get a pint of. While in Britain try some out to wash down your 'Pub Grub': lunches or dinners served in pubs where the food is invariably good home-cooking, and at a low price.

British cuisine has improved dramatically recently and restaurants are now on a level with any European country's. In Britain Indian and Chinese meals can be easily found due to the many Commonwealth citizens who came to live in Britain in the 1960s. Typically British dishes to look out for include roast beef and Yorkshire pudding; Scottish beefsteak, Scottish salmon; roast lamb and game dishes. Bakery is of a high standard, particularly in Scotland, and the great British institution of 'Afternoon Tea' should be sampled whenever the occasion arises. This is served in all good hotels, country houses, and cafés and consists of a pot of tea, scones, cream, jam and assorted cakes and biscuits. Even in the most exclusive of hotels the cost is only a few pounds.

Breakfast is generally served from 0700–0930; lunch from 1200–1400; tea from 1400–1730; and dinner from 1900–2200.

London

INTERNATIONAL AIRPORTS – HEATHROW (LHR)
– GATWICK (LGW)

HEATHROW

15 miles west of London lies Heathrow, the world's busiest international airport. Over 70 airlines fly direct scheduled services to more than 200 destinations from Heathrow, and in excess of 27 million passengers use this airport annually. There are 4 terminals.

Terminal 1 handles mainly British Airways domestic and European routes, together with Aer Lingus and a variety of domestic carriers.

Terminal 2 handles non-UK airlines operating services to Europe.

Terminal 3 handles long-haul and inter-continental flights.

Terminal 4 handles all British Airways inter-continental flights, including Concorde, and BA Paris and Amsterdam services. KLM and Air Malta also use Terminal 4.

AIRPORT FACILITIES

● **Terminal 1:**

Information Desk	0700–2200 (tel. 01-745 7702/3/4).
Bank/Foreign Exchange	0700–2300. Seven days.
Hotel Reservations Service	Arrivals hall. Accommodation anywhere in Britain can be booked from here. Tel. 01-759 2719. Open 0700–2300.
Problems and Insurance Facilities	Any of the following companies will help with travel problems (visas, documents, sort out flight delays, etc.) and insurance:

	Airport Assistance Ltd (tel. 01-897 6884); Tate Aeroservice (tel. 01-897 3408); Thomas Cook Ltd (tel. 01-897 8249).
Bar	All bars operate 1100–1400, 1730–2230 except those in the International Departures Lounges, located after Passport Control, which are open from 0700–2230 daily.
Restaurant/Buffet	There is a restaurant and grill for most of the day, and a buffet open 24 hours.
Post Office	Post box and stamp machines available.
Baggage Deposit	25 kilos weight limit and opening of baggage may be demanded for security reasons. Open 0645–2200. Do not leave baggage unattended at any time.
Nursery	0700–2200 daily. If closed apply to airline or Information Desk.
Shops	'Skyshops' on both sides of Immigration Control. Food, magazines, gifts, tobacco etc. all available.
Medical Centre	Medical Centre in Queen's Building staffed 24 hours a day. Tel. 01-745 7211 or ask Airport Information Desk in emergency.
Toilets	Open 24 hours.
Meeting Point	Airport Information Desk.
Car Rental Desks	Avis, Hertz, Europcar and Budget all have desks. 0700–2300 with telephone links outside these hours is the norm.
Lost Property	Ground floor of car park 2, at exit end, opposite Terminal 2.

	Open 0900–1600 daily (tel. 01-745 7727).
Public Telephones	Coin boxes, card phones, credit card phones, in terminal. Open 24 hours.
International Business Centre	Provides full range of business services including telephones, telex, computers, photocopying, translation, conference rooms etc. Situated next to Terminal 2 (tel. 01-759 2434).
Airline Lounges	Private lounges provided by following airlines: Aer Lingus, British Airways, ElAl and South African Airways.
Porters and Trolleys	Free service available 24 hours.
London Transport Desk	Open 0700–2100 daily.
British Rail Desk	Open 0800–2100 daily.

• Terminal 2:

Information Desk	0700–2200 (tel. 01-745 7115/6/7).
Bank/Foreign Exchange	0700–2300. Seven days.
Hotel Reservations Service	Arrivals hall. Accommodation anywhere in Britain can be booked from here (tel. 01-897 0821).
Problems and Insurance Facilities	Any of the following companies will help out on travel problems (visas, documents, sort out flight delays etc.) and insurance: Airport Assistance Ltd (tel. 01-897 6884); Tate Aeroservice (tel. 01-897 3408); Thomas Cook Ltd (tel. 01-897 8249).
Bar	All bars operate 1100–1400, 1730–2230 except those in the

	International Departures Lounges, located after Passport Control, which are open 0700–2230 daily.
Restaurant/Buffet	A restaurant, grill and buffet are open most of the day.
Post Office	In passenger terminal. Open 0830–1800 Monday–Saturday. (Opens 0900 Fridays.)
Baggage Deposit	25 kilos weight limit and opening of baggage may be demanded for security reasons. Open 0645–2200.
Nursery	0700–2200. If closed apply to airline or Information Desk.
Shops	'Skyshops' on both sides of Immigration Control. Food, magazines, gifts, tobacco, etc. all available.
Toilets	Open 24 hours.
Meeting Point	Airport Information Desk.
Car Rental	Avis, Hertz, Europcar and Budget all have desks.
Lost Property	Ground floor of car park 2, at exit end, opposite Terminal 2. Open 0900–1600 daily (tel. 01-745 7727).
Public Telephones	Coin boxes, card phones and credit card phones in terminal. Open 24 hours.
International Business Centre	Provides full range of business services including telephones, telex, computers, photocopying, translation, conference rooms, etc. Situated next to Terminal 2 (tel. 01-759 2434).
Airline Lounges	Private lounges provided by following airlines: Air France, Iberia, Lufthansa, and SAS.

• **Terminal 3:**

Information Desk	Arrivals: 0600–2230 (tel. 01-745 7412/3/4); Departures: 0830–1730 (tel. 01-745 7067).
Bank/Foreign Exchange	Arrivals: open 24 hours, seven days; Departures: 0630–2130, seven days.
Hotel Reservations Service	Arrivals hall. Accommodation anywhere in Britain can be booked from here (tel. 01-897 0507).
Problems and Insurance Facilities	Any of the following companies will help out on travel problems (visas, documents, sort out flight delays etc.) and insurance: Airport Assistance Ltd (tel. 01-897 6884); Tate Aeroservice (tel. 01-897 3408); Thomas Cook Ltd (tel. 01-897 8249).
Bar	All bars operate 1100–1400, 1730–2230 except those in the International Departures Lounges, located after Passport Control, which open from 0700–2230 daily.
Restaurant/Buffet	There is a restaurant and grill open for most of the day, and a buffet service open 24 hours.
Post Office	In passenger terminal. Pillar boxes and coin-operated stamp machines only.
Baggage Deposit	25 kilos weight limit and opening of baggage may be demanded for security reasons. Open 0600–2230. Do not leave baggage unattended at any time.

Nursery	0700–2200 daily. If closed apply to airline or Information Desk.
Shops	'Skyshops' on both sides of Immigration Control. Food, magazines, gifts, tobacco, etc. all available.
Toilets	Open 24 hours.
Car Rental	Avis, Hertz, Europcar and Budget all have desks.
Meeting Point	Airport Information Desk.
Lost Property	Ground floor of car park 2, at exit end, opposite Terminal 2. Open 0900–1600 daily (tel. 01-745 7727).
Public Telephones	Coin boxes, card phones, credit card phones in terminal. Open 24 hours.
International Business Centre	Provides full range of business services including telephones, telex, computers, photocopying, translation, conference rooms, etc. Situated next to Terminal 2 (tel. 01-759 2434).
Airline Lounges	Private lounges provided by following airlines: Air Canada, Air India, British West Indian Airlines, Ghana Airlines, Japan Air Lines, Middle East Airlines, Pakistan International Airlines, Pan American, Saudia, Singapore Airlines and Trans World Airlines.
Porters and Trolleys	Free service available 24 hours.

• **Terminal 4:** Split-level terminal with check-in hall, ticket desks, Passport Control and Departure concourse on upper floor, and Arrivals area, transfers, Immigration, Customs and baggage hall on lower floor.

Information Desk	Open 0530–2230 (tel. 01-745 7139).

Bank/Foreign Exchange	Seven days, 24 hours.
Hotel Reservations Desk	Open 0600–2300.
Insurance Facilities	In International Departures Lounge, open 0700–2200.
Bar	All bars operate 1100–1400, 1730–2230 except those in the International Departures Lounges, located after Passport Control, which are open from 0700–2230 daily.
Restaurant/Buffet	There is a restaurant and grill open for most of the day, and a buffet open 24 hours.
Post Office	Pillar boxes and stamps available.
Baggage Deposit	25 kilos weight limit and opening of baggage may be demanded for security reasons. Open 0530–2230. Do not leave baggage unattended at any time.
Nursery	0700–2200 daily. If closed apply to airline or Information Desk.
Shops	'Skyshops' on both sides of Immigration Control. Food, magazines, gifts, tobacco, etc. all available.
Toilets	Open 24 hours.
Car Rental	Avis, Hertz, Europcar and Budget all have desks.
Meeting Point	Airport Information Desk.
Lost Property	Ground floor of car park 2, at exit end, opposite Terminal 2. Open 0900–1600 daily (tel. 01-745 7727).
Public Telephones	Coin boxes, card phones and credit card phones in terminal. Open 24 hours.
International Business Centre	Provides full range of business services including telephones, telex, computers, photocopying,

translation, conference rooms, etc. Situated next to Terminal 2 (tel. 01-759 2434).

Air Lounges   Private lounges provided by the following airlines: British Airways and KLM.

Porters and Trolleys   Free service available 24 hours.

● **Common to all Terminals:** For use by all passengers, regardless of terminal of departure or arrival, are the following facilities:

Medical and First Aid   There is a 24-hour medical
Centre   centre staffed by British Airports' nursing sisters, and there are doctors on call who can be reached in an emergency. In some cases a call-out fee is charged. Contact the Airport Information Desk.

Chapel   St George's Chapel is underground opposite the entrance to car park 2, in the centre of the airport (tel. 01-745 4261). There are services as follows:
                               Church of England Eucharist – Sunday 0930 and Wednesday 1300.
                               Free Church Prayer and Meditation – Thursday 1300.
                               Roman Catholic Mass – Sunday 0800, 1100, 1200 and 1800. Also Monday to Saturday 1230.

Spectator Viewing   From the roof gardens of the
Facilities   Queen's Building you may watch the activities of the airport. Open 1000–1800 in summer and 1000–1630 in winter, all year except December 25 and 26. Adults

60p, children 20p. Park in the
Long-term car park and take the
free bus to Terminal 1, from
where you walk to the Queen's
Building.

AIRPORT INFORMATION

Check-in Times

Average for all airlines:
international 90 minutes;
domestic 30 minutes.

Airport Tax

Nil.

Duty Free Shops

Located in Terminals 1, 2, 3 and
4. Sell: cigarettes, cigars,
tobacco, wines, aperitifs, spirits,
liqueurs, lighters, watches,
perfumes and gifts.

Take: convertible currencies,
traveller's cheques, all the
following credit cards:
Eurocard, Master Charge,
American Express, Visa, Diners
Club, Carte Blanche, Vantage
and Access.

You must produce your
airline boarding card or ticket
when making duty free
purchases.

Transferring Flights

The baggage claim check
attached to your luggage shows
the destination airport of your
baggage. The letters LHR or
LON mean it has been labelled
only to London and *must* be
claimed there and re-registered
for your next flight. If your
baggage has been labelled to
your final destination, follow the

yellow overhead TRANSFERS signs to the Transfer Desk for your check-in information. Before arriving at the Transfer Desk you will go through a security check where you and your hand baggage will be screened. If your flight leaves from another terminal there are frequent transfer coaches. If your baggage has been labelled on to your final destination it will automatically be transferred on to your onward flight.

If your baggage has been labelled for London only, follow the ARRIVALS signs to reclaim it before proceeding to re-register. If you are arriving at a different terminal from where your connection departs you will take one of the transfer buses. There are 2 separate bus services connecting the terminals. One serves mainly those who are starting or ending their journeys elsewhere in the UK – the 'landside' service – and the other serves those transferring between international flights – the 'airside' service. Both are free and run every 10 minutes or so. Your luggage may travel with you on the buses.

At Terminals 1 and 2 the airside transfer bus operates from a gate adjacent to the Eurolounge which connects terminals 1 and 2. It operates from Gate 12 in Terminal 3 and from the Transfer Gate in Terminal 4.

The landside bus calls at the North Door in Terminal 1; the west end of Terminal 2 at the Departures forecourt, the arrivals coach station in Terminal 3, and the Arrivals forecourt in Terminal 4.

International-to-Domestic Transfer

If you are transferring from an international flight to one for a UK destination, follow the yellow overhead signs to ARRIVALS. After completing immigration formalities collect your baggage, *even if it is labelled to your final UK destination*, and clear Customs.

Immediately outside Customs in Terminal 3 are the Transfer Desks where you should deposit luggage for your domestic flight. Then all you need to do is take the courtesy coach or walk to the first floor departure level of Terminal 1.

International Transfers

If your luggage is checked through to your final destination all you need do is transfer terminals (if applicable) in the way described above.

INTER-AIRPORT TRANSFER

To get from Heathrow to London Gatwick (LGW):
Jetlink Coach – 60 minutes, £3 fare. Every 30–60 minutes from 0530–2030. Board the bus at the airport bus station.
Taxi – 70 minutes, costing approx. £36.

AIRPORT HOTELS

● First Class:
Heathrow Penta – Bath Road, Hounslow (tel. 01-897 6363). Courtesy coach to hotel.

● Super Club Class:
Hotel Ibis – Bath Road, Hayes (tel. 01-759 4888).
Cottage Hotel – Royal Lane, Hillingdon (tel. 0895 35995).
Arlington Hotel – Shepiston Lane, Hayes (tel. 01-573 6162).

● Economy:
Shepiston Guest House – 31 Shepiston Lane, Hayes (tel. 01-573 1266).
Stanwell Halls Hotel – 171 Town Lane, Stanwell (tel. 0784 252292).
Hounslow Hotel – 41 Hounslow Road, Feltham (tel. 01-890 2109).

CITY LINKS

Heathrow is 15 miles from the centre of London.

● **Rail:** London Underground takes 50 minutes to the centre, costing £1.50. The airport is linked by the Piccadilly line, and the station is under the terminal. Stop for Terminal 4 first, then stop for Terminals 1, 2, and 3.

   Quick and cheap, but not recommended for travellers with large amounts of baggage.

● **Bus:** London Transport Airbus. There are 3 routes: the A1 to Victoria Railway Station; the A2 to Paddington Railway Station, and the A3 to Euston Railway Station. A convenient and inexpensive way to get in to London. Operates from all terminals. £3.

● **Taxi:** To the city £15. Ranks for authorized (black) cabs are outside each terminal. All journeys in the area of London are controlled by the Metropolitan Police, and must be charged according to the meter. Taxi drivers may refuse hire if the distance is over 20 miles. Do not use unlicensed cabs which are touted inside the terminal buildings.

● **Car Hire:** See the terminal facility tables for details of the different car hire firms available.

GATWICK

27 miles from London is Gatwick Airport, the fourth busiest in the world, running the flights of over 90 airlines and numerous tour operators' charter flights throughout the year. There is only one main terminal, and all departures are checked in by one of three handling agents: British Caledonian, British Airways and Gatwick Handling Ltd.

No flight departure announcements are made at Gatwick, except in the event of a delay, so keep a close check on your flight's progress on the departure board and flight information television monitors. When boarding commences make your way to the relevant gate – do not expect anyone to instruct you to do so.

- **International Flight Departures:** After checking in you normally go straight into the International Departures Lounge, which is reached by way of the 'International Departures and Satellite channel'. Show your boarding card, go through the security checks and Passport Control, and wait in the seating area until your gate number is showing.

The Duty and Tax Free shop is located in the international Departures Lounge. Other shops serve Gates 23–26, and Satellite gates 31–38. If you have spare time before boarding there is a shopping centre – Gatwick Village – on the third floor of the terminal, before you reach the International Departures and Satellite channel.

If the information for your flight shows up as 'Go to Satellite', you should go through security and Passport Control to the main Departures Lounge, and follow the signs to the Satellite. This is a circular building connected to the main terminal by a rapid transit link. Baggage trolleys are not allowed on the transit for safety reasons. At the Satellite walk around the circular lounge to find your gate number (31–38). If you need help there are staff at the Gatwick Handling desk, just on your left as you enter the Satellite.

Boarding the aircraft takes place between 30 and 60 minutes before departure.

- **Domestic Flight Departures:** Passengers travelling to UK destinations, Eire or the Channel Islands are not subject to Passport Control and use the domestic departure gates.

Flights to Cork, Dublin or Jersey check in on the main concourse.

Flights to Belfast follow the signs to 'South Pier check in', located down the stairs marked 'Domestic Flights' and turn left (lift available).

Many other UK flights check in at the departure gate. Check in luggage with the handling agent in the main concourse; those with only hand luggage should proceed to the departure gate.

The domestic departure channel leads from the British Caledonian check-in area on the departure concourse.

• **International Flight Arrivals:** After arrival follow the black and yellow signs for Baggage Reclaim which lead to Immigration Control. Passengers transferring from one international flight to another should follow the signs for transfer passengers which will take them to a desk where they check in for the next leg of their journey.

When you reach the Immigration Hall you will see signs showing which desk to go to for your nationality. Non-British passengers are required to complete a landing card. The handling agent in this hall will give you one.

After Immigration you enter a seating area. Wait here until your baggage has been delivered to the Reclaim Hall on the floor above. When this happens your flight number and airport of departure is displayed on one of the television monitors. The television will show the number of the reclaim carousel your baggage will be on, and an arrow indicates the easiest access.

In this area of waiting toilets are available, and a British Rail desk where you can buy train tickets is operational at busy periods.

Once up in the Baggage Reclaim Hall check your luggage *is* yours (many cases look similar), and if you have any difficulties go to the baggage services desk of your handling agent, located at the end of the hall. (The letters following your flight number on the TV monitor indicate which handling agent is responsible for your baggage delivery.)

After reclaiming your baggage go through Customs. After Customs you arrive at the main Arrivals concourse, which is on the second floor of the terminal.

AIRPORT FACILITIES

Information Desk

In International Arrivals Hall, open 24 hours. General advice and airport information. Also some tourist information. For flight information consult your handling agent – all three have desks in the Arrivals concourse. Alternatively telephone your airline direct:

Aer Lingus (0293) 502074
Air Europe (0293) 502060
Air New Zealand (0293) 518033*
Air Zimbabwe (0293) 518033*
American Airlines (0293) 502078
Britannia Airways (0293) 502075
British Air Ferries (0293) 25555
British Airtours (0293) 518033*
British Airways (0293) 518033*
British Caledonian (0293) 25555
Cathay Pacific (0293) 518033*
Dan Air (0293) 502068
Delta Air Lines (0293) 502113
Eastern Airlines (0293) 25555
Garuda Indonesian (0293) 502025
Monarch Airlines (0293) 502066
NLM City Hopper (0293) 502070
North-West Orient (0293) 502079
People Express (0293) 502061
Philippine Airlines (0293) 518033*
SAS Scandanavian (0293) 518033*
Virgin Atlantic (0293) 502105
Wardair Canada (0293) 33161

(recorded message on 0293
502123 from 0600–1700).
World Airways (0293) 50207
All Other Airlines (0293) 31299
* = recorded message 2300–
0700.

Bank/Foreign Exchange

In both Departures and Arrivals
Halls (second floor), banks
provide exchange and banking
service. Banks stay open on
alternate nights 24 hours (closed
25 December).

Hotel Reservations

The Hotel Plus desk books your
hotel accommodation either at
hotels located near the airport
or anywhere else in Britain.
Open 0700–2300, or tel. (0293)
34851/2 and 28822 ext. 2798/9.
Gatwick Hilton International
(tel. 518080) is linked to the
terminal building and reached
by covered walkways. The
Gatwick Penta (tel. 785533) is
also at the airport. The Penta
and other local hotels operate
courtesy coaches. Follow the
signs for 'courtesy coaches' to
the lower forecourt at the exit to
the terminal.

Insurance Facilities

Flight insurance available (tel.
0293 21046).

Catering

The Country Table is a 24-hour
self-service restaurant; the
Village Inn is a real-ale pub
serving hot and cold pub grub
and drinks during the normal
licensing hours; coffees and
pastries served outside licensing
hours. Shortstop Burgers is a 24-
hour fast-food unit; The

Panorama Restaurant opens
0630–2200 daily, with adjoining
cocktail bar. Baskin Robbins Ice
Cream sells ice cream in
numerous flavours, and
Healthworks sells freshly
squeezed orange juice, nuts,
fruit etc.

Post Office

In Gatwick Village, open 0900–
1730 Monday–Friday; 0900–1300
Saturday. Stamp machines and
post box available outside these
hours.

Baggage Deposit

Arrivals concourse. Open 24
hours.

Nursery

Four nurseries are available: one
downstairs in the International
Departures Lounge, one in the
Satellite, and two in Gatwick
Village.

Shops

'Skyshops' located on the main
check-in concourse, to the right
of the entrance to International
Departures. On third floor of
terminal Gatwick Village has
many more shops.

Medical Centre

Near Gatwick Village, on the
third floor of the terminal,
above International Arrivals
concourse, is a 24-hour medical
centre. Doctor's call-out fee may
have to be charged, but nursing
sisters always available. In
emergency dial 2222 on any grey
or white airport telephone for
ambulance.

Car Hire

Desks in the concourse and
reception buildings, next to the
terminal. Avis, Hertz, Kenning

	and Godfrey Davis Europcar all have desks.
Toilets	Located throughout terminal, open 24 hours.
Public Telephones	In various parts of the terminal. Also ten British Telecom card phones available. Cards on sale in Post Office or Skyshops.
Showers	In toilets close to the Tie-Rack shop. Towel and soap may be hired. Dial 2968 on any white or grey airport phone.
Lost & Found	Downstairs below the Departures concourse. Open 0830–1630 every day (tel. 0293 503162). Items left on the aircraft should be traced via the handling agent.
Chapel	In Gatwick Village, on third floor. Open 24 hours. Services – RC Mass: Saturday 1200 and 1430; Sunday 0800, 0930, 1200; Monday–Friday as announced. Anglican Eucharist: Sunday 0700 (May–September) and 1030. Other faiths requiring minister of their religion, contact Airport Information Desk.
Spectator Viewing Facilities	On the roof of the terminal building is the spectators' gallery overlooking the airfield. Take one of the lifts from the Arrivals concourse to the fourth floor. Open 0800–2000 daily in summer. Further information tel. (0293) 503843.

INTER-AIRPORT TRANSFER

Airliner operates a door-to-door service between Heathrow and Gatwick. Tel. 01-759 4741 and a minibus will collect you at your door. At Gatwick follow the yellow and black signs to the coach station and an airliner bus will be called for you.

There is a Speedlink coach as a cheaper alternative. This takes 50 minutes and costs only a few pounds. They run every 20 minutes between 0600–2000, and then at 2100 and 2200. Speedlink stops at each terminal at Heathrow, and passengers should check in at Gatwick at the waiting area at the Arrivals concourse.

A taxi takes approx. 75 minutes and costs around £40.

AIRPORT HOTELS

• **First Class:**
Gatwick Hilton International – connected by walkway to the terminal (tel. 0293 518080). A most comfortable hotel, with the Hilton touches.
Gatwick Penta – Povey Cross Road, Horley (tel. 0293 785533). Courtesy coach to this lower priced, but still first class hotel.

• **Super Club Class:**
Gatwick Concorde – Lowfield Heath, Crawley (tel. 0293 33441).
Gatwick Manor – London Road, Lowfield Heath (tel. 0293 26301). (Courtesy coach.)
Gatwick Wena Hotel – Russ Hill, Charlwood (tel. 0293 862171).

• **Economy:**
Ifield Court – Ifield Avenue, Crawley (tel. 0293 34807). (Courtesy coach.)
Mill House – Salfords, Nr Redhill (tel. 0737 67277).
Skylane Motor Hotel – Brighton Road, Horley (tel. 0293 786971). (Courtesy coach.)

CITY LINKS

• **Rail:** The British Railway 'Gatwick Express' is the easiest way to get out to Gatwick from London. It operates between London

Victoria and Gatwick every day at 15-minute intervals, and the non-stop journey takes just 30 minutes. Trains leave the airport at 5 minutes, 20 minutes, 35 minutes and 50 minutes past the hour, between 0620 and 2235, and operate hourly throughout the night. Another service connects Gatwick and London Bridge station now. Trains run hourly from 0909 to 2209 with additional services at peak times. The first train of the day leaves Gatwick at 0702.

The British Rail station is part of the terminal building. The station entrance leads from the international Arrivals concourse. Lifts available. No trolleys are allowed on the platforms but porters are available, and once in the terminal there are plenty of trolleys.

If you are travelling with British Caledonian you can check in your luggage at their air terminal in Victoria Station, and be free of it until your final destination.

• **Bus:** There are direct express coaches between Gatwick coach station and London's Victoria coach station. Service 777 connects the two and this operates half-hourly for most of the day. Lifts from coach station set-down points to concourse level.

• **Taxi:** Approximately £30 to the city centre.

• **Car Hire:** See the car hire details under 'Facilities' section for details of the four companies available.

For those driving in to Gatwick there are open and under cover car parks; long- and short-stay. Passengers may be set down at the entrance to the terminal building on the upper forecourt level, but no waiting allowed.

LONDON

London is a must in any world tour. There are three Londons to take into account: the CITY of London (the financial and administrative centre of Great Britain), WESTMINSTER (the political, royal and religious centre), and the WEST END (home of British theatre and cinema, smart shops and clubs). Each area has a different feel to it, and the combination of all three with over a thousand years of history and traditions, plenty of open green spaces and the buzz of Europe's largest city, makes a visit here unforgettable.

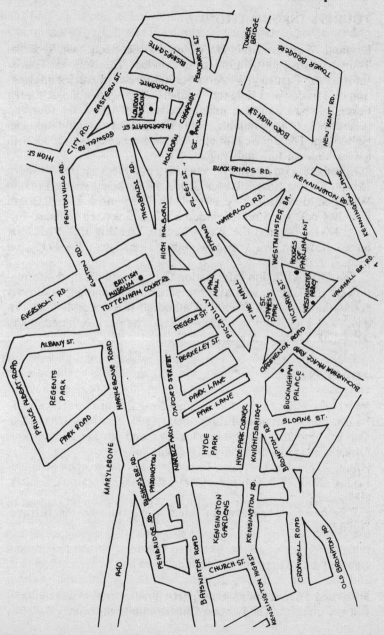

TOURIST INFORMATION

England, Northern Ireland, Wales and Scotland have separate Tourist Boards, all with offices in London. The National Tourist Information Centre at Victoria Station forecourt carries information on London and England. Leaflets, maps, guidebooks, tourist tickets for buses and the underground, and sightseeing tour and theatre tickets are available. Same-day hotel accommodation can be booked. The Centre is open seven days a week, 0900–2030, with longer hours in July and August.

Information on Northern Ireland is available from the Northern Ireland Tourist Board, Ulster Office, 11 Berkeley Street, London W1, open Monday–Friday, 0905–1715. The Scottish Tourist Board is at 19 Cockspur Street, London SW1, and is open Monday–Friday, 0900–1700; and the Wales Tourist Board is at 2–3 Maddox Street, London W1, open Monday–Thursday, 0915–1715 and Friday, 0915–1700.

The City of London Information Centre, with detailed information on the City as well as more general information, is directly across the road from St Paul's Cathedral. It is open Monday–Friday, 0930–1700, Saturday, 0930–1300 during April–September and 0930–1200 October–March.

ADDRESSES

Post Office – King Edward Building, King Edward Street (tube, St Paul's), open Monday–Friday, 0800–1900, Saturday 0900–1230. This is where all poste restante mail will end up. The 24-hour Post Office is at St Martin's Place, Trafalgar Square.

Amex – 6 Haymarket (tube, Piccadilly). Exchange open Monday–Friday, 0900–1700, Saturday, 0900–1800 (2000 in season), Sunday, 1000–1800.

US Embassy – 24 Grosvenor Square, W1 (tel. 499 9000) (tube, Bond Street).

CITY TRANSPORT

• **Bus and Tube (London Transport):** Transportation in London is fast and efficient. The London Underground runs from 0600–2400, and like the red double-decker buses operates on a zone system. Tickets for the underground (the 'tube') are bought in the stations, where large maps are located showing the extensive network which covers all the capital and environs. Bus tickets are bought on the buses. The single-decker Red Arrow buses operate with ticket machines on board. There are some night buses running midnight to 0500. London Transport will supply details of the Go-As-You-Please tourist tickets available.

• **Taxis:** Taxis are everywhere and no problem to hire in the street. The fares are metered. For journeys outside the metropolitan area the fare should be agreed with the driver first.

• **Car Hire:** All the international car hire companies have offices in London. The Tourist Board will put you in touch, or alternatively contact the Car Hire Centre International, 23 Swallow Street, Piccadilly (tel. 734 7661). They will fix you up anywhere in Britain with a hire car.

SIGHTS

London has swallowed many villages into its bulk in the course of its development, but even today each village (now district) has its own character and traditions. Soho, Hampstead and Chelsea are as different from each other as individual towns. It's easy to divide London into its three sections but this would neglect the areas that fall between, like the fashionable COVENT GARDEN, or the intellectual centre of BLOOMSBURY where the BRITISH MUSEUM and London University are located. Don't forget either the wonderful days out you can have at the maritime centre of GREENWICH, or at the Royal Botanical Gardens at KEW, or HAMPTON COURT PALACE, and many more. This rundown is just a small sample of what you can see, but once you've made your visit to Tourist Information, you should be in a position to work out your own best itinerary.

Many sightseeing tours exist: London Transport's bus tours from Victoria are perhaps the best value, but if it's luxury you're after, try the Harrods Bus Tours. The Tourist Office has all the details.

The London of the 11th century is that area known as 'the City'. In this 'square mile', the wheelings and dealings of the Stock Exchange and big business take place, and the Bank of England and Royal Exchange have their headquarters here. The sights include: the beautiful Renaissance cathedral of ST PAUL'S (the one Charles and Di chose for their wedding in 1981), where Nelson and Wellington are buried; FLEET STREET, the home of the British press; the INNS OF COURT and the OLD BAILEY – the heart of the British legal system; and the TOWER OF LONDON which dates back to William the Conqueror and has served as prison, palace and mint. The Crown Jewels, the White Tower and Tower Green where Henry VIII had Anne Boleyn and Catherine Howard executed, are among some of the sights to see here.

Roughly, Westminster and the West End stretch from HYDE PARK (the famous expanse with Speakers' Corner – a national venue for impromptu free speech on Sundays) to WESTMINSTER ABBEY, the incredible gothic church so central to the country's history. WHITEHALL and the HOUSES OF PARLIAMENT, the centres of British government and administration, are along here, and so is the timekeeping landmark of London, Big Ben. To go in and listen to Parliament (a fascinating experience), line up at St Stephen's entrance opposite the Abbey.' THE MALL is the boulevard leading from TRAFALGAR SQUARE, home of the NATIONAL GALLERY, to BUCKINGHAM PALACE, the home of the monarchy, which is not open to the public. The hub of the capital is PICCADILLY CIRCUS with its statue of Eros, and SOHO, the seamy cosmopolitan entertainment district that comes alive after dark. The museums to look out for in this part of London are: the TATE GALLERY at Millbank (a fine collection of modern masterpieces and sculpture); the VICTORIA AND ALBERT at Cromwell Road; the BRITISH MUSEUM, which is worth at least a day of anyone's time (everything, from the Elgin Marbles from the Acropolis to Magna Carta, is here); and MADAME TUSSAUD'S wax museum, where the famous are immortalized. The famous department store HARRODS where you can buy 'absolutely anything', is close to KNIGHTSBRIDGE. Wander round the food hall there – they sell every type and variety of eats you've ever imagined. Other shops worth taking in for their sheer entertainment value are LIBERTY'S (the neo-Tudor building on Regent Street) and FORTNUM AND MASON, Piccadilly.

ACCOMMODATION

London has some wonderful hotels – institutions such as the Ritz, Waldorf, Savoy, and Claridge's, steeped in tradition and offering unbeatable facilities. However London is also one of the most expensive cities in the world for a hotel bed, and in high season the 14 million visitors who descend on the capital lead to an accommodation crisis, so pre-booking is wise.

● **First Class:** (Double over £100)
The Hilton – Park Lane, W1 (tel. 493 8000). Fine views, excellent location and all the first class facilities one would expect, including particularly good restaurants and bars.

Mayfair Inter-Continental – Stratton Street, W1 (tel. 629 7777). A wonderful hotel in the very centre of the capital. Truly de luxe service – many little extras, well appointed rooms, and restaurants and bars as exclusive as you'll find anywhere in the West End. Surprisingly this first class establishment has remained one of London's best kept secrets, so a pleasant feeling of peace predominates. Booking is advisable, though not always necessary.

The Savoy – Strand, WC2 (tel. 836 4343). One of the world's great luxury hotels, situated between the City and the West End. A favourite with the theatrical crowd and noted for its fine restaurant and grill. Booking essential.

● **Super Club Class:** (Double £40–£70)
Regent Palace – 12 Sherwood Street, W1 (tel. 734 7000). The position of this hotel is its biggest plus – right in the centre of London, on Piccadilly Circus.

Great Western Hotel – Praed Street, Paddington, W2 (tel. 723 8064). Next to Paddington Station. A comfortable and tastefully restored hotel.

Royal Court – Sloane Square, SW1 (tel. 730 9191). Handy for the fashionable Chelsea area, and comfortably fitted out.

London Tara – Wrights Lane, W8 (tel. 937 7211). Off Kensington High Street. Not much atmosphere, but very comfortable and well priced.

• **Economy:** (Double £20–£40)

YMCA – 112 Great Russell Street, WC1 (tel. 637 1333). Excellent facilities in a central location.

Manor Court – 35 Courtfield Gardens, SW5 (tel. 373 8585). Basic but comfortable, and good value by London standards.

Vicarage Hotel – 10 Vicarage Gate, W8 (tel. 229 4030). Again good value and handy for Kensington and the centre.

Elizabeth – 37 Eccleston Square, SW1 (tel. 828 6812). As good a place as you will get at low prices in this smart location.

Oxford House – 92 Cambridge Street, Pimlico, SW1 (tel. 834 6476). Very good prices for London, and a clean central base for sightseeing trips.

White House Hotel – 12 Earls Court Square, SW5 (tel. 373 5903). One of the most attractive economy bases in London.

St Margaret's Hotel – 26 Bedford Place, Bloomsbury, WC1 (tel. 636 4277). Handy for the British Museum and central shopping.

Court Lodge Hotel – 7 Sussex Place, Paddington, W2 (tel. 723 0418). Basic but acceptable.

DINING OUT

There is no food that cannot be had in London. Restaurants of every cuisine and nationality exist, and the choice is quite staggering. Menus are generally posted outside. Credit cards are not always accepted, so check first. Lunch is usually a lighter affair, and cheaper than dinner, which is the main meal of the day. Tourist menus can be easily found. Check that cover charges and all taxes are included, and note that eating out on a Sunday is restricted by the number of restaurants which close.

Soho is *the* area for restaurants, especially good Chinese cuisine. Indian restaurants can be found all over the capital, and French and Italian are the mainstay of many of the smart restaurants. Singapore, Japanese, Turkish, Greek . . . the list goes on. Head into the West End area to sample the more exotic.

• **First Class:** (£50–£70 for two)
Langan's Brasserie – Stratton Street, W1 (tel. 493 6437). Reservations essential to ensure a place in this fashionable London bistro which does its main trade in after-theatre dinners.

Connaught Hotel Restaurant – Carlos Place, W1 (tel. 499 7070). Exclusive and steeped in tradition, the restaurant here is world-renowned for its excellent menu and wine list.

Shogun Restaurant – Britannia Inter-Continental, Grosvenor Square, W1 (tel. 493 1877/1255). Generally regarded as the finest Japanese restaurant in London. A gastronomic experience not to be missed. The yakitori is particularly good. Book ahead.

• **Super Club Class:** (£30–£50 for two)
Le Bistingo – A bistro chain with restaurants all over central London. Well priced and full of 'trendies'. Try the branches at 235 King's Road, SW3 (tel. 352 2350); Lower Grosvenor Place, SW1 (tel. 834 0722); and 57 Old Compton Street, W1 (tel. 437 0784).

Fredericks – Camden Passage, N1 (tel. 359 2888). Good food, good wines and an imaginative setting (the conservatory is worth a look).

Wind in the Willows – 4 Elliot Road, W4 (tel. 995 2406). Wonderfully imaginative dishes served in this tiny 'inglenook' restaurant.

• **Economy:** (£15–£30)
Poons – 4 Leicester Street, WC2 (tel. 437 1528). Chinese food at its best in the heart of Soho.

Khans – 13 Westbourne Grove, W2 (tel. 727 5420). Excellent Indian cuisine for very reasonable prices in atmospheric restaurant. Booking advisable.

Blooms – 90 Whitechapel High Street, E1 (tel. 247 6001). Kosher restaurant which comes to life on Sunday mornings when the Petticoat Lane Market is on. Cheap and interesting.

Neal's Yard – Neal's Yard Lane, Covent Garden, WC2 (tel. 836 3233). Wonderfully healthy soups and wholefoods here for very low prices. No need to book, but queues start early in the lunchtime period.

Afternoon tea, the great British institution, can be best sampled at: *Harrods*, Knightsbridge; *Liberty's*, Regent Street; or *Fortnum & Masons*, Piccadilly.

NIGHTLIFE

Nightlife in London can be anything you want. It's all here: shows, theatre, ballet, opera, concerts, discos, dinners, films. . . . Nightclubs offer temporary membership for visitors and are generally licensed until 2 a.m. All are expensive – a night can easily cost £50, and it's advisable to phone in advance. These few suggestions can be augmented by getting hold of a copy of *What's On*, *Time Out* or *City Limits*. The newspapers also carry listings of concerts, films, musical and theatrical events.

● **Nightclubs:**
Annabel's – 44 Berkeley Square, W1 (tel. 629 2350). Pricey to get in to this very select disco, but all the names and faces await you inside!

Hilton Hotel Rooftop Restaurant – 22 Park Lane, W1 (tel. 493 8000). Good entertainment laid on, and excellent cuisine. Suited to the older market.

Hippodrome – Leicester Square, WC2 (tel. 437 4311). The young will enjoy this super, high-tech disco designed by Peter Stringfellow. Two nights a week are specifically 'gay' here.

Ronnie Scott's – 47 Frith Street, Soho, is a famous jazz club well worth a visit if you're into jazz music.

Pubs and wine bars offer cheaper forms of entertainment and a way to meet Londoners. These few suggestions merely scratch the surface. (Licensing hours 1100–1500, 1730–2300; Sunday 1200–1400, 1900–2230.)

Brahms & Liszt – 19 Russell Street, WC2. Fun place with good food and loud music.

The Crusting Pipe – 27 The Market, Covent Garden (downstairs). Full of after-work execs; trendy, a bit pseudy but attractive.

El Vino's – 47 Fleet Street, EC4. Unofficial office for most Fleet Street journalists, plus the legal lot from courts down the road. Loads of atmosphere and a great man-watching haunt.

The Sun Inn – Lamb's Conduit Street, WC1. Historic pub with character.

London has over 4000 pubs and food is served in many of them. A pub lunch is a cheap and enjoyable way to fill up and meet the locals. Pubs are so much a part of the British scene that one has to visit some when in London.

EXCURSIONS

Whilst it is technically possible to make a day trip to places as far flung as Edinburgh, Inverness or Cardiff (by using shuttle flights) the suggestions here concentrate on the places within a 20-mile radius of the capital. For further-flung suggestions see the section on *Major Sights of the Country* in the Great Britain section on page 568.

HAMPTON COURT PALACE was the Tudor palace residence of Henry VIII. It is surrounded by beautiful gardens and with an authentic Tudor maze. Rail, green-line coach or boat can take you the 12 miles out of London to the palace.

WINDSOR CASTLE in the town of Windsor will be of interest to the historically minded. The reception rooms, royal mausoleum and St George's Chapel are well worth seeing in this still much-used royal residence. A walk away is the famous ETON COLLEGE, the most famous of England's 'public' schools. There are several buses daily to Windsor, and the train journey takes 35 minutes.

RICHMOND PARK, west of London, makes for a relaxing day's walking in the countryside looking on to the capital. An ideal summer picnic venue.

GREENWICH is best reached by boat. Charing Cross Pier, Victoria Embankment, is where boats leave in summer to take you the 50-minute trip down the Thames to Greenwich village. Alternatively, if you've no sea legs, you can take the train from Charing Cross or Waterloo to Maze Hill. The fruits of both Inigo Jones and Christopher Wren can be seen here, along with a vast collection of astronomical and navigational equipment.

BRIGHTON, the popular 18th-century seaside resort, makes an interesting day trip. Only 50 minutes from London, the sights here include the opulent Royal Pavilion and the shops of the 'Lanes'.

Italy

RED TAPE

• **Passport/Visa Requirements:** Most travellers only require a full passport to enter Italy. You will generally not have to obtain a visa or produce proof of a return ticket.

CUSTOMS

• **Duty Free:** The following may be brought into Italy without incurring customs duty:

By residents of European countries travelling from an EEC country: 200 cigarettes or 50 cigars or 250g of tobacco; 1 litre of spirits or 2 litres of fortified or sparkling wine or 2 litres of still wine; 50g of perfume and 250g of toilet water, 750g of coffee; 150g of tea; and goods to the value of L340,000.

By residents of European countries travelling from a non-EEC country: 200 cigarettes or 50 cigars or 250g of tobacco; 2 litres of alcoholic beverages up to 22 per cent or 0.75 litres over 22 per cent; 50g perfume and 250g of toilet water; 500g of coffee; 100g of tea; and goods to the value of L15,000.

By other passengers: 400 cigarettes or 100 cigars or 500g of tobacco. Other allowances as for residents of the EEC from a non-EEC country.

HEALTH

1. There are no risks from malaria, cholera or yellow fever, though inoculation against typhoid/polio is advised.

2. Water is drinkable in most places. In some rural areas you will need to boil drinking water.
3. Reciprocal health agreement with EEC covers general medical costs (UK travellers should obtain form E111 from the DHSS). Insurance is advised for specialist treatment.

CAPITAL – Rome. Population – 3 million.

POPULATION – 58 million.

LANGUAGE – Italian. German is spoken in the far north and some French and German understood in most big cities.

CURRENCY – Lira (L). Coins – L 100, 200, 500 and 1000. Notes – L 500, 1000, 5000, 10,000, 20,000, 50,000 and 100,000. £1 = L2000; US$1 = L1500.

BANKING HOURS – 0830–1300 and 1500–1600 (Monday–Friday). Money can be exchanged at a slightly lower rate at exchange offices (cambio) which remain open until 1800.

POLITICAL SYSTEM – Parliamentary democracy.

RELIGION – Roman Catholic.

PUBLIC HOLIDAYS

January 1	New Year's Day
March/April	Easter Monday
April 25	Liberation Day
August 15	Assumption of the Virgin
November 1	All Saints' Day
December 8	Immaculate Conception
December 25, 26	Christmas

Local feast days are held annually in honour of a town's patron saints.

CLIMATE – The north has pleasant summers and cool wet winters, while the south is mild all year round, getting very hot in the summer, especially in the extreme south. Nearly all of Italy is very

604   The Round the World Air Guide

pleasant from spring through till autumn, though avoid the south in the summer if you don't like the heat. In the north, the climate in the mountains can be quite hostile during winter with heavy snowfalls.

You should take lightweight cottons and linens during summer, except in the mountains where warmer clothes will be required. During winter you will need light to medium weights in the south, warmer clothes elsewhere and alpine wear in the mountains.

TIME DIFFERENCE – GMT + 1 hour.

COMMUNICATIONS

● **Telephone:** There is full IDD service in Italy, but you need to phone from a special international call box. These have yellow signs and also require special tokens (gettoni). The IDD code for Italy is 39. To phone out of Italy the international access code is 00.

● **Post:** Letters up to 200g: L600. Postcards: L400.

ELECTRICITY – 220v AC.

OFFICE/SHOPPING HOURS – Offices are open 0830–1300 and 1400–1730 (Monday–Friday). Shops are open 0900–1300 and 1600–1930 in winter and 0900–1300 and 1600–2000 in summer.

● **Best Buys:** Some of the best and most exclusive (designer) clothes can be bought in Italy, and dresses, stockings, hats, linen, shoes, gloves, silk ties and shirts, and knitwear will all be of the highest quality. Other suggestions include: lace; leather goods (handbags, luggage, shoes); cloth (silk, linen, wool, cotton); pottery; gold and silverware; marble and alabaster objects; woodwork; straw and raffia works; glass and crystal; wines and spirits; art books and reproductions; and local handicrafts.

INTERNAL TRAVEL

● **Air:** Italy has around 30 domestic airports, of which 10 handle international traffic. Services are operated mainly by Alitalia, the national carrier. All parts of the country are covered and there are reductions of up to 50 per cent for family travel and 30 per cent if you travel at night. Students get a 25 per cent discount and full details can be obtained from the airline offices or a local travel agent.

• **Rail:** There is an extensive network which criss-crosses the whole country. The fastest and most comfortable trains are the air-conditioned Super-Rapido trains which contain only first class seats with reservation being compulsory. 'Travel-at-will' tickets can be bought for periods of 8, 15, 21, and 30 days, and these represent extremely good value for money. There is also the 'chilometrico' ticket which is valid for 3000 kilometres and which can be used by up to 5 people at the same time, for a maximum of 20 journeys. Price: L90,000 (second class); L160,000 (first class). Circular returns (return journey by a different route) are also available and tourists can get discounts on day and 3-day returns.

• **Road:** There are nearly 4000 miles of motorway in Italy, providing excellent routes to all parts of the country. Tolls are imposed on many roads to pay for the upkeep of the system. In case of emergency, dial 116 from the nearest phone box for the free tourist breakdown service. Tourists can get a reduction on petrol, but only if their vehicles are registered outside Italy (i.e. this won't apply to cars hired in Italy). Fuel cards can be ordered through CIT (England) Ltd at 50/51 Conduit Street, London W1, or any RAC or AA regional main office. They are also available on the Italian border, but you will save valuable holiday time getting them in advance. As a tourist, you can even get reductions on toll charges.

Good coach services run between towns and cities and there are numerous local buses. In more remote areas, buses will normally connect with rail services. Hire cars are available in most cities and resorts from about L500,000 for a week (unlimited mileage). Remember that local firms will be cheaper than the big international firms. Drivers must carry an International Green Card or some other form of insurance. A British driving licence is valid if accompanied by a translation, which is available, free of charge, from the AA, RAC, ACI frontier and provincial offices of the Italian Tourist Board. Scooters are an inexpensive and convenient way of getting round the resorts and can be hired from around L15,000 daily. Traffic proceeds on the right.

Taxis are available in and between all towns and cities, and all major towns have extensive networks of public transport including buses, trams, trolley-buses, and in the larger cities, metros.

Anybody intending to travel extensively in Italy should obtain a copy of *Italy: A Traveller's Handbook* (published by the Italian State Tourist Office) which is available from Tourist Offices. It contains all manner of useful tips on travelling in Italy, ranging from instructions on the highway code to prices of air, rail and ferry tickets.

MAJOR SIGHTS OF THE COUNTRY

As befits the most visited country in Europe, Italy has an enormous range of sights, spread over the whole country.

• **The North:** In the districts of Piedmont and Valle d'Aosta in the extreme north-west lie the ITALIAN ALPS, featuring some of the highest and most spectacular mountains in Europe including the MATTERHORN. Together with the DOLOMITE range further east, the Italian Alps provide some of the finest skiing in the world, as well as a host of other winter sports. Excellent winter resorts are to be found in all of Italy's northern provinces, from CERVINIA in the west to CORTINA D'AMPEZZO in the east. At the foot of the Alps in the regions of Piedmont and (especially) Lombardy, lie some of Europe's most beautiful lakes. LAKE COMO is bordered by many attractive towns and villages; LAKE GARDA is dominated by towering peaks; and LAKE MAGGIORE snakes all the way to the Swiss Alps with there being numerous opportunities for scenic cruises. Smaller lakes such as LAKE ORTA are also becoming increasingly popular with tourists and locals alike.

Piedmont's capital, TURIN, is situated on the banks of the Po and surrounded by the majestic Alps. There is an unmistakably French feel to the city, which takes great pride in being known as the 'Paris of Italy'. The city is characterized by its elegant architecture and magnificent squares, with the Piazza San Carlo considered to be one of the finest in Italy. Apart from several good (and diverse) museums, Turin's most famous attraction is the Holy Shroud, which is said to have been the very shroud in which Jesus was wrapped when he was taken from the cross. Neighbouring Lombardy's capital is MILAN, Italy's northern centre of business, art and fashion. At the heart of the city is the Piazza del Duomo with its imposing gothic cathedral, which is the second biggest church in the world. Near here is the smart gathering place of the Galleria Vittorio Emanuele, and the Piazza de la Scala, with its world-famous opera house, the Teatro della Scala. There are many fine art galleries in the city, notably the Palazzo di Brera which contains one of the finest collections in Italy, and the Palazzo dell' Ambrosiana, which features works by all the great painters of the Renaissance, including Leonardo da Vinci, whose epic 'Last Supper' can be seen elsewhere in the city, on the wall of the refectory of Santa Maria delle Grazie.

South of Piedmont the twin rivieras of Liguria stretch along the Mediterranean coast for 217 miles with fine beaches and lively resorts such as SAN REMO. Despite bad pollution problems, these resorts can get terribly crowded during the summer months, especially the chief attraction of GENOA. This is a fine old city with an attractive medieval quarter and over 400 churches, and is at its best in spring during the opera season – before the hordes arrive.

Over to the east coast, and VENICE: possibly the most beautiful city in the world. Everybody knows its main sights: St Mark's Square, regal and magnificent with its great Basilica, one of the finest churches in the world with its incredibly rich interior; the Doge's Palace, next door to the Basilica and also possessing a rich interior with vast rooms in pink and white marble; and, of course, the Bridge of Sighs, which is, to be honest, rather dwarfed by the other attractions of the city. If you are prepared to splash out, you can take a tour in a gondola down Venice's 200 canals. Otherwise, there are cheaper motorboat excursions around the main sights, and most of these can be reached on foot too (remember that no cars are allowed in the city). Try to avoid visiting Venice in the summer when both the crowds and the prices are monstrous. Many find that the city is at its serene best around Christmas, when the ancient and decaying 'streets' take on a strange ethereal presence in the hazy winter sunshine.

The Cipriani is *the* hotel in Venice. For seclusion, sumptious surroundings and general five-star luxury, book your room ahead (tel. 707744).

Much of the splendour of Venice is echoed in the other cities of the Veneto. PADUA, 20 miles west of Venice (you can take a lengthy canal trip to reach it) is a fine medieval city with a famous university, and both VICENZA and VERONA contain buildings of great architectural merit. Visitors should take the opportunity of experiencing open-air opera in the splendid Roman arena at Verona. Further east, the area around TRIESTE has a strong Slavic influence, and with its varied scenery and good beaches, which are incidentally far cleaner than those around Venice, the area is well worth exploring.

In Emilia, BOLOGNA has splendid Renaissance buildings and a fine gothic cathedral, the great Church of San Petronio. It is also the home of that most Italian of dishes, spaghetti bolognese, and the city contains any number of excellent restaurants. Further up the Emilian Way, the old Roman road which connects Milan with Rimini on the Adriatic, is PARMA, another city with both an artistic and culinary reputation, which was the home of Verdi. His operas are still regularly performed in the charming opera house. Near Rimini, RAVENNA, once the capital of the Byzantine Empire, is famous for the mosaics which adorn its principal churches.

Perched on top of imposing Mount Titano on the Adriatic coast, the tiny republic of SAN MARINO ekes out a living solely from its stamps and from tourism. Its medieval fortresses are still in good condition, and it's worth the trip up from the Adriatic resorts for the view alone.

● **The Centre:** FLORENCE, superbly crammed with treasures of architecture and art, is one of the finest cities in the world. Everywhere there are churches, palaces, bridges, and statues, all of outstanding beauty, which bear tribute to a host of famous Florentines. The celebrated Uffizi Gallery contains perhaps the finest collections of Old Masters in the world, and there is a good modern gallery too. Statuary is also well represented and the Accademia di Belle Arti, near to the Uffizi, contains several examples of Renaissance sculpture including the most well known: Michelangelo's sublime 'David'. There are numerous architectural delights including the cathedral, with its distinctive marble layers and giant frescoed dome. Next to the cathedral, Giotto's 14th-century campanile has been called the most beautiful bell tower in the world. The Pitti and Strozzi palaces are both outstanding, as are the churches of San Lorenzo, with the famous tombs of the Medici nearby, and San Marco, whose museum contains the most important works of Fra Angelico, including his 'Annunciation'.

One of the highlights of any European tour is a stay in the Villa San Michele, a magnificent Michelangelo-designed monastery, now turned into a luxury hotel. Situated 15 minutes' drive from Florence city centre, this small piece of Tuscan paradise needs pre-booking. The prices certainly reflect the jacuzzi-in-every-room type of luxury, but for a couple of days' relaxation or a honeymoon-type picturesque break, this is one of Europe's finest locations. It is on the via Doccia (tel. 05559451).

But Florence is not the only attraction in Tuscany, the whole region is full of historic towns and cities, and with its varied scenery of snow-capped mountains, lush countryside and wide, sandy beaches, it is not surprising that this is one of the most visited regions in all Italy. West of Florence, there are at least three delightful towns (LUCCA, PISTOIA and the city of PRATO) before you get to PISA, where all the major monuments, including the world-famous Leaning Tower which 'leans' around 14 feet off-centre due to a slight movement of the land during construction, are conveniently situated in the great Piazza del Duomo.

Also worth a visit are the charming towns of SIENA, perhaps the most complete medieval city in Italy and very popular with tourists, and AREZZO, whose delightful hilly streets contain many treasures, including della Francesca's great series of frescoes in the Church of San Francesco, 'The Story of the True Cross', one of the most important frescoes in the world.

Off the Tyrrhenian (Tuscan) coast, ELBA is a little island with pines and good beaches in abundance. Napoleon was, of course, exiled here although he apparently spent all his endeavours actually trying to get off the island. Elba is so pleasant that you really wonder why.

The region of Umbria to the south-east of Tuscany has fewer places of interest but ORVIETO, at the top of an island of volcanic rock in the Tiber Valley, is an atmospheric city with a fine cathedral, PERUGIA has well preserved medieval streets of which the Via delle Volte is the most renowned and photogenic, and ASSISI's basilica on the Hill of Paradise which contains the tomb of St Francis and numerous other relics is a shrine for pilgrims from all over the world.

South of Tuscany and Umbria is Latium and, of course, ROME, one of the most historic cities in the world. Please turn to our *City Guide* to Rome on p. 613 for more details.

• **The South:** The major city of the south is NAPLES, and a city of contrasts. On the one hand there are fine squares and buildings, notably the sumptuous Capodimonte Royal Palace and the National Museum, which contains some of the finest treasures of the ancient world, while on the other, the city contains some of the worst slums in Europe. The people are friendly and exuberant, however, and are one of the chief attractions of the city. Naples is shadowed by MOUNT VESUVIUS, which erupted in AD 79, engulfing the towns of POMPEII and HERCULANEUM in red hot cinders and molten mud, and preserving these Roman communities virtually intact until archaeologists discovered them nearly 2000 years later on. Many other good excursions can be made from Naples: you can visit the tomb of Virgil on the outskirts of the city; the Roman amphitheatre at POZZUOLI which is smaller but better preserved than the Colosseum; LAKE AVERNUS, the entrance to the Underworld with the Greek colony of CUMA nearby; after Cuma, BAIA's hot springs made it into the largest and most dissolute spa of the Roman Empire. Also worth a visit, but a lot further south, is the Greek colony of PAESTUM whose imposing temples are considered among the best preserved Greek architecture.

The playgrounds of rich Neapolitans are the beautiful islands of CAPRI and ISCHIA. Capri is the more celebrated with its fine medieval remains and wonderful grottoes but both islands are equally crowded all summer.

In the extreme south, Calabria is one of the most unspoilt areas in all Italy with uncrowded beaches with clear water, and high mountains with picturesque villages where traditional handicrafts are still practised. Off the south coast, SICILY is a beautiful and varied island with a long history of colonization. Some of the finest Greek ruins are to be found on the island, including AGRIGENTO and its temples; SYRACUSE and its amphitheatre; and SELINUNTE with its huge Temple of Apollo. The cathedral at MONREALE, with its 6000 square yards of mosaics, is the most significant of all Norman buildings in Italy and the cathedral at CEFALÙ is not far behind. The capital of the island is PALERMO which also has a long history and many opulent buildings, but it is to beautiful TAORMINA that most tourists go. The still active volcano of ETNA bubbles in the distance and the beaches are clean and lovely.

Italy's second biggest island is SARDINIA which has a startling wild beauty. The rugged countryside is fringed with 800 miles of coastline, featuring countless deserted beaches with white sand and clear waters. This is possibly the best place in Italy to really get away from it all.

HOTELS

There are 40,000 hotels of all kinds in Italy ranging from international luxury hotels right down to cheap family pensions. Hotels are classified into 5 categories: Deluxe, First, Second, Third and Fourth; and pensions into 3: First, Second and Third. No hotel reservations can be made through the offices of the National Tourist Board (ENIT), though lists of available accommodation can be obtained. Reservations made through travel agents or hotel representatives tend to be for Deluxe or First Class hotels. Service charges and taxes are usually included in your bill, but you should double check this when you book. Hotel rates are generally reasonable but hotels in Milan, Rome and above all Venice can be very expensive. Those wishing to stay in converted historic buildings can obtain a list of such establishments from the Tourist Board.

NIGHTLIFE AND RESTAURANTS

All the big cities in Italy have a varied and lively nightlife, and the numerous resorts scattered along Italy's 15,000 or so miles of coastline come alive in the summer months. Two of these resorts, Venice and San Remo on the Italian Riviera, have casinos, and there are two more, at St Vincent in the Alps and Campione on the shore of Lake Lugano.

As the home of opera, Italy has several splendid opera houses, notably La Scala in Milan, the Teatro dell' Opera in Rome, La Fenice in Venice, the Teatro Comunale in Florence and the San Carlo in Naples. Genoa and Parma also possess quality opera houses. The season lasts from December to May or June and varies from city to city. There are summer seasons at cities with suitable outdoor auditoria such as Verona and Maccrata (both in July).

Film is well catered for and the most important film festivals take place in the crowded resorts of Venice (August–September), Sorrento (October) and Messina and Taormina in Sicily (July).

Italian restaurants are generally very good indeed – from a top notch 5-star establishment right the way down to a simple trattoria. In fact, as most Italian cooking is based on peasant and family traditions there is usually no need to frequent the most expensive restaurants, as you can eat just as well in the cheaper ones. In tourist cities many restaurants offer a limited-choice, fixed-price 'menu turistico' which includes the cover and service charges which would normally increase your bill by anything up to 20 per cent. Fish and truffle dishes tend to be quite expensive. It is best to reserve a table in advance for your evening meal and people generally eat later the further south you go.

Italian cuisine is varied, delicious and healthy, and is finally being recognized as one of the world's best. The most famous dishes are derivatives of pasta and pizza, which originate from the south while polenta (maize dumplings) and risottos are more popular in the north. Pasta is probably the staple diet in the south, and contrary to popular opinion, is not actually fattening – although some of the sauces are. In the south the sauces rely heavily on tomatoes as a flavouring while further north, pesto, made from basil, oil and garlic, is Genoa's famous variation. Grated Parmesan cheese is used everywhere as a topping for pasta dishes. Pasta is also used as a starter (antipasto) and in several soups, the most famous of which is minestrone. Pizzas are probably as popular as they are because you can choose just about any topping. The most common is probably Pizza Margherita, with tomatoes, oregano and mozzarella cheese topping, and most other pizzas add various other savoury goodies to this basic combination. Meat and fish dishes are popular as main courses, with veal, pork, chicken and lamb being the most popular meats used, while swordfish and mullet remain the most popular fish. These are usually served with deliciously fresh vegetables or salads, which are available from local markets along with excellent fruit.

Italy is also the home of ice cream, and there are any number of different flavours, with the most well known being a combination of vanilla, chocolate and strawberry: the Neapolitan.

A vast array of drinks is available in Italy. The wines are good, and generally speaking, the best reds tend to come from the north with Lambrusco, Valpolicella, and Barolo all well known as wines of quality. Chianti, Italy's best known wine, comes from central Italy, but you should also try the dry white Orvieto and the fruity, yellow Frascati from this region. Italy's sparkling whites such as Asti Spumante are worthy alternatives to champagne, and decidedly cheaper.

There is also a huge variety of aperitifs, sweet liqueurs, and fierce digestivi most of which tend to be variations of the throat-burning grappa, which is made from the third or fourth grape pressing, and distilled to at least 70° proof.

For a pleasant, non-alcoholic drink you can have a spremata which is basically freshly squeezed fruit juice, or a frullato which is a milkshake made with real fruit. In one of the many cafés you can have a frothy cappuccino coffee or just a plain coffee, of a blend far smoother than its French counterpart.

Rome

LEONARDO DA VINCI (FIUMICINO) INTERNATIONAL AIRPORT

Fiumicino Airport lies 21 miles to the west of Rome. It is served by 74 airlines and around half a million passengers use the airport annually. The buildings are on 3 levels: on the ground floor – International Arrivals, Domestic Arrivals and Departures; first floor – International Departures; second floor – catering facilities.

There are 2 terminals, Terminal 1 being International, and Terminal 2 Domestic. The terminals are linked by escalators.

AIRPORT FACILITIES

● **International Terminal:**

Information Desk   The main office is in the International Departures area on the ground floor and is open 0700–2400 daily. Tourist information is provided by CIT and ENIT offices in the International

	Arrivals Hall. CIT: open 0700–2400 daily (tel. 612318). ENIT: open 0900–1900 daily (tel. 6011459).
Restaurant	On the second floor. Self-service. Open 1100–1800 daily. There is a restaurant in the Domestic Terminal which is open 0600–2400 daily.
Snack Bar/Bars	The snack bar on the first floor is open 0600–2400 daily, and there are a total of 5 bars spread across both terminals.
Foreign Exchange	Currency exchange facilities are open 0700–2130 daily.
Bank	The Banco di Santo Spirito on the ground and first floors handles transactions. Open 0745–1945 daily.
Duty Free/Shops	There are 3 duty free shops in the International Terminal, open round the clock. Shops selling souvenirs, books, gifts and toys are to be found on the ground ﬂoor and are open 0700–2315 daily.
Chemist	On the first floor in the Departures Area.
First Class Lounge	There are 5 airline club lounges.
Lost Goods	Athe the 'Ufficio Oggetti Rivenuti' counter in the Arrivals Area. Open 24 hours.
Toilets	Throughout terminals.
Hotel Reservation	From CIT office in Arrivals.
Post	There is a Post Office on the first floor in Departures. Open 24 hours.
Medical	There is a vaccination centre in Arrivals.
Disabled Facilities	There are special toilets and rest rooms for disabled people, as well as ramps.
Meeting Point	At the Roman Catholic Chapel on the ground floor.
Left Luggage	Office located in Arrivals Area and open 24 hours.
Nursery	Two nurseries in the Domestic Terminal only. Open 0700–2315 daily.

Conference Rooms	None.
Car Rental	Avis, Europcar, Hertz, InterRent/ Autotravel, Italy by Car, and Maggiore have desks in Arrivals. Avis is open 24 hours (Monday–Friday) and 0700–2300 at weekends.
Taxis	From ranks outside. Beware pirate operators.

AIRPORT INFORMATION

Check-in Times	International – 45 minutes; Domestic – 25 minutes.
Airport Tax	Nil.
Transferring Flights	Proceed to the Transit Area. You should be able to get an international connection in 45 minutes. Domestic connections take around an hour.

AIRPORT HOTELS

None. The Hilton, Excelsior, Grand, and Holiday Inn all run courtesy bus shuttles, however, and the 'Intermezzo' bus does the rounds to several city centre hotels.

CITY LINKS

Leonardo da Vinci (Fiumicino) Airport is 21 miles west of the city centre.

• **Rail:** There are no direct connections at present, but you can take a taxi to the nearby underground station of Cinecitta, from where you can get to any station in town. The taxi fare is around L500, and the underground closes around 2330.

• **Taxi:** The quickest, if most expensive, way to the city centre. The journey takes around 40 minutes and you will pay up to L50,000, which is twice what the meter will read but there you go. Beware of illegal taxi drivers who do not drive the regulation yellow cabs and who will charge the earth to take you to Rome if they can get you in their cars.

• **Bus/Coach:** There is a bus service to the main railway terminal which leaves the airport every 15 minutes until 0015, then every half hour until 0800. Tickets cost L4000 and can be bought at the Acrotal bus company booking window near the airport exit at Fiumicino. The 'Intermezzo' coach travels to many city centre hotels and the top hotels run courtesy coaches.

• **Car Hire:** Cars can be hired from the airport 24 hours a day except at weekends, when the offices shut at 2315. Prices from around L500,000 per week (unlimited mileage).

TOURIST INFORMATION

The EPT (Provincial Tourist Organization) is based at Via Parigi 11 (tel. 461851) and has offices at Via Parigi 5 (tel. 463748); Termini Station (tel. 465461/475078); Autostrada del Sole, Roma Nord (tel. 691995); Roma Sud (tel. 9420050); and Fiumicino Airport (Arrivals) (tel. 6011255).

ENIT (Italian National Tourist Organization) has its office at Via Marghera 2 (tel. 49771).

You can find out what's going on by consulting *This Week In Rome*, available everywhere from newsagents.

ADDRESSES

UK Embassy – Via XX Settembre 80a (tel. 4755441).
US Embassy – Via Vittorio Veneto 119.
Emergency – Phone 113 for police, fire brigade, or ambulance.

GETTING ABOUT

• **Taxis:** Taxis wait on ranks or can be called by phone (tel. 3875). Use only the yellow, official cabs as you are likely to get badly ripped off by pirate operators. Prices are around average for a major city (i.e. expensive) and there are extra charges for night service, luggage, Sundays and holidays.

• **Metro:** There are 2 metro lines: the fast A line and the slower line B. Fares are around L400 and you must either have exact change for the ticket machines, or buy books of tickets in advance from tobacconists or newsagents. There is also a 28 km network of trams, consisting of 8 routes.

• **Bus:** The city's extensive bus network is operated by ATAC. The ATAC booth in front of Termini Station provides information and also sells maps, books of tickets and cheap tours. Fares are around L400 and you have to buy tickets in advance. It is more convenient to buy books rather than single tickets. Avoid buses during the rush hour when it will be quicker and doubtless more comfortable to walk to your destination.

• **Car Hire:** Cars can be hired at the airport or through hotels from around L500,000 per week (unlimited mileage), and scooters are an inexpensive, if risky, way of exploring Rome's narrow streets. Prices are from around L15,000 daily.

SIGHTS

Make sure you leave yourself plenty of time for sightseeing as there's an awful lot to see. Start at the PIAZZA VENEZIA, right at the heart of the city. Here is the grandiose Palazzo Venezia, from where Mussolini regaled the nation, and the huge Victor Emmanuel Monument, which is the site of the war memorial. Behind the monument is the Church of St Mary of Aracoeli. Next to this, and halfway up the celebrated Capitoline Hill, is the PIAZZA DEL CAMPI-DOGLIO, based on the plans of the great Michelangelo. In the Piazza you can see his elegant statue of Marcus Aurelius and visit his magnificent Capitoline Palace, now Rome's City Hall. The square also has 2 good museums and a gallery and directly behind it lie the

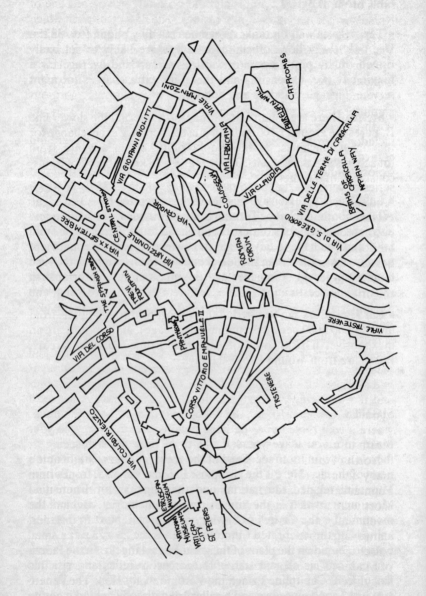

ruins of the Imperial Forums and the ROMAN FORUM itself, one of Rome's greatest architectural treasures. The best place from which to view the Roman Forum is the terrace reached by going down the Via del Campidoglio from the right side of the Senators' Palace.

From the Forum it is a short walk past the impressive Basilica of Maxentius and Constantine to the most famous of all Rome's monuments: the COLOSSEUM. This was originally an enormous amphitheatre, capable of holding some 50,000 people, but only the north-east side has really withstood the ravages of time which have included a major earthquake. It's still worth seeing, however, and you can climb to the top tier for an impression of how large the Colosseum used to be and you can also explore its bowels where a series of corridors, cells and passages have been unearthed, which used to serve for the organization of the spectacles.

Next to the Colosseum, the ARCH OF CONSTANTINE has 3 richly decorated arches of large proportions, but is suffering badly from air pollution. Also near here are the Trajan Markets, Column and Forum (the most impressive of the Imperial Forums which were erected by various Emperors whose egos were a sight larger than the original Forum); the ruins of the great Baths of Caracalla; and the imperial palaces of the Palatine and Celian Hills which are also ruined.

North of the Piazza Venezia runs the Via del Corso, the principal street of ancient Rome, which is today lined with churches and palaces. The PIAZZA COLONNA is a lively meeting place for Romans and also provides the location for the Column of Marcus Aurelius and the impressive Palazzo Montecitorio. Near here is the most famous fountain in Rome, the beautiful, baroque Trevi Fountain, where a coin tossed into the huge bowl is said to guarantee your return to toss another one.

North of the Fountain is one of the most picturesque of Rome's many squares, the Piazza di Spagna, complete with its Bernini Fountain and, of course, the famous SPANISH STEPS. From here it's a short walk to the Pincio, Rome's original public gardens, and the lovely VILLA BORGHESE PARK, with its delightful fountains, glades, statues and museums which include the Casino Borghese, a small palace containing numerous Old Masters, and the National Gallery of Modern Art. At the south of the park you can enter the famed VIA VITTORIO VENETO through the Porta Pinciana. The Via Veneto is Rome's great cosmopolitan boulevard, where a lot of the nightlife is concentrated. At the other end of the boulevard you can view the grisly subterranean chapels of the Church of the Capuchin Monks which are filled with skeletons.

South of the Via Veneto is the Piazza del Quirinale with its grand palace, which used to be the summer residence of the Popes, and now houses the President of Italy. Nearby is the National Museum with its important archaeological collections, and half a mile to the north-east the Porta Pia stands testament to the architectural genius of Michelangelo. If you continue along the Via Nomentana from here, you soon come to the Church of Sant' Agnuse, whose maze of 3rd-century catacombs provided one of the few places of refuge for the early Christians.

On the other side of the Villa Borghese Park, the PIAZZA DEL POPULO is a sizeable and harmoniously symmetrical square, where you can find the Church of Santa Maria del Populo which possesses one of the richest collections of art of all Rome's churches. Near here is the imposing Barbarini Palace, one of the finest baroque monuments in all Italy.

To the west of the Piazza Venezia lies the Church of Gesu, which is well worth a visit, as is the splendid PIAZZA NAVONA with yet another fine Bernini fountain as its centrepiece. Beyond the square stands one of the most venerable and best preserved monuments of Roman antiquity: the excellent PANTHEON. This was built (in its present form) by Hadrian and, as a pagan monument to a Christian cult, neatly interlaces the two cultures which have dominated the history of Rome. Hadrian also built the Castel Sant' Angelo on the western banks of the Tiber and there are panoramic views of all Rome from the castle.

The final destination left to visit, and one that should not be missed at all costs, is the independent and sovereign state of the VATICAN CITY, which is situated a mile and a half to the west of the city centre. You can see the great sights of the city without formalities, though large areas of the Vatican remain closed to outsiders. You arrive first at the immense and majestic ST PETER'S SQUARE, which took Bernini 10 years to complete. At one end of the square, which can hold anything up to half a million people, lies the most imposing basilica in Christendom, ST PETER'S: the biggest church in the world. The interior, featuring works by Raphael, Michelangelo (the celebrated Pietà) and Bernini, to name but three, is simply stunning, especially when viewed from the rooftop gallery, and the grottoes of the crypt are also well worth a visit. Don't miss the SISTINE CHAPEL, reached through the Vatican Museum, decorated with Michelangelo's unrivalled frescoes, notably 'The Last Judgement'.

ACCOMMODATION

Rome is well provided with accommodation but it is always a good idea to book well in advance. Make sure the quotation proffered is inclusive of service and taxes. Prices will be somewhat higher than those in the rest of Italy.

• **First Class:** (over L200,000 for a double)
The Grand Hotel – Via Vittorio Veneto (tel. 04709). Rome's most elegant and expensive hotel. Palatial rooms and superb service. Sophisticated grill room and restaurant.

Cavalieri Hilton – Via Cadolo 101, Monte Mario (tel. 063151). Situated on a hill in 7 acres of parkland, the Hilton has panoramic views over the whole of Rome. Pool, comfortable business facilities and excellent rooftop nightclub/restaurant.

Sheraton Roma – Viale del Pattinagio (tel. 05453). Very well equipped modern hotel situated between the airport and the city centre. Lacking the character of Rome's numerous older hotels, the Sheraton nevertheless has excellent restaurants and sports facilities and conference facilities for up to 2000 delegates.

• **Super Club Class:** (L75,000–150,000 for a double)
Hotel Lord Byron – Via de Notaris 5 (tel. 3609541). Classy 19th-century hotel with a relaxed, intimate atmosphere due to its shunning of large group bookings. The Le Jardin restaurant is one of the best in town and the hotel's private gardens offer peace and quiet in an otherwise noisy city.

Hotel Forum – Via Tor' de Conti 25 (tel. 6792446). A former Renaissance palace and now an elegant hotel right in the heart of the ancient city. The rooftop dining terrace has breathtaking views over the Roman Forum and the rest of the city.

Hotel Gregoriana – Via Gregoriana 18 (tel. 6794269). Delightful hotel which used to be a convent. Very small, intimate and reasonable. Book well in advance and ask for a room at the back.

• **Economy:** (under L60,000 for a double)
Dinesden – Via Porta Pinciana 18 (tel. 4751524). Old-fashioned and spacious, and surprisingly cheap considering the surroundings.

Aventino – Via San Dominica 10 (tel. 572831). Attractive and quiet location on the Aventine Hill.

Ivanhoe – Via del Ciancaleoni 49 (tel. 480186). Small, central hotel which is basic but pleasant and very cheap.

Sicilia Daria – Via Sicilia 24 (tel. 493841). Good pension in part of a palazzo near the Via Veneto.

DINING OUT

There are many first-class restaurants in Rome but you certainly have to pay for the privilege of eating in one of them. Many Romans prefer to eat in a simple trattoria, where the food will be good, the service friendly and the bill cheap. Tourist menus can often be dull and overpriced in comparison. Many restaurants close for the August holiday.

• **First Class:** (over L130,000 for two)
El Toula – Via della Lupa (tel. 6781196). Closed Sundays and August. Superb decor, cuisine and service. An outstanding link in the exclusive chain of restaurants belonging to Alfredo Beltrame.

Rallye – At the Grand Hotel (tel. 4709). Quality restaurant, elegant setting.

Carmelo alla Rosetta – Via della Rosetta 9 (tel. 6561002). All kinds of seafood flown in daily from Catania and exquisitely prepared by the Sicilian chef. Choice wine list.

• **Super Club Class:** (around L80,000 for two)
Trattoria del Pantheon (aka Da Fortunato) – Via del Pantheon 55 (tel. 6792788). Classic Italian cuisine served at tables which directly overlook the best preserved ancient monument in Rome. Good veal and fish, and extensive wine list.

L'eau Vive – Via Monterone 85 (tel. 6541095). Curious but classy establishment run by nuns in traditional garments. Mixture of Italian and French colonial cuisine. Closed on Sundays, funnily enough.

Al Moro – Vicolo della Bolletta (tel. 6782395). Popular restaurant near the Trevi Fountain. Book in advance.

• **Economy:** (under L40,000 for two)
La Campana – Vicolo della Campana 18 (tel. 6567820). Traditional family restaurant which is crowded with regulars who know they're on to a good thing. Try the red mullet, baby lamb cutlets, vignarola (vegetable soup), or shellfish risotto. Excellent cooking considering the price.

Padrino – Spaghetti Notte – Via Arno 38 (tel. 855535). Closed Mondays and August. Great late-night eaterie with over 30 different kinds of pasta.

Buca di Ripetta – Via Ripetta 36 (tel. 6789578). Closed Fridays. Tiny but popular restaurant near the Piazza del Populo.

Vecchia Roma del Severino – Via Monserrato 96 (tel. 6569383). Closed Mondays. Excellent family-run trattoria.

NIGHTLIFE

There are plenty of CLUBS to suit all types: The Cabala is a pleasant if dated spot on top of the Hostaria dell'Orso; more modern, and still frequented by the odd celebrity or two, is Jackie 'O' in the Via Boncompagni; for the energetic and youthful there is a blastingly loud disco at Via Ovidio 17 called Supersonic. Other clubs which attract a younger crowd include Much More, at Via Luciani 56, and the Veleno in Via Sardegna; Club 84 just off the Via Veneto is always lively and closes late; and Easy Going is a fun disco for gays at Via Purificazione.

You can relive the Hemingway era at the eponymous club in the Piazza delle Coppelle, near the Pantheon, and the pleasures of eating can be combined with entertainment at the glittering Open Gate restaurant/piano bar at Via San Nicolo, or the elegant Bella Blu at Via Luciani 21.

New clubs are always opening and some shut for the August holiday, so it is best to check in advance before putting on your dancing shoes.

Organized Rome-By-Night tours are not really worth bothering with.

For music lovers, the OPERA house is at Via Viminale and performances take place in the winter only. In the summer, however, it is possible to see open-air opera in the numerous parks and piazzas of Rome, along with theatre, folk and pop music, and circus performances. JAZZ lovers can attend the nightly Dixieland concerts at the Mississippi Jazz Club at Borgo Angelico 16, near St Peter's, and the Music Inn in Largo dei Fiorentini also puts on concerts. Programmes for all events can be found in the local press or in the *This Week In Rome* bulletin, available from newsagents.

EXCURSIONS

50 miles along the coast to the north-west of Rome lies TARQUINIA with its splendid medieval monuments including the Palazzo Vitelleschi, whose museum houses a major collection of Etruscan antiquities. The chief attraction of the town, however, is its necropolis, whose interesting frescoes give a rare insight into the customs and character of the ancient Etruscan people. Halfway to Tarquinia, CERVETERI also has an interesting Etruscan necropolis and you can take a pleasant dip at the nearby lakeside resort of BRACCHIANO. VITERBO, 20 miles to the north-east of Tarquinia, is another charming medieval city with many fine fountains. The main building of interest is the Papal Palace in the gothic style, but the whole of the medieval quarter makes for a pleasant walk.

20 miles to the east of Rome is TIVOLI, famed since antiquity as a patrician holiday resort and celebrated for its villas and waterfalls. Nearby is the VILLA ADRIANA, one of the most interesting archaeological complexes of Roman times, consisting of the ruins of an imperial villa built for Hadrian, with baths, temples and a small theatre. Continuing east, you come to the picturesque medieval town of SUBIACO, high in the mountains, where St Benedict founded 13 monasteries before moving on to MONTECASSINO further south, which is also worth a visit. At Subiaco, don't miss the main monastery of St Benedict, built around the Sacred Cave where the

saint passed the first few years of his monastic existence. The lower church consists of a series of chapels cut out of the mountain rock and has some splendid 13th-century frescoes.

To the south-east of Rome are the delightful Roman castles, which are dotted around the lovely lakes of ALBANO and NEMI. The most famous of these is FRASCATI, and after you have seen the castle you can enjoy a glass of the town's renowned crisp white wine. Continuing south-east along the historic APPIAN WAY there are many ancient monuments and Roman tombs.

If you continue travelling south-east, you come to a number of charming historical towns and resorts in the ALBAN HILLS. VELLETRI has a beautiful cathedral and the superb Trivio Tower, and the ABBEY DI FOSSANOVA, near Priverno, is considered one of the most beautiful Cistercian monasteries in all Italy. On the coast, SANT FELICE CIRCEO, besides being a lovely resort, is known for its caves, and TERRACINA, further down the coast, was a resort cut into the cliffs by the Romans. The imposing TEMPLE OF JUPITER ANXUR is nearby on the top of the cliff. Further south still, GAETA, gathered on a promontory under a fortress, has a noteworthy cathedral and there are some interesting caves close by, notably the CAVE OF TIBERIUS.

Also to the east of Rome, the area of LA CIOCIARIA is worth exploring. At PALESTRINA, 25 miles east of Rome, the magnificent ruins of the Temple of Fortune are to be found on the southern slopes of Mount Ginestro. There are more imposing ruins and an excellent Archaeological Museum on the upper slopes of the mountain, with a fine medieval cathedral further down. Further along the Via Prenestina, ANAGNI has a stunning romanesque cathedral with excellent frescoes. Other interesting buildings here include the medieval Town Hall, the Palace of Boniface VIII, and the well restored Barnekow House. FERENTINO preserves the ruins of some pre-Roman walls with some extremely ancient gates, and the fine medieval church and romanesque cathedral are also worth a visit. 65 miles from Rome, ALATRI is an ancient town with a splendid church at its centre. The town also features the best preserved hill fort in Italy, on the acropolis, and the interesting grotto of COLLEPARDO is nearby.

The coast of Lazio (Latium) has provided resorts for the Romans for thousands of years. Seaside towns of all ages are dotted along the coast and good resorts include ANZIO, now totally rebuilt after severe destruction during World War II, SANTA MARINELLA, GAETA and FORMIA, though all of these are packed solid during the summer season and at Easter. At OSTIA, the contrast between the beauty of the ancient town and the ugliness of the modern is rather saddening. The old town has several important archaeological sites and is well worth a visit, but avoid the new town.

Finally, you can take a boat trip to PONZA, around 25 miles from the coast of Lazio. This delightful volcanic island is crammed with tourists in the summer season but exceedingly pleasant off-season.

All major tourist agencies in Rome feature bus tours through both the environs of Rome and the Lazio area, and the local tourist board, while acknowledging the splendours of the capital, is trying to push other areas in Lazio as being worthy of equal attention.

The Netherlands

RED TAPE

• **Passport/Visa Requirements:** All most people need for a stay in the Netherlands not exceeding 3 months is a valid passport, and members of the EEC do not even need one of these provided they have an Identity Card, or a British Visitor's Passport for UK nationals. EEC members do not even need a work/residence permit for stays exceeding 3 months.

CUSTOMS

• **Duty Free:** The following may be brought into the Netherlands without incurring Customs duty:

By European travellers from EEC countries: 300 cigarettes or 75 cigars or 400g of pipe tobacco (persons over 17 years); 4 litres non-sparkling wine; 1.5 litres alcoholic beverages (over 22 per cent) or 3 litres under 22 per cent; 75g perfume; 750g coffee; 150g tea. Other goods up to the value of 720 Guilders.

By travellers from other countries within Europe: 200 cigarettes or 50 cigars or 250g tobacco; 2 litres non-sparkling wine; 1 litre alcoholic beverages (over 22 per cent proof) or 2 litres under 22 per cent; 50g perfume, and 0.25 litre eau de cologne and other lotions; 500g coffee.

By travellers from countries outside Europe: 400 cigarettes or 100 cigars or 500g of tobacco (same age restriction). Other limits as above depending upon country of origin.

HEALTH

There are no risks from the following diseases and immunization certificates are not required: yellow fever; malaria; typhoid/polio; cholera. The water is perfectly safe to drink and hospitals are excellent.

CAPITAL – Amsterdam. Population 700,000. (Although the government sits at The Hague.)

POPULATION – 14.3 million.

LANGUAGE – Dutch, with English, French and German widely spoken.

CURRENCY – Guilder (or Florin), divided into 100 cents. Notes are in denominations of 5, 10, 50, 100, and 1000 NLG. Coins – 5, 10, 25, 50 cents, and 1, 2.50 NLG.
£1 = 3.18 NLG; US$1 = 2.27 NLG.

BANKING HOURS – 0900–1600 hours, Monday–Friday. Money exchange offices (GWK) at Dutch border towns are open through Saturday, often in the evening and on Sunday as well.

POLITICAL SYSTEM – Constitutional monarchy.

RELIGION – Mainly Protestant.

PUBLIC HOLIDAYS

January 1	New Year's Day
March/April	Good Friday, Easter Monday
April 30	Koninginnedag (Queen's Birthday)
May	Ascension Day, Whit Monday
December 25	Christmas Day

CLIMATE – The Netherlands has a pleasant maritime climate, with average temperatures from 16° to 26°C (60°–80°F) in the spring and summer, and −4° to 16°C (24°–60°F) in the autumn and winter. The best time to visit is in the late spring when the days are sunny and the tulips are in full bloom. In the winter you will need a heavy overcoat, and a light coat is advisable in summer too, as the Dutch climate is every bit as unpredictable as that of Britain.

TIME DIFFERENCE – GMT + 1 hour (+2 in the summer).

COMMUNICATIONS

• **Telephone:** IDD service from anywhere. Public phone booths are easy to use and cheap, with instructions in English.

• **Post:** Fast and efficient. Post Offices are open from 0900 to 1700 hours (Monday–Friday) and some are also open from 1900 to 2030 on Thursdays and from 0900 to 1200 on Saturdays.

ELECTRICITY – 220v AC.

OFFICE/SHOPPING HOURS – Offices are open from 0800 or 0900 to 1700 hours (Monday–Friday). Shops are open from 0900 to 1800 hours (Tuesday–Friday). Many shops are closed on Monday mornings and most shut at 1700 on Saturdays.

• **Best Buys:** The blue and white porcelain from Delft is a popular buy, and leatherwork, pewter, crystal and silver are also worth shopping for. Amsterdam is excellent for shopping expeditions and the distances between shops are not great. You can arrange to send home flower bulbs as an unusual gift, or opt instead for the more traditional Dutch souvenirs of cheese, cigars or wooden clogs. Remember, too, that Amsterdam is the world centre for uncut diamonds.

INTERNAL TRAVEL

• **Air:** The distances in the Netherlands are too short to warrant travelling by air.

• **Rail:** The trains are fast, comfortable and clean. The extensive network is among the most efficient in the world, and all the lines are electrified. 'Rail Rover' tickets, which are valid for 3–7 days and offer unlimited rail travel, are very good value indeed. These can be offered with 'Link Rover' tickets which entitle the traveller to unlimited travel on public transport in all major cities.

• **Road:** Comprehensive network covers the country. Bus and rail timetables are integrated and there is a common fare structure. Luxury coaches operate between major cities as well as scheduled buses. Taxis are metered and available everywhere. Self-drive cars are widely available and comparatively cheap for Europe. An International Driving Licence is required, together with full insurance. Drive on the right-hand side of the road, watch out for the tricky one-way systems to be negotiated in many towns, and give way to cyclists coming from the right, of whom there will be many.

• **Other:** You can use ferries to get up and down the coast or up rivers. Amsterdam and Rotterdam have metros and there are still trams in many towns. With its near total lack of hills and highly developed cyclo-routes, the Netherlands is *the* place to exercise a bit of pedal power. Bicycles can be hired very inexpensively everywhere, so here's your chance to get fit while you take in the sights!

MAJOR SIGHTS OF THE COUNTRY

Low-lying and tiny, the Netherlands lacks the rugged, splendid scenery to be found in other countries. However, its golden North

Sea beaches, numerous lakes, 5000 miles of canals and fields of flowers ablaze with colour have attractions of their own. The landscape is dotted with picturesque villages and windmills, and ancient churches and castles bear testament to the country's rich and varied past. The Dutch are obviously proud of their cultural heritage and there are more museums in the Netherlands per square mile than in any other country.

After you have had your fill of colourful and cosmopolitan AMSTERDAM (see p. 632 for details in the *City Guide* section) you are ready to experience the 'real' Netherlands. Distances are not great and travel is cheap and convenient so there's no real need for guided tours. North of the capital are many unspoilt and beautiful villages such as historic MONNICKENDAM (8 miles) and MARKEN, where the inhabitants still wear traditional costume. 15 miles to the west lies HAARLEM with its preserved gothic buildings, featuring the oldest museum in the Netherlands. You shouldn't miss THE HAGUE, 45 miles south-west of Amsterdam, with its Houses of Parliament, Peace Palace, excellent museums and model city of Madurodam, which has been visited by well over 30 million people since it was first opened in 1952.

On the coast is the island entertainment complex of SCHEVEN-INGEN, one of many fine resorts along the coast. The casino here is the largest and most beautiful on the coast. The giant inland port of ROTTERDAM is another great place to spend your cash. Far more lively at nights than its close neighbour The Hague, Rotterdam has around 600 cafés which are open well into the early hours, after which you can dance till dawn at one of the city's throbbing nightclubs. During the day you can go to the fine zoo, scale the 607-ft Euromast Spacetower and take in the stunning views, or simply potter around the several good museums.

Between The Hague and Rotterdam lies the historic and beautiful city of DELFT, world-famous for its blue and white china produced there since the 17th century. Only 12 miles north-east of Rotterdam, GOUDA is famous for its delicious cheese, but also has many houses built in Early Dutch styles, particularly its Weighing Station and ancient Town Hall. One of the Netherlands' most noted landmarks is KINDERDIJK, with its 19 windmills, also around half an hour's drive from Rotterdam. Nature lovers should head north-east, where there are many lakes and forests with abundant wildlife. GRONINGEN is the ideal base from which to explore the north.

HOTELS

Dutch hotels are excellent, and while many are not that cheap, they generally tend to be spotlessly clean and provide efficient and courteous service, no matter how modest, especially the small but charming hotels to be found in the smaller cities, which are often family-run. There are two systems of grading: the national 5-star system and the newer Benelux 4-star grading system. 'H' on the national system represents a Hotelette which has not satisfied the conditions for a star classification. An open star is given to hotels which are outstanding for their group. Several good chains are represented in the major cities, and the Dutch Tourist Organization (NNTO) publishes a useful booklet which lists every town and city of importance, and nearly all Dutch hotels and their prices. English is spoken by hotel staff nearly everywhere.

NIGHTLIFE AND RESTAURANTS

The nightlife in the two biggest cities, Amsterdam and Rotterdam, is tremendous. Theatres, cinemas, concerts, cafés, bars, nightclubs (many open well into the night) – you should never be at a loose end in the evenings in these two cities. The Hague is well served by a selection of top-class theatres and numerous festivals take place throughout the year at nearby Scheveningen. In fact, there is plenty to do at night in every city in the Netherlands, though some places do close early.

The Dutch tend to eat early, and many restaurants are closed by 10.30 p.m. although you can get a snack in the big cities throughout the night. There are plenty of top-class restaurants, particularly in Amsterdam. The Netherlands is noted for its outstanding selection of Indonesian restaurants, and a good tip here is to ask for 'Grote Rijsttafel' (ricetable) which consists of a selection of up to 30 spicy dishes, served with rice. Less exotic is the Dutch cuisine. Various hot-pots are popular, as is pea soup (snert), and 'broodjeswinkels', which are basically soft bread rolls filled with all manner of tasty fillings and sold at street cafés. However, its dairy produce is excellent and justly famous. Try the butter and delicious cheeses at breakfast, when the Dutch like to eat a hearty meal. Wash down a meal with the excellent Dutch beer and afterwards sample one of the many Dutch liqueurs. The indigenous spirit is 'jenever' – the Dutch version of gin.

Amsterdam

SCHIPHOL INTERNATIONAL AIRPORT

Situated 9 miles south-west of Amsterdam, Schiphol is repeatedly voted the best airport in the world by leading air travel magazines. It is spacious, handling only 12 million passengers per year as against its capacity of 18 million, and relaxed, with a marked lack of announcements and obtrusive advertising. It has the biggest and cheapest duty free shopping centre in Europe and most facilities are open 24 hours per day. Around 65 airlines use the airport, and its city links are good. There is one terminal.

AIRPORT FACILITIES

Many facilities are open 24 hours.

Information Desk	Tourist Information (VVV) Office at extreme right of Arrivals near exits and information can also be obtained from the desk opposite the coffee shop to the left. Tel. 020-5110432.
Restaurant	3, including 5-star and Indonesian. Open 0830–2100 hours.
Snack Bars/Bars	6 bars and snack bars, 5 coffee shops.
Foreign Exchange/Banks	Adjacent to exits from main areas of Arrivals. Open 24 hours for exchange. Banks are open 0600–2300.

Duty Free/Shops	Massive tax-free shopping centre containing all kinds of goods. Shops at Piers A and D and at the lounge. Access restricted to departing travellers.
First Class Lounge	Open 0600–2200.
Lost Goods	Ask at Information
Toilets	On all floors of terminal.
Hotel Reservations	2 counters in Arrivals. Near main exits, opposite banks.
Chemist	Basement, open 0800–2100.
Medical Facilities	24 hours, under D Pier.
Meeting Point	In central area of Arrivals, next to lifts to multi-storey car parks and railway station.
Left Luggage	0600–2300 in Departures, cost 1 NLG per item.
Nursery	Situated to the left of Pier A in Arrivals. Free. KLM Junior Jet lounge for unaccompanied minors open 24 hours at D Pier.
Day Rooms	Between Piers A and B, behind nursery.
Conference Rooms	To the right of Pier B in Arrivals. 30–60 NLG per hour. Open 0700–2300. Tel. 020-5172180.
Disabled Facilities	Excellent facilities are provided for handicapped people in the terminal building. For special assistance, passengers should notify their agents well in advance.
Art Galleries	1 open 1130–2200 on 3rd floor. Other in lounge with mezzanine floor.
Aviation Museum	1000–1700, 750 metres from terminal. There is a bus, cost: 4.25 NLG.
Chapel	Lounge with mezzanine floor. Open 0530–2300.

Car Rental	6 offices situated near left-hand exits of Arrivals, all open from 0700 to 2300 hours.
Taxi Hire	Outside right-hand exits of Arrivals.

AIRPORT INFORMATION

Check-in Times	Domestic – 1 hour before departure International – 1½ hours before departure
Airport Tax	Nil.
Transferring Flights	There is a KLM Transfer Desk in Departures opposite Piers A and B, open 0600–2030.

AIRPORT HOTELS

• **First Class:** (over 350 NLG for a double)
Schiphol Hilton – Schiphol-C (tel. 5115911). The only airport hotel right at the airport. Two minutes' walk, or use the complimentary shuttle bus. The hotel has an indoor heated swimming pool and complete health club. There are conference rooms and 24-hour business facilities.
Sheraton Schiphol Inn – 195 Kruisweg, Hoofdorp (tel. 02503 15851). Further out, but slightly cheaper than the Hilton.

• **Super Club Class:** (150–300 NLG double)
Ibis Hotel – 181 Schipholweg, Badhoevepdorp (tel. 02968 1234).
The Golden Tulip – South of the airport on the Amsterdam/Hague motorway.

All the above hotels operate courtesy buses to and from the airport.
   Alternatively, the weary traveller could do worse than stay in one of the 16 excellent rest rooms at Schiphol. These are situated beneath the lounge area on the ground floor (Arrivals) between Piers A and B (tel. 020-174944). These cost just over 100 NLG per night for a double.

CITY LINKS

Schiphol International Airport is approximately 9 miles from Amsterdam.

● **Rail:** At last there is a direct link with Amsterdam Central Station (ACS), and given the comfort and efficiency of Dutch trains and the relative expense of hiring a taxi from the airport, this would seem to offer the best way of getting to central Amsterdam. The station is underneath the terminal, and there are lifts and escalators connecting it with Arrivals and Departures. Buy your ticket before you board or you will be charged extra. The fare is around 3 NLG. Until late at night 4 trains run to ACS (0515–0100) and it should be noted that there are direct links with The Hague, Rotterdam and Utrecht as well.

● **Bus:** The Dutch airline, KLM, operates a luxury coach service of great frequency (see timetable at airport) to and from ACS. The fare is 8 NLG and the first bus leaves Schiphol at 0410 and the last bus at 2315. There are also buses operated by Centraal Nederland which continue till 0013. You pay the driver (around 10 NLG) and the trip lasts 30 minutes. There are also direct buses to Utrecht every half-hour.

● **Taxi:** From the ranks outside Arrivals. These are available round the clock and the journey to the centre of Amsterdam takes 25 minutes. There is a flagfall of 3.60 NLG (over £1.00) and fares to the city are quite expensive (over 45 NLG). Tel. 150834.

● **Car Hire:** Cars can be hired at Schiphol from the following: Avis; Budget; Europcar; Hertz; InterRent; and Van Wijk European. All the counters are near the exits from Arrivals. Cars cost from 45 NLG for unlimited mileage.

TOURIST INFORMATION

The National Tourist Office (NBT) is at Vlietweg 15, 2266KA Leidschendam and open from 0900 to 2200 hours daily from Easter to October. For the rest of the year it is open from 1030 till 2100 (1800 on Sundays). In addition to this there is a local information office (VVV) at the Central Station (most VVV offices in the

Netherlands are at or near stations). This is open daily from 0845 till 2300 (Easter–October) and, from October–Easter, 0900–1900 (Monday–Saturday) and 1000–1730 on Sundays. The staff are courteous and all speak English. You can get helpful literature on hotels and the sights of Amsterdam.

ADDRESSES

UK Embassy – Koningslaan 44, The Hague (tel. 645800).
UK Consulate – Johannes Vermeerstraat 7, Amsterdam (tel. 764343).
US Embassy and Information Service – Lange Voorhout 102, The Hague (tel. 624911).
US Consulate – Museumplein 19, Amsterdam (tel. 790321).
GPO – Head Office, 182 Nieuwezijds Voorburgwal.
Emergency – In case of accident phone 555555 for ambulance.

GETTING ABOUT

Amsterdam is quite small and ideal for exploring on foot. *Taxis* are generally hired from ranks (the flagfall is 3.60 NLG) and are relatively cheap for Western Europe, but most people use public transport and there is a choice of *bus*, *tram* or *metro*. A zonal fare system is used. Tickets are purchased from automatic dispensers for the metro and you pay the driver on trams and buses. Strips of tickets can be purchased for all three and, even better, tickets which offer unlimited travel. These cost: 7.85 NLG for 1 day; 10 NLG for 2; and 12.25 NLG for 3. A good way of getting round is to hire a *bicycle*. These are very cheap and handy for negotiating Amsterdam's many narrow streets. Main thoroughfares generally have cycle lanes. Remember that local *car hire* firms tend to be slightly cheaper than the big international firms.

SIGHTS

There are lots of sights to see in the city, and the good news is that you won't have to travel around for hours to see them all as the distances in Amsterdam are not very great. Indeed, two of the best

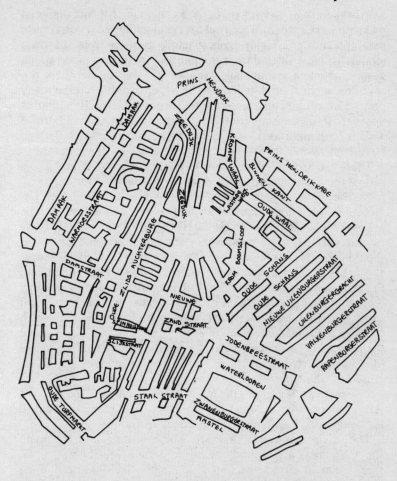

ways to see the city are on foot (start at Dam Square) or on a bicycle
(available from the Central Station). Another popular way to see
the sights, and one most tourists seem unable to resist, is a BOAT
TRIP round the canals. There are a number of starting points and all
are central: Damrak; Rokin; Amstel; and Nassaukade, near
Leidseplein. Make sure your boat has a glass roof and, if travelling
with a partner, consider one of the romantic candle-light boat trips
along the illuminated canals, complete with wine and cheese.

Visit the ROYAL PALACE on the Dam, built in 1640 and designed by Jacob van Campen. Watch out for the mantelpiece which depicts several scenes of a highly explicit nature from the lives of former monarchs! Near the Palace is the interesting NIEUWE KERK, which despite its name was actually founded in 1408. In fact there are countless architectural delights to be experienced: from the many pretty 17th-century almshouses dotted around, such as Begijnhof at Spui with its picturesque courtyard; to the modern work of Berlage and his contemporaries, such as the Stock Exchange which Berlage built from 1898–1903. You can go inside and view the galleries.

There are around 50 MUSEUMS in Amsterdam alone, and if this sort of thing is your cup of tea, then do purchase a 'Museumcard' from the VVV, which covers entrance fees to dozens of top museums (including many elsewhere in the Netherlands). The prices are 7.50 NLG (under 25); 20 NLG (over 25); and 12.50 NLG (senior citizens). The most important museums, and ones you should definitely not miss, are the RIJKSMUSEUM (National Gallery) at 42 Stadhouderskade, which contains many fine Dutch and Flemish paintings from the 15th–19th centuries, including possibly the world's largest collection of Rembrandts; and the VAN GOGH MUSEUM at 7 Paulus Potterstraat, near to the Rijksmuseum, which contains a magnificent selection of the master's work, covering all the periods of his career. Next door is the STEDELIJK (Municipal Museum) which has a very fine collection of modern art. Other museums which may be of interest include the Nederlands Historisch Scheepvart Museum – the maritime museum – and the Holland Arts and Craft Centre, which has permanent exhibitions of about 30 arts and crafts, including many live demonstrations.

The city's many MARKETS are worth visiting and the main shopping areas are around Nieuwendijk and Kalverstraat, while there are many attractive antique shops along the Munttoren. Even if you can't afford a diamond, you can arrange a visit to one of the diamond-cutting houses and a guide will show you round.

ACCOMMODATION

Accommodation can be a little hard to find during the flower season (April–May) and summer, although the situation is nothing like as bad as in some cities.

● **First Class:** (400–500 NLG for a double)

The Amstel Inter-Continental – 1 Professor Tulpplein (tel. 226060). The best hotel in town, with all facilities. Fine position near the Amstel, so ask for river view when booking. La Rive restaurant is exceptional, and the bar has great views. Recommended for those who want and can afford the best.

The Amsterdam Hilton – 138–40 Apollonaan (tel. 780780). Situated on a canal in the green heart of the city. All the usual business and sports facilities, plus the classy Diamond restaurant, but a bit pricey really.

American Hotel – Leideskade 97 (tel. 245322). City centre hotel of character. Two speciality restaurants and good business facilities.

● **Super Club Class:** (150–350 NLG for a double)

Amsterdam Sonesta – 1 Kattengat (tel. 212223). Interesting hotel with plenty of character and excellent facilities. There is a superior restaurant and coffee shop, and the conference hall is a converted church.

Grand Hotel Krasnapolsky – 9 Dam (tel. 554911). Good hotel in very central position. Three good restaurants, including top-class Japanese.

Rembrandt Crest – 255 Herengracht (tel. 221727). For those who want a taste of old Amsterdam, this hotel is in a row of fine restored houses.

● **Economy:** (40–150 NLG for a double)

Trianon – 3 J.W. Brouwerstraat (tel. 732073). Good position near to the Rijksmuseum and Van Gogh Museum and next to the Concertgebouw. Popular choice.

Sander – 69 Jac. Obrechtstraat (tel. 722495). Nice family atmosphere and good food.

Schiller – 26–36 Rembrandtsplein (tel. 231660). For those who want a decent hotel near the 'action'.

Canal House – 148 Keizersgracht. Splendid restored building with bags of character. Intimate hotel – only 14 bedrooms, all with shower, most with canopied double beds – and very central.

Wiechmann – 328 Prinsengracht (tel. 263321). Friendly hotel and handy for the Central Station.

Cok Young Budget Hotel – 30 Koninginneweg (tel. 646111). Don't be put off by the name, this is a nice hotel near Vondelpark and thus handily situated for culture-vultures.

In addition to those, the VVV office at the Central Station has a list of really cheap, central accommodation, usually dorms or twins, and failing this you can always take your chances on one of the houseboats behind the Central Station.

DINING OUT

Amsterdam has traditionally been a haven for refugees from all around the world, and they have certainly left their culinary mark on the city. In addition to the unparalleled range of cuisines on offer, most restaurants are very reasonable by Western European standards. You should be mindful of the fact that many will not serve food after 9 p.m.

• **First Class:** (over 200 NLG for two)
La Rive – At the Amstel Inter-Continental (tel. 226060). French cuisine of great class and sophistication at a hotel with a reputation to live up to.

Bali – 95 Leidestraat (tel. 227878). Expensive but well worth it. Best Indonesian food in town.

Vijif Vlieghen (Five Flies) – 294–302 Spuistraat (tel. 245214). The authentic 17th-century decor is possibly the main attraction here, but the place is always full.

• **Super Club Class:** (50–150 NLG for two)
Dorrius – 336–42 N.Z. Voorburgwal (tel. 235875). Probably best Dutch food you'll find, with the accent on fish. Popular with businessmen, closed Saturdays.

Fong Lie – 80 P.C. Hooftstraat (tel. 716404). Chicken and fish specialities and very tasty they are too. You probably won't get better Chinese food anywhere else in the city – certainly not at these prices.

De Groene Lanterne – 43 Haarlemmerstraat (tel. 241952). Very odd establishment: only 5 feet wide, with tables on 3 floors. Not for the overweight.

● **Economy:** (under 50 NLG for two)

Basically, the best advice we can give is head for Leidseplein/Jordaan area. Good, cheap restaurants abound, and you can find food from all round the world here in these lively surroundings. Beware of places advertising 'tourist menus', for there are plenty of excellent restaurants in Amsterdam and consequently no need to risk the food served by some of these establishments. Alternatively, have a meal in one of the city's famous *Brown Cafés*. These are sparsely decorated pub-like affairs, but full of character and well worth visiting.

Café Pacifico – 31 Warmoestraat (tel. 242911). Established Mexican café, and still the best of the ten or so Mexican restaurants which proliferated in recent years.

Het Paleis – 16 Paleisstraat (tel. 260600). Just behind the Royal Palace and excellent value. Good range of Dutch/Indonesian food and quality salads.

De Eettuin – 10 Tweede Tuindewarsstraat (tel. 237706). Cosy, inexpensive bistro with good self-service salad bar.

De Oesterbar – Leidseplein. As the name suggests, good fish specialities, and a central location.

NIGHTLIFE

There are certainly no problems finding something to do at night in Amsterdam. Apart from being one of the liveliest cities in Europe, there is the added bonus of not having to travel far to reach the various nightspots. There is a wide variety of bars, nightclubs and cabarets, with many to be found in the areas around the Leidseplein and Rembrandtsplein squares, which also happens to be prime red-light territory. The floorshow at the PICCADILLY at 6 Thorbeckeplein is popular with tourists, while the trendy BOSTON club is based in the Sonesta hotel at 1 Kattengat. At Halvemaansteeg, near to Rembrandtsplein the AMSTEL TAVERN is a lively bar with music. Other nightclubs open till 4 a.m. include the BLUE NOTE at 71–3 Korte Leidsedwarstraat and the MOULIN ROUGE at 5 Thorbeckeplein, and from 11 p.m. there is live salsa and modern jazz at DE KROEG at 163 Lijnbaansgracht.

There are classical music concerts at the renowned CONCERTGE-BOUW, 98 Van Baerlestraat (tel. 718345), and its equally famous orchestra also gives concerts at the remarkable THEATRE CARRE. Both classical and rock concerts are put on in the VONDELPARK throughout the summer.

There is both opera and dance at the STADSSHOUWBURG, the main municipal theatre, while modern dance can be experienced at the SHAFFY THEATRE at 324 Keizersgracht (tel. 231311), and smaller studios such as the DANCE LAB on the Wibautstraat.

THEATRE is thriving in the city, and apart from the Shaffy and Stadsshouwburg, two companies put on plays in English: The English Speaking Theatre Amsterdam which performs at various venues around the city, and The American Repertory Theatre at 4 Kerkstraat (tel. 259495). The Mickery at 117 Rozengracht (tel. 236777) is well known and progressive, and presents more alternative works. Every 2 years the FESTIVAL OF FOOLS takes place in Amsterdam, providing a wealth of street entertainment. Cinema is well represented too, and the best cinemas are the TUSCHINSKI at 26 Reguliersbreestraat, the biggest and most ornate cinema in Amsterdam, and THE MOVIES, at 161 Haarlemmerdijk, which is the best of the few independent cinema complexes in the city.

Finally, if all this isn't enough, those who prefer a more dubious form of pleasure can take comfort in the fact that Amsterdam is one of the few places in the world where cannabis is legal.

EXCURSIONS

As distances in the Netherlands are so small you could really go anywhere in the country (see section entitled *Major Sights of the Country* for details of cities such as The Hague and Rotterdam). Trips can be arranged through Holland International at Central Station, Damrak and Dam Square. The following are suggestions for day trips other than those to major cities. Most are pretty rural towns.

8 miles north of Amsterdam lies the charming town of MONNICK-
ENDAM and past here MARKEN and VOLENDAM, 2 picturesque small
towns where the inhabitants still wear traditional costume with
pride and not just for the tourists. EDAM is worth a visit, especially if
you appreciate its mild, round cheeses. There are more attractive
places further north in Westfriesland, such as the well preserved
port of ENKHUIZEN on the Ijsselmeer, and ALKMAAR, popular for its
fine old buildings and cheese markets. 15 miles to the west of the
capital lies HAARLEM, with many excellent gothic buildings, including the oldest museum in the Netherlands, the Teylers Museum.
Along the whole North Sea coast and islands are many fine
beach-resorts, all with excellent water-sport facilities. The fishing is
good at IJMUIDEN, while there is motor-racing at ZANDVOORT and a
good beach and a casino at KENNEMERDUINEN. At LISSE, 11 miles
south of Haarlem, there are attractive gardens, and from the end of
March till the end of May, a very popular open-air flower show.

West Germany

RED TAPE

• **Passport/Visa Requirements:** Nationals from EEC countries need
only their ID permits. A British Visitor's Passport is acceptable.
Most other nationals need only a valid passport. If you do need a
visa (most don't) it will cost 10 DM for an entry visa and 4 DM for a
transit. You can stay for 3 months, and residence permits can be
obtained from the local Aliens Office should you wish to stay
longer, but you must apply within 3 months of arriving.

CUSTOMS

• **Duty Free:** The following goods may be brought into the country
without incurring Customs duty:

By residents of EEC countries: 200 cigarettes or 50 cigars or 250g of tobacco; 2 litres sparkling wine to 22 per cent or 1 litre if above 22 per cent, and 2 litres non-sparkling wine; 50g perfume and 0.25 litre of toilet water; 100g tea and 250g coffee; goods to the value of 640 DM.

By non-European residents: The same except that goods to the value of 460 DM only may be brought into the country, with only 115 DM of goods from non-EEC countries.

The limits are increased by 50 per cent if you have paid duty on your goods.

HEALTH

There are no risks from yellow fever, malaria, typhoid/polio or cholera, although vaccination certificates are required if arriving from an infected country. The water is perfectly safe to drink and German health care is outstanding. There are also over 250 officially recognized spas with medical facilities which are open to visitors seeking therapeutic treatment.

CAPITAL – Bonn. Population 285,000.

POPULATION – 61 million.

LANGUAGE – German.

CURRENCY – Deutschmark (DM) = 100 Pfennig. Notes are in denominations of DM 5, 10, 20, 50, 100, 500, and 1000. Coins are in 1, 2, 5, 10 and 50 Pfennigs and DM 1, 2, and 5.
£1 = DM2.81; US$1 = DM2.

BANKING HOURS – 0830–1200 and 1330–1600 (Monday–Friday). Open to 1730 in main cities.

POLITICAL SYSTEM – Parliamentary democracy.

RELIGION – Approx. 45 per cent Roman Catholic and 45 per cent Protestant.

PUBLIC HOLIDAYS

January 1	New Year's Day
March/April	Good Friday, Easter Monday
May 1	Labour Day
May	Ascension Day, Whit Monday
June 17	Day of Unity
November 21	Day of Prayer and Repentance
December 25, 26	Christmas

In addition to these, there are public holidays in some regions on:

January 6	Epiphany
May/June	Corpus Christi
August 15	Assumption of the Virgin
November 1	All Saints' Day

CLIMATE – Temperate throughout the country with cold winters, especially in the south, and warm pleasant summers. Rain falls throughout the year but mainly in winter. The average temperatures are from 1.5°C in the lowland areas to −6°C in the mountains during January, the coldest month; and from 17/18°C in the north to 20°C in the Rhine valley during July, the warmest month. You will need a heavy coat in the winter, especially in the mountains where conditions can be quite severe, and lightweight clothes plus a raincoat in the summer. Waterproofing is advisable all year round.

TIME DIFFERENCE – GMT + 1 hour.

COMMUNICATIONS

• **Telephone:** Full IDD service. International calls can be made either from call boxes with the green sign 'Inland Ausland' or 'National International', or direct from your hotel.

• **Post:** Fast and efficient. 1 DM for a letter, 70 Pf. for a postcard.

ELECTRICITY – 220v AC.

OFFICE/SHOPPING HOURS – Offices are open 0800–1700, while shops are generally open 0900–1830. Some close between 1300 and 1500 for lunch, and others close early on Saturdays at 1400.

● **Best Buys:** There is an excellent range of goods available from large department stores, although prices can be quite steep. Good, quality buys are clocks/watches; field glasses; photographic equipment and tape recorders. For the souvenir hunter, ornaments, toys, ceramics and wood carvings all offer reasonable value for money.

INTERNAL TRAVEL

● **Air:** There are now 11 international airports in West Germany, with another 10 handling domestic flights only. Frankfurt is the focal point of internal air services, and all West German airports can be reached in 50 minutes' flying time at least 4 times daily. Services are operated by the efficient national carrier Deutsche Lufthansa (DLH).

● **Rail:** The Federal Railway System – the Deutsche Bundesbahn (DB) – is the largest public transport system in West Germany, and over 20,000 passenger trains run daily in the Federal Republic. The inter-city network connects 50 major cities with fast trains running at hourly intervals. All these trains are air-conditioned and extremely comfortable. There are various fare reduction offers open to the traveller. There are special rates for the young, old, and those travelling in groups, and any non-West German with a valid passport can purchase a DB Tourist card, which allows unlimited travel over the whole network for 4, 9 or 16 consecutive days. There are also 'Rail Rover' tickets which permit travel over a restricted area, usually about 200 km. These are ideal for exploring large areas of the country such as the Black Forest, south-east Bavaria, or central Rhineland, although there are 73 regions to choose from. Those under 23 (26 if still a student) can take advantage of the Tramper Monthly Ticket scheme which allows unlimited travel for a month and is exceptionally good value.

• **Road:** There is an extensive network covering the country featuring many Autobahns, which are the fastest roads in Europe. Coaches run by Europabus and the National Bus Company connect most cities and there is a rural network operated by the Federal Railway. Taxis are available everywhere and the use of meters is compulsory. The initial charge is 3.60 DM plus 0.80 – 1.5 DM per kilometre depending on time and distance. Self-drive cars are universally available. Many bus and train stations possess car hire facilities. Price: From 50–150 DM per day, plus petrol and mileage. An International Driving Licence is recommended and traffic travels on the right.

MAJOR SIGHTS OF THE COUNTRY

• **The North:** HAMBURG is the focal point of the north, and the second largest city in West Germany. There are many fine buildings around St Michael's Cathedral and to its east most notably the Renaissance Rathaus, and you can take an excellent trip around the largest port in the country – but it is Hamburg's outstanding nightlife which is the principal attraction. All the hot-spots are centred around the city's (in)famous St Pauli Reeperbahn district, where there is a phenomenal concentration of clubs and bars. To the north-east of Hamburg, and well worth a visit, is LÜBECK, with its beautiful medieval buildings and historic taverns, and 14 miles from Lübeck TRAVEMÜNDE is a lively Baltic resort with a luxurious casino. Further south, HANNOVER, a modern industrial city with a long cultural tradition, has 2 interesting castles and a world-famous zoo. West of Hannover lies HAMELN with its palatial, timbered Renaissance houses including the residence of the famous Pied Piper.

• **The Centre:** The Rhine valley is West Germany's heartland: its importance symbolized by the preponderance of healthgiving thermal and mineral springs in the area. As well as being the industrial powerhouse of the nation, the region is also an area of great beauty, its wooded slopes having long associations with German culture and wine-growing. BONN, the capital, is the gateway to the Rhine valley. It has buildings dating back to the 12th century and a rich musical heritage, being associated with both Beethoven and Schumann. There are plenty of country excursions from Bonn and the nearby Drachenfels, with its romantic castle ruins, is one of the most visited mountains in Europe. AACHEN to the west is a historic spa. Many of the later Roman emperors were crowned here and the great Charlemagne is buried in the cathedral. Further down the Rhine COLOGNE (Köln) is another city dating back to Roman times. Go during carnival time and don't miss its splendid selection of medieval churches, particularly the huge and magnificent cathedral with its Lochnar triptych and golden reliquary of the Three Magi. DÜSSELDORF is a centre of world fashion today, although it was an important cultural centre in the past as is evidenced by the Goethe Museum and outstanding Municipal Art Museum.

The most logical entry point for most people is FRANKFURT. The city has excellent international and internal communications but also many attractions of its own (see p. 651 for our guide to Frankfurt). The road north-east to GÖTTINGEN is liberally endowed with historic old towns, enchanting castles and medicinal spas. Hereabouts, old traditions and customs still survive and there is much to interest the lover of folklore. South of Frankfurt, the beautiful university town of HEIDELBERG is dominated by its impressive 14th-century castle. In the cellar, a 'Giant Cask' has a capacity of 48,422 gallons, which must have been sufficient to satisfy the most avid ancient drinker. The renowned drama festival takes place in July and there are plenty of open-air concerts. Or one can simply relax on a boat trip along some of the loveliest stretches of the river NECKAR. On another tributary of the Rhine, the Moselle, lies Germany's oldest town: TRIER. This was the famed Roman imperial capital of Porta Nigra and its remains are still worth visiting. Some of the best wines in Germany are produced near here on the banks of the MOSELLE.

• **The South:** Tucked into the south-western corner of West Germany lies the magical BLACK FOREST. Splendid scenery, a host of charming hillside resorts and the best climate in Germany combine to make this one of the most popular areas in the land. FREIBURG is the largest city/resort in the Black Forest and has a historic castle and lovely market squares. The country's oldest inn, the Röter Baren, is in the heart of the old town and the city is noted for its trout and game dishes. Take a cable car up the 4200-ft Schauinsland mountain and admire the stunning views. Further north, BADEN BADEN is an elegant mountain spa resort, with plenty of sights and excellent sports facilities. To the east ULM, with magnificent churches and preserved city walls, is just one of the many interesting places in this region. However, for concentrated picture-postcard beauty, just cross into Bavaria and take one of the special buses along the so-called 'Romantic Road' which connects alpine FÜSSEN with WÜRZBURG to the north. This is a trail of over 200 miles featuring some of the best scenery and picturesque medieval resorts in Europe. AUGSBURG, on the lovely Lech river which follows the early part of the route, is probably the finest, but there are so many places of note, that your only problem is going to be how long you devote to each.

MUNICH is the capital of Bavaria and a great centre of art and culture. Apart from its sights, the city appears to have something to celebrate all year round: from the winter Fasching (carnival), through the summer seasons of the State Opera and Theatre, to the famous Oktoberfest at the end of September, when beer drinkers and brewers descend on Munich from all over the world for a couple of weeks of revelling. The Germans drink more beer per head than any other national on earth and most of it seems to get consumed by the hearty inhabitants of Bavaria around this time. Fans of Wagner shouldn't miss the Richard Wagner Festival which takes place from July to August in BAYREUTH. Bavaria's other international festival only takes place once every 10 years when the inhabitants of OBERAMMERGAU present the Passion Play. The village is worth a visit for its dramatic scenery even if the play is not being performed, as are the ancient cities of PASSAU and REGENSBURG, which also makes a fine base from which to explore the Bavarian Forest.

Finally there is WEST BERLIN, the former capital and now cut off from the rest of the country through the partition of Germany after World War II. Unless you fly, you will need a transit visa to get across East Germany, but it's worth the effort. Its most famous sight is the 2-mile long Kurfürstendamm, which is both an ideal shopping and nightlife centre. There is no better place to go to sample German culture as the city has 18 theatres, the German National Opera, 14 museums and some 50 art galleries. Nightlife is excellent and accommodation is cheaper than in other large German cities.

HOTELS

There are around 45,000 establishments offering accommodation in the Federal Republic of West Germany, ranging from family boarding houses through inns up to the large international standard hotels. There are many good hotel chains in the country including the fascinating 'Romantik Hotels' which are all over a hundred years old and offer a high degree of service and comfort in buildings of great character.

NIGHTLIFE AND RESTAURANTS

There is certainly no shortage of things to do, especially in the larger cities of Germany. Hamburg, Berlin and Munich cater for all tastes and even in smaller cities there will usually be plenty to keep you entertained at nights, especially during summer festivals.

Although there is strictly no such thing as a national German cuisine, each region has evolved its own specialities. Most are meaty and all tend to be rich. There are countless variations of wurst (sausage) which Germans consume at any hour of the day, usually served with dumplings, bread or potatoes, and washed down with a glass (or three) of beer. Specialities include Falscher Hase (meat-loaf); Schweinebraten (roast knuckle of pork); Sauerkraut (pickled cabbage accompaniment to pork or beef) and Schnitzel, which are fried escalopes of pork, veal, or beef. There is a positive cornucopia of sweets to choose from and they are all slimmers' nightmares. Schwarzwälder kirschtorte is Black Forest cherry cake liberally soaked in cherry schnaps; Apfelkuchen is a spicy apple pie; and Käsekuchen is a rich and delicious cheesecake.

Both German beers and wines are excellent. Helles is light lager while dunkels is dark. The German house wine served in most restaurants is the excellent Mosel which is characteristic of most German wines: dry, light and fruity. Menus are generally displayed outside restaurants and service is included in the price, as is tax. Try eating in one of the numerous bier kellers when in the south, as many of the local culinary specialities are available within.

Frankfurt

RHEIN-MAIN INTERNATIONAL AIRPORT

The Rhein-Main airport is the third busiest passenger airport in Europe with an annual turnover approaching 18 million passengers. More than 75 airline companies use the airport, which has direct connections with 185 destinations in some 80 countries. This large airport is located 6 miles from the centre of Frankfurt, and is a favourite destination for those transferring flights, as transfers are guaranteed within 45 minutes. There is one terminal.

AIRPORT FACILITIES

Blue signs give information to arriving/departing passengers; green signs direct to service installations, and silver pictographs guide to various commercial facilities. All major facilities are open 24 hours.

Information Desk	Tel. 690 3051 for information. There are desks in Arrival Hall B, Transit Hall B and 2 in Departure Hall A. Some of these shut at 2100.
Restaurants/Snack Bars	There are 9 restaurants in the terminal and a total of 30 establishments where you can get a drink or a bite to eat at any time of the day.
Foreign Exchange/Banks	Money can be exchanged at all banks in Halls A, B, and C. Money-changing facilities are available round the clock, and the banks have extended hours for business travellers.
Duty Free/Shops	An extensive array of products is available from the 100-plus shops

which stock everything from antiques to marital aids. These are situated in Departures A, B, and C and also in the Transit Hall. Passengers should remember to fill in VAT refund forms on purchases made in the airport. Once home, the shops will arrange for 14 per cent of the cost of your goods to be refunded.

Chemists
In Departure Hall B and on Level 0 – 'Unterm Flughafen' (tel. 690 2880).

Post Offices
In Departures B and Transit Hall B.

First Class Lounge
This is the Europe City Club Lounge situated in Departure Hall B (tel. 690 3718). There is also a British Airways Executive Lounge in Departure Hall B (tel. 690 2970). VIP travellers can book CIP (Commercial Important Persons) treatments (tel. 690 3659 or 690 3751 in advance).

Toilets
Throughout terminal.

Left Luggage
The offices are located on the Departure level between Halls B and C and on the Arrival level between Halls A and B.

Lost Luggage
The lost and found office is in Arrival Hall A and open 0700–1900 hours (tel. 690 6359). There is also a baggage tracing service operated by the airport company (tel. 690 6358) and other airlines. To contact the Airport Police, tel. 110.

Airport Clinic
Situated between Halls B and C on the Departure level and open 24 hours (tel. 690 2030).

Nursery
Day nurseries are provided by airlines as well as the service for

Unaccompanied Minors (UM). Tel. 690 5061 for assistance from Social Services in the Departure area. Baby rooms are available for changing nappies and nursing in Halls A, B and C.

Disabled Facilities	There are special parking spaces in the car park from where supervisors can be called to provide assistance. Lifts are located in Hall B. Further information and assistance provided by airlines.
Baggage Transport	Porters available in Hall B. Call 690 3469.
Meeting Point	Is located in Arrival Hall B.
Hotel Reservations	These are provided by the airport travel agency in Arrival Hall B (tel. 690 6211 or 690 6212).
Conference Rooms	These can accommodate up to 150 persons and are located in the Departure area between Halls A and B. For reservations tel. 690 5229 or 690 3088.
Bus Tours	Guided tours of the airport are organized by Flughafen Frankfurt/ Main AG. For advance booking tel. 690 4013.
Cinemas	'Unterm Flughafen', Hall C.
Sightseeing	Gallery in Departure Hall B. Price 3 DM (2 DM for children under 16).
Discotheque	
Ninepin Bowling	
Airport Exhibitions	In the Gallery between Departure Halls A, B and C.
Car Rental	By several companies in Arrival Hall A. Companies with offices here are: Schuldt; InterRent; Eurorent; Europcar; Avis; and Auto-Sixt, the cheapest.
Taxi Hire	From ranks outside Arrivals.

AIRPORT INFORMATION

Check-in Times	Domestic – 30 minutes.
	International – 30 minutes.
Airport Tax	Nil.
Transferring Flights	The facilities at Frankfurt Rhein-Main are unrivalled in Europe for speed and efficiency. The airport guarantees a transfer time of 45 minutes, unique for airports of this size.

AIRPORT HOTELS

• **First Class:** (around 250 DM for a double)
Frankfurt Sheraton – Opposite Terminal Building and reached via a pedestrian bridge (tel. 69770/69811).
Steigenburger Airport Hotel – 300–4 Flughafenstrasse (tel. 69851). The hotel is 5 minutes from the airport and it operates a courtesy bus shuttle.

There are no Economy hotels, but the centre of Frankfurt is only 6 miles distant.

CITY LINKS

The airport's links with the city centre and also the rest of the country are excellent.

• **Rail:** The train station below the terminal is served by inter-city trains, regional trains and the Lufthansa Airport Express. Information and tickets can be obtained at the Deutsche Bundesbahn counter in Arrival Hall B (tel. 0611/691844). The train ride into Frankfurt by 'S-Bahn' (Routes 514 and 515) takes about 10 minutes, with services approximately every 10 minutes. The fare is around 3.50 DM, depending on hour/day, with a first class supplement of 2 DM. Remember that you *must* obtain your ticket *before* you board the train.

• **Road:** Road links are excellent too, with the 'Frankfurter Kreuz' – the intersection of the most important highways from north to south – being only a few hundred metres from the airport. The bus terminal is located at the Arrival level in front of the terminal and the buses take you either to Frankfurt South or Frankfurt Schwanheim. The taxi ranks are located on the same level and the fare to the centre is around 30 DM.

TOURIST INFORMATION

There are 2 main offices of the Official Tourist Service. One is at the Main Station (Hauptbahnhof), situated opposite platform 23. It is open from 0800 to 2100 (2200 in the summer), Monday–Saturday, and from 0930 to 2000 on Sundays and holidays (tel. 231055). The other is in the Hauptwache Passage and is open 0900–1800 (Monday–Friday) and 0900–1400 on Saturdays (tel. 287486/ 281018). The offices supply tourist information (their brochure on Frankfurt is excellent) and also give details of where to find accommodation. You can also book city tours here as well as tickets for major cultural events. The staff all speak English.

ADDRESSES

UK Consulate-General Office – Bockenheimer Landstrasse 51–53 (tel. 720406).
US Consulate-General Office – Sies Mayerstrasse 21 (tel. 740071).
24-Hour Post Office – At the Main Railway Station.
Police – Tel. 110.

GETTING ABOUT

• **Bus:** Bus services are fast and efficient and a 24-hour season ticket costing 7 DM can be purchased from automatic ticket machines. The tickets are valid for travel within the central zone of the city's public transportation network. Many companies offer bus/coach tours, and details of these can be obtained from the Official Tourist Offices at the Main Station (tel. 231055), and at Hauptwache Passage (tel. 287486).

● **Rail:** An extensive network of underground and surface trains covers the city, and details of both train *and* bus timetables can be obtained by contacting Deutsche Bundesbahn on 230333.

● **Taxis:** Radio taxis are available day and night, at the same price, either from taxi stands or by phoning 250001/230033/545011. There is no charge for collection and the fare payable is the total on the taxi's meter, regardless of the number of passengers or amount of luggage. The basic fare is 3.60 DM – plus 1.60 DM for each kilometre travelled.

● **Car Hire:** Hiring a car is a good way to explore the surrounding countryside and cars can be hired from the airport or the Main Central Station. Prices start from around 50 DM, excluding petrol and mileage.

SIGHTS

Many of the sights of Frankfurt are concentrated in the area from the HAUPTWACHE, which is the city centre, to the river, a few hundred yards to the south. Do not miss the RÖMER, which is one of Frankfurt's most famous landmarks. The picturesque City Hall with its triple-gabled front dates back to the 14th century and has been lovingly restored after extensive damage during World War II. Also in this area are 3 important churches: the impressive Dom (Cathedral of St Bartholomew) with its 400-ft tower, which the more energetic can ascend for a magnificent view of the city; the ancient Church of St Nicholas; and the later Paulskirche which today stages a number of important public functions.

Some of the chief tourist attractions are in the Old Town – the ALTSTADT – and these include Goethe's house, which has been carefully restored after destruction in the war; St Leonard's Church; the Steinernes House which houses an art collection; the Saalhof, once the palace of Frederick Barbarossa; and the famous Börse – the stock exchange – which dates back to 1585.

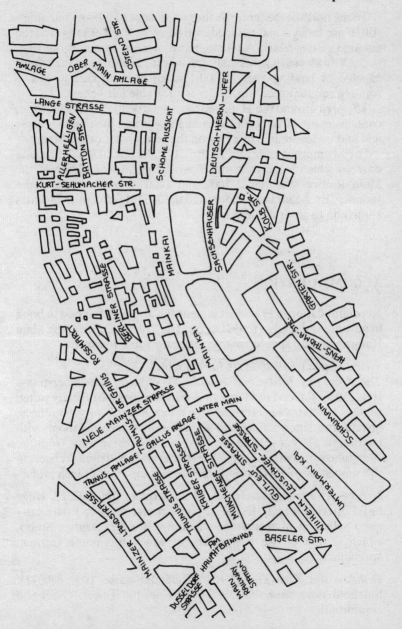

To the north of the centre lie the picturesque old OPERA building – still in use today – and the medieval storybook tower known as the ESCHENHEIMER TURM. Another, more modern tower, is the HENNIGER TOWER which is basically the tallest storehouse in the world, capable of holding over 15,000 tons of brewing barley, with a rotating restaurant on top, and a comfortable bar beneath.

The area around the Hauptwache, in particular KAISERSTRASSE, contains many of Germany's leading stores and the museum lover will find no less than 7 in a row on the south bank of the Main.

For a comprehensive tour of the city, take one of the sightseeing coaches which leave from the Tourist Information Office at the Main Railway Station at 1000 and 1400 hours throughout the summer. Each tour lasts 3 hours and the 24 DM ticket price includes admission to several museums.

ACCOMMODATION

Accommodation in Frankfurt is plentiful, although it is best to book in advance if there is a trade fair on. The Tourist Office at the Main Railway Station should be able to secure you a room.

• **First Class:** (over 250 DM for a double)
The Frankfurt Inter-Continental – 43 Wilhelm-Leuschnerstrasse (tel. 230561). Good modern hotel with facilities particularly suited to the businessman. Business facilities include private offices, instant translation service and several rooftop meeting rooms with panoramic views over the city. There are 4 restaurants, from the Bierstube which offers simple bar snacks and good draught beer, to the sophisticated Rotisserie, which serves top-class French grills.

Steinberger Frankfurter Hof – 17 Kaiserplatz (tel. 20251). Huge hotel offering a high degree of comfort and service. Particularly good selection of restaurants, featuring the Frankfurter Stubb, which is one of the best places in which to sample German specialities.

Holiday Inn City Tower – 1 Mailänderstrasse (tel. 680011). Splendid views over the Old Town, from the Tower. Quiet and comfortable.

• **Super Club Class:** (120–200 DM for a double)
Frankfurt Savoy – Wiesenhütten'strasse 42 (tel. 230511). Has a fine bar and restaurant, a disco and a sauna.

Parkhotel – 28/38 Wiesenhüttenplatz (tel. 26970/26971). A very comfortable older-style hotel in the centre of the city.

Savigny Hotel – 14/16 Savignystrasse (tel. 75330). Elegant modern hotel with a nice atmosphere.

• **Economy:** (40–100 DM for a double)
Admiral – 25 Hölderlinstrasse (tel. 448021). Near the zoo.

Ebel – 26 Taunusstrasse (tel. 252736). Central, but no restaurant.

Zentum – 7 Rossmark (tel. 295291). Cosy little hotel.

Maingau – 38 Schifferstrasse (tel. 617001). Very quiet considering its position near the Main Station.

Rex – 31 Berlinerstrasse (tel. 287290).

Vera – 118 Mainzer Landstrasse (tel. 745023).

DINING OUT

Frankfurt possesses a number of good international restaurants and it is possible to eat very well indeed during your stay in the city.

• **First Class:** (100–150 DM for two)
Erno's Bistro – 15 Liebigstrasse (tel. 721997). Nouvelle cuisine à la Paul Bocuse in this intimate restaurant furnished in the style of a French bistro. Impressive wine list and highly recommended.

Gutsschanke Heuhof – At Neuhof Manor, in Dreieich Gotzendam, just outside Frankfurt (tel. 06102 3214). Excellent reputation which lures droves of diners from the city centre. Beautiful setting.

Frankfurter Stubb – At the Steinberger Hotel (tel. 215679). Venerable cellar restaurant serving regional German specialities such as beef loin stuffed with goose liver.

● **Super Club Class:** (40–100 DM for two)
Henniger Turm – 60/64 Hainerweg (tel. 610471). Revolving restaurant at the top of a tower 1067 feet high. Stunning views and choice from snacks up to good 4-course meals. Not for those who suffer from vertigo.

Da Claudio – 10 Zum-Jungenstrasse (tel. 565471). Friendly restaurant whose owner personally chooses a new menu daily. Italian specialities.

Alt Frankfurt – 10 Berlinerstrasse (tel. 281064). Romantic older-style location. Has a beer fountain and its speciality is roast suckling pig.

● **Economy:** (up to 40 DM for two)
Zum Anker – 9 Grusonstrasse (tel. 439027). Sausages, sausages and more sausages! All kinds, massive portions, and very cheap.

Sudpfanne – 20 Eschenheimer Landstrasse (tel. 550001). More meaty specialities.

Dippegucker – 40 Eschenheimer Anlage (tel. 551965). For those who truly believe sausages to be the wurst thing since sliced bread, this rustic tavern serves wonderfully crisp salads.

'Imbiss' Stands – These are quick service stands that can be found all over the city. This is the way the locals eat their sausages, so why not join them?

NIGHTLIFE

While not having the extensive range to be found in the larger German cities, Frankfurt does offer a wide variety of entertainments at night. Municipal THEATRES present a complete range of opera and drama, while the Kleines Theatre im Zoo; the Komodie; and the Theatre am Turm present the work of modern authors. There are half a dozen good concert halls in the city and all types of music from pop to opera to chamber music can be sampled regularly. JAZZ is thriving and a visit to one of numerous clubs such as the Schlachthof at 36 Deutschherrnufer, specializing in Dixie and Swing, is highly recommended.

There are plenty of nightclubs ranging from the more elegant hotel clubs to the many hot-spots in the area around the Main Station. Clubs like Die Schmiere and Die Maininger present more sophisticated cabaret, and there are gambling casinos at nearby Bad Homberg and Wiesbaden. At present there are 78 cinemas in Frankfurt and for details of programmes, together with other information on the city's nightlife, consult *Frankfürter Wochen-scham* or the local newspaper, *Frankfürter Verkehrsverein*.

EXCURSIONS

Frankfurt's central location and excellent communications mean that it is not unrealistic to travel to any outlying point in the whole of West Germany. However, there is a rich variety of interesting places not far from the city itself. Chief of these is probably HEIDELBERG with its beautiful old town and imposing castle. The city is situated 53 miles south of Frankfurt and is very lively during the summer when it hosts a number of festivals. The surrounding countryside is also very pleasant and a boat trip along the Neckar is thoroughly recommended. Also lively is RÜDESHEIM which is a thriving village 35 miles distant.

To the west lies MAINZ (24 miles), capital of the Rhineland Palatinate, an ancient city dominated by the great tower of its 1000-year-old romanesque cathedral. Near Mainz is TAUNUS, a beautiful region of pine forests which is a paradise for nature lovers. The region has many spas of which the most renowned is WIESBADEN, 25 miles from Frankfurt. Boat trips down the Rhine are very popular, and the one from Mainz to historic KOBLENZ, in the shadow of the famous Ehrenbreitstein Fortress, encapsulates most of the attractions of this great river. You can even float down to BONN, 120 miles from Frankfurt, at the Gateway of the Rhine valley, but it is more practical to take one of the fast inter-city trains from Frankfurt, which will whisk you to the nation's capital in under 2 hours.

To the north, MARBURG (70 miles) is within reach, and lovers of folklore will be delighted at this medieval town where old customs and traditions still flourish. To the east, WÜRZBURG in Bavaria lies at the end of the famous Romantic Road which proceeds in its magical way right down to the Alps.

5. THE MIDDLE EAST

Bahrain

RED TAPE

• **Passport/Visa Requirements:** You will need the following to enter Bahrain: a valid passport, proof of return ticket, and a visa. Only British nationals do not require a visa, although they do if travelling on a British Visitor's Passport. Visas are obtainable at the airport, cost £3 and are valid for one month. Those not travelling on business require a letter from friends/relatives resident in Bahrain, a photo, and a 'no objections' certificate from the Immigration Office. Otherwise you will need a business visa, which costs £10 upon production of a letter from your company, a photo, and a 'no objections' certificate. Long-term business visas (1–2 years) are also available if the company in Bahrain obtains a 'no objections' certificate on behalf of the individual. Applications should be made to the Embassy of the State of Bahrain at least 72 hours in advance.

CUSTOMS

The following goods may be imported into Bahrain without incurring any duty: 400 cigarettes; 50 cigars; 8 oz tobacco in opened packets; 8 oz perfume; 2 bottles wine or spirits (non-Muslims only); and gifts up to the value of BD50. Unpolished pearls produced outside the Gulf are under strict import regulations and some goods are boycotted by members of the Arab League.

HEALTH

1. There is no yellow fever risk, but a certificate of immunization is required from those travelling from an infected area.
2. There is no malaria risk but to be on the safe side, travellers can be vaccinated at the airport 24 hours daily.
3. There are risks of both cholera and typhoid/polio, and immunization is advised, though not essential.
4. Water is safe to drink in the hotels, but caution is recommended when away from hotels.

Visitors are advised to take sensible precautions against the heat and also to ensure that they have some sort of medical insurance as only private treatment is available in the hospitals.

CAPITAL – Al Manama. Population – c.100,000.

POPULATION – 360,000.

LANGUAGE – 90 per cent Arabic, with local dialects. English is commonly the language of business.

CURRENCY – Dinar, divided into 1000 Fils. Notes are in denominations of 0.5, 1, 5, 10, and 20 Dinars. Coins are in denominations of 5, 10, 25, 50, and 100 Fils.
£1 = BD0.54; US$1 = BD0.40.

BANKING HOURS – 0700 to 1300 Saturday–Thursday.

POLITICAL SYSTEM – The country is governed by the Amir and his cabinet of appointed ministers.

RELIGION – Muslim, with Christian, Bahai, Hindu and Parsi minorities.

PUBLIC HOLIDAYS

January 1   New Year's Day
December 16   National Day

All other holidays follow the Muslim calendar and many depend upon sightings of the moon. In December–January: Prophet's

Birthday; July–August: Eid el-Fitr (3-day celebration at the end of the month of strict fasting called Ramadan, when visitors may well experience difficulties conducting business, travelling around and finding restaurants open during the daylight hours); September–October: Eid el-Adha; October–November: Muslim New Year; October–November: Al Ashoura.

CLIMATE – The summer months (June–September) are best avoided as temperatures of 43°C (110°F) are not uncommon. It is far cooler and generally more pleasant in the winter (December–March), particularly in the evenings, and the little rain that falls does so around this time. From spring to autumn you will require the lightest of cottons and linens, while it is advisable to take warmer clothes for the winter evenings. Sunglasses are almost essential.

TIME DIFFERENCE – GMT + 3 hours.

PROHIBITION – Bahrain is not as strict as other Arab states, and alcohol is available in hotels and restaurants. However you are advised to follow the restrictions imposed during Ramadan.

COMMUNICATIONS

• **Telephone:** The telephone network is one of the most modern in the Gulf, and there is a full IDD service. The international access code is 00 and the country code is 973.

• **Post:** Airmail service to UK takes 3–4 days. Internal service is reliable.

ELECTRICITY – Manama: 230v AC; Awali: 120v AC.

OFFICE/SHOPPING HOURS – Government offices are open 0700–1300. Companies are open 0730–1230 and 1500–1800. Shops are open 0800–1300 and 1600–1900. Friday is the weekly holiday.

• **Best Buys:** Gold (discs in the shape of Dilmun seals in particular), pearls and jewellery. Material and clothing. Antiques and Persian carpets, brass, copper and silver utensils and decorative items. Red pottery from A'ali.

INTERNAL TRAVEL

• **Air:** There are no internal air services.

• **Rail:** There are no railways.

• **Road:** Manama is served by an excellent modern network and most of the mainland towns and villages are now connected by bus, with a standard fare of 50 Fils. Taxis are available and fares should be agreed in advance, as drivers pay little attention to government limits. Fares increase by 50 per cent after midnight.

You can hire a car from the following firms: Avis (c/o Bahrain International Travel on 253315/6); Gulf Car Hiring Company (713288); Hilton Garage (255026); and Husain Ali Slaibikh (252570). You must apply in person for a permit from the police at Isa Town. Holders of licences for the UK, USA and Australia are not required to take a driving test, but must apply for a permit and take a sight test. All others must take a driving test. Traffic travels on the right.

• **Sea:** Bahrain's islands are connected by motorboat or dhow. For details, contact local travel agents.

MAJOR SIGHTS OF THE COUNTRY

Bahrain actually comprises 35 islands, most of which are uninhabited and barren. Most of the attractions are archaeological digs (the country's history dates back nearly 3000 years) and good beaches. Apart from the island of BAHRAIN, featuring the towns of MANAMA – with the ancient capital BALAD AL-QUADIM just outside, and picturesque RIFAA, the lake of AIN AL-QASARI, and the burial mounds at A'ali, all featured in our *City Guide* to Manama on p. 668 – there are only a couple of other islands of interest. MUHARRAQ is connected to Manama by road. It has a characteristic bustling Arab

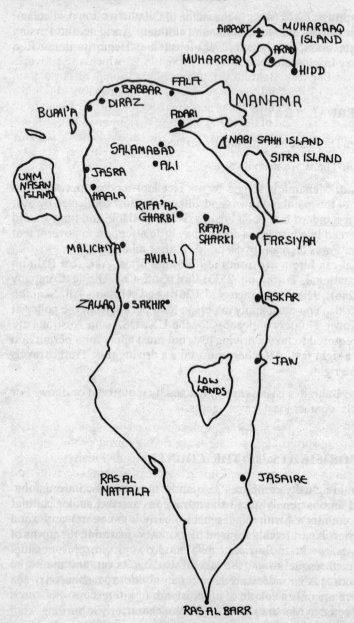

AIRPORT
MUHARRAQ ISLAND
MUHARRAQ
ARAD
HIDD
FALA
BABBAR
DIRAZ
MANAMA
BUPAI'A
ADARI
NABI SAHH ISLAND
SITRA ISLAND
SALAMABAD
ALI
UNM NASAN ISLAND
JASRA
HAALA
RIFA'AL GHARBI
RIFAJA SHARKI
FARSIYAH
MALICHIYA
AWALI
ZALLAQ
SAKHIR
ASKAR
JAW
LOW LANDS
RAS AL NATTALA
JASAIRE
RAS AL BARR

main town of the same name, and the attractive town of HEDD. which is built on the south-east promontory and features many preserved ancient houses. The island's strategic importance is reflected in the number of forts on the island, which also provides the location for Bahrain's modern international airport. NABI SALIH, a tiny island south of Manama, is probably the most attractive, with its little lakes and ponds and luxuriant vegetation. The northern coast of industrial SITRA – linked by road to Bahrain – is pleasant with its springs and palms. The other islands are mainly barren and difficult to reach.

HOTELS

Bahrain has numerous first-class hotels, catering mainly for the business community, but there is little in the way of cheaper accommodation. For details contact the Bahrain Tourist Office at the airport, tel. 21648. There is no official hotel rating system. Hotels get very crowded during the 2-week period either side of Eid el-Adha.

NIGHTLIFE AND RESTAURANTS

There are cinemas showing English and Arabic films in the main towns and cultural and social events are organized by the Alliance Française. Manama has a number of nightclubs, many at hotels, but dining out seems to be the main feature of evening social life and there are a number of good restaurants serving all kinds of food. Arab food is mainly spicy and strongly flavoured. Lamb is popular and often served with salads and dips. Arabic sweets are very sweet and possibly too sickly for western tastes. Beer and the Arab spirit arak (grape spirit flavoured with aniseed) are the most common forms of alcohol available, and all alcoholic beverages tend to be very expensive indeed. Tea is common and you should try the exceedingly fierce Arabic coffee, served in tiny cups and often stewed for hours to extract maximum flavour.

Manama

MUHARRAQ INTERNATIONAL AIRPORT

Bahrain's airport lies on the island of Muharraq, 4 miles north-east of Manama, and it is now served by a total of 69 airlines. Around 3 million passengers use the airport yearly. There is one terminal.

AIRPORT FACILITIES

All important facilities are open 24 hours.

Information Desk	In Arrivals. For flight information, and general information about the airport, telephone Bahrain Airport Services on 321444. There are also 5 travel agencies in Arrivals who can supply information.
Restaurants/Snack Bars	Open 24 hours.
Foreign Exchange/Banks	24-hour facilities. The telephone number of the National Bank of Bahrain is 321352.
Duty Free/Shops	Duty free open round the clock. The airport's duty free shops compare favourably with those elsewhere in the Gulf. Alcohol, perfume and traditional Arab clothing are good buys.
Left Luggage	Contact Bahrain Airport Services on 321444.
Hotel Reservations	Contact Bahrain Airport Services (PAX Handling).
Meeting Point	Sign in International Arrivals concourse.
Conference Rooms	CAD conference room.
Car Rental	Via Avis, tel. 234423.

Taxi Hire   Directly outside Arrivals. Available
                                 24 hours. Turn right outside
                                 Arrivals.

AIRPORT INFORMATION

Check-in Time   60 minutes.
Airport Tax   Nil.
Transferring Flights   There are convenient transfers to
                                 other destinations and the Transit
                                 Lounge has been enlarged for the
                                 convenience of passengers. In the
                                 transit area there is a branch of the
                                 National Bank of Bahrain, a good
                                 restaurant, and snacks and
                                 refreshments are available. Airport
                                 procedures are quite simple to
                                 follow, though baggage retrieval is
                                 quite haphazard and can lead to
                                 delays. You should be able to get a
                                 transfer in an hour.

AIRPORT HOTELS

• **First Class:** (around BD40 for a double)
The nearest is *The Holiday Inn* – King Faisal Road (tel. 241112).

CITY LINKS

Muharraq Airport is 4 miles north-east of Manama.

• **Road:** The taxi fare is officially BD1, but most drivers charge
BD3. Arrange a price before you go and remember that fares
increase by 50 per cent after midnight. The journey to Manama
takes around 10 minutes.
    From the hours of 0510 until 2300 you can take bus nos. 4, 6 or 10
to Muharraq bus station, and from there a 1, 2 or 19 will take you to

the city station. Buses leave the airport every 20–30 minutes and the fare is 100 Fils. The journey to the city centre takes about half an hour.

TOURIST INFORMATION

Contact the Tourist Information Office at the airport, tel. 21648. Alternatively contact a travel agent in Manama such as Thomas Cook, Unitag House, Government Road, tel. 257444/258000. They will give you leaflets and book tours for you.

ADDRESSES

British Airways Office – Tel. 254621.
UK Embassy – Al Mathaf Square, PO Box 114, tel. 254002/253446 and 257155 (commercial).
US Embassy – Shaikh Isa Road, PO Box 431, tel. 714151.

GETTING ABOUT

The bus network is efficient both around Manama and to other destinations around the island. The standard fare to any destination outside Manama is 100 Fils. Taxis can be hired readily, but do agree on a price before embarking on your journey.

SIGHTS

Manama is a modern business town, rapidly acquiring a Manhattan-style skyline. The oldest relic of the past is the TOMB OF SHAIKH AHMAD AL-KHALIFAH, who recovered the island from the Persians, and this dates from the end of the 18th century. The focal point of the town is SHAIKH SULMAN SQUARE and nearby towers the minaret of the JUMA MOSQUE, the tallest on the island. The historic BAZAAR begins here, extending the whole length of Bab al-Bahrain Street. An extraordinary array of goods can be haggled over here and the bazaar, with its traditions stretching back over many thousands of years, is well worth a visit. Running along the sea front, Government Road possesses some handsome buildings, notably the National Bank and Government House. One of the town's most impressive buildings is the PALACE near Guadibiya Gardens. This was built in the 1930s in a U-shape, and has a large dining hall used for state banquets.

ACCOMMODATION

Accommodation in Manama is expensive and geared almost exclusively towards the businessman (and his family if he is an Arab). All the hotels are modern and purpose-built, and cheap accommodation is almost impossible to come by due to the high cost of living in Bahrain, and the government policy of building only luxury hotels.

● **First Class:** (over BD50 for a double)
Bahrain Inter-Continental – (tel. 231777). Superbly equipped luxury hotel catering for every need. Fine sports and business facilities, and excellent choice of international restaurants.

Bahrain Hilton – King Faisal Road, PO Box 1090 (tel. 250000). Luxurious modern hotel in the city centre. Every room has views of the island and the Gulf. Full range of executive facilities, choice of 4 restaurants and lively piano bar.

Bahrain Sheraton – PO Box 30 (tel. 233233). Central, coastal location. Full conference facilities. Choice of 2 good restaurants, or barbecue food and snacks available all day by the pool. Good sports facilities including 2 tennis courts and an air-conditioned squash court.

● **Super Club Class:** (BD40–50 for a double)
The facilities provided by these hotels are extremely good and there is little or no difference between these and the first-class hotels listed.

Gulf Hotel – PO Box 580 (tel. 712881). Fine position overlooking Quadibiya Bay, 5 minutes from the centre of Manama. Full business facilities. 24-hour coffee shop. Swimming and tennis.

Ramada Manama – PO Box 5750 (tel. 58100). Right at the city centre opposite the Guest Palace. Restaurant with lobster and seafood tank, nightclub and pool.

Middle East – Shaikh Isa Road, PO Box 838 (tel. 54733). Another modern, luxurious hotel in the centre of Manama, convenient for the main business and shopping districts.

There is no accommodation that could really be classified as 'Economy'.

DINING OUT

There are plenty of good restaurants in Bahrain. As dining out is such a major feature of Bahrain's social life, it is advisable to reserve tables in advance, especially if dining in hotel restaurants. As with hotels, there aren't really any restaurants which could be classed as 'Economy'.

● **First Class:**
Bazaar Grill – At the Hilton (tel. 250000). Elegant surroundings and fine international cuisine.

Al Safir – At the Sheraton (tel. 233233). Speciality dishes from both eastern and western traditions. Formal restaurant with tremendous views over the Gulf.

Falcon Room – At the Gulf (tel. 712881). Excellent reputation.

● **Super Club Class:**
Keith's Restaurant – Quadibiya Road (tel. 713613). French nouvelle cuisine.

The Chinese Restaurant – New Palace Road, Quadibiya.

Dreamland Restaurant – Isa al-Kabir Road (tel. 250122). Continental, Chinese and Indian specialities.

● **Economy:**
Visitors may be able to purchase relatively inexpensive take-away food, but that's about all.

NIGHTLIFE

Nightlife in Bahrain is not especially wonderful. The only real 'hot-spot' is the beach at midday. NIGHTCLUBS tend to be sophisticated affairs, usually based at the top hotels, such as Juliana's at the Delmon Hotel, Government Road, or the Zartaji near the Bristol Hotel, Shaikh Isa Road. Hotels like the Sheraton run supper clubs where you can combine a meal with an evening's entertainment. You can take out temporary membership of the British or American CLUBS and make use of their social facilities, or contact the ALLIANCE FRANÇAISE, which is basically a cultural organization which organizes social activities such as dances, excursions, and film-shows. Other films, in Arabic and English, are shown at the cinemas, but the main nightly recreation in Bahrain is eating out.

EXCURSIONS

A few miles south-west of Manama, Lake AIN AL-QASARI, with its lush banks, is a pleasant spot to while away an evening far from the bustle of the main town. Continuing west along Shaikh Sulman Road you come to the village of BALAD AL-QADIM, easily recognizable by the twin minarets of the SUQ AL-KHAMIS MOSQUE. This dates from the 14th century (at least) and is the most interesting of the 3 mosques at the former medieval capital of Bahrain. Half a mile beyond the village is the AIN ADARI (Pool of the Virgin), whose cool gardens and groves have made it a favourite resort for many Bahrainis. The northern part of the island has many archaeological sites of interest, most notably the now dilapidated Portuguese fort known as the QALAAT AL-BAHRAIN, near BUDAIYA on the north-west tip of the island, and the remains of the Bronze Age stronghold of DILMUN close by.

The old town of RIFAA, 10 miles south of Manama, is undoubtedly the most picturesque on the island. The old Amir's fort dominates the town, although in its present form it dates only from the middle of the 18th century. The lush countryside surrounding the town is nourished by the purest water in the land, which flows from the HANANI spring, situated at the foot of the fort. Along the road from A'ALI, famous for its red pottery, to ZALLAQ lie thousands of intriguing burial mounds. These date back to the third millennium BC, and form the largest Bronze Age cemetery in the world.

Along the western coast there are some fine beaches with excellent sports facilities, especially SHAIKH'S BEACH, where the Amir has his country residence. Nearby is the JEBEL DUKHAN, the 'Mountain of Smoke', from the top of which there are fine views across the whole of the southern half of the island and across to Saudi Arabia and Qatar. Right at the southern tip of the island, RAS AL-BARR can only be visited with police permission, but there is exotic wildlife to be seen here, such as pink flamingoes and various gazelle, and the seagull eggs which cover the shores at certain times of the year are a local delicacy. It is easier to view the wildlife at the AL AREEN wildlife park.

The only two islands worth visiting are the pleasure islet of NABI SALIH, which pilgrims used to swim to from Manama, and MUHAR-RAQ, a mile to the north-east of Manama and connected to it by road. Bahrain's MUSEUM is situated here and some of the exhibits, such as the gold seals used by the merchants of the ancient town of Dilmun, date back some 4000 years. On the south-eastern promontory, HEDD has some nice old buildings.

Sightseeing tours can be arranged through hotels and travel agents. Bahrain Explored (tel. 742211) offer good tours of either the archaeological sites of Bahrain, or around the island of Muharraq.

The United Arab Emirates

RED TAPE

• **Passport/Visa Requirements:** Most people need only a valid passport to enter the United Arab Emirates (UAE) but it is worth having a return/onward ticket in advance in order to avoid delay and interrogation. You can stay in the UAE for 1 month and this period can be extended to 3 upon application. However, travel and visa requirements are liable to change at short notice and passengers can keep themselves abreast of further developments in this area by contacting the Ministry of the Interior, Department of Nationality, Passports and Residence, PO Box 228, Abu Dhabi (tel. 41280).

CUSTOMS

• **Duty Free:** The following goods may be brought into the UAE without incurring Customs duty:

By passengers to Dubai: 1000 cigarettes or 50 cigars or 1 kilo of tobacco; 1 litre toilet water and 50g perfume; 3 litres of alcohol less than 22 per cent (only non-Muslims).

By passengers to Sharjah: no restrictions on tobacco products or perfumes, but only 1 litre of alcohol permitted.

By passengers to Abu Dhabi: 200 cigarettes or 50 cigars or 0.5 kilo of tobacco; gifts up to the value of ADH10; alcohol is only permitted for residents with permits.

HEALTH

1. Yellow fever vaccination certificate required by all travellers coming from infected areas.
2. Vaccination against smallpox is essential.
3. Cholera vaccination certificate required if arriving within 5 days after leaving or transiting countries with infected areas.
4. Water precautions advisable. Tap water is purified in Abu Dhabi, Dubai and Sharjah, but boiled water may be preferable.
5. Health insurance is vital, for while health care in the UAE is good, it does not come cheap.

CAPITAL – Abu Dhabi. Population – c.300,000.

POPULATION – 1.1 million.

LANGUAGE – Arabic and Urdu, with English widely used in commerce.

CURRENCY – Dirham (ADH) = 100 Fils. Notes – ADH 1, 5, 10, 50, 100, and 1000. Coins – 1, 5, 10, 25, and 50 Fils and ADH1. £1 = ADH5.3; US$1 = ADH3.8.

BANKING HOURS – Abu Dhabi: 0800–1200 (Saturday–Wednesday) and 0800–1100 (Thursday). In the Northern Emirates banks remain open until midday on Thursdays too.

POLITICAL SYSTEM – A Union Council of Ministers responsible to the Supreme Council has executive authority and implements Union laws.

RELIGION – Islam (mainly Sunni), with Christian, Hindu and Parsi minorities.

PUBLIC HOLIDAYS

January 1	New Year's Day
May/June	Ramadan
August 6	Anniversary of Shaikh Zayed Sultan al-Nahan (Abu Dhabi only)
September	Eid el-Adha
September/October	Ashoura
October/November	Muslim New Year
December 2	National Day
December 4	Prophet's Birthday
December 25	Christmas Day

It can be difficult to travel or find restaurants open during Ramadan.

CLIMATE – Blisteringly hot summers with temperatures reaching 44°C (112°F) in July/August. In the winter (December–March), it is cooler, especially in the evenings. Little rain falls during the year. Take lightweight, light-coloured clothes, with an extra layer if travelling in winter, and a pair of sunglasses.

TIME DIFFERENCE – GMT + 4 hours.

PROHIBITION – The UAE is not as strict as other countries and non-Muslims can buy alcohol in bars and hotels, or in licensed shops in Dubai. However, it is advisable to respect local customs, particularly during Ramadan.

COMMUNICATIONS

• **Telephone:** IDD service available. International access code: 010; country code: 971. Good internal network. Local calls are free.

• **Post:** Airmail letters and parcels take about 5 days to reach the UK. Post Offices are usually open 0800–1300 and 1600–1800.

ELECTRICITY – 220v AC (Northern States); 240v AC (Abu Dhabi).

OFFICE/SHOPPING HOURS – Office hours: 0700–1300 and 1600–1800 (Saturday–Wednesday) and 0700–1200 (Thursday). Government offices are open: winter, 0800–1400 (Saturday–Wednesday) and 0800–1200 (Thursday); summer, 0700–1300 (Saturday–Thursday). All offices are closed on Fridays throughout the year, and some offices shut on Thursday afternoons. Shops: 0800–1300 and 1600–2000. Friday is the weekly holiday.

• **Best Buys:** Electrical goods; hi-fi and stereo equipment; cameras; gold and jewellery; carpets; antiques; oriental and Middle Eastern clothing (Dubai). Try shopping in the souks (markets) and don't forget to haggle.

INTERNAL TRAVEL

• **Air:** Gulf Air runs flights to all internal airports. The main airports are Dubai, Abu Dhabi, Sharjah (all international), and Ras-al-Kyaymah. Distances are not vast and flights are quick but quite expensive. There is a daily shuttle between Abu Dhabi and Dubai. It is important to remember that flights between the various Emirates are regarded as international.

• **Rail:** No railways.

• **Sea:** Coastal commercial and passenger services serve all ports.

• **Road:** Road links are good and a limited bus service connects major towns. Taxis are easily available throughout the UAE and can be hired on an hourly basis. Long distance trips can be arranged and the fare should be agreed in advance. You should pay no more than ADH200 to get from Dubai to Abu Dhabi.

There are numerous car hire firms and visitors wishing to drive hired cars must obtain a temporary licence from the traffic police. A current driving licence, a passport and 2 passport photos must be produced to obtain this. The licensing laws are quite complex and the car hire firms will help you through the mass of bureaucracy. Traffic proceeds on the left.

MAJOR SIGHTS OF THE COUNTRY

The UAE is not really a tourist country and there are hardly any sights worth seeing. When not conducting business, you are better off on the beach or in the major cities. Much of the old city of ABU DHABI, the capital, has been demolished to make way for numerous commercial buildings, and the Old Palace is just about the sole surviving remnant of the city's past. However some of the modern buildings are not unattractive: the Trade Centre is a spectacular feat of modern architecture, and the interior of Shaikh Mohammed's palatial residence is very impressive. You can see burial mounds at UMMAR-NAL, and Mesopotamian pottery at JEBEL-HAFIT. Near to Abu Dhabi, AL-AIN has parks, a zoo, and an interesting camel market, while the Omani village of BURAMI has a couple of interesting forts and the Gardens of Hilli.

DUBAI has suddenly sprung up from virtually nothing into one of the most important commercial centres of the Middle East. Near Dubai, SHARJAH has a lovely new souk and AJMAN a historic palace. KHOR KALBA beach is famous for its shells, and that's about it.

HOTELS

There is plenty of first-class accommodation but hardly anything that could be classed as 'Economy'. There is no official rating system but many international chains have outlets here, such as Hilton, Inter-Continental, Sheraton and Hyatt. Prices are quite reasonable for the type of accommodation on offer.

NIGHTLIFE AND RESTAURANTS

The major cities contain several nightclubs of the exclusive variety, to be found mainly in the top hotels, and also English language cinemas. Traditional dances are performed on public holidays, and those determined to seek out local culture can contact the Ministry of Information and Culture at PO Box 17, Abu Dhabi (tel. 26000); or PO Box 5010, Deira, Dubai (tel. 225994).

One of the main pastimes at night in the UAE is dining out and there are a number of good international restaurants in both Abu Dhabi and Dubai especially. Restaurants outside hotels are not licensed. Bills contain a 10 per cent service charge and a 5 per cent government tax.

Dubai

DUBAI INTERNATIONAL AIRPORT

Dubai's airport lies just 2.5 miles and 10 minutes' drive from the city centre. The airport is very modern and is considered one of the best in the Gulf. By 1983, the airport was being used by 44 airlines and 3.5 million passengers every year. A new terminal is under construction for arrivals. There is one terminal at present.

AIRPORT FACILITIES

Most facilities are open 24 hours.

Information Desk	For flight information, tel. 232233. There is a desk in Arrivals, and all airport staff are courteous and efficient.
Restaurant/Snack Bar	There are 2 restaurants (open 24 hours) and several stand-up snack bars (also open 24 hours).

Bar	There are 2. Only non-Muslims served.
Foreign Exchange/Banks	There are banking facilities with the National Bank of Dubai (tel. 224622) in the Duty Free Complex and Arrivals, and money-changing facilities available round the clock.
Duty Free/Shops	There are 25 duty free shops at the airport's Dubai Duty Free Shopping Complex offering an extensive range of goods at the 'lowest prices in the world' – or so we're told. Actually, they're not far wrong and certainly the prices in the huge liquor and tobacco shop are hard to match. The Complex is beneath the Transit Lounge.
Nursery	In the Transit Lounge.
Medical	There is a well equipped medical centre in the Transit Lounge. There are also facilities for disabled travellers.
Day Rooms	Available in the Transit Lounge.
Museum	The 'Arab Heritage' enclosure has exhibitions highlighting the culture and traditions of the area, and a film is shown as well as the exotic display of antiques and artefacts.
Conference Rooms	Contact Airport Exchange on 224222.
Car Rental	Avis, Budget and Gulf National all have offices in Arrivals.
Taxi Hire	Outside the terminal (24 hours).

AIRPORT INFORMATION

Check-in Times	International – 60 minutes. Domestic – 45 minutes.
Airport Tax	Nil.

Transferring Flights

Dubai is becoming an increasingly popular stop-over point for many travellers due to its excellent duty free facilities and smooth transfer. The minimum time for any connection (domestic or international) is a swift 45 minutes and passengers are very well looked after during their wait.

AIRPORT HOTELS

• **First Class:** (ADH400 for a double)
Dubai International – At the airport (tel. 285111). 5-star hotel with fine sports facilities and a restaurant open 24 hours.

There are rest rooms available in the airport, and the city centre is only 10 minutes away.

CITY LINKS

The International Airport is 2.5 miles south-east of the city.

• **Taxi:** 5–10 minutes to the city centre. Vouchers can be obtained outside the terminal for taxis and the fare is ADH20.

• **Coach:** Hotel courtesy coaches run to the Carlton Tower; Chicago Beach; Dubai International; Excelsior; Hilton; Hyatt Regency; Inter-Continental; and Sheraton hotels.

TOURIST INFORMATION

There is a desk at the airport, but no tourist board as such. For information, contact the Ministry of Information and Culture, PO Box 5010, Deira, Dubai (tel. 225994). Hotels can generally offer assistance (with excursions etc.).

ADDRESSES

UK Embassy – Tariq bin Zayed Street, PO Box 65 (tel. 431070).
US Consulate – Al Futtaim Building, Creek Road, PO Box 5343 (tel. 229003).
Emergency – Fire: 222222; Police: 221111; Ambulance: You cannot call one. Get in touch with your hotel immediately.

GETTING ABOUT

There is a limited bus network, but taxis are easily available.

SIGHTS

Dubai has little in the way of sights though it is an attractive enough modern town. The 150-year-old AL-FAHIDI FORT now contains an interesting museum and the GRAND MOSQUE is an impressive sight, night or day. BASTAKIA is a district of fine old wind towered houses and basically, that's your lot. Students of modern architecture may find much to enthuse about (95 per cent of the city is less than 20 years old) but there really isn't anything else to do except perhaps to take a boat up the lovely CREEK, while away some time in Dubai's excellent souks, or lounge around on one of its splendid beaches.

ACCOMMODATION

Dubai has a number of international quality hotels and a few cheaper establishments, but little in the way of 'Economy' accommodation.

• **First Class:** (over ADH400 for a double)
The Inter-Continental – PO Box 476 (tel. 227171). Luxury hotel only a couple of minutes from the city centre. Fine selection of restaurants, featuring the cuisines of France, Thailand and Italy. All mod cons, and superb service.

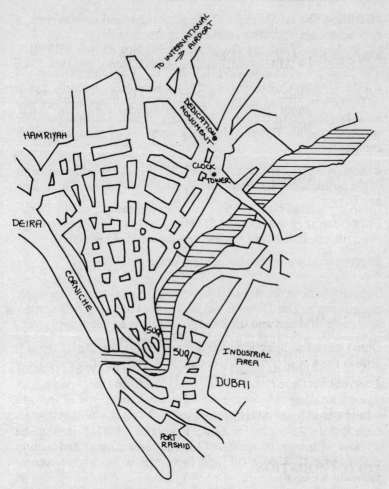

The Hilton – PO Box 927, Deira (tel. 470000). Situated around 5 miles from the main shopping area in the residential district of Deira (complimentary bus shuttle), the Hilton is a superior luxury hotel with comfortable business facilities and its own exclusive and well equipped Beach Club (free shuttle).

Hyatt Regency – (tel. 238000). Fine position overlooking the sea with superb views from the hotel's excellent revolving rooftop restaurant, the Al-Dawaar. There are 2 other good restaurants, a cocktail lounge and disco, and good sports facilities.

• **Super Club Class:** (ADH200–350 for a double)
The Sheraton – PO Box 4250 (tel. 281111). Conveniently situated overlooking the Creek, and possibly the most architecturally stylish of Dubai's numerous modern luxury hotels. All the facilities you would expect and a conference capacity of 800. Seasonal poolside speciality nights. Better value than some of its more expensive competitors.

Phoenicia Hotel – PO Box 4467 (tel. 227191). Located in the heart of the business district. Philippine speciality restaurant, coffee shop and bar.

Dubai Marine Hotel – PO Box 5182 (tel. 434140). Smaller hotel with good rooms, Italian and English restaurants and nightclub.

There is hardly any accommodation under ADH200.

DINING OUT

Dubai has a fine selection of first-class restaurants. Again there is little in the way of 'Economy' restaurants, although there are some very reasonable Indian and Chinese take-aways.

• **First Class:** (over ADH250 for two)
Café Royal – At the International Hotel (tel. 285111). Restaurant of class with true atmosphere. International cuisine and nightly entertainment. Always full and there can be no higher recommendation than that.

Al-Boom – Dhow Restaurant – Moored in the Creek opposite the British Embassy (tel. 433330/5). Delicious fresh seafood and kebabs in air-conditioned dining room in ship's hold. Complimentary boat from the Sheraton, and boat trips in a smaller dhow with coffee. Recommended.

Al-Dawaar – At the Hyatt Regency (tel. 238000). Elegant revolving rooftop restaurant with spectacular views of the city and Gulf. The hotel has 2 other good restaurants.

• **Super Club Class:** (ADH150–250)

Talay Thong Restaurant – At the Inter-Continental (tel. 227171). Open-air poolside restaurant.' Seafood specialities cooked and served in authentic Thai style. All the restaurants at the Inter-Continental are worth considering.

Estanbouli Restaurant – Next to the Jumairah Fire Station roundabout (tel. 452418). Arabian atmosphere with Lebanese and international specialities. Live Arabic folk music.

The Golden Dragon – Opposite the Palm Beach Hotel (tel. 435517). Oriental decor and atmosphere. Good food but a trifle expensive.

While there are no Economy restaurants as such, you can get moderately priced take-away food from places like the *Tandoor*, opposite the Marine Hotel (tel. 436098/216).

NIGHTLIFE

Most nightclubs – and there are quite a few of them – are to be found in the top hotels and they are all pretty much of an 'exclusive' muchness. There are many sports and social clubs which welcome foreign visitors as either guests of a member or as temporary members. THE DUBAI COUNTRY CLUB on Aweer Road and the DARJEELING CRICKET CLUB (tel. 222034) are a couple of clubs to consider. There are English language cinemas in Dubai but, as with many eastern countries, the prime night-time pastime is eating out.

EXCURSIONS

It is worth taking a boat trip up the famous CREEK and you can book these and other trips through your hotel. DNATA World Travel (tel. 220217/21170) offer half-day tours around Dubai and to SHARJAH and AJMAN, to see the beautiful new souk and old palace respectively. Various desert safaris can be booked, or you can choose to visit a beach resort instead such as KHOR FUKKEN to the east, or the famous KHOR KALBA where you can find many beautiful shells. Also to the east lies the desert oasis of DHAYD. It is certainly possible to fly to ABU DHABI and spend a lively night there, but most visitors will probably be content to remain near Dubai for the duration of their stay.

6. NORTH AMERICA AND THE CARIBBEAN

Antigua, Barbados and Bermuda

RED TAPE

• Passport/Visa Requirements:

For Antigua – In addition to a full passport, visas are required by nationals of all countries except: Austria, Brazil, Finland, Japan, Liechtenstein, Malta, Mexico, Monaco, Norway, Peru, Portugal, Spain, Surinam, Sweden, Switzerland, Turkey, USA and Venezuela; also, nationals of all EEC and British Commonwealth countries.

For Barbados – In addition to a full passport, visas are required by nationals of all countries except: Austria, Belgium, Colombia, Denmark, Finland, West Germany, Greece, Iceland, Republic of Ireland, Israel, Italy, Liechtenstein, Luxembourg, Netherlands, Norway, Peru, San Marino, Spain, Surinam, Sweden, Switzerland, Tunisia, Turkey, USA and Venezuela; also, nationals of all British Commonwealth countries. NB: Nationals of almost all other countries (except Communist countries) can stay without a visa in transit and in possession of an onward ticket for a period of up to 21 days.

For Bermuda – Visas are not required except by nationals of a Communist country or a Chinese resident of Taiwan. All travellers must have sufficient funds and hold onward travel tickets. NB: Travellers visiting the USA directly after Bermuda must hold tickets to a destination beyond the US, and any necessary entry documents for that country.

CUSTOMS

Antigua – Visitors can take in 200 cigarettes or 50 cigars or 250g (8 oz) of tobacco; also 1 litre of wine or spirits, and 6 oz of perfume. Visitors are prohibited from taking in weapons or non-prescribed drugs.

Barbados – Visitors can take in 200 cigarettes or 50 cigars or 8 oz of tobacco; also 1 quart of spirits and 150g of perfume.

Bermuda – Visitors can take in 200 cigarettes or 50 cigars or 1 lb of tobacco; also 1 quart of spirits and 1 quart of wine.

HEALTH

Antigua – A yellow fever vaccination certificate is required from visitors over 1 year of age coming from an infected area.

Barbados – An International Certificate of Vaccination against smallpox is required, and also a yellow fever certificate from those coming from an infected area.

Bermuda – An International Certificate of Vaccination against smallpox is required.

CAPITALS

Antigua – St John's. Population – 38,000.
Barbados – Bridgetown. Population – 100,000.
Bermuda – Hamilton. Population – 5000.

POPULATION

Antigua – 78,241.
Barbados – 265,000 (1978).
Bermuda – 60,000 (1978).

LANGUAGE – English on all islands.

CURRENCY

Antigua – Eastern Caribbean Dollar, divided into 100 EC cents. Notes – 1, 5, 10, 20, 50 and 100 dollars; coins – 1, 5, 10, 25, and 50 cents.
£1 = EC$3.64; US$1 = EC$2.60.

Barbados – Barbados Dollar, divided into 100 cents. Notes – 1, 5, 10, 20 and 100 dollars; coins – 1, 5, 10, 25 cents, and 1 dollar.
£1 = B$2.68; US$1 = B$1.91.

Bermuda – Bermudian Dollar, divided into 100 cents. Notes – 1, 5, 10, 20 and 50 dollars; coins – 1, 5, 10, 25 cents.
£1 = B$2.7; US$1 = B$1.93.

BANKING HOURS

Antigua – 0800–1200 Monday–Thursday, 0800–1300 and 1500–1700 Friday; closed Saturday except Bank of Antigua 0800–1230.

Barbados – 0800–1300 Monday–Thursday, 0800–1300 and 1500–1730 Friday.

Bermuda – 0930–1500 Monday–Thursday, 0930–1500 and 1630–1800 Friday.

POLITICAL SYSTEM

Antigua – Constitutional monarchy.
Barbados – Independent democracy.
Bermuda – Constitutional monarchy.

RELIGION

Antigua – Methodist, Moravian, Anglican, Roman Catholic.
Barbados – Anglican (70 per cent), Methodist, Moravian, Roman Catholic.
Bermuda – Anglican, Methodist, Roman Catholic.

PUBLIC HOLIDAYS

Antigua

January 1	New Year's Day
March/April	Good Friday, Easter Monday
Early May	Labour Day (date varies)
May	Whit Monday (date varies)
June 7	Queen's Birthday
Late July/early August	Carnival (date varies)
November 1	Independence Day
December 25, 26	Christmas

Barbados

January 1	New Year's Day
May 1	May Day
June 7	Queen's Birthday
November 30	Independence Day
December 25, 26	Christmas

Other holidays for which the dates vary are Good Friday, Easter Monday and Whit Monday. Also CARICOM Day in early July, and United Nations Day in early October.

Bermuda

January 1	New Year's Day
May 24	Commonwealth Day
November 11	Remembrance Day
December 25, 26	Christmas

Other holidays recognized are Good Friday, and the Cricket Cup match (2 days in July/August).

CLIMATE – In Antigua the climate is a very pleasant tropical one, and stays warm and relatively dry throughout the year. In Barbados the temperature ranges from around 24°C (75°F) to 30°C (86°F), and rainfall occurs mainly in the period from June to November. In Bermuda the climate is sub-tropical with an annual average temperature of around 21°C (70°F). Summer is from April to mid-November, and peak temperatures occur in July and August, reaching around 30°C (86°F); winter and spring temperatures rarely fall below 10°C (50°F).

TIME DIFFERENCE – All islands are GMT − 4 hours.

COMMUNICATIONS

In Antigua there is a full internal and international phone service. Public phones are easily found in built-up areas, and the charge of a call is 10 EC cents per unit of time. In Barbados, the telephone system is also a well developed one, and direct calls can be made both internally and internationally. The same applies to Bermuda, where there is an automatic telephone system, and public phone kiosks are located all over the island. All islands have international telegram and telex facilities, and postal services are efficient and reliable on each.

ELECTRICITY

Antigua – 220/110v AC.
Barbados – 110v AC, 50 Hz.
Bermuda – 115/230v AC, 60 Hz.

OFFICE/SHOPPING HOURS

Antigua – Government offices are open 0800–1200 and 1300–1700 Monday–Friday. Shops are open 0830–1200 and 1300–1600 Monday–Saturday. Early closing on Thursday.

Barbados – Government offices are open 0815–1630 Monday–Friday. Shops are open 0800–1600 Monday–Friday, and 0800–1200 on Saturdays.

Bermuda – Government offices are open 0900–1700 Monday–Friday. Shops are open 0900–1700 Monday–Friday.

• **Best Buys:** Among the traditional souvenirs available in Antigua are pottery goods, batik and silkscreen printed fabrics, jewellery incorporating semi-precious Antiguan stones, and an enormous variety of quality straw goods. In Barbados souvenirs to look out for are leather goods, clothing unique to the island, and also straw goods and other handicrafts. Handicrafts also feature in Bermuda's souvenir goods, and among them are cedarwood ornaments, baskets, shell and copper enamel jewellery, and various straw hats.

Antigua

ST JOHN'S COOLIDGE INTERNATIONAL AIRPORT

St John's Coolidge International Airport is around 6.5 miles from Antigua's capital, St John's. It handles direct flights to and from several major cities around the world. There is one terminal.

AIRPORT FACILITIES

All the following facilities exist:

Information Desk
Bank/Foreign Exchange
Hotel Reservations Service
Bar
Restaurant/Buffet
Post Office
Baggage Deposit
Shops
Duty Free – shops have limited stock
Toilets
Meeting Point Location
Car Rental Desks
Lost Property
Public Telephones

AIRPORT INFORMATION

Check-in Times   Average for all airlines:
                  International – 90 minutes.
                  Domestic – 60 minutes.
Airport Tax   £4/US$6 equivalent.

CITY LINKS

• **Taxis:** Taxis are the most available and reliable method of transport from the airport to anywhere around the island. They are not metered, and rates are fixed. The usual fare from the airport to St John's is around US$5, and to Nelson's Dockyard US$50.

ANTIGUA

Antigua was discovered in 1493 by Christopher Columbus who, while falling short of landing on the island, did name it – after Santa Maria la Antigua of Seville. It wasn't until some 130 years later that a group of Englishmen sailed from St Kitts and claimed the island for Great Britain, under whose control it has remained right up to the present day (except for the year 1666 when the French invaded and took possession of the island; it was subsequently returned to the British a year later).

Today Antigua is an island of beauty and charm, with locals (there are 78,000 of them) and visitors alike enjoying access to secluded bays, small inlets, and some 360 white sand beaches. The culture on the island, like that of others in the Caribbean, is tinged with more than a hint of Britishness; however, a slower pace of life, calypso, limbo, steel bands and carnival, among other things, ensure that its character is nevertheless distinctly Caribbean.

TOURIST INFORMATION

For details of things to do, sights, events, accommodation-listings etc., contact: *Antigua-Barbuda Department of Tourism* – High Street, St John's, Antigua (tel. 20029/20480).

ADDRESSES

Main Post Office – Located at the corner of High and Long Streets, St John's.
British High Commission – 38 St Mary's Street, St John's (tel. 20008/9).
US Embassy – St John's, Antigua (tel. 23505).

GETTING ABOUT

The bus system in Antigua is very casual; buses don't run to any set schedule, and services are patchy. A more reliable method of getting around the island is by taxi – these are always available at the airport, the deep water harbour, St John's, and at hotels. They're not metered and rates are fixed; a usual fare from, say, the airport to St John's is around US$5.

Car hire is perhaps the best method of travel around the island if you're staying any length of time. Cars can be hired from several companies (all local) in operation all over Antigua, and details can be obtained from the Tourist Office.

SIGHTS

The most common starting point for sightseeing around Antigua is St John's, the capital, in the north-west of the island. There are several interesting sights here, among them the PUBLIC MARKET and ST JOHN'S CATHEDRAL; the market is on the southern edge of town, and provides an ideal opportunity to sample some of the unusual foods of Antigua; it is completely outdoor, full of colour and is usually bustling with people, especially on Saturday mornings. The cathedral is on Newgate Street; originally built in 1683, it was replaced in 1745, destroyed in the earthquake of 1843 and then reconstructed. Built of stone, its interior is cased in pitch pine, which has enabled the building to survive several earthquakes; it's an interesting place to view, both from the outside and interior.

THE BOTANICAL GARDENS in St John's provide an ideal opportunity both to relax and to enjoy an exotic range of natural beauty; it's rather a small area compared with some botanical gardens, but

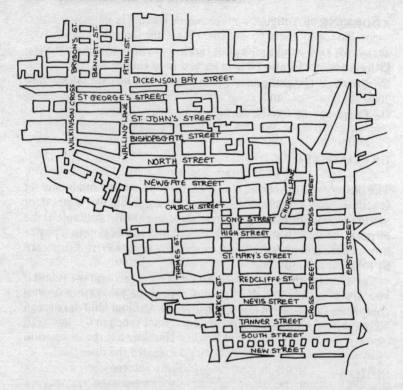

contains an ample amount of various tree types, native and tropical, and also flowering shrubs. FORT JAMES dates back to 1704, and is an intriguing place to visit if only for its historical significance – it was the main look-out for the former British troops stationed in St John's. Among the other attractions well worth taking in while in St John's are the COURT HOUSE, noted for its portraits of King George III and Queen Caroline which are said to have been painted by the celebrated Sir Joshua Reynolds in the mid-18th century, the INDUSTRIAL SCHOOL FOR THE BLIND where it's possible to buy various unique pieces of straw work, the ARAWAK CRAFT CENTRE which sells Antiguan pottery, and the LOCAL HANDICRAFT CENTRE where the handicrafts on sale are very impressive. There's also the CENOTAPH MEMORIAL, built in honour of the Antiguans who died serving in World Wars I and II, and the WESTERBY MEMORIAL which was erected in 1888.

Elsewhere in Antigua, a place worth visiting is NELSON'S DOCK-YARD. On the southern coast of the island, the British Navy used the dockyards here from the start of the 18th century to the end of the 19th. Admiral Horatio Nelson served here (hence its name), and the area's attractions include the ADMIRAL'S HOUSE, which is a nautical museum, and the restored OFFICERS' QUARTERS. Also CLARENCE HOUSE overlooks the dockyard – this was built as the residence of Prince William Henry while he was in command of *Pegasus* in the late 18th century.

The area of SHIRLEY HEIGHTS is located in the town of English Harbour, just north of Nelson's Dockyard. Shirley Heights are the hills above English Harbour, and they were named as such after being fortified by General William Shirley in 1787; this was one of the principal fortifications of the British troops, and today it's possible to view the various battlements, barracks and powder magazines used by the troops guarding the dockyard. There are many other relics of forts on Antigua used by troops to protect the island from invaders. As well as Fort Shirley on Shirley Heights and Fort James in St John's, FORT GEORGE was a retreat for women and children during attacks, FORT BARRINGTON on Goat Hill was named after Admiral Barrington who defeated the French in the late 18th century, and FORT BERKELY at English Harbour has the distinction of being one of the first to be fortified to guard the dockyard.

A couple of sights in Antigua which are interesting for the fact that they reflect the island's distant Indian heritage are DEVIL'S BRIDGE in Indian Town (a national park in the north-east) and also the MEGALITHS OF GREENCASTLE HILL; the former makes for fascinating viewing – it's a natural bridge with blow-holes spouting surf; the latter were erected centuries ago, and are well worth the climb up Greencastle Hill to see.

ACCOMMODATION

Winter rates in most Antigua hotels are almost double the summer rates, winter being from December to April.

● **First Class:** (double US$90–$120 in winter, and US$60–$90 in summer)
Curtain Bluff – Old Road, Antigua (tel. 31067). Luxurious hotel where facilities include tennis courts (and a resident professional),

direct access to 2 good beaches, and a yacht available for sailing during the day; all water sports are also catered for. Fine dining is available in the restaurant.

The Inn – Freeman's Bay, Antigua (tel. 31014). Located right at the water's edge at English Harbour, the rooms here are attractive and very comfortable, and the service is excellent. All water sports are catered for, and other facilities include a beach bar, a fine restaurant, and live entertainment.

Long Bay – Long Bay, Antigua (tel. 32005). Right on the water's edge, this hotel is somewhat isolated on Antigua's north-eastern coast; the rooms are extremely comfortable and have balconies facing a lagoon. All water sports are catered for by the hotel.

● **Super Club Class:** (double US$50–$80 in winter, US$30–$50 in summer)
White Sands – Hodge's Bay, Antigua (tel. 4622300). On an attractive stretch of beach, this small hotel has a very relaxed atmosphere, and its situation makes it ideal for water sports. The staff are friendly, and facilities are very good.

Castle Harbour Club and Casino – St John's, Antigua (tel. 21266). Comfortable establishment, noted for its casino and restaurant more than anything else. Facilities include a swimming pool, and frequently live entertainment is laid on.

Admiral's Inn – Nelson's Dockyard, English Harbour, Antigua (tel. 31027). Located in the Nelson's Dockyard area, the rooms here are small but comfortable and service is good; among the facilities is an excellent restaurant, and free transport is provided to a nearby beach.

Anchorage Hotel – Dickinson Bay, Antigua (tel. 20267). Very much at the upper end of the Super Club price range, this hotel is right on the beach, and has facilities for all water sports. The rooms are very comfortable, and there's entertainment and dancing nearly every night.

● **Economy:** (US$40–$50 in winter, US$20–$40 in summer)
Falmouth Beach Apartments – Falmouth Harbour, Antigua (tel. 31027 or 31534). Attractive location in Falmouth Harbour; facilities are good and the rooms comfortable.

Dian Bay Resorts Apartments – Long Bay, St John's, Antigua (tel. 32425 or 32003). Very comfortable with good facilities.

Courtland Hotel – Upper Gambles Street, St John's, Antigua (tel. 21395). Convenient location in the capital, the atmosphere here is pleasant, the surroundings comfortable, and the facilities good.

Catamaran Hotel – Falmouth Harbour, Antigua (tel. 31036). Excellent facilities. The staff are friendly, too, and it is convenient for points of interest along the southern shore.

Antigua Beach Hotel – Country Club Road, Hodges Bay, Antigua (tel. 22069). Attractively located in Hodges Bay, the rooms here are very comfortable, and the facilities excellent.

Silver Dollar Inn – All Saints' Road, St John's, Antigua (tel. 21275). Excellent value, both for its comfortable rooms and adequate facilities.

DINING OUT

From beach-side salad bar to luxury hotel dining room, there is a wide selection of establishments in Antigua serving an impressive range of cuisines. Antiguan cuisine is featured in many places . . . rather spicy, most dishes are influenced by the West Indian taste for delicate sauces. The island speciality is lobster with red snapper; also worth trying are suckling pigs, free-range chickens and charcoal grills. Most menus around the island also offer a wide variety of curries, and in the large hotels various imported delicacies are available. Among the local drinks that are served in virtually all restaurants are cold fruit and sugar cane juice, and coconut milk. Look out also for the Antiguan-produced red and white rums.

• **First Class:** (US$25–$30 for two)
Cockleshell Inn – Fort Road, Nr St John's, Antigua (tel. 20471). Dining is available both indoors and out in this popular establishment. The atmosphere here is very pleasant, and the menu consists mainly of fine seafood dishes. Among the house specialities is cockles done in a mixture of island spices.

L'Auberge de Paris – Halcyon Heights, Antigua (tel. 21223). A very elegant restaurant where the panoramic terrace overlooks Dickinson Bay; there's also a piano bar, a swimming pool and a tropical garden. The menu is French, and the range of dishes wide and very good indeed. Excellent service, too.

Bach-Lien – Hodges Bay, Antigua (tel. 23293). The only place on the island serving Vietnamese cuisine, this restaurant offers either outdoor dining on the verandah, or indoors amid a relaxed and intimate atmosphere. Dishes worth trying here are beef and fish prepared Vietnamese style.

● **Super Club Class:** (US$15–$25 for two)
Darcy's – Kensington Court, St John's, Antigua (tel. 21323). Popular outdoor restaurant where the menu is varied, and includes typical West Indian dishes among other cuisines. A steel band plays during lunch.

St James Club (Rainbow Lounge) – St John's, Antigua (tel. 31430). Sophisticated establishment in the St James Club Hotel. Tables are candle-lit, a band plays soft music, and the food is excellent. Service is impeccable, and there's also an extensive wine list.

Admiral's Inn – Nelson's Dockyard, English Harbour, Antigua (tel. 31027). Set on the ground floor of a 200-year-old inn, this restaurant offers classic dining. it's also possible to eat on the terrace at the water's edge, and the food served is splendid, especially the seafood.

● **Economy:** (US$10–$15 for two)
Shirley Heights Lookout – Shirley Heights, Antigua. Located in an historic area, this restaurant offers superb views of Nelson's Dockyard and English Harbour. The food is also splendid, notably the seafood and grilled steaks.

Kim Sha – Church Street, St John's, Antigua (tel. 24505). Quiet, elegant Chinese restaurant, with attractive Oriental decor. The food is good, and the service excellent.

China Garden – Newgate Street, St John's, Antigua (tel. 21298). Oriental dishes are the house speciality, but excellent Antiguan specialities are also featured.

Pelican Club Restaurant – Hodges Bay, Antigua. Good Italian food served in a relaxing atmosphere. Guests are able to eat either indoors or on the sea terrace, and evening entertainment is also laid on frequently. Seafood is also served.

NIGHTLIFE

Most of Antigua's nightlife is to be found in the island's hotels, the majority of which offer nightly entertainment. Steel bands, limbo dancing, fire-eating, calypso and various other entertainments, traditional or otherwise, are available. There's at least one casino on the island, several music clubs, and a string of discotheques. Quiet, intimate bars also feature in the major tourist areas.

● **Nightclubs:**
Castle Harbour Club and Casino – St John's, Antigua (tel. 21266). One of the island's few casinos, if not the only one; it features roulette, blackjack, craps and one-armed bandits. There's also entertainment in a pleasant lounge nearby.

Halcyon Cove – Dickinson Bay, Antigua (tel. 20256). One of the island's more expensive hotels, there are various traditional entertainments on offer here every night, as well as dancing. Lively atmosphere.

Admiral's Inn – Nelson's Dockyard, English Harbour, Antigua (tel. 31027). Not just a fine hotel with an excellent restaurant, the bar here and the pleasant tabled courtyard provide one of Nelson's Dockyard's favourite attractions for locals, seamen and tourists alike. The atmosphere in this 200-year-old inn is very friendly indeed, and the clientele from all walks of life.

Golden Peanut – St John's (centre), Antigua (tel. 21415). An excellent restaurant serving a range of food from hamburgers to splendid West Indian dishes, there is also a range of entertainment on offer here in the evenings, from the traditional Antiguan to the more internationally flavoured. There is a cover charge in the evenings.

EXCURSIONS

SEA EXCURSIONS from Antigua are a popular method of exploring the enormous range of marine beauty that surrounds the island. Various trips, cruises and jaunts in glass-bottomed boats all enable visitors to view the splendid tropical fish and coral beneath the waters of the Caribbean, and the animal life above. Also available are buffet and barbecue cruises, which include live entertainment. Below are listed some of the trips available.

The *Jolly Roger*, a 2-masted 'tall ship' schooner built in 1944, offers a fun pirate cruise around the waters of the Caribbean. The trip includes dancing to calypso, a free bar (serving Jolly Roger Pirate Rum Punch among other things), a barbecue steak or lobster lunch, a chance to 'walk the plank' and, perhaps most interesting of all, guests are able to snorkel over a wreck underneath the water surface. For information phone 22064.

Falcon, a 61-foot catamaran, offers a choice of 2 day-charters. On one of these, guests depart from Halcyon Cove for Barbuda, where it's possible to tour the bird sanctuary, to snorkel on beautiful reefs, and there's a beach buffet laid on. The other option is to depart from Halcyon Cove and sail for English Harbour, entering the harbour just as Lord Nelson did in the 18th century; from there, guests can tour the historic buildings of Nelson's Dockyard, lunch in a local restaurant, go shopping with Antiguan women and swim at one of the island's beaches. Both make for a full day's pleasant activity and sightseeing. For details, phone 20256 (Hotel Activity Desk at the Halcyon Cove Hotel).

Franco's Calypso and Glass Bottom Boat offers a 2½-hour cruise during which guests can watch the pelicans at Pelican Island and also examine underwater innumerable species of tropical fish, conch and coral forests. There's an open bar on board, and calypso entertainment. For information phone 20061 (Hotel Activity Desk at the Jolly Beach Hotel).

See By Sea offer private yacht charters on fully equipped luxury yachts. These trips include exploring tiny islets on unspoiled beaches, snorkelling on reefs, discovering Arawak caves, underground sea passages and bird sanctuaries, and also a barbecued lunch. There's an open bar on board with free drinks. For details, contact Basil Hill Tours on 24882.

Barbados

GRANTLEY ADAMS INTERNATIONAL AIRPORT

Grantley Adams International Airport is located 11 miles south-east of Bridgetown, the Barbados capital. It handles all flights in and out of Barbados, both to the Caribbean islands and other international destinations. There is one terminal.

AIRPORT FACILITIES

Information Desk	Located in the terminal building.
Bank/Foreign Exchange	There is a branch of the Barbados National Bank which offers currency exchange.
Hotel Reservations Service	There is an office of the Barbados Board of Tourism which can assist with hotel bookings. This is located within the terminal.
Bar	There is a bar in the terminal.
Restaurant/Buffet	A restaurant is located in the terminal building.
Post Office	Located in the terminal.
Shops	There is a total of 15 shops in the terminal selling gifts, books, newspapers, magazines, etc.
Duty Free	There are several duty free shops in the terminal building selling a variety of goods, such as liquor, bone china, perfume, electronic equipment, cameras and binoculars, watches, and jewellery. There are also a number of duty free shops in various parts of the island.

Toilets	These are all over the terminal building.
Car Rental Desks	Several car hire firms have counters in the terminal.
Public Telephones	These are all over the terminal.

AIRPORT INFORMATION

Check-in Times	Domestic – 60 minutes on average. International – 90 minutes on average.
Airport Tax	BD$16 (US$8). Visitors remaining in Barbados for less than 24 hours are exempt from such tax.

CITY LINKS

• **Taxi:** A well organized taxi service operates between the airport and the rest of the island, and taxis are available round the clock. A usual fare to Bridgetown is around BD$23, and the Barbados Hilton around BD$18.

BARBADOS

The name Barbados comes from the Portuguese 'los barbados' – 'the bearded ones' – which was given by Portuguese explorer Pedro da Campa, who on discovering the island in 1536 was evidently struck by the shaggy, exposed roots of the banyan trees he sighted on the shore. Campa didn't claim Barbados for Portugal, and subsequently it was the British who, on landing on its west coast in 1627, became the island's first settlers. They ruled for over 350 years, and it was only in 1966 that Barbados gained its independence. Today this island, 1 mile wide and 21 in length, has virtually everything for the perfect holiday: pink and white beaches, clear ocean, year-round sunshine, and a culture that combines modern-day Caribbean living with an atmosphere of 18th-century England. From calypso music and limbo dancing to quiet, restful beaches and stunning tropical scenery, Barbados is an island to satisfy most.

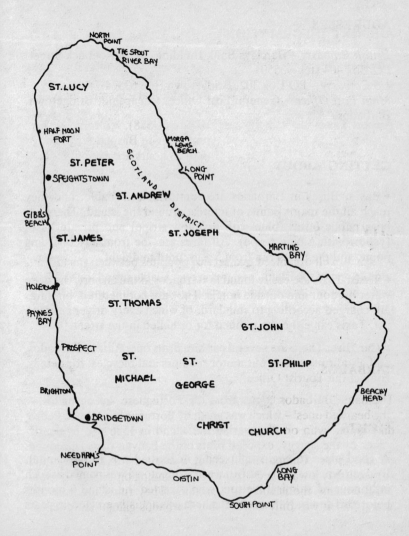

TOURIST INFORMATION

For details of things to do, sights, events, accommodation-listings, etc., contact: *Barbados Board of Tourism*, PO Box 242, Harbour Road, Bridgetown, Barbados (tel. 427-2623/4).

ADDRESSES

British Embassy – Barclays Bank Building, 147/9 Roebuck Street, PO Box 404 (tel. 93550).
US Embassy – PO Box 302, Bridgetown (tel. 63574-7).
Main Post Office – General Post Office, Cheapside, Bridgetown, Barbados.

GETTING ABOUT

• **Buses:** Buses in Barbados are comfortable, reliable, and they reach all the major points of interest around the island. There are both public buses (blue with a yellow stripe) and private buses (yellow with a blue stripe). All fares are 75c from any boarding point, and the buses run from 5 a.m. until midnight.

• **Taxis:** Taxis are easily found in Barbados at the airport, the deep water harbour and outside hotels. They are not metered, but fares are charged according to standard, of which every driver carries a list. Taxis can either be phoned for or hailed in the street.

• **Car Hire:** There are several car hire firms operating in Barbados, and also firms renting out motor scooters and bicycles; for details, contact the Tourist Office.

SIGHTS

A good place to begin sightseeing in Barbados is in the capital, Bridgetown. TRAFALGAR SQUARE in Bridgetown was named as such in honour of Admiral Nelson, who'd visited the island 6 months before his death; Nelson's statue here was actually erected 36 years before the one in London. THE OLD SYNAGOGUE AND CEMETERY is interesting for its historical significance: it was the Jews coming from Brazil in the early 1620s who introduced sugar cane into Barbados, and their synagogue dates back to the mid-17th century; it is the oldest synagogue in the western hemisphere, and the tombstones in the adjoining Jewish cemetery go back as far as 1630. ST PATRICK'S CATHEDRAL began construction in 1840 and was completed 9 years later; the original building was destroyed by fire, and the cathedral that stands today was built in 1899. As well as being the hub of Roman Catholicism in Barbados, the building is interesting for its architecture.

A fascinating place to stroll around in Bridgetown is PELICAN VILLAGE; near the deep water harbour, it's an arts and crafts centre located in an attractive landscaped area . . . there are several shops here where visitors can buy the goods on show. QUEEN'S PARK is the former residence of the general in charge of the British troops in the West Indies. On the withdrawal of the British regiment, it was turned into a park – among its points of interest is one of the largest trees in Barbados – a baobab, which is 61½ feet in circumference and estimated to be 1000 years old. THE FOUNTAIN GARDENS in Bridgetown came about when a fountain was erected in Barbados after piped water was introduced to the island; the actual fountain was completed in 1865, and work on the gardens began in 1882.

Away from Bridgetown there is much of interest around the island. HARRISON'S CAVE at St Thomas is a series of underground caverns with stalagmites, stalactites, underground streams and waterfalls; visitors can travel through the caves on an electric tram. HOLETOWN in St James is the site where Barbados' original settlers first landed in 1627, and there is a Holetown monument commemorating their discovery; a good time to visit is mid-February when the Holetown Festival takes place in celebration of the landing. OUGHTERSON NATIONAL WILDLIFE PARK in St Philip is an interesting place to examine various fauna and flora that include monkeys, alligators, snakes and turtles. There's also a nature trail through a large orchard, and tours are available of Oughterson House, which is a typical Barbadian plantation Great House.

SOUTH POINT LIGHTHOUSE in Christchurch is unique in Barbados since it is made entirely from cast iron; built in England during the 19th century, it was dismantled, shipped across the Atlantic and put back together on its present-day site.

A visit to TURNER'S HALL WOODS in St Andrew is a trip into what Barbados looked like to its first settlers; these woods are a remnant of the tropical forest that covered the island in the early part of the 17th century, and they are full of interesting species such as the trumpet tree, and the macaw palm.

THE COTTON TOWER in St Joseph is one of several old island forts and military signal towers; they used to be in wide use before the introduction of modern communications to the island, and the Cotton Tower is open to public viewing. GUN HILL SIGNAL STATION at St George is another military installation which not only re-creates Barbados' early days but also affords an excellent panorama of the complete southern half of the island, a view that's particularly impressive in early evening.

MOUNT HILLABY in St Andrew, at 1115 feet above sea level, is the highest point on Barbados; it's possible to reach the summit by taking a narrow road from the village of Hillaby, and once there one can view the east and west coasts and also the northern section of the island.

The affluent lifestyle of people in 17th- and 18th-century Barbados can be sampled at VILLA NOVA in St John; a well preserved mansion from those days, it used to be the home of Edmund Haynes, a sugar baron of the 19th century, and visitors are able to tour the building, which is set in a tropical garden.

MORGAN LEWIS MILL in St Andrew is interesting both for its status as the only windmill on the island in perfect working order, and for the reason behind its appearance; it strongly resembles the windmills of Holland due to the Dutch Jews who settled in Barbados and were behind the beginning of the island's cane sugar industry.

ANDROMEDA GARDENS in St Joseph is internationally renowned for its beauty, and provides the perfect opportunity to view some of the tropical world's most exotic plants. There's also a bubbling stream winding through the gardens which is the source of various pools and waterfalls . . . all adding to a stunning environment. WELCHMAN HALL GULLY in St Thomas is also an ideal spot to take in some exotic plants and trees; this natural gully is ¾ mile long and, besides its plant life, it offers excellent views of the north end of the island, especially at dawn and dusk. There's also the chance to see some monkeys here too.

ACCOMMODATION

Hotel prices in Barbados vary according to the season, with winter prices in many places being as much as double the summer prices.

● **First Class:** (double over US$70 in summer, and over US$170 in winter)

Hilton International Barbados – PO Box 510, Bridgetown, Barbados (tel. 426-0200). Located at Needham's Point in Bridgetown on the south-west coast of the island, this particularly attractive hotel is built around a central court which is packed with tropical gardens. Excellent facilities include 2 fine restaurants, a bar/lounge and nightclub, a swimming pool, a fully equipped fitness centre complete with sauna, and there's also good access to the beach and water sports.

Sandy Lane – St James, Barbados (tel. 21311). Very elegant hotel with first-class facilities for tennis and golf, and with easy access to an excellent beach. There is also superb dining in the restaurant, and the service is good.

Cobblers Cove – St Peter, Barbados (tel. 22291). A fairly small hotel which offers villa rooms with balconies or patios. It was once a private home, and the atmosphere tends to be pleasant and personal. Facilities include a swimming pool, excellent bar, fine terrace dining, and the beach adjacent.

● **Super Club Class:** (double over US$55 in summer, and over US$90 in winter)

Buccaneer Bay – St James, Barbados (tel. 21362). This is a fine hotel right on the beach, with facilities including a comfortable bar, an excellent à la carte restaurant, and room service. Water and land sports are also easily arranged.

Crane Beach – St Philip, Barbados (tel. 36220). Beautifully situated overlooking the Atlantic, the facilities here include a pillared pool and surf beach. The excellent restaurant is also noted for its fine dining (especially seafood) and extensive wine list. As well as standard rooms, there are antique-decorated apartments with four-poster beds, tiled baths, etc.

Southern Palms – Christchurch, Barbados (tel. 86101). A series of houses lining a length of beach. Accommodation available here varies from twin-bedded rooms to housekeeping apartments. The restaurant is noted for its barbecues which feature the local (Bajan) cuisine; there's often live music at night too.

Sandy Beach – Christchurch, Barbados (tel. 80933). An attractive hotel where the atmosphere is distinctly Bajan, due mainly to the traditional entertainment and the local dishes served in the fine restaurant. There are good facilities for water sports, and the staff are friendly.

● **Economy:** (double over US$35 in summer, and over US$45 in winter)
Treasure Beach – St James, Barbados (tel. 21346). Somewhat at the top of the economy price range, the good facilities here include a swimming pool, live entertainment and an excellent West Indian restaurant. There's also good access to the beach.

Tides Inn – St Peter, Barbados (tel. 22403). Located a short walk from the beach, the atmosphere here is very relaxed and the facilities are good; they include the free use of snorkel gear.

Island Inn – St Michael, Barbados (tel. 60057). Close to Carlisle Bay beach, the atmosphere here is friendly, the rooms clean and the facilities adequate.

Ocean View – Christchurch, Barbados (tel. 77821). Right next to the sea, good facilities here include a Bajan dining room overlooking the ocean.

Maresol – St Lawrence, Christchurch, Barbados (tel. 89300). Friendly atmosphere, and well located next to the sea. Clean and comfortable.

Sandridge – St Peter, Barbados (tel. 22361). Very comfortable rooms complete with air-conditioning and balconies amid attractive surroundings, with a large garden. Facilities include an excellent restaurant, and an on-the-beach bar.

DINING OUT

Restaurants in Barbados offer a variety of cuisines, from familiar continental dishes to exotic and interesting Bajan delicacies. The local speciality is flying fish (the symbol of Barbados) and it's served in various forms – deep-fried, baked, broiled, stuffed and in stew – at a range of establishments, from first-class restaurant to seaside stall. Other popular seafood dishes are the sea egg – the roe of a sea urchin, Crane chub – dolphin (the pelagic fish variety), red snapper, and also fresh lobster.

Among the tasty Bajan dishes well worth trying are black pudding and souse, and suckling pig; there's also a wide variety of tropical fruit available in most Bajan restaurants, including mango and Bardados cherries.

After dinner, Barbados rum is not to be forgotten; probably the smoothest and richest in the world, it is served in various ways – but usually in punches. Continental restaurants around the island tend to be much more expensive than Bajan establishments.

● **First Class:** (over US$60 for two)
Greensleeves – St Peter, Barbados (tel. 22275). One of the island's most expensive restaurants, but offering quality to match the price. Dining is outdoors beside a lit pool, and the food is reputed to be the best on the island. A very elegant dining experience.

Bagatelle – Highway 2A, St Thomas, Barbados (tel. 02072). Located in the hills, this is an extremely elegant establishment in the cellars of a once private house. An intimate atmosphere is created by lantern-lit tables and hand-crafted furniture. An excellent menu includes both local and continental dishes; stuffed flying fish is a house speciality. There's also an extensive wine list.

Brown Sugar – St Michael, Barbados (tel. 67684). Pleasant surroundings in which to enjoy some excellent Bajan cuisine. Dishes worth looking out for are the pumpkin soup and pepperpot.

● **Super Club Class:** (US$30–$60 for two)
Château Creole – St James, Barbados (tel. 24116). The menu here is excellent, and covers a range of cuisine that includes Creole and Bajan dishes. Seafood is a speciality, and the homemade ice cream is worth trying too.

Flower Drum – St James, Barbados (tel. 04394). Intimate Chinese restaurant with lanterns lighting the tables. The Szechuan and Peking cuisine served is excellent, and the service impeccable.

Crane Beach Hotel – St Philip, Barbados (tel. 36220). Prices here are at the upper end of the Super Club range, but for the house specialities of seafood, fresh fish and langoustine alone, it's worth every penny. The wine list is also extensive.

• **Economy:** (US$10–$30 for two)
Atlantis Hotel – St Joseph, Barbados (tel. 31526). Overlooking Tent Bay, this restaurant is attractively located and the Bajan cuisine served is splendid. House specialities include turtle steak, flying fish, and spinach cakes.

Mike's Place – St Peter, Barbados (tel. 22001). Located just outside Speightstown, this place has a very relaxed atmosphere; best on the menu are the fresh fish and also the turtle steaks.

Peter's Patio – St Michael, Barbados (tel. 68684). Good outdoor dining in the porch; the food is excellent – mainly Bajan cuisine.

The Pebbles – St Michael, Barbados (tel. 64668). Located at the edge of Carlisle Bay, this restaurant is popular for its beachside lunches.

NIGHTLIFE

The emphasis in Barbados' nightlife is on quality, and most if not all nightspots are well kept and offer good entertainment or comfortable facilities or both. Many of the hotels have Floorshow Nights, which involve various traditional entertainments such as steel bands, belly dancing, fire-eating and other Bajan acts. Numerous music clubs around the island offer everything from reggae to calypso to jazz; there are also clubs with various cabaret acts, usually involving much song, dance, folklore and traditional music. Otherwise there is a wide selection of quiet bars and cocktail lounges available, and there is a lively discotheque in every town.

For details of what's going on around the island, consult *The Visitor*, which is distributed free in most hotels.

● **Nightclubs:**

Belair Jazz Club – Bay Street, Bridgetown, Barbados. One of the oldest and most popular nightspots on the island, this New Orleans-style jazz club (complete with tables on balconies overlooking the street) has top jazz acts and a tremendous atmosphere well into the early hours.

The Carlisle – Bay Street, St Michael, Barbados (tel. 79772). An open-air disco/bar which also has a fine restaurant. The atmosphere here is very lively.

1627 and All That Sort of Thing – Barbados Museum. Every Sunday and Thursday this show is presented in the courtyard of the museum; it's dinner theatre, and includes a Bajan buffet, wine, Afro-Barbadian music and various dance shows covering 400 years of the island's history. Tickets cost around $20.

Unicorn One – Southern Palms Hotel, St Lawrence Gap, Christchurch (tel. 87171). A very intimate discotheque open into the early hours. The decor here is very elegant, with a clientele to match.

EXCURSIONS

Most of the sights to be seen around Barbados are listed in the *Sights* section, as the island's size means that to go anywhere doesn't require an excursion. There are, however, day-long trips and activities laid on for visitors. The renting of boats is organized by many hotels, and for a day it's possible to sail out into the ocean on an individual charter, on a party cruise, or on various other sailboat deals. If they don't rent boats at your hotel, try the Barbados Yacht Club (tel. 71125), or the Barbados Cruising Club (tel. 64434).

Other water sports and activities are also available to visitors. Snorkelling and scuba equipment are rented at most hotels, and provide the ideal opportunity to go diving and spearfishing in the reefs of the west and south coasts. Also worth trying while on the island are water-skiing, parasailing, and deep-sea fishing; if your hotel doesn't offer facilities for any of these, it will put you in touch with someone who does.

Bermuda

BERMUDA KINDLEY FIELD AIR TERMINAL

Located 12 miles from city centre.

AIRPORT FACILITIES

Number of Terminals	One terminal handles all flights.
Information Desk (Visitors Service Bureau)	Normally 1100–1800 dependent upon flight schedules. Arrivals Hall 1100–1600 except weekends and public holidays. Main Lobby.
Hotel Reservation/ Accommodation	Same as Information Desk.
Insurance Facilities	Not available.
Bar	Varies depending upon flight schedules. Normally 1000–1900. Three bars available – 1 in public area, 1 in sterile Departure Lounge and 1 in Transit Lounge.
Buffet (Cafeteria)	Located in main lobby, 1st floor adjacent to viewing terrace.
Restaurant	Varies depending upon flight schedules – normally 1000–1900.
Post Office	Not available.
Baggage Deposit	Not available.
Nursery	Not available.
Shops	Normally 0900–2300. Dependent on flight schedules. Three shops/1 in main lobby (public area), 1 in sterile departure area, 1 in transit lounge.
Medical Center	Not available on airport. There is a medical room available as needed.
Toilets	Open during operational hours in all areas of the terminal.

Meeting Point Location	Eastern end of terminal outside arrivals/Bermuda Customs area.
Car Rental Desks	Not available. There are no car rentals in Bermuda.
Additional Facilities	Travel agents desk situated in Arrivals Hall adjacent to Bermuda Immigration desks. All flights are International. The airlines recommend check-in time 1 hour 15 minutes prior to scheduled departure time.
Airport Tax	A departure head tax is charged by the Bermuda Government. $10 per adult, $5 per child between the age of 2–12 years.
Duty Free Shops	None available on the airport.
Transfer Flights	The majority of passengers do not transfer flights in Bermuda.
Airport Hotels	Not available. The closest hotel is Grotto Bay Hotel less than five minute's drive. No courtesy coaches available. Taxi $2.30. Limo $1.75 per person.
City Links	Taxi approximately $13. Limousine bus $6 per person. Public bus $2 per person.

BERMUDA

Bermuda is named after Juan de Bermudez, the Spanish explorer who passed the islands on his way to the Caribbean in 1503. Just as he didn't stay, neither did the next person on Bermuda, who simply carved the initials T.F. and the date 1543 on a rock, then disappeared. It was 50 years later that the islands became known to the British, courtesy of Captain Henry May, who was wrecked on Bermuda in 1593 and managed to make his way back to England to reveal its existence.

The first Englishmen who came to Bermuda to settle arrived in 1612, and it was in 1684 that it became a British colony, which it has remained to this day.

The islands cover an area of 21 square miles, and the local population of some 70,000 find themselves native to a beautiful Caribbean nation full of green hills, pastel houses, rainbow-coloured flowers, fine beaches and clear ocean. It's tailor-made for the tourist, and the Bermudians themselves, with their friendly attitude towards visitors, do much to enhance its charm.

TOURIST INFORMATION

The Bermuda Department of Tourism is at Front and Court Streets, Hamilton (tel. 20023).

ADDRESSES

Deputy Governor's Office (Britain) – Government House, Hamilton (tel. 23600).
US Consulate – Vallis Building, Front Street, Hamilton (tel. 295-1342).
Amex – LP Gutteridge Ltd, Harold Hayes Frith Building, PO Box 1024 (tel. 295-4545).
Main Post Office – 56 Church Street, Hamilton, Bermuda (tel. 55151).

GETTING ABOUT

Public transport in Bermuda is well organized and efficient, and getting around on the island is easy.

• **Bus:** The bus service covers all the major routes around Bermuda and links points of interest; they usually run to schedule, and all buses leave from the Central Bus Terminal on Washington Street in Hamilton City. The fare for any trip within 3 zones (the island is divided into 14 zones) is 55c, and 85c is charged for anything longer; exact change is required when boarding a bus.

• **Taxis:** Taxis are always available around Bermuda, especially at the airport or at any harbour when there's a cruise docking. They are metered, and carry a maximum of 4 people. A usual fare from the airport to Hamilton is around $9; there is a 25 per cent surcharge for trips between midnight and 6 a.m., and for luggage carried in the boot there is a charge of 25c per item (to a maximum of $2 per trip).

• **Car Hire:** There is no car rental in Bermuda; this is because officials want to limit the number of cars on the islands (because of their size).

• **Moped Hire:** A very popular method with visitors of touring the island. This can be arranged at most hotels, and prices range from around $15 for 4 hours to about $25 for one day. It's also possible to rent bicycles, which are slightly cheaper.

SIGHTS

An interesting place to begin sightseeing around Bermuda is its capital, HAMILTON. Located in Pembroke Parish on the inner shore of the island's fishhook, not only does it have a string of shops, pubs and attractive residential areas, but there are also numerous interesting and beautiful attractions. The CENOTAPH, between Parliament and Court Streets, was built in honour of Bermudians who died during World Wars I and II. In the park behind the cenotaph is the CABINET BUILDING, where Bermuda's Legislative Council sits, and there are a number of government offices here.

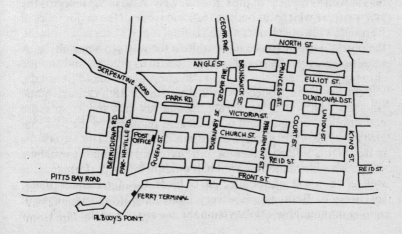

The House of Assembly sits at SESSIONS HOUSE, an imposing building in the middle of the park to the right of Reid Street; this is also home to the Supreme Court, where the judges still wear white wigs as in British courts. Architecturally, Sessions House is interesting for the clock-tower on its south-west corner which was built to commemorate Queen Victoria's Jubilees in 1887 and 1897.

The CITY HALL of Hamilton is an intriguing place both to view and to visit; it was built in 1960 and has a modern wind-clock tower outside, while inside it houses a small theatre, the Mayor's Parlour, and various offices of the Corporation of Hamilton; upstairs in the building is the BERMUDA SOCIETY OF ARTS, which contains many interesting works by local and international artists and sculptors. The BERMUDA HISTORICAL SOCIETY is located in Par-la-Ville gardens, and is well worth visiting for its enormous range of exhibits of Bermudiana; in the gardens too is the PUBLIC LIBRARY, which boasts a collection of island newspapers dating back to 1787 among other things. Also worth taking in while in Hamilton is FORT HAMILTON, a restored fortress from Victorian days, which is of much historical significance and provides excellent views of the city and harbour.

Elsewhere in Bermuda, a major attraction is the town of ST GEORGE, in the St George parish which is in the northern section of Bermuda. Founded in 1612, it was the first capital of Bermuda, and today offers a wide selection of sites from the past. Among these is FORT ST CATHERINE, whose exhibits include various historic dioramas as well as replicas of the Crown Jewels. Also in St George is the STATE HOUSE which was built in 1620 and is one of the major relics of Bermuda's historical past; worth visiting, too, is ST PETER'S CHURCH, the oldest Anglican place of worship in the western hemisphere. A stroll around KING'S SQUARE, complete with its pillories and antique ship replicas, often helps to create an atmosphere of old Bermuda.

VERDMONT, on Collectors Hill Road, is an 18th-century home which is well worth wandering around not just for its splendid collections of antiques and other elegant remnants of the past, but also for its beautiful gardens and stunning sea view. The AQUARIUM in tiny Flatt's Village makes for some excellent marine-life watching – there's a wide range of sea animals on show and in performance, as well as a zoo and a fine collection of birds, too. On Ireland Island, just west of Bermuda, is a very interesting MARITIME MUSEUM; among innumerable exhibits from the sea are the celebrated Teddy

Tucker's treasures, which were once sunken treasures. There are also many fine BEACHES worth visiting around Bermuda, some of the better ones being found at Stonehole, Warwick, Long, Chaplin and Horseshoe Bay.

ACCOMMODATION

Accommodation in Bermuda falls into 4 categories: hotels, cottage colonies, housekeeping (self-catering) apartments and guest houses. In the First Class section below, 2 hotels and 1 cottage colony are listed; in the Super Club category 2 hotels, 1 cottage colony and 1 housekeeping apartment are listed; in the Economy section there is 1 hotel and the other recommendations are either holiday apartments or guest houses.

Many of the hotels, especially the smaller ones, encourage half board accommodation (bed, breakfast and dinner) which is no bad thing as a moped and the Bermudan roads after a few glasses of wine is not to be looked for.

● **First Class:** (double over $90)
Princess Hotel – Hamilton, Bermuda (tel. 53000). Right at the edge of Hamilton Harbour, first-class facilities here include a luncheon terrace, 2 pools by the ocean, shopping arcades and a beauty salon. Free transport is laid on to the South Shore Beach Club, and also to its own golf course. Excellent dining is available in the 'Tiara Room' restaurant, and there's also live entertainment on most nights.

Castle Harbour Hotel, Beach and Golf Club – Tucker's Town, Hamilton Parish, Bermuda (tel. 38161). Situated on a large estate, guests here can enjoy 6 tennis courts, 2 swimming pools, a golf course, and 2 private beaches. All water sports are catered for, and there's a yacht club and marina.

Cambridge Beaches (cottage colony) – Somerset, Bermuda (tel. 40331). In a somewhat remote location, this cottage colony not only has attractive surroundings that include a 25-acre garden, but also excellent private beaches, a heated pool, tennis courts and facilities for all water sports. Occasionally there's also live entertainment and dancing. Convenient for the ferry to Hamilton.

● **Super Club Class:** (double $65–$85)
Grotto Bay Beach Hotel and Tennis Club – Hamilton Parish, Bermuda (tel. 38333). Next to the ocean, the rooms here are very comfortable and offer excellent sea views from their balconies. Good facilities include tennis courts, boating and 2 private beaches. There are also caves on the premises which provide unique sightseeing.

Belmont Hotel, Golf and Beach Club – Warwick, Bermuda (tel. 51301). Attractively located overlooking Hamilton Harbour, facilities here include an 18-hole golf course on the premises, tennis courts, transport to the South Shore Beach Club and a swimming pool.

Horizons (cottage colony) – Paget, Bermuda (tel. 50048). On top of a hill, the facilities here include a heated pool, a sun terrace, a putting green and tennis courts. It's also possible to swim in the ocean at nearby Coral Beach Club.

Marley Beach Cottages (holiday apartments) – Warwick, Bermuda (tel. 51151). Luxury housekeeping cottage units above the South Shore beach which belongs to them. A terrace and gardens make the environment attractive; rooms are air-conditioned, and there is a daily maid service.

● **Economy:** (double $30–$55)
Rosedon – Nr Hamilton, Bermuda (tel. 51640). Rooms are in an old manor house which is set in attractive gardens. There's a heated pool on the premises, and it's close to restaurants and the ferry terminal.

Pretty Penny (guest house) – Paget 6, Bermuda (tel. 21194). In a largely residential area in Paget Parish, the self-contained studios and self-contained apartments here are very comfortable indeed; there's also a private pool and it's close to golf, beaches and the ferry.

Salt Kettle House (guest house) – Salt Kettle, Paget 6–10, Bermuda (tel. 20407). Attractive location, and the facilities here are good. There are private beaches, and the Hamilton ferry is close.

Garden House (guest house) – 4 Middle Road, Somerset Bridge, Sandys 9–21, Bermuda (tel. 41435). Comfortable guest house in the pleasant Somerset Parish.

Green Bank and Cottages (guest house) – Paget 6, Paget Parish, Bermuda (tel. 63615). Comfortable rooms are well kept by friendly staff, and the atmosphere of the whole place is very relaxed and informal.

Munro Beach Cottages – Southampton 8, Southampton Parish, Bermuda. Convenient location overlooking Whitney Bay and adjacent to a golf course. Quiet and relaxing environment.

DINING OUT

There is a range of cuisines available almost wherever you go in Bermuda and seafood is an island speciality. Worth sampling perhaps before anything else is Bermudian food itself, which has proved popular with most visitors to these islands. Among the local dishes that come highly recommended are large tiger shrimp, tangy mussel pie, sweet Bermuda lobster (when in season, from September to March), and the traditional 'Hoppin' John' which consists of black-eyed peas and rice. Look out also for Bermuda fish chowder, which is done with sherry peppers and black rum, and 'Bermuda Fish', which features on most menus, is fish that's been caught fresh the same day, served either pan-fried or broiled. Besides the islands' many restaurants, there are numerous British-type pubs which provide lunch and supper as well as a suitably stocked bar in a relaxed and informal atmosphere . . . the prices at these establishments are usually reasonable. It's worth noting that in most restaurants in Bermuda men are required to wear jackets at dinner, and in several cases a jacket and tie. It's a good idea to check with the restaurant beforehand.

● **First Class:** (over $40 for two)
Papillon – Church and Barnaby Streets, City of Hamilton, Pembroke Parish (tel. 50333). Elegant establishment where the menu includes superb continental dishes, as well as a range of Bermudian cuisine. A house speciality is fish with bananas and almonds.

Waterlot – off Middle Road, Nr Riddell's Bay, Southampton Parish (tel. 26517). An elegant and intimate place to enjoy numerous excellent dishes on an extensive menu. The restaurant is in a restored inn, and candle-lit tables add to the tasteful decor and the atmosphere to make dining a traditionally Bermudian experience.

Fourways – junction of Cobbs Hill Road and Middle Road, Paget Parish, Bermuda (tel. 26517). One of the islands' most popular restaurants, this place was built as an inn in the early 18th century, which is reflected in the elegant atmosphere. The menu includes superb continental and seafood dishes; among the best are lobster bisque with cognac, and lamb and veal.

● **Super Club Class:** ($20–$40 for two)
Miramar – Mermaid Beach, Warwick Parish, Bermuda (tel. 55031). A popular place with Bermudians, this restaurant's menu is noted for excellent charcoal-broiled sirloin, and filet mignon.

Henry VIII Pub-Restaurant – South Shore Road, Southampton Parish (tel. 81977). Rather a lively atmosphere in which to enjoy a fine English and Bermudian menu; dishes range from Yorkshire pudding to mussel pie. The service here is excellent and the staff friendly.

Lobster Pot – Bermudiana Road, City of Hamilton, Pembroke Parish (tel. 26898). Noted for its excellent Bermuda fish dishes; also worth sampling here are the spicy fish chowder and lobster.

● **Economy:** ($10–$20 for two)
Dennis Lambe's Hideaway – St David's Island, St George's Parish (tel. 70044). Excellent menu includes seafood stews, fish chowders and conch fritters among other seafood dishes.

Hog Penny Pub – Burnaby Street, City of Hamilton, Pembroke Parish (tel. 22534). A basic menu, but tasty nonetheless – bangers and mash is a house speciality. Other English dishes are available too.

Rum Runners – Front Street, City of Hamilton, Pembroke Parish (tel. 24737). The economy part of this place is the pub, with its balcony overlooking the harbour. Piano entertainment is laid on in the evenings.

The Crown and the Anchor – Somers Wharf, St George's Parish, Bermuda (tel. 71730). Intimate atmosphere complete with candle-lit tables. The very good menu includes shrimp and prime beef, and there's also an extensive salad bar.

NIGHTLIFE

After-dark entertainment in Bermuda offers much the same diversity as other Caribbean islands. There are no nude shows, and little in the way of large-scale cabaret, but in the larger hotels innumerable after-dinner shows are on offer, from the traditional limbo, fire-eating and calypso to performances by top entertainers. In the guest houses and smaller hotels, the accent is more on intimacy, and often a calypso singer or piano player will perform over dinner. Pubs are much in evidence around Bermuda, and discotheques are everywhere. The once-every-2-weeks *Preview of Bermuda Today* offers information on what's going on around the islands.

● **Nighclubs:**

The Clay House Inn – North Shore Road, Devonshire (tel. 23193). One of the liveliest shows on the island is here, and no holds are barred in a series of performances that involve steel bands, calypso, limbo and other dancing.

The Club – Bermudiana Road, Hamilton (tel. 56693). Up-market nightclub where the clientele are mostly over 30. The surroundings are quiet and comfortable, and dress is usually formal.

Gazebo Bar – Princess Hotel, Hamilton, Bermuda (tel. 53000). Exquisite place for cocktails from where guests can watch the sunset, and see all around the Great Sound. The clientele here in one of Bermuda's most expensive hotels are elegant and refined.

Ram's Head – Pitts Bay Road, Hamilton, Bermuda (tel. 56098). One of the liveliest pubs on the islands, the atmosphere here is friendly and relaxed, and the clientele always very jolly.

EXCURSIONS

There are various excursions available using different methods of transport to tour the islands.

TAXI TOURING is an ideal way to get to know Bermuda. You are able to plan your own route, tell the driver (drivers with small blue flags on their taxis are qualified tour guides), and he'll take you along it, giving a commentary on the various sights. The drivers are almost always good at what they do, and they are usually friendly and ever-informative (he'll help you plan your route). An average cost for a 6-hour daylight tour is around $70 per taxi; one company which offers excellent tours (preset routes) is Penboss Taxi Tours (tel. 53927) – their itinerary takes in Harrington Sound, Somerset and St George's Island – all at length.

SEA EXCURSIONS in all types of craft ranging from yachts to catamarans to glass-bottomed boats are available in several directions from Hamilton Harbour. Cruises taking from 2 hours to a whole day are operated by several companies, and as well as offering the opportunity to explore the marine life, coral reefs and other beauty-at-sea, included on many trips is lunch, a free bar, and various calypso, limbo and other Caribbean entertainments. Among the companies dealing in different types of cruises are Williams Marine (tel. 53727) and Kitson & Company (tel. 52525).

FERRY SERVICES, which are operated by the Bermudian government and travel across the Great Sound between Paget, Warwick, Hamilton and Somerset, are an ideal opportunity to travel the waters around Bermuda for the price of about $1. Often taking the same, or covering part of the routes taken by cruisers, a ride on a government ferry offers sightseeing at a bargain price (minus the frills, however). For information phone 54506.

SIGHTSEEING BUS TRIPS are another excellent way to get to know Bermuda. These are operated by several companies and information will be available at most hotels.

Canada

RED TAPE

• **Passport/Visa Requirements:** In addition to a full, valid passport, visas are required by nationals of Andorra, Argentina, Austria, Barbados, Belize, Brazil, Cyprus, Dominica, Finland, Gambia, Iceland, Jamaica, Leichtenstein, Malta, Mexico, Monaco, New Zealand, Norway, Panama, Papua New Guinea, Paraguay, Peru, Portugal, Singapore, Spain, Sweden, Switzerland, Tanzania, Tonga, Zambia and Zimbabwe.

Visas are normally provided for a period up to 3 months, to be decided by the Immigration officers on arrival. Nationals of the USA do not require a passport or visa to enter Canada.

CUSTOMS

• **Duty Free:** No Customs duty will be charged on the following goods being taken into Canada: 200 cigarettes and 50 cigars and 2 lb of tobacco (over 16 years); 1 bottle (40 fl oz) spirits or wine or 24 cans (12 fl oz) of beer or equivalent, to 8.2 litres per person (over 18) entering Alberta, Manitoba, Prince Edward Island and Quebec and per person (over 19) entering British Columbia, North West Territories, the Yukon, New Brunswick, Newfoundland, Ontario, Saskatchewan and Nova Scotia. A small amount of perfume for personal use is allowed. Also, gifts not exceeding C$25 per item.

HEALTH

No vaccinations are required for entry into Canada.

CAPITAL – Ottawa.

POPULATION – 24,750,000.

LANGUAGE – Bilingual: French and English. English is spoken by most people in the larger cities of French-speaking areas, such as Quebec.

CURRENCY – Canadian Dollar = 100 cents. Notes – 1, 2, 5, 10, 20, 50, 100, 500, 1000; coins – 1, 5, 10, 25 and 50 cents, and 1 dollar (silver coin).
£1 = C$1.94; US$1 = C$1.39.

BANKING HOURS – 1000–1500 Monday–Friday.

POLITICAL SYSTEM – Constitutional monarchy.

RELIGION – 46.2 per cent Roman Catholic, 17.5 per cent United Church of Canada, 11.8 per cent Anglican, 24.5 per cent others.

PUBLIC HOLIDAYS

January 1	New Year's Day
March/April	Good Friday, Easter Monday
May (Monday before May 25)	Victoria Day
July 1	Canada Day
September (1st Monday)	Labour Day
October (2nd Monday)	Thanksgiving Day
November 1	Remembrance Day
December 25, 26	Christmas Day, Boxing Day

CLIMATE – The climate in Canada varies between regions. As a general guide, however, spring is warm with cool nights, summers are sunny and hot everywhere, autumn is cool with frost in most regions and from December through to February the weather is wintry with heavy snowfall in most provinces.

TIME DIFFERENCE – There are 6 time zones across the breadth of Canada:

Pacific Standard Time	GMT − 8 hours.
Mountain Standard Time	GMT − 7 hours.
Central Standard Time	GMT − 6 hours.
Eastern Standard Time	GMT − 5 hours.
Atlantic Standard Time	GMT − 4 hours.
Newfoundland Standard Time	GMT − 3½ hours.

(+1 hour April–October, except in Saskatchewan.)

COMMUNICATIONS

● **Telephone:** Public coin-operated telephones are countrywide. Local calls normally cost 25c and can be dialled directly. Calls to the USA can usually be made direct, although to phone anywhere else outside Canada, dial '0' and ask for the operator. Reduced rates for telephone calls are from 1800–0800 Monday–Friday, and from 1200 on Saturday till 0800 on Monday.

City telephone codes in Canada as follows: Montreal 514; Toronto 416; Vancouver 604.

• **Post:** There's no extra airmail charge for letters or postcards sent within Canada or to the USA. International mail is automatically air-lifted. Stamps can be bought in any Post Office, or from coin-operated vending machines in hotels, banks, railway stations and chemists.

ELECTRICITY – 110v AC.

OFFICE/SHOPPING HOURS – Offices open to the public 0900–1700 Monday–Friday. Shops open 0900–1800 Monday–Friday. Most are also open on Saturdays, and late-night shopping in some stores until 2100 on Thursdays and Fridays.

• **Best Buys:** Each province in Canada has its own individual souvenir range. In western provinces such as Alberta, souvenirs are typically western, with stetsons, cowboy boots and feather headbands proving popular among visitors. In the northern provinces a wide range of Eskimo art is available, such as sculptures, soapstones etc. Hand-embroidered Eskimo clothes can also be bought, as well as a variety of furs. While souvenirs in most eastern provinces are typical of their fishing environment, Quebec offers some with a distinctly French flavour, covering most aspects of its culture from French-Canadian cuisine to high fashion. All over Canada it's possible to buy the celebrated Maple Syrup (a must for any visitor), and to indulge in the Canadian institution of Laura Secord chocolate and confectionery.

INTERNAL TRAVEL

• **Air:** Air Canada, CP Air, Eastern Provincial Airways, Norcanair, Nordair, Pacific Western Airlines and QuebecAir provide extensive domestic services around Canada, serving most cities, and offering a comprehensive service to many towns in the northern regions.

• **Rail:** Via Rail Canada operates a Transcontinental service, as well as providing services within the provinces. There are no rail services in the North West Territories or the Yukon.

• **Road:** Several coach lines operate a wide range of long-distance services, taking in nearly every town in the country, however small. Taxis are available in every town. Most of the major international hire-car agencies are present in all towns, as well as many smaller ones. Drivers not holding a Canadian or US driver's licence should carry an International Driving Licence. Traffic in Canada moves on the right side of the road.

MAJOR SIGHTS OF THE COUNTRY

Canada's vastness, and consequent large distances between points of interest, mean that sightseeing around the country inevitably involves a fair amount of travelling. The major cities of Toronto, Montreal, and Vancouver are perennially popular with tourists for their abundance of things to see and do; away from these centres, however, Canada has a very wide and diverse range of attractions.

For sheer spectacle, Canada's jewel in the crown is undoubtedly the NIAGARA FALLS. One of the world's outstanding natural wonders, the falls are located between Lake Erie and Lake Ontario on the US border, and their 186-feet-high booming white chutes of water not only possess a unique visual splendour – especially at night when illuminated – but the power of the water also fills the atmosphere with a near-frightening roar, which can make a visit there quite awe-inspiring.

QUEBEC CITY, the capital of Quebec province, is about two and a half hours from Montreal. Canada's focal point for its French culture, the city is divided into two main sections, each possessing a distinct flavour more of old France than modern North America. The cliff-top 'vieux Quebec', with its castle, cathedral and other grand architecture, dominates the historical lower town, where the narrow streets and buildings from the past evoke a quaint charm. 95 per cent of locals speak French, although most are bilingual, and communication is usually quite easy.

Culture of a more Celtic nature can be sampled on Nova Scotia's picturesque island of CAPE BRETON. In keeping with the Nova

Scotians' Scottish ancestry, Cape Breton's rugged highland scenery, old fishing villages, and its inland 'Bras d'Or' lakes combine to give the island a definitive Celtic character. Scottish tradition is kept alive here by many of the very friendly local residents who still speak Gaelic, and often indulge in bagpipe-playing or highland dancing. Travel to Cape Breton can be by air, rail, or car.

Between Nova Scotia and New Brunswick, in the Gulf of St Lawrence, lies PRINCE EDWARD ISLAND, Canada's smallest province. Originally inhabited by the MicMac Indians (represented today on four reservations), Prince Edward Island is noted for its rich natural beauty – its south shore made up of flourishing green fields and trees atop red sandstone cliffs, with the north shore renowned for its white silken sand, making a visit to the island very pleasant and worthwhile.

Travellers with a real taste for adventure, however, will revel in Canada's NORTH WEST and YUKON TERRITORIES, where temperatures drop as low as −32°C in winter (15°C in summer), and the tourist trade is still in its infancy, enabling visitors to sample the provincial lifestyle on a more authentic, if slightly less comfortable, basis.

The North West Territories are divided into three Districts: the District of Franklin is renowned for Baffin Island, where there is good hiking, fishing, winter sports, mountaineering and superb scenery to enjoy; the District of MacKenzie has excellent hunting and fishing as well as the mighty MacKenzie River for canoeists and cabin-cruisers alike; while embracing the great Hudson Bay is the DISTRICT OF KEEWATIN. Not so much activity here as dramatically scenic country. Almost uninhabited, the Keewatin is spectacular because of the tundra that sweeps over it, where the rock and low willows are home to vast caribou herds, and the countless lakes are teeming with fish and waterfowl. Beautiful sunsets and the Northern Lights also provide spectacular displays in Keewatin's clear skies.

The Yukon Territory, too, boasts a wide range of natural rugged delights. Its winters are long, dark and bitterly cold, but in summer the sun shines on picturesque jagged mountains, streams and a large variety of wildlife from mink to moose.

Travel to the North West and Yukon Territories is by road (weather permitting), sea and air. Numerous package tours of the

Territories are available, and these are the most comfortable way of getting to know the regions.

HOTELS

Hotels in Canada cover a wide price range. On average, a double room in a first-class hotel costs around C$90 a night, with some economy hotels charging about C$30. Standards vary according to cost, and are very high in the upper price range. Most of the major hotel chains operate across Canada, including Hilton, Inter-Continental, Holiday Inn and Travelodge.

For the economy traveller, Canada has an extensive network of bed-and-breakfast and farm holiday accommodation. Both operate along the same lines, and are a good way of getting to know real Canadians in their true environment – for around C$15 (single) a night, Canadians will let you sleep in their homes and cook you breakfast. With a 'B&B' you stay in a house, whereas farm holiday accommodation is on a farm. In the cities, 'B&B's are known as guest houses.

Comfortable, clean and inexpensive, hostels are open to all age groups (families as well). For around C$7 a night, guests can stay up to 3 nights in any of Canada's 60 hostels, many of which are found in the country's less frequented parts. Membership is required for entry to youth hostels.

Camping is very popular among both the natives and visitors to Canada. Facilities are extensive, and there are innumerable camping grounds across the country.

Another common practice among travellers in Canada which is reasonably priced is the hiring of mobile trailers or motorhomes. For details, contact the Tourist Information Offices.

NIGHTLIFE AND RESTAURANTS

Most entertainment in Canada is to be found in the larger provincial cities, where there is an immense variety of after-dark pursuits to choose from. Theatre in Canada has grown considerably over the years, and now enjoys worldwide acclaim. Toronto has emerged as the country's focal point for English-speaking theatre, although there's much to view elsewhere too, often during festivals.

Dance has also risen in prominence, and as well as the celebrated National Ballet of Toronto and the Royal Winnipeg Ballet, there is a lot more to this aspect of Canadian culture on a regional basis too.

The Canadian music scene is renowned worldwide. Symphony orchestras are the country's forte, and this is well reflected in the performances of both the Toronto and Montreal Symphonies. Cinema is also very popular all over the country, and most towns have at least one cinema house.

The nightclub scene in Canada is a particularly thriving one. Though only really found in the large cities, the range of nightclubs, casinos and discotheques is extremely wide and varied. There are also numerous jazz clubs to choose from wherever you go.

Canadian cuisine is as varied as the country itself and the nationalities that have settled in it. On the coast the speciality is seafood fresh from two oceans and several seas-worth of coastline. In the Central Plains beef and agricultural products are the favoured dishes with Canadians, and are highly recommended. Among the typical Canadian seafood dishes are King Crab, oysters, shrimp and other shellfish, as well as cod, haddock and salmon. Traditional dishes inland include first-class beef, partridge, prairie chicken, wild duck and goose.

In the major cities (particularly in Ontario) restaurant specialities read like an international cookbook, since most nationalities among Canada's immigrant population are represented in the restaurant trade. In Quebec, there are many restaurants which specialize in French cuisine.

In general, restaurants in Canada's cities tend to be rather expensive, and restaurants featuring foreign cuisine often fall into this category.

Alcohol is sold in nearly all hotels in Canada, as well as in the restaurants and bars, with most offering a wide selection of international beverages. Some restaurants display the sign 'Licensed Premises' if alcohol is served there, since a lot of establishments allow customers to bring their own.

Montreal

Montreal has 2 airports: Mirabel International, which deals with all international flights to and from the Montreal area, and Dorval, which handles domestic flights, and those to the US.

MIRABEL INTERNATIONAL AIRPORT

Montreal's Mirabel International Airport is 34 miles north-west of the city, and is used by around 40 airlines, both domestic and international. Mirabel deals with all international flights to and from the Montreal area, as well as some connecting flights between major cities. It has 1 main passenger terminal which has 3 levels.

AIRPORT FACILITIES

Information Desk	An Information Desk is located on the main floor of the terminal.
Bank/Foreign Exchange	Main floor.
Insurance Facilities	Travel insurance counter is located on the main floor.
Bar	There are bars and cocktail lounges on the main floor and mezzanine levels.
Restaurant/Buffet	There is a restaurant and dining room on the mezzanine level.
Baggage Deposit	Baggage lockers are located on the main floor.
Shops	Shops selling a wide variety of goods are on the main floor and main levels. Food, tobacco, newspapers, gifts, etc. are all available.
Duty Free	Located on the main floor, several duty free shops sell cigarettes, cigars,

	gifts, spirits, liqueurs etc. Most credit cards and traveller's cheques are accepted, and an airline boarding card or a ticket is required when making a purchase.
Toilets	These are on all levels.
Post Office	Stamps can be bought in shops around the terminal.
Car Rental Desks	Avis, Tilden, Budget and Hertz all have desks on the main and third floors.
Public Telephones	These are all around the terminal.
Medical Service	A doctor is available in the terminal from 1430 until 2300 daily.

CITY LINKS

Mirabel is 34 miles from downtown Montreal.

● **Bus:** A rapid bus service operated by the Montreal Transport Commission runs between Mirabel and downtown Montreal. For information, phone the Transport Commission on 476-3470.

● **Taxi:** Taxis are easily found at the taxi ranks in front of the passenger terminal. The fare to Montreal is around C$49.

MONTREAL INTERNATIONAL AIRPORT – DORVAL

Montreal International Airport – Dorval was built in 1940 and today is used by travellers bound for Canadian or American destinations. 14 miles west of the city, Dorval deals with some 80 per cent of air passenger traffic in the greater Montreal area, with 21 airlines operating there.

The airport has 1 passenger terminal, which is 8 storeys high. The ground floor and first floor are reserved for passenger handling, the latter for departures, the former for arrivals.

AIRPORT FACILITIES

Information Desk	First floor.
Bank/Foreign Exchange	Ground and first floors.
Hotel Information	Ground floor.
Insurance Facilities	Flight insurance counter on the first floor.
Bar	There are bars on the ground, first and third floors.
Restaurant/Buffet	There are restaurants and a diningroom on the second floor.
Nursery	First floor.
Shops	There are shops selling a variety of goods on the basement, ground, first and second floors.
Duty Free	Located on the first floor, this sells the usual duty free goods such as tobacco, gifts, liquor and perfume. Most major credit cards are accepted, and a ticket or airline boarding card must be presented before a purchase can be made.
Medical Clinic	On the first floor.
Toilets	These are located all around the terminal.
Car Rental Desks	Avis, Budget (Sears), Budget, Hertz, Thrifty/Canada Holiday and Tilden all have desks on the ground floor.
Public Telephones	On all levels.
Airline Lounges	Two VIP lounges owned by Transport Canada are available on request, and some airlines have their own lounges, including CP Air and Delta Air.

CITY LINKS

• **Bus:** A bus service operates from various points around the city to Dorval. The fare is C$5.50, and the pick-up points are Le Château Champlain, Queen Elizabeth Hotel and the Sheraton Centre and Towers.

MONTREAL

Montreal is a city which shouldn't be missed by visitors to Canada. Originally an Indian village by the name of 'Hochelaga' when it was discovered by the French explorer Jacques Cartier in 1535, the Montreal of today is a city which has grown to become not only one of Canada's most important industrial centres (being a busy port on the St Lawrence river), but also one of the country's major intellectual and artistic capitals. The name Montreal is derived from Mont Royal, the extinct volcano dating back around 350 million years which rises up from the heart of the city.

The rich history of this more-French-than-Canadian metropolis can be lived in the Old Montreal (Vieux Montreal) district – cobbled streets, renovated old buildings and market-places, not to mention fine street and indoor entertainment, all make for a charming old-world atmosphere coupled with a lively entertainment scene.

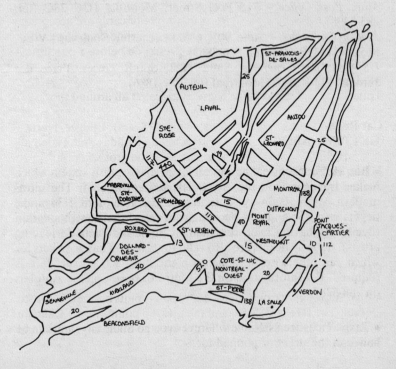

The city's more modern sections are also packed with their own unique attractions; whatever your taste in amusement or culture, by daylight or after dark, you're liable to find it here.

TOURIST INFORMATION

For details of sightseeing tours, events, things to do, accommodation-listings, etc., contact: *Greater Montreal Convention and Tourism Bureau*, Place Bonaventure, Mart F-1 Frontenac, PO Box 889, Montreal, Quebec H5A 1E6 (tel. 871-1595).

ADDRESSES

Main Post Office – 715 Peel Street, Montreal H3C 28C (tel. 283-5398).
British Consulate – Suite 901, 635 Dorchester Boulevard West, Montreal H3B 1R6 (tel. 866-5863).
US Consulate-General – Suite 1122, South Tower, Place des Jardins, PO Box 65, Montreal (tel. 281-1886).

GETTING ABOUT

• **Bus/Métro:** Montreal has an excellent mass-transit system which makes travel around the city quick and convenient. The ultra-modern Métro (subway) runs from 5.30 a.m. until 1.30 a.m.; tickets cost 85c and can be bought in the stations (sights within themselves having been designed by some of Quebec's leading artists). Subway tickets are also valid for travel on buses, tickets for which can otherwise be bought on the bus itself – exact fare is required. For information on the Métro or buses, phone Autobus on 288-6287.

• **Taxis:** Taxis are available wherever you go in the city, and can be hailed in the street or phoned for.

• **Car Hire:** All the major hire firms have branches at the 2 main airports, Central Station and in the city's main hotels. They also have central offices.

SIGHTS

A favourite area with visitors to Montreal is the OLD MONTREAL district. Whether you go there on foot, by Métro or by horse-drawn carriage, it is well worth spending some time exploring around. Old Montreal's major attraction is undoubtedly JACQUES-CARTIER SQUARE, one of the city's oldest market-places, which is complete with sidewalk cafés, flower stalls, and old-world architecture, as well as street musicians and other assorted performers. Among the area's other points of interest is CHÂTEAU RAMEZAY, a restored house which dates back to Montreal's days under French colonial rule – a museum in the house contains exhibits depicting life during that period. The NOTRE-DAME-DE-BON-SECOURS church is a chapel which was formerly used for sailors, and the building next door is the BONSECOURS MARKET, which today houses municipal government offices – both these buildings are interesting to visit. Elsewhere in Old Montreal, places worth taking in include the PLACE D'ARMES, a square commemorating the founding of Montreal; the NOTRE-DAME BASILICA, a splendid building in neo-gothic style dating back to the last century; the HÔPITAL DES SOEURS GRISES (Grey Nuns' Hospital) which is one of the city's oldest buildings, being constructed in 1644; and also YOUVILLE SQUARE, where the surroundings create a centuries-old atmosphere.

Away from the Old Montreal area, there is much more on offer in the way of sights. Rising from the heart of Montreal is MONT ROYAL PARK; known locally as 'the mountain', the park is a year-round playground, with its slopes providing facilities for skiing, cycling, skating and other activities. There's also a fine view of the city to be had from its summit. Other parks in the city are LAFONTAINE PARK, which contains a fairyland-children's zoo and a lagoon for various water activities, and the BOTANICAL GARDENS, which houses more than 25,000 different varieties of plants.

JEAN-TALON MARKET in the centre of the city's Italian district is worth wandering through. Open all year round, the market is very popular among Montrealers for its wide selection of fresh produce, meat, fish, pastries and handicrafts, and the outdoor stalls and noisy vendors create a true market atmosphere. Other markets which you might find interesting to stroll around are ATWATER MARKET, which deals in meat, cheeses and speciality foods, and GREATER MONTREAL CENTRAL MARKET which caters largely to the wholesale trade but nevertheless welcomes all shoppers.

Museums and art galleries in the city exhibit a diverse range of culture. The MONTREAL MUSEUM OF FINE ARTS, in Sherbrooke Street West, houses world-class exhibitions such as a superb collection of pre-Columbian figures, and one of Eskimo sculpture; the MUSEUM OF MODERN ART, in the Cité-du-Havre, displays contemporary art both from Canada and from around the world; SAINT-JOSEPH'S ORATORY MUSEUM, inside the main building of Saint-Joseph's oratory on Mont Royal, houses a collection of stained-glass windows, bronzes and mosaics; and LE MUSÉE D'ART SAINT-LAURENT, on the Boulevard Sainte-Croix, boasts some fine works reflecting the cultural heritage of the Quebec province.

Among the many other museums, those worth visiting include LE MUSÉE DES ARTS DÉCORATIFS on Sherbrooke Street opposite the Botanical Gardens (exhibitions on the decorative arts from the mid-19th century to today), the SAIDYE BRONFMAN CENTRE on the Chemin Côte Sainte-Catherine (contemporary works by national and international artists), and the MUSÉE DU CINÉMA on the Boulevard de Maisonneuve East has a display of film-making equipment dating back to last century among other interesting exhibits.

A unique feature of Montreal is its large number of underground complexes, which are linked together by pedestrian walkways and by Métro, and which make up between them quite a sizeable 'underground city', not only providing weatherproof access to hotels and offices, etc., but also housing an extensive range of shops, boutiques, bars, cinemas and various other attractions which make this city beneath a city well worth spending some time in.

Among the other attractions around the city is the DOW PLANETARIUM, at 1000 St Jacques Street West, which presents 5 different audio-visual displays every year, each very spectacular; the observatory at the city's SAINT-LAMBERT LOCK provides visitors with a chance to examine the locking procedures of the St Lawrence Seaway; and the OLYMPIC PARK, built for the 1976 Olympic Games, hosts events all year round which range from 'Expos' baseball matches on the actual park to exhibitions, fairs and shows in the Velodrome.

ACCOMMODATION

● **First Class:** (double over C$150)
Le Centre Sheraton Hotel and Towers – 1201 Dorchester West, Montreal, H3B 2L7 (tel. 878-2000). The Sheraton Towers are luxurious suites located on floors 32–36 of Le Centre Sheraton. These offer all the facilities of Le Centre Sheraton plus a private lounge serving continental breakfast and an evening bar service. Le Centre Sheraton is itself a fine establishment, with guest facilities including 3 lounges, 4 restaurants, an indoor heated pool, a health club, sauna and shopping arcade. The hotel's location makes it convenient to Place Ville Marie, Mont Royal Mountain, and Ste Catherine Street.

Bonaventure Hilton International – 1 Place Bonaventure, Montreal, H5A 1E4 (tel. 878-2332). First-rate facilities include 3 restaurants, an entertainment lounge, pool-bar, and 24-hour room service, as well as a 2½ acre landscaped rooftop garden, a health club, and a year-round heated outdoor pool. There is also direct indoor access to the famous underground city.

Hotel Du Parc – 3625 Avenue du Parc, Montreal, H2X 3P8 (tel. 288-6666). Conveniently located next to Mont Royal Park, and 10 minutes from downtown. Facilities include indoor and outdoor pools, exercise rooms, squash, tennis and handball courts, and a fine restaurant.

● **Super Club Class:** (double C$70–C$100)
Le Grand Hotel – 777 University Street, Montreal (tel. 879-1370). Excellent facilities include a rooftop revolving restaurant, as well as an in-house dinner theatre.

Hotel Ruby Foo's – 7655–7815 Boulevard Decarie, Montreal, H4P 2H3 (tel. 731-7701). Only minutes from downtown by subway, this hotel is noted for its fine restaurant and friendly service. Facilities are also good.

Manoir Shangri-La – 157 Sherbrooke Street East, Montreal, H2X 1C7 (tel. 285-0895). Luxurious hotel located close to business and shopping districts.

Maritime Travelodge – 1155 Guy Street, Montreal, H3H 2K5 (tel. 932-1411). Excellent facilities include an indoor pool and sauna.

• **Economy:** (double C$20–C$40)
Hotel de Touristes St-Norbert – 40 St Norbert Street, Montreal, H2X 1G3 (tel. 844-4263). Clean with adequate facilities.

Hotel Karukera – 311 Ontario Street East, Montreal, H2X 1H7 (tel. 845-7932). Comfortable, and conveniently located near to city sights.

Maison De Touristes Jolicoeur – 1700 Ontario Street East, Montreal, H2L 1S7 (tel. 522-3223). Good facilities including television in some rooms. Friendly staff.

Hotel Ville De France – 57 Ste Catherine Street West, Montreal, H2X 1K5 (tel. 849-5043). Convenient for sightseeing.

Maison Jay Tourist Rooms – 1083 Rue St Denis, Montreal, H2X 2J3 (tel. 844-6068). In one of the city's liveliest areas for nightlife, this hotel is good value. Friendly staff.

Hotel Le Plateau – 438 Mont Royal Avenue East, Montreal, H2J 1W7 (tel. 843-7396). Clean with reasonable facilities.

DINING OUT

Montreal is renowned as one of North America's centres of culinary delight, since its 2000-odd restaurants boast not only the best in authentic French and French-Canadian cuisine, but also a range of ethnic gastronomy from some 30 nationalities. As well as restaurants Montreal has a wide selection of sidewalk cafés and tearooms, and good food is also served at the many café-concerts and café-theatres. Menus and prices are always posted outside any eating place, and major credit cards are accepted in most establishments, although it is advisable to check first. Among the Quebec specialities which shouldn't be missed are Matane shrimp, Gaspe salmon, maple syrup and lobster from the Magdalen Islands.

● **First Class:** (over C$60 for two)
Le Saint-Amable – 188 St Amable Street, Place Jacques-Cartier, Montreal (tel. 861-4645). Set in an old house, this is one of the city's most renowned French establishments, both for its superb food and elegant surroundings.

Festive du Gouverneur – Old Fort, Sainte-Hélène Island, Montreal (tel. 879-1141). Traditional French fare amid medieval banquet atmosphere. Due to the restaurant's beautiful setting, eating here is a very pleasant experience.

Bill Wong's – 7965 Boulevard Decarie, Montreal (tel. 731-8202). Situated in Montreal's North End, this restaurant serves some of the best Chinese food in town amid pleasant decor. Friendly staff.

● **Super Club Class:** (C$40–C$60 for two)
Les Halles – 1450 Crescent Street, Montreal (tel. 844-2328). Good food in an authentic Parisian environment.

Peking Garden – 5339 Queen Mary Road, Montreal (tel. 484-9139). Excellent Chinese cuisine in Montreal's North End. Try the spicy dishes.

Lanterna Verde – 1560 Herron (Dorval), Montreal (tel. 631-6434). Fine continental and Italian food served in pleasant surroundings. Friendly service.

● **Economy:** (C$20–C$40 for two)
La Mer a Boire – 429 St Vincent Street, Montreal (tel. 866-8307). Excellent French food in an intimate, cosy atmosphere.

Le Muscadin – 100 St Paul Street West, Montreal (tel. 842-0588). Fine Italian food served by friendly staff. Probably the best pasta in town.

Auberge Handfield – St Marc-sur-le-Richelieu, Montreal (tel. 670-0284). Traditional Canadian fare in tastefully decorated restaurant.

Au Quinquet – 354 St Joseph Boulevard, Montreal (tel. 272-4211). An excellent menu includes many typical Quebec dishes.

NIGHTLIFE

Montreal offers some of the best after-dark entertainment in the whole of Canada. Renowned for its classical and contemporary music concerts, ballets, opera and shows featuring internationally famous performers, the city also has an enormous range of sidewalk cafés, bars, discotheques, nightclubs and other nightspots to suit every taste and budget. Two of the city's liveliest areas for nightlife are OLD MONTREAL and SAINT-DENIS STREET, the latter providing for the young, with the former catering for all ages with almost everything available in the way of night-time pursuits. For specific details of events and things to do in the evening, consult the English-language morning newspaper the *Gazette*.

● **Nightclubs:**
L'Air du Temps – 191 St Paul, Old Montreal (tel. 842-2003). Very popular nightclub among both visitors and locals.

Arthur Dinner Theater – Queen Elizabeth Hotel, 900 Dorchester Street (tel. 861-3511). Excellent entertainment laid on most nights in the form of lavish full-size shows and cabarets.

Disco Constellation – Four Seasons (Quatre Saisons) Hotel, 1050 Sherbrooke Street West, Montreal (tel. 248-1110). A lively disco-theque in one of Montreal's finest hotels. Strictly for the energetic.

The Caf'Conc' – Château Champlain, Montreal (tel. 878-1688). Lavish Parisian-style cabarets nightly amid traditional French decor.

EXCURSIONS

The LAURENTIDES (Laurentians) are a range of mountains one hour's drive north of Montreal, and to visit here is to sample some of Canada's most spectacular scenery. The mountains, lakes and valleys of the Laurentides were carved out 8000 years ago, and today the area's natural beauty is complemented by excellent sports facilities (swimming, boating, golf, skiing, riding, etc.) to make it an ideal place either to get away from it all, or to enjoy more active pursuits. Well worth visiting in the area is the Trappist monastery at OKA which produces the famous Oka cheese, and also the artists' colony at VAL-DAVID.

RICHELIEU-RIVE SUD, 30 minutes' drive south of Montreal, is a valley steeped in history, the Richelieu River which runs through the valley having been witness to many a colonial battle and to Indian wars. Otherwise, the area today is very tranquil; while there are a number of historic sites and forts to visit, it's a good idea to take in a pleasure cruise up the river or take a walk around the elegant old residences or country churches which exist, particularly in Chambly. The quiet towns on the banks of the Richelieu River also offer a diverse range of other attractions: there's a safari park at Hemmingford, popular apple festivals at Saint-Antoine-Abbé and Rougemont, and a superb cruise among the islands at Sorel is offered to visitors.

Half an hour's drive north-east of Montreal is LE LANAUDIERE, a region with great variety in its range of things to see and do. Centuries ago the region lay under water, and today this is reflected in the innumerable lakes, rivers and waterfalls which provide a wealth of natural beauty and make for superb sightseeing, as well as providing facilities for sports such as fishing and windsurfing. In the regional capital of JOLIETTE it's well worth taking in the art museum, which contains medieval sculptures, Renaissance works, and many traditional Quebec carvings. The nearby town of RAWDON boasts a restored Canadiana village, interesting not only for its aesthetic qualities, but also for its cultural value.

Just across the Jacques-Cartier Bridge from Montreal is the ÎLE SAINTE-HÉLÈNE, which provides excellent facilities for picnics and swimming in summer, and for snow-shoeing and cross-country skiing in winter. Other attractions on the island include the Alcan Aquarium, the Old Fort and La Ronde, an amusement park which offers craft workshops, restaurants and boutiques as well as amusement rides.

Toronto

LESTER B. PEARSON INTERNATIONAL AIRPORT

The Lester B. Pearson International Airport lies 18 miles north-west of Toronto, and deals with a total of 16 airlines, both international and domestic. There are 2 terminals.

Terminal 1 handles Wardair, Eastern Provincial, KLM, Olympic, PEM Air, Republic, American, US Air, Eastern Pilgrim, Aeromexico, Arrow Air, QuebecAir, MALL, United, Nordair, BWIA International, CP Air and Alitalia.

Terminal 2 handles Air Canada, Air France, Air Jamaica, Air Ontario, Austin Airways, British Airways, Comair, Commuter Express, Lufthansa, Pacific Western, Swissair, Toronair, Voyageur and Yugoslav.

AIRPORT FACILITIES

Information Desk	Arrivals level in Terminals 1 and 2.
Bank/Foreign Exchange	Arrivals and Departures levels in Terminals 1 and 2. American Express machine in Terminal 1 Departures level.
Hotel Information	Arrivals level Terminal 1.
Bar	Cocktail lounge in Terminal 1 Arrivals level, and bar/cocktail lounge in Terminal 2 Arrivals level.
Restaurant/Buffet	Restaurant and snack bar in Terminal 1 Departures level, and in Terminal 2 Departures there is a restaurant/lounge as well as several fast-food outlets and coffee shops.
Nursery	Available in Terminal 2 Departures level and in Terminal 1 basement 0800–2359.

Shops	Various shops on all levels in both terminals sell food, gifts, magazines, etc.
Duty Free	Located in both terminals, they sell gifts, perfumes, liquor and a wide range of other goods. They accept most credit cards and, when making purchases, you need to show an airline boarding card or ticket.
Medical Clinic	In basement level of Terminal 1, and Terminal 2 Departures level.
Toilets	Widely available in both terminals.
Car Rental Desks	Avis, Budget, Hertz and Tilden have desks in the Arrivals level.
Insurance Facilities	Flight insurance desk on the Departures level in Terminal 2 and in Terminal 1.
Public Telephones	These are found all over the airport.
Barber Shop	On Terminal 2 Arrivals level and Terminal 1 Departures level.
Chapel	In the Terminal 2 Departures level.
Terminal Transfer	A shuttle bus service is available between Terminal 1 and Terminal 2 parking lot every 15 minutes, fare: 50c.

AIRPORT HOTELS

● **First Class:**
Toronto Airport Hilton International – 5875 Airport Road, Mississauga (tel. 677-9900). Complimentary shuttle service to and from Terminals 1 and 2.

● **Super Club Class:**
Holiday Inn – Toronto West – 2 Holiday Inn Drive (tel. 621-2121).
Howard Johnson's-Toronto Airport Hotel – 801 Dixon Road, Rexdale (tel. 675-6100).
Constellation Hotel – 900 Dixon Road, Rexdale (tel. 675-1500).

● **Economy:**
Heritage Inn – 385 Rexdale Boulevard, Rexdale (tel. 742-5510).
Ascot Inn – 534 Rexdale Boulevard, Rexdale (tel. 675-3101).
Plaza Hotel-Airport – 240 Belfield Road, Rexdale (tel. 241-8556).

CITY LINKS

Lester B. Pearson International Airport is 18 miles from the centre of Toronto.

● **Bus:** Gray Coach provide an express bus service to the airport from the Islington, York Mills and Yorkdale subway stations. Time: 30 minutes, fare: C$3.75–C$4.75. Gray Coach also operate an express service which uses as its pick-up points the Hilton Harbour Castle, Delta Chelsea Inn, Holiday Inn Downtown, L'Hotel, Royal York and the Sheraton Centre Hotel and Towers.

● **Limousine:** Several companies offer limousine services to and from the airport. Among these are Airlift Limousine (222-2525), and Carey Limo (485-6544).

● **Taxi:** Taxis can be found at ranks outside each terminal, and fares will be charged according to the price on the meter. Be wary of unlicensed cabs.

TORONTO

Situated on the north-west shore of Lake Ontario, Toronto is a major commercial and industrial port on the St Lawrence Seaway system. Originally called York by the area's first settlers in the mid-18th century, the town quickly grew in importance, and adopted the name of Toronto when it was incorporated as a city in 1834; today it is the capital of the Ontario province and is Canada's largest city.

The contrast between past and present in Toronto is a very striking one; while the downtown area is packed with tall buildings and bustling commercial districts, a lot of Victorian architecture, tree-lined streets and sidewalk cafés are to be found in many parts of the city, and all help to evoke a charming historical flavour.

Being home to a population of 3 million, Toronto is also one of Canada's liveliest centres of culture and entertainment. Both are represented on a very grand scale, and from theatre, cinema, concerts and opera to a fine selection of restaurants, nightclubs and coffee houses, there is an enormous range of both night-time and daytime pursuits on offer in the city.

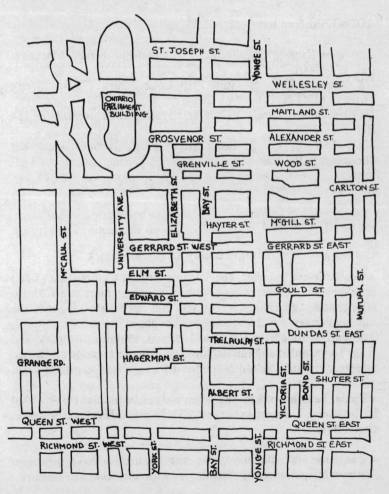

TOURIST INFORMATION

For maps, details of sightseeing tours and events, accommodation-listings, trailer sites, etc., contact: *Metropolitan Toronto Convention and Visitors Association*, Toronto Eaton Centre Galleria, Box 510, Suite 110, 220 Yonge Street, Toronto, Ontario (tel. 979-3143).

ADDRESSES

American Express Canada Inc. – 101 McNabb Street, Markham (tel. 474-8000).
UK Consulate-General – Suite 1910, College Park, 777 Bay Street, Toronto M5G 2G2 (tel. 593-1290).
US Consulate-General – 360 University Avenue, Toronto M5G 1S4 (tel. 595-1720).
Main Post Office – 21 Front Street West, Toronto. Customer Services tel. 369-4626.

GETTING ABOUT

Getting around in Toronto is easy and usually quick.

● **Bus/Streetcar/Subway:** The Toronto Transit Commission (TTC) operates bus, streetcar and subway services; fares are C$1 for adults, and exact change is required. Bus tickets are bought on the bus, and tickets for the subway are bought in the subway stations. The subway runs from 6 a.m. to 1.30 a.m. Monday–Saturday, and from 9 a.m. until 1.30 a.m. on Sundays. For information on all bus, streetcar and subway routes, phone TTC Information on 393-4636.

● **Taxis:** Taxis are widely available, and can be phoned for or hailed in the street. The initial charge is C$1.30, and 20c every 274 metres thereafter.

● **Car Hire:** All the major car hire companies have offices in Toronto as well as many smaller – and usually cheaper – ones.

SIGHTS

The centrepiece of Toronto's tourist attractions is undoubtedly the CN (CANADIAN NATIONAL) TOWER. At a height of 544 metres, it is the highest free-standing structure in the world, and it's been well adapted to suit its many visitors, with glass elevators, the 'Top of Toronto' revolving restaurant and tower-top nightclub, as well as 2 observation decks which provide panoramic views of up to 75 miles on a clear day. In the tower's basement is the TOUR OF THE UNIVERSE, a spaceport set in the year 2019, which features flights to Jupiter among other space adventures.

For a taste of old Toronto, there are several places worth visiting. BLACK CREEK PIONEER VILLAGE, at the junction of Jane Street and Steeles Avenue, is an authentic reflection of life in the mid-19th century, complete with costumed villagers, restored buildings, animals and gardens. FORT YORK, in Garrison Road off Fleet Street, was built in 1793, destroyed in the war of 1812, rebuilt, and today its role in that war is re-created through tours, displays and demonstrations by the Fort York Guard, dressed in British uniform of that era. At the corner of King and Jarvis Streets is the ST LAWRENCE HALL, a popular meeting place for Torontonians of the late 19th century which has been restored to its former elegance.

Among the other places of historical interest are the MARINE MUSEUM in Exhibition Place, recalling the days of Great Lake shipping, MONTGOMERY'S INN in Dundas Street West, which was built last century and today maintains its old character with the help of suitably costumed staff, THE ENOCH TURNER SCHOOLHOUSE in Trinity Street, which depicts school-life as it was in the middle of last century, and the HOCKEY HALL OF FAME in Exhibition Place, which traces the history of Canada's national sport, displaying films, photos, trophies and other memorabilia.

CASA LOMA, in Austin Terrace, is a fairytale castle which was built at the beginning of this century to incorporate all the typical features of European castles under one roof, and its secret passages, spooky towers and various other romantic aspects provide for some unique sightseeing.

Beside the lake at Queen's Quay West is the HARBOURFRONT – a recreational complex, 90 acres in size, it caters for a wide range of activities from water sports to theatre and dance, and also contains some fine restaurants and shops. One of Toronto's sights which is not to be missed is ONTARIO PLACE, a collection of 3 man-made islands rising out of Lake Ontario on which are built theatres, amusement rides, gift shops, boutiques and numerous other cultural and entertaining attractions.

Where museums and art galleries are concerned, Toronto is home to some of Canada's most important. Among those of particular interest are the ROYAL ONTARIO MUSEUM, at the junction of Avenue Road and Bloor Street, where exhibits include Chinese art and artefacts, as well as an extensive depiction of the evolution of civilization. The McLAUGHLIN PLANETARIUM adjoins the museum and is itself interesting. THE ART GALLERY OF TORONTO is well known as home to the works of many Canadian artists, as well as a notable collection of Henry Moore sculptures; and also of interest is the ONTARIO SCIENCE CENTRE in Don Mills Road, which has innumerable scientific and technological displays, many of which can be operated by visitors.

In downtown Toronto, CITY HALL on Nathan Phillips Square is worth wandering through for its prize-winning modern architecture, which incorporates elevated walkways and a reflecting pool used as a skating rink in winter.

There are several parks in Toronto, providing ideal facilities for an active or relaxing afternoon. With the latter in mind, HIGH PARK is suitably tranquil and scenic, as are EDWARDS GARDENS, JAMES GARDENS and the old farm property COLBORNE LODGE. TORONTO ISLANDS PARK, on the other hand, has facilities for swimming, boating and also contains an animal park.

ACCOMMODATION

• **First Class:** (double over C$130)
Bradgate Arms – 54 Foxbar Road, Toronto (tel. 968-1331, or toll free 800-268-7171). Elegant small hotel with excellent service, covered atrium, piano lounge and first-rate restaurant.

The Sheraton Centre of Toronto, Hotel and Towers – 123 Queen Street West, Toronto M5H 2M9 (tel. 361-1000). The Sheraton Towers is a luxury hotel within a hotel; on the 20th to 23rd floors of the Sheraton Centre, 102 luxury skyline view suites offer superb facilities for the executive traveller, including exclusive Towers Club and Lounge. The Sheraton Centre itself provides first-class facilities and service; it has 4 restaurants and lounges (2 of which offer live entertainment and dancing), indoor/outdoor heated swimming pools, saunas, jacuzzis, an exercise room, 65 speciality shops and boutiques, 2 theatres, a 2-storey waterfall and a 2-acre landscaped garden.

Toronto Hilton Harbour Castle – 1 Harbour Square, Toronto M5J 1A6 (tel. 869-1600). Situated on the edge of Lake Ontario, this hotel is convenient to business and entertainment centres, with a courtesy minibus provided for travel downtown. Superb facilities include 3 restaurants (1 revolving rooftop restaurant), a nightclub, 2 lounges, a pool, health club with gym, sauna, squash court and an exercise room.

● **Super Club Class:** (double C$70–C$100)
Town Inn Hotel – 620 Church Street, Toronto M4Y 2G2 (tel. 964-3311). Good facilities with excellent service. As well as a dining room and lounge, this hotel has an indoor/outdoor swimming pool, saunas and tennis court.

Ramada Hotel Toronto – 111 Carlton Street, Toronto M5B 2G3 (tel. 977-8000). Conveniently located downtown, this hotel is home to the splendid Royal Pheasants Dining Room, and has lounges which feature dancing and live entertainment. Also on offer is a heated outdoor pool, saunas and in-house movies.

Hampton Court Hotel – 415 Jarvis Street, Toronto M4Y 2G8 (tel. 924-6631). Facilities comprise a heated outdoor pool, a boutique and in-house movies among other things. Close to good shopping.

Brownstone Hotel – 15 Charles Street East, Toronto M4Y 1S2 (tel. 924-7381). Comfortable surroundings with facilities including a fine bar and restaurant. Convenient downtown location.

● **Economy:** (double C$30–C$60)
Neill-Wycik College-Hotel – 96 Gerrard Street East, Toronto M5B 1G7 (tel. 977-2320). A wide range of facilities for such a low-priced place . . . there's a sauna available as well as tennis courts and a swimming pool. The Italian restaurant serves a good lunch.

University of Toronto – Business Affairs Dept, University of Toronto, Toronto M5S 1A1 (tel. 978-8735). Clean with good facilities. Accommodation only available between May and August.

Metro Inn – 2121 Kingston Road, Toronto M1N 1T5 (tel. 267-1141). Convenient to downtown, with good restaurants and lounges.

Executive Motor Hotel – 621 King Street West, Toronto M5V 1M5 (tel. 362-7441). Facilities include a dining lounge, cocktail lounge and coffee shop.

Woodlawn Residence YWCA – 80 Woodlawn Avenue East, Toronto M4T 1C1 (tel. 932-8454). Clean, with reasonable facilities.

Toronto International Hostel – 223 Church Street, Toronto M5B 1Z1 (tel. 368-0207/1848). Cheapest in town, although clean and comfortable.

Motel 27 – 650 Evans Avenue, Toronto (tel. 255-3481). Clean accommodation with reasonable facilities.

Seashore Motel – 2095 Lakeshore Boulevard West, Toronto M8V 1A1 (tel. 255-4433). Pleasant location, with comfortable rooms.

DINING OUT

Like most of Canada's large cities, an influx of immigrants in the last decade has meant that the range of cuisine available in Toronto's restaurants today constitutes a very cosmopolitan choice, so much so that Toronto is now considered one of the best dining cities on the American continent. There's no one area of the city where restaurants are concentrated, but a wander downtown will lead you to a wide selection. American Express, Visa and MasterCard as well as other credit cards are accepted by most restaurants, but it's a good idea to check first. There is a 7 per cent sales tax on meals, and a 10 per cent sales tax on liquor.

• **First Class:** (over C$60 for two)
Winston's – 104 Adelaide Street West, Toronto M5C 1K9 (tel. 363-1627). Renowned for its excellent food which comes beautifully

presented. Service is excellent, and there's also live entertainment. Closed Sundays.

Babsi's – 1371 Lakeshore Drive West, Toronto. A very pleasant environment in which to try delicious local dishes. Popular, so book ahead.

Montreal Bistro – 65 Sherbourne Street, Toronto. First-class French-Canadian cuisine, with quick, friendly service. The 'Tortiere' is a must.

● **Super Club Class:** (C$40–C$60 for two)
The Courtyard Café (The Windsor Arms Hotel) – 22 St Thomas Street, Toronto M5S 2B9 (tel. 979-2212). More than just a café, this restaurant serves great food, especially where fish dishes are concerned. Tastefully decorated, too.

Scaramouche – 1 Benvenuto Place, Toronto M4V 2L1 (tel. 961-8011). One of Toronto's finest restaurants, it not only boasts good food but also a spectacular view of the city skyline.

La Scala Dining Lounge – 1121 Bay Street, Toronto M5S 2B3 (tel. 964-7100). Fine Italian food in very elegant surroundings, with an extensive wine cellar. Closed Sunday.

Anesty's – 16 Church Street, Toronto. Fine Greek food served amid white-walled decor.

● **Economy:** (C$25–C$40 for two)
Muddy York – 5 Church Street, Toronto M5E 1C9 (tel. 364-5758). Good food and friendly service; also a lounge with dancing.

Le Petit Gaston's French Restaurant – 35 Baldwin Street, Toronto M5T 1L1 (tel. 364-0706). Classic French cuisine in a quiet atmosphere.

Copenhagen Room (Danish Food Centre) – 101 Bloor Street, Toronto M5S 1P7 (tel. 920-3287). An authentic Danish restaurant with tasty Danish fare served by friendly staff. Music and sing-along on Tuesday nights. Closed Sunday.

Gasthaus Schrader – 120 Church Street, Toronto M5C 2G8 (tel. 364-0706). A wide range of German food is served here, amid decor similar to that of a German country inn.

NIGHTLIFE

Toronto has much to offer in the way of nightlife, and there is something to suit everyone. The performing arts are represented on a grand scale, and the Toronto Symphony, Canadian Opera Company and the National Ballet of Canada give prestigious performances year-round. There's also a varied selection of night-clubs, discotheques, and assorted wine and piano bars to choose from as well as numerous jazz clubs. For up-to-the-minute details of all events, check the daily newspapers: *Globe*, *Mail* and *Sun* in the morning, and the *Star* in the morning and evening.

● **Nightclubs:**
Imperial Room – Royal York Hotel, 100 Front Street West. One of the biggest and most expensive clubs in the city, frequently featuring big-name entertainers.

Meyer's Deli – Yorkville Avenue. A very lively nightspot which features live jazz of all kinds well into the early hours. Usually crowded.

El Mocambo – 464 Spadina Avenue. Extremely popular with lovers of blues music, and the live bands on show here are usually well worth taking in.

Aquarius 51 – 55 Bloor Street West. A quiet, plush roof lounge on top of one of Toronto's skyscrapers. Very comfortable, with excellent views.

EXCURSIONS

One of the joys of Toronto is that it doesn't take long to get out beyond the city limits, making day trips a popular pursuit among Torontonians and visitors alike.

CANADA'S WONDERLAND, 20 miles north-west of Toronto, is a vast theme park containing fantastic delights such as the Happyland of Hanna-Barbera and Smurf Forest. There's a wealth of special theme amusement rides on offer which cater for the more adult visitors as much as for children. Wonderland also provides an enormous range of live entertainment and visitors are frequently treated to elaborate Broadway-like shows.

PARKWOOD in Oshawa, east along the bank of Lake Ontario, is a magnificent 55-room heritage mansion which is the estate of the late Colonel and Mrs R.S. McLaughlin, the founder of General Motors of Canada. Tours of the estate take visitors through some of the country's most splendid art galleries, gardens and greenhouses, and allow for the viewing of a fascinating collection of antiques. There's a quaint summer tea house for refreshments.

CULLEN GARDENS AND MINIATURE VILLAGE in Whitby, around 20 miles north-east of Toronto, contains a wealth of natural beauty on its 50 acres. Combined with the gardens' trees and flowers is a one-twelfth scale miniature village which features over 100 buildings and a country fair, all of which provides a pleasant setting for a relaxing afternoon.

PICKERING ENERGY INFORMATION CENTRE in Pickering, around 10 miles east along the bay of Lake Ontario, is a generating station which caters for visitors with a wealth of interesting and entertaining displays, films and exhibits that explain how electricity is made from uranium. Admission is free, and in-plant tours can be arranged by phoning the Information Centre in advance (Pickering 839-0465). An adjacent 100-acre park also offers good picnic facilities.

Vancouver

VANCOUVER INTERNATIONAL AIRPORT

Vancouver International Airport is situated 11 miles south-west of the city. 24 different airlines, international and domestic, operate direct scheduled flights to and from it.

The airport building has 3 levels: Level 1 handles international and trans-border arrivals. Level 2 handles domestic arrivals and US departures. Level 3 handles domestic and international departures.

AIRPORT FACILITIES

Information Desk	Levels 2 and 3.
Bank/Foreign Exchange	Levels 1, 2 and 3. Open 0830–1900 Mon.–Thurs. and Sat. 0830–2300 Fri.–Sun., and 0630–2400 respectively. Automatic bank machine on level 3, also. Level 1 open 0900–2300.
Hotel Directory	Level 2. Hotel phone on level 1.
Insurance Facilities	Level 3. Open 0630–1900.
Bar	Chieftain Lounge on level 2, and cocktail lounge on level 3.
Restaurant/Buffet	Gourmet Grill and snack bar on level 2, and on level 3 there is a dining room and snack bar. Level 1 also has a snack bar.
Post Office	Level 3. Open 0900–1200, 1300–1600 Mon.–Fri.
Shops	There are shops on all levels selling everything from speciality foods to gifts.
Duty Free	Located on levels 2 and 3, the shops sell tobacco, liquor, gifts, perfumes etc. Most major credit cards are accepted. A ticket or airline boarding card is required before making a purchase.
Toilets	On every level.
Car Rental Desks	Avis, Budget, Hertz, Tilden, Holiday and Dominion all have desks on levels 1 and 2.
Lost Property	Level 1.
Public Telephones	On every level.
Airline Lounges	Private lounges are provided by CP Air and Western Airlines.
Barber Shop	Level 3.
Chaplaincy	Level 3.

AIRPORT INFORMATION

Airport Tax	Adults – C$12.50, children (2–12 years) – C$6.25.
Shuttle Service	Buses run from Main Terminal Building to South Terminal. Airline shuttle buses free, but perimiter transportation buses require payment.

AIRPORT HOTELS

None yet at airport, but these are all close.

● **First Class:**
Delta River Inn – 3500 Cessna Drive, Richmond (tel. 278-1241). Bus every 15 minutes.

● **Super Club Class:**
Coast Vancouver Airport Hotel – 1041 SW Marine Drive (tel. 263-1555).

● **Economy:**
Airport Inn Resort – 10251 St Edward's Drive, Richmond (tel. 278-9611). Shuttle available.

CITY LINKS

The International Airport is 11 miles from the centre of Vancouver.

● **Bus:** A half-hourly shuttle bus links the airport with downtown Vancouver. Pick-up points for the service are the Century Plaza Hotel, the Four Seasons Hotel, Georgia Hotel, Holiday Inn Harbourside, Hyatt Regency Vancouver on Discovery Square, Bayshore, the main bus terminal, the Sandman Inn-Georgia Street, Sheraton Landmark Hotel, Vancouver Hotel and the Westin Hotel. Fare for the bus is C$5.75, C$4 for children (2–12).

● **Taxi:** Taxis are widely available at the airport, and a usual fare for a trip to downtown Vancouver is around C$15.

● **Car Hire:** See the *Airport Facilities* section for details of the agencies located at the airport.

VANCOUVER

Cultured, cosmopolitan, and with a touch of class, Vancouver is fronted by the Burrard Inlet and backed by the snow-capped Coast Mountains, making it one of the world's most attractive cities. The city itself is the commercial/industrial hub of British Columbia, and its fine weather, breathtaking surrounds and varied menu of things to see and do make it a city to suit most tastes.

Vancouver's mild year-round climate provides excellent conditions for sightseeing both in and around the city. It also allows visitors to take full advantage of some superb outdoor facilities, which cater for everything from golf to alpine skiing within minutes of the downtown area.

There's a lot on offer in Vancouver indoors as well. Where culture's concerned, the city has many fine museums and galleries displaying art and history on an impressive scale. Lighter pursuits can be enjoyed among extensive shopping facilities, cafés and a lively theatre scene; there's also a wide selection of restaurants, nightclubs, cabarets and other assorted nightspots.

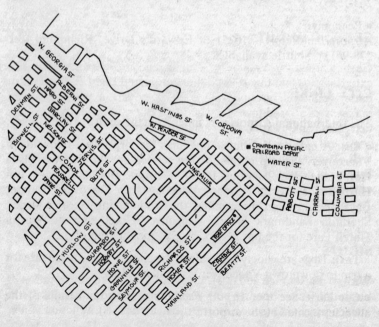

TOURIST INFORMATION

For maps, accommodation-listings, details of things to do etc., contact: *Greater Vancouver Convention and Visitors Bureau*, 1055 West Georgia Street, No. 1625, Royal Centre, Vancouver, BC (tel. 682-2222). Open 0900–1700, Monday–Friday. Or: *Tourism BC*, 800 Robson, Robson Square, Vancouver, BC (tel. 668-2300). Open 0830–1900 except Friday and Sunday, when it's open till 2300.

ADDRESSES

Main Post Office – 349 West Georgia, Vancouver, BC.
UK Consulate-General – 1075 West Georgia, 21st Floor, Vancouver (tel. 685-4311).
US Consulate-General – Suite 800, 1111 Melville Street, Vancouver V6E 3V6 (tel. 683-4421).

GETTING ABOUT

Getting around in Vancouver is quick and convenient. Besides an extensive bus and taxi service, the automated Light Rapid Transit underground/overground rail network covers a wide area and makes trips around town easy and efficient. All bus fares are C$1; taxi fares can be expensive over long distances.

All the major car hire companies have offices in Vancouver, as well as many smaller firms. Details can be found at the Visitors Bureau. The use of a car is recommended in touring this city and environs.

SIGHTS

With so much to see and do, it's a good idea to take one of the city's bus tours. These operate both within the city and to various scenic attractions nearby (see Visitors Bureau for details). Whether you're being driven or not, though, a day's sightseeing around Canada's 'gateway to the Pacific' is a full itinerary.

Vancouver has a very large selection of museums and art galleries. THE VANCOUVER ART GALLERY, at 750 Hornby Street, is noted for its works of the famous west-coast painter Emily Carr, including her depictions of the British Columbia forests and Indian life. North-west coastal Indian culture from the Stone Age to totemic art is featured in the CENTENNIAL MUSEUM in Vanier Park, where there is also an exhibition on the history of the province; right next door is the PLANETARIUM, with its stars, light and sound show. The adjoining MARITIME MUSEUM displays the historic schooner *St Roch*, the first ship to navigate the North-west Passage in both directions, and to circumnavigate the continent.

More Indian culture can be found at the University of British Columbia's MUSEUM OF ANTHROPOLOGY, which contains one of the world's greatest collections of north-west coast Indian arts, including replicas of Haida long houses.

There are 115 parks within Vancouver's boundaries. One of the largest is STANLEY PARK, which is only 5 minutes from downtown, situated next to the sea, and its 1000 acres incorporate picnic and playground sites, sports fields, a zoo, beaches, and the popular Vancouver aquarium, complete with its performing whales. Among the city's other parks is EXHIBITION PARK, host to the Pacific National Exhibition in late August (agricultural fair, loggers' festival, rodeo etc.), and QUEEN ELIZABETH PARK, which accommodates a conservatory with tropical plants, fish and birds. Also of interest is the FORT LANGLEY NATIONAL HISTORICAL PARK, a partially reconstructed Hudson's Bay Company post of the 1840s.

The delights of nature are also to be found in Vancouver, notably in the BOTANICAL GARDENS at the University of British Columbia, well known for their alpine flora from every continent. The VAN DUSEN BOTANICAL DISPLAY GARDEN, which features MacMillan Bloedel's conceptual pavilion 'A Walk in the Forest', is also well worth a visit.

Vancouver's sporting attractions are many and varied. Probably the most notable of these is the covered BRITISH COLUMBIA STADIUM, which is home to American football's BC Lions, and to soccer's Vancouver Whitecaps. Among the sporting events in the surrounding area which usually provide a good day's entertainment are the auto-racing at Westwood circuit; harness-racing at Ladner

(20 minutes from downtown), an annual rodeo at Cloverdale; and the BC Salmon Derby each July at Horseshoe Bay. There's also an International Air Show at Abbotsford every August.

To sample the spirit of early Vancouver, a wander through old GASTOWN is a good idea. As well as its restored buildings, shops and boutiques dealing in everything from leatherwork to antiques, Gastown also has many cafés, restaurants and pubs. There's an antique market and a fleamarket there on Saturdays and Sundays, too.

In the city's West End, west of Burrard, is ROBSONSTRASSE. Originally Robson Street, its name changed in the 1950s when thousands of German immigrants arrived. The street has now developed into a shoppers' paradise, and boasts dozens of international restaurants, boutiques, speciality shops and hotels.

Another interesting area of Vancouver is Chinatown. Spread over several blocks in the city's east central area, Vancouver's Chinese community is Canada's largest, and here one finds a wide range of food markets, restaurants and curiosity shops selling oriental imports. Also of interest is the DR SUN YAT-SEN ORIENTAL GARDEN, where the scenery is typically oriental, and the atmosphere one of peace and tranquillity.

ACCOMMODATION

● **First Class:** (C$150–C$250 for two)
The Vancouver Mandarin – 645 Howe Street, Vancouver (tel. 687-1122). Central location, with superb facilities. As well as a lounge bar and 2 splendid restaurants, it has a health club, squash and racquetball courts, a billiard room and sauna. A first-class establishment.

Holiday Inn City Centre Harbourside – 1133 West Hastings Street, Vancouver (tel. 689-9211). Located downtown with excellent views of the city and harbour. Good service.

The Denman Hotel – 1733 Comox Street, Vancouver (tel. 688-7711). Just 2 blocks from English Bay and Stanley Park, this hotel offers excellent facilities, including a first-rate restaurant and lounge.

● **Super Club Class:** (C$50–C$150 for two)

Nelson Place Hotel – 1006 Granville Street, Vancouver (tel. 691-6341). Situated downtown, this hotel is near theatres, shopping and the bus terminal.

Bosman's Motor Hotel – 1060 Howe Street, Vancouver (tel. 682-3171). Comfortable hotel, includes restaurant, piano bar and heated outdoor swimming pool (seasonal).

Kingston Hotel – 757 Richards Street, Vancouver (tel. 684-9024). A comfortable hotel, close to Pacific and Vancouver centres, bus depot and shopping.

Austin Motor Hotel – 1221 Granville Street, Vancouver (tel. 685-7235). Ideal downtown location close to Stanley Park, BC Stadium and beaches.

● **Economy:** (C$20–C$50)

YMCA Hotel – 955 Burrard Street, Vancouver (tel. 681-0221). Comfortable with good facilities, in a central location. Couples and women welcome.

Woodbine Hotel – 786 East Hastings Street, Vancouver (tel. 253-3244). Minutes from downtown on city bus routes, this hotel has light housekeeping and sleeping units, with a full maid service.

Hazelwood Hotel – 344 East Hastings Street, Vancouver (tel. 687-9126). Bright and clean renovated rooms, this hotel is on most major bus routes, 12 blocks from Chinatown, and close to good shopping.

YWCA – 580 Burrard Street, Vancouver (tel. 683-2531). Within walking distance of all tourist attractions, this hotel is comfortable with good facilities. Couples and families are welcome.

Sylvia Hotel – 1154 Gifford, Vancouver (tel. 681-9321). Situated on English Bay, a quaint place which is comfortable. Good value.

Blue Boy Motor Hotel – 725 South East Marine Drive, Vancouver (tel. 321-6611). Comfortable hotel, in an ideal location for touring. At the upper end of this price range.

DINING OUT

Vancouver takes a great pride in its wide and cosmopolitan range of restaurants. Whatever the nationality, whatever the dish, it's bound to be served in Vancouver.

While beef and fish are favourites among Vancouverites, seafood fresh from the Pacific Ocean is a speciality in many restaurants, and so it comes highly recommended.

The 'Robsonstrasse' is Vancouver's main centre of attraction for discerning diners. With a choice of, among others, German, Lebanese, Indian, Vietnamese, Italian, Japanese, Danish and French cuisine, you're bound to find one restaurant to suit you there.

Not all restaurants accept credit cards, so check first; also, most are closed on Sundays.

● **First Class:** (over C$40 for two)
The Beach House – in Stanley Park on Beach Drive (tel. 682-2888). Top-class continental cuisine in a beautiful setting.

The Cannery Seafood Restaurant – 2205 Commissioner Street, Vancouver (tel. 254-9606). One of the best restaurants in town for the local speciality – seafood.

Cristal – Vancouver Mandarin Hotel, 645 Howe Street, Vancouver (tel. 687-1122). Situated in one of Vancouver's finest hotels, this French restaurant is world-renowned for its high standards in cuisine, service and presentation.

● **Super Club Class:** (C$30–C$40 for two)
Café de Paris – 751 Denman, near Stanley Park and the Bayshore Hotel (tel. 687-1418). Good food in authentic Parisian bistro setting. Excellent value.

Château Madrid – 1277 Howe Street, Vancouver (tel. 684-8814). Tasty Spanish dishes in traditional surroundings.

Maiko Gardens – 1077 Richards, Vancouver (tel. 683-8812). Fine Japanese cuisine in a quiet, friendly atmosphere.

● **Economy:** (below C$20 for two)
Orestes – 3116 West Broadway, Vancouver (tel. 732-1461). Authentic Greek cuisine, with good service.

The Noodle Makers – 122 Powell Street, Vancouver (tel. 683-9196). First-rate Chinese restaurant.

Yang's – 4186 Main Street, Vancouver (tel. 873-2116). Chinese food. Try the Peking duck.

Schnitzel House – 1060 Robson Street, Vancouver (tel. 682-4850). Traditional German food.

NIGHTLIFE

Whatever your fancy in after-dark entertainment, the chances are good that you'll find something suitable in Vancouver, since it is one of the more lively cities by night on the west coast.

While a lot of the popular nightspots are housed in some of the more expensive hotels, Vancouver has many nightclubs, large and small, often with big-name entertainers appearing. The city also has a variety of discotheques, cabarets, coffee houses and pubs. For details of what's on and where to go, check the daily newspapers the *Province* and the *Sun*.

• Nightclubs:

Champers – in the Denman Hotel. Lively nightspot for those with up-market tastes.

English Bay Café – 1795 Beach Avenue, Vancouver. A charming place, where you can take in the ocean views when your glass is empty.

Hot Jazz Society – 2120 Main Street, Vancouver. It's got a dancefloor, a bar, and it's good value. One of the livelier clubs in town.

Pelican Bay – Granville Island Hotel. A pleasant singles bar by the water.

EXCURSIONS

For a memorable trip aboard a legendary train, the ROYAL HUDSON STEAM TRAIN along the coast is not to be missed. Starting in North Vancouver, the engine winds its way along the edge of the spectacular Howe Sound to its destination of Squamish – a port and forestry town – 80 miles away. You can have lunch in Squamish, then reboard the train for the return journey to Vancouver. It's also possible to travel one way by sea on the MV *Britannia*. Contact the Visitors Bureau for details.

GRANVILLE ISLAND is only a short boat trip away from Vancouver. The island is famous for its public market, where an old warehouse section of Vancouver has been restored to house shops and restaurants. Be sure to try the market's bread and doughnuts, home-made pasta and wide selection of fish and seafoods.

A 15-minute ride from downtown, GROUSE MOUNTAIN is packed with the delights of nature in summer, and is one of Canada's most popular ski areas in winter, with slopes for everyone. A major attraction on the mountain is the 'Skyride', which covers the 1 mile from lower terminal level to 1230 metres in 5 minutes, giving its riders a fantastic view. There's also a restaurant on the top half of the mountain, where the views are as good as the food.

British Columbia Ferries offer a day-long cruise aboard their *Queen of the North* ferry through the INSIDE PASSAGE, which takes you in great comfort through some of the world's most beautiful scenery. The trip is a very popular one, and it's a good idea to book in advance. Definitely an excursion to remember.

A great advantage of Vancouver's location on the west is its close proximity to the ROCKY MOUNTAINS, which stretch through some of Canada's most scenic National Parks.

To get to the Rockies from Vancouver, a commonly used and certainly recommendable route is via the city of CALGARY – renowned as much for its ranching and farming as for its oil industry. Air Canada operate several flights daily between Vancouver and Calgary.

A good time to be in Calgary is in early July for the world-famous CALGARY EXHIBITION AND STAMPEDE, a stirring 10-day celebration of the west with everything from bacon breakfasts to bucking broncos and chuckwagon races. Within Calgary itself, there's a lot to see and do. For outdoor activity, the city has 2000-hectares worth of parks to enjoy, notably FIRST CREEK PARK for its fishing, horse-riding and cross-country skiing, and GLENMORE PARK for its sailing. Also, try and visit CALAWAY PARK for its amusement rides – less greenery here, but plenty of thrills and spills.

More sedate fresh-air pursuits can be enjoyed in HERITAGE PARK, where the original buildings and vehicles re-create the west of long ago – they even sell penny candy in the general store. Also worth visiting is the CALGARY ZOO AND PREHISTORIC PARK, where the life-size models of pre-historic creatures are as intriguing as the 1400 live exhibits.

There's much to be found in Calgary's indoors, too. In the ENERGEUM, at 618 5th Avenue SW, visitors can review the history of western Canada's energy industry. There's also FORT CALGARY, where you can gain an insight into the North-west Mounted Police, the SAM LIVINGSTONE FISH HATCHERY AND REARING STATION, at 1440 17A Street, for aquaculture Alberta-style, and also interesting is the GLENBOW MUSEUM, which houses excellent art and historical exhibitions.

For a complete vista of Calgary and its surrounding beauty, a jaunt up the Calgary tower is recommended: its 188 metres afford a spectacular panoramic view.

For more details of things to see and do in and around Calgary, contact: *Calgary Tourist and Convention Association*, 1300 6th Avenue SW, Calgary, Alberta T3C 0H8.

CALGARY ACCOMMODATION

• **First Class:** (C$150–C$250 for two)
Westin Hotel Calgary – 4 Avenue and 3rd Street SW, Vancouver (tel. 266-1611). Probably the finest establishment in Calgary. Its dining room is one of the best in the country.

• **Super Club Class:** (C$45–C$80 for two)
Calgary Center Inn – 202 4th Avenue SW, Vancouver (tel. 262-7091). Excellent facilities, including bar, pool and beer parlour.

• **Economy:** (below C$20 for two)
Hotel Empress – 219 6th Avenue SW, Vancouver. Located in the centre of the downtown area, this is a comfortable and clean hotel.

From Calgary, onward travel to the National Parks is by Greyhound bus, 'Via Rail' train, by car, or even by bicycle (which can be hired).

There are several National Parks within striking distance of Calgary: four of the most popular with visitors are KOOTENAY (hanging glaciers, alpine lakes, deep canyons, with Rocky Mountain goats); BANFF (gondola lifts to the top of its mountains from where you can view the sandstone statuary, mineral hot springs, glaciers, wildlife and wilderness . . . the magnificent Lake Louise is also nearby); JASPER (mountain ranges, icefields, with a scenic drive through the Rockies on the icefields parkway); and GLACIER (steep and challenging trails for the fit outdoor enthusiast, famous for its grizzly bears).

As well as offering commercial accommodation, all these parks provide extensive camping facilities all year round, catering for tents, trailers, campervans or motorhomes. For details of what type of camping is available on specific campgrounds within these four National Parks and others (each park has several campgrounds – only one type of camping is permitted on each individual ground), contact the park's information office.

United States of America

RED TAPE

• **Passport/Visa Requirements:** In addition to a full, valid passport, almost all visitors to the United States require a visitor's visa. Exceptions are Canadian nationals who are normally exempt from passport and visa requirements when arriving in the US from countries in the western hemisphere, citizens of Mexico with a form I-136 coming from Canada or Mexico who are likewise exempt, and British citizens resident in Canada or Bermuda arriving from countries in the western hemisphere. Visas are normally provided for a 3-month stay – an expiry date will be decided by Immigration officers on arrival.

CUSTOMS

• **Duty Free:** Visitors can bring the following articles into the US free of duty and internal revenue tax: all personal effects (clothes, etc.); 1 litre of alcoholic beverage (wine, beer or liquor) if the visitor is a non-resident and over 21; 200 cigarettes or 50 cigars or 3 lbs of tobacco, or proportionate amounts of each. Articles to be used as gifts up to $100 in value may be brought in free of duty and tax if the visitor stays in the US for at least 72 hours and has not claimed his gift exemption in the last 6 months. Up to 100 cigars may be included in this exemption.

HEALTH

Most visitors to the United States don't require a vaccination certificate, although depending on the areas a visitor has previously travelled in a vaccination may be required for diseases such as cholera or yellow fever. Check with any American consulate or embassy if in doubt.

CAPITAL – Washington DC.

POPULATION – 232 million.

LANGUAGE – English. Spanish is widely spoken in some southern areas, and among many immigrant communities in cities.

CURRENCY – The dollar, which is divided into 100 cents. Notes – 1, 2, 5, 10, 20, 50, 100, 500 and 1000 dollars; coins – 1, 5, 10, 25 and 50 cents. £1 = US$1.4.

BANKING HOURS – 0900–1500, Monday–Friday.

POLITICAL SYSTEM – Constitutional democracy.

RELIGION – Predominantly Protestant, but with substantial minority religions, notably Roman Catholic.

PUBLIC HOLIDAYS

January 1	New Year's Day
February (3rd Monday)	Washington's Birthday
May (last Monday)	Memorial Day
July 4	Independence Day
September (1st Monday)	Labor Day

October (2nd Monday)	Columbus Day
November 11	Veterans' Day
November (4th Thursday)	Thanksgiving
December 25	Christmas Day

NB: Some states observe George Washington's Birthday on February 22 and Columbus Day on October 12.

CLIMATE – Excluding Hawaii, Alaska and other outlying territories, the US can be divided into 5 climatic regions. The North Pacific area is the wettest part of the country, and in winter there is a considerable amount of snowfall; summers here are fairly hot, with temperatures rising to peaks of 90°F (32°C). The mid-Pacific and Rockies area is dry and very sunny for most of the year, with temperatures varying according to altitude – as high as 115°F (46°C) in some places, as low as −66°F (−55°C) in others. The south-west region is the hottest and the driest in the United States, with summer temperatures of 110°F (43°C), and crisp winters with scattered frost. The mid-west is fairly dry with hot summers and very cold winters, while the eastern sector of the country has an average amount of rain, usually pleasant although often humid summers, with snow in winter.

TIME DIFFERENCE – The United States spans 4 major time zones:

Eastern Time	GMT −5 hours.
Central Time	GMT −6 hours.
Mountain Time	GMT −7 hours.
Pacific Time	GMT −8 hours.
Hawaii	GMT −10 hours.

(+1 hour April to late October, except in Hawaii.)

COMMUNICATIONS

● **Telephone:** Public telephones are widely found in America, and long-distance and many international calls can be dialled direct, although long-distance calls cost more from a pay phone than from a private one. Cheap rates (private phones only) are in the evening (after 1700) and at night (after 2300); weekend rates are also lower. Local calls usually cost 10 to 25 cents.

Hotels levy up to 300 per cent charges on calls, so charge to your private charge card or use a public phone when possible. 914 will get you emergency services in most communities and for information on toll-free services dial 800-555-1212. Most major hotels, car rental and airline companies in the US have toll-free numbers.

The telephone codes for American cities which are destinations in this book are as follows:

Boston	617
Dallas	214
Los Angeles	213
Miami (and Miami Beach)	305
New York	212
San Francisco	415
Seattle	206
Tampa	813
Washington DC	202
Honolulu (and Hawaii)	808

Remember that any telephone number beginning with 800 in place of the city code will be toll-free, the call being charged to the number you are ringing.

• **Post:** There is no additional airmail charge for mail destined for Canada or somewhere within the US. International mail is automatically sent by airmail unless 'surface' is specified. Post Offices are open 0830 or 0930 to 1700 or 1730, Monday–Friday, and from 0800 or 0900 till 1200 or 1300 on Saturdays. Stamps can be bought from vending machines in travel terminals, drugstores and other public places.

ELECTRICITY – 110v AC; 60 Hz.

OFFICE/SHOPPING HOURS – Office hours: 0900–1700, Monday–Friday; in Hawaii: 0730 or 0800–1600. Shops open 0930 or 1030–1750 or 1800. Most major department stores have one late-night closing per week, usually on a Thursday or Friday, until 2130.

● **Best Buys:** Souvenirs on offer in the United States vary from region to region. In New Mexico and Texas, for example, shops are full of stetson hats, leather cowboy boots and various other clothes and souvenirs of the wild west. From the Rocky Mountains, jade jewellery is available on a wide scale; in Colorado buckskin jackets are popular and from Arizona, Indian jewellery, basketry and hand-woven rugs make attractive souvenirs; north-western areas also deal largely in Indian souvenirs, selling model totem poles, clay pipes and the like. These are just an example of the more traditional souvenirs available in the country; for more details on a particular area's souvenir market, contact the local Tourist Office. General good buys are computer software, casual clothing, sportswear, guitars – particularly Martin acoustic guitars. Californian wines are also good value. Look out for the Beaulieu label for good vintages, and Domaine Chandon for sparkling wines.

INTERNAL TRAVEL

● **Air:** Air travel is by far the quickest and most convenient way of getting around the United States, and due to the large number of airlines operating domestic services, it's often the cheapest. Airlines linking all the major cities are American, Continental, Delta, Eastern, National, North West Orient, Trans World (TWA), Western and United Airlines. Airlines which are concerned with certain regions only include Texas International Frontier, Republic, Piedmont and US Air. United and American Airlines operate services to various Hawaiian destinations, and Hawaiian and Mid-Pacific Airlines offer inter-island flights.

Correct at time of going to press but likely to change.

● **Rail:** Amtrak, America's National Railroad Passenger Corporation, operates an extensive network linking 500 major cities and towns daily.

● **Road:** The two big coach companies, Greyhound and Trailways USA, offer extensive services linking all the major cities.

Taxis operate in all towns, however small. In the larger cities (except Washington DC) they all have meters, and can be phoned for or hailed in the street. When no meters exist, agree a price beforehand.

Hire car agencies operate in all the major cities, and in many small towns. The motorway system covers all well populated areas; driving is on the right, and foreign visitors are advised to obtain an International Driving Licence, although it is not essential. Hertz are big in the US and can be found at every airport, offering special deals for foreign visitors. Campervans (known as RVs) are particularly useful for touring in the US. Ask at American Express offices in the UK. They offer an excellent service and can supply luxury vans for all major destinations in the US.

To rent a camper after arrival in the US check the Yellow Pages of the telephone book under 'Recreational Vehicles' for the names of local rental agencies.

MAJOR SIGHTS OF THE COUNTRY

In many people's book the most breathtaking natural wonder of the United States, if not the world, is the famous GRAND CANYON, Arizona's mile-deep gorge whose sides show millions of years of earth erosion, and whose vistas simply have to be seen to be believed. The Grand Canyon National Park has 3 main areas – South Rim, North Rim and the canyon gorge itself. First-time visitors should go to the South Rim, which is more accessible than the North, and is also where the Grand Canyon Village is located, with hotels and cabins as well as good camping facilities. The Park headquarters at the village also provides information on bus tours of the main Rim drive, bicycling around the rim, hiking down the canyon or riding a mule, and also on taking a rubber raft ride along the Colorado River at the bottom of the canyon. Make reservations well in advance if visiting in summer.

Some 100 miles from the Grand Canyon, and about 240 miles north-east of Los Angeles, lies the gambling mecca of LAS VEGAS. While everyone should see Vegas once, a lengthy stay isn't recommended; casinos, fruit machines, girlie-shows, quickie-marriage chapels . . . it's all here, and all adding to the town's reputation as a den of avarice and vice. There's nothing quite like it anywhere else, however, and for that reason it's a good idea to spend at least one night viewing the various sights and sampling some of the town's very unique entertainments.

Two of America's most interesting and entertaining man-made spectacles, at least one of which is well worth a visit, are DISNEYLAND, 27 miles south-east of downtown LA, and WALT DISNEY WORLD, 20 miles south-west of Orlando in Florida. Both are theme parks devised by movie-maker Walt Disney; Disneyland is a mini-version of the real thing – Disneyworld, which is thousands of acres worth of fantasy and escapism. Highlights in Disneyland include 'Adventureland' which takes you on a boat through Asia, Africa, and the South Pacific complete with plastic alligators, stuffed elephants and hairy gorillas; Disneyworld's showpiece is its EPCOT Center – a massive entertainment centre where visitors can enjoy Disney-eyed views of the world's past and future.

Well linked to Boston on America's north-east coast is CAPE COD, a 65-mile-long hook protruding out into the Atlantic, which is home to many splendid ocean beaches and other attractive scenery. Famed as the former holiday retreat of the Kennedy family, the Cape is a protected area, and thus offers a very pleasant and natural environment in which to get away from it all on a day or weekend trip, provided you stay away from the tourist centre of Hyannis.

YELLOWSTONE NATIONAL PARK, in the north-west corner of Wyoming, provides some of the most dramatic sightseeing in the country. Not only is it a vast landscape of mountains, valleys, forests and river, it also contains geysers shooting high into the air, bubbling hot springs, volcanic mudpots and waterfalls cascading from incredible heights. To view nature at its most spectacular, visiting here is a must.

Probably the most popular area among visitors to the United States are the Hawaiian Islands. As near to a dream-like paradise as anywhere, the 7 islands boast an exotic range of natural beauty, with each island offering its own unique attractions. While the capital Honolulu on the island of Oahu is the most commonly visited by tourists, it's well worth taking in some of the others too. The island of Hawaii, or Big Island, is renowned as much for its volcanoes, one of which – Kilauea Crater – is still active, as it is for its good beaches, waterfalls and beautiful sunsets; MAUI is the second most popular island among tourists, and is home to superb beaches as well as the famous Haleakala, a dormant volcano 21 miles in circumference and hundreds of feet in height; KAUAI is known locally as the 'Garden Isle' for its lush greenery – not much nightlife here, but plenty of stunning mountain scenery and wildlife; the island of MOLOKAI is largely free of tourists and commercialism, and it's well known for the Makanalua peninsula on its north coast – victims of leprosy were isolated there in the mid-1800s. Finally, LANAI is ideal for a quiet holiday; there are no lively nightspots or luxurious accommodation, but there is the opportunity for mule-trekking, taking bumpy jeep trips or hiking around the island.

HOTELS

Hotels in the United States can be expensive, with the average price for a room in a first-class hotel being around $100, and $30 in an economy. Standards are high, however, and most hotel rooms are well furnished and service is generally good. All the large hotel chains are represented across the country. Ask for, and expect, reductions at weekends and in summertime in virtually all major business cities.

Tourist homes (guest houses) and Bed-and-Breakfast establishments are widely available in major cities and in many small towns. These operate on usual B&B principles – guests stay in the home of an American family for a reasonable nightly fee which also includes a cooked breakfast. B&B and Tourist Home lists can be found at local Tourist Offices.

Hostels: both the YMCA/YWCA and American Youth Hostels (AYH) offer inexpensive hostel accommodation across the US. AYH hostels charge $3–$8 per person a night for a maximum of 3 nights. YMCA/YWCA hostels charge from $12 to $32 for a single room, and from $18 to $46 for a double.

Camping is one of the cheapest, most popular forms of accommodation among travellers in the US, and camping facilities across the country are extensive. National Parks, State Parks and forests provide public campgrounds, and elsewhere private sites are common – both are inexpensive. Recreational vehicles such as motorhomes, caravans, etc. are well catered for in all campgrounds.

NIGHTLIFE AND RESTAURANTS

Every major city in America boasts a wide range of after-dark entertainment, with most night-time pursuits usually represented on a grand scale. New York is undoubtedly the place with the most diverse entertainments list; whatever your tastes in music, dance, theatre or the cinema, you're bound to find something suitable here, with the American Ballet Theater, the New York City Opera, and the New York Philharmonic leading their own individual fields; and Times Square and Broadway offering the newest and the best in film and theatre respectively. The nightclub scene here is also thriving, and from small-time folk singers to top-flight cabaret acts, there's virtually everything on offer; discotheques are popular, and there's also a large selection of wine and piano bars to choose from. All the other cities in the US offer pretty much the same entertainments as New York, although there are some regional variations worth looking out for, such as in Texas where some nightclubs offer mud-wrestling and electronic bucking broncos, or in New Orleans where live jazz of all kinds not only fills the clubs and bars, but spills on to the streets too.

Due to its immigrant heritage, America has a wide and cosmopolitan selection of restaurants to offer in all its major cities. Also, cities large and small have a lot of coffee shops and cafeterias (offering hamburgers, sandwiches, etc.), delicatessens (a cross between a restaurant and a grocery store, selling large sandwiches, salads, etc.), traditional American 'diners', fast-food outlets, health-food restaurants and juice bars (vegetarian food, fruit and vegetable juice).

As far as traditional American food is concerned, the most typical dishes countrywide are usually beef-orientated – American beef being the world's best – and top-quality steaks and hamburgers come highly recommended across the country. Favourite regional dishes among visitors to the US include San Francisco Dungeness crab, New England clams, Florida baked red snapper, Long Island scallops, and New York shad and shad roe.

Breakfast is usually served from 7 to 10 a.m.; lunch from 11 a.m. to 2.30 p.m.; and dinner from 5 or 6 until around 9.30 p.m. 'Brunch' (breakfast/lunch) is served on Sundays from 11 a.m. to 3 p.m.

Boston

LOGAN INTERNATIONAL AIRPORT

Logan International Airport lies 2½ miles east of Boston. Many international and domestic airlines offer flights to and from Logan, making it one of the USA's busiest airports. There are 4 terminals. The John A. Volpe International Terminal handles international flights. The North, South, and South West terminals handle domestic flights.

AIRPORT FACILITIES

Information Desk	These can be found in the lower levels of the North and John A. Volpe terminals.
Bank/Foreign Exchange	Available in the lower level of the John A. Volpe terminal.
Hotel Reservations Service	In the lower level of the John A. Volpe terminal.
Insurance Facilities	Available in the lower levels of the John A. Volpe and North terminals, and the upper levels of the South and South West terminals.
Bar	There are bars in the upper levels of the John A. Volpe, the South West and North terminals.
Restaurant/Buffet	There are restaurants in the upper levels of the John A. Volpe, the South, and South West terminals.
Baggage Deposit	Available on the lower levels of the John A. Volpe and North

	terminals, and on the upper levels of the South and South West terminals.
Shops	A variety of shops exist in all the terminals selling gifts, books, newspapers, confectionery, etc.
Duty Free	Located in the flight departure areas, these sell cigarettes, cigars, tobaccos, wines, liquor, gifts, jewellery etc. Only local and Canadian currencies are accepted, along with Mastercharge, American Express and Visa credit cards.
Toilets	These can be found all over in every terminal.
Meeting Point Location	The Information Desk in the John A. Volpe and North terminals (lower levels), and in the baggage reclaim areas of the South and South West terminals (upper levels).
Car Rental Desks	Avis, Hertz, Budget, Dollar and National have desks on the lower levels of the John A. Volpe and North terminals, and on the upper levels of the South and South West terminals.
Public Telephones	These are widely available on all levels of each terminal.

AIRPORT INFORMATION

Check-in Times	Average for all airlines: international – 60 minutes; domestic – 45 minutes.
Airport Tax	Nil.

CITY LINKS

Logan International Airport is 2½ miles east of Boston.

• **Rail:** A Rapid Transit Train runs to the city every 15 minutes from 0530 to 0030 hours. The train can be boarded at the airport subway station, which can be reached by taking the Massport inter-terminal shuttle bus. Train fare $0.75.

• **Coach:** Every 30 minutes a coach runs to and from the airport, making pick-ups at Park Plaza, Sheraton, Statler Hilton and other major hotels. The service operates from 0730 to 2300 hours, and the fare is $3.25.

• **Taxi:** A normal taxi fare into the city is around $6.50.

BOSTON

A visit to the US would be incomplete without taking in Boston, the place where Americans of the 18th century fought against British rule to gain their nation's independence. The city is very proud of its role in that struggle, and from the famous Boston Tea Party ship where the war began, to the Old State House where independence was first declared, all the sites from the days of colonialism and revolution are here, preserved to look just as they did in their finest hour.

Since its days of rebellion Boston has blossomed to become the bustling capital of New England, and today the city's historical significance combines with a good deal of scenic beauty and a wealth of culture to provide visitors with a wide and varied choice of itinerary when touring the city.

While Boston is considered one of America's more conservative cities, it is also a lively and cosmopolitan centre. Besides the Anglo-Saxon descendants of its original settlers, the city's population is made up of large Italian, black and Irish communities as well as the students of some 70 colleges, each section adding a different flavour to Bostonian life.

It's a city well worth getting to know, and its old-world charm coupled with a range of things to see and do make a visit here both interesting and entertaining.

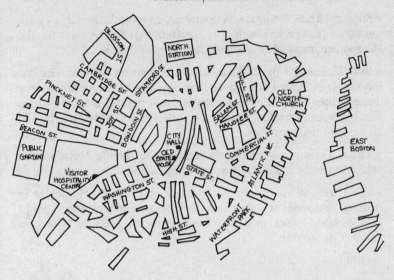

TOURIST INFORMATION

There are 2 major tourist offices in Boston. For maps, tour information, accommodation-listings, details of things to do in and around Boston etc., contact: *Massachusetts Tourist Information Center*, 100 Cambridge Street, Boston, MA 02202 (tel. 727-3201). Also the *Greater Boston Convention and Tourist Bureau*, Prudential Towers, Box 490, Boston, MA 02199 (tel. 543-4100).

ADDRESSES

British Consulate-General – 4740 Prudential Towers, Boston, MA 02199 (tel. 437-7160).

GETTING ABOUT

Public transport in Boston consists of a subway system and a bus network. Both are quick, efficient, and extensive.

778 The Round the World Air Guide

• **Subway:** The subway trains operate round the clock and fares are moderate (tickets are bought in the stations). Route maps for the subway are on display in every station.

• **Bus:** Tickets for the city's buses are bought on the bus. The bus service runs regular services in the city and its surrounding area through the day, while a skeleton service operates after midnight. The Massachusetts Bay Transport Authority will provide details of all bus and train services.

• **Taxis:** Taxis are available throughout the Boston Metropolitan area and can be hailed in the street or phoned for.

• **Car Hire:** All the major international car hire firms operate in Boston, as well as many smaller ones. Contact the Tourist Information Center, or look in the Classified Telephone Directory under 'Car Rentals'.

SIGHTS

One of the most attractive cities in North America, Boston achieves an attractive blend between the old and the new. While Boston has grown considerably over the years, to the extent that Greater Boston currently covers an area of some 1050 square miles, the city itself is clustered around its harbour, making its sights fairly easy to negotiate. Consequently, Boston is ideal for touring on foot, and a recommended route for the sightseer is the FREEDOM TRAIL, a red line painted on the city's pavements which follows a one and a half mile path taking in 16 of Boston's most famous colonial and revolutionary landmarks. The trail starts at the Freedom Trail Information Center on Tremont Street, and the first stop is the PARK STREET CHURCH of 1809, where 'America' was sung for the first time on 4 July 1831. Subsequent stops along the Freedom Trail include the OLD SOUTH MEETING HOUSE where the colonists plotted revolution, the BOSTON TEA PARTY SHIP AND MUSEUM which is a replica of the ship where the revolt was sparked, and the OLD STATE HOUSE from where the Declaration of Independence was first read in 1776. Among the trail's other points of interest, all connected with the fight for American independence, is PAUL REVERE HOUSE, the OLD NORTH CHURCH, FANEUIL HALL and also the GRANARY BURYING GROUND which contains the graves of the revolutionaries John Hancock, Paul Revere, Samuel Adams and Robert Paine, and also the parents of Benjamin Franklin.

To further sample the Boston of yesteryear, it's a good idea to walk around the city's BEACON HILL area, where the gas-lit streets, cobbled roads and Victorian terraced houses make a stroll through the area reminiscent of the 19th century. At the edge of Beacon Hill, on Beacon Street, is the golden-domed NEW STATE HOUSE, which was built in 1798 and today is the seat of the Massachusetts state government. The house was designed by Charles Bullfinch and boasts a beautiful interior design, well worth viewing.

Of more recent historical significance is the JOHN F. KENNEDY NATIONAL HISTORIC SITE, at 83 Beals Street, where visitors can tour the house where President Kennedy was born, left much as it was in his day.

Amid all this historical splendour, Boston isn't without its modern attractions. Among the most modern is FANEUIL HALL MARKETPLACE, which offers excellent shopping facilities, various stalls, and comfortable restaurants and bars. Street entertainers are also commonplace here.

More selective shopping can be done along the fashionable NEWBURY STREET, where the boutiques house only the most chic styles, and other shops sell a wide range of quality goods. There is also a selection of fine restaurants in this area.

Where culture is concerned, Boston has much to offer. The city's range of museums includes the wonderful CHILDREN'S MUSEUM; the MUSEUM OF FINE ARTS at 465 Huntington Avenue; the MUSEUM OF SCIENCE where among the exhibits is a space capsule and a giant dinosaur; and the MUSEUM OF TRANSPORTATION at 300 Congress Street, where the displays reflect on 300 years of Bostonian transport.

Adjacent to the Museum of Science is the CHARLES HAYDEN PLANETARIUM which has elaborate shows, and also worth visiting is the NEW ENGLAND AQUARIUM on the Central Wharf, where dolphins and sea lions feature in daily displays.

For a bird's-eye view of Boston and its environs, go up either the JOHN HANCOCK TOWER (New England's tallest building) or the PRUDENTIAL BUILDING. Both have observation levels near their tops, and each affords a spectacular panoramic view.

Across the Charles River from Boston is the city of CAMBRIDGE, which is worth the subway ride across if only to visit Harvard Square, home to the celebrated HARVARD UNIVERSITY (which you can take a walk around). Also here is a variety of entertainment which goes on well into the night. Take a stroll around the square at night and watch the street entertainers.

If you can find time to relax from touring around Boston, a good place to visit is the peaceful BOSTON COMMON, a wide expanse of grass and trees right in the middle of the downtown area, which is ideal for a picnic or simply strolling in the sun. The adjoining PUBLIC GARDEN is also very pleasant with its willow trees, lakes, and swanboat rides, as is the CHARLES RIVER EMBANKMENT, on the banks of the Charles River between Science Park and the Boston University bridge, where there is parkland, fishing sites, and the famous music shell where the Boston Pops Orchestra gives its summer concerts.

ACCOMMODATION

Boston has a wide range of hotel accommodation that covers every price bracket, and hotel styles range from the old and the grand to newly built multi-storey buildings. Most hotels tend to be rather expensive, especially in summer when thousands of tourists descend on the city. Advance booking is recommended.

● **First Class:** (double over $100)
The Ritz-Carlton – corner of Arlington and Newbury Streets (tel. 536-5700). Total luxury in very elegant surroundings. As well as fine restaurants and bars, this hotel can offer guests all the trimmings that might be expected of a first-class hotel.

Sheraton Boston Hotel and Towers – Prudential Center (tel. 236-0330). The top 4 floors of the Sheraton Boston Hotel are designated luxury class. Only 5 miles from the airport, this is the city's most comfortable and luxurious hotel, with particularly good facilities for businessmen. An 'intimate European flavour' is what they advertise for this hotel, and certainly all the little touches are laid on, with excellent service to complement.

Bostonian Hotel – Faneuil Hall Marketplace (tel. 523-3600. Toll-free 800-343-0922). De luxe small hotel in city centre with excellent rooftop restaurant 'Seasons'. Book ahead.

● **Super Club Class:** (double $40–$70)
Lenox – 710 Boylston Street (tel. 536-5300). A small yet comfortable place, this hotel is conveniently located near Copley Square and the Prudential Center, and is only a short pleasant walk from downtown. There is a restaurant and a bar here.

Eliot – 370 Commonwealth Avenue. A small, cosy establishment in the Back Bay area.

Ramada Inn-Airport – 225 McClellan Highway, East Boston (tel. 569-5250). Close to the airport, this hotel is also only a short trip from downtown. As well as a restaurant and bar, there is also a swimming pool. Good service.

Holiday Inn-Government Center – 5 Blossom Street (tel. 742-7630). Situated next to the attractive Beacon Hill area, all the comforts are provided here from swimming pool to first-rate restaurant and bar.

● **Economy:** (double $20–$40)
Greater Boston YMCA – 316 Huntington Avenue (tel. 536-7800). A short trip from the downtown area by subway, this hotel provides good facilities, with shared bathrooms. Both men and women welcome.

Berkley Residence Club (YWCA) – 40 Berkley Street (tel. 482-8850). Good facilities with comfortable, clean rooms. Not far from downtown.

Beacon Inn – 1087 or 1750 Beacon Street, Brookline (tel. 566-0088). Small hotel in a quiet area.

Suisse Chalet Motor Lodge – Wm. T. Morrissey Boulevard, Dorchester (tel. 287-9100). Basic but comfortable.

Guest House – 625 Commonwealth Avenue (tel. 247-7682). A nursing school during term time, rooms are only available here from mid-May to September.

Cambridge YMCA – 820 Massachusetts Avenue (tel. 876-3860). Situated just across the Charles River and on a direct subway line from downtown. Men only.

DINING OUT

Dining out in Boston is a very popular pursuit among Bostonians and visitors alike, and this is a fact reflected in the city's wide selection of fine restaurants.

Seafood is the local speciality, and dishes such as freshly boiled lobster, swordfish steaks, clam chowder, oysters and cheese-gilded scallops are among the New England delicacies that shouldn't be missed. The cuisine of old Boston is also represented by the popular Boston baked beans, and Indian pudding.

Boston's immigrant population also contributes a great deal to the local restaurant scene. All sorts of international dishes from Italian to Chinese are available around town.

Cambridge, just a subway ride across the Charles River, has a varied selection of international restaurants to choose from, and the North End area of the city is renowned for its food, particularly its Italian dishes.

● **First Class:** ($50–$70 for two)
Julien – in the Hotel Meridien, Post Office Square (tel. 451-1900). Fine French food served in the luxurious surroundings of one of Boston's newest hotels. The veal kidneys and the sole mousse are especially recommended.

Locke-Ober – 3 Winter Place (tel. 542-1340). Stop in here for a taste of old Boston, where both the surroundings and the menu reflect a distinctly Victorian flavour.

Grill 23 – 161 Berkley Street (tel. 542-2255). A first-rate steak house in true American style. Excellent food and good service.

● **Super Club Class:** ($30–$50 for two)
Kai-Seki – 132 Newbury Street (tel. 247-1583). A Japanese sushi bar, this establishment also serves other splendid authentic Japanese dishes.

Tiger Lilies – 23 Joy Street (tel. 523-0609). A charming environment in which to sample an American menu, with fireplaces and patio dining in summer.

Fedele's – 30 Fleet Street. One of the city's most popular spots for Italian food.

Athenian Taverna – 567 Massachusetts Avenue, Cambridge. Traditional Greek food in equally traditional surroundings, with live Greek music in the evenings.

● **Economy:** ($15–$30)
Durgin Park – 340 Faneuil Hall Marketplace (tel. 227-2038). Seating in long tables where diners sit elbow to elbow. Seafood a speciality.

Bangkok Cuisine – 177a Massachusetts Avenue. The best Thai restaurant in Boston with excellent food, comfortable surroundings and friendly service.

Dolphin Seafood – 1105 Massachusetts Avenue (tel. 354-9332). Good seafood in large portions.

Oh! Calcutta! – 468 Massachusetts Avenue (tel. 576-2111). Large portions of Indian food, with friendly service.

NIGHTLIFE

Boston offers a lot in the way of after-dark entertainment and between what goes on in the city and Cambridge, across the Charles River, there is enough scope to suit every taste. From jazz clubs through discotheques to quiet cafés, it's all here, and prices are reasonable in many establishments. There's also a thriving theatre and music scene in the city.

For full details of what's on, look in the *Boston Phoenix*, or *Panorama* magazine (distributed free in hotels).

● **Nightclubs:**
The Regatta Bar – Charles Hotel, Harvard Square, Cambridge. Talented local jazz acts perform here in very modern and comfortable surroundings.

Spinnaker – the Hyatt Regency Hotel, Memorial Drive. A revolving lounge on top of the hotel, with superb views of both the Charles River and the city's skyline.

Quincy Market – Formerly a warehouse complex, Quincy Market's fast-food counters make it a bustling lunch centre every afternoon. In the evening, however, it takes on a very pleasant, almost romantic atmosphere, and its quiet, intimate restaurants and outdoor piano bars make for a relaxing evening's entertainment.

Hampshire House – 84 Beacon Street. Located in the quaint Beacon Hill area, Hampshire House has an elegant bar and lounge, with excellent views of the public garden with its lakes and willow trees. A very pleasant atmosphere.

EXCURSIONS

The town of LEXINGTON, 12 miles north-west of Boston, is well worth visiting because of its much-revered role in the American War of Independence. It was through Lexington that Paul Revere rode on the night of 18 April 1775 to warn the American revolutionary leaders of a British offensive, and it was on Lexington Green where minutemen spilled blood for the first time in the name of freedom. Visitors can look back to revolutionary America in the VISITORS CENTER, which has a diorama depicting the battle, and the HANCOCK-CLARKE HOUSE, at 3 Hancock Street. This is where the celebrated rebels John Hancock and Samuel Adams slept the night of 18 April. THE MUSEUM OF NATIONAL HERITAGE, at 33 Marriett Road, features exhibits from all periods of American history. Travel to Lexington is most convenient by subway.

During the summer, BAYSTATE-SPRAY AND PROVINCETOWN STEAMSHIP COMPANY operate very pleasant harbour cruises from the city's docks. Stops during the cruise can be made at either GEORGE'S ISLAND STATE PARK, where there are good beaches for swimming, or at the picturesque PROVINCETOWN on the tip of Cape Cod (well worth the trip for a day's relaxation). Cruises leave from 20 Long Wharf. For more information, telephone 723-7800.

The town of CONCORD, easily accessible from Boston, has a wealth of history and beauty for any visitor. Besides its War of Independence relics, such as the Minute Man National Historical Park, Concord has a host of other bygone and present-day attractions. There are the homes of writers Nathaniel Hawthorne and Louisa May Alcott, the RALPH WALDO EMERSON HOUSE, and also an ANTIQUARIAN MUSEUM. Away from Concord's history, current natural delights around town include the GREAT MEADOWS WILDLIFE REFUGE and also WALDEN POND, the scene of Thoreau's famous 'return-to-nature' hermitage.

For a taste of both the brighter and darker sides of New England history, take a trip to the town of SALEM. Famous for its beautiful architecture, the town is equally well known for its controversial 17th-century witch trials, an aspect of its history vividly re-created at the Salem Witch Museum. For an authentic depiction of early colonial days, visit the PIONEER VILLAGE, which is a full-scale replica of the lifestyle of early settlers. Also of interest is the SALEM MARITIME NATIONAL HISTORIC SITE (wharves, nautical homes, etc.). The ESSEX INSTITUTE is an intriguing complex of houses dating back to the late 17th century, and CHESTNUT STREET contains some of America's most beautiful, old-world architecture.

Dallas

DALLAS/FORT WORTH INTERNATIONAL AIRPORT

Dallas/Fort Worth International Airport is one of the world's largest and busiest airports, handling more than 37 million passengers every year. The airport is 17 miles north-west of Dallas, and deals with a total of 31 airlines, both international and domestic.

There are 4 terminals. Terminal 2E handles Altus, American, American Eagle, Continental, Eagle, Eastern, Frontier, General Aviation, Jet America, Lufthansa, Midway, Midwest Express, Ozark, Piedmont, TWA and Western. Terminal 2W handles Braniff, British Caledonian, Mexicana, North West Orient, Pan American, People Express, Republic, Thai International, United and USAir. Terminal 3E handles American and American Eagle. Terminal 4E handles Air Canada, Delta and Rio.

AIRPORT FACILITIES

Information Desk	Near the baggage claim areas of all terminals. Airport Assistance Center in Terminal 2E (tel. 574-4420, 24 hours).
Bank/Foreign Exchange	Deak Perrera Foreign Currency Exchange: Terminal 2E 0830–2030; Terminal 2W 0830–1800.
Hotel Reservations Service	Near the baggage claim area of every terminal.
Bar	There are bars and cocktail lounges in every terminal. Open 0800–2100 Monday–Saturday, 1200–2200 Sunday.
Restaurant/Buffet	Restaurants and snack bars in every terminal. Open 0530–2100 or 2200.
Post Office	Located on International Parkway access road. Monday–Friday 0700–2000.
Shops	Shops selling gifts, newspapers, magazines, etc. are in all terminals.
Duty Free	Located in terminals 2E (0745–1810) and 2W (0900–1700). They sell liquor, cigarettes, cigars, perfumes etc. All major credit cards accepted.
Toilets	All over every terminal.
Car Rental	Located in all terminals near baggage claim area, and in the north and south reduced rate parking lots (24 hours). Avis, Hertz, Budget and National.
Lost Property	Phone 574-4454.
Public Telephones	All over every terminal.

AIRPORT INFORMATION

Check-in Times	Average for all airlines: international – 60 minutes; domestic – 30 minutes.
Transferring Flights	Airtrans Airport Transit operates between terminals. Can be boarded on the lower level of each terminal building. The service also operates to remote parking lots.

AIRPORT HOTELS

● **First Class:**
Hyatt Regency Hotel – located in the airport (tel. 453-8400). Luxury hotel with good facilities. Booking advisable.

● **Super Club Class:**
Marriott Airport – 7750 LBJ Freeway (tel. 258-4800). Comfortable hotel offering standard US facilities.

CITY LINKS

● **Bus:** 'The Link' is a shuttle bus service operating between the airport and downtown, and several major suburban hotels. The fare is $8. The Surtran Coach operates between the airport and downtown every 30–60 minutes (24-hour service); fare $5.50. There is also a Surtran service to major hotels, fare $7.50. Tickets can be bought at Surtran ticket counters near the baggage claim area of each terminal.

● **Taxi:** Taxis are easily found at the airport, and operate round the clock. Usual fare to downtown Dallas is around $25.

DALLAS

Next to Houston, Dallas is the second biggest city in Texas. Situated in Texas' north-east, Dallas was originally a trading post, and rapid development over the years has today made it one of the world's major commercial centres, counting oil, banking and fashion among its important money-spinners.

It's also one of America's most worthwhile tourist towns: built on a flat prairie, the high-rise Dallas skyline, fine restaurants, elegant shopping areas, and diverse cultural attractions that encompass theatre, music, and the arts, all go to make a packed itinerary for the visitor. A distinct southern identity also gives the city a character of its own . . . stetson hats and cowboy boots are very much the order of the day: go there to capture a génuine flavour of the Southwest.

TOURIST INFORMATION

For information on things to do, events, accommodation-listings etc., contact: *Dallas Convention and Visitors Bureau*, 1507 Pacific Avenue (3rd Floor), Dallas (tel. 954-1482).

ADDRESSES

Main Post Office – 400 North Ervay Street, Dallas (tel. 760-7200). *British Consulate-General* – 813 Stemmons Tower West, 2730 Stemmons Freeway, Dallas (tel. 637-3600).

GETTING ABOUT

• **DART:** Public transport in Dallas is quick and cheap. The Dallas Area Rapid Transit (DART) operates a reliable service which covers all areas of the city as well as most suburbs. The service runs from 5 a.m. until midnight, and the downtown fare is 50c. Maps of DART routes are available at Main and Akard Streets.

• **Taxi:** Taxis are widely available around Dallas, and they can either be phoned for or hailed in the street.

• **Car Hire:** All the major car hire firms operate in Dallas, and can be found under 'Car Rentals' in the Classified Telephone Directory.

SIGHTS

One of the most popular places with visitors to Dallas is the STATE FAIR PARK, at Parry and Second Avenue, which contains several museums and attractions. Among those is the DALLAS GARDEN

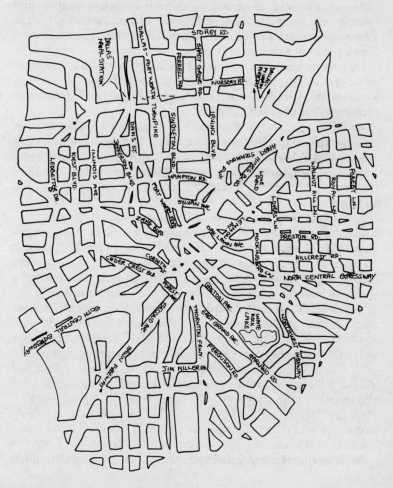

CENTER, which boasts a tropical garden, a solarium, a rose garden and other plant exhibits. The AQUARIUM is also in the park, and features various freshwater, tropical and coldwater fish . . . there's also a harbour seal on show. Museums in the State Fair Park include the DALLAS HEALTH AND SCIENCE MUSEUM AND PLANETARIUM, the AGE OF STEAM RAILROAD MUSEUM, which houses a collection of various types of train from 1900 to 1950, and the DALLAS MUSEUM OF FINE ARTS, home to various art works including pieces from ancient Greece. Also of interest in the park is the DALLAS MUSEUM OF NATURAL HISTORY, which has exhibitions of Texan animals and birds in their natural habitat, and the TEXAS HALL OF STATE, built in 1936 as a celebration of Texan independence, which is remembered here by various exhibits, murals and other displays.

Elsewhere in Dallas, it's worth visiting the JOHN F. KENNEDY MEMORIAL PLAZA; on the corner of Main and Market Streets, this 9-metre-high structure was built in remembrance of the former president who was shot in Dallas.

At the intersection of Houston and Elm Streets, passers-by can view the TEXAS SCHOOL BOOK DEPOSITORY, from where assassin Lee Harvey Oswald fired the shot that killed the president. There's also a plaque at the corner of Houston and Main Streets which describes the route of President Kennedy's motorcade on the day of the shooting.

Just across from the memorial is the JOHN NEELY BRYAN CABIN, which is interesting as the first ever log cabin built in Dallas, in the year 1841. The first log cabin school in Dallas, meanwhile, is to be found in OLD CITY PARK, at St Paul and Ervay Streets. Among other buildings and exhibits from early Dallas, the park also contains a southern mansion from 1885, complete with white columns.

DALLAS CITY HALL, on Akard Street, is worth viewing for its sheer size – it rises 560 feet into the air. The square it surrounds, with fountains and plantlife, is very pleasant, too. There are 2 buildings in Dallas where the observation decks offer panoramic views of the city. One is the FIRST NATIONAL BANK, at the corner of Elm and Akard Streets, and visitors can view Dallas and its surrounds from the terrace on the 50th floor. The other is the REUNION TOWER on Houston Street, which has 50 storeys, and offers a revolving restaurant and cocktail lounge as well as a top-floor observation deck.

Well worth taking in is the DALLAS ZOO, at 621 East Clarendon

Drive. It's one of the top zoological parks in America, and houses an enormous collection of mammals, birds, reptiles and amphibians.

THE BIBLICAL ARTS CENTER, at 8909 Boedecker and Park Lane, is noted for its popular light and sound presentations of 'Miracle at Pentecost'.

Another museum in Dallas which is renowned for its architecture as much as for its exhibits is the DALLAS MUSEUM OF ART, at 1717 North Harwood Street. Among the exhibits, pre-Columbian art is heavily featured; the outdoor sculpture garden provides an ideal spot for lunch.

ACCOMMODATION

● **First Class:** (double over $150)
Sheraton Dallas Hotel and Towers – 400 North Olive Street, Southland Center, Dallas (tel. 922-8000). The Sheraton Towers are luxury suites atop the Sheraton Dallas Hotel. The most luxurious of facilities include a private breakfast/cocktail lounge. The facilities in the Sheraton Dallas Hotel, which are also open to guests of the Towers, include 3 fine restaurants and 3 lounges with live entertainment. The hotel is also conveniently located near to the fine arts district and other downtown attractions.

Loews Anatole Dallas – 2201 Stemmons Freeway, Dallas (tel. 748-1200). Luxurious hotel whose setting includes 2 splendid atria. Among the facilities are several fine restaurants and comfortable lounges. The service is excellent.

Westin Galleria Dallas Hotel – 13340 North Dallas Parkway, Dallas (tel. 934-9494). The best in luxury and comfort. Excellent facilities as well as friendly and efficient staff.

● **Super Club Class:** (double $100–$150)
The Plaza Hotel – 1933 Main Street, Dallas. Conveniently located downtown, across from City Hall, this hotel has good facilities including a restaurant, lounge and beauty shop. The staff are friendly.

Dallas Hilton – 1914 Commerce Street, Dallas. Centrally located, this hotel is noted for its restaurants and lounges. Excellent service.

Holiday Inn – Downtown – 1015 Elm Street, Dallas. Excellent facilities include a swimming pool and lounge with live entertainment. Also good dining in the restaurant.

Grenelefe Hotel – 1011 South Akard Street, Dallas. Good facilities. Noted for its fine restaurant on the top floor, which affords excellent views of the city and surrounds.

• **Economy:** (double $40–$100)
Town House Motor Hotel – 2914 Harry Hines Boulevard, Dallas (tel. 748-9567). Half a mile from downtown, this hotel is clean with good facilities.

Grande Lodge Motel – 1401 North Zang Boulevard, Dallas (tel. 946-5144). A bus ride from downtown, this hotel is old but clean with a restaurant and pool.

Rodeway-Central – 4150 North Central Expressway, Dallas. Downtown location, and the facilities are good.

Travelers Inn – 3243 Merrifield, Dallas (tel. 826-3510). Four miles from downtown. Clean and comfortable, however, and well linked by bus.

Deluxe Inn – 9737 Harry Hines Boulevard, Dallas (tel. 357-2411). Somewhat removed from downtown, but linked by bus. Comfortable with friendly staff.

Days Inn – 9386 LBJ Freeway, Dallas. Good facilities include a fine restaurant.

DINING OUT

Restaurants in Dallas offer a wide variety of both international and American dishes. Being America's cattle centre, beef dishes are featured in many establishments, and most come highly recommended. As well as steaks and hamburgers, it's worth looking out for spicy barbecued Texan beef, and the local speciality 'Texas Fried' – a breaded deep-fried cut of beef. Mexican restaurants are much in evidence around the city, and there's also a wide selection of European and Oriental establishments. Greenville Avenue is one of Dallas' main dining centres, and offers a wide and varied choice of places to eat, from the cheapest to the most expensive. McKinney and Mockingbird Streets, and Northwest Highway, also provide a selection of restaurants. Reservations are advised in the more expensive places.

● **First Class:** (over $50 for two)
Il Sorrento – 2821 Turtle Creek, Dallas. Excellent Italian food amid pleasant decor. Also fine views.

Café Royal – Plaza of the Americas Hotel, 650 North Pearl Street, Dallas. Dining at its most elegant, with superb food and tasteful decor. The service is excellent.

L'Ambiance – 2408 Cedar Springs, Dallas. Splendid French cuisine in a very pleasant atmosphere. Good wine list.

● **Super Club Class:** ($25–$40 for two)
Royal Tokyo – 7525 Greenville Avenue, Dallas. Excellent sushi bar with American/Japanese atmosphere.

Southern Kitchen – 6615 East Northwest Highway, Dallas. All-you-can-eat restaurant, with excellent chicken and steaks. Friendly staff.

Ruth's Chris – 4940 Greenville Avenue, Dallas. Best steak in town, with equally good hospitality.

● **Economy:** ($15–$25)
Sahib – 9100 North Central Expressway, Dallas. Superb Indian cuisine at a reasonable price.

Stuart Anderson Cattle Co. – 7102 Greenville Avenue, Dallas. Excellent steaks.

China Star – 5027 West Lovers Lane, Dallas. Good Chinese food.

Rib – 5741 West Lovers Lane, Dallas. Noted for its barbecued dishes.

NIGHTLIFE

The nightlife scene in Dallas is a lively one. Clubs, corner pubs, cabarets, live music, singles bars . . . there's no shortage of any around the city. Some clubs are listed as 'Private' – this means you need a membership before you can be served alcohol; membership is easily available for a reasonable fee at these establishments. Greenville Avenue is where the largest choice of nightspots is to be found, although McKinney Avenue is also lively. For details of what's going on around town, consult the *Dallas Times*, *Herald*, or the morning news.

● Nightclubs:

Aw Shucks – 3601 Greenville Avenue, Dallas (tel. 821-9449). Pleasant outdoor seafood bar. Very popular with locals, and the ideal spot for raw oysters and cold beer on a warm evening.

Adair's Saloon – 2624 Commerce Street, Dallas (tel. 939-9900). Nothing if not typically Texan, complete with pool table, games of shuffleboard, and beer served by the jug.

Acapulco – 5111 Greenville Avenue, Dallas (tel. 692-9855). Fashionable singles bar, with a pleasant, intimate atmosphere.

EXCURSIONS

SIX FLAGS OVER TEXAS is an amusement park 15 miles from downtown Dallas. As the name suggests, Texas and its history comes under the spotlight, and 6 sections in the park reflect on 6 different state-ruling governments. Incorporated in these sections are a wide variety of amusement rides, shops, restaurants and entertainment theatres, making a day spent here action-packed.

SOUTHFORK RANCH, home of the popular American soap opera 'Dallas', is a short drive north-east of downtown Dallas, and for a small fee visitors can walk around the grounds (the actual house is closed to the public). Unmissable for fans of the TV series.

INTERNATIONAL WILDLIFE PARK, near to Six Flags Over Texas, is home to hundreds of wild animals roaming free in their natural habitat. Visitors can drive through the park and examine them all at close quarters.

Los Angeles

LOS ANGELES INTERNATIONAL AIRPORT

Los Angeles International Airport deals with some 70 airlines,
domestic and international, and the airport's 34 million passengers
every year make it the third busiest travel centre in the world. The
airport is 14 miles south of downtown Los Angeles. There are 9
terminals.

The Tom Bradley International Terminal (TBIT) handles most
international departures and arrivals. All the other terminals
handle domestic flights, including flights to Canada, Hawaii and
Mexico.

AIRPORT FACILITIES

Information Desk	In TBIT 0830–2100 daily. In other terminals, use the telephone on Information Display at Arrivals level.
Bank/Foreign Exchange	Automatic bank tellers in the Theme Building (centre of terminal area) and in Terminals 1, 4 and 7.
Hotel Reservations Service	Hotel/motel phones are located in the baggage claim area of all terminals.
Insurance Facilities	In all terminals.
Bar	Bars and cocktail lounges in all terminals.
Restaurant/Buffet	There are cafeterias in all terminals. Full service restaurant in the Theme Building, and a buffet in TBIT.
Post Office	No Post Office in the terminals

	(although there is one on the airport property), but stamps can be bought and there are mail boxes in all terminals.
Baggage Deposit	Lockers in all terminals. Long-term storage available on TBIT Departure level.
Nursery	All terminals except TBIT.
Shops	A wide variety of shops selling gifts, newspapers, magazines, etc. are in all terminals.
Duty Free	Located in the ticketing and departure areas of Terminals 2, 3, 4, 5, TBIT and the Imperial Terminal. They sell wines, liquor, tobacco, cigars, perfumes, gifts, etc. Also some drugstore items are sold. Accepted credit cards are Visa, Mastercharge, Diners Club, American Express, and most traveller's cheques are OK.
Medical Centre	In TBIT and on airport property.
Toilets	These are all over every terminal.
Meeting Point Location	On TBIT Departure level.
Car Rental	Avis, Budget, Dollar, Hertz and National have counters in all baggage claim areas.
Lost Property	Contact airline, or phone 646-2260.
Public Telephones	These are all over each terminal.
International Business Centres	In Terminals 1, 4 and 7. They include secretarial service, conference rooms, photocopying, bag storage etc.
Showers/Sleeping Rooms	TBIT.
Observation Deck	In the Theme Building, 0900–1700.

AIRPORT INFORMATION

Check-in Times	Average for all airlines: International – 2 hours; Domestic – 1 hour.
Airport Tax	$3.
Flight Transfers	Free connecting shuttle buses are available for passengers transferring flights.

AIRPORT HOTELS

● **First Class:**
Hyatt House at Los Angeles International Airport – 6225 West Century Boulevard, LA 90045 (tel. 670-9000).
Ramada Inn – 9620 Airport Boulevard, LA 90045 (tel. 670-1600).

● **Super Club Class:**
Marriott Hotel – 5855 West Century Boulevard, LA 90045 (tel. 641-5700).
Hacienda International Hotel – 525 North Sepulveda Boulevard, El Segundo (tel. 322-1212).
Marina Hotel – 3130 Washington Boulevard, Venice (tel. 821-5086).
Airport-Marina Hotel – 8601 Lincoln Boulevard, LA 90045 (670-8111).
Travelodge International – 9750 Airport Boulevard, LA 90045 (tel. 645-4600).

CITY LINKS

Los Angeles International Airport is 14 miles south of downtown LA.

● **Bus:** There are a number of bus services which operate from the airport to downtown Los Angeles and to other areas in the vicinity. Buses should be boarded on the lower level islands in front of each terminal; information and tickets for many lines are available at booths directly in front of the terminals. Otherwise, you pay the bus driver. Fare is $3.50, and exact change is required. Courtesy buses are usually provided for hotels in the airport area.

• **Taxi:** Taxis are easily available at the airport, and the fare to most downtown areas is around $15–$17.

• **Car Hire:** See *Airport Facilities* for details.

LOS ANGELES

Known as the 'City of Angels', Los Angeles has come a long way since its days as a late 18th-century settlement of some 50 people. Today it stretches over an area of around 470 square miles, and is home to a population of over 7 million.

There's lots more to Los Angeles than just beaches and surfing, and the various districts of the city all have their own unique attractions: Hollywood, of course, is the mecca of movies and television; Beverly Hills is home to the celebrities as well as to all things expensive and luxurious; downtown contains the quaint charms of Chinatown and Little Tokyo; and the city's celebrated coastline is well deserving of its reputation as having some of the world's biggest waves and most golden sand. There's culture in Los Angeles, too, and a great many art galleries and museums are to be found around the city. There's also a lively concert and theatre scene among the wide range of after-dark entertainments.

TOURIST INFORMATION

For information on things to do, tours, sightseeing, accommodation-listings etc., contact: *Greater Los Angeles Visitors and Convention Bureau*, 505 South Flower Street, Los Angeles 90071 (tel. 239-0204).

ADDRESSES

Main Post Office – 901 South Broadway at 9th Street (tel. 894-2290). Open 0830–1700 Monday–Friday, and 0830–1200 on Saturdays.

British Consulate-General – 3701 Wilshire Boulevard, Los Angeles 90010 (tel. 385-7381).

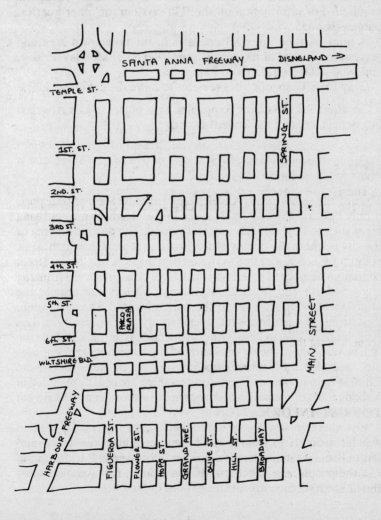

GETTING ABOUT

Getting around Los Angeles if you don't have a car can be quite an inconvenience.

● **Bus:** The Southern California Rapid Transit District (RTD) is a bus service which covers a wide area, but the system can be complex. Basic fare for the RTD is 85c, and exact change is required. For information on the RTD system, or other queries, phone 626-4455.

A minibus (line no. 602) operates in the downtown area and serves most points of interest; it runs 0700–1750 Monday–Friday, and 0900–1600 on Saturdays. Fare is 25c.

Gray Line Tours offer bus services to more distant attractions.

● **Car Hire:** All the major companies have offices in Los Angeles. For details, contact the Tourist Board.

SIGHTS

Touring the sights of Los Angeles requires some form of transport, if only because the city sights spread from downtown to outlying areas such as Beverly Hills and Hollywood. The downtown area of the city is where the history of Los Angeles is most in evidence. EL PUEBLO DE LOS ANGELES STATE HISTORIC PARK along Main Street contains a number of buildings which have been preserved from the city's Spanish and Mexican beginnings; visitors can sample the atmosphere of those days in the park's Merced Theater, where 'Spectrum' is a photographic documentary on the history of Los Angeles from 1860 to 1940. Other attractions in the park include the OLD PLAZA, where the fig trees around the bandstand are centuries old, and also the former gambling and opium dens of the old Chinese immigrants in the catacombs – these are usually included in walking tours of the park which start at the visitors' centre nearby at 130 Paseo de la Plaza.

Elsewhere in downtown Los Angeles, an interesting area to wander around is CHINATOWN. Mainly centred around Hill and North Broadway Streets, Chinatown is full of typical Eastern charm . . . the people, the street sounds, the food markets, and certainly the fine restaurants, are all straight out of the Orient.

LITTLE TOKYO is another area worth visiting. Found between 1st and 3rd, and Main and Central Streets, it not only contains more than 50 excellent restaurants, but also the JAPANESE VILLAGE PLAZA, on East 2nd Street, an America-goes-Japanese shopping mall where the stores sell all sorts of exotic jewellery, gifts and cookware. The JAPANESE AMERICAN CULTURAL AND COMMUNITY CENTER, at 244 South San Pedro Street, is worth spending some time in, and the MUSEUM OF NEON ART, at 704 Traction Avenue, provides some interesting exhibitions, as do other smaller art galleries on the eastern edge of Little Tokyo.

Hollywood is a perennial favourite with visitors to Los Angeles. Some of the area's sparkle is captured in HOLLYWOOD BOULEVARD: the WALK OF FAME with its concrete and bronze stars commemorating old famous names is here; there's also the celebrated GRAUMAN'S CHINESE THEATER, at 6925 Hollywood Boulevard, where cinema personalities first started leaving their foot and palm prints in 1927. To sample Hollywood's traditional movie-making, it's possible to go on tours around various studios and film sets – details of these can be obtained from the Tourist Office. Hollywood's GRIFFITH PARK covers an area of more than 4000 acres, and boasts several attractions: the LOS ANGELES ZOO is here, as well as the outdoor GREEK THEATER which has concerts year round and the GRIFFITH OBSERVATORY AND PLANETARIUM. There is also a bird sanctuary and hiking trails among the park's mountains. Among other Hollywood attractions is the famous SUNSET STRIP; on the west of the Hollywood area, it's not quite the glamorous strip it used to be, and today it plays host to various discos, rock clubs, girlie-shows etc. It's still worth viewing, however.

The Beverly Hills area west of Hollywood is home not only to stars of stage and screen, but also to some of America's most magnificent architecture and expensive shops. RODEO DRIVE has a bit of all three, and a stroll along here offers excellent window shopping . . . a favourite pastime also of famous locals.

In WESTWOOD, near Beverly Hills, is the sprawling campus of the UNIVERSITY OF CALIFORNIA AT LOS ANGELES (UCLA). As well as containing some prestigious academic departments, the campus also houses the FRANKLIN D. MURPHY SCULPTURE GARDEN, where large 20th-century works are on display; the JAPANESE GARDENS also provide an ideal setting for a quiet stroll. Elsewhere on the campus is the MUSEUM OF CULTURAL HISTORY, in Haines Hall, which

has on display numerous archaeological and anthropological artefacts, as well as a range of historical and contemporary art.

ACCOMMODATION

• **First Class:** (double $120–$150)
Westin Century Plaza – 2025 Avenue of the Stars, Beverly Hills, Los
Angeles (tel. 277-2000). Located in the attractive Beverly Hills area
of Los Angeles, this hotel offers the very best in hospitality. The
rooms are well decorated and most have excellent views. Facilities
include several fine restaurants, and comfortable bars.

Sheraton Grande Hotel – 333 South Figueroa Street, LA 90071 (tel.
617-1133). Facilities in this luxury hotel include 4 motion picture
theatres, 2 lounges with live entertainment, an outdoor pool and
health club, as well as butler service on every floor. The hotel is also
conveniently located in the downtown financial and cultural centre,
close to Chinatown..

Hyatt Regency – 711 Hope Street, Los Angeles (tel. 683-1234).
Situated downtown, this hotel offers superb facilities and service.
Noted for its gourmet dining in 'Hugo's V', as well as a rooftop
revolving restaurant and lounge.

• **Super Club Class:** (double around $100)
Los Angeles Hilton – 930 Wilshire Boulevard, Los Angeles (tel.
629-4321). Conveniently located downtown, with comfortable
surroundings and excellent service. Superb facilities include 6 fine
restaurants.

The Ambassador – 2400 Wilshire Boulevard, Los Angeles (tel.
387-7011). Located downtown with good facilities which include
several excellent restaurants, a health club and tennis complex.

The Bonaventure – Corner of 5th and Figueroa Streets, Los Angeles
(tel. 624-1000). An elegant piece of architecture with its round
towers, this hotel boasts splendid facilities as well as excellent
service.

L'Ermitage – 9291 Burton Way, Beverly Hills, Los Angeles (tel. 278-3344). In the Beverly Hills area of Los Angeles, this hotel is noted especially for its superb Café Russe. Otherwise, the facilities are excellent and the service very good.

• **Economy:** (double $30–$60)
Figueroa Hotel – 939 South Figueroa Street, Los Angeles (tel. 627-8971). Conveniently located downtown, with good facilities.

Oasis Motel – 2200 West Olympic Boulevard, Los Angeles (tel. 385-4191). A quiet hotel in the downtown area. Friendly staff.

Gala Inn Towne – 925 South Figueroa Street, Los Angeles. Conveniently located downtown.

Holiday Lodge – 1631 West 3rd Street, Los Angeles (tel. 482-4920). Small hotel, with good facilities and friendly staff.

City Center Motel – 1135 West 7th Street, Los Angeles (tel. 628-7141). Central location in downtown Los Angeles.

Alexandria – Corner of Spring and 5th Streets, Los Angeles (tel. 626-7484). Centrally located, with good facilities.

DINING OUT

Like many of America's major cities, Los Angeles' dining scene benefits from the range of different nationalities that live there and have opened restaurants. Whatever the dish from whatever the country, the chances are good that it'll be found somewhere in Los Angeles: Mexican restaurants are centred mainly in the east of the city, Jewish and Eastern European food is most easily found in the Fairfax area, and Japanese, Thai, Chinese and Vietnamese restaurants are found, not surprisingly, in Chinatown and Little Tokyo.

Among the various Los Angeles specialities which aren't to be missed is tofu (found in burgers at vegetarian restaurants), a California Roll at a sushi bar (made of rice, seaweed, cucumber, raw fish and avocado), and also the celebrated snack of tortilla chips and salsa.

Restaurants tend to be busy in the Los Angeles area, and it is advisable to reserve in advance.

• **First Class:** (over $70 for two)
The Palms – 9001 Santa Monica Boulevard, Los Angeles (tel. 550-8811). Traditional American food served in very comfortable surroundings. Excellent steaks.

La Scala – 9455 Little Santa Monica Boulevard, Beverly Hills, Los Angeles (tel. 275-0579). Noted as one of the finest Italian restaurants in LA. A wide selection of superb dishes is served by very friendly and efficient staff.

Scandia – 9040 Sunset Boulevard, West Hollywood, Los Angeles (tel. 278-3555). Superb Scandinavian cuisine served amid tasteful decor. A favourite among locals.

• **Super Club Class:** ($50–$70 for two)
Jade West – 2040 Avenue of the Stars, Los Angeles (tel. 556-3888). Superb Szechuan cuisine served in authentic Chinese surroundings.

Jimmy's – 201 Moreno Drive, Beverly Hills, Los Angeles (tel. 879-2394). Classic French dishes with an excellent wine list. Friendly service.

Maison Magnolia –2639 South Magnolia Avenue, Los Angeles. Fine Continental cuisine served in very elegant surroundings which are filled with art and antiques.

• **Economy:** ($20–$40 for two)
Hard Rock Café – 8614 Beverly Boulevard, Los Angeles (tel. 276-7605). Fashionable place to try some traditional American ribs, chillis and burgers.

Gorky's – 536 East 8th Street, Los Angeles (tel. 627-4060). Russian/American cuisine served round the clock in the city's Soho district. Lively atmosphere.

Mon Kee – 170 North La Cienega Boulevard, Los Angeles (tel. 628-6717). Considered to be one of the best Chinese restaurants in the LA area. A favourite among locals.

El Cholo – 1121 South Western Avenue, Los Angeles (tel. 734-2773). Excellent Mexican food. The Margaritas are a house speciality which shouldn't be missed.

NIGHTLIFE

Most hotels and restaurants in Los Angeles house bars and cocktail lounges that offer either quiet, intimate relaxation, or lively entertainment, depending on which you choose. Otherwise, the nightclub scene around the city is an extensive one, catering largely for live entertainment, and on any given evening, several clubs have big-name pop, jazz, rock and country and western entertainers giving performances. For up-to-the-minute details of events and entertainment in the Los Angeles area, consult the calendar section of the *Los Angeles Times* (Sunday edition) or the local magazines.

● **Nightclubs:**

The Palomino – 6907 Lankershim Boulevard, North Hollywood, Los Angeles. Live country and western shows are given here most evenings by talented musicians. The atmosphere is lively, and there is also dancing.

Ye Little Club – 455 North Canon Drive, Beverly Hills, Los Angeles. A quiet, intimate spot where cocktails are served, and entertainers play suitably soft music. Tasteful decor.

Chippendales – 3739 Overland Avenue, West LA. Trendy discotheque frequented by lovers of punk, new wave and other music – all of which is played at full volume. Very lively atmosphere.

Donte's – 4269 Lankershim Boulevard, North Hollywood, Los Angeles. Top jazz entertainers give nightly performances here. The music is excellent, and the atmosphere is both friendly and lively.

EXCURSIONS

PASADENA is a suburb of Los Angeles, 10 miles from downtown, and has a range of attractions that are both interesting and entertaining. The world-famous Huntington Library, Art Gallery, and Botanical Gardens are here. The library houses treasured collections of English and American literature, the art gallery is noted for its centuries-old British paintings and the gardens contain some of the world's rarest and most beautiful plants. Also in Pasadena is the Pacific Asia Museum (displaying various forms of Asian art), the Norton Simon Museum of Art (a range of diverse international art is on show here), and also the Southwest Museum, which has exhibitions depicting the history and culture of California's early settlers. New Year's Day in Pasadena is renowned for the Tournament of Roses Parade, and the Rose Bowl.

The area of MALIBU, a narrow stretch of coastline just north of Santa Monica, is a region of scenic cliffs and beautiful beaches. On a cliff above the ocean, just east of Malibu Beach, is the famed J. Paul Getty Museum (17985 Pacific Coast Highway); built as a replica of a first-century villa at Herculaneum, the plants and gardens are done in the style of the Romans. Inside are paintings, tapestries, and furniture from the Renaissance period, as well as Greek and Roman sculpture. (Note, you must reserve a place in the parking lot a day in advance and in summer, a week in advance. Alternately you can take a bus from Malibu or Santa Monica.) Another of Malibu's attractions which shouldn't be missed is the Malibu Creek State Park, which is 4000 acres in size, and has some 15 miles of trails to wander along.

VENICE, up the coast from Los Angeles, was once the subject of an unsuccessful attempt to turn it into a second Venezia, and today it is a bustling centre of attraction for the (even)-more eccentric in Los Angeles. What were once the grand hotels and buildings that it was hoped would turn the town into a high-class tourist resort, have all made way for health-food shops, sidewalk cafés and juice bars. Ocean Front Walk is worth strolling along: sights here include the bodybuilders on muscle beach, and an army of roller-skaters, cyclists and joggers. The lively atmosphere in general is what makes Venice tick, and it's well worth sampling.

SANTA MONICA, a short drive north of Los Angeles, is an area of some charm and attraction. Just south of the Santa Monica mountains the area used to be a beach resort, and while the Santa Monica beach is still much frequented by Los Angelians, major attractions in the area are the Old Santa Monica Mall, an outdoor shopping centre which is noted for its bargain-priced clothes and cheap ethnic foods, and the more up-market Santa Monica Place, which is much the same only on a higher price scale. The Santa Monica Pier isn't to be missed either, complete with its early 20th-century carousel which was recently restored.

Miami

MIAMI INTERNATIONAL AIRPORT

Miami International Airport is 8 miles west of downtown Miami; it handles some 23 airlines, both domestic and international. There is 1 terminal.

AIRPORT FACILITIES

Information Desk	Located on the first floor.
Bank/Foreign Exchange	On the first floor.
Insurance Facilities	Available on the first floor.
Bar	There are several bars on the first floor.
Restaurant/Buffet	There are snack bars and a restaurant on the first floor.
Baggage Deposit	Available on the ground and first floors.
Shops	On the first floor there are shops selling flowers, confectionery, books, gifts, toys, etc.
Duty Free	Located in Flight Departures, selling cigarettes, cigars, tobacco, wines, aperitifs, spirits, liqueurs, cameras, lighters, watches, radios, jewellery, glass, china and fashion accessories.
Toilets	These are on all floors of the terminal.
Meeting Point Location	The concourse E information counter on the first floor.
Car Rental Desks	Avis, Hertz, National, Dollar, Greyhound and Budget have counters on the first floor.
Barber Shop	On the ground floor.

AIRPORT INFORMATION

Check-in Times

Average for all airlines:
International – 90 minutes;
Domestic – 60 minutes.

Airport Tax

$3.

AIRPORT HOTELS

• **First Class:**
Sheraton River House – 3900 NW 21st Street, Miami (tel. 871-3800).

• **Super Club Class:**
Miami Airport Inn – 1550 LeJeune Road, Miami (tel. 871-2345).

CITY LINKS

• **Coach:** A coach service is available between the airport and downtown. It runs every 25 minutes and operates round the clock; fare is $6. The service to the airport runs from the city's Greyhound bus station; pick-ups can be made at hotels by phoning 526-5764 24 hours in advance.

• **Bus:** Bus No. 20 runs from the airport to downtown every 30 minutes from 0600 to 0100 hours. The fare is 75c, and the bus can be boarded at the lower level bus loop outside Customs at concourse E.

• **Taxi:** Taxis are easily found at the airport, and a usual fare to downtown Miami is around $15; to Miami Beach, anything between $19 and $25 depending on the area desired.

• **Car Hire:** For details, see *Airport Facilities*.

MIAMI

Gateway to the state of Florida, the Greater Miami area is divided into two cities – Miami and Miami Beach. Separated from each other by Biscayne Bay, but linked by virtue of several causeways

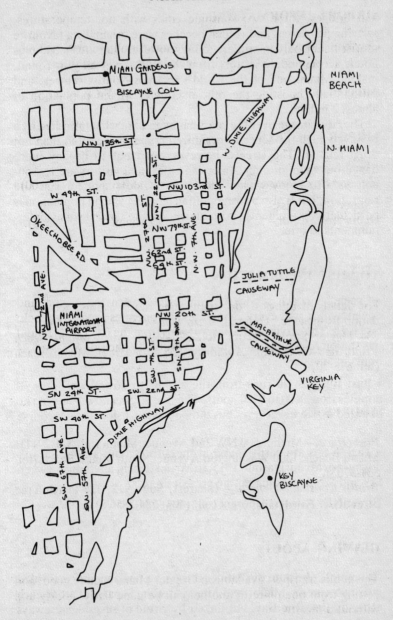

and bridges, these two sunshine cities with hot temperatures, swaying palm trees and golden beaches were originally a favourite tourist haunt only in winter; today, however, the area's 800-plus hotels accommodate visitors from the world over all year round, making Miami one of the world's foremost tourist centres, and substantially boosting the official Greater Miami population of almost 2 million.

The city's image over the years has been somewhat tarnished by a relatively high incidence of organized crime, more often than not drugs-related. The streets, however, tend not to be any more dangerous than in other American cities, and visitors are reasonably safe to enjoy what is not only an ideal spot for sun and relaxation, but is also a cosmopolitan city (the Cuban population is particularly prominent), with much culture and diverse entertainments to offer.

TOURIST INFORMATION

For details of things to do, sightseeing tours, events, accommodation-listings etc., contact: *Metro Dade Department of Tourism*, 234 Flagler Street, Miami (tel. 375-4694). Also: *Miami Beach Visitor and Convention Authority*, 555 17th Street, Miami Beach (tel. 673-7070).

ADDRESSES

Post Offices – Miami: 500 NW 2nd Avenue, Miami (tel. 371-2911). Miami Beach: 1300 Washington Avenue, South Miami Beach (tel. 531-3763).
British Consulate-General – (nearest) Suite 912, 225 Peach Tree Street NE, Atlanta, Georgia (tel. (404) 524-5856/8).

GETTING ABOUT

The public transport available in Greater Miami is quite good, and getting from one place to another can be done fairly quickly and without difficulty.

• **Bus/Train:** As well as an extensive Metrobus system which links downtown with the various municipalities (fare 75c, runs 0600–1800; till 2300 on major routes), there is an elevated rail system – Metrorail – operating downtown. The fare for Metrorail is $1, and a rail-bus transfer costs 25c. Also, the Metromover is an amusement park-style network of moving platforms, linked to Metrorail, which provides relaxing elevated transport around downtown.

• **Taxi:** Taxis are widely available around the city and can be hailed in the street or phoned for. They can be found under 'Taxicabs' in the Classified Telephone Directory.

• **Car Hire:** All major car rental firms have offices in the Miami metropolitan area. Many of the major hotels can arrange for immediate car hire.

SIGHTS

Getting round the sights of Miami and Miami Beach can be done in various ways. Among the sightseeing tours available, it's possible to take helicopter trips for a bird's-eye view of the whole area (phone the Miami Helicopter Service on 377-0934, or Skylark Helicopters on 377-3344), boat tours offer a relaxing way of sampling the region's scenic attractions (several companies run cruises, among them 'Spirit of Miami' from October to June – phone 379-5119), and there are also various bus tours run by companies such as Greyhound (538-0381) and Gray Line (573-0550).

There is a wide range of sights and attractions in the area which are well worth taking in. Located on Virginia Key is the SEAQUA-RIUM, which has a unique range of attractive marine life, including performing porpoises, sea lions, dolphins and killer whales. There's also a monorail which gives aerial tours of the complex. Across the Rickenbacker Causeway from the Seaquarium is PLANET OCEAN – more educational, it has a vast range of scientific exhibits, connected largely with the mysteries of the sea; the permanent ocean exposition deals with man's dependence on water for the survival both of himself and his earth. More animal life is on view in the

PARROT JUNGLE at 11000 SW 57th Avenue; amid the jungle leaves, a variety of tropical birdlife can be spotted, including flamingos and macaws. There are also displays given by trained birds.

VIZCAYA at 3521 South Miami Avenue is the former home of International Harvester heir James Deering, and today visitors can tour it for a small fee. A palace 'in the style of old Venice', its 70 rooms housing a magnificent collection of various pieces of furniture and art dating back to the first century, it is worth a visit; a light-and-sound show is also laid on for guests at night.

A very interesting place to visit is the SPANISH MONASTERY OF ST BERNARD at 16711 West Dixie Highway. It was originally built in Spain in the mid-12th century, then in true American fashion it was dismantled, the pieces shipped to the US, and built on the site where it stands today.

Where cultural attractions are concerned, Miami can boast a wide and interesting selection of museums and art galleries. At 3280 South Miami Avenue are two museums: THE HISTORICAL MUSEUM OF SOUTHERN FLORIDA is full of exhibits and displays depicting local historical and marine exhibits, and the adjoining MUSEUM OF SCIENCE AND SPACE TRANSIT PLANETARIUM has a wide range of things worth viewing, such as coral reef exhibits, various under-water finds that were made both in Florida and the Caribbean, and Indian artefacts. THE METROPOLITAN MUSEUM AND ART CENTER at 1212 Anastasia Avenue, Coral Gables, offers frequently changing exhibitions as well as its permanent collection; the BASS MUSEUM OF ART at 2100 Collins Avenue (Miami Beach) has an intriguing collection of various works from throughout the ages; and the LOWE ART MUSEUM at 1301 Miller Drive, Coral Gables, is noted for its collections of Oriental and European paintings, among other things.

An area of Miami where it's a good idea to spend some time strolling around is LITTLE HAVANA. Not only home to Cuban business, this area of the city has an endless number of Cuban cultural attractions that range from restaurants (some of the best Cuban cuisine in the country can be found here) to museums. One place to look out for is the CUBAN MUSEUM OF ARTS AND CULTURE at 1300 SW 12th Avenue, which is a renovated house containing some of the best Cuban works of art around. Otherwise, Little Havana's charm lies in its streets, its people, and generally Cuban atmosphere.

ACCOMMODATION

● **First Class:** (double over $100)
Sheraton River House – 3900 NW 21st Street, Miami (tel. 871-3800). Located next to Miami International Airport, this offers the best in luxury, and the widest range in facilities. Available to guests is an outdoor heated pool, a health club, saunas, jacuzzis, 3 lighted tennis courts and a golf course adjacent. There's also excellent dining in 'Daphne's' restaurant, and live entertainment is laid on in at least one of the 3 lounges.

Hyatt Regency – 400 SE 2nd Avenue, Miami (tel. 358-1234). Very modern hotel whose facilities include 2 fine restaurants and comfortable lounges. There's a magnificent ballroom, and also various shops and boutiques on the premises.

Doral-on-the-Ocean – 4833 Collins Avenue, Miami Beach (tel. 532-3600). In the attractive Miami Beach area, this hotel is not only architecturally stunning, but it also boasts splendid facilities and hospitality. Noted for its rooftop supper club.

● **Super Club Class:** (double $75–$95)
Miami Lakes Inn and Country Club – NW 154th Street, Miami (tel. 821-1150). Excellent facilities include a pool, tennis courts and golf facilities as well as fine restaurants and bars. There's also dancing in the evenings.

Biscayne Bay Marriott Hotel and Marina – 1633 N Bayshore Drive, Miami (tel. 374-3900). Conveniently located downtown, there is excellent dining in the restaurant and very comfortable bars, some of which offer live entertainment.

Pan American – 17875 Collins Avenue, Miami Beach (tel. 932-1100). In the Miami Beach area, this hotel offers guests good facilities and the beach is on the doorstep.

Versailles – 3425 Collins Avenue, Miami Beach (tel. 531-6092). Excellent facilities include a private beach and swimming pool. The staff are friendly.

● **Economy:** (double $30–$70)
Waves Hotel – 1060 Ocean Avenue, Miami Beach (tel. 531-5835). Well placed on the beach front, this hotel is clean and the facilities good. Friendly atmosphere.

Miramar Hotel – 1133 Ocean Avenue (tel. 394-3731). In Santa Monica area. Clean and comfortable.

Dixie Court Motel – 762 South Dixie Highway, Coral Gables (tel. 661-4286). Situated near the University of Miami, facilities here include a swimming pool. Air-conditioning in rooms.

Miami Airways Motel – 5001 36th Street, Miami (tel. 883-4700). Near the airport, facilities here are quite good, and the surroundings clean.

Collins Plaza Hotel – 318 20th Street, Miami Beach (tel. 531-7301). A short walk from the beach, this hotel is pleasant both in surroundings and atmosphere.

DINING OUT

As well as boasting an international selection of restaurants, Miami and the Miami Beach area are renowned country-wide for being home to some of the best seafood and Cuban restaurants in America. There are over 300 places to eat in Miami and Miami Beach, and they range from the elegant and expensive to the basic and economical. Washington Avenue in Miami Beach is a centre for eating establishments, and elsewhere restaurants are scattered all around. Local specialities not to be missed include stone crabs, Florida lobster and crawfish. Among the recommended Cuban dishes are 'media noche' sandwiches and mamey ice cream; cafe cubano is also worth tasting. Most Cuban establishments are found in the Little Havana area of Miami.

Otherwise, there is a variety of French, German, Chinese, Scandinavian and other international places serving their own traditional fare; American cuisine is widely featured too.

● **First Class:** ($40–$60 for two)
King Arthur's Court – Viscount-Miami Hotel, 500 Deer Run, Miami Springs (tel. 871-6000). Elegant establishment with decor reminiscent of Old England. The atmosphere is pleasant and the service excellent. Included on a fine menu are some memorable beef dishes.

Joe's Stone Crab – 227 Biscayne Street, Miami Beach (tel. 673-0365). Very popular restaurant which serves some of the best seafood in the area, with stone crab a house speciality. Open October to May.

Dominique's – 5225 Collins Avenue, Miami Beach (tel. 861-5252). French cuisine of the highest quality. The restaurant has an attractive decor, and the atmosphere is intimate. Also excellent service.

● **Super Club Class:** ($20–$40 for two)
Brasserie De Paris – 244 Biscayne Boulevard, Miami (tel. 374-0122). A pleasant atmosphere in which to sample a menu of classical French cuisine. Good wine list.

Port of Call – 14411 Biscayne Boulevard, Miami (tel. 945-2567). One of Miami's most popular restaurants, this place is owned by fishermen, and it's their catch which often graces the menu. The food is excellent, and the atmosphere lively.

Gatti's Restaurant – 1427 West Avenue, Miami Beach (tel. 673-1717). Excellent continental/Italian cuisine served in a pleasant atmosphere. Chicken dishes are a house speciality.

● **Economy:** ($10–$20 for two)
Crab House – 1551 79th Street Causeway, North Bay Village (tel. 868-7085). An all-you-can-eat seafood/salad place. Rather lacking in elegance, but the fresh seafood is excellent value.

Olympic Flame Greek Restaurant – 904 Lincoln Road Mall, Miami Beach (tel. 538-2745). Very good authentic Greek dishes served at bargain prices, at the cheaper end of the economy range.

Sorrento – 3058 SW 8th Street, Miami. Good Italian cuisine in a relaxed atmosphere. The Chicken Florentine is well worth trying.

S & S Diner – 175 NE 2nd Avenue, Miami (tel. 373-4291). Typical American diner which serves excellent beef dishes among other things. Good value.

NIGHTLIFE

Miami and Miami Beach are both areas where night entertainment is the toast of locals and visitors alike.

Most of the nightclubs in Miami are found in the larger resort hotels. There, a wide range of entertainment is on offer, from Latin-style revues to lively discotheques, to the intimate atmosphere of a piano bar. Otherwise, there is a good selection of bars, jazz clubs, and various other live music spots. It's also a good idea to take in a Cuban supper club. For details of what's going on, consult the *Miami-South Florida Magazine* or the *Miami Herald*.

• Nightclubs:

Our Place Restaurant – 830 Washington Avenue, Miami Beach (tel. 674-1322). An excellent restaurant for most of the week, this place converts to the 'Folk Club' from Wednesday through till Saturday. The atmosphere is always lively, and the music usually good.

The 30s Café – 622 Lincoln Road Mall, Miami Beach (tel. 532-5882). Very lively nightspot that captures a 30s atmosphere with nightly performances of music from that era. Friendly atmosphere.

Garden Lobby Bar – Fontainebleau Hotel, 4441 Collins Avenue, Miami Beach (tel. 538-2000). Very elegantly decorated, this is one of Miami's more up-market lounge bars. The clientele are a sophisticated crowd, and the atmosphere is suitably intimate.

The Gallery – Omni International Hotel, Biscayne Boulevard, Miami (tel. 374-0000). Pleasant lounge bar atop one of Miami's tallest structures. The staff here are friendly, the atmosphere pleasant, with unbeatable views of Miami and its surrounds adding extra sparkle.

EXCURSIONS

KEY BISCANE, 6½ miles from downtown Miami across the Rickenbacker Causeway, is an ideal spot for any number of pursuits, however relaxing or active. Crandon Park on the Key not only contains fine beaches which are often deserted, but there's also a zoo, a miniature train ride, cabanas and bath-houses among other things. To the south of the Key is Bill Baggs Cape Florida State Park, which provides the perfect setting and facilities for fishing, boating, swimming and picnicking.

MONKEY JUNGLE, around 20 miles south of Miami, is a 10-hectare tropical rain forest which offers visitors the chance to see a range of different types of monkeys in their natural environment. While the monkeys (mostly from Asia and South America – all are wild) roam free, visitors walk along routes through the park which are covered by cages. It's an interesting and often amusing place to spend some time – made all the more intriguing, of course, by the fact that the monkeys are completely at home in the park, and act according to their natural environment.

FAIRCHILD TROPICAL GARDEN, 8 miles from downtown Miami at 10901 Old Cutler Road, is not only an ideal spot for getting away from the bustle of the city, but it also provides one of the most prestigious collections of tropical plant life in the country. The garden covers an area of some 100 hectares, and contains thousands of varieties of tropical flowers, trees and plants. Tram tours through the garden are available.

The SERPENTARIUM, 11 miles south of Miami at 12655 South Dixie Highway, is well worth taking in. On show here is a wide variety of reptilian life from the most harmless to the deadly; among the outdoor attractions that guests can view are snakes, tortoises, iguanas and crocodiles. A favourite with visitors to the Serpentarium is the 'milking' of snake venom which is demonstrated during every tour.

New York

New York has 3 airports: John F. Kennedy International, Newark International and La Guardia.

JOHN F. KENNEDY INTERNATIONAL AIRPORT

JFK International Airport is located in the borough of Queens around 15 miles south-east of Manhattan; it handles domestic as well as international flights all around the world. It has 9 terminals.

The International Arrivals Building handles all international arrivals. All the other terminals are owned by the various airlines, and each is used by that airline for their flights.

These terminals are: American Airlines Terminal; United Airlines Terminal; Eastern Airlines Terminal; Northwest/Delta Terminal; Pan American Airlines Terminal; TWA International Terminal A/TWA Domestic Terminal B; British Airways Terminal.

AIRPORT FACILITIES

Information Desk	A central desk is on the first floor of the main lobby of the International Arrivals Building. All the other terminals have desks too.
Bank/Foreign Exchange	Located in most terminal buildings.
Hotel Reservations Service	Located in the International Arrivals Building (24 hours). Also desks in other terminals or courtesy phones.
Insurance Facilities	Available in all terminals.
Bar	There are bars and cocktail lounges in every terminal.
Restaurant/Buffet	Available in all terminals.
Post Office	Located in the east wing of the International Arrivals Building. Also, postboxes and stamp vending machines in every terminal.
Baggage Deposit	Available in the International Arrivals, American, United, and Eastern Airlines terminals.
Nursery	Located on the second floor of the International Arrivals Building. Also in the British Airways and TWA terminals (those are restricted to

	passengers travelling on these airlines).
Shops	Shops selling a wide variety of goods are in all the terminal buildings.
Duty Free	There are duty free shops in all the terminals selling perfume, cigarettes, cigars, liquor, gifts etc. Major credit cards, and only local currency are accepted. Duty free goods are not available for flights with intermediate stops in the US.
Medical Centre	A medical clinic is located in Building No. 198 at 150th Street and South Cargo Road, tel. (718) 656-5344.
Toilets	These are all over every terminal building.
Car Rental Desks	There are car rental desks and counter phones in all terminals.
Lost and Found	Passengers should contact their airline representative first for any lost property; alternatively, the main office can be reached on (178) 656-4120.
Public Telephones	These are available all over every terminal.

AIRPORT INFORMATION

Check-in Times	Average for all airlines: International – 60 minutes; Domestic – 45 minutes.
Airport Tax	Nil.
International–Domestic Transfers	On arriving at JFK, passengers should claim their baggage and proceed through Customs and

Domestic–International
Transfers

Immigration. After clearance, luggage should be checked with the airline representative at the baggage collection point. Passengers arriving on a domestic flight should arrange with their travel agent for their luggage to be 'interlined' – it will then be transferred automatically.

INTER-AIRPORT TRANSFER

● **To New York–La Guardia Airport:**
There is a coach service every 30 minutes from 0730 up to 2120. The fare is $3.50 and the journey takes 60 minutes. The coach can be boarded on the Arrivals level of each terminal. A taxi to La Guardia takes around 30 minutes and the fare is usually about $13.

● **To New York–Newark Airport:**
There's a coach service every 60 minutes from 0800–2030. The journey takes 90 minutes, and the fare is $12. Reservations should be made at the service desk in the main lobby of the International Arrivals Building. A taxi to Newark takes around 75 minutes and costs about $50.

In addition, many of the airlines operate helicopter and limousine services to La Guardia and Newark. For details, contact your airline representative.

AIRPORT HOTELS

There is an International Hotel at the airport (tel. (718) 995-9000 on a courtesy phone). Other hotels can be reached on courtesy phones or through travel agents or airline representatives.

CITY LINKS

• **Bus:** The JFK Express operates from all terminals to the Howard Beach–JFK subway station, and from there a special subway service goes to several places around the city. Journey time is around one hour, and the fare is $6 each way ($5.10 plus 90c subway fare).

The Carey Bus Service runs every 30 minutes from the airport to Grand Central Station and the Port Authority Terminal. Fare is $8 one way and $15 round-trip.

• **Taxi:** Taxis are available outside every terminal; during peak hours, there are uniformed taxi dispatchers outside the International Arrivals Building and at the other central terminal area buildings. A usual fare is around $25.

• **Car Hire:** For details, see *Airport Facilities*.

NEWARK INTERNATIONAL AIRPORT

Newark International Airport is 16 miles from Manhattan in New Jersey, and handles both international and domestic flights. There are 4 terminals.

Terminals A, B and C handle international and domestic flights. Terminal C handles incoming international flights. The North Terminal, located 3½ miles from the Central Terminal Area, handles domestic and charter flights.

AIRPORT FACILITIES

Information Desk	Near the centre door on the Arrivals level of each terminal.
Bank/Foreign Exchange	Available in all terminals.
Hotel Reservations Service	In all terminals.
Insurance Facilities	Available in all terminals.
Bar	There are bars and cocktail lounges in all terminals.
Restaurant/Buffet	Each terminal has either a buffet or similar eating place.

Baggage Deposit	There are baggage lockers in the 3 satellite areas of Terminal B.
Nursery	Child-care nurseries are provided in the ladies' restrooms in Terminal B on the concourse level near satellites A and C, and in the ladies' restroom within satellite C.
Shops	There are shops selling confectionery, books, gifts, toys, newspapers, magazines, etc. in all terminals.
Duty Free	Duty free shops at the airport sell cigarettes, cigars, tobacco, wines, aperitifs, spirits, liqueurs, watches, lighters, and electronic goods. Major credit cards and local currency are accepted.
Medical Centre	Medical services for passengers requiring inoculation are located in building No. 5 near the North Terminal.
Toilets	In every terminal.
Car Rental Desks	Avis, Budget, Dollar, Hertz and National all have counters in Terminals A and B. In Terminal C and in the North Terminal there are telephones for these counters.
Lost Property	The airport recommend you contact your airline representative first; failing that, phone (201) 961-2235.
Public Telephones	They are all over every terminal.

AIRPORT INFORMATION

Check-in Times	Average for all airlines: International – 45 minutes;

	Domestic – 30 minutes.
Airport Tax	Nil.
Transferring Flights	There is an inter-terminal bus from Terminals A and B to the North Terminal and vice-versa; it's free of charge and runs from 0600–0130 (until 2300 on Saturdays).

The connecting service between Terminals A and B runs every 7 minutes 0700–2300; it's also free.

INTER-AIRPORT TRANSFER

● **To New York–J.F. Kennedy Airport:**
There is a coach service every 60 minutes 0800–1830, Monday–Saturday. The journey takes 75 minutes and the fare is $12. By taxi the journey takes around 75 minutes and costs about $50.

● **To New York–La Guardia Airport:**
There is a coach service every 60 minutes 0800–1830. The journey takes around 60 minutes and costs $12. The taxi journey takes around 50 minutes and costs about $50.

AIRPORT HOTELS

Hotels situated near to the airport can be contacted via courtesy telephones, or through travel agents or airline representatives.

CITY LINKS

● **Rail:** There is a train service to Manhattan which leaves from Penn Station in Newark; to board it, passengers can get on the Airlink minibus at all terminals every 30 minutes from 0620–2315 (Monday–Friday) and from 0640–0010 (Saturday and Sunday). The train leaves Penn Station every 25 minutes from 0620–2355, and goes to

Pennsylvania Central Station in Manhattan. Fare for the minibus is $2, and for the train $1.25. A Rapid Transit Train also operates a service between Penn Station in Newark and the World Trade Center/Wall Street area, and the Pennsylvania Station area. This runs every 25 minutes between the same hours as the other rail link. Passengers should take the Airlink minibus to Penn Station in Newark as before ($2); fare for the Rapid Transit Train is $0.30.

● **Bus:** An Airport Express Bus operates a service to the Port Authority Terminal in Manhattan every 15 minutes from 0630–2400. The fare is $4.

There is a coach service (Newark Minibus) to major hotels in Manhattan every 30 minutes from 0700–0010. Journey time is 25 minutes, and the fare is $9.

Also, the MTA bus No. 107 runs from the airport to Manhattan; fare is $2.15 in exact change.

● **Taxi:** Fares to midtown Manhattan range from $25 to $26 plus tolls. Between 0800 and midnight 'Share and Save' taxi rates allow 4 passengers to share a taxi to Manhattan, cutting the cost for each individual. For details, ask the taxi dispatchers who work outside every terminal.

● **Car Hire:** For details, see *Airport Facilities*.

LA GUARDIA AIRPORT

La Guardia Airport is located on the East River in the borough of Queens, 8 miles east of Manhattan; it handles both international and domestic flights. There are 5 terminals.

Airlines handled by the Main Terminal are Air Canada, Allegheny Commuter, American, Braniff, Continental, Eastern, Empire, Frontier, Horizon, Midway, New York Air, Ozark, Pan American, Piedmont, Pilgrim, Republic, Trans World, United and US Air.

Airlines handled by the Eastern Airlines Shuttle Terminal are Air North, Bar Harbor, Brockway Air, Command, Eastern, New Air, Precision, Provincetown and Boston.

Airlines handled by the Delta Airlines Terminal are Delta, Northwest and Ransome.

Airlines handled by the Marine Air Terminal are Catskill, East Coast, East Hampton, Aire, Ford Aire, Montauk-Caribbean, Resorts International, Starflite, Tropicana and Trans East International.

AIRPORT FACILITIES

Information Desk	Located in all terminals.
Bank/Foreign Exchange	A bank with a currency exchange service is located in the Main Terminal.
Hotel Reservations	Available at desks in the American, Trans World, and Eastern Arrivals areas.
Insurance Facilities	Available in the Main Terminal area.
Bar	There are bars or similar refreshment facilities in each terminal.
Restaurant/Buffet	There are various eating points in each terminal.
Post Office	Located in the lower level of the Main Terminal, central lobby area. Open 0900–1500 Monday & Tuesday, and from 0900–1600 Wednesday–Friday.
Nursery	Provided in the ladies' restroom, on the lower level of the Main Terminal, near the central lobby area.
Shops	Shops selling books, gifts, toys, newspapers, magazines, etc. are in all terminals.
Duty Free	Duty free shops at the airport sell cigarettes, cigars, tobacco, wines, spirits, perfume etc. Major credit cards and local currency are accepted; duty free

	goods can only be bought for flights to Canada.
Medical Centre	Medical services are available at an office in the central part of Hangar 7, in the Marine Terminal. Open weekdays 0800–1600, tel. (718) 476-5575.
Toilets	Located all over every terminal.
Car Rental Desks	Avis, Budget, Dollar, Hertz and National all have counters in the lower or Arrivals areas of the Main Terminal.
Lost Property	The airport recommend that any lost property be reported to airline representatives in the first instance; failing that, phone the lost property office on (718) 476-5115.
Public Telephones	These are located all over every terminal.

AIRPORT INFORMATION

| Check-in Times | Average for all airlines: International – 45 minutes; Domestic – 30 minutes. |
| Airport Tax | Nil. |

INTER-AIRPORT TRANSFER

• To New York–J.F. Kennedy Airport:

There's a coach service every 60 minutes from 0830–1230, and every 40 minutes from then until 2215. The journey takes 60 minutes and the fare is $3.50. The usual taxi fare is around $13.

• To New York–Newark Airport:

There's a coach service every 60 minutes from 0830–2230. The journey takes around 60 minutes, and the fare is $12. A taxi journey takes around 50 minutes, and the fare is about $50.

CITY LINKS

• **Bus:** Carey Bus Service operates a service every 30 minutes from 1100–1800 (Monday–Friday) from the airport to the Port Authority Bus Terminal in Manhattan. The fare is $6 one-way, and $10 round-trip. You can also take the MTA 'Q48' bus to the Eighth Avenue subway in Queens, and from there the E or F train goes to Manhattan.

• **Taxi:** Uniformed taxi dispatchers are on duty at all taxi stands 0800–midnight. From the airport to mid-Manhattan the fare is around $12.

• **Car Hire:** For details, see *Airport Facilities*.

NEW YORK

Situated at the mouth of the Hudson River in America's north-east, what started as a small Dutch trading post has grown to a bustling metropolis covering some 23 square miles, accommodating a population of nearly 8 million . . . New York is today the largest city in America, and the third largest in the world.

Everything about the city is striking: visually, there is nothing but skyscrapers as far as the eye can see; culturally, it couldn't be more diverse, with inhabitants from every corner of the globe; and for speed, activity and excitement, there's nowhere like it. The title 'city that never sleeps' is apt indeed – wherever you are at whatever time, there's always something to see or do.

The Big Apple, of course, isn't without its dangers. It has a relatively high crime rate, and certain parts of the city are virtual no-go areas for New Yorkers and tourists alike. Following general rules of street safety, however, such as planning your route before going anywhere (and staying to the beaten track), not carrying any loose valuables, and not drawing attention to yourself as a visitor, should guarantee a safe passage around what is a truly fascinating place.

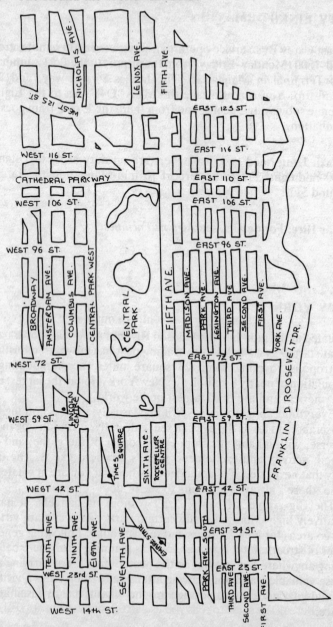

TOURIST INFORMATION

For details of things to do, events, accommodation-listings etc., contact: *New York Convention and Visitors Bureau*, 2 Columbus Circle, New York City (tel. 397-8222).

ADDRESSES

Main Post Office – 33rd Street and Fifth Avenue, New York City (tel. 971-7731). Open Monday–Saturday, 0900–1700.
British Consulate – 845 Third Avenue, New York City (tel. 752-8400).

GETTING ABOUT

New York's roads are on a grid system. All numbered streets go in one direction and the avenues are at 90 degrees to them. Both the public bus service and subway system in New York are extensive.

● **Subway:** The subway is the quickest method of travel if you're travelling up and down Manhattan as opposed to across, and the trains also go as far as the outer boroughs; the subway does have its drawbacks, however – many of the stations are old and run-down, its size means that making a connection can be confusing, and between the hours of 2300 and 0700 it's a dangerous place to wander. A one-way fare on the subway is 90c. To ride on the subway you need to buy tokens which are sold in the subways. A token is valid for a journey of an unlimited length.

● **Bus:** The fare on the buses is also 90c, and while they are cleaner and safer than the subway, they take longer to reach their destination, especially during rush hour; buses run a full service till midnight, then a reduced service after that. Exact charge is required for the buses. The same tokens you use on the subway are also valid.

• **Taxi:** Taxis are widely available around the city; it's advisable to take only the yellow painted cabs, since they are the ones licensed by the city of New York. Taxis are metered, and the fare starts at around $1, with an extra 10c charged for every ninth of a mile. They can be phoned for or hailed in the street. It's worth noting, however, that there is fierce competition for them in bad weather or during the rush hour.

• **Car Hire:** All the major international car hire companies operate in New York as well as many smaller ones though car hire in New York is more expensive than in any other city in the USA. It's advisable to use public transport in getting around the city, since parking a car is either extremely difficult or very expensive.

SIGHTS

Because of the enormous range of sights in New York, it's a good idea to go on one of the many sightseeing tours of the city that are available. One such is the CIRCLE LINE – a 3-hour, 35-mile boat tour around Manhattan, which takes you past all the different sections of the city, and affords excellent views of its skyline as well as the bustling New York docks; a commentary on the various sights is provided by a guide on board.

New York City is made up of 5 boroughs – Manhattan, Brooklyn, The Bronx, Queens and Staten Island. In this section we shall concentrate on the sights of Manhattan. There is, however, a wide range of attractions worth visiting in the other boroughs, and full details of these are available at the Tourist Office.

A must on every visitor's itinerary to Manhattan is the EMPIRE STATE BUILDING on 34th Street at 5th Avenue. The world's tallest building on its construction, it's since lost that title, but still offers spoctacular views of Manhattan and its surrounds from 2 observation decks near its top; also, on the concourse level of the building is the GUINNESS WORLD RECORD EXHIBIT HALL, which is well worth taking in. Another architectural attraction is the ROCKEFELLER CENTER, a complex of buildings (mostly skyscrapers) from 48th to 52nd Streets and between 5th and 6th Avenues. The Center's most popular spot is the outdoor café on the Lower Plaza, which converts to an ice rink in winter; there are scenic roof gardens, the RCA building, the famous RADIO CITY MUSIC HALL and the National Broadcasting Corporation (NBC) studios in the complex too.

The WORLD TRADE CENTER in Church and Vesey Streets is made up of twin skyscrapers which are the tallest twin buildings in the world; it's worth a visit not just for its structural significance, but there are also elevators taking guests to an observation deck, open promenade and restaurant near the top, each affording excellent views of both the city and New York Harbor. Along the East River at 16 Fulton Street is SOUTH STREET SEAPORT; an outdoor nautical museum, the atmosphere of 'Old' New York is re-created here by restored buildings, several market-places, and 6 old ships docked in the port – all making for an attractive and historic area to explore.

Two other areas of Manhattan worth strolling around for their distinct characters and numerous attractions are CHINATOWN and GREENWICH VILLAGE. Chinatown is in lower Manhattan bordered by Baxter, Worth and Canal Streets, and the Bowery. It's home to the second largest Chinese community in the US (San Francisco has the largest), and for Oriental charm and atmosphere, there are few places like it: from the locals in traditional dress to the pagoda-like telephone booths, not to mention the enormous selection of restaurants, visitors can enjoy a varied range of eastern attractions. Greenwich Village, meanwhile, stretches from 14th Street to Houston Street in lower Manhattan, and is the city's haven of counter-culture – students, musicians, struggling artists, New York's largest gay population and various Bohemian types are counted among the area's residents. Wandering around listening to street musicians and taking in the sights can give you an authentic feel for the place, as well as enabling you to visit some of the Village's more specific points of interest such as the former residence of Louisa May Alcott (author of *Little Women*) at 132 MacDougal Street, and the LIBERAL CLUB at No. 137 on the same street, where leftists like Emma Goldman and Upton Sinclair used to meet years ago. Similar to Greenwich Village in atmosphere is SOHO, bounded by Broadway, Canal and Houston Streets and West Broadway. This is the current haunt of many city artists, and there are lofts and galleries here to browse around, as well as quaint cafés, boutiques and restaurants.

CENTRAL PARK is another place worth exploring. Bordered by 5th Avenue, Central Park West, 59th and 110th Streets, it's a vast parkland which is attractive for its lakes, trees and other greenery, and also offers visitors a winter ice-skating rink, outdoor restaurants, a boating lake and a zoo; it's also possible to rent horse-drawn carriages and bicycles to tour the park. A word of warning, however – the park is very dangerous after dark, and even for New Yorkers is a virtual no-go area.

An area of Manhattan often avoided by tourists is HARLEM, due mainly to its reputation as the slum part of town. Ghettos there certainly are, but Harlem today isn't without its middle-class areas, and also various tourist attractions, among them the MALCOLM SHABAZZ MASJID MOSQUE, where black leader Malcolm X was once minister. Parts of Harlem are unsafe for tourists, and so exploring the area is perhaps best done on a tour (one company operating them here is Penny Sightseeing Co., tel. 246-4220).

The centre of entertainment in New York is TIMES SQUARE and BROADWAY. Broadway, home to theatres hosting world-renowned stage shows, runs into Times Square, which is a mass of neon lights, cinemas and other varied forms of entertainment. It's also another area where it's advisable not to be walking around after the streets have emptied.

Among the many interesting museums in New York are the METROPOLITAN MUSEUM OF ART, on 5th Avenue at 82nd Street, which is the largest art museum in the western hemisphere, and houses a suitably grand collection of exhibits; the MUSEUM OF THE AMERICAN INDIAN on Broadway at 155th Street contains the world's largest collection of items relating to Indian culture; and the MUSEUM OF THE CITY OF NEW YORK on 5th Avenue and 104th Street recounts the story of New York's development from being a Dutch trading post to the metropolis it is today.

As a shopper's paradise New York is hard to beat. You can buy anything you like here, so long as you have the dollars or plastic. One very NY place to visit is the food line in Zabar's Deli, Broadway and 80th Street, or its more up-market rival Balducci's on 6th Avenue and 8th Street. For speciality shopping ask at Tourist Info. They can point you towards the best areas for different types of goods.

It's truly a vast city, and while this section has covered the major points of interest as well as some of the lesser ones, details of anything else to view and visit around the city can be found at the Tourist Office.

ACCOMMODATION

Note – look out for the reductions you can get at weekends when business travellers have left the city.

- **First Class:** (double $175)
Barclay Inter-Continental – 111 East 48th Street, New York City 10017 (tel. 755-5988). In Manhattan, close to Park Avenue, this hotel is among the city's older establishments, and accordingly has an elegant atmosphere and traditional comforts. Superb facilities include the renowned 'King's Court' restaurant and an added attraction is the aviary in the lobby.

Vista International Hotel at the World Trade Center (Hilton) – 3 World Trade Center, New York City 10048 (tel. 938-9100). Situated between the twin towers of the World Trade Center in the financial district, there are excellent views from the hotel of New York Harbor, the Statue of Liberty, the Hudson River, and the World Trade Center's landscaped plaza complete with sculptures. First-class facilities include 2 superb restaurants and bar lounges with live entertainment, an executive fitness centre complete with an indoor pool, gym, steam bath, racquetball courts and jogging tracks, and there are also walking tours of lower Manhattan arranged for guests.

The Sheraton Center Hotel and Towers – 52nd Street and 7th Avenue, New York City 10019 (tel. 581-1000). The Sheraton Towers is atop the Sheraton Center, and its 151 luxury suites offer the very best in comfort and in facilities, which include many thoughtful extras; the private club with cocktail lounge is particularly exquisite. The Sheraton Center itself is also one of New York's finest first-class hotels; among the attractions here are the superb Rainier's restaurant, the Café Fontana with live entertainment, and also 'La Ronde' club with dancing. Both the Towers and the Center are conveniently located in midtown Manhattan, close to the Rockefeller Center, Radio City and 5th Avenue.

- **Super Club Class:** (double $100–$150)
Penta – 401 7th Avenue, New York City (tel. 736-5000). Directly across from Penn Station in downtown Manhattan, this hotel offers guests modern, extremely comfortable rooms and good general facilities.

The Westin Plaza – 5th Avenue and 59th Street, New York City 10019 (tel. 759-3000). Located in midtown Manhattan overlooking Central Park, this hotel is an elegant Edwardian-style building with rooms, facilities and atmosphere to match. There are 6 fine restaurants and bars (including the elegant Edwardian with its excellent views of Central Park), tennis facilities nearby, limousine and theatre ticket services, and also various stores (jewellery, boutiques etc.) on the premises.

Park Central – 7th Avenue and 56th Street, New York City 10019 (tel. 247-8000). A popular hotel with personalities of TV and stage, the facilities here are excellent and the rooms luxurious, as are the surroundings in general. Service in the hotel is very good, and its location is convenient for Carnegie Hall, the Coliseum, and the theatre district.

Elysee – 60 East 54th Street, New York City 10022 (tel. 753-1066). Conveniently located for various sights, this place is renowned for its comfort and luxury; rooms are given names rather than numbers, service is excellent, and the 'Monkey Bar' is very popular.

• **Economy:** (double $50–$75)
YMCA – Vanderbilt – 224 East 47th Street, New York City 10017 (tel. 755-2410). In a safe neighbourhood in midtown Manhattan, this is a clean and very comfortable establishment, with facilities including a gym and a swimming pool. Co-ed.

YMCA – West Side – 5 West 63rd Street, New York City 10022 (tel. 787-4400). Located close to Lincoln Center, the rooms here are comfortable and well cared for; good facilities are offered to guests, among them an indoor track, 2 pools, racquet courts and Nautilus equipment.

Franklin Hotel – 164 East 87th Street, New York City (tel. 289-5958). Located in a side street close to Lexington Avenue, the surroundings here are clean and the facilities adequate. Pleasant atmosphere.

Pickwick Arms Hotel – 230 East 51st Street, New York City (tel. 355-0300). In east midtown Manhattan, the decor here consists of much brass and leather furniture. The rooms are comfortable, and the atmosphere pleasant.

Murray Hill Hotel – 42 West 35th Street, New York City (tel. 947-0200). Tastefully decorated establishment where the atmosphere is elegant. Conveniently located opposite Penn Station in midtown Manhattan.

Excelsior Hotel – 45 West 81st Street, New York City 10024 (tel. 362-9200). Situated in one of Manhattan's best neighbourhoods, this hotel is at the top end of the economy range, but the service and comfort on offer are appropriate to the price.

DINING OUT

The dining capital of the United States, New York has over 10,000 restaurants of all kinds offering a range of cuisines as wide as anywhere in the world . . . you name it, and it'll be somewhere in the city. Around Manhattan there are various areas noted for their restaurants: Little Italy is home to the city's best Italian places, while Chinatown has restaurants accounting for every part of the Orient; on the Upper West Side of Manhattan along a stretch of Broadway is a selection of establishments that serve cuisines as varied as French, Spanish, Indian, Turkish, Thai, Jewish and Cuban; Yorkville, around East 86th Street, between 3rd and 2nd Avenues, features numerous Czech, Hungarian, and German places; for Mexican food, and also Spanish and Italian, Greenwich Village is a good place to try, although prices here can be slightly more expensive.

Prices generally in New York can range from anything over $80 for two people at the lavish and magnificent restaurants to around $10 for two at the more basic, though usually good quality establishments.

● **First Class:** (over $100 for two)
Lutece – 249 East 50th Street (between 2nd & 3rd Avenues), New York City (tel. 752-2225). One of the best French restaurants in the city, the atmosphere here is elegant, and the cuisine superb; among the dishes specially worth trying are the soufflé glacé, médaillons de veau aux morilles, and the salmon en croûte. A jacket and tie is required.

'21' Club – 21 West 52nd Street (between 5th & 6th Avenues), New York City (tel. 582-7200). Classic American and continental cuisine in suitably plush surroundings. An excellent varied menu incorporates innumerable superb dishes, and among the house specialities are English sole, baby pheasant, terrapin and veal charleroi. The wine list is extensive too, and the service is impeccable.

Il Caminetto – 1226 2nd Avenue (between 64th & 65th Streets), New York City (tel. 758-1775). Some of the finest Northern Italian cuisine is served here in tastefully decorated rooms which have an intimate atmosphere. Worth looking out for on the superb menu are the homemade pastas and the 'plume de veau' veal dishes, as well as some imaginative appetizers. There's also an excellent wine list.

● **Super Club Class:** ($50–$100)
The Four Seasons – 99 East 52nd Street, New York City (tel. 754-9494). A truly excellent restaurant serving international cuisine where the menu changes with the seasons. The decor is very tasteful and consists of several works of art such as the world's largest Picasso. There's a complete wine cellar here too.

Imperial Dragon East – 148 East 46th Street, New York City (tel. 986-4676). Superb Chinese and Szechuan dishes served by very friendly staff in a continental setting. House specialities include Peking duck, seafood basket and orange beef.

Mormando – 541 Lexington Avenue, New York City (tel. 935-9570). An American/continental restaurant specializing in steaks, seafood and pasta. The atmosphere is pleasant, and the service very good.

● **Economy:** ($15–$50 for two)
Oliver's – 141 East 57th Street (between 3rd and Lexington Avenues), New York City (tel. 753-9180). Cosy restaurant with open fire and picture window where the menu is mainly American. Piano played during dinner.

O'Lunney's Steak House – 12 West 44th Street (between 5th & 6th Avenues), New York City (tel. 840-6688). Hearty American and Irish food served in an informal atmosphere. The staff are friendly, and there's either a pianist or guitarist playing nightly.

Patsy's Italian – 236 West 56th Street (between Broadway and 8th Avenue), New York City (tel. 247-3491). Good Italian food in simple, well lit surroundings. Worth trying are the linguini mare-chiare and the chicken contadino.

Kaplan's Delicatessen – West 47th Street (between 5th & 6th Avenues), New York City (tel. 391-2333). A Jewish-style deli restaurant, the atmosphere is informal, and an excellent menu includes chicken in the pot, stuffed cabbage, and corned beef and pastrami.

NIGHTLIFE

Where nightlife's concerned, New York has everything. Night-clubs, discos, bars, lounges, comedy clubs, 'singles bars' – the list of things to do is endless. Among the nightclubs, a very pleasant evening can be spent in a 'supper club' – very plush establishments which offer first-class food and host nightly shows by top-name performers. Otherwise, the bars (ranging from quiet piano bars to live rock music joints) are usually open till 4 a.m., the discos boast some of the world's most elaborate lighting systems and novel dance routines, jazz clubs are everywhere, and each evening there is an enormous range of shows and cabaret acts performing around the city, on Broadway as well as off. For up-to-the-minute details of what's going on around New York, check with the *New Yorker* or *Village Voice* magazines as well as the local press. Friday and Sunday editions of the *NY Times* have good information.

● **Nightclubs:**
Knickerbocker Saloon – 33 University Place, New York City (tel. 228-8490). Lively jazz club which features famous bassists and pianists nightly. Excellent American cuisine is also served, and there's a bar too. A popular spot with local jazz connoisseurs.

Bill's Gay Nineties – 57 East 54th Street, New York City (tel. 355-0243). 50 years ago this establishment was a speakeasy complete with peephole and secret storage room for liquor; it hasn't changed since those days, and to sample the New York nightclub atmosphere of yesteryear, this place is well worth a visit. Lunch, dinner, cocktails and after-theatre supper are served, and continuous entertainment is laid on.

Top of the Tower – 3 Mitchell Place, New York City (tel. 355-7300). On the top floor of the Beekman Tower, this piano bar boasts a panoramic view of the whole of Manhattan as well as a relaxed, intimate atmosphere.

Something Different – 1488 1st Avenue, New York City (tel. 570-6666). As the name would suggest, this nightclub offers unique entertainment: the waiters and waitresses are all professional performers, and each performs to and serves guests.

EXCURSIONS

A trip on a ferry through New York Bay to STATEN ISLAND not only offers the delights of the island itself, but also provides passengers with an excellent view both of New York Harbor and the Manhattan skyline. The ferry leaves from Whitehall Terminal in Battery Park (lower Manhattan), and for a very low price it's possible to make the 25-minute journey to the island, where attractions include the Richmondtown restoration, which is a restored village covering some 100 acres. Among the buildings here is the Vorleezer House, America's oldest elementary school, the Staten Island Historical Society Museum, and also the Snug Harbor Cultural Center overlooking New York Harbor, which used to be a sailors' retirement home, but nowadays houses a gallery theatre and concert hall.

On Liberty Island in New York Harbor is the STATUE OF LIBERTY, one of the world's tallest and most revered statues. It was a gift to the US from France in 1884, and today visitors are able to go to the top of 'Miss Liberty's' torch, from where the views of New York Harbor and Manhattan are stunning. In the statue's base is the American Museum of Immigration, where the story of the millions of immigrants to the US is told.

Nearby ELLIS ISLAND was the arrival point in the US for the majority of these immigrants, and today there can be seen remnants of its significant past, such as the reception room and main hall that greeted the immigrants.

FIRE ISLAND is a small island about 45 miles from New York, and it's attractive for its excellent beaches and scenery. A 40-mile strip of sand dunes and barrier beach, the island is unique for the fact that there are no roads on it, and the local population of 25,000 get around either on foot or by bicycle. All public areas on the island can be reached by ferry, and once there, visitors can enjoy superb facilities for hiking, bicycling, swimming and nature tours in a very pleasant setting. To get to the island, you can take a ferry from a port in Long Island; for details, contact Fire Island Ferries on 665-5045.

Around 30 miles from New York on Long Island is JONES BEACH, the most popular beach with New Yorkers, and an ideal spot either to relax or be entertained. Officially Jones Beach State Park, it covers some 2500 acres worth of woods and beach area; there's room for over 100,000 swimmers, either in the ocean or in salt water pools, as well as a 2-mile boardwalk, good fishing facilities, restaurants, and also the outdoor Marine Theater, which hosts various musicals, theatrical and water shows during the summer.

San Francisco

SAN FRANCISCO INTERNATIONAL AIRPORT

Located 16 miles from the city's downtown area, San Francisco International Airport is the world's sixth busiest, and deals with a total of 41 international and domestic airlines. The airport is made up of 3 buildings: the North, South and International Terminals, each inter-connected by convenient passageways as well as a complimentary shuttle bus service.

AIRPORT FACILITIES

• **South Terminal:**

Information	White courtesy phone for any information on upper level, in

operation 0900–2100, 7 days a week. Number to dial 7-0118.

Hotel Reservations

Free hotel/motel phone service located in the baggage claim area.

Bar

Cocktail lounges are located in every boarding area.

Restaurant/Buffet

There is a cafeteria serving breakfast, lunch and dinner, as well as a few snack bars.

Post Office

Stamps are available from a machine located across from the Continental Airlines ticket counter. Post boxes are in the ticket lobby area.

Baggage Deposit

Baggage lockers are located behind the ticket counter area and in the boarding areas.

Shops

Located on the Departure level, numerous shops in South Terminal sell a variety of gifts and souvenirs.

Toilets

Located behind ticket counters, near baggage claim; also in all boarding areas.

Car Rental Desks

Avis, Budget, Dollar, Hertz, and National have counters in the baggage claim area.

Public Telephones

Located throughout the terminal. Telephone for the deaf is available by calling 7-0285 on a white courtesy telephone.

Baggage Carts

Located at racks in front of and throughout the terminal. Cost is $1, with a refund of 25c when the cart is returned to the rack.

● **North Terminal:**

Information

White courtesy phones on upper level. Dial 7-0118, 0900–2100, 7 days a week.

Bank/Foreign Exchange

Bank of America located on the mezzanine level, open 0830–1700,

Monday–Friday. Automated teller machine behind the Air Canada ticket counter.

Hotel Reservations	Free hotel/motel phone service located in the baggage claim area.
Bar	There are several bars and lounges to choose from.
Restaurant/Buffet	A wide range of snack bars, dining rooms and restaurants are available.
Post Office	Stamps are available from a machine behind the American Airlines ticket counter, next to the Delta Air Lines baggage claim area. A machine is also located in the boarding area F rotunda. Post boxes are in the ticket lobby area of the terminal.
Baggage Deposit	Lockers are located behind the ticket counter area and in the boarding areas.
Nursery	Nursery rooms are available in the mezzanine level above the Eastern Airlines ticket counter. Call 6-2135 on a white courtesy phone to have a room unlocked. Available 24 hours a day.
Shops	A number of shops in the North Terminal sell a wide range of gifts and souvenirs. Try The California Shoppe for some fine California wines.
Toilets	Located behind the ticket counters near baggage claim, and in all boarding areas.
Car Rental	Avis, Budget, Dollar, Hertz and National all have counters in the baggage claim area.
Public Telephones	Located throughout the terminal. A telephone for the deaf is available by calling 7-0285 on a white courtesy telephone.
Baggage Carts	Located at racks in front of and

throughout the terminal. Cost is $1, with a refund of 25c when the cart is returned to the rack.

Video Games Room — Located behind the Eastern Airlines ticket counter. Open 0800–midnight.

● International Terminal:

Information — White courtesy phones located on lower level. Dial 7-0118, 0900–2100 7 days a week.

Bank/Foreign Exchange — Bank of America branch behind the Pan Am ticket counter. Open 0830–1700, Monday–Friday. Foreign exchange is available here 0700–2300 7 days a week, and in boarding area D from 0800–2000 7 days a week. Automated teller machines are located adjacent to the Bank of America. Citicorp foreign exchange office is next to the security checkpoint on upper level, 0700–2200, 7 days a week. A 24-hour automated teller is located in the lower lobby.

Hotel Reservations — Free hotel/motel phone service located in the baggage claim area.

Bar — The Barbary Coast Saloon is the terminal's main cocktail lounge.

Restaurant/Buffet — There is a varied selection of food on offer in several restaurants.

Post Office — A stamp machine is located in front of the Gift Shop in the concession concourse. Post boxes are in the terminal's ticket lobby area.

Baggage Deposit — Lockers are located behind the ticket counter area and in the boarding areas.

Shops — A number of shops offer a range of gifts and souvenirs. Try the concourse gallery for framed art and posters, or the Western Shop for western apparel

	and other gifts from the old west.
Duty Free	Located in the concession lobby on the upper level of the terminal and in the international flight departure area. Small duty free carts are located at the boarding gates of Western Airlines and Air Canada, and these are open when international flights depart. All purchases must be made 45 minutes before departure.
Toilets	Located behind the ticket counters near baggage claim and in all boarding areas.
Car Rental	Avis, Budget, Dollar, Hertz and National have counters in the baggage claim area.
Lost Property	Located at the Police Desk next to the China Airlines ticket counter.
Public Telephones	Located throughout the terminal. Telephone for the deaf is available by calling 7-0285 on a white courtesy telephone.
Baggage Carts	Located at racks in front of and throughout the terminal. Cost is $1, with a refund of 25c when the cart is returned to the rack.

AIRPORT INFORMATION

| Check-in Times | International flights – 90 minutes; Domestic flights – 60 minutes. |

FACILITIES COMMON TO ALL TERMINALS

Available to all passengers, whatever their terminal of departure or arrival, are the following facilities:

| Medical Clinic | This clinic is located on the lower level of the International Terminal, |

	and it's open 24 hours a day. Dial 7-0444 on a white courtesy phone.
Barber Shop/Showers	Located in the connector between the North and International Terminals. Open 0730–1800 Monday–Friday, and 0730–1700 on Saturdays. Closed Sundays.
Terminal Shuttle	Running every 5 minutes from 0500–midnight is the 'Terminal Shuttle', a brown bus that stops in front of each terminal on the upper level roadway at designated bus shelters. Free of charge.

CITY LINKS

San Francisco International Airport is 16 miles from the centre of San Francisco.

• **Bus:** There are 2 main bus services operating from the airport to downtown San Francisco. For a $6 fare, the SFO Airporter runs every 15 minutes from 0600–2200, then every 20 to 40 minutes until 0320. Services to various other points in the city are operated by several private companies, including Supershuttle, every 45 minutes until about 2100, for a $7 fare. Just turn up and tell them where you want to go. These buses stop at designated SFO Airporter stops on the lower level roadway in front of all terminals so you are bound to see them. The San Trans bus service also operates between the airport and downtown. The 7B and 7F lines go to the city, and buses run every 30 minutes from 0600–1900, then every hour until 0100. Stops for these buses are located in front of Eastern Airlines in the North Terminal and Continental Airlines in the South Terminal, on the upper level roadway. Fare up to $1.15 depending on the distance travelled, and exact change is required.

• **Taxi:** Available 24 hours a day, taxis to San Francisco from the airport cost around $30. Taxis can be found at cab stands (identified by a yellow-striped pillar) on the centre island of the lower level roadway in front of all terminals. Only use taxis which display the gold San Francisco International Airport medallion.

• **Car Hire:** See the *Airport Facilities* tables for details of car hire firms in operation at the airport. Hertz at 433 Mason Street (tel. 771-2200) offer one of the best deals in town. From the airport to downtown limousines can be hired. A shared rental to a city centre hotel can work out at as little as $8 each if there are enough of you, so it is worth checking out this option.

SAN FRANCISCO

As the city whose Golden Gate has been the gateway to America for travellers since the early 19th century, San Francisco is today home to a population taken from almost every corner of the earth, and to a culture which is consequently full of diversity. Whether you're walking through Chinatown (the largest Chinese community outside Asia), Japantown or Little Italy, 'Frisco's cosmopolitan atmosphere is ever-evident; the fact that it's the gay capital of the world adds yet another dimension to the city's character.

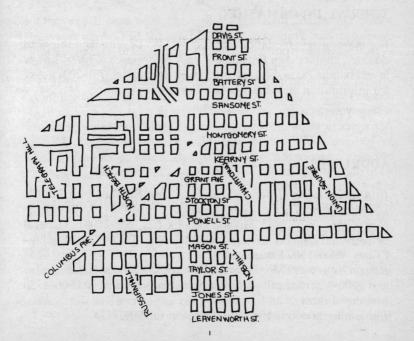

One of America's most attractive cities, San Francisco offers a range of both natural and man-made beauty. After the great earthquake of 1906 which caused half the city to be razed to the ground, 'Frisco was rebuilt around those Vicitorian beginnings which remained, with the result that the steep hills on which the city is built today show an attractive blend of the old and the new, from the famous cable cars and Victorian residences, to the fashionable Japan Center and celebrated Golden Gate Bridge. Other attractions include the picturesque Bay area, the panoramic views which can be seen from any one of the city's hills, and the cool summers and warm winters of the Northern Californian climate.

The city also boasts a very wide range of things to do; as well as countless museums and other daytime pursuits on offer, there's a lively after-dark entertainment scene, with something to suit most tastes.

TOURIST INFORMATION

For maps, accommodation-listings, details of events and things to do, etc., contact: *San Francisco Visitor Information Center*, Lower level Hallidie Plaza, Market and Powell Streets (tel. 391-2001). Ask for information on B&Bs – a San Francisco speciality.

ADDRESSES

British Consulate-General – The Equitable Building (9th Floor), 120 Montgomery Street, San Francisco, CA 94104 (tel. 981-3030).
Post Office – 7th and Mission Streets (tel. 556-2600). General delivery and Express services available. Open 0730–1730, Monday–Friday, 0900–1300 Saturday.
Rincon Annex – 99 Mission Street, open 0800–2200 Monday–Friday and 0900–1700 Saturdays. Other branches open at least 0900–1750 Monday–Friday.
Babysitting Service – Bay Area Agency, tel. 991-7474.

GETTING ABOUT

There are several forms of public transport in San Francisco. The cheapest method of getting around the city is by taking a bus, cable car, or a street car, which all operate a fairly extensive network (have exact change ready). For trips further afield, the Bay Area Rapid Transit underground and overground rail system links the city with surrounding communities. Taxis are widely available in San Francisco and can be phoned for or hailed in the street. All the major national car rental firms operate in San Francisco, as well as several smaller ones. Rental desks can often be found at major hotels; otherwise, look in the Classified Telephone Directory under 'Car Rentals'.

SIGHTS

Sightseeing in San Francisco can be a full-time occupation for 2 or 3 days – there's much to see and do. Probably the city's most famous attraction is its cable cars, and riding on them is not only a convenient way of touring the downtown sights, but it can also be an exhilarating way of getting around, particularly if you stand on the rear platform. Further investigation into this San Franciscan institution can be pursued in the CABLE CAR BARN MUSEUM, at the corner of Mason and Washington Streets, which contains the huge steel cables and machinery that powers the cable cars.

Another museum which houses treasures from old 'Frisco is the SAN FRANCISCO MARITIME MUSEUM, the main building of which is in Aquatic Park at the foot of Polk Street, though the exhibits stretch to PIER 43, where *The Balclutha*, one of the great sailing ships and the last survivor of the Cape Horn fleet, is docked. Also of nautical interest is the HYDE STREET PIER, where 4 restored ships from America's sea-faring past are docked: a wooden steamer, a side-wheel ferry boat, a work scow and a 3-masted schooner.

Other Bay-side attractions include FISHERMAN'S WHARF, THE CANNERY and PIER 39. Fisherman's Wharf is at the foot of Taylor Street, and being the docking area for local fishing boats, it has a lot of restaurants, fish markets and sidewalk stalls selling assorted seafood. The Cannery is close to Fisherman's Wharf, and gets its name from its former role as a fruit cannery. Today, however, it's been converted into a complex of art galleries, speciality shops and restaurants, and it's also a popular area with street musicians and performers. Pier 39 is a major shopping and restaurant complex, too, whose main attraction lies in the fact that its design reflects the San Francisco of last century; it offers excellent views of the city and its surrounds. Also worth visiting for its views over the Bay and city and its exclusive shops is GHIRARDELLI SQUARE, a former chocolate factory which has been converted to a Victorian-style deluxe shopping and restaurant centre. Whilst there sample a San Franciscan legend – delicious chocolates and ice-cream sundaes in Ghirardelli's Ice Cream Parlor.

To sample the cultural as well as the cosmopolitan aspects of San Franciscan life, it's a good idea to wander through the city's CHINATOWN, LITTLE ITALY and JAPANTOWN. Chinatown in San Francisco is the largest Chinese community outside of Asia, and its sights and people give it a truly authentic Oriental atmosphere. As well as the Buddhist temples and endless selection of fine Chinese restaurants, the area's points of interest include the CHINATOWN WAX MUSEUM, the CHINESE CULTURE CENTER and the CHINESE HISTORICAL SOCIETY OF AMERICA. The focal point of Japantown is the JAPAN CENTER, which is 3 square blocks in size, and houses a complex of shops, coffee houses, a Japanese steam bath, tempura bars and Oriental gardens. Also found here is the PEACE PLAZA, which is home to colourful festivals such as the SPRING CHERRY BLOSSOM FESTIVAL and the AKI MATSURI festival in the autumn. The city's Little Italy area is located at North Beach and is well worth visiting, if not for its sidewalk cafés and restaurants, then for its off-Broadway threatres, its nightclubs and numerous other forms of entertainment.

San Francisco is also home to one of America's finest city parks – THE GOLDEN GATE PARK. Besides its beautiful lakes, the exquisite JAPANESE TEA GARDEN, botanical gardens and paddock fields with herds of buffalo, the park also contains some fine museums, including the MORRISON PLANETARIUM, the ASIAN ART MUSEUM and the CALIFORNIA ACADEMY OF SCIENCES.

Other museums around the city include the SAN FRANCISCO MUSEUM OF MODERN ART in the Civic Center at Van Ness Avenue, the OLD MINT, which is a museum displaying coins and other related exhibits, and the CALIFORNIA PALACE OF THE LEGION OF HONOR at Lincoln Park, which houses various forms of French art.

Shopping can be a joy in San Francisco. The choice is endless, but watch out for the hefty 6½ per cent state tax added on to everything, but not shown on the price tag.

ACCOMMODATION

Beware: all hotels charge additional for use of in-room telephones. The telephone company charges here are very heavy, and they charge for every phone call – even if there is no reply. No weekend or summer reductions in this city.

● **First Class:** (double over $100)
Westin St Francis – Union Square, San Francisco (tel. 397-7000). Conveniently situated downtown in the heart of the city, this hotel offers first-rate facilities and excellent service. The nightlife and restaurant facilities are exceptionally fine, and within the States this is regarded as one of *the* top hotels.

Mark Hopkins Inter-Continental – Number One Nob Hill, San Francisco (tel. 392-3434). Another of the US's great hotels, in superb location overlooking the Bay area. Close to Chinatown, Fisherman's Wharf and the Golden Gate Bridge, and offering a choice of excellent restaurants and cafés including the 'Top of the Mark', one of the city's landmarks offering panoramic views while you eat Sunday brunch. All rooms have wide ranging views. Business centre in hotel.

Mandarin Oriental – 221 Pine Street, San Francisco, CA 94104 (tel. 885-0999). A brand-new luxury hotel in good central location.

● **Super Club Class:** (double $80–$100)
Sheraton Palace Hotel – 639 Market Street, San Francisco, CA 94105 (tel. 392-8600). Conveniently located in the centre of the financial district, this hotel is 4 blocks from Chinatown. Excellent facilities include 4 restaurants and several bars.

The Donatello – 501 Post Street, San Francisco, CA 94102 (tel. 441-7100). Very comfortable surroundings with excellent service, and fine dining in the Donatello restaurant.

Holiday Inn – Union Square, 480 Sutter Street, San Francisco, CA 94108 (tel. 398-8900). Comfortable hotel with friendly service. Central location.

Huntington – 1075 California Street, San Francisco, CA 94108 (tel. 474-5400). Near downtown, this hotel's facilities include a fine restaurant and bar.

• **Economy:** (double $40–$80)
King George – 334 Mason Street, San Francisco, CA 94102 (tel. 781-5050). Comfortable surroundings with facilities including a tea-room. Central location.

Embarcadero YMCA Center – 166 The Embarcadero, San Francisco, CA 94105 (tel. 392-2191). Pleasant location, with facilities including a pool.

Pensione International – 875 Post Street, San Francisco, CA 94109 (tel. 775-3344). Complimentary breakfast in this clean, central guest house.

Pension San Francisco – 1668 Market Street, San Francisco, CA 94102 (tel. 964-1271). Central location, with room fee including morning coffee.

Hotel Essex – 684 Ellis Street, San Francisco, CA 94109 (tel. 474-4664). Clean and comfortable.

Temple Hotel – 469 Pine Street, San Francisco, CA 94109 (tel. 781-2565). Clean with reasonable facilities. Convenient location.

DINING OUT

San Francisco has a wide selection of fine restaurants with most nationalities being represented in the city. Chinatown is obviously the place to go for Chinese food, North Beach is home to innumerable Italian restaurants, and for seafood it's best to head for Fisherman's Wharf. French and Japanese cuisine are also well represented in the city – Japantown is the centre for the latter, while the French restaurants are scattered around. There are also numerous restaurants which feature local specialities – these include Crab Louis, abalone steak, crusty sourdough bread, Bay shrimp and artichoke dishes. Celebrated California wines and cheeses are also available in many establishments. The great American tradition of Sunday brunch can be found in many restaurants and cafés in San Francisco – a blend of breakfast and lunch, brunch is usually preceded by a Bloody Mary or a Screwdriver, and typically includes eggs, steak, ham, breads and coffee.

● **First Class:** ($70–$90 for two)
Ernie's – 847 Montgomery Street (tel. 397-5969). Superb food in a pleasant atmosphere enhanced by the elegant Victorian decor. Also offers a fine wine list.

Nob Restaurant – Mark Hopkins Inter-Continental, 1 Nob Hill (tel. 392-3434). A wonderful restaurant for innovative American cuisine. Excellent starters and desserts and a most impressive wine list featuring the best of Californian vintages.

The Torga – Fairmont Hotel, 950 Mason Street (tel. 772-5278). A South Sea extravaganza, complete with floating band and hourly thunderstorms. The Chinese food is particularly good and it's an 'all-American' experience. Dancing to live music.

● **Super Club Class:** ($50–$70 for two)
Amelio's – 1630 Powell Street (tel. 397-4339). High-class Italian restaurant with excellent pasta.

Gaylord – Ghirardelli Square (tel. 771-8822). Fine Indian cuisine with comfortable surroundings and friendly service. Good views of the Bay.

Trader Vic's – 20 Cosmo Place (tel. 776-2232). Renowned for its superb Polynesian dishes, and a very fashionable place to have lunch.

● **Economy:** ($30–$50 for two)
Sam's – 347 Bush Street (tel. 421-0594). Excellent fish fresh from the ocean. Reservations required.

Yamoto – 717 California Street (tel. 397-3456). One of the best Japanese restaurants in town, with great food and friendly service. Try the sushi.

Scoma's – Pier 47 (foot of Jones Street) (tel. 771-4383). Some of the best seafood in the city, and very popular with locals. Reservations are recommended.

New San Remo – 2237 Mason Street (tel. 673-9090). Italian and seafood dishes served amid Victorian decor.

NIGHTLIFE

San Francisco has a very lively after-dark entertainment scene. From its selection of bars to a wide range of nightclubs hosting everything from fruit machines to big-name live entertainment, there's something to suit most tastes. The city also boasts a lively theatre and concert scene. Full details of all events can be found in the entertainment sections of the daily newspapers, or in the *San Francisco Restaurants and Nightlife*, which is distributed at the Visitors Bureau. As 'gay' capital of the world it is difficult not to notice the plethora of gay bars and clubs, but if this offends you these places are easily avoidable.

• Nightclubs:
Venetian Room – The Fairmont Hotel, corner of California and Mason Streets. An expensive and high-class establishment which provides drinks, dinner, and often features top stars in cabaret.

Pier 23 – Embarcadero, down on the waterfront. Lively, fashionable yuppie type nightclub in good nightlife area.

Washington Square Bar and Grill – 1707 Powell Street. As well as being a popular dining spot serving excellent fish and pasta, this is a place well patronized for its saloon atmosphere. A favourite haunt of many political and theatrical names.

Harry's Bar and American Grill – 500 Van Ness Avenue. Apart from excellent lunches and dinners, this is *the* place to be seen at nights. After-theatre snacks and drinks are good here, but book ahead.

EXCURSIONS

An increasingly popular method of travel among tourists in the United States today is the use of motorhomes, which are particularly suited to exploring the great outdoor potential of California. Leading the field in motorhome rental in recent years has been American Express, who offer vehicles suitable in size for as little as 2 adults to as many as 8. The American Express motorhomes are equipped with all mod cons, including showers, flush toilets, ovens, fridges, etc., and they provide a very comfortable and convenient way of getting around.

Because of San Francisco's proximity to many of America's most famous tourist attractions and most popular National Parks, there are many advantages in renting a motorhome here. Within striking distance of the city by driving are the YOSEMITE and LASSEN VOLCANIC NATIONAL PARKS, and also LAKE TAHOE, all showing California at its most beautiful. Yosemite is home to deep valleys, mountain streams, trees, waterfalls and mountain peaks; Lassen Volcanic National Park contains fascinating hot springs and cold lakes with German brown trout; and Lake Tahoe is one of the USA's most celebrated spectacles, with fine beaches and excellent countryside around the lake.

These attractions offer extensive camping facilities to visitors, and all cater to a large extent for the motorhome traveller, with designated overnight parking areas well equipped with a range of amenities. Book ahead in July/August for the most popular campsites, especially in Yosemite.

Prices for renting a motorhome are reasonable, and it often works out cheaper than car hire and motel accommodation, particularly where 4-6 people are concerned. Various travel packages are available concerning American Express motorhomes (bookable in the UK) and for details of these and other general enquiries, contact any American Express Travel Service Office.

The Tourist Office will hand out leaflets on the various organized tours available. Among some of the best excursions are those to the Muir Woods, Monterey Bay Aquarium, Carmel and 17 Mile Drive, and Sacramento. The Gray Line Co. are the most popular company.

ALCATRAZ ISLAND is located in San Francisco Bay off the Fisherman's Wharf area. The island's prison is one of the country's leading tourist attractions. Once home to notorious criminals such as Al Capone and 'Machine Gun' Kelly, the penitentiary was closed down in 1963, but today its forbidding corridors and eerie cells are open to the public, and are well worth visiting. To get to the 'Rock', take the round-trip ferry service which departs from Pier 41 (foot of Stockton Street); reservations are required. Admission to the prison is free of charge.

SAUSALITO is a fairly small town 10 miles north of San Francisco, and from its bygone days as a fishing village it has become home to a wide and diverse range of fine restaurants, antique shops and art galleries, and the local population today consists mainly of artists, sculptors and writers, most of whom gather in the No Name Bar. The town has a very quaint feel and a relaxing atmosphere, and it's a good idea to have a wander around. There's also a spectacular view of the San Francisco skyline to be had from here. To get to Sausalito, take either a ferry, or drive north via the Golden Gate Bridge.

About 15 miles north-west of San Francisco, the MUIR WOODS consist of a magnificent collection of towering redwood trees which are centuries old. They provide an ideal opportunity to see at least some of California's awesome natural wonders. Walking trails taking you through some spectacular natural sights are marked out, and are not too physically demanding.

South of San Francisco, and hidden from the Bay area sprawl by low coastal mountains, is SAN MATEO COUNTY, where the cliffs, the greenery and the excellent beaches are light years away from the hustle and bustle of life in the nearby cities. The peace and quiet and attractive scenery here make it a good place to relax and get away from it all. The county can be reached either by car or by using the San Mateo County Transit.

Seattle

SEATTLE–TACOMA INTERNATIONAL AIRPORT

Seattle–Tacoma International Airport is 13 miles south of the centre of Seattle. It deals with around 20 airlines, both domestic and international. There are 3 terminals.

The Main Terminal handles Braniff, Western, Pacific Western, Continental, Hughes Airwest, Alaska, Eastern, SAS, United, Cascade, Commuters, Northwest and Pan Am. The North Satellite Terminal handles United and SAS. The South Satellite Terminal handles Northwest, Pan Am and Pacific Western.

AIRPORT FACILITIES

Information Desk	Located in the Main Terminal upper level.
Bank/Foreign Exchange	Upper level of the Main Terminal.
Hotel Reservations Service	Main Terminal, upper level.
Insurance Facilities	Located on the upper level of the Main Terminal.
Bar	There are several bars in every terminal.
Restaurant/Buffet	There is a restaurant on the upper level of the Main Terminal, and various eateries in the other terminals.
Baggage Deposit	Upper level of the Main Terminal.
Nursery	Upper level of the Main Terminal.
Shops	In every terminal, selling confectionery, gifts, books, toys, etc.
Duty Free	Located in the Main Terminal. They sell cigarettes, cigars, tobacco, wines, spirits, liqueurs, watches, jewellery, leather goods, cameras, luggage, radios, and various designer accessories. Major convertible currencies are accepted, as are Master Charge, American Express and Visa credit cards.

Toilets	All over every terminal.
Meeting Point Location	The meeting point is in the South Satellite in the Customs area on the third floor.
Car Rental	Avis, Hertz, Airways, Budget, National and Dollar all have desks on the lower level of the Main Terminal.
Public Telephones	All over every terminal.

AIRPORT INFORMATION

Check-in Times	Average for all airlines: International – 90 minutes; Domestic – 45 minutes.
Airport Tax	Nil.
Transferring Flights	There is an inter-terminal underground automated transit system, which runs every 2 minutes.

AIRPORT HOTELS

● **First Class:**
Hilton Inn – 17620 Pacific Highway South, Seattle (tel. 244-4800).
Hyatt House – 17001 Pacific Highway South, Seattle (tel. 244-6000).
Marriott Hotel Seattle – 3201 South 176th Avenue, Seattle (tel. 241-2000).

● **Super Club Class:**
Red Lion Inn – 18740 Pacific Highway South, Seattle (tel. 246-8600).

CITY LINKS

• **Bus:** Metro bus No. 174 runs from the airport to downtown every half hour daily 0600–0100 (fare 90c during peak hours, 75c off-peak). On returning to the airport, the bus can be boarded at the Metro bus station, 3rd and Union Streets.

Gray Line coaches (and limousines) also operate between the airport and downtown. The coach runs every 20 minutes 0700–2100, and every 30 minutes 2100–0100. The fare is $3.60. Pick-up points for the journey to the airport are Gray Line Tours terminus, 5th and University Streets, and the Olympic and Washington Plaza Hotels.

• **Taxis:** Taxis are easily found at the airport, and a usual downtown fare is around $18.

• **Car Hire:** For details, see *Airport Facilities*.

Various hotels around the city have courtesy coaches operating to and from the airport.

SEATTLE

With the Olympic Mountains to the west, the Cascade Range to the east, and Elliott Bay stretching the length of its waterfront, Seattle is a city unique both in character and beauty. Named after Chief Seathl, leader of an old Indian nation, Seattle's first settlers arrived in the area in 1851, and the city's development since then has been a rapid one.

The city grew up around its harbour, and to sample Old Seattle a wander around the waterfront area takes in a wide range of old-world curio shops, sidewalk seafood bars and various other antiquated sights that create an atmosphere of years ago.

Today the city is known as the rain capital of the US . . . true to an extent (although some American cities have more rain), but it's fair to say that Seattle's physical and cultural attractions far outweigh its climatic drawbacks; there are innumerable places to see and visit around town, and for theatre, music, art galleries, after-dark entertainment and the like, Seattle is a very lively city.

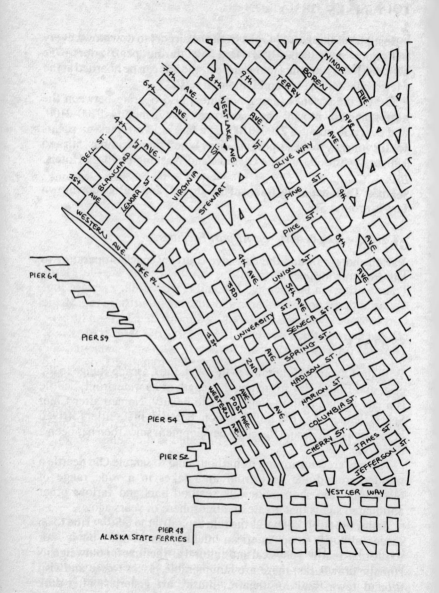

TOURIST INFORMATION

For details of things to do, places to visit, events, accommodation-listings etc., contact: *Seattle-King County Visitors Bureau*, 666 Stewart Street, Seattle (tel. 447-4240).

ADDRESSES

Main Post Office – Corner of Union Street and 3rd Avenue, Seattle (tel. 442-1978).
British Consulate – 820 1st Interstate Center, 999 3rd Avenue, Seattle, Washington 98104 (tel. 622-9255).

GETTING ABOUT

The public transport in Seattle is excellent. The Seattle Metro Transit offers an inexpensive bus and electric trolley service that covers both the downtown area and outlying suburbs. In the 'Magic Carpet Zone', which is bordered by Stewart and Jackson Streets, 6th Avenue and the waterfront, travel is free of charge. Otherwise, a fare for travel within the city limits is 60c during peak hours, and 50c off-peak; buses operate from 0600 to 0100 or 0200 daily, and there is a skeleton night service between 0130–0430. A monorail operates between downtown and Seattle Center.

Taxis are easily available around the city – they can be phoned for or hailed in the street. There are around 12 major car rental firms operating in Seattle and they can be found in the Yellow Pages.

SIGHTS

A good place to start sightseeing in Seattle is at the SEATTLE CENTER, on 5th Avenue North, bounded by Mercer Street and Denny Way. The Center is a large park which was home to the World's Fair in 1962, and which today has numerous attractions. THE PACIFIC SCIENCE CENTER is here, at 200 2nd Avenue North, complete with films, space shows, a model of the moon and other aerospace exhibits. THE CENTER HOUSE is worth visiting while in the park, too – it's a market-place with an international flavour, where there's a beer garden and live entertainment as well as interesting shops and museums. At 370 Thomas Street is the FUN FOREST AMUSEMENT PARK: open from June to September, it has amusement rides and various fun and games suitable for all ages. There are several interesting museums in the Seattle Center too; the SEATTLE ART MUSEUM-MODERN ART PAVILION houses a range of works by artists from the Washington area; the WASHINGTON STATE FIRE MUSEUM has on display innumerable pieces of antique fire apparatus, and also has exhibits which involve visitor participation; the NORTHWEST CRAFT CENTER AND GALLERY and the MUSEUM OF FLIGHT are well worth visiting too. Elsewhere in the park, THE SPACE NEEDLE is a structure 185 metres tall which has high-speed elevators to the top where there's an observation deck and revolving restaurant which offer a view of the city.

Away from the Seattle Center, there is much more around the city to see and visit. A pleasant area to stroll through is PIONEER SQUARE, bounded by 1st Avenue, Yesler Way and James Street. Seattle was founded here in 1851, and today the restored buildings of the Square house restaurants, art galleries, theatres and bookshops; there are also some interesting shops and boutiques, as well as the PIONEER SQUARE AREA WAX MUSEUM, at 112 1st Avenue South, which includes exhibitions to do with both Seattle and American history. PIKE PLACE MARKET, at 1431 1st Avenue, is a market-place which is worth strolling through and at least viewing the various stalls and stall-holders selling everything from seafood to antiques and crafts.

At the south end of the market is a set of stairs (or an escalator) which lead to the WATERFRONT area, where there are many sea-related attractions to enjoy. On Pier 59 is the SEATTLE AQUARIUM, which among other things has exhibits which reflect the history of sealife in the nearby Puget Sound. Upstairs from the aquarium is the MUSEUM OF SEA AND SHIPS, which houses extensive collections of nautical treasures. THE GOLD RUSH STRIP, running from Pier 50 to 59, is a centre for fish markets and various shops selling imported goods; 'Ye Olde Curiosity Shop' is also found here, selling a wide range of arts, crafts and curios. Other waterfront attractions include FISHERMAN'S TERMINAL (dock of the world's largest salmon fleet), CHITTENDEN LOCKS (locks that are raised and lowered for the transport of ships), and Pier 70, a docking berth packed with shops selling various imports.

THE UNIVERSITY OF WASHINGTON, the main entrance of which is on 17th Avenue, has a vast campus which contains many centres of cultural importance: there's the THOMAS BURKE MUSEUM, the HENRY ART GALLERY and the FISHERIES CENTER among others – all open to the public and well worth visiting.

THE KLONDIKE GOLD RUSH NATIONAL HISTORIC PARK, at 117 Main Street, offers an interesting reflection on the exploits of the miners of the 1800s; the SEATTLE ART MUSEUM, at 14th Street, is noted for its fine collection of Asian art among other exhibits.

It's worth spending some time exploring Seattle's INTERNATIONAL DISTRICT (Chinatown). Home to immigrants from all parts of Asia, the area's attractions include the NIPPON KAN THEATER, where there's often a show of Asian culture, and the WING LUKE MUSEUM, at 414 8th Street, where the exhibitions are always of a distinctive Asian nature and very interesting. The shops in this area are full of rare imports and various Oriental gifts and the restaurants offer fine authentic Japanese and Chinese cuisine.

Seattle's other points of interest are the WOODLAND PARK ZOOLOGICAL GARDENS at Phinney Avenue North, the JAPANESE GARDEN at East Helen Street (bus No. 43 from downtown), and not to be missed is an UNDERGROUND TOUR, which can be arranged at 610 1st Avenue – in 1889, there was a big fire in Seattle, and an area of the street was reconstructed and raised 3 metres above its original level; these tours take you above and below the current level.

ACCOMMODATION

● **First Class:** (double over $90)
Seattle Hilton – 6th Avenue and University Street, Seattle (tel. 624-0500). Attractive location overlooking Freeway Park, and excellent facilities include a first-class dining room and coffee shop, with a cocktail lounge offering live entertainment.

The Westin Hotel – 5th and Westlake Avenues, Seattle (tel. 728-1000). A massive hotel downtown which offers the best in hospitality and the most luxurious surroundings and facilities. Excellent restaurants and cocktail lounges.

Seattle Sheraton Hotel and Towers – 1400 6th Avenue, Seattle (tel. 621-9000). The towers are on 3 floors on top of the Sheraton Hotel; as well as offering the facilities of the Sheraton Hotel itself, various exclusive extras are laid on, among the most notable of which is the Towers lounge/club on the 32nd floor. The Sheraton Hotel itself counts a health club, sauna/jacuzzi, indoor pool and 3 lounges among its first-class facilities.

● **Super Club Class:** (double $60–$80)
Continental Plaza Motel – 2500 Aurora Avenue North, Seattle. (tel. 284-1900) Fine establishment noted for its excellent hospitality. Facilities include an indoor pool.

Ramada Inn – 2140 North Northgate Way, Seattle (tel. 365-0700). Large hotel with good facilities which include a pool.

Sheraton-Renton Inn – 800 Rainier Avenue South, Seattle (tel. 621-9000). Large hotel which boasts excellent hospitality as well as good facilities, including a swimming pool.

Sorrento Hotel – 900 Madison Street, Seattle (tel. 622-6400). Small hotel in downtown Seattle. Facilities are excellent, and the views of the city are splendid.

● **Economy:** (double $20–$40)
YMCA (AYH) – 909 4th Avenue, Seattle (tel. 382-5000). Clean with good facilities which include a TV lounge on each floor, and a swimming pool.

YWCA – 1118 5th Avenue, Seattle (tel. 447-4888). Clean with good facilities and security. Women only.

The College Inn – 4000 University Way NE, Seattle (tel. 633-4441). Plush accommodation for the economy traveller.

Pacific Hotel – 317 Marion Street, Seattle (tel. 622-3985). Clean hotel in a safe location. Good facilities, and friendly staff.

Motel 6 – 18900 47th Avenue South, Seattle (tel. 246-5520). A bus ride from downtown (No. 170), this hotel is clean with adequate facilities.

St Regis Hotel – 116 Stewart Street, Seattle (tel. 622-6366). Clean hotel in a convenient location for sights.

DINING OUT

Being a city by the ocean, the cuisine in Seattle centres mainly around seafood. Excellent seafood it is too, and local delicacies such as shrimp, salmon and clams are well worth trying. Pike Place Market and the waterfront area are where the most seafood restaurants are found, and they also provide an attractive setting for eating out. Seafood also features elsewhere in the city, and there is a cosmopolitan selection of restaurants on offer, among them French, German, Italian, Chinese, Japanese and Polynesian. Establishments vary in elegance and price, from the very top to the very bottom of the market.

Major credit cards are accepted in most restaurants, as are traveller's cheques. Although there's always space somewhere, it's a good idea to reserve in advance if you're heading for one of the more popular establishments around the waterfront area.

● **First Class:** (over $50 for two)
Canlis – 2576 Aurora Avenue, Seattle (tel. 283-3313). Located in an attractive setting overlooking Lake Union, the decor here is plush, and the atmosphere pleasant. Noted for its fine seafood and steaks.

The Other Place – 319 Union Street, Seattle (tel. 623-3340). Pleasant downtown restaurant, where the menu includes some of the best fish and game in the city.

Rossellini's Four-10 – 2515 4th Avenue, Seattle (tel. 728-0410). The menu here is superb and offers several recipes typical of years ago. The decor is very elegant, and the service is excellent.

● **Super Club Class:** ($20–$40 for two)
Ivar Captain's Table – 333 Elliott Avenue West, Seattle (tel. 284-7040). Excellent seafood in this fine restaurant situated by the harbour.

Ray's Boathouse – 6049 Seaview Avenue NW, Seattle (tel. 623-7999). Fresh seafood served in this pleasant restaurant. The staff are friendly and there is a fine view of Shilshole Bay.

Benihana of Tokyo – 5th Avenue and University Streets, Seattle (tel. 628-4686). Superb authentic Japanese cuisine in a quiet, intimate atmosphere.

● **Economy:** ($10–$20 for two)
Ying Hei Restaurant – 644 South King Street, Seattle (tel. 622-4229). Superb Oriental food in appropriately decorated establishment. The barbecue and soy sauce chicken come highly recommended.

El Puerco Lloron – 1507 Western Avenue, Seattle (tel. 624-0541). The best Mexican food in town.

Ivar's Acre of Clams – Pier 52, Marion Street, Seattle. Good seafood. Baked salmon a house speciality.

Kokeb Restaurant – 926 12th Avenue, Seattle (tel. 322-0485). Good Ethiopian restaurant, where the hot and spicy meat stews are well worth trying.

NIGHTLIFE

Nightclubs, jazz, other live music, dancing, theatre, the arts – all are represented in Seattle after dark. While groups such as the Seattle Symphony Orchestra and the Seattle Repertory Theater give performances at the Opera House and the Seattle Center Playhouse respectively, more contemporary entertainment can be found in most of the city's major hotels and supper clubs, where big-name stars frequently appear. For details of what's going on around Seattle, consult *The Weekly* newspaper.

● **Nightclubs:**
Jazz Alley – 4135 University Way NE, Seattle (tel. 632-7414). One of the most popular centres of jazz with both locals and visitors, with live jazz (mostly traditional) being featured every night. Dinner is also available here.

Virginia Inn – 1937 1st Avenue, Seattle (tel. 624-3173). Interesting bar frequented by all kinds of Seattlites. A much-revered place with those who know it, and it's always reasonably full.

Murphy's Pub – 2110 North 45th Street, Wallingford, Seattle (tel. 634-2110). Quaint little Irish pub just west of the university district. There's an extensive beer list, and also live folk music every night. Very warm atmosphere.

Tugs Belltown – 2207 1st Avenue, Seattle (tel. 441-4297). Pleasant tavern, with a wide selection of drinks to choose from, and also a varied clientele.

EXCURSIONS

CHÂTEAU SAINTE MICHELLE is 15 miles north-east of Seattle on Highway 202. A winery on a large estate, the wines here are produced from European grapes which are grown in a nearby valley. The setting is beautiful, and during the daily tours guests are encouraged to sample the estate produce. Tours are laid on, and tasting is available.

THE PUGET SOUND is an area of water up the coast from Seattle which is home to a wide and varied selection of marine and bird life. Day trips of the Sound are available (details from the Tourist Office), and with the help of spotters, it's possible to view puffins, eagles, porpoises, seals, sea lions, and the chances are good (75 per cent) that killer whales (the orcas) will also be spotted.

The MUSEUM OF FLIGHT, just south of Seattle at 9404 East Marginal Way South, houses a fascinating collection of exhibits reflecting the history of aviation. The museum is in the famous, and by now restored, Red Barn, which is where the Boeing Aircraft Industry was founded in 1916 by William E. Boeing. 25 miles north of Seattle, in Everett, it's possible to go on a guided tour of a present-day Boeing plant (for information phone the Everett Tour Center on 342-4801).

Cruises to TILLICUM VILLAGE in BLAKE ISLAND STATE PARK provide guests with an enjoyable insight into Indian culture. They leave from Pier 56, and included in the 4–5 hour trip are displays of North Coast Indian interpretive dancing and an authentic Indian Baked Salmon feast.

Tampa

TAMPA INTERNATIONAL AIRPORT

Tampa International Airport is 5 miles west of the city, and deals
with a number of airlines, both international and domestic. There is
1 terminal, Central Terminal, which handles all passengers. The
terminal has 3 levels.

AIRPORT FACILITIES

Information Desk	Level 3.
Bank/Foreign Exchange	Level 2.
Hotel Reservations Service	Level 3.
Insurance Facilities	Located on level 2.
Bar	There is a bar on the third level.
Restaurant/Buffet	There is a restaurant and snack bar on level 3.
Baggage Deposit	Baggage lockers are on level 1.
Nursery	Level 3.
Shops	On the third level there are shops selling flowers, confectionery, books, gifts, toys, etc.
Duty Free	Located in Flight Departures, they sell cigarettes, cigars, tobacco, wines, aperitifs, spirits, liqueurs, lighters, watches, radios, jewellery, glass, and china. All major credit cards are accepted, although only Canadian and local currency is taken.
Meeting Point	Level 3 (at the escalators).
Toilets	Every level.

Car Rental Desks	On the first floor. Avis, Hertz, Dollar and National all have counters.
Public Telephones	All over the terminal.
Barber Shop	Level 3.

AIRPORT INFORMATION

Check-in Times	Average for all airlines: International – 60 minutes; Domestic – 30 minutes.
Airport Tax	Nil.

AIRPORT HOTELS

• **First Class:**
Tampa Marriott – Located in the airport.

• **Super Club Class:**
Holiday Inn – 4500 Cypress Street, Tampa.

CITY LINKS

• **Bus:** To get to downtown Tampa, you can take HARTline bus No. 30; this runs every 35 minutes from 0510 to 2030, Monday–Friday, and every 70 minutes from 0600 to 2035 on Saturdays. There's also a 24-hour bus/van service called Airport Connection. Fare to Tampa is $7.25.

• **Taxi:** Taxis are available at the airport, and a usual fare to downtown Tampa is around $8.

• **Car Hire:** See *Airport Facilities* for details.

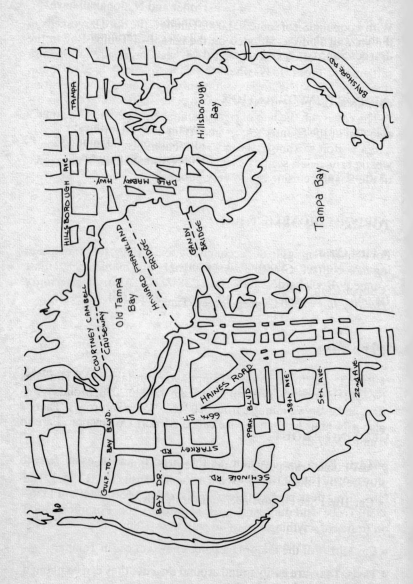

TAMPA

With a population of some 300,000, Tampa is the third largest city in the state of Florida. Situated on the corner of Tampa Bay in the middle of Florida's west coast, it was originally a Spanish settlement. From 1539 when the first Spaniard landed there, through its growth in the late 19th century as a cigar-manufacturing city, up to the present day, Tampa has retained a Latin flavour.

The city is still the hub of cigar-manufacturing in the US, and it's also one of the country's most important industrial ports.

For visitors to Tampa, the city's attractions lie mainly in its sunny weather, its quiet, scenic beaches and picturesque harbours. Some of the Spanish cuisine is also very popular.

TOURIST INFORMATION

For details of things to do, accommodation-listings, tours, sightseeing etc., contact: *Greater Tampa Chamber of Commerce*, 801 East Kennedy Boulevard, Tampa (tel. 228-7777). Also: *St Petersburg Chamber of Commerce*, 225 4th Street, Tampa (tel. 821-4715).

ADDRESS

British Consulate-General (nearest) – Suite 912, 225 Peachtree Street NE, Atlanta, Georgia 30303 (tel. 404-524-5856).

GETTING ABOUT

● **Bus:** Public transport in Tampa centres around the bus service provided by Hillsborough Area Regional Transit (HARTline). The fare during peak periods (Monday–Saturday, 0630–0900 and 1530–1830) is 60c, and during off-peak periods it's 40c. For information on routes or anything else to do with the system, phone 254-4278.

● **Car Hire:** All the major companies have offices in Tampa.

● **Taxis:** Taxis are easily found around the city; they can be phoned for or hailed in the street.

SIGHTS

The true flavour of Tampa is probably best sampled at the WATERFRONT. The docks at 139 Twiggs Street are still well used by ships from around the world delivering cargo ranging from bananas to tobacco . . . the whole unloading process can make for interesting viewing. Elsewhere on the waterfront, the *Jose Sasparilla* is a replica pirate ship which has all the trappings; there's also the USS *Requiem*, a submarine which saw action during World War II – both are open to the public.

An area of Tampa which was home to the city's cigar factories late last century is YBOR CITY. Today called the Latin Quarter, Ybor City's cigar legacy is represented in YBOR SQUARE, a 19th-century factory where cigars are still rolled by hand; otherwise, the square presently houses expensive shops and restaurants. Other attractions in Ybor City include the YBOR CITY STATE MUSEUM, at 1818 9th Avenue, where visitors can learn about the development of Ybor City as prompted by the cigar industry. There are several good restaurants to be found there, too, and some of the Spanish cuisine available in the area is of the highest quality.

The second most popular attraction with visitors to Florida is Tampa's vast amusement park, BUSCH GARDENS (THE DARK CONTINENT), at 3000 Busch Boulevard. The park has 7 African theme sections, and some 3000 animals roaming free (you can watch them from the Safari Monorail). There are also stage shows, restaurants, bizarre shops, dolphin shows and amusement rides such as the rollercoaster which goes through a 360° loop.

The TAMPA BAY HOTEL, at 401 West Kennedy Boulevard, is interesting for its historical significance. It was once Florida's most fashionable hotel, and is today remembered as the place where Teddy Roosevelt stayed while he trained his 'Rough Riders' for the Spanish–American war in the backyard.

ADVENTURE ISLAND, at 4545 Bougainvillea Avenue (near Busch Gardens), is an attractive spot to spend some time exploring. It's a water theme park, and its attractions include water flumes, diving platforms, a swimming pool and a wave pool for body and surf rafting; there's also a children's section with water slides, water cannon and spray fountains. Next to Ybor Square, at 1205 8th Avenue, is THE WINES OF SAINT AUGUSTINE, Florida's very first large-scale winery. Guests can sample the winery's products, some of which come from California, in a quaint garden annexe.

ST PETERSBURG, adjacent to and almost as large as Tampa, is famous for its attractive beaches. The two best ones are the PASS-A-GRILLE BEACH, and the MUNICIPAL BEACH at Treasure Island. The SUNKEN GARDENS, at 1825 4th Street North, are full of natural beauty, and boast some 7000 varieties of exotic plants and flowers. At 1000 3rd Street South is the SALVADOR DALI MUSEUM, which houses the largest collection in the world of Dali's works and various other mementoes of his distinguished career. Also well worth a visit in St Petersburg is the *Bounty*, the wooden ship built for the film *Mutiny on the Bounty*. Docked downtown at 345 2nd Avenue, next to the municipal pier, the ship is a maritime museum and contains many interesting displays and exhibits depicting life at sea.

ACCOMMODATION

● **First Class:** (double over $150)
Tampa Hyatt Regency – 2 Tampa City Center, Tampa (tel. 225-1234). Conveniently located in the centre of Tampa, this hotel offers very modern and luxurious surroundings, as well as warm hospitality.

Bay Harbor Inn – 7700 Courtney Campbell Causeway, Tampa (tel. 885-2451). In an attractive setting by the beach, this hotel has excellent facilities which include a heated pool and rental sailboats, as well as a first-class restaurant and comfortable cocktail lounge.

Hilton Inn – 200 Ashley Drive, Tampa (tel. 223-2222). Comfortable rooms have balconies overlooking the river. Also excellent restaurant and lounge, together with a convenient downtown location.

● **Super Club Class:** (double $120–$150)
Admiral Benbow Inn – 1200 North Westshore Boulevard, Tampa. Excellent facilities include heated pools and a sauna. There's also a fine restaurant, and a lounge which has live entertainment.

Inn on the Point – Campbell Causeway, Tampa. Noted for its large swimming pool as much as for its superb restaurant. Live entertainment on selected evenings.

Holiday Inn – 111 West Fortune Street, Tampa. Located downtown, good facilities include a pool, restaurant and bar. Service is efficient and quick.

Quality Inn – 2905 North 50th Street, Tampa. On the east of the city, this hotel has a swimming pool and an excellent restaurant, as well as friendly staff.

• **Economy:** (double $20–$60)
Econo Lodge Motel – 11414 Central Avenue, Tampa. Clean, with good facilities. Air-conditioning in every room.

AAA Motel – 6345 4th Street North, St Petersburg (tel. 525-5900). Comfortable, with basic facilities. Located in St Petersburg, the area adjoining Tampa.

YMCA – 116 5th Street South, St Petersburg (tel. 822-3911). Small, comfortable rooms. Clean, with friendly staff.

Grant Motel – 9046 4th Street North, St Petersburg (tel. 576-1369). Located in St Petersburg, adjacent to Tampa, this motel is comfortable and clean.

Windjammer – 10450 Gulf Boulevard, St Petersburg Beach. Clean and comfortable in an attractive beach setting.

Days Inn – 701 East Fletcher, Busch Boulevard, Tampa. Facilities include swimming pool and restaurant.

DINING OUT

Restaurants in Tampa offer a wide range of international dishes. Many nationalities are represented, most notably Spanish, Cuban and French. Eating out in Florida generally tends to be expensive, and Tampa is no exception; the food is usually worth whatever you pay, however, and seafood is especially highly recommended. Stone crabs are the pride and joy of local seafood restaurateurs: nowhere else in the US are they caught fresh from the sea, or, consequently, served as tender or as tasty as they are all over Florida. Look out also for the various fish, shellfish and shrimp dishes on offer – dozens of varieties of each are available.

- **First Class:** (over $50 for two)
Selena's – 1623 Snow Avenue, Tampa. Fashionable establishment where French cuisine is at its best. Excellent service, too.

Bern's Steakhouse – 1208 South Howard Avenue, Tampa (tel. 251-2421). Splendid steaks served as well as a good selection of wines and cheeses. There's also a cocktail lounge here.

The Scandia – 19829 Gulf Boulevard, Indian Stores (tel. 595-5525 or 595-4928). Tasteful decor dates back to Denmark of centuries ago, and the Scandinavian menu offers some excellent dishes.

- **Super Club Class:** ($20–$30 for two)
Rollande et Pierre – 2221 4th Street North, St Petersburg (tel. 822-4602). Excellent French cuisine served in château-like surroundings. Friendly service.

Mama Mia – 4732 North Dale Mabry, Tampa. Good Italian food. The atmosphere here is very relaxed, and the staff good-humoured.

Columbia Restaurant – 2117 East 7th Avenue, Ybor City, Tampa (tel. 248-4961). Delicious Spanish food served amid appropriate decor. There's also a nightly flamenco revue.

- **Economy:** ($10–$20 for two)
JD's – 2029 East 7th Avenue, Ybor City, Tampa (tel. 247-9683). Good value soups, sandwiches and traditional Spanish dishes.

Crawdaddy's – 2500 Rocky Point Drive, Tampa (tel. 885-7407). Noted for its seafood and Creole specialities. Bizarre decor, too.

Duff's Smorgasbord – 8805 North Florida Avenue, Tampa (tel. 932-2313). Relaxed, all-you-can-eat restaurant. Friendly staff.

The Verandah – 5250 West Kennedy Boulevard, Tampa. Elegant dining at the expensive end of the economy scale. The food is well worth the extra, however.

NIGHTLIFE

Nightclubs in Tampa are rather few and far between, and live entertainment is largely confined to the city's more plush hotels, which lay on everything from local jazz bands to big-name entertainers. Ybor City is worth exploring at night: there are several quaint piano bars and sidewalk cafés there, as well as other night-time attractions. The St Petersburg area also comes alive after dark. For details of what's going on around the city, consult the local newspapers and magazines.

● **Nightclubs:**

Seaman's Cove – Maximo Moorings, St Petersburg. Not just an excellent seafood restaurant, there is a bar here which is popular both for its sea-faring decor and good views of the yacht harbour.

CK's – Tampa Marriott Hotel, Tampa Airport. If you can bear the 5-mile trip, this revolving penthouse restaurant and lounge atop the airport's luxury hotel offers a relaxing environment in which to enjoy impressive views of the city and surrounds.

Rough Riders – Ybor City, Tampa. Named after Teddy Roosevelt's Rough Riders in the Spanish–American war, this restaurant with cocktail lounge has appropriate photos and antiques everywhere. The atmosphere is pleasantly relaxing.

EXCURSIONS

TARPON SPRINGS, some 20 miles north-west of Tampa, is a village by the seaside which has a quaint old-world charm that reflects its beginnings as a Greek community. Encompassing the scenic Spong Docks, the village has a range of small ethnic restaurants, attractive bayous, a freshwater lake, and golden beaches. It's a very beautiful and relaxing environment, and presents an ideal opportunity to get away from the bustle of the city.

The TAMPA FRONTON, 15 miles north-west of Tampa, is an interesting and, for many, a novel place to visit. There you can watch and place bets on players of jai-alai. It's a game which basically involves throwing a pelota (a ball) at a wall, and the players on show are able to do it at speeds of up to 150 miles per hour. It's fascinating to watch, and makes for a good day out.

Washington DC

Washington DC has 3 airports: Dulles International, National and Baltimore–Washington International.

DULLES INTERNATIONAL AIRPORT

Washington–Dulles International Airport is located in Virginia, 26 miles west of downtown Washington DC. The airport handles more than 15 airlines, both domestic and international. The main terminal handles all airlines.

AIRPORT FACILITIES

Information	Phone 471-7838. Otherwise, the international visitors' Information Service Counter is on the ground floor.
Bank/Foreign Exchange	There is a bank on the ground floor, open 0900–1300, and 1500–1700 Monday–Friday. Currency exchange is available at the bank, and at counters on the main and ground floors. An American Express Traveller's Cheque Machine is on the ground floor.
Hotel Reservations Service	Phones are on the ground floor.
Insurance Facilities	At the east and west ends of the main floor.
Bar	Bars and cocktail lounges are on the main floor.
Restaurant/Buffet	There is a restaurant on the main floor, and snack bars on both floors.

Post Office	Located on the ground floor. Open 24 hours daily.
Baggage Deposit	Storage lockers are available on the ground floor.
Shops	Shops selling gifts, newspapers, magazines, books, etc. are on the main floor.
Duty Free	Located on the main floor, they are open 0700–2300 daily, and sell cigarettes, cigars, aperitifs, spirits, liqueurs, cameras, lighters, watches, radios, jewellery, perfume, glass and china. Local currencies accepted, as well as Canadian, Japanese and Western European. Most major credit cards are accepted.
Medical Services	Located on the ground floor, phone 661-9234.
Toilets	On both floors.
Meeting Point Location	On the ground floor at the Information Service Counter.
Car Rental Desks	Avis, Hertz, National, Dollar and Budget all have desks on the ground floor.
Lost Property	Phone 471-4114.
Public Telephones	On both floors.
Business Centre	On the ground floor. Services include telex/telegram, photocopy, secretarial services, etc.
Porters	Available throughout the airport. A special 'Skycap' call button is located inside the building at parking ramp entrances.
Barber Shop	Main floor.

AIRPORT INFORMATION

Check-in Times   Average for all airlines:
                                International – 60 minutes;
                                Domestic – 45 minutes.
Airport Tax   Nil.

INTER-AIRPORT TRANSFER

● **To Baltimore–Washington Airport:**
There is a coach service which operates from 0600 until 2200. Fare is
$14.75. Journey takes 120 minutes. The usual taxi fare is around
$48, and the journey takes 90 minutes.

● **To Washington–National Airport:**
There is a coach service every 60 minutes, from 0615 until 2315, the
journey takes 60 minutes. The usual taxi fare is $28, and the journey
takes around 45 minutes.

AIRPORT HOTEL

● **First Class:**
Sheraton National Hotel – Columbia Pike and Washington Boule-
vard, Washington DC 22204 (tel. (703) 521-1900). 1 mile from
Washington–National Airport.

CITY LINKS

● **Bus:** A coach service operates from the airport to downtown every
60 minutes from 0630 to 2400. The fare is $7.75, and the journey
takes 50 minutes. Pick-ups for the trip to the airport are at the
Washington Hilton, the Capitol Hilton and Sheraton Washington
Hotels.

● **Taxi:** Taxis are easily found at the airport, and a usual fare to
downtown is around $28.

● **Car Hire:** For details, see *Airport Facilities*.

• **Limousine:** British Airways Concorde offer a limousine service to downtown for $30.

WASHINGTON–NATIONAL AIRPORT

Washington–National Airport is located in Virginia 4 miles from downtown Washington, and deals with a total of around 20 domestic and commuter airlines. There are 7 terminals.

The Main Terminal handles Braniff, Eastern Air, Ozark, United, US Air, and Midwest Express Airlines. American Terminal handles New York Air and American Airlines. North Terminal handles Delta Air, Empire Airlines, Pan American World Airways, and People Express. NW/TWA Terminal handles Midway Airlines, Northwest, Republic, Trans World, Midwest Express and Western Airlines. Piedmont Terminal handles Piedmont Aviation.

AIRPORT FACILITIES

Information Desk	Main Terminal, phone (703) 684-3472.
Bank/Foreign Exchange	Bank on upper level of Main Terminal, Room 274. Currency exchange in Main, North and NW/TWA terminals, 0700–2300 daily. American Express Traveller's Cheques machine in Main Terminal, and on the North concourse.
Hotel Reservations Service	All terminals.
Insurance Facilities	Available in Main, North and NW/TWA terminals, 0700–2300 daily.
Bar	Cocktail lounges in the Main and North terminals. Open 0700 to 2200, or from 0900 to 2300 daily.
Restaurant/Buffet	Restaurant in Main Terminal, and Buffeterias in the North,

	Aviation, NW/TWA and Main terminals.
Post Office	Main Terminal. Open 0830–1700 Monday–Friday, and 0830–1200 on Saturdays.
Baggage Deposit	Baggage storage lockers are available behind security checkpoints.
Shops	Shops selling gifts, newspapers, books, etc. are in the Main Terminal (news-stands in all terminals).
Medical Centre	Lower level of Main Terminal, Room 70, tel (703) 892-6240.
Toilets	All over every terminal.
Car Rental Desks	Avis, Hertz, National, Budget and Dollar have counters in the Main and North terminals. Rental phones are in the Main, North and Commuter terminals for Americar, Thrifty and Value (all off-airport).
Lost Property	Main Terminal, lower level, Room 72.
Public Telephones	All over every terminal.
Business Centre	Main, North and Main (South) terminals. Provide currency exchange, secretarial services, telex/telegram, conference rooms, etc.
Barber Shop	Main Terminal.
Porters and Trolleys	All airline terminals.

AIRPORT INFORMATION

Check-in Times	???
Airport Tax	???
Transferring Flights	Shuttle bus service operates between terminals.

INTER-AIRPORT TRANSFER

● **To Baltimore–Washington Airport:**
A coach service from 0600 to 2200. Fare is $8.60. Journey takes 90 minutes. Usual taxi fare is around $35, and the journey takes 60 minutes.

● **To Washington–Dulles International Airport:**
There is a coach service every 60 minutes from 0730 to 2330. Fare is $7.75 and the journey takes 60 minutes. Usual taxi fare is around $28 and the journey takes 45 minutes.

AIRPORT HOTEL

● **First Class:**
Sheraton National Hotel – Columbia Pike and Washington Boulevard, Washington DC 22204 (tel. (703) 521-1900). 1 mile from airport.

CITY LINKS

Washington–National Airport is 3 miles south-west of the city.

● **Rail:** Metrorail service from the airport to downtown every 5 minutes from 0600 to 2400 hours. The fare is 80c, and a courtesy shuttle bus operates between the terminals and the metro station. Return train can be boarded at the Metro Center.

● **Bus:** There is a coach service to the city every 30 minutes from 0700 to 2200. The fare is $3.50. Return pick-ups are at the Washington Hilton, Capitol Hilton and Sheraton Hotels, every 60 minutes from 0600 until 2000.

● **Taxi:** Taxis are easily found at the airport, and the usual fare to downtown Washington is $8.

● **Car Hire:** For details, consult *Airport Facilities*.

● **Limousine:** For information on limousine services to downtown phone (301) 859-3000.

BALTIMORE–WASHINGTON INTERNATIONAL AIRPORT

Baltimore–Washington International is located 10 miles south-west of Baltimore, 30 miles north-east of Washington DC. There is 1 terminal.

AIRPORT FACILITIES

Information	Telephone 787-7111.
Bank/Foreign Exchange	Upper level.
Hotel Reservations Service	Upper level.
Insurance Facilities	Upper level.
Bar	Upper level.
Restaurant/Buffet	Upper level.
Post Office	Upper level.
Baggage Deposit	Upper level.
Shops	Upper level.
Duty Free	Selling cigarettes, cigars, tobacco, wines, aperitifs, spirits, liqueurs, lighters, watches, jewellery, perfume, clocks.
Meeting Point Location	Upper level.
Car Rental Desks	Lower level: Avis, Hertz, National, Dollar.
Airline Club Lounges	Ionosphere, Red Carpet.

AIRPORT INFORMATION

Check-in Times	Average for all airlines: International – 60 minutes; Domestic – 45 minutes.
Airport Tax	Nil.

INTER-AIRPORT TRANSFER

● **To Washington–National Airport:**
Coach journey takes 90 minutes, costs $8.60, for connecting flights from 0700 to 1625. Taxi takes 60 minutes and usual fare is $35.

• **To Washington–Dulles Airport:**
Coach takes 120 minutes, costs $14.75, for connecting flights from 0600 to midnight. Taxi takes 90 minutes and usual fare $48.60.

CITY LINKS (TO/FROM BALTIMORE)

• **Coach:** To city takes 25 minutes and costs $4.50. Coach leaves every 30 minutes from 0600 to midnight.

Returns from Baltimore Hilton Hotel (Hannover and Fayette Streets) from 0635 to 2235, and picks up at Lord Baltimore, Holiday Inn and Hyatt Regency Hotels.

• **Train:** To city takes 17 minutes and costs $3.90 by Amtrak line; $2.25 by Conrail line. 8 times daily from 0630–1940. There is a free shuttle bus service between the airport terminal and BWI Airport station, the journey taking 10 minutes.

Returns from Penn Station, 1500 North Charles Street.

• **Bus:** To city takes 60 minutes and costs $1 on the No. 16, which runs 3 times daily (twice a day at weekends) from 0600–1915.

Returns from Howard and Baltimore Streets from 0645–1823.

• **Taxi:** 20 minutes to city, usual fare about $10.

CITY LINKS (TO/FROM WASHINGTON DC)

• **Coach:** To city takes 60 minutes and costs $8. Coaches leave every 45–60 minutes 0520–0230.

Return from Capitol Hilton Hotel (16th and K Streets NW) from 0615–0320 and pick up at Sheraton and Carlton Hotels.

• **Train:** To Washington DC takes 35 minutes and costs $7 by Amtrak line, $5 by Conrail. Service 8 times daily (6 on Sundays) from 0630–1940. There is a free shuttle bus service between the airport terminal and BWI Airport station, taking 10 minutes.

Return from Union Station, 50 Massachusetts Avenue NE.

• **Taxi:** To city takes 60 minutes and costs about $30.

WASHINGTON DC

It was in 1791 that President George Washington commissioned French engineer Pierre L'Enfant to design a future capital of the US to rival European capitals, and today Washington DC is testimony to a fine effort on L'Enfant's part. Situated at the head of the Potomac River on America's east coast, Washington DC – District of Columbia – is a capital as famous for its beauty as much as for its history.

The city's centre is where its charm lies – The Mall with its museums, Capitol Hill with its political significance, and an endless variety of monuments, culture and entertainment nearby. Many of Washington's neighbourhoods, however – home to a large number of the city's sizeable black population – tend to be run down, the north-east, south-east and south-west sections being particularly dilapidated and, indeed, dangerous.

Overall, though, Washington DC is a joy to explore and shouldn't be missed on a trip to the United States.

TOURIST INFORMATION

For maps, details of events, sightseeing tours, things to do, accommodation-listings etc., contact: *Visitor Information Center*, Great Hall of Department of Commerce, Pennsylvania Avenue NW, Washington DC (tel. 789-7038), or: *Convention and Visitors Association* NW, 1575 I Street, Washington DC (tel. 789-7000).

ADDRESSES

Post Office – Corner of North Capitol Street and Massachusetts Avenue NE (across from Union Station). Open 24 hours, 7 days.
British Embassy – 3100 Massachusetts Avenue NW, Washington DC (tel. 462-1340).

GETTING ABOUT

Public transport in Washington DC is quick and efficient.

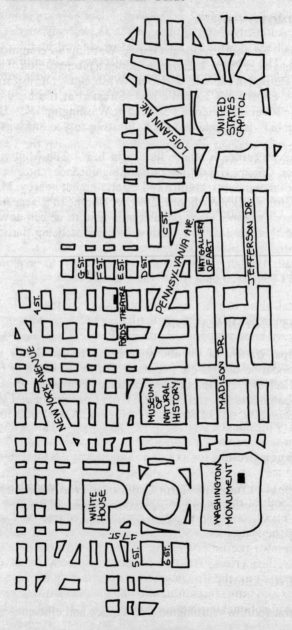

• **Metro Bus and Subway:** The Washington Metropolitan Area Transit Authority (Metro) offers a bus and subway service which covers all the downtown and city areas as well as the outlying suburbs. The subway system, Metrorail, runs daily until midnight (except Sunday when it runs from 1000–1800), and the normal fare is 80c. The bus system, Metrobus, is far-reaching, and the normal fare is 75c. Fares on the bus and subway vary during the rush hour.

• **Taxis:** They are easily found around the city, and can be hailed in the street or phoned for (look under 'Taxicabs' in the Classified Telephone Directory). Taxi fares are charged according to zones (the more zones you cross, the higher the fare).

• **Car Hire:** All the major car hire firms can be found in Washington. Look under 'Car Rentals' in the Classified Telephone Directory.

SIGHTS

A logical place to start sightseeing in the city that's the hub of American politics is on CAPITOL HILL, an 85-acre park on Pennsylvania Avenue which is the site of the CAPITOL BUILDING – one wing is occupied by the Senate, the other by the House of Representatives, and the central white dome is home to the ROTUNDA and STATUARY HALL. Tours are available of the building, during which visitors can watch the House and the Senate in action. THE WHITE HOUSE, the 3-storey mansion that has been home to every US president except George Washington, is at 1600 Pennsylvania Avenue, and it's possible to take a tour of the building which is as interesting for its art and antiques as it is for its historical significance.

THE MALL in Washington is well worth strolling along both for its beauty and for the museums and art galleries that are part of the SMITHSONIAN INSTITUTION, a vast complex of culture on The Mall. Among the institution's attractions are the NATIONAL MUSEUM OF HISTORY AND TECHNOLOGY, the NATIONAL MUSEUM OF NATURAL HISTORY, the NATIONAL SCULPTURE GARDEN, the NATIONAL AIR AND SPACE BUILDING, the HIRSHORN MUSEUM AND SCULPTURE GARDEN, the ARTS AND INDUSTRIES BUILDING and the FREER GALLERY OF ART – all are of national importance, and each is extremely interesting.

Other museums around the city well worth spending some time in are the FORD'S THEATER AND LINCOLN MUSEUM, at 511 10th Street – where Abraham Lincoln was fatally shot, and among other things the pistol and diary of the assassin are on display. The HOUSE WHERE LINCOLN DIED, across from the Ford's Theater, has been restored to look the way it did in the 1860s.

The FEDERAL BUREAU OF INVESTIGATION (FBI) HEADQUARTERS is on Pennsylvania Avenue, and tours of the building are available. Exhibits include firearms from the past and present, FBI techniques for crime-solving and the FBI forensic laboratory; there's also a section on notorious criminals.

The BUREAU OF ENGRAVING AND PRINTING, on 14th and C Streets, is worth exploring; this is where the government prints new money and destroys the old. Tours are available of the various presses which also print bonds and postage stamps.

THE NATIONAL GEOGRAPHIC EXPLORERS' HALL, at 17th and M Streets NW, houses exhibits which reflect famous expeditions sponsored by the *National Geographic* magazine. Prehistoric life features heavily, and there are cartography demonstrations as well as exhibits on space exploration.

Two churches in Washington which are among America's most significant are the WASHINGTON NATIONAL CATHEDRAL and the NATIONAL SHRINE OF THE IMMACULATE CONCEPTION. The Cathedral is on Wisconsin and Massachusetts Avenues NW, has been under construction since the early 1900s, and is now almost complete; one of the world's largest churches, its gothic-style architecture, beautiful stained glass windows and grounds which include a gold-plated statue of George Washington on horseback make it well worth exploring. The National Shrine, on 4th Street and Michigan Avenue NE, is notable for its Byzantine/romanesque architecture, including an impressive gold and blue dome.

There are several monuments in Washington DC. Among these are the LINCOLN MEMORIAL at the foot of The Mall – particularly impressive when lit at night. The Gettysburg Address and second Inaugural Address of Abraham Lincoln are on the memorial's walls; it was here that Martin Luther King Jr delivered his 'I have a dream . . . ' speech. The JEFFERSON MEMORIAL was built in honour of President Thomas Jefferson and is impressive in its architecture, and the WASHINGTON MONUMENT on The Mall is a marble structure that rises nearly 170 metres into the sky; it's possible to take an elevator to the top, from where there is a superb view of the city. The VIETNAM WAR MEMORIAL, engraved with the names of more than 50,000 war victims, is on Constitution Avenue.

Other points of interest around Washington include the NATIONAL ZOOLOGICAL PARK in Rock Creek Park, EMBASSY ROW on Massachusetts Avenue, where 150 foreign embassies are located, and the GATEWAY TOUR CENTER, at 4th and E Streets SW, where AMERICAN ADVENTURE (depicting the country's past) and the NATIONAL HISTORICAL WAX MUSEUM can be found.

Parks in the city which are particularly attractive are ROCK CREEK PARK (hiking, jogging, picnic facilities, etc.), the US NATIONAL ARBORETUM – at 3501 New York Avenue NE (landscaped grounds), and the US BOTANIC GARDEN CONSERVATORY on Maryland Avenue which has excellent displays of tropical plants.

One area of Washington it's a good idea to spend some time exploring is GEORGETOWN, west of Rock Creek Park, where the university, the nightspots, street musicians, arts and crafts shops, unusual boutiques and attractive residential streets all create an atmosphere worth sampling.

ACCOMMODATION

Washington being one of America's tourist capitals (some 16 million come here every year), the accommodation situation in the city is tight, especially during the spring, when hordes of schoolchildren descend on the city. In the summer there is virtually no business travel and Congress is out for most of August, but it is also oppressively hot and humid. It's a good idea to reserve in advance if at all possible.

● **First Class:**(double over $140)
Vista International Hotel – 1400 M Street NW, Washington DC (tel. 429-1700). Recently built hotel which has superb facilities including an Executive Fitness Center with sauna, massage and various exercise equipment available. There are also 3 fine restaurants and 2 comfortable bar lounges. The hotel is noted for its 14-storey glass-enclosed atrium which is quite dramatic; it's centrally located, too – downtown and close to the White House, Lafayette Square, and the new Washington Convention Center among other sights.

Complete luxury is available in any of the 6 Givenchy Suites and 2 Executive Floors.

The Sheraton Grand on Capitol Hill – 525 New Jersey Avenue NW, Washington DC (tel. 628-2100). Conveniently located near the city sights, this hotel has first-class facilities which include an atrium café and a fine restaurant featuring American cuisine. There are also plush lobby and wine bars which have live entertainment, a 24-hour room service and cable movies piped into the rooms.

The Willard Inter-Continental Hotel – 1401 Pennsylvania Avenue, Washington DC (tel. 293-1171). Located in the heart of Washington, this hotel is within walking distance of many of the city's major points of interest. Recently restored to the elegance of its early days in 1847, it's thought by many to be the city's grandest hotel. Facilities include exquisite restaurants and bars, same-day laundry and valet service, and Peacock Alley – a promenade of unique shops and boutiques.

● **Super Club Class:** (double $110–$140)
Georgetown Inn – 1310 Wisconsin Avenue NW, Washington DC (tel. 333-8900). In Washington's oldest and probably most attractive section, Georgetown, this hotel has excellent facilities and the rooms are very comfortable and well decorated. Friendly staff.

Washington – Corner of 15th Street and Pennsylvania Avenue NW, Washington DC (tel. 424-9540). An old and rather elegant hotel which counts among its facilities a roof garden from where guests can enjoy views of city monuments (splendid at night). There's also a selection of good restaurants.

Washington Hilton – 1919 Connecticut Avenue NW, Washington DC (tel. 483-3000). Situated close to the business section of the city, this hotel has good facilities and excellent service. There's a swimming pool and tennis courts.

The Westin Hotel – 2401 M Street NW, Washington DC (tel. 429-2400). Located between Georgetown and the White House, this hotel has superb facilities which include a complete fitness centre and an indoor pool, a ballroom, and 'The Colonnade' – an excellent restaurant, as well as a bistro-style bar/restaurant.

- **Economy:** (double $20–$50)
Harrington Hotel – Corner of 11th and E Streets NW, Washington DC (tel. 424-8532). Located downtown, this enormous hotel's facilities include an excellent cafeteria.

Columbia Guest House – 2005 Columbia Road NW, Washington DC (tel. 265-4006). Clean with good facilities. Located in a safe area.

Connecticut-Woodley – 2647 Woodley Road NW, Washington DC (tel. 667-0218). In an attractive area, this hotel is run by very friendly staff. Clean and comfortable.

The Reeds – 1310 Q Street NW, Washington DC (tel. 387-8877). A Victorian mansion complete with antique furniture.

Allen Lee Hotel – 2224 F Street NW, Washington DC (tel. 331-1224). Clean with adequate facilities.

Bellevue Hotel – 15 E Street NW, Washington DC (tel. 638-0900). Located near to Capitol Hill, facilities include a cafeteria and pub.

DINING OUT

Like most cities in the US, Washington DC has a selection of restaurants as cosmopolitan as the city's population. Afghan, Chinese, Japanese, Mexican, French – whatever your taste you're liable to find it somewhere in Washington. The local speciality is fresh seafood straight from the Chesapeake Bay, which is found in many establishments; American beef also features on numerous menus around the city. Downtown is where most restaurants are to be found, and the attractive Georgetown area of the city is home to many places too. Because dining out is a popular pursuit among both locals and visitors, city restaurants tend to be crowded (especially the best ones), lunch being the worst time. Reserving in advance is strongly recommended.

- **First Class:** (over $70 for two)
The Prime Rib – 2020 K Street NW, Washington DC (tel. 466-8811). One of the best places for American cuisine in the city. The decor is tasteful, and the menu includes excellent beef and seafood selections.

Dominique's – Corner of 20th Street and Pennsylvania Avenue NW, Washington DC (tel. 452-1126). Elegant dining amid decor reminiscent of 19th-century France. Popular with theatre-goers, the atmosphere here is very intimate, the menu classically French and the service superb.

Cantina D'Italia – 1214A 18th Street NW, Washington DC (tel. 659-1830). One of the city's finest Italian restaurants. The food here really is excellent, and any pasta dish is highly recommended. Friendly staff.

• **Super Club Class:** ($50–$70 for two)
Yenching Palace – 3524 Connecticut Avenue NW, Washington DC (tel. 362-8200). Excellent Chinese cuisine in a quiet atmosphere. The menu offers a selection of dishes from all over China, and the staff are very friendly.

Billy Martin's Carriage House – 1238 Wisconsin Avenue NW, Washington DC. Located in attractive Georgetown, the menu here consists of good American food, and seafood too.

Jacqueline's – 1990 M Street NW, Washington DC (tel. 785-8877). One of the best French restaurants in the city. The decor is attractive and the atmosphere pleasant; the menu has a fine selection of French cuisine.

• **Economy:** ($10–$20 for two)
Vietnam-Georgetown Restaurant – 2934 M Street NW, Washington DC (tel. 337-4536). Excellent Vietnamese restaurant in Georgetown. The staff are pleasant, and the atmosphere is quiet and intimate.

Iron Gate Inn – 1734 N Street NW, Washington DC (tel. 737-1370). Popular restaurant which serves excellent Middle Eastern cuisine. The atmosphere is lively and the courtyard is delightful in the evening.

Sholl's Colonial Cafeteria – 1990 K Street NW, Washington DC (tel. 296-3065). American cuisine served in generous portions for a bargain price. Good atmosphere, and the staff here are very hospitable.

The Thai Room – 5037 Connecticut Avenue NW, Washington DC (tel. 244-5933). Good place to try spicy Thai food. The chicken dishes are especially recommended.

NIGHTLIFE

The liveliest area of Washington for nightlife is Georgetown. As well as a range of bars, clubs and discotheques to suit everyone, the streets there at the weekend are full of musicians, flower-sellers and various other sights and sounds which make it a pleasant place to stroll through. Clubs in the area offer jazz, theatre, other live music and cabaret. Elsewhere in the city there is much to do after dark downtown. Details of what's going on can be found in most of the daily newspapers.

● **Nightclubs:**
The Blues Alley – 1073 Wisconsin Avenue NW, Washington DC (tel. 337-4141). A converted carriage house where guests can enjoy all kinds of live jazz and blues in an intimate environment.

Comedy Café – 1520 K Street NW, Washington DC (tel. 638-5653). One of the city's best comedy clubs where the acts are very funny and the atmosphere is, naturally, lively. Dinner is also available here.

F. Scott's – 1232 36th Street NW, Washington DC. A very elegant bar where the clientele is older and more composed than in some city bars. Tasteful decor, and dining is also available in the garden room.

Bit O'Ireland (Matt Kane's) – 1118 13th Street NW, Washington DC. A popular Irish pub where the drinks list is extensive, and the atmosphere and clientele very lively indeed. Irish folk groups play here on most evenings.

EXCURSIONS

The CHESAPEAKE AND OHIO CANAL NATIONAL HISTORIC PARK is a vast area stretching as far as Maryland. There's much to do in the park – not only is there nearly 200 miles of bicycle and hiking trails, but visitors are also able to rent canoes and boats to navigate their own passage along the park canal (rentals of boats and bikes from Fletcher's Boat House, 4940 Canal Road NW). Visitors to the park can also ride on a 19th-century canalboat, *The Georgetown*, which is drawn by mules.

The ARLINGTON NATIONAL CEMETERY in Arlington (across the Memorial Bridge from Washington) is the resting place of some of America's favourite sons and bravest soldiers. There are around 175,000 tombs here, and among them are those of ex-President John F. Kennedy, his brother Robert, Joe Louis and Oliver Wendell Holmes; there is also the Tomb of the Unknown Soldier in honour of America's war dead. Memorial services are often held in the Memorial Amphitheater or in the Curtis-Lee Mansion, both of which are on the premises.

Across the 14th Street bridge from Washington is ALEXANDRIA, Virginia. It's a town with a history, and the restoration of many of its 18th-century buildings has served to preserve its old-world atmosphere. Besides its charm, Alexandria's attractions include George Washington's Masonic Memorial, the Torpedo Factory Art Center and Gadsby's Tavern Museum.

Around 10 miles south of Alexandria is MOUNT VERNON, formerly home of George Washington. Today the house and gardens are as beautiful and full of natural delights as they were in the president's day, and visitors are able to tour the grounds. The whole place is made doubly interesting by the fact that it used to be a typical Southern tobacco plantation, complete with imported slaves.

Hawaii

CLIMATE – Very little seasonal variation makes Hawaii's climate close to perfect. The warmest months of August and September have an average temperature of 81°F (28°C) while the 'coldest' month of February's average is 72°F (22°C). Rainfall at the coast is about 20 inches annually but the mountains receive up to 185 inches. The islands are consistently bathed with a gentle trade-wind breeze which brings a refreshing cool to the heat of the day.

TIME DIFFERENCE – GMT – 13 hours.

COMMUNICATIONS

Hawaii is the communications hub of the Pacific. Undersea cable and satellite systems provide 2-way voice, data and TV services to the USA, Australia and Asia.

• **Telephone:** The Hawaiian Telephone Company provides a telephone service throughout Hawaii. Local directory assistance can be obtained by dialling 1-411 and international calls by dialling 0.

• **Television:** Satellite and relay stations provide the state with 13 commercial and 2 public TV channels. Radio stations are also ample.

• **Newspapers:** Several of the daily and weekly newspapers are printed in English, Japanese, Korean and Chinese. The 2 major ones are the morning *Honolulu Advertiser* and the afternoon *Honolulu Star Bulletin*.

OFFICE/SHOPPING HOURS – Post Offices are open from 0830 to 1630 hours, Monday to Friday and 0800–1200 hours Saturday. The main branch is in Ala Moana (tel. 423-3990) and there are 2 in Waikiki, on Saratoga Road (tel. 941-1062) and Royal Hawn (tel. 926-3710).

Opening hours for shops vary considerably in downtown Honolulu and Waikiki. 0900–2200 hours opening is quite common.

• **Best Buys:** Such a multi-cultural spot as Hawaii is bound to produce a wealth of products and being the crossroads of the Pacific adds to this. Goods from India, China, Japan, Hong Kong, Sri Lanka, the Philippines and Thailand are sold alongside those specifically Hawaiian. Art objects made from coral, ivory, lava, rope, tapa (Polynesian hand-pounded cloth), coconuts, wood (native koa and monkeypod) and many other materials, plus local landscape paintings, are sold everywhere. Fabrics are also abundant in Hawaii – the distinctively loud cotton prints seem to suit the climate and atmosphere of the islands! Hawaiian flowers are a very popular buy, but do check with Customs if you wish to take any fruit or flowers out of the country. Muumus, those versatile, comfortable, flowing dresses, are well worth buying at the beginning of your stay here as they are ideal for day or evening wear, as are aloha shirts for men. To really get into the Hawaiian spirit buy a grass skirt or lava-lava. Jewellery, perfumes and local spirits (especially a light whiskey called Okolehao) are among the many other items sold.

Shopping centres abound in Waikiki and Honolulu, providing places to eat, shop and be entertained. The Ala Moana Center (between Ala Moana Boulevard and Kona, Atkinson and Piikoi Streets) is one of the largest complexes with department stores, boutiques, galleries, restaurants and snack bars. Kahala Mall on Waialae Avenue (between Kilauea and Hunakai) sells first-class merchandise rather than tourist trinkets. The Cultural Plaza in downtown Honolulu sells goods from a huge variety of countries and also has some interesting restaurants, including a Chinese theatre-restaurant. In Waikiki's centre is the International Market Place where stalls and open-fronted shops sell all sorts of things. This is a good late-night entertainment spot.

Pearlridge (Aiea/Pearl City) sports a monorail which transports shoppers along a route passing 90 shops and department stores. In contrast King's Alley (Kaiulani Street, one block from Kalakaua Avenue) is nostalgic of the monarchal days with clock-towers, cobblestone paths, belfry and guardhouse, complete with a daily changing of the guard.

For retail stores, wholesale facilities and light industry merchandise the Ward Warehouse in Ala Moana (across from Kewalo Basin) is the place to go. Giant photomurals of old Honolulu add an interesting touch. There are other malls, lanes and squares full of a variety of shops worth looking into.

Honolulu

HONOLULU INTERNATIONAL AIRPORT

Honolulu International Airport caters for Hawaii State's foreign and domestic overseas flights plus inter-island travel and commercial, military and private aircraft. Smaller airports on the other islands primarily handle inter-island flights. Just short of 4 miles from Honolulu City, the airport's one international passenger terminal deals with up to 18 million passengers per annum and has ample facilities for the 55 airlines which use it. The terminal is divided into Arrivals (ground level) and Departures (second level) with the Inter-Island Terminal to the right of these.

● **Arrivals Level:**
International Arrivals is to your left as you approach the hall from the Arrivals gates. Domestic Arrivals is straight ahead and to the right. Baggage claim areas, telephones and Information Desks are all clearly signposted in the area.

Snack Bars	Open 0600–2330 hours.
Cocktail Lounge	Open 0730–0200. Continental breakfasts are served here.
Bank	Bank of Hawaii (tel. 537-8561), open 0830–1500. Situated beyond the International Arrivals block, down the escalator to the parking lot.
Car Rental	Beyond the baggage claim areas are Budget Rent-A-Car and Hertz desks.
Lei and Flower Stand	To the right of the parking lot escalator.
Toilets	Beside the central baggage claim, beside International Arrivals and beyond the right-hand baggage claim areas.
Buses/Taxis	Straight ahead from the baggage claim areas.
Re-ticketing	For ongoing flights there is a desk beyond the International Arrivals area.

● **Departures Level:**
Baggage and ticket check-in counters and airline reservation desks are right along the front of the hall as you enter. Telephones are just to the right of each check-in counter and there is an Information Desk in front of the Y-concourse leading to gates 14–22. The main

waiting lobby is slightly to your left beyond the check-in area and two more waiting areas are beyond this, on either side of the Information Desk. A departures information board is adjacent to the main waiting lobby.

NB: Departing travellers will have their baggage checked by Customs for certain fruits, plants and insects. This is to prevent the spread of plant diseases. A list of the banned items may be obtained before you leave (tel. 836-1491).

Restaurant	Above the Y-concourse (on the third level). Serves lunch 1100–1600 and dinner 1700–2200.
Cocktail Lounge	Next to the restaurant. Open 1100–2330.
Snack Bar	To the right of the main lobby. Open 0600–2330.
Coffee Shop	In the Y-concourse. Open 0600–2330 and sells a wide variety of foods and beverages.
Shops	Food stores, gift and jewellery shops and duty free shops are all around the main lobby. Most open at around 0700 for the morning and open in the evening according to flight departure times.
News-stand	On the left-hand side of the main waiting lobby (open 24 hours) and in the Y-concourse (open 0700–2300).
Currency Exchange	Opposite the entrance to gates 14–16. Open 0800–0100 daily.
Insurance	Near the right-hand baggage check-in counter.
Baggage Lockers	Next to the insurance desk or opposite gates 13 or 25.
Toilets	Around the waiting lobbies or directly to your right as you enter the departure level.
Showers	Beyond the left-hand check-in counter, with a barber shop next door.

● **Inter-Island Terminal:**

Situated to the right of the main, international terminal, this deals with flight services to the other islands of Hawaii. Aloha Airlines has a check-in and ticket counter along the left limb of the terminal and Hawaiian Airlines has one in the right limb. Baggage claim areas are at either end and in the centre of the terminal. Telephones and Information Desks are next to the baggage claim areas and the check-in counters.

Restaurant	In the centre of the terminal, next to baggage claim area two. Serves lunch 1100–1600 and dinner 1700–2200.
Snack Bar	In the centre, opposite the restaurant. Open 0600–1900.
Bar	Next to the restaurant. Open 1100–1930.
Toilets	In the central area, beside Aloha Airlines baggage check-in, beside the entrances to gates 52–55 and gates 56–59.
Car Rental	Desks are dispersed throughout the terminal.
News-stand	In the central area, next to the snack bar and at the entrance to gates 52–55.
Buses/Taxis	The road for transport from the airport runs along the left-hand side of the terminal (i.e. opposite the baggage check-in counters).

AIRPORT INFORMATION

Check-in Times	60 minutes before flight departure time for inter-island flights, 90 minutes before flight departure time for international flights.
Airport Tax	Nil.

Medical Centre	24-hour service with registered nurses on duty and doctors on call. There is a fee for service. Located on the Arrivals (ground) floor of the main terminal, next to stairs and elevator to the second level. On inter-airport phones dial 782 for the medical office or 711 for emergency services. From outside the airport you can contact the medical office on 836-3341.
Transferring Flights	On arrival go to the Re-ticketing Desk beyond the International Arrivals area.

AIRPORT HOTELS

● **Super Club Class:**
Holiday Inn – Honolulu Airport – 3401 Nimitz Highway (tel. 836-0661). Adequate facilities and handy for the airport.

● **Economy:**
The Shower Tree – Second level of the main terminal (tel. 836-3044). Actually a 'mini hotel', which means you can stay there for a short time only while you await onward travel. Comfortable resting, sleeping and showering facilities and you can check into and out of your room at any time of the day or night.

CITY LINKS

Airport buses or limousine services are available and better than the rather expensive taxicabs. You can 'share' cabs if several of you are going to the same hotel. Privately operated motorcoach transportation goes from the airport to Waikiki with stops at the major hotels from 0700–2100 daily. Car rental companies based at the airport provide a transport alternative.

HONOLULU

Capital of the Hawaiian Islands since King Kamehameha III made
it his residence in 1845, Honolulu is a thriving, modern metropolis
and one of the United States' most popular holiday resorts. It is a
harbour city situated on the south-east coast of Oahu, one of the 8
main islands which make up Hawaii State. Although it is believed
that Oahu was populated in AD 1000 by Polynesians from Tahiti, or
even before that by the Marquesas Islanders, Captain James Cook
first sighted Oahu in 1778 and introduced the islands to the western
world. He actually landed on Kauai, north-west of Oahu, and
named the archipelago the Sandwich Islands. It was on the island of
Hawaii, the largest and furthest south of the string, that Cook was
slain in a fight with the Hawaiians in 1779. King Kamehameha I,
from the island of Hawaii, established the kingdom by conquering

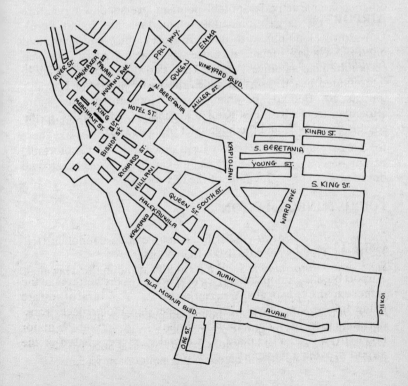

the other islands one by one. The Kingdom of Hawaii survived until 1893 when a bloodless revolution led to formation of a provisional government and, in 1898, annexation by the USA.

With its fine harbours Oahu became the state's political, economic, military, educational and cultural centre. Honolulu Harbor was a key Pacific port for whalers and sandalwood and fur traders, while nearby Pearl Harbor became a strategic military base. Sugar and pineapple industries resulted in large-scale immigration from several countries during the 19th century, notably Japan, the Philippines, Korea, Portugal and Puerto Rico. The 1941 Japanese bombing of Pearl Harbor brought the US into World War II. Interestingly, the Japanese Hawaiians in the 442nd Regimental Combat Team, who served in Europe, collected the most US decorations of the entire war.

Today the major industries of Oahu are tourism, construction, manufacturing and agriculture. It is the state's only island where other economic activities, notably tourism, overshadow agriculture (even so, the largest pineapple plantations are found here). Downtown Honolulu, with its multi-storey office and apartment blocks, is Hawaii's financial centre where nearly every Hawaiian corporation has an office. A mere 3 miles down the coast is Waikiki – the famed beach resort to which the vast majority of Hawaii's tourists go. Behind and inland from Honolulu are the more attractive, tropically green Koolau Mountains; a few miles up the coast is the airport and the huge inlet of Pearl Harbor.

TOURIST INFORMATION

Hawaii Visitors Bureau – 2270 Kalakaua Avenue, Honolulu (tel. 923-1811). Open weekdays 0800–1630 hours.
State Visitor Information Service – Booths at the major Hawaiian airports. Open weekdays 0800–1630 (tel. 847-9413).
Oahu Bus Information – Tel. 531-1611.
Emergency Number – 911 for police, ambulance or fire brigade. It can be dialled free on public pay phones.
Medical Services – The Honolulu County Medical Society (24-hour service, tel. 536-6988) will give you the names of physicians.

GETTING ABOUT

As tourism is the big money-maker in Hawaii, transport is laid on to every conceivable corner of the state. Within the city of Honolulu buses, cabs and hire cars are available.

• **Buses:** Mass Transit Lines buses run an extensive network of routes across the city. They all show route numbers and destinations and the driver will give you a free transfer ticket for another route should you mistakenly take the wrong bus. 'The Bus', as these bright yellow buses are known, will not accommodate luggage. For schedule information ring 531-1611.

• **Taxi:** These are plentiful but quite expensive. Random cruising is not allowed in Honolulu so you must phone for a taxi instead of being able to hail one in the street. Recommended companies are Charley's Taxi (tel. 946-7032 or 531-1333), Sida (tel. 836-0011) and Gray Line Hawaii (tel. 834-1033).

• **Car Rental:** Available from the airport or numerous places on Kalakaua Avenue, the main street in Waikiki. Drivers must have a valid US or International Driving Licence and may have to be over 25 years old. Avis are at 148 Kaiulani Avenue, in the Outrigger East Hotel. Budget Rent-A-Car are at 2379 Kuhio Avenue and Hertz are at 233 Keawe Street, Suite 625.

SIGHTS

On Pier 9 in downtown Honolulu, the ALOHA TOWER, a harbour-side landmark built in 1926, is now dwarfed by skyscrapers but used to be the tallest building in Honolulu. An observation balcony is open to the public 0800–2100 daily (free).

Falls of Clyde is a 4-masted, square-rigged ship on Pier 5, near Aloha Tower. It was built in Scotland in 1878 and sailed the Hawaiian waters. Now used as a maritime museum, the ship is open 0930–1600 daily with an admission charge.

DIAMOND HEAD is an extinct volcanic crater which forms an outstanding coastal landmark near Waikiki. The site is used regularly for rock concerts and folk festivals and has a lighthouse at the foot of its 760-ft peak.

In the Marva Valley stands the University of Hawaii campus with several distinctive buildings including an Oriental teahouse and garden. Tours of the EAST-WEST CENTER are given free during the week, starting from Jefferson Hall.

The FOSTER BOTANIC GARDENS at 180 North Vineyard Boulevard are open daily for picnicking or just sauntering around. On view is a collection of rare plants native to the tropics including a wide variety of palm trees and a wild orchid garden. Free tours begin at 1330 hours on Mondays and Wednesdays. There is an admission charge to the gardens. The HONOLULU ZOO is at 151 Kapahulu Avenue, in Kapiolani Park, Waikiki. A well stocked, fairly spacious zoo with snack bars and picnic grounds, it is open 0830–1600 daily with an admission charge.

IOLANI PALACE, on the corner of King and Richards Streets, downtown Honolulu Civic Center, is an Italian Renaissance-style royal palace (the USA's only one) completed in 1882 for King Kalakaua. It was used by Hawaii's governments until 1969 and has since been restored to its 1880 style. Tours from 0900–1415 hours Wednesday–Saturday (children of 5 years or less are not allowed in the palace). Its limited capacity and huge popularity mean it is wise to book in advance (tel. 523-0141). IOLANI BARRACKS was the former home of the Royal Household Guards and Royal Hawaiian Band concerts are now performed here. Located in the palace grounds, the concerts take place in the pavilion each Friday noon. Free.

KAPIOLANI PARK is a leisure park near Diamond Head. Tennis courts, softball diamonds, jogging paths and areas for bowling, football, rugby and polo are set amongst lawns and shade trees. Free Sunday afternoon concerts are given at an outdoor bandstand, while the Waikiki Shell, an outdoor amphitheatre, hosts the Kodak Hula Show.

The KAWAIAHAO CHURCH, 957 Punchbowl Street (near the Civic Center), is built of coral and steeped in Hawaiian regal splendour and history. Sunday morning services are followed by conducted tours. The Chancel is open daily.

The NATIONAL MEMORIAL CEMETERY OF THE PACIFIC is at Puowaina Drive (via Pali Highway turnoff). Also known as 'Punchbowl', this volcanic crater has become a memorial for US war casualties. It's worth visiting for its World War II and Korean battle-map murals, Ernie Pyle's grave (a famous war correspondent) and a terraced shrine for the 'Courts of the Missing'. A viewpoint looks out over the city and shoreline of Honolulu. Open daily.

A showpiece of tropical birds and flowers in Marva Valley (at the top of Marva Road) is PARADISE PARK. Many of the rare birds have been trained to perform in shows, or to perch on shoulders. Open 1000–1700 hours daily. Restaurant and snack bar inside.

Hawaii is rich in museums and art galleries also. ALICE COOKE SPALDING HOUSE, 2411 Makiki Heights Drive, is full of Asian decorative arts, notably the Michener collection of ancient Japanese woodblock prints. Open daily except Mondays. BISHOP MUSEUM, 1355 Kalihi Street, has Pacific arts and crafts, Hawaiian royal artefacts and natural history, arts and science displays. Open Monday–Saturday 0900–1700, with charges for the planetarium show.

The HONOLULU ACADEMY OF ARTS, 900 South Beretania Street, exhibits Asian, European, American and Pacific art. Open 1000–1630 Tuesday–Saturday and 1300–1700 Sunday. Admission free.

EMMA'S SUMMER PALACE, at 2913 Pali Highway, was the home of King Kamehameha IV's widow and is fully furnished with displays of her treasures. Finally, the TENNANT ART FOUNDATION GALLERY at 203 Prospect Street is worth a visit, showing Madge Tennant's art works. (One of Hawaii's most respected artists.)

ACCOMMODATION

As one would expect of a huge holiday destination, there is a great diversity of accommodation. Recent investment has gone into 'polishing up' this age-old Pacific resort and new hotels have sprung up while existing ones have been extensively upgraded. Booking in advance is strongly advised.

• **First Class:** (double $100–$140)
Kahala Hilton – 5000 Kahala Avenue, Honolulu (tel. 734-2211). On a secluded, sandy beach 15 minutes from Waikiki and overlooking lush, landscaped gardens, this is one of the luxury hotels of the world. Complete business facilities, 3 restaurants, an outdoor pool and private beach with boats and snorkel gear for hire. The Hilton's Hala Terrace is *the* place for Sunday brunch.

The Westin Ilikai – 1777 Ala Moana Boulevard, Waikiki (tel. 949-3811). On Waikiki beach and within walking distance of the Ala Moana Shopping Center, this is very well priced for its high standards. The complex houses Champeaux's restaurant and Annabelle's nightclub plus swimming pools, tennis courts (with resident coaches) and a tropical lagoon.

Sheraton Waikiki – 2255 Kalakaua Avenue, Waikiki (tel. 922-4422). Also on the beach with a rooftop restaurant giving superb views. All the expected first-class facilities are here in this, one of the 10 largest hotels in the world.

● **Super Club Class:** (double $60–$100)
Hyatt Regency – 2424 Kalakaua Avenue, Waikiki (tel. 922-9292). The newest hotel in Waikiki and a definite asset to the revitalized image of the resort. Home to one of the best restaurants in Honolulu, Bagwell's 2424, and one of the trendiest nightclubs, Trappers.

Moana – 2365 Kalakaua Avenue, Waikiki (tel. 922-3111). First on the beach in 1901 and still the archetypal South Seas hotel. Moana's Banyan Court is a well known place to go for cocktails or dinner to watch the 'Tahiti Polynesian Revue' staged twice nightly.

Waikiki Beachcomber – 2300 Kalakaua Avenue, Waikiki (tel. 922-4646). Set back from the beach, on the main shopping street of Waikiki. Comfortable accommodation and good service, with its own pool and restaurants.

Holiday Inn Waikiki Beach – 2570 Kalakaua Avenue, Waikiki (tel. 922-2511). At the Diamond Head end of the beach; all the standard Holiday Inn facilities.

● **Economy:** (double $20–$60)
Hawaiian King – 417 Nohonani Street, Waikiki (tel. 922-3894). Attractive suites in central Waikiki (one block from the beach). A pool and shops are among the facilities.

Ilima – 445 Nohonani Street, Waikiki (tel. 923-1877). In central Waikiki with pool and restaurant. The studio-type rooms all have kitchens.

Outrigger East – 150 Kaiulani Avenue, Waikiki (tel. 922-5353). Good accommodation in a very handy spot – on the market-place one street away from the beach.

Reef Lanais – 225 Saratoga Road, Waikiki (tel. 923-3881). A short walk from the beach and the shops. Suites with kitchen facilities. Restaurant, pool and cocktail lounge.

Royal Grove – 151 Uluniu Avenue, Waikiki (tel. 923-7691). A smaller hotel in central Waikiki with studio accommodation (sitting-room which converts to bedroom) and kitchen facilities.

Waikiki Circle – 2464 Kalakaua Avenue, Waikiki (tel. 923-1571). Good location on the beach front with lovely views. Studio accommodation but no kitchen facilities.

Waikiki Surf West – 412 Lewers Street, Waikiki (tel. 923-7671). Bedrooms or family apartments (2 rooms) with kitchenettes at very reasonable rates. In central Waikiki, a short walk from the beach.

Waikiki Terrace – 339 Royal Hawaiian Avenue, Waikiki (tel. 923-3253). Very well priced one-bedroomed apartments (full kitchen). There is a minimum stay of two days. Central Waikiki.

DINING OUT

Hawaiian restaurants serving the local cuisine are actually in the minority in Honolulu: there are so many other nationalities to vie with. Korean, Filipino, German, French, Thai, Mexican, Greek, Indian and Japanese restaurants abound and it's quite common to find yourself eating a cosmopolitan array of dishes within one meal. The price range is equally diverse, ranging from the cheaper lunch wagons parked on beaches, or traditional 'luaus' (Hawaiian feasts) where you can eat as much as you like, to expensive haute cuisine in the elegant restaurants.

● **First Class:** ($60–$90 for two)
Michel's – Colony Surf Hotel, 2895 Kalakaua Avenue (tel. 923-6552). Exquisite French cuisine, beautifully served in elegant surroundings with a terrific beach view. Well worth the expense for a blow-out dinner.

The Third Floor – Hawaiian Regent Hotel, 2552 Kalakaua Avenue (tel. 922-6611). Fine international cuisine and superb service. Recently voted 'No. 1' in Honolulu.

Bagwell's 2424 – Hyatt Regency Hotel, 2424 Kalakaua Avenue (tel. 922-9292). One of the best in Honolulu with a French and continental menu including many island foods (such as opakapaka) enhanced by delicious sauces. An adjacent wine bar permits tastings from the formidable wine list.

● **Super Club Class:** ($40–$60 for two)
Willows – 901 Hausten Street (tel. 946-4808), or its new branch, *Banyan Gardens* in Waikiki (2380 Kuhio Street, tel. 923-2366). Noted for Polynesian dishes, excellent musicians and plenty of island atmosphere.

Chez Michel – 444 Hobron Lane, Eaton Square (tel. 955-7866). Michel himself presides over this French Riviera-type setting and produces classic French cuisine.

Canlis – 2100 Kalakaua Avenue (tel. 923-2324). One of the oldest restaurants in town with interesting architecture, a pleasant atmosphere and good food.

● **Economy:** ($10–$30 for two)
It's Greek To Me – 2201 Kalakaua Avenue, in the Royal Hawaiian Center. Inexpensive Greek food and atmosphere.

Ono Hawaiian Foods – 726 Kapahulu Avenue. The locals recommend it and usually crowd it out.

Matteo's – 364 Seaside, in the Marine Surf Hotel. Fine Italian food for moderate prices.

Kanraku Tea House – 750 Kohou Street, in Kalihi. Japanese in style and atmosphere – join the locals sitting cross-legged on the floor.

With most restaurants it is advisable to book in advance. Dress is usually casual in Honolulu but some of the top-class restaurants expect more formal wear.

NIGHTLIFE

The entertainment capital of the Pacific must surely be Waikiki. All the major hotels have shows of some description, accompanied by dinner and dancing. Typical Polynesian shows are slick and flashy productions with the verve and fire of Tonga, Fiji or Tahiti. Hawaiian music and dancing is softer, more gentle and melodious. Nightclubs usually lay on 2 performances each night – a buffet-dinner show then a cocktail show later. Dancing and disco venues are to be found all over Waikiki and many stay open until 4 a.m. The penthouse-level clubs on hotel top floors are the most popular. Bars vary from the outdoor beach bars to smarter lounge bars. Most stay open until 1 or 2 a.m. and have cocktail happy hours in the early evenings. Traditional Hawaiian luaus may not quite be the feasts they once were, but they're still well worth a visit. The commercial ones tend to be stingier on the native dishes and less authentic than the charitable or church luaus. If you are visiting one of the other islands the luaus will be better value there. Other special events like the Filipino shows, aquacades and hukilau are usually good fun.

For information on night entertainment the *Waikiki Beach Press*, *Hawaii Tourist News*, *Snooper*, *Where* and *This Week* are useful publications or the daily newspapers will have entertainment pages. Some events and venues to note are:

The Tahiti Polynesian Revue – In Moana's Banyan Court twice nightly: plenty of grass skirts and war chants.

Danny Kaleikini's Polynesian Show – At the Kahala Hilton. Very slick.

Neal S. Balidell Center – Puts on top-flight shows and concerts, often with world-renowned performers.

Honolulu Concert Hall – A magnificent building where the Honolulu Symphony Orchestra plays.

Annabelle's Nightclub – Westin Waikiki Hotel. A high-class and sophisticated nightspot.

Trappers – Hyatt Regency Hotel. Chic bar and disco provides great jazz and attracts the trendiest late-night crowds on the beach.

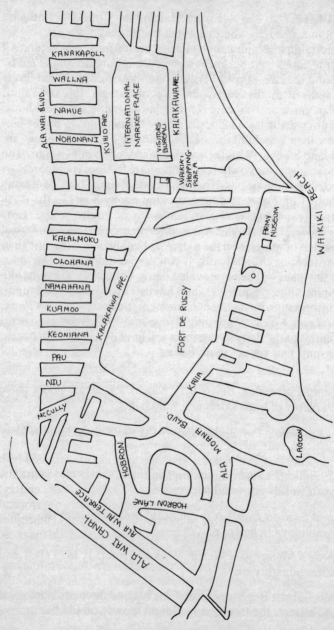

House Without A Key – In the Halekulani Hotel. An intimate cocktail lounge where you can watch the dramatic sunsets.

The Rose and Crown – In King's Village. A good 'pub' atmosphere (noisy, crowded and full of high spirits!).

EXCURSIONS

Getting away from the bustle of city and beach is very quick and easy here. Rural areas and remote beaches on Oahu are only a short drive away. In fact, a circuit drive of the whole island can be accomplished in one day. Tour information is freely available at the Hawaii Visitors Bureau (HVB) or hotel tour desks. Some of the more major sights of Oahu are PEARL HARBOR, the ARIZONA MEMORIAL (on top of the sunken battleship *Arizona* in Pearl Harbor), the BYODO-IN TEMPLE in the Valley of the Temples on Kahekili Highway, HANAUMA BAY, the KAHUKU SUGAR MILL (on the north shore), the SEA LIFE PARK (Makapuu Point) and the KOKO HEAD BLOW HOLE.

Inter-island travel is also quickly and easily accomplished via numerous air-taxis or one of the 3 scheduled airlines, Hawaiian, Aloha and Mid-Pacific. All provide regular services. Non-jet air-taxis have the advantage of including 'flightseeing' transportation which gives you a fantastic view of the islands and ocean. Brandt Air, Air Molokai and Air Hawaii do this, as does the Royal Hawaiian Air Service (they are slightly more expensive). Each island airport has car rental desks and hiring a car is the best way of doing any extensive travelling on your own.

KAUAI, the 'Garden Island', offers magnificent scenery and lush vegetation, waterfalls, canyons and valleys. Places to note are the Waimea Canyon, the 'hidden' valley of Kalalau, Hanalei Bay, Wailua River, Nawiliwili Bay and Poipu Beach. Colourful tropical plants and flowers make this island quite spectacular. Helicopter flightseeing excursions are available and show you some of the more inaccessible spots. For information go to the HVB.

MOLOKAI, the 'Friendly Isle', is only just waking up to tourism. Consequently the 6500 inhabitants are still extremely friendly towards visitors and it's a lovely place for a day trip. Pineapple plantations, ranching and a surprising African Game Reserve take up most of the island. Do try the delicious Molokai bread while you are here.

LANAI is rightly called the 'Pineapple Island' as most of it is planted by the Dole Company. Still a lovely island to visit for a peaceful, relaxing time.

MAUI, the 'Valley Isle', boasts the largest dormant volcano crater in the world – Haleakala – which is really quite a spectacular sight. Notable spots are Lahaina (Hawaii's capital before 1845 and an old whaling town), the Kaanapali resort area and Hana and Iao Valleys.

HAWAII is the 'Big Island' and one of many contrasts, from snow-clad Mauna Kea (13,796 ft) to the Ka'u Desert. Tropical forests and splendid waterfalls are just some of the natural phenomena to be seen. Sugar, coffee, cattle and macadamia nuts are grown on the island. Good places to visit are the Hawaii Volcanoes National Park, Kealakekua Bay, Kailua-Kona, Kawai-hae, Parker Ranch and Waipo Valley.

Kahoolawe Island is uninhabited and used by the US Navy and Airforce as a target. Niihau Island is privately owned. To stay on any of the other islands for more than a day you should book accommodation in advance (advice from the HVB).

7. SOUTH AMERICA

Brazil

RED TAPE

• **Passport/Visa Requirements:** As well as a full passport, visas are required by nationals of all countries *except*: Argentina, Austria, Barbados, Belgium, Bolivia, Canada, Chile, Colombia, Costa Rica, Denmark, Dominican Republic, Ecuador, Finland, France, West Germany, Greece, Guatemala, Guyana, Haiti, Honduras, Iceland, Republic of Ireland, Italy, Jamaica, Liechtenstein, Luxembourg, Mexico, Morocco, Netherlands, Nicaragua, Norway, Panama, Paraguay, Peru, Philippines, Portugal, El Salvador, Spain, Sweden, Switzerland, Trinidad and Tobago, United Kingdom (includes Guernsey and Jersey), Uruguay, USA and Venezuela. Visas are granted for a stay of up to 3 months, which can be extended for a further 3 months.

CUSTOMS

• **Duty Free:** Visitors can take in clothing and articles for personal use such as cameras, radios, tape recorders, etc., provided there is not more than one of each. Also 400 cigarettes, 3 litres of wine, 25 cigars, 2 litres of spirits, 2 litres of champagne, 280g of perfume, and 700g of toilet water. There is no limit to the amount of currency allowed to be taken into Brazil, but visitors must not leave the country with more money than when they arrived.

Liable to duty: commercial samples for which the owner is bound to pay duty should the samples not be re-exported.

HEALTH

An International Certificate of Vaccination against smallpox is required before entry can be permitted.

CAPITAL – Brasilia. Population – 900,000.

POPULATION – 120 million.

LANGUAGE – Portuguese. English is widely understood.

CURRENCY – Cruzeiro (Crs), divided into 100 centavos. Notes – 1, 5, 10, 50, 100 and 500 cruzeiros; coins – 1, 2, 5, 10, 50 centavos and 1 cruzeiro.
£1 = 20; US$1 = 15.

BANKING HOURS – 1000–1600, Monday–Friday.

POLITICAL SYSTEM – Military government; the country is ruled by presidential decree.

RELIGION – Roman Catholic.

PUBLIC HOLIDAYS

January 1	New Year's Day
4 days before Ash Wednesday (February)	Carnival/Mardi Gras
March/April	Good Friday
April 21	Tiradentes Day
May 1	Labour Day
September 7	Independence Day
November 2	All Souls' Day
November 15	Proclamation Day
December 25	Christmas Day

CLIMATE – Because most of the country lies just south of the equator, the Brazilian climate is generally unchanging year-round. The climate is comfortable in most of the country, with temperatures usually ranging from 65° to 85°F (18° to 30°C), and coastal towns benefit from a refreshing sea breeze. Light clothing is suitable for almost every region at any given time of year.

TIME DIFFERENCE – GMT – 3 hours (the only major city which differs is Manaus, at GMT – 4 hours).

COMMUNICATIONS

• **Telephone:** Public telephones are widely available in the street, hotels, railway stations and other public places. They are coin-operated, and accept metal tokens, 'fichas', which can be bought at news-stands or in various shops. Almost all the main cities in Brazil are connected by a modern microwave communications system and can be reached by dialling direct; it's possible to dial direct to North America, Japan and most of Europe, although not from some public phones which are fitted with a blocking device; international calls are expensive. A 40 per cent tax is added to the cost of all telephone communication.

• **Post:** The internal mail operation is rather unreliable, and many deliveries are thus subject to delays. Letters abroad can be sent either by land or air – airmail is recommended.

ELECTRICITY – Rio de Janeiro and Sao Paulo: 110v AC, 60 Hz. Brasilia: 220–240v AC, 60 Hz.

OFFICE/SHOPPING HOURS – Government offices are open to the public 0930–1800, Monday–Friday. Shops are open 0900–1800, Monday–Friday; 0900–1300 on Saturdays.

• **Best Buys:** Brazil offers a range of traditional handicrafts and souvenirs. Among the more popular are leather and embroidered goods – crocodile-skin bags and belts, leather handbags; Indian handicrafts – wood carvings and native paintings. There's also a wide range of jewellery on offer in all cities, large or small. Precious and semi-precious stones corner much of Brazil's souvenir trade: the country produces 90 per cent of the world's colourful minerals, and stones such as aquamarine, topaz, opal and agate are readily available in many shops.

INTERNAL TRAVEL

• **Air:** Four national airlines – Varig, Cruzeiro, Transbrasil and Vasp – operate domestic air services around the country. The internal air system is well developed, and these airlines between them offer flights to almost every populated area in Brazil.

• **Rail:** Train services are good from Rio to Sao Paulo and to Belo Horizonte; services inside the state of Sao Paulo are also adequate. Otherwise, train services to southern and central regions tend to be slow, and any one journey often requires several train changes.

• **Road:** Bus services linking cities in Brazil are good; they are fast and comfortable, and next to flying offer the most convenient method of travel.

Taxis are available in all towns, and can be hailed in the street or reserved in advance by phone. In Rio and Sao Paulo they are fitted with meters; elsewhere they can be hired by the journey or by the half-hour.

Car hire companies operate in all the main cities and towns. An International Driving Licence is required, and traffic travels on the right-hand side of the road.

MAJOR SIGHTS OF THE COUNTRY

An area which shouldn't be missed is the AMAZON FOREST, in the state of Amazonas in Brazil's north-east. Trees of up to 45 metres cover what is one of the world's largest natural reserves, where the fauna, flora, animal and plant life is as exotic and fascinating as it is unique. Various trips into the forest are available from the city of Manaus – it's possible to take a trip in a long-boat up small rivers, and stay in basic hotels in the middle of the jungle, take a canoe through the jungle marshes, or cut your way through the forest with a machete knife under the guidance of an experienced leader, sampling an enormous range of natural delights along the way.

The cities of SALVADOR and RECIFE are the largest in the north-east of the country, and both are well worth taking in for their own unique attractions. Salvador is one of Brazil's more exotic cities, and is a centre for folklore with mysticism and various historical and cultural traditions. One such local tradition is the 'capoeira' (once a fight but now a dance), and another is the local spicy cuisine (try vatapa, acaraje, chicken xinxim) which is sold on the streets by locals (Bahianas) in long white skirts and fancy necklaces. Salvador is also noted for its innumerable churches and fine beaches.

The city of Recife was originally founded by the Dutch, and as well as being beautiful (it's known as the 'city of bridges and rivers'), it's a good base from which to explore nearby historical landmarks such as the city of OLINDA, IGARACU and the island of ITAMARACA to the north.

SAO PAULO, Brazil's most prosperous city in the country's south-east, is also one of its most worthwhile tourist centres. Not only is it an active cultural centre, with 3 major universities and a range of interesting museums, it is also intriguing for its history (it was founded in 1554 as a mission station by 2 Jesuit priests), which is reflected in the city's architecture, such as the 19th-century opera house, and in the charming residential areas; there's also a copy of the original Jesuit settlement in the city centre. Sao Paulo is also one of Brazil's liveliest after-dark cities, with an enormous selection of restaurants, nightclubs, and different entertainments.

BRASILIA is the capital of Brazil, situated in the country's central-west region; it is worth visiting for its immense cultural (it's home to the national theatre), political (it's the seat of government) and academic (there are 4 universities here) significance. The architecture in Brasilia is also interesting to view for its ultra-modernity and in parts futurity.

The ARAGUAIA RIVER is also in Brazil's central-west region, and from the little town of Aruana it's possible to sail down the river on 'boatels' (floating motels), to the island of Bananal which is known for its Indian villages. The river also has excellent beaches, which are ideal for visiting in summer.

FOZ DO IGUACU, at the border town of Iguacu in the south where Brazil, Argentina and Paraguay meet, is a famous set of waterfalls; there are 275 falls in total here, and some are almost 100 metres high, making them one of Brazil's most spectacular natural wonders.

GRAMADO and CANELA MOUNTAINS (around 90 miles from Porto Alegre) are part of the scenic Gaucho mountain range in the country's south; both make for excellent sightseeing, which is due in part to their tiny settlements where the alpine-style cottages resemble those of a Bavarian village.

These are just some of the worthwhile sights and places around Brazil, each reflecting either the immense natural beauty, vast culture, fascinating history or radical modernity of the country.

HOTELS

In all the major Brazilian cities, hotel accommodation covers a wide price range. In a first-class hotel, two people can expect to pay something around US$50 a night, while economy hotels charge anything from US$10 to US$40 for a double room. Hotels, especially the more expensive ones, often include breakfast in their prices, and this is frequently served in guests' rooms; breakfast in Brazilian hotels can range from juice, rolls and coffee to a full meal complete with fruit, cheese, warm rolls and coffee.

There are several large international hotel chains in operation around Brazil, among them Sheraton and Hilton; Sheraton have hotels in Rio de Janeiro and Sao Paulo, while Hilton have hotels in Belem, Sao Paulo, and Belo Horizonte.

For the economy traveller, most of Brazil's cities, certainly the larger ones, have Youth Hostels. A Youth Hostel card is needed to get into many of them, and because they are so cheap (some charge as little as US$3 for one person for one night), they are often crowded, and getting a place can be difficult – especially at peak periods in the summer. Also, student houses (casas de estudante) sometimes offer cheap accommodation, for which a student card is needed.

It is essential to make advance reservations during Carneval.

NIGHTLIFE AND RESTAURANTS

The larger cities are where Brazil's nightlife and entertainment, cultural or otherwise, are to be found. Rio de Janeiro is renowned the world over for its bubbling nightlife; there's virtually everything available, and after around 11 p.m. when dinner is eaten the whole city comes alive, and from strip-show to disco to a celebrated samba cabaret show, most nightspots stay open until dawn. A measure of the city's entertainment diversity is the fact that several cinemas around town show obscure English-language films. Where culture is concerned, Rio's Municipal Theatre (Teatro Municipal) is a centre of attraction for its opera, ballet and various musical concerts.

The nightlife in other Brazilian cities offers much the same as Rio. In Sao Paulo it is perhaps more varied, however. There is a wide selection of nightclubs, many of which play host to big-name international entertainers ahead of Rio. The theatre scene is particularly vibrant here, and the Sao Paulo Municipal Theatre is a centre for theatrical entertainment (as well as opera), as are several excellent theatres around the city.

The cuisine available in Brazil constitutes a choice as cosmopolitan as you'd find almost anywhere. The large cities are where the choice is widest due to innumerable international restaurants, among them Chinese, Japanese, French, Italian, German, Swiss and English. There are also many typically Brazilian establishments in all towns and cities, whatever their size, and their traditional cuisine is well worth trying. Often unusual but usually tasty, national (Bahian) dishes include different fish and seafood done in various ways. 'Feijoada' is the most typical of Brazilian dishes, and consists of black beans and rice, with pork and sausages added to it when served on Saturdays, for reasons of tradition. Also worth trying is 'churrasco' – meat grilled over an open fire in true gaucho fashion, and xinxim de galinha which features pieces of chicken done in a white sauce. There's also, of course, delicious, rich Brazilian coffee, served in tiny cups with vast quantities of sugar.

Rio de Janeiro

RIO DE JANEIRO INTERNATIONAL AIRPORT

Rio de Janeiro International Airport is 12½ miles north-west of the city, and it handles all international and many domestic flights into and out of the Rio area. There is 1 terminal, divided into 3 sectors. Sector A handles domestic flights. Sectors B and C handle international flights.

AIRPORT FACILITIES

Information Desk	Open 24 hours.
Bank/Foreign Exchange	Both available in the terminal. Open 24 hours.
Hotel Reservations Service	Available 0600–midnight.
Bar	There are bars open round the clock in the terminal. There's also a Beer House in sector C of Airport Observation Terrace.
Restaurant/Buffet	A restaurant and buffet is available 24 hours a day. Fast food bars operate 24 hours on 3rd floor of sectors A, B and C.
Post Office	Open 24 hours.
Baggage Deposit	Available round the clock.
Shops	Shops selling confectionery, books, gifts, toys, etc. are open 0600–midnight.
Duty Free	There are 2 duty free shops in the Departure level and 4 in the Arrival level; both are international. In the International Departure level, there are 9. They sell cigarettes, liquor, perfumes, electronic material and various gifts. Most currencies are accepted, as are the following credit cards: Visa, Mastercharge, American Express and Diners Club.
Medical Centre	A medical centre is in operation 24 hours a day.
Toilets	These are all over the terminal, and are open 24 hours.
Car Rental Desks	Avis, Localiza, Locabras, and Nobre have counters. Available 24 hours a day.
Public Telephones	These are all over the terminal.

Lost Property   Located in Departure sector A,
                                     on the 2nd floor (tel. 398-4152).

AIRPORT INFORMATION

Check-in Times   Average for all airlines:
                                     International – 90 minutes;
                                     Domestic – 60 minutes.
Airport Tax   International: US$8.83.
Transferring Flights   The time needed for transfer
                                     from an international to a
                                     domestic flight is 90 minutes.
                                     For domestic to international, 45
                                     minutes is required.

INTER-AIRPORT TRANSFER

• **To Santos Dumont Airport:** *Bus* – there is a service every 15
minutes from 0515 until 2400. Fare – Crs50, journey takes 40
minutes. *Taxi* – A usual taxi fare to Santos Dumont Airport is
around Crs600. Journey takes 30 minutes.

AIRPORT HOTELS

There are 2 hotels located within the terminal premises: *Luxor
Hotel* (14 rooms); *Pousada Galeao* (15 rooms).

CITY LINKS

• **Bus:** There is a bus service to Santos Dumont downtown airport
every 15 minutes from 0515 until midnight. This doubles as a service
downtown. Fare is Crs50.

• **Taxi:** Tickets for airport taxis can be bought at company desks on
the Arrivals level of the terminal. Usual fare is around Crs600. City
taxis are also available at the airport, and fares on them are
metered.

RIO DE JANEIRO

Rio de Janeiro in English means 'river of January' – this was the name given to the area in 1502 when a Portuguese expedition landed on Brazil's east coast. Rio in its early days came alternately under French and Portuguese control until 1822, when Brazil's independence was declared; until 1960 it was the country's capital,

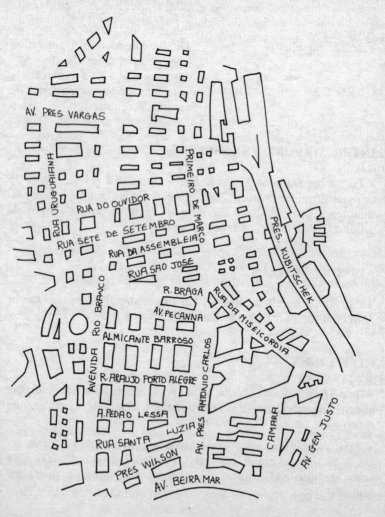

and while today it's the capital only of the state of Rio de Janeiro, it is still one of Brazil's most important commercial and industrial cities, as well as being the country's cultural centre.

It's also a very beautiful city; not only is it blessed with a location on the western banks of the Guanabara Bay, and near to the Tijuca Mountains, Rio counts Sugar Loaf Mountain and Corcovado Mountain (complete with its Christ the Redeemer statue) among its sights. Its year-round summer climate also increases its appeal, and serves to boost considerably the local population of 5 million with a large influx of visitors every year.

TOURIST INFORMATION

For maps, general information, accommodation-listings etc., contact: *Riotur*, Rua Sao Jose 90, 10th floor, Rio de Janeiro (tel. 232-4320). Information is given in English from here by phoning (021) 580-8000.

ADDRESSES

Main Post Office – Rua Primeiro de Marco (at the corner with Rua do Rosario), Rio de Janeiro.
American Express – Kontik-Franstur, Avenida Atlantica 2316, Copacabana.
British Consulate – Praia do Flamengo 284, Rio de Janeiro (tel. 225-7552).

GETTING ABOUT

Public transportation in Rio is adequate.

• **Bus:** The cheapest way of getting around is by bus; you tell the conductor where you want to go and he charges you accordingly – fares start at around 10c, and a usual fare to go to most sections of the city is about 40c. There are also trolleys in operation in some parts of the city, mostly in Santa Teresa, and they provide a fun method of travel. A normal fare for a trolley ride is around 4c; they are also popular with pickpockets, so extra precaution is advised on a trolley.

• **Taxis:** Taxis are easily found around the city; they tend to be rather run-down vehicles, usually with the front seat missing, and the drivers are renowned for their aggression behind the wheel. There is a surcharge after 10 p.m.

• **Car Hire:** International companies which have offices in Rio are Hertz (265-9204), and Avis (205-5796). It's worth noting that petrol can't be sold between Friday night and Monday morning.

SIGHTS

One of Rio's most popular tourist attractions is SUGAR LOAF MOUNTAIN, or Pao de Acucar as it's known locally. Situated at the entrance to Guanabara Bay, it stands at a height of some 1300 feet and its peak offers breathtaking views of Rio and its surrounds. Visitors are able to reach the top of the mountain and a sister peak in glass-enclosed cable cars – the ride takes 5 minutes and is in itself quite exhilarating. The cable car rides start at Praia Vermelha station, 25 minutes from the city centre (take bus 511 from Copacabana, or 107 from downtown).

More centrally, there are a host of sights worth taking in around the city itself. Interesting areas to stroll around downtown are the MAUA PLAZA (PRACA MAUA) and the PRACA XV; the former is intriguing for the aged, elegant architecture in the streets nearby and the ocean liners which are anchored there, while the latter is Rio's oldest square, and is surrounded by quaint buildings in different colours as well as 16th-century churches.

Also, CARIOCA SQUARE (LARGO DA CARIOCA), near the main shopping area, is interesting for its faith healers and shoe-shiners. Nearby is the SAN ANTONIO CONVENT AND CHURCH (CONVENTO E IGREJA DE SANTO ANTONIO), one of Rio's oldest buildings, dating back to the early 17th century, which is worth viewing for its architecture and visiting for the paintings inside. Among the other churches of interest is the CHURCH OF ST FRANCIS OF THE PENITENCE

(IGREJA DE SAO FRANCISCO DA PENITENCIA) which houses carved altars and roof paintings by Jose de Oliveira, one of Brazil's most celebrated artists. The NEW CATHEDRAL (CATEDRAL) on the Avenida Chile is widely known for its avant-garde architecture.

FLAMENGO PARK (PARQUE FLAMENGO), which stretches along the shore of Rio's Flamengo area, is home to various activities: there are children's playgrounds, sports fields, an old DC-3 aeroplane that visitors (usually children) can climb upon, bandstands which host musical displays and a small train which takes visitors from place to place. Also in the park is the NATIONAL WAR MEMORIAL (MONUMENTO DOS MORTOS DA II GUERRA), which consists of 2 pillars 150 feet high on top of which is a curved bowl with an eternal flame; the crypt beneath houses the tomb of the unknown soldier and the remains of Brazilian soldiers who fought with the Allies in the Second World War. The MILITARY MUSEUM (MUSEU MILITAR) nearby contains memorabilia from World War II, including weapons, photographs and murals. The MUSEUM OF MODERN ART (MUSEU DE ARTE MODERNA), which is regarded by many as Rio's best, is also in Flamengo Park, and contains works by famous artists both from Brazil and around the world; the ceramic and metal sculptures are particularly impressive. Other museums in Rio well worth visiting are the MUSEUM OF THE REPUBLIC (MUSEU DA REPUBLICA), at Rua do Catete 179, a historical museum which used to be the home of Brazil's presidents, the PHARMACY MUSEUM at Rua Santa Luzia 206, which contains various old pharmaceutical equipment, and the POLICE ACADEMY MUSEUM at Rua Frei Caneca 162, which has a range of exhibits on fingerprinting, ballistics and other crime-fighting equipment.

There are several beaches in the Rio area: FLAMENGO and BOTAFOGO are the nearest to downtown, and there is also LEBLON, GAVEA and BARRA DA TIJUCA. The most popular beach communities, however, are COPACABANA and IPANEMA. Copacabana boasts the longest and widest beach area in Rio, and it's the centre of attraction on most weekends, both at night and during the day; the beach front is packed with hotels, shops, sidewalk cafés, restaurants etc., and as you go into the city from the beach, there are antique shops, tree-lined streets, art galleries and cinemas.

Ipanema is narrower and less crowded than Copacabana. The area is noted for its HIPPIE MARKET (MERCADO HIPPIE) which takes place every Sunday in the Praca General Osorio; it's the local version of a flea-market, and on sale here is everything from copper wall plates to blowpipes. Otherwise, Ipanema is an area of good hotels and restaurants, but it's primarily residential.

ACCOMMODATION

• **First Class:** (double over US$100)
Hotel Inter-Continental Rio – Avenida Prefeito Mendes de Morais, Praia de Gavea 222, Rio de Janeiro (tel. 322-2200). A very luxurious hotel where the rooms' balconies face either the ocean or the hotel grounds, which contain tennis courts and a double pool (there's a bar in between). Located close to downtown, the hotel has a courtesy coach service to the various beaches nearby. Facilities include excellent restaurants, snack bars and lounges, as well as in-house shops, beauty salons and a range of entertainment in the evenings.

Rio Sheraton – Avenida Niemeyer 121, Rio de Janeiro (tel. 274-1122). Attractively located on a private beach available exclusively to guests, first-rate facilities here include tennis courts, a health club, saunas, shops, boutiques, 2 swimming pools, fine restaurants and intimate bars. The service is excellent, and the rooms luxurious, many with splendid views of Ipanema.

Hotel Meridien Copacabana – Avenida Atlantica 1020, Copacabana (tel. 275-9922). Stylish hotel which is noted particularly for Le St Honore, a rooftop restaurant which serves classic French cuisine and offers panoramic views of the surrounding area. Otherwise everything is luxurious: facilities include a swimming pool, sundeck, comfortable bars and a quaint French-style café on the main floor.

• **Super Club Class:** (double US$50–US$70)
Trocadero – Avenida Atlantica 2064, Copacabana (tel. 257-1834). Conveniently located next to the Copacabana beach strip, this hotel has excellent facilities, good service, and is noted for its Bahian restaurant The Moenda – one of Rio's finest.

Sol Ipanema – Avenida Viera Souto 320, Ipanema (tel. 227-0060). As well as a swimming pool and roof solarium, guests here can enjoy excellent facilities amid typical Brazilian decor.

Bandeirantes – Rua Barata Ribeiro 548, Copacabana (tel. 255-6252). Situated in a quiet, pleasant neighbourhood with antique stores and various small restaurants, this hotel offers very good hospitality and excellent facilities.

Debret – Rua Almirante Goncalves, Copacabana (tel. 255-9992). Besides its good facilities and service, this hotel is noted for its tasteful decor: the lobby alone is filled with excellent sculpture and paintings. It's also conveniently located close to the sidewalk cafés and lively nightlife of Avenida Atlantica.

• **Economy:** (double under US$40)
Canada – Avenida Copacabana 67, Copacabana (tel. 257-1864). In the Copacabana Beach area, this hotel is clean with adequate facilities, although nothing luxurious.

Florida – Rua Ferreira Viani 81, Flamengo (tel. 245-8160). Located in the Flamengo section of town, this place is comfortable and well looked after by the staff.

Novo Mundo – Praia do Flamengo 20, Flamengo (tel. 225-7366). Also in the Flamengo section of the city, this hotel is clean, and noted for its outstanding views of Guanabara Bay and Pao de Acucar.

Vermont – Rua Visconde Piraja 254, Ipanema (tel. 247-6100). On the Main Street of Ipanema, this hotel's somewhat at the upper end of the economy range, but its clean, comfortable rooms and good facilities are worth it.

Guanabara Palace – Avenida Presidente Vargas 392, Rio de Janeiro (tel. 253-8622). Situated in Rio's banking district, this hotel's facilities include a restaurant and bar.

Argentina – Rua Cruz Lima 30, Rio de Janeiro (tel. 255-7233). Conveniently located downtown and near to sights.

DINING OUT

Eating out is very popular among Brazilians themselves, and the restaurant scene in Rio flourishes accordingly. There are as many different international restaurants as there are establishments serving typical Brazilian food – Chinese, German, French, English and Italian among them. Places with traditional Brazilian menus are well worth trying, and some of the national dishes are highly recommended: among the best is 'feijoada' – consisting of black beans and rice (feijoada completa is the Saturday version and includes sausage and pork), 'siri' is a spicy stuffed crab dish, 'frango con arroz' is the local version of chicken and rice, and 'vatapa' consists of shrimp or fish served in coconut milk. Some of the local drinks worth sampling are a 'batida' (a cocktail made with a strong cane liquor), and 'guarana', the national soft drink made with the seeds of an Amazonian fruit.

Most restaurants in Rio serve lunch from noon till 3 p.m., and dinner is usually served after 9 p.m. A cover charge is common in many establishments, and covers a side dish of bread, butter, quail eggs and a cold vegetable platter. Most places are often crowded, so reserving in advance is a good idea.

● **First Class:** (US$50–US$70 for two)
Castelo da Lagoa – Avenida Epitacio Passoa 1560, Lagoa (tel. 287-3514). This very elegant restaurant is set in a private home overlooking a lagoon. The decor is stylish and the atmosphere intimate. The menu is mainly French, and includes excellent duck dishes among other delicacies. Live organ music adds an extra French flavour.

Moenda – Avenida Atlantica 2064, Copacabana (tel. 257-1834). For typical Brazilian food, this is one of the restaurants in Rio most worth trying. It's on the second floor of the Hotel Trocadero overlooking Copacabana Beach, and the menu offers some of the best in Bahian cuisine. The decor is tasteful, and the staff are friendly and delighted to explain the different dishes. There's live music on weekends.

La Tour – Rua Santa Luzia 651, Rio de Janeiro (tel. 242-3221 or 242-2221). The setting of this restaurant is what makes it one of Rio's most popular. Near the top of an office building, it revolves once every hour, and views range from the Christ the Redeemer statue to the downtown skyline. The menu includes dishes from Italy, Germany and France on a wide and varied scale – all are excellent.

• **Super Club Class:** (US$35–US$50 for two)

New Mandarin – Rua Carlos Gois 344, Leblon (tel. 247-6574). One of the best places in the city for Chinese food. A converted private home, the atmosphere in each of the 3 small dining rooms here is quiet and intimate. Open until midnight.

O Pirata – Rua Carlos Gois 83, Leblon (tel. 267-5365). Excellent Italian dishes served by waiters clad as pirates. The decor is of a nautical nature, and the atmosphere generally relaxed. Guests are able to choose hors d'oeuvres from an antipasto/salad bar before the main course from an extensive choice of pasta dishes.

Lucas – Avenida Atlantica 3744, Copacabana (tel. 247-1606). Traditional German food served both indoors and on an outdoor terrace covered by a roof. Dangling wine bottles and sausages make for a relaxed atmosphere outdoors, and included on an interesting and extensive menu is 'Weiner Schnitzel' – a breaded and fried veal cutlet – which comes highly recommended.

• **Economy:** (under US$25 for two)

Garota de Ipanema – Rua Montenegro 39, Ipanema. An attractive sidewalk café around the beach area, where the food is good, and the benign weather makes eating here a pleasant experience. It's the place where the hit song 'The Girl From Ipanema' was composed.

Oriento – Rua Bolivar 64, Copacabana (tel. 257-8765). Good value Chinese food served amid appropriate decor. Huge portions.

Akasaka – Avenida Copacabana 1391, Copacabana (tel. 287-3211). One of the best Japanese restaurants in Rio, the atmosphere here is intimate and the food excellent. Some dishes are cooked at your table on small stoves.

Helsingor – Rua General San Martin 983, Ipanema (tel. 294-0347). Charming Danish place which specializes in sandwiches, the choice of which is enormous.

NIGHTLIFE

Rio's world-renowned after-dark entertainment scene caters for virtually every taste, and from quiet piano bars and English pubs to

German beer halls and erotic cabaret shows, nothing is unavailable. Because Brazilians eat dinner after 9 p.m., most places come alive around midnight and keep going almost all night. Nightclubs with shows usually charge a cover of something around US$10; dress for most places is informal. Brazilian nightclubs as a rule only admit couples – but this has changed a little in recent years, and some admit either single men or women, especially if they are tourists.

Cinelandia is the centre of entertainment downtown and its main street, Rua Senador Dantas, is several blocks long.

• Nightclubs:

Caneao – Avenida Venceslau Braz 215, Botafogo (tel. 295-3044). With a capacity of 2000, this is regarded as one of Rio's top nightclubs, and frequently hosts shows by big-name Brazilian and international entertainers. It's also a lively dancing spot. There's a cover charge at weekends, when reservations are recommended.

Bierklause – Rua Ronald de Carvalho 55, Copacabana (tel. 235-7727). Popular Bavarian beer hall which offers German food, beer and music on one floor, and on the other level is another club featuring samba shows. There's a cover charge on both levels.

A Desgarrada – Rua Barao da Torre 667, Ipanema (tel. 287-8846). A romantic, dimly-lit Portuguese restaurant and nightclub which features quiet guitar music to which guests can dance.

Oba Oba's – Rua Visconde de Piraja 499, Ipanema (tel. 227-1289). On the entertainments bill here is the famous show featuring the celebrated mulatto showgirls in skimpy outfits as well as samba dancers.

EXCURSIONS

HUNCHBACK MOUNTAIN (CORCOVADO) is one of Rio's most famous attractions. This is the mountain on which stands the statue of Christ the Redeemer, 120 feet in height; the mountain itself is around 2400 feet high. A steep climb to the statue is well worth enduring for the stunning view of the beach areas, Guanabara Bay and Sugar Mountain. The statue can also be reached by riding on an open-sided cog railroad leaving from Cosme Velho station. The mountain itself has other attractions besides the statue. There is a road up the mountain, and along the route are several good look-out points and picnic spots. There's also Largo do Boticario, a collection of colonial houses.

TIJUCA FOREST (FLORESTA DE TIJUCA) is a short drive from downtown Rio, and is a tropical forest full of trees and interesting plant life. Visitors can wander along paths through the woods, small waterfalls and other natural delights that include a 3000-foot-high mountain – Pico de Tijuca. There are several ideal spots for a picnic in the forest, and generally, the environment provides the perfect escape from the bustle of the city.

PAQUETA ISLAND (ILHA PAQUETA) is a small island in Guanabara Bay, and a trip here provides the opportunity to take a pleasant boat journey through the Bay, to see Rio from a different angle and to explore what is an attractive place. Once the summer residence of the imperial Brazilian family, the island's population of something over 5000 consists mainly of fishermen, and any activity to do with the sea is a favourite pastime of the locals. No cars are allowed on the island, and the methods of transport available to tourists are rented bicycles or horse-drawn carriages; once there, visitors can enjoy good beaches, and some first-rate seafood restaurants among many other things.

SANTA TERESA is in the suburbs of Rio de Janeiro, and is a very beautiful area which reflects what the city looked like in its colonial days. Narrow, tree-lined streets contain houses that were built in the 19th century – all in stark contrast to the architecture of modern Rio. There's also a trolley service in operation in this area – Rio's last.

Peru

RED TAPE

• **Passport/Visa Requirements:** For entry to Peru, a visa is required by nationals of all countries *except*: Argentina, Austria, Belgium, Bolivia, Brazil, Canada, Colombia, Denmark, Ecuador, Finland, France, West Germany, Greece, Italy, Japan, Liechtenstein, Luxembourg, Netherlands, Norway, Spain, Sweden, Switzerland,

United Kingdom (including Jersey and Guernsey), Uruguay and the USA, for a stay of up to 90 days. Nationals of Portugal do not require a visa for a stay of up to 60 days.

CUSTOMS

● **Duty Free:** Visitors can take into Peru 400 cigarettes or 50 cigars or 50g of tobacco, and 2 kg of food free of duty. Also items for personal use or gifts up to a value of US$200. There is no limit to the amount of foreign currency which can be taken into or out of Peru, but a maximum of 5000 Peruvian soles may be taken in or out.

Liable to duty: samples of commercial value can be imported temporarily for 6 months on payment of a cash deposit or bond guarantee; if the samples are re-exported within 6 months, the deposit is returned or the bond cancelled.

NB: Radios, record players and tape recorders may be confiscated if any attempt is made to import them.

HEALTH

An International Certificate of Vaccination against smallpox is required for entry into Peru.

CAPITAL – Lima. Population – 3,900,000.

POPULATION – 16,900,000 approx.

LANGUAGE – Spanish is the official language of the country, Quechua is the second official language.

CURRENCY – Sol, divided into 100 centavos. Notes – 5, 10, 50, 100, 200, 500 and 1000 soles; coins – 5, 10, 20, 25, 50 centavos; and 1, 5 and 10 soles.
£1 = 14; US$1 = 10.

BANKING HOURS – From January–March, 0800–1130, Monday–Friday; April–December, 0915–1245, Monday–Friday.

POLITICAL SYSTEM – Military junta.

RELIGION – Roman Catholic.

PUBLIC HOLIDAYS

January 1	New Year's Day
March/April	Maundy Thursday, Good Friday
May 1	Labour Day
June 29	SS Peter and Paul
July 28, 29	Independence Days
August 30	Santa Rosa de Lima
October 9	National Dignity Day
November 1	All Saints' Day
December 8	Immaculate Conception
December 25	Christmas Day

CLIMATE – In Peru's coastal regions, the climate is fairly cool from June to November – there is virtually no rain during this period, but humidity is high and there is little sunshine. The eastern Sierra region has heavy rains between October and April, and temperatures here vary considerably between night and day. The Montana region, east of the Sierra, and the Selva – a jungle area of the Amazonian basin – both have tropical climates.

TIME DIFFERENCE – GMT – 5 hours.

COMMUNICATIONS

• **Telephone:** The internal telephone system in Peru is adequate, and public telephones are available in the street as well as in shops, railway stations, and other public places. There are 3 different kinds of telephone boxes, and each accepts a different size and weight of soles. Local calls cost 5 soles, except for a cheap rate on Sunday when they cost 4.

• **Post:** The internal postal services in Peru are unreliable, and deliveries can be erratic and subject to delays; for this reason, it's a good idea to use a private delivery service, many of which exist in the larger cities; these are efficient, but they only operate within a particular city, and are prohibited from undertaking inter-city deliveries. In Lima, the main Post Office is on Jiron Junin, west of the Plaza de Armas.

ELECTRICITY – Lima: 220v AC, 60 Hz. Arequipa: 220v AC, 50 Hz. Iquitos: 110v AC.

OFFICE/SHOPPING HOURS – Government offices are open to the public: January–March, 0930–1130 Monday–Saturday; April–December, 0930–1100, 1500–1700 Monday–Friday, 0930–1130 Saturday. Shops are open: January–March, 0830–1130, 1500–1830 Monday–Friday; April–December, 0830–1230, 1500–1830 Monday–Friday.

• **Best Buys:** Among the souvenirs to be bought around Peru are a wide range of silver and gold handicrafts, as well as jewellery often produced in pre-Columbian designs. Also available are various Indian hand-spun and hand-woven textiles, and manufactured textiles in Indian designs. Worth looking out for, too, are the various fine leather products – many unique to Peru – and llama and alpaca wool products, which include ponchos, sweaters, slippers, blankets, hats and rugs.

INTERNAL TRAVEL

• **Air:** Domestic air travel in Peru is quite comprehensive: Aeroperu and the Compania de Aviacion Faucett are the principal operators, and services are available in and out of Andahuaylas, Anta, Arequipa, Ayacucho, Bellavista, Cajamarca, Chiclayo, Chimbote, Cuzco, Huanuco, Iquitos, Juanjui, Juliaca, Moyobamba, Piura, Pucallpa, Puerto Maldonado, Rioja, Tacna, Talara, Tarapoto, Tingo Maria, Trujillo, Tumbes, and Yurimaguas. In comparison with other countries, domestic air travel in Peru is relatively inexpensive. It's worth noting that Aeroperu and the Compania de Aviacion Faucett are notorious for overbooking their flights – it's a good idea, therefore, to re-confirm your flight 24 hours in advance.

• **Rail:** The Central and Southern Railway operates into inland Peru from the coast. There is a service from Lima to Oroya, with connections available to Cerro de Pasco in the north and Huancayo in the south. Arequipa and Puno in the south are linked by rail, and a connection is available to Cuzco via Juliaca. Beware of pickpockets at railway stations.

• **Road:** The major road in Peru is the Pan-American highway which runs north from Lima along the coast to Ecuador, and south to Arequipa and Chile. Otherwise, very few roads in the country are paved. Regular daily bus services are available from Lima to the major coastal towns as well as to many places inland.

Taxis are widely available all over Peru, and it's a good idea to agree on a fare in advance. Also available are 'colectivos' – vehicles which will take you almost anywhere in the country; they can be booked in advance and a pick-up point arranged.

Car hire companies operate in all the major cities (chauffeur-driven cars are also for hire); an International Driving Licence is required, and traffic travels on the right-hand side of the road.

MAJOR SIGHTS OF THE COUNTRY

One of Peru's most celebrated attractions for visitors is the railway journey on 'EL TREN DE LA SIERRA' from Lima north into the mountains of the Andes. This unforgettable trip takes passengers through 65 tunnels, over 61 bridges and climbs a mountain pass around 4800m above sea level – prompting a bout of altitude sickness for many (a guard supplies bags of air). The journey provides an excellent opportunity to view the mountain world of the old Inca tribes – impressive both in beauty and character – and travelling through places such as the awe-inspiring Javja Valley, striped with coloured furls of mountain, is simply breathtaking.

The train journey takes passengers to the town of HUANCAYO in the central Andes, an important market centre which is well worth spending some time in. The town has a very unique flavour – it was here that the native Huanca tribe fought with the Incas back in the 15th century, and a cultural legacy from those days has resulted in colourful costumes and traditional dances. Huancayo's own particular history is well represented around the town.

High in the Andes mountains, and linked to civilization by train, is the lost city of MACHU PICCHU. Although its location was given in various records for many years, Machu Picchu remained a 'lost city' until 1911, when it was rediscovered by an American professor, and since then it has been proclaimed 'The Lost City of the Incas'. Thousands of feet above sea level and on top of one of the highest peaks in the Andes, a visit here not only presents an opportunity to sample the Inca-controlled Peru of centuries ago, but the scenery surrounding the city provides some of the most stunning sights in the world.

In the southern part of Peru, on the border with Bolivia, is LAKE TITICACA. Covering an area of 3200 square miles, it is the highest navigable waterway in the world, some 12,500 feet above sea level. A fascinating feature of the lake is the resident Urus tribe, who live on thick carpets of reed scattered on the surface; a visit to these floating islands is highly recommended, not just for their spectacle value, but also to examine the lifestyle and culture of the Urus tribe, one of the oldest in the country.

TRUJILLO, Peru's second largest city with a population of 400,000, is in the northern part of the country, set against the brown foothills of the Andes. The city has a character reminiscent of colonial times – old churches, monasteries and homes are much in evidence around the city squares and streets. There are a number of interesting places to visit in the city, among them the Archaeological Museum (Calle Bolivar 446) which is noted for its exhibits of Chimu and Mochica pottery, and the 18th-century house inhabited by General Iturregui when he pronounced Trujillo's freedom from Spain in 1820.

CHAN-CHAN, the imperial city of the Chimu civilization, is a short drive from Trujillo and though today a crumbling ruin, its citadels and sacred enclosures provide a fascinating insight into the culture and traditions of the Chimus as they were centuries ago – for example, a burial mound was excavated recently revealing the skeletons of 13 young girls who'd sacrificed their lives to be buried alongside a Chimu king.

The third largest city in Peru in the country's south is AREQUIPA. At the foot of El Misti volcano, the city is known for the fact that its Spanish-style buildings and old churches are made from sillar, a pearl-white volcanic substance. The city grew with the Incas, and among its points of interest is the Santa Catalina Convent; almost a city within a city, it was opened in 1970, covers an area of 2 hectares and is filled with various interesting furniture, paintings etc.

HOTELS

To meet the demands of an increasing number of tourists, hotels of every type and price have been springing up in all of Peru's major cities within the last few years. The standard varies widely, and while the more expensive places offer all the comforts that might be expected, cheaper hotels can sometimes be rather too basic, often with erratic water supplies.

The price per night for two people in an expensive city hotel can be as much as US$80, while a good economy hotel will charge around US$20 for the same. Several large international chains have hotels in Peru – Sheraton and Hilton among them.

Hostels are another aspect of travel accommodation that has experienced a growth in line with that of the country's tourist trade. There is a range of hostels available – most are cheap, and the facilities and conditions depend on just how cheap they are. To stay in most youth hostels subscribing to the Youth Hostel Association a membership card is needed, but there are many hostels, especially in the major cities, which are open to all ages where only payment is required.

Camping is catered for in Peru, although compared to other countries where camping is popular, the facilities provided are usually rather basic.

A word of warning – tap water shouldn't be drunk untreated in many parts of the country; check with the local Tourist Office about the situation in any place you visit.

NIGHTLIFE AND RESTAURANTS

The major cities are where the nightlife in Peru is to be found. Lima is perhaps the liveliest of all, with a range of entertainments on offer to rival many places around the world. There are plenty of clubs, pubs and discos here, most of which are well frequented by both locals and tourists, especially on weekends. There are 2 main theatres in the city: the Teatro Municipal (at Jiron Ica 355) and the Teatro Segura (at Huancavelica 250) – both stage prestigious theatrical performances in Spanish. English-language theatre in Lima is provided by The Good Companions (tel. 41-99-50).

Very popular in Lima are displays of traditional Peruvian folklore; these are found in some of the larger hotels and theatres, and also in some bars and small nightclubs. They involve musical entertainment and dancing along traditional lines, complete with national costume in most cases.

Nightlife in other Peruvian cities has much the same things on offer, only on a different scale.

Food is very important to Peruvians, and this fact is reflected in the restaurant scene in most cities. Many have a wide selection of international restaurants – certainly Lima – and the cuisine of most countries is available wherever you go. Native Peruvian establishments are plentiful in all cities, large or small. The national cuisine, criolla, is a combination of Spanish and Indian cooking, and basic ingredients consist of native spices and vegetables. Restaurants vary in quality and atmosphere; some of the larger hotels in any city house excellent restaurants serving both local and international dishes; otherwise, an expensive city restaurant will charge around US$50 for two people, while cheaper places will charge anything under US$20 for two. A 10 per cent service charge is included in the bill in all establishments, and a 5–10 per cent tip is customary.

Lima

JORGE CHAVEZ INTERNATIONAL AIRPORT

Lima's Jorge Chavez International Airport is 10 miles north-west of the city; it handles all flights to and from the area, both domestic and international. It has 1 terminal.

AIRPORT FACILITIES

Information Desk	Located within the terminal, offering both flight and tourist information.
Bank/Foreign Exchange	A bank offering all services including currency exchange is located in the terminal.
Hotel Reservations Service	Available in the terminal.
Insurance Facilities	Available in the terminal.
Bar	There is a bar in the terminal.
Restaurant/Buffet	Both are available in the terminal.
Post Office	All postal services are available in the terminal.
Baggage Deposit	Available in the terminal.
Nursery	Nursery facilities are available.
Shops	Several shops are located around the terminal selling flowers, confectionery, books, gifts and toys.
Duty Free	There is a duty free shop selling tobacco, wines, aperitifs, spirits, liqueurs, watches, lighters, cameras, radios, jewellery, electrical goods, glass and china. Cigarettes are not sold.
Vaccination Centre	This is located within the terminal (an International Certificate of Vaccination against smallpox is required for entry into Peru).
Toilets	These are located all around the terminal building.
Car Rental Desks	Avis, Hertz, Budget, Europcar, Nova and Safari all have counters in the terminal.
Public Telephones	These are located all over the airport.

AIRPORT INFORMATION

Check-in Times	Average for all airlines: International – 60 minutes; Domestic – 45 minutes.
Airport Tax	US$10.
International–Domestic Transfers	International–domestic takes 60 minutes. Domestic–international takes 60 minutes.

CITY LINKS

• **Bus:** An airport bus service to the city runs every 15 minutes round the clock. The journey takes 60 minutes, and the fare is 77 soles. Return from Camana, Block 8.

• **Taxi:** Taxis are easily available at the airport (ticket touts are everywhere), and a usual fare to the city is around 1700 soles.

• **Coach:** There is a coach service every 5 minutes to the city; it takes 30 minutes and the fare is 90 soles. Return pick-ups at Le Paris movie stop, La Colmena Avenue, Block 7, and the Hotel Crillon.

Colectivos also operate between the airport and the city. They are quite cheap, and are easily available.

LIMA

First established by Spanish conquistador Francisco Pizarro as the 'City of Kings', Lima was the capital of Spain's South American empire right up until it gained independence at the start of the 19th century. The name of Lima was given to the city quite by accident – it was situated along a river and valley which the Indians knew as 'Rimac'; this was understood by the Spanish as 'Limac', and subsequently shortened to Lima.

Today Lima is very much the political and cultural focus of Peru; from government and industry to education and the media, everything is centralized here – a fact that has prompted a population boom in the capital (4½ million live here today compared with 500,000 in 1940).

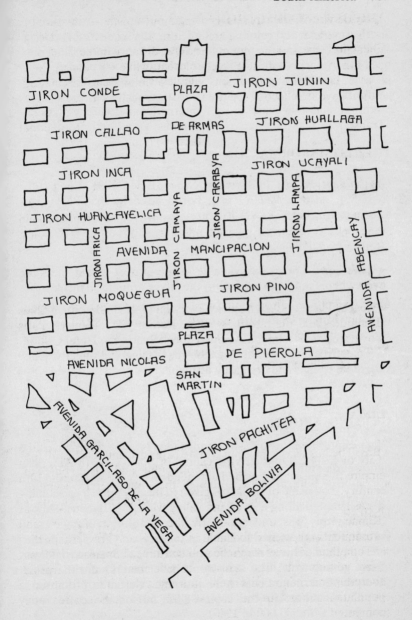

For the visitor, the city has its own unique appeal. A mixture of South American and colonial architecture, the scenic resorts along the Pacific coast and the mountains in the distance make Lima one of South America's most attractive cities, while its people, their lifestyle, customs and traditions give it a unique and fascinating cultural flavour reflecting the area's past as much as its present.

TOURIST INFORMATION

Government Tourist Information Office, Belen 1066, Lima (tel. 32-35-59). Also: *ENTUR Peru*, Portal de Zela 965, Plaza San Martin (tel. 27-40-77).

ADDRESSES

Main Post Office – Jiron Junin (west of the Plaza de Armas). Open Monday–Friday, 0800–1915, Saturday and Sunday 0800–1200.
Amex – Lima Tours, Belen 1040 (tel. 27-66-24).
British Vice-Consulate – Saenz Pena 154, PSNC, Calle Independencia 150 (Casilla 368) (tel. 29-90-40).

GETTING ABOUT

• **Bus:** The bus service in Lima is quite extensive and reaches all the major parts of the city. There are both public and private buses in operation – both are OK, although the public service is more extensive. A standard bus fare for a trip within the city limits is US$0.10.

• **Taxi:** Taxis are widely available in the city, and are perhaps the safest method of travel for those who don't speak Spanish (in terms of not getting lost). The taxis don't have meters, and the price should be determined before the journey. A usual fare is around US$0.50 for a short trip, and around US$1.50 from the centre to the suburbs.

• **Car Hire:** Firms operate in all the major hotels and at various points around the city. International firms include Avis, Hertz, Budget and National. Car rental can be expensive in Lima. Colectivos also operate in Lima along much the same lines as taxis; they can be reserved in advance (pick-up points can be arranged), and will take you anywhere in the country, as well as on short trips around town.

SIGHTS

An ideal place to begin sightseeing in Lima is at the PLAZA DE ARMAS, its main square. In the heart of the city, its sights include the PRESIDENTIAL PALACE, the ARCHBISHOP'S PALACE, and city hall. A good time to arrive here is at 1 p.m., when it's possible to view the changing of the presidential guard. THE CATHEDRAL (CATEDRAL) is also here; it dates back to the mid-18th century, and its architecture is interesting, as are its carved choir stalls (a gift of Charles V to Peru), and the remains of Pizarro, the planner of the Plaza de Armas, which are kept in a glass case.

There are a number of interesting colonial churches within walking distance of the Plaza de Armas, among them the CHURCH AND MONASTERY OF SANTO DOMINGO (IGLESIA Y MONASTERIO DE SANTO DOMINGO), at Jiron Camana 170, Plazuela Santo Domingo; this was built in 1549, and today belongs to the Dominican friars. Its architecture is typically colonial, and the building is also interesting as the site of the founding of South America's oldest university, San Marcos, in 1551. Also near the Plaza de Armas at Jiron Ica 225 is the CHURCH OF SAN AGUSTIN (IGLESIA DE SAN AGUSTIN) – noted especially for its finely carved stone facade, it is a beautiful building. Other churches in Lima worth a visit both for their beauty and historical significance are the CHURCH OF SAN PEDRO (IGLESIA DE SAN PEDRO) at Jiron Ucayali 300, the CHURCH AND MONASTERY OF ST FRANCIS (IGLESIA Y MONASTERIO DE SAN FRANCISCO) at Jiron Ancash 300 and the CHURCH OF LA MERCED (IGLESIA DE LA MERCED) at Jiron Ica 621.

THE ACHO BULLRING (PLAZA DE TOROS DE ACHO) in the Plaza de Acho north of Balta Bridge, is an unmissable attraction in Lima, not just for its status as focal point for the intense national passion for bullfighting. It was built in the mid-18th century and restored in 1945 – today it still has its original facade, preserved and protected. The bullfighting season takes place during October and November, and big names from around the world come to fight here, on Sundays and holidays during these months.

At the Palacio de Gobierno in the district of Rimac is the PROMENADE OF THE BAREFOOT FRIARS (LA ALAMEDA DE LOS DESCALZOS). This was inaugurated at the start of the 17th century by the viceroy, Marquis de Montesclaro, and was a fashionable spot of that period – elegantly attired upper-class ladies and eligible gentlemen used to come here to meet. This is also the location of the LOS DESCALZOS church which is run by Carmelite friars; the monastery is closed to visitors, but its typical 17th-century beauty can be sampled from the outside.

There are several museums worth looking out for around Lima. One is the MUSEUM OF ANTHROPOLOGY (MUSEO DE ANTROPOLOGIA Y ARQUEOLOGIA), at the Plaza Bolivar in Pueblo Libre, which houses various exhibitions and displays including rare weavings, pottery and mummies, as well as tapestries from Paracas and Nazca. Similar displays can be found at the MUSEUM OF ART (MUSEO DE ARTE) at Paseo Colon 125, where Peru's culture through the pre-Inca, Inca, colonial and republican periods is illuminated with the help of a wide range of exhibits. The MUSEUM OF THE INQUISITION (MUSEO DE LA INQUISICION) at Jiron Junin 548 (Plaza Bolivar), once the base of torture and various grisly goings on during the 19th century, houses one of the best collections of wood carvings in the city. It's also possible to visit prisoners' galleries and cells. The LARCO HERRERA ARCHAEOLOGICAL MUSEUM (MUSEO ARQUEOLOGICO LARCO HERRERA) at the Avenida Bolivar 1515 houses the famous Larco Herrera collection of pottery which reflects an era of Peruvian culture (called the 'fluorescent era') from AD 200 to 600. The ceramics on show are mainly from cultures on Peru's northern coast. One other museum in Lima worth taking in is the GOLD MUSEUM (MUSEO DEL ORO) at the Avenida Alonso de Molina 1100, Monterrico, which houses some 7000 pieces of worked gold, such as cups, images and ceremonial objects.

An area of Lima where it's a good idea to take a stroll is CHINATOWN (BARRION CHINO). Though not as exotic as it once was, this area around the Plaza de Armas still has its Oriental charms, including some excellent restaurants.

ACCOMMODATION

• **First Class:** (double US$50–US$80)
Lima Sheraton Hotel and Towers – Paseo de la Republica 170, Lima (tel. 32-86-76 & 32-90-50). The Sheraton Towers is located atop the Lima Sheraton Hotel, and offers luxurious extra facilities such as a private breakfast/cocktail lounge exclusive to guests. The rooms in the Towers are superb, and suites are also available. The Lima Sheraton Hotel is itself a first-class establishment, and its excellent facilities include an outdoor heated pool, a sauna, tennis courts, 24-hour room service, a coffee shop, and 2 fine restaurants and cocktail lounges with live entertainment. It's also conveniently located downtown and near to sights.

Hotel Crillon – Avenida Nicolas de Pierola 589, Lima (tel. 28-32-90). In the heart of Lima, the rooms and suites of this 22-storey hotel are all comfortable and air-conditioned. It's noted for its roof-garden restaurant which serves both Peruvian and international cuisine, and the top floor 'Sky Room' offers both live entertainment in the evenings as well as a superb view of the city and surrounds.

Gran Hotel Bolivar – Plaza San Martin, Lima (tel. 27-64-00). Conveniently located in the central Plaza San Martin, this place has a strong British influence, evidence of which is the afternoon tea served in the glass-domed rotunda every day. Facilities include an excellent bar and a fine restaurant which is noted for its excellent native dishes.

• **Super Club Class:** (double US$30–US$50)
Hostal Miraflores – Avenida Petit Thouars 5444, Miraflores (tel. 45-87-45). Located close to the centre of Miraflores, the rooms here are very comfortable, and include a bath and telephone. There is an excellent in-house cafeteria, and the service is very good.

El Plaza – Avenida Nicolas de Pierola 850, Lima. Close to the Plaza San Martin, this small establishment offers comfortable rooms and excellent hospitality. Facilities include an intimate cocktail lounge and good restaurant. All rooms are air-conditioned.

Hostal Barranco – Malecon Osma 104, Barranco (tel. 67-17-53). 10 minutes from the centre of Lima, this converted mansion overlooks the ocean and includes among its facilities a swimming pool, sauna, dining room, piano bar and fitness room. The atmosphere here is very relaxed.

• **Economy:** (double under US$30)

Hostal Polonia – Avenida Republica de Panama 6599, Miraflores (tel. 45-65-90). Modern, well furnished hotel, which has a good restaurant.

Hostal San Francisco – Jiron Ancash 340, Lima (tel. 28-36-43). Centrally located, this hotel is at the cheaper end of the economy range. It's clean, and facilities are adequate.

Hostal San Sebastian – Jiron Ica 712, Lima (tel. 23-27-40). Clean and comfortable with friendly staff who speak English. There is a restaurant, and laundry facilities are available. Can be a bit noisy, however.

Residencial Beech – Los Libertadores 165, San Isidro (tel. 40-55-95). Rooms have baths, and breakfast is available. Located in San Isidro, one of Lima's most pleasant residential districts.

Pension San Antonio – Paseo de la Republica 5783, Miraflores (tel. 47-78-30). Clean and comfortable hotel, although guests must share a bathroom. Ask for hot water.

Katmandu – Avenida Grau 181, Miraflores (tel. 45-17-60). Price includes breakfast. This hotel is clean, and the staff are friendly. English is spoken.

DINING OUT

Where a choice of restaurants is concerned, Lima is probably the most cosmopolitan city in the whole of South America. Among the international cuisines to be found around the city are Chinese, French, Spanish, Italian, German, Arab, Argentinian, Mexican, Swiss, Jewish and Japanese, and there are also numerous vegetarian restaurants. Peruvian cuisine, called criolla, is a mixture of Spanish and Indian cooking and native spices and vegetables feature heavily in most dishes. There are innumerable criolla in Lima. Whatever their nationality, the restaurants in Lima vary considerably in their size, quality and atmosphere. Some of the best and expensive restaurants can be found in the more expensive hotels, while on the street establishments vary from the most elegant to the stall. Eating out is a popular pursuit among locals, so many establishments are often crowded and reserving in advance is advisable.

● **First Class:** (US$40–$50 for two)
Las Trece Monedas – Jiron Ancash 536, Lima (tel. 27-65-47). Very elegant mansion built in 1787 is home to what is one of Lima's finest Peruvian restaurants. The atmosphere is pleasant and the food superb; international dishes are served as well as criolla. All major credit cards are accepted. Reservations are necessary.

La Costa Verde – Barranquito Beach, Barranco (tel. 45-14-92). Recognized locally as Lima's best seafood restaurant, this place is right on the beach, and it's possible to eat at beach-side tables – as relaxing as it is romantic. Reservations are not necessary. Major credit cards are accepted.

Blue Moon – Pumacahua 2526, Lince (tel. 71-13-89). In the residential area of Lince, this restaurant serves excellent Italian dishes amid tasteful decor. The atmosphere is pleasant. Reservations are not necessary, and most major credit cards are accepted.

● **Super Club Class:** (US$25–$40 for two)
Chalet Suisse – Avenida Nicolas de Pierola 560, Lima (tel. 31-29-85). Superb Swiss and Viennese cuisine served amid appropriate decor. Reservations are advised, and most major credit cards are accepted.

Casa Vasca – Avenida Nicolas de Pierola 734 (tel. 23-66-90). Fine Basque restaurant serving different dishes; one not to be missed is the Peruvian speciality 'cebiche', which involves raw fish pickled in hot pepper and lemon juice. Reservations are advised, and most major credit cards are accepted.

Fidel – Jiron Salaverry 282, Magdalena (tel. 61-77-44). Very lively restaurant which serves typical Peruvian food and has live entertainment, which guests are encouraged to join in. Reservations are not usually needed, and credit cards are *not* accepted.

• **Economy:** (under US$20 for two)

Bircher Benner – Schell 598, Miraflores (tel. 47-71-18). Inside a quaint old house, this restaurant serves some of the best vegetarian food in the city, as well as fresh juices and herb teas. It's closed on Sundays; reservations are not necessary, and credit cards are *not* accepted.

Rosita Rios – Cajatambo 100, La Florida, Rimac (tel. 81-41-05). Good Peruvian restaurant which offers a wide variety of local dishes as well as live Peruvian music. Good atmosphere. It's closed on Mondays; reservations are advised, and credit cards are *not* accepted.

La Colina – Schell 727, Miraflores. Good value local dishes served in a relaxed atmosphere.

Latin Brothers – Avenida Jose Leal 1277-81, Lince (tel. 71-02-60). In the suburb of Lince, this is a rather basic establishment, where the speciality is communal dishes of seafood at the tables. There are salsa paintings on the walls, and live salsa music is often laid on.

NIGHTLIFE

The nightlife in Lima is very lively, and from loud discotheques to piano bars there is something for everyone. Prominent amid the city's nightlife are 'penas', where it's possible to enjoy some traditional folklore – which is mainly music from the Highlands – other music such as criolla, or typical sounds from the coastal regions. Going out to nightspots is not recommended for women on their own, especially into bars called cantinas. There are no singles bars in Lima.

• **Nightclubs:**

La Miel – Pardo 120, Miraflores (tel. 45-03-22). An elegant dinner/disco in Miraflores which is well worth taking in for its good food, lively disco atmosphere and general ambiance. It's also an excellent place to sample some traditional folklore.

Johann Sebastian Bar – Schell 369, Miraflores (tel. 46-52-53). A very elegant Tudor building in which to enjoy a quiet drink in a relaxing atmosphere, enhanced by taped classical music.

New Ed's Bar – Avenida Miguel Dasso 176, Lima (tel. 22-07-56). Comfortable surroundings in which guests can relax at tables or dance. Rock music is played.

Las Guitarras – Manuel Segura 295, Barranco. One of the area's better penas which has live criolla music. Ideal for sampling some traditional Peruvian entertainment.

EXCURSIONS

The towns of CHACLACAYO and CHOSICA, close to each other around 19 miles from Lima, provide a worthwhile day trip from the city – mostly for reasons of climate and character. Some 80 years ago, Chosica was the top holiday resort in winter for the people of Lima – a fact well reflected in the Victorian houses here. In time, it was taken over as the select resort by Chaclacayo, nearby, where the climate is even better due to its higher altitude. Today, Chosica counts among its attractions not only its climate, but a range of very charming architecture, including its central plaza surrounded by palm trees. Chaclacayo's points of interest include its traditional public market, typical of the mountain markets to be found around Peru.

PARK OF THE LEGENDS (PARQUE DE LAS LEYENDAS) at Avenida de la Marina in San Miguel, a suburb of Lima, is a relatively small zoological park, which offers a clear picture of the geography of the country through its various displays and exhibits, live and otherwise. The 3 principal geographical regions of Peru are represented: the desert coast, the Andes and the Amazon jungle.

The town of BARRANCO, 2 miles south of Miraflores, is a very beautiful place where the architecture and character are reminiscent of the Victorian era. A stroll around Barranco will take you past splendid old mansions, through quiet attractive parks with a charming range of trees and plantlife, and in the summer to a slightly cooler climate which is due to the ocean nearby.

LA HERRADURA BEACH, just south of the popular Costa Verde, is just as attractive, and less crowded than its more celebrated neighbour. The shape of the bay here is that of a horseshoe, and it's an ideal spot to practise water sports or simply to relax. Along the shore there are various food stalls and restaurants selling a range of local delicacies.

Please write to us and let us know if you have any tips or personal recommendations to make after your business trip or holiday round the world. We hope that you've found this guide a useful travelling companion.

Your opinions, whether praising or criticizing, are welcomed in order to make the *Round the World Air Guide* even better.

Thank you.

Please write to:

Katie Wood and George McDonald,
Fontana Paperbacks,
Collins Publishers,
8 Grafton Street,
London W1X 3LA.

or:

E. P. Dutton Inc.,
2 Park Avenue,
New York,
NY 10016,
USA.

Part Three

Appendix

Airline Two-Letter Codes

It is useful to know these two-letter codes as they are used extensively in time-tables, brochures and tickets to identify airlines. The list below is not complete but covers the main ones you are likely to encounter on an around the world journey.

Code	Airline
AA	American Airlines
AC	Air Canada
AF	Air France
AH	Air Algerie
AI	Air India
AM	Aermexico
AN	Ansett Airlines of Australia
AR	Aerolineas Argentinas
AY	Finnair
AZ	Alitalia
BA	British Airways
BD	British Midland Airways
BR	British Caledonian Airways
CI	China Airlines
CO	Continental Airlines, Inc.
CP	CP Air
CX	Cathay Pacific Airways
DL	Delta Air Lines
EA	Eastern Air Lines
EI	Aer Lingus (Irish)
FI	Flugfelag-Icelandair
FJ	Air Pacific
GA	Garuda Indonesian Airways
GE	Guernsey Airlines
GF	Gulf Air
GH	Ghana Airways
GJ	Ansett Airlines of South Australia
HA	Hawaiian Airlines
HB	Air Melanesie
HN	NLM – Dutch Airlines
IA	Iraqi Airways
IB	Iberia
IC	Indian Airways
IQ	Caribbean Airways
IS	Eagle Air
IT	Air Inter
JL	Japan Air Lines
JM	Air Jamaica
KE	Korean Airlines
KL	KLM – Royal Dutch Airlines
KM	Air Malta
KQ	Kenya Airways
KU	Kuwait Airways
LB	Lloyd Aero Boliviano
LG	Luxair – Luxembourg Airlines
LH	Lufthansa German Airlines
LV	LAV – Linea Aeropostal Venezolana
LY	El Al Israel Airlines
ME	Middle East Airlines/ Airliban
MH	Malaysian Ayrline System
MK	Air Mauritius
MS	Egyptair

MX	Mexicana de Aviacion	RJ	ALIA – Royal Jordanian
ND	Nordair		Airlines
NE	Executive Airlink	'RH	Air Afrique
NH	All Nippon Airways	SA	South African Airways
NI	American International	SK	SAS – Scandinavian
	Airways		Airlines
NU	Southwest Airlines		System
NW	Northwest Orient Airlines	SN	Sabena – Belgian World
NZ	Air New Zealand		Airlines
OA	Olympic Airways	SQ	Singapore Airlines
OS	Austrian Airlines	SR	Swissair
PA	Pan American World	SV	Saudi Arabian Airline
	Airways	TC	Air Tanzania Corp.
PC	FijiAir	TE	Air New Zealand –
PE	People Express Airlines		International
PH	Polynesian Airlines	TN	Trans-Australia Airline
PK	Pakistan International	TP	TAP Air Portugal
	Airlines	TW	TWA – Trans World
PL	Aeroperu		Airlines, Inc.
PR	Phillipine Airlines	UA	United Airlines
PV	Eastern Provincial Airways	UB	Burma Airways Corp.
PW	Pacific Western Airlines	UE	United Air Services
PZ	LAP – Lineas Aereas	UK	Air UK
	Paraguayas	UL	Air Lanka
QF	Quantas Airways	UP	Bahamasair
QZ	Zambia Airways	UT	UTA
RA	Royal Nepal Airlines	UZ	Air Resorts Airlines
RB	Syrian Arab Airlines	VT	Air Polynesie
RG	Varig, SA	WA	Western Airlines
RH	Air Zimbabwe	ZV	Air Midwest
RI	Eastern Airlines of	ZP	Virgin Air
	Australia		

Principal Airports Around the World

City Name	3 Letter Code	Name of Airport/s	Distance from City Centre	
			Miles	K/m
AFRICA				
Algiers	ALG	Houari Boumediene	12.5	20
Capetown	CPT	D F Malan	9	14
Casablanca	CAS	Mohamed V	19	30
Dar-es-Salaam	DAR	International	8	13
Djibouti	JIB	Djibouti	3	5
Durban	DUR	Louis Botha	12	19.5

City Name	3 Letter Code	Name of Airport/s	Distance from City Centre Miles	K/m
Freetown	FNA	Lungi Intl.	18	29
		Hastings	15	24
Harare	HRE	Harare	7.5	12
Johannesburg	JNB	Jan Smuts	15	24
Nairobi	NBO	Jomo Kenyatta	4.5	7
		Wilson	2	3
Tangier	TNG	Boukhalef Souahel	9	15

AMERICA

City Name	3 Letter Code	Name of Airport/s	Distance from City Centre Miles	K/m
Atlanta	ATL	William B Hartsfield	9	14.5
Barbados	BGI	Grantley Adams	11	18
Bermuda	BDA	Kindley Field	12	19
Boston	BOS	Logan Int.	2.3	3.6
Buenos Aires	BUE	Ezeiza	31.5	50
		Aeroparque Jorge Newbery	5	8
Chicago	CHI	O'Hare Intl.	21	35
		Midway	10.5	17
		Meigs Field	1	1.6
Cleveland	CLE	Cleveland Hopkins	12	19
Dallas/Fort Worth	DFW	Regional	17	17
		Love Field	6	10
Denver	DEN	Stapleton Intl.	6.5	10
Detroit	DTT	Metropolitan	20	32
		City Airport	5.5	9
Edmonton	YEG	International	17.5	28
		Municipal Airport	3	5
Halifax	YHZ	International	23	37
Houston	HOU	Intercontinental	20	32
		Hobby Airport	10	16
Kansas City	MKC	International	17	27
Las Vegas	LAS	McCarran Intl.	9	14.5
Los Angeles	LAX	International	15	24
		Burbank	21	34
Memphis	MEM	International	10	16
Mexico City	MEX	Benito Juarez Intl.	8	13
Miami	MIA	International	7	11
Minneapolis/St Paul	MSP	Minneapolis-St Paul Intl.	10	16
Montreal	YUL	Dorval	14.5	23.3
		Mirabel	33	53
Nassau	NAS	International	10	16
New Orleans	MSY	International	13	21

City Name	3 Letter Code	Name of Airport/s	Distance from City Centre Miles	K/m
New York	NYC	J F Kennedy Intl.	14	22.5
		La Guardia	8	13
		Newark	16	26
Ottawa	YOW	Uplands Intl.	11	17.5
Panama City	PTY	Omar Torrijos H.	17	27
Philadelphia	PHL	International	8	13
		North Philadelphia	12	19
Pittsburgh	PIT	Greater Pittsburgh	16	26.5
Quebec	YQB	Quebec	9	14.5
Rio de Janeiro	RIO	International	12.5	20
		Santos Dumont	1	1.6
St Louis	STL	Lambert Intl.	15	24
Salt Lake City	SLC	International	7	11
San Diego	SAN	Lindbergh Intl.	3	4.8
San Francisco	SFO	International	13	21
Seattle	SEA	Seattle/Tacoma Intl.	14	22
Toronto	YYZ	Lester B. Pearson Intl.	18	29
Vancouver	YVR	International	9	15
Washington	DC	Dulles Intl.	27	43
		National	5	8
Winnipeg	YWG	International	4	6.5

ASIA

Bangkok	BKK	International	15.5	25
Beijing	PEK	Capital	16	26
Bombay	BOM	Bombay	18	29
Calcutta	CCU	Calcutta	8	13
Colombo	CMB	Colombo Intl.	20	32.2
Delhi	DEL	Delhi	9	14
Hong Kong	HKG	Kai Tak	4.5	7.5
Karachi	KHI	Civil	12	19
Kuala Lumpur	KUL	Subang Intl.	14	22.5
Osaka	OSA	International	10	16
Singapore	SIN	Changi	12.4	20
		Seletar	12	19
Tokyo	TYO	Haneda	12	19
		Narta	40	65

AUSTRALASIA

Adelaide	ADL	Adelaide	5	8
Auckland	AKL	International (Mangere)	14	22.5
Brisbane	BNE	Brisbane Intl.	4	6.5
Canberra	CBR	Canberra	4	6.5
Honolulu	HNL	International	6	10

City Name	3 Letter Code	Name of Airport/s	Distance from City Centre Miles	K/m
Melbourne	MEL	Melbourne	13.5	21
		Essendon	7	11
Perth	PER	Perth	6	10
Sydney	SYD	Kingsford Smith (Mascot)	6.8	11
Wellington	WLG	International	5	8

EUROPE

Amsterdam	AMS	Amsterdam-Schiphol Intl.	9.3	15
Athens	ATH	Hellinikon	6	10
Belgrade	BEG	Belgrade	12	20
Berlin, West	BER	Tegel	5	8
Brussels	BRU	National	7.5	12
Copenhagen	CPH	Kastrup	6	10
Dusseldorf	DUS	Dusseldorf	5	8
Frankfurt	FRA	Frankfurt Intl.	6	10
Geneva	GVA	Geneva	2.5	4
Hamburg	HAM	Fuhlsbuttel	7.5	12
Helsinki	HEL	Helsinki-Vantas	12	19
Istanbul	IST	Yesilkov	15	24
Lisbon	LIS	Lisbon	4.5	7
London	LON	Heathrow	15	24
		Gatwick	27	43
		Stansted	34	55
Madrid	MAD	Barajas (Mad.)	10	16
Malta (Valletta)	MLA	Luga	3	5
Marseille	MRS	Marignana	18.6	30
Milan	MIL	F. Forlanini-Linate	6.25	10
Nice	NCE	Cote d'Azur	4	7
Oslo	OSL	Gardermoen	32	51
Paris	PAR	Orly	9	14
		Charles de Gaulle	14.5	23
Prague	PRG	Ruzyne	11	17
Rome	ROM	Leonardo da Vinci (Fiumicino)	22	35
Stockholm	STO	Arlanda	25	41
Vienna	VIE	Schwechat	11	18
Zurich	ZRH	Zurich	7.5	12

MIDDLE EAST

Abu Dhabi	AUH	Abu Dhabi Intl.	23	37
Bahrain	BAH	Muharraq	4	6.5
Beirut	BEY	International	10	16

City Name	3 Letter Code	Name of Airport/s	Distance from City Centre	
			Miles	K/m
Cairo	CAI	International	14	22.5
Dubai	DXB	Dubai	2.5	4
Jeddah	JED	King Abdulaziz Intl.	11	17.5
Jersualem	JRS	Atarot	5.6	9
Kuwait	KWI	International	10	16
Riyadh	RUH	King Khaled Intl.	22	35
Tel Aviv	TLV	Ben Gurion Intl.	12	19

Foreign Tourist Boards in the United Kingdom

Where there is no tourist office given, try the relevant embassy or consulate.

Algeria	6 Hyde Park Gate, London SW7	221 7800
Andorra	63 Westover Rd, London SW18 2RF	874 4806
Antigua	Antigua House, 15 Thayer St, London W1M 5DL	486 7073
Australia	4th Floor, Heathcoat House, 20 Savile Row, London W1X 1AE	434 4371
Austria	30 St George St, London W1R 9FA	629 0461
Bahamas	23 Old Bond St, London W1X 4PQ	629 5238
Barbados	263 Tottenham Court Rd, London W1 PA4	636 9448
Belgium	38 Dover St, London W1X 3RB	499 5379
Bermuda	9–10 Savile Row, London W1X 2BL	734 8813/4
British Virgin Islands	48 Albemarle St, London W1X 4AR	629 6355
Canada	Canada House, Trafalgar Sq, London SW15 5BJ	629 9492
Cayman Islands	Hambleton House, 176 Curzon St, London W1Y 7FE	493 5161
China	4 Glentworth St, London NW1	935 9427
Denmark	Sceptre House, 169/173 Regent St, London W1R 8PY	734 2637
Eastern Caribbean	10 Kensington Court, London	937 9522
Egypt	168 Piccadilly, London W1Y 9DE	493 5282
Finland	66/68 Haymarket, London SW1Y 4RF	839 4048
France	178 Piccadilly, London W1V 0AL	491 7622
West Germany	61 Conduit St, London W1R 0EN	734 2600
Gibraltar	Arundel Great Court, 179 The Strand, London WC2R 1EH	836 0777/8

Greece	195/7 Regent St, London W1R 8DL	734 5997
Hong Kong	125 Pall Mall, London SW1Y 5EA	930 4775
Iceland	73 Grosvenor St, London W1X 9DD	499 9971
India	7 Cork St, London W1X 2AB	437 3677/8
Indonesia	PO Box 4ZG, W1A 4ZG	629 0862
Israel	18 Great Marlborough St, London W1V 1AF	434 3651
Italy	1 Princes St, London W1A 7RA	408 1254
Jamaica	Jamaica House, 50 St James's St, London SW1A 1JT	493 3647
Japan	167 Regent St, London W1R 7FD	734 9638
Jordan	211 Regent St, London W1	437 9465
Kenya	13 New Burlington St, London W1X 1FF	839 4477/8
Korea	Vogue House, 1 Hanover Square, London W1R 9RD	408 1591
Luxembourg	36/37 Piccadilly, London W1V 9PA	434 2800
Macao	35 Piccadilly, London W1V 9PB	734 7282
Malawi	33 Grosvenor St, W1	491 4172/7
Malaysia	17 Curzon St, London W1Y 7FE	499 7388
Malta	Suite 207, College House, Wrightscane W8 5SH	938 1140
Mauritius	49 Conduit St, W1	434 4375
Mexico	7 Cork St, London W1X 1PB	734 1058
Morocco	174 Regent St, London W1R 6HB	437 0073/4
Netherlands	143 New Bond St, London W1Y 0QS	499 9367
New Zealand	New Zealand House, 80 Haymarket, London SW1Y 4QT	930 8422
Norway	20 Pall Mall, London SW1Y 5NE	839 6255
Philippines	199 Piccadilly, London W1	439 3481
Portugal	New Bond Street House, 1/5 New Bond St, London W1Y 0NP	493 3873
Seychelles	50 Conduit St, London W1A 4PE	439 9699
Singapore	33 Heddon St, London W1	437 0033
South Africa	Regency House, 1–4 Warwick St, London W1R 5WB	439 9661
Spain	57/58 St James's St, London SW1A 1LD	499 0901
Sri Lanka	52 High Holborn, London WC1V 6RB	405 1194
Sweden	3 Cork St, London W1X 1HA	437 5816
Switzerland	Swiss Centre, 1 New Coventry St, London W1V 8EE	734 1921
Tanzania	77 South Audley St, London W1Y 5TA	499 7727
Thailand	9 Stafford St, London W1X 3FE	499 7670
Trinidad & Tobago	20 Lower Regent St, London SW1 4PH	930 6566
Tunisia	7a Stafford St, London W1	499 2234
Turkey	1st Floor, 170/173 Piccadilly, London W1V 9DD	734 8681/2
Turks & Caicos Islands	48 Albemarle St, London W1X 4AR	629 6355
USA	22 Sackville St, London W1	439 7433
US Virgin Islands	25 Bedford Square, London WC1B 3HG	637 8481
Zambia	163 Piccadilly, London W1V 9DE	493 0848
Zimbabwe	Colette House, 52/55 Piccadilly, London W1V 9AA	629 3955

Foreign Tourist Offices in the United States

Australia	1270 Ave of the Americas, New York, NY 10020	489 7550
Austria	545 5th Ave, New York, NY 10017	697 1651
Bermuda	Rockefeller Center, 630 5th Ave, New York, NY 10111	397 7700
Brazil	551 5th Ave, New York, NY 10017	682 1055
British Virgin Islands	370 Lexington Ave, New York, NY 10017	696 0400
Caribbean	20 E 46th St, New York, NY 10017	682 0435
Chile	1 World Trade Center, Suite 5121, New York, NY 10048	
China	159 Lexington Ave, New York	725 4950
Colombia	140 E 57th St, New York, NY 10022	688 0151
Eastern Caribbean	220 E 42nd St, New York, NY 10017	986 9370
Ecuador	167 W 72nd St, New York, NY 10023	873 0600
Egypt	630 5th Ave, New York, NY 10111	246 6960
French Polynesia	200 E 42nd St, New York, NY 10017	757 1125
France	610 5th Ave, New York, NY 10020	757 1125
	Also covers the French West Indies.	
Gambia	19 E 47th St, New York, NY 10003	759 2323
West Germany	747 3rd Ave, New York, NY 10017	308 3300
Haiti	1270 Avenue of the Americas, New York, NY 10020	757 3517
Hong Kong	548 5th Ave, New York, NY 10036	947 5008
Iceland	75 Rockefeller Plaza, New York, NY 10019	582 2802
India	30 Rockefeller Plaza, New York, NY 10020	586 4901
Indonesia	5 E 68th St, New York, NY 10021	564 1939
Israel	350 5th Ave, New York, NY 10118	560 0650
Ivory Coast	c/o Air Afrique, 1350 Ave of the Americas, New York, NY 10019	
Jamaica	2 Dag Hammarskjold Plaza, New York	688 7650
Japan	45 Rockefeller Plaza, New York, NY 10020	757 5640
Kenya	15 E 21st St, New York, NY 10022	486 1300
Korea	460 Park Ave, New York, NY 10016	688 7543
Mexico	630 5th Ave, New York, NY 10020	265 4696
Morocco	521 5th Ave, New York, NY 10175	557 2520
New Zealand	630 5th Ave, New York, NY 10020	586 0060
Panama	630 5th Ave, New York, NY 10020	246 5841
Philippines	556 5th Ave, New York, NY 10036	575 7915
St Lucia	41 E 42nd St, New York, NY 10017	867 2950
St Vincent & the Grenadines	220 E 40th St, New York	986 9370
Senegal	200 Park Ave, New York, NY 10003	682 4695
South Africa	610 5th Ave, New York, NY 10020	245 3720
Spain	665 5th Ave, New York, NY 10022	759 8822

Sri Lanka	609 5th Ave, New York	935 0369
Switzerland	608 5th Ave, New York, NY 10020	757 5944
Tanzania	201 E 42nd St, New York, NY 10017	986 7124
Thailand	5 World Trade Center, New York, NY 10048	432 0433
Tunisia	630 5th Ave, Suite 863, New York, NY 10020	582 3670
Turkey	821 United Nations Plaza, New York, NY 10017	687 2194
Uganda	801 2nd Ave, New York	
United Kingdom	680 5th Ave, New York, NY 10019	
USSR	45 E 49th St, New York, NY 10017	371 6953
Venezuela	450 Park Ave, New York, NY 1101	355 1101
Zambia	150 E 58th St, New York, NY 10022	758 9450
Zimbabwe	535 5th Ave, New York, NY 10017	307 6565

Foreign Tourist Offices in Australia

Austria	19th Floor, 1 York St, Sydney NSW 2000	
Canada	8th Floor, AMP Centre, 50 Bridge St, Sydney NSW 2000	
Denmark	60 Market St, PO Box 4531, Melbourne, Victoria 3001	
West Germany	c/o Lufthansa German Airlines, Lufthansa House, 12th Floor, 143 Macquarie St, Sydney NSW 2000	
Greece	51–57 Pitt St, Sydney NSW 2000	
Hong Kong	Bligh House, 4–6 Bligh St, Sydney NSW 2000	
India	Carlton Centre, Elizabeth St, Sydney NSW 2000	
Macao	Suite 604, 135 Macquarie St, Sydney NSW 2000 or GPO Box M973, Perth, Western Australia 6001	
Malaysia	12th Floor, R & W House, 92 Pitt St, Sydney NSW 2000	
Mexico	24 Burton St, Darlington, Sydney NSW 2000	
South Africa	AMEV-UDC House, 115 Pitt St, Sydney NSW 2001	231 6166
Singapore	8th Floor, Gold Fields House, 1 Alfred St, Sydney Cove NSW 2000	
Sri Lanka	FP Leonard Advertising Pty Ltd, 1st Floor, 110 Bathurst St, Sydney 2000	
Switzerland	203–233 New South Head Rd, PO Box 82, Edgecliff, Sydney NSW 2027	
American Samoa	327 Pacific Highway, North Sydney NSW 2060	
Thailand	12th Floor, Royal Exchange Building, Corner Bridge and Pitt Streets, Sydney NSW 2000	

Foreign Tourist Boards in Canada

Antigua	Suite 205, 60 St Clair Ave East, Toronto, Ontario M4T 1L9
Australia	120 Eglington Ave East, Suite 220, Toronto, Ontario M4P 1E2
Austria	2 Bloor St East, Suite 3330, Toronto, Ontario M4W 1A8 *or* Suite 1220–1223, 736 Granville St, Vancouver, BC *or* 1010 Ouest Rue Sherbrooke, Montreal, Quebec
Barbados	615 Dorchester Blvd West, Suite 960, Montreal, Quebec H3B 1P5 *or* Suite 1508, Box 11, 20 Queen St West, Toronto, Ontario M5H 3R3
Bermuda	Suite 510, 1075 Bay St, Toronto, Ontario M58 2B1
British Virgin Islands	Mr W. Draper, 801 York Mills Road, Suite 201, Don Mills, Ontario M3B 1X7
Cayman Islands	234 Eglington Ave East, Suite 600, Toronto, Ontario
Denmark	PO Box 115, Station 'N', Toronto, Ontario M8V 3S4
Eastern Caribbean	Suite 205, 60 St Clair Ave East, Toronto, Ontario M4T 1L9
France	1 Dandas St West, Suite 2405, Box 8, Toronto, Ontario M5G 123
West Germany	2 Fundy, PO Box 417, Place Bonaventure, Montreal PQ, H5A 1B8
Greece	1233 Rue de la Montagne, Montreal QC, H3G 1Z2
Israel	102 Bloor St West, Toronto, Ontario M5S 1M8
Jamaica	2221 Yonge St, Suite 507, Toronto, Ontario M4S 2B4
Jordan	181 University Ave, Suite 1716, Box 28, Toronto, Ontario M5H 3M7 *or* 1801 McGill College Ave, Suite 1160, Montreal, Quebec H3A 2N4
Kenya	Gillin Building 600, 141 Laurier Ave, West, Ottawa, Ontario
Macao	Suite 601, 700 Bay St, Toronto, Ontario M5G 1Z6 *or* 475 Main St, Vancouver, British Columbia V6A 2T7
Mexico	1 Place Ville Marie, Suite 2409, Montreal 113, Quebec *or* 1008 Pacific Centre, Toronto Dominion Bank Tower, Vancouver 1 British Columbia
Morocco	2 Carlton St, Suite 1803, Toronto, Ontario M5B 1K2
Peru	Mr Raziel Zisman, 344 Bloor St West, Suite 303, Toronto, Ontario
Portugal	Suite 1150, 1801 McGill College Ave, Montreal, Quebec H3A 2N4

South Africa	Suite 1001, 20 Eglington Ave West, Toronto, Ontario M4R 1K8
Spain	60 Bloor St West, Suite 201, Toronto, Ontario M4W 3B8
Switzerland	PO Box 215, Commerce Court, Toronto, Ontario M5L 1E8
Trinidad & Tobago	York Centre, 145 King St West, and University Ave, Toronto, Ontario M5H 1J8
USSR	2020 University St, Suite 434, Montreal, Quebec H3A 2A5
US Virgin Islands	11 Adelaide St West, Suite 406, Toronto, Ontario M5H 1L9

Foreign Tourist Offices in New Zealand

Australia	15th Floor, Quay Tower, 29 Customs St, Auckland 1 (PO Box 1646, Auckland)
Great Britain	PO Box 3655, Wellington
Fiji	47 High St, Auckland
Hong Kong	General Buildings, G/F Corner Shortland St and O'Connell St, Auckland (PO Box 1313, Auckland)
Malaysia	Malaysian Airline System, Suite 8, 5th Floor, Air New Zealand House, 1 Queen St, Auckland 1
Singapore	c/o Rodney Walsh Ltd, 87 Queen St, Auckland

Embassies, High Commissions and Consulates in the United Kingdom

Algeria	6 Hyde Park Gate, London SW7 1QQ	221 7800
Antigua	Antigua House, 15 Thayer St, London W1M 5DL	486 7073
Argentina	Brazilian Embassy, Argentine Interest Section, 111 Cadogan Gardens, London SW3 2RQ	730 7173
Australia	Australia House, Strand, London WC2B 4LA	438 8000
Austria	18 Belgrave Mews West, London SW1X 8HU	235 2731
Bahamas	39 Pall Mall, London SW1 5JG	930 6967
Bahrain	98 Gloucester Rd, London SW7 4AU	370 5132/3
Bangladesh	28 Queen's Gate, London SW7 5JA	584 0081/4
Barbados	1 Great Russell St, London W1	235 8686
Belgium	103 Eaton Square, London SW1W 9AB	235 5422

Bolivia	106 Eaton Square, London SW1W 9AD	235 4255
Brazil	Consular Section, 6 Deanery St, London W1Y 5LH	499 7441/4
Burma	19a Charles St, Berkeley Square, London W1X 8ER	499 8841
Canada	38 Grosvenor Street, London W1X 0AA	409 2071
Chile	12 Devonshire St, London W1N 2DS	580 6392
China	13 Weymouth Mews, London W1N 3FQ	636 5726
Denmark	55 Sloane St, London SW1X 9SR	235 1255
Ecuador	3 Hans Crescent, Knightsbridge, London SW1X 0LS	584 1367
Egypt	19 Kensington Palace Gdn Mews, London W8 4QL	229 8818
Fiji	34 Hyde Park Gate, London SW7 5BN	584 3661
Finland	38 Chesham Place, London SW1X 8HW	235 9531
France	College House, 29/31 Wright's Lane, London W8	937 1202
Federal Rep. Germany	23 Belgrave Square, London SW1X 8PZ	235 0165
Greece	1A Holland Park, London W11 3TP	727 8040
Hong Kong	6 Grafton St, London W1X 3LB	499 9821
Iceland	1 Eaton Terrace, London SW1W 8EY	730 5131
India	India House, Aldwych, London WC2B 4NA	836 8484
Indonesia	38 Adams Row, London W1	499 7661
Rep. Ireland	17 Grosvenor Place, London SW1X 7HR	235 2171
Israel	15 Old Court Place, Kensington, London W8 4QB	937 8050
Italy	38 Eaton Place, London SW1	235 9371
Jamaica	50 St James's St, London SW1A 1JT	499 8600
Japan	43/46 Grosvenor St, London W1X 0BA	493 6030
Jordan	6 Upper Phillimore Gdns, London W8 7HB	937 3685
Kenya	45 Portland Place, London W1N 4AS	636 2371/5
Korea Rep.	4 Palace Gate, London W8 5NF	581 0247
Kuwait	46 Queen's Gate, London SW7	589 4533
Luxembourg	27 Wilton Cres, London SW1X 8SD	235 6961
Malawi	33 Grosvenor St, London W1X 0HS	491 4172/7
Malaysia	45 Belgrave Square, London SW1X 8QT	235 8033
Malta	16 Kensington Square, London W8 5HH	938 1712/6
Mauritius	32/33 Elvaston Place, Gloucester Rd, London SW7	581 0294/8
Mexico	8 Halkin St, London SW1X 7DW	235 6393/6
Morocco	49 Queen's Gate Gardens, London SW7 5NE	581 5001/4
Nepal	12a Kensington Palace Gdns, London W8 4QU	229 1594/6231
Netherlands	38 Hyde Park Gate, London SW7 5DP	581 5040
New Zealand	New Zealand House, Haymarket, London SW1Y 4QT	930 8422
Norway	25 Belgrave Square, London SW1X 8QD	235 7151
Oman	44A/B Montpelier Square, London SW7 5DN	584 6782
Pakistan	34 Lowndes Square, London SW1X 9JN	235 2044
Papua New Guinea	14 Waterloo Place, London SW1R 4AR	930 0922/7
Paraguay	Braemar Lodge, Cornwall Gdns, London SW7 4AQ	937 1235
Peru	52 Sloane St, London SW1X 9SP	235 1917

Philippines	1 Cumberland House, Kensington High Street, London W8	937 3646
Portugal	72 Brompton Rd, London SW3 1BJ	235 6216
Qatar	115 Queen's Gate, London SW7 5LP	581 8611
Saudi Arabia	30 Belgrave Square, London SW1X 8QB	235 0831
Senegal	11 Phillimore Gdns, London W8 7QG	937 0925/6
Seychelles	50 Conduit St, 4th Floor, PO Box 4PE, London W1A 4PE	439 0405
Sierra Leone	33 Portland Place, London W1N 3AG	636 6483/6
Singapore	5 Chesham St, London SW1X 8ND	235 9067/9
South Africa	Golden Cross House, Duncannon St, London WC2	839 2211
Soviet Union	5 Kensington Palace Gdns, London W8 4QS	229 3215
Spain	20 Draycott Place, London SW3 2RZ	581 5921
Sri Lanka	13 Hyde Park Gdns, London W2 2LX	262 1841/7
Sweden	11 Montagu Place, London W1H 2AL	724 2101
Switzerland	16/18 Montagu Place, London W1H 2BQ	723 0701
Syria	8 Belgrave Square, London SW1X 8PH	245 9012
Tanzania	43 Hertford St, London W1Y 7TF	499 8951/4
Thailand	30 Queen's Gate, London SW7 5JB	589 2857
Tongo	New Zealand House, 12th Floor, Haymarket, London SW1Y 4TE	839 3287
Trinidad & Tobago	42 Belgrave Square, London SW1X 8NT	245 9351
Tunisia	29 Prince's Gate, London SW7 1QG	584 8117
Turkey	Rutland Lodge, Rutland Gardens, Knightsbridge, London SW7 1BW	589 0949
United Arab Emirates	48 Prince's Gate, London SW7 2QA	589 3434
United States	5 Upper Grosvenor Street, London W1A 2JB	499 7010
Uruguay	48 Lennox Gdns, London SW1X 0DL	589 1735
Venezuela	71a Park Mansions, Knightsbridge, London SW1X 7QU	589 9916
Zambia	2 Palace Gate, London W8 5NG	589 6655
Zimbabwe	Zimbabwe House, 429 Strand, London WC2R 0SA	836 7755

Embassies, High Commissions and Consulates in the United States

Algeria	2118 Kalomama Rd, NW, Washington DC 20008	328 5300
Argentina	1600 New Hampshire Ave, NW, Washington DC 20009	387 0705
Australia	1601 Massachusetts Ave, NW, Washington DC 20036	797 3000
Austria	2343 Massachusetts Ave, NW, Washington DC 2008	483 4474
Bahamas	600 New Hampshire Ave, NW, Washington DC 20037	338 3940
Bahrain	2600 Virginia Ave, NW, Washington DC 20037	324 0741
Bangladesh	3421 Massachusetts Ave, NW, Washington DC 20007	327 6644
Barbados	2144 Wyoming Ave, NW, Washington DC 20008	387 7373
Belgium	3330 Garfield St, NW, Washington DC 20008	333 6900
Bolivia	3012 Massachusetts Ave, NW, Washington DC 20008	483 4410
Brazil	3006 Massachusetts Ave, NW, Washington DC 20008	797 0100
Burma	2300 S St, NW, Washington DC 20008	332 9044
Canada	1746 Massachusetts Ave, NW, Washington DC 20036	785 1400
Chile	1732 Massachusetts Ave, NW, Washington DC 20036	785 1746
China	2300 Connecticut Ave, NW, Washington DC 20008	328 2500
Colombia	2118 Leroy Place, NW, Washington DC 20008	387 5828
Costa Rica	2112 S St, NW, Washington DC 20008	234 2945
Denmark	3200 Whitehaven St, NW, Washington DC 20008	234 4300
Dominican Rep.	1715 22nd St, NW, Washington DC 20008	332 6280
Ecuador	2535 15th St, NW, Washington DC 20009	234 7200
Egypt	2310 Decatur Place, NW, Washington DC 20008	232 5400
Fiji	1629 K St, NW, Washington DC 20006	296 3928
Finland	3216 New Mexico Ave, NW, Washington DC 20016	363 2430
France	2535 Belmont Rd, NW, Washington DC 20008	328 2600
Fed. Rep. of Germany	4645 Reservoir Rd, NW, Washington DC 20007	298 4000
Great Britain	3100 Massachusetts Ave, NW, Washington DC 20008	462 1340
Greece	2221 Massachusetts Ave, NW, Washington DC 20008	667 3168
Haiti	2311 Massachusetts Ave, NW, Washington DC 20008	332 4090
Honduras	4301 Connecticut Ave, NW, Washington DC 20008	966 7700
Iceland	2022 Connecticut Ave, NW, Washington DC 20008	265 6653
India	2107 Massachusetts Ave, NW, Washington DC 20008	265 5050
Indonesia	2020 Massachusetts Ave, NW, Washington DC 20036	293 1745
Ireland	2234 Massachusetts Ave, NW, Washington DC 20008	462 3939
Israel	3514 International Drive, NW, Washington DC 20008	364 5500
Italy	1601 Fuller St, NW, Washington DC 20009	328 5500
Jamaica	1850 K St, NW, Washington DC 20009	452 0660
Japan	2520 Massachusetts Ave, NW, Washington DC 20008	234 2266
Jordan	2319 Wyoming Ave, NW, Washington DC 20008	265 1606
Kenya	2249 R St, NW, Washington DC 20008	387 6101
Korea	2370 Massachusetts Ave, NW, Washington DC 20008	483 7383
Kuwait	2940 Tilden St, NW, Washington DC 20008	966 0702

Luxembourg	2200 Massachusetts Ave, NW, Washington DC 20008	265 4171
Malawi	1400 20th St, NW, Washington DC 20036	296 5530
Malaysia	2401 Massachusetts Ave, NW, Washington DC 20008	328 2700
Malta	2017 Connecticut Ave, NW, Washington DC 20008	462 3611
Mauritius	4310 Connecticut Ave, NW, Washington DC 20008	244 1491
Mexico	2829 16th St, NW, Washington DC 20009	234 6000
Morocco	1601 21st St, NW, Washington DC 20009	462 7979
Nepal	2131 Leroy Place, NW, Washington DC 20008	667 4550
Netherlands	4200 Linnean Ave, NW, Washington DC 20008	244 5300
New Zealand	37 Observatory Circle, Washington DC 20008	328 4800
Nigeria	2201 M St, NW, Washington DC 20037	223 9300
Norway	2720 34th St, NW, Washington DC 20008	333 6000
Oman	2342 Massachusetts Ave, NW, Washington DC 20008	387 1980
Pakistan	2315 Massachusetts Ave, NW, Washington DC 20008	332 8330
Panama	2862 McGill Terrace, NW, Washington DC 20008	483 1407
Papua New Guinea	1140 19th St, NW, Washington DC 20036	659 0856
Paraguay	2400 Massachusetts Ave, NW, Washington DC 20008	483 6960
Peru	1700 Massachusetts Ave, NW, Washington DC 20036	833 9860
Philippines	1617 Massachusetts Ave, NW, Washington DC 20036	483 1414
Portugal	2125 Kalorama Rd, NW, Washington DC 20008	265 1643
Qatar	600 New Hampshire Ave, NW, Washington DC 20037	338 0111
Saudi Arabia	1520 18th St, NW, Washington DC 20036	483 2100
Senegal	2112 Wyoming Ave, NW, Washington DC 20008	234 0540
Seychelles	820 Second Ave, New York, NY 10017	687 9766
Singapore	1824 R St, NW, Washington DC 20009	667 7555
South Africa	3051 Massachusetts Ave, NW, Washington DC 20008	232 4400
Spain	2700 15th St, NW, Washington DC 20009	265 0190
Sri Lanka	2148 Wyoming Ave, NW, Washington DC 20008	483 4025
Sweden	600 New Hampshire Ave, Washington DC 20037	298 3500
Switzerland	2900 Cathedral Ave, NW, Washington DC 20008	462 1811
Syria	2215 Wyoming Ave, NW, Washington DC 20008	232 6313
Tanzania	2139 R St, NW, Washington DC 20008	232 0501
Thailand	2300 Kalorama Rd, NW, Washington DC 20008	667 1446
Trinidad & Tobago	1708 Massachusetts Ave, NW, Washington DC 20036	467 6490
Tunisia	2408 Massachusetts Ave, NW, Washington DC 20008	234 6644
Turkey	1606 23rd St, NW, Washington DC 20008	667 6400
USSR	1125 16th St, NW, Washington DC 20036	628 7551
United Arab Emirates	600 New Hampshire Ave, NW, Washington DC 20037	338 6500
Uruguay	1918 F St, NW, Washington DC 20006	331 1313
Venezuela	2445 Massachusetts Ave, NW, Washington DC 20008	797 3800
Western Samoa	211 E 43rd St, New York NY 10017	682 1482
Yemen Arab Rep.	600 New Hampshire Ave, NW, Washington DC 20037	965 4760

| Zaire | 1800 New Hampshire Ave, NW, Washington DC 20009 | 234 7690 |
| Zambia | 2419 Massachusetts Ave, NW, Washington DC 20008 | 265 9717 |

Embassies, High Commissions and Consulates in Australia

Argentina	1st Floor, Suite 102, MLC Tower, Woden, ACT 2606
Austria	107 Endeavour St, Red Hill, Canberra
Bangladesh	43 Hampton Circuit, Yarralumla, Canberra, ACT 2600
Belgium	19 Arkana St, Yarralumla, Canberra, ACT 2600
Brazil	11th Floor, 'Canberra House', 40 Marcus Clarke St, Canberra City, ACT 2601
Burma	85 Mugga Way, Red Hill, Canberra, ACT 2603
Canada	Commonwealth Ave, Canberra, ACT 2600
Chile	93 Endeavour St, Red Hill, Canberra, ACT 2603
China	14 Federal Highway, Watson, Canberra, ACT 2602
Colombia	PO Box 391, Double Bay (NSW), Sydney 2028
Cyprus	37 Endeavour St, Red Hill, ACT 2603, Canberra
Denmark	24 Beagle St, Red Hill, ACT 2603, Canberra
Egypt	125 Monaro Crescent, Red Hill, ACT 2603, Canberra
Fiji	9 Beagle St, Red Hill, PO Box E159, Canberra, ACT 2600
Finland	10 Darwin Ave, Yarralumla, Canberra, ACT 2600
France	6 Darwin Ave, Yarralumla, Canberra, ACT 2600
Fed. Rep. of Germany	119 Empire Circuit, Yarralumla, Canberra, ACT 2600
Greece	1 Stonehaven Crescent, Red Hill, Canberra, ACT 2603
Iceland	2 Montalto Ave, Toorak 3142
India	3–5 Moonah Place, Yarralumla, Canberra, ACT 2600
Indonesia	Piccadilly Court, 3rd Floor, 222 TITT, PO Box 6, Sydney
Rep. Ireland	200 Arkana St, Yarralumla, Canberra, ACT 2600
Israel	6 Turrana St, Yarralumla, Canberra, ACT 2600
Italy	12 Grey St, Deakin, ACT 2600
Japan	112 Empire Circuit, Yarralumla, Canberra, ACT 2000
Jordan	20 Roabuck St, Red Hill, Canberra, ACT 2603
Korea	113 Empire Circuit, Yarralumla, Canberra, ACT 2600
Malaysia	71 State Circle, Yarralumla, Canberra, ACT 2600
Malta	261 La Perouse St, Red Hill, Canberra, ACT 2603
Mauritius	16 National Circuit, Suite 6, Barton, Canberra, ACT 2600
Mexico	14 Perth Ave, Yarralumla, Canberra, ACT 2600
Netherlands	120 Empire Circuit, Yarralumla, Canberra, ACT 2600
New Zealand	Commonwealth Ave, Canberra, ACT 2600

Norway	3 Zeehan St, Red Hill, Canberra, ACT 2603
Pakistan	59 Franklin St, Forrest, PO Box 198, Manuka, Canberra, ACT 2603
Papua New Guinea	Forster Crescent, Yarralumla, Canberra, ACT 2600
Peru	94 Captain Cook, Canberra, ACT 2603
Philippines	1 Moonah Place, Yarralumla, Canberra
Portugal	8 Astrolabe St, Red Hill, Canberra, ACT 2603
Seychelles	127 Commercial Rd, South Yarra, Victoria 3141
Singapore	81 Mugga Way, Red Hill, Canberra, ACT 2603
South Africa	Rhodes Place, Yarralumla, Canberra, ACT 2600
Soviet Union	78 Canberra Ave, Griffith, ACT 2603
Spain	15 Arkana St, Yarralumla, ACT, PO Box 256, Woden, Canberra
Sri Lanka	35 Empire Circuit, Forrest, Canberra, ACT 2603
Sweden	9 Turrana St, Yarralumla, Canberra, ACT 2600
Switzerland	7 Melbourne Ave, Forrest, ACT 2603
Thailand	111 Empire Circuit, Yarralumla, Canberra, ACT 2600
Turkey	60 Mugga Way, Red Hill, Canberra, ACT 2603
United States	Yarralumla, Canberra, ACT 2600
Venezuela	Suite 106 MLC Tower, Woden, Canberra, ACT

Embassies, High Commissions and Consulates in Canada

Antigua	Suite 205, 60 St Clair Ave East, Toronto, Ontario M4T 1L9
Argentina	130 Slater St, 6th Floor, Ottawa
Australia	The National Building, 13th Floor, 130 Slater St, Ottawa K1P 5H6
Austria	445 Wilbrod St, Ottawa, Ontario K1N 6M7
Bangladesh	85 Range Rd, Suite No 1007, Sandringham Apartments, Ottawa
Barbados	Suite 700, 151 Slater St, Ottawa, Ontario K1P 5HE
Belgium	The Sandringham, 6th Floor, 85 Range Rd, Ottawa
Brazil	255 Albert St, Suite 900, Ottawa K1P 6A9
China	415 St Andrews, Ottawa
Costa Rica	No 2902, 1155 Dorchester Blvd West, Montreal
Denmark	85 Range Rd, Apt. 702, Ottawa K1N 8J6
Eastern Caribbean	112 Kent St, Suite 1701, Ottawa, Ontario K1P 5P2
Egypt	454 Laurier Ave, East Ottawa, Ontario
Finland	222 Somerset St West, Suite 401, Ottawa, Ontario, K2P 2G3

France	1 Dundas St West, Suite 2405, Box 8, Toronto 0NT MSG 123
Fed. Rep. Germany	1 Waverley St, Ottawa, Ontario K1N 8VA
Greece	80 Maclaren Ave, Ottawa, Ontario K2P 0KG
Iceland	5005 Jean Talon St West, 3rd Floor, Montreal, Quebec H4P 1W7
India	325 Howe St, 1st Floor, Vancouver, BC
Indonesia	225 Albert St, Suite 101, Kent Sq Building CPO, Box 430, Terminal A, Ottawa, Ontario
Rep. Ireland	170 Metcalfe St, Ottawa K2P 1P3, Ontario
Israel	Laurier Ave West, Ottawa K1R 7T3
Italy	275 Slater St, 11th Floor, Ottawa K1P 5H9
Jamaica	Sandringham Apt, Suite 202–204, 85 Range Rd, Ottawa, Ontario
Japan	255 Sussex Drive, Ottawa, Ontario K1N 9E6
Kenya	Gillin Building Suite 600, 141 Laurier Ave, West Ottawa, Ontario K1P 5J3
Korea	151 Slater St, Suite 608, Ottawa, Ontario K1P 5H3
Malawi	112 Kent St, Suite 905, Ottawa, Ontario K1P 5P2
Malaysia	60 Boteler St, Ottawa, Ontario K1N 8Y7
Mexico	130 Albert St, Suite 206, Ottawa, Ontario K1P 5G4
Morocco	38 Range Rd, Ottawa
Netherlands	3rd Floor, 275 Slater St, Ottawa, ONT K1P 5H9
New Zealand	Metropolitan House, Suite 801, 99 Bank St, Ottawa, ONT K1P 6G3
Norway	Suite 932, Royal Bank Centre, 90 Sparks St, Ottawa, ONT K1P 5B4
Pakistan	2100 Drumond St, Apt 505, Montreal H3G 1X1
Peru	170 Laurier Ave West, Suite 1007, Ottawa, ONT K1P 5V5
Philippines	130 Albert St, 606–607 Ottawa, Ontario
Portugal	645 Island Park Drive, Ottawa K1Y 0B8
Saudi Arabia	Suite 901, 99 Bank St, Ottawa, K1P 5P9
South Africa	15 Sussex Drive, Ottawa K1M 1M8
Soviet Union	285 Charlotte St, Ottawa K1N 845
Spain	350 Spark St, SUIR802, Ottawa, Ontario K1R 758
Sri Lanka	85 Range Rd, 'The Sandringham', Suites 102–104, Ottawa, Ontario, K1N 8J6
Sweden	441 Maclaren St, Ottawa, Ontario K2P 2H3
Switzerland	5 Malborough Ave, Ottawa, Ontario K1N 8E6
Tanzania	50 Range Rd, Ottawa, Canada K1N 84
Thailand	85 Range Rd, Suite 704, Ottawa, Ontario K1N 8J6
Trinidad & Tobago	73 Albert St, Room 508, Ottawa, Ontario K1P 5R5

Tunisia	115 O'Conner St, Ottawa
Turkey	197 Wurtenburg St, Ottawa, Ontario K1N 8L9
United States	100 Wellington St, Ottawa K1P 5T1
Venezuela	Suite 2000, 320 Queen St, Ottawa K1R 5A3
Zambia	130 Albert St, Suite 1610, Ottawa, Ontario
Zimbabwe	112 Kent St, Suite 915 Place deVille, Tower B, Ottawa, Ontario K1P 5P2

Embassies, High Commissions and Consulates in New Zealand

Argentina	IBM Center, 151–165 The Terrace, 5th Floor, PO Box 1033, Wellington
Australia	72–78 Hobson St, Thorndon, Wellington
Belgium	Williston St 1, PO Box 3841, Wellington
Canada	PO Box 12–049 Wellington N, ICI Building, 3rd Floor, Molesworth St, Wellington
Chile	Robert Jones House, 12th Floor, Jervois Quay, Wellington
China	No 226 Glenmore St, Wellington
Denmark	18th Floor, Challenge House, 105–109 The Terrace, PO Box 10035, Wellington 1
Fiji	Robert Jones House, Jervois Quay, Wellington N2
France	1 Williston St, DBP 1695, Wellington
Fed. Rep. Germany	90–92 Hobson St, Wellington
Hong Kong	General Building, G/F Corner Shortland St & O'Connell St, Auckland
India	Princes Towers, 10th Floor, 180 Molesworth St, Wellington
Israel	13th Level, Williams City Centre, Plymmet Steps, PO Box 2171, Wellington
Italy	38 Grant Rd, PO Box 463, Wellington
Japan	7th Floor, Norwich Insurance House, 3–11 Hunter St, Wellington 1
Korea	12th Floor, Williams Parking Centre Building, Corner of Boulcoutt St & Gilmer Terrace, Wellington N2
Malaysia	163 Terrace, PO Box 9422, Wellington
Netherlands	Investment House, 10th Floor, Ballance and Featherstone St, Wellington
Norway	38–42 Waring Taylor St, PO Box 1392, Wellington
Papua New Guinea	Princes Towers, 11th Floor, 180 Molesworth St, Thorndon, Wellington

Peru	3rd Floor 36/37 Victoria St, Wellington
Philippines	Level 30, Williams City Centre, Boulcott St, Gillmer Terrace, Wellington
Portugal	47–49 Fort St, Auckland
Singapore	17 Kabul St, Khandallah, Wellington
South Africa	Molesworth House, 101–103 Molesworth St, Wellington, PO Box 12045
Soviet Union	57 Messines Rd, Karori, Wellington
Sweden	PO Box 1800, Wellington 1
Switzerland	22–24 Panama St, 7th Floor, Wellington 1
Thailand	2 Burnel Ave, PO Box 2530, Wellington 1
United States	29 Fitzherbert Terrace, Wellington

London Area Airline Offices of Major Airlines

Airline	Address	Fares	Telephone numbers Reservations	Admin. & Enqs.
Aer Lingus	223 Regent Street, London W1		437 8000	
Aeromexico	Morley House, 320 Regent Street, London W1R 5AD	637 4108	637 4108	637 4107
Air Afrique	117 Piccadilly, London W1	493 4881	629 6114	493 4881
Air Canada	140 Regent Street, London W1	759 2636	759 2636	759 2636
Air France	158 New Bond Street, London W1Y 0AY	499 9511	499 9511	499 9511
Air India	17 New Bond Street, London W1Y 0AY		491 7979	493 4050
Air Jamaica	6 Bruton Street, London W1		493 4455	
ALIA Jordanian	177 Regent Street, London W1		734 2557	437 9465
Alitalia	205 Holland Park Ave, London W11 4XB	602 7111	759 2510	745 8200

Airline	Address	Fares	Telephone numbers Reservations	Admin. & Enqs.
American Airlines	7 Albermarle Street, London W1	629 8817	629 8817	629 8817
Austrian Airlines	50 Conduit Street, London W1		439 0741	
Avianca	2 Hanover Street, London W1	408 1889	408 1889	408 1889
British Airways	PO Box 10, Heathrow Airport, Hounslow Middlesex TW6 2JA	370 4255	370 4255	759 2525
British Caledonian	215 Piccadilly, London W1V 0PS		668 4222	434 1501/2
British Midland	Heathrow Airport, Hounslow, Middlesex		581 0864	745 7321
CP Air	62 Trafalgar Square, London WC2		930 5664	930 5664
Caribbean Airways	6 Bruton Street, London W1		493 6251	491 3817
Cathay Pacific Airways	123 Pall Mall, London SW1	930 444	930 7878	930 7878
Delta Airlines	140 Regent Street, London W1	688 0935	688 0935 688 9135	688 0935
Eastern Airlines	49 Old Bond Street, London W1	409 3376	409 3376	491 7879
Egypt Air	296 Regent Street, London W1		580 5477	580 5477
El Al	185 Regent Street, London W1	437 8237	437 9255	439 2564
Finnair	130 Jermyn Street, London SW1Y 4UJ	930 3941	930 3941	930 3571
Gulf Air	73 Piccadilly, London W1	409 1951	409 1951	409 1951
Iberia	29 Glasshouse Street, London W1		437 5622 439 7539	437 9822
Icelandair	73 Grosvenor Street, London W1X 9DD	499 9971	499 9971	499 9971

Airline	Address	Fares	Telephone numbers Reservations	Admin. & Enqs.
Japan Airlines	Hanover Court, 5 Hanover Street, London W1R 0DR	629 9244	408 1000	629 9244
KLM	Time and Life Bldg, New Bond Street, London W1Y 0AD	560 6155	568 9144	568 9144
Kenya Airways	16 Conduit Street, London W1	409 0185	409 0277	409 3121
Korean Airlines	66 Haymarket, London SW1	930 6513	930 6513	930 6513
Kuwait Airlines	52 Piccadilly, London W1	409 3191	499 7681	409 3191
Lufthansa	23–26 Piccadilly, London W1	408 0322	408 0442	408 0322
Malaysian Airline System	25/27 St George Street, Hanover Square, London W1R 9RE		491 4542	499 6286
Middle East Airlines	80 Piccadilly, London W1	493 6321	493 5681	493 6321
New Zealand Air	15 Charles Street II, London SW1		930 1088	930 4951
Northwest Orient	Reservations: 37 Sackville Street, London W1 Sales Office: 49 Albermarle Street, London W1	409 3422	439 0171	
Olympic Airways	141 New Bond Street, London W1Y 0BB		493 1233	493 7262
Pakistan International	45 Piccadilly, London W1	741 8066	734 5544	759 2544
Pan Am	193 Piccadilly, London W1	409 0688	409 0688	409 0688
People Express Airlines	North Roof Office Block, Gatwick Airport, London Gatwick, Sussex RH6 0BX		0293 38100	

| Airline | Address | Telephone numbers | | |
		Fares	Reservations	Admin. & Enqs.
Philippine Airlines	Centrepoint, 103 New Oxford Street, London WC1A 1QD	379 6855	379 6855	379 6855
Qantas	169 Regent Street, London W1	995 4811	995 7722	955 1361
Sabena	36 Piccadilly, London W1	437 6960	437 6950	437 6950
Saudia/Saudi Arabian	171 Regent Street, London W1	995 7755	995 7777	995 7755
SAS	52 Conduit Street, London W1	437 7086	734 4040	734 6777
Singapore Airlines	143–147 Regent Street, London W1R 7LB	439 8111	995 5411	439 8111
South African Airways	251–259 Regent Street, London W1R 7AD	437 0932	734 9841	437 9621
Swiss Air	Swiss Centre, 10 Wardour Street, London W1X 3FA	734 6737	439 4144	439 4144
Tap Air Portugal	38 Gillingham Street, London SW1	828 2092	828 0262	828 2092
Thai International	41 Albemarle Street, London W1	499 9113	499 9113	499 7953
Trans Australia	49 Old Bond Street, London W1X 4DU	995 1344	995 1344	493 2557
TWA	Reservations: 200 Piccadilly, London W1 Administration: 214 Oxford Street, London W1	636 5411	636 4090	636 4090
United Airlines	7/8 Conduit Street, London W1	997 0179	997 0179	734 9282
UTA	177 Piccadilly, London 1	493 4881	629 6114	493 4881
Virgin Atlantic	2 Woodstock Street, London W1	409 2882	409 2429	409 2882

Note: symbol ■ means a visa is required.

Country Travelling To:	VISA REQUIREMENTS AND RESTRICTIONS				
	UK	USA	Canada	Australia	New Zealand
Algeria	■ Permit de sejour needed if you wish to stay more than 3 mths	■ Permit de sejour needed if you wish to stay more than 3 mths	■ Permit de sejour needed if you wish to stay more than 3 mths	■ Permit de sejour needed if you wish to stay more than 3 mths	■ Permit de sejour needed if you wish to stay more than 3 mths
Andorra					
Antigua	must have a return ticket	must have a return ticket	must have a return ticket	must have a return ticket	must have a return ticket
Argentina	■	■	tourists don't require visas, others do	■	■
Australia	■	■	■		
Austria	can stay up to 6 mths	can stay up to 3 mths	can stay up to 3 mths	can stay up to 3 mths	can stay up to 3 mths
Bahamas					
Bahrain	■	■		■	■
Bangladesh	■	■	only needed if stay exceeds 30 days	■	■
Barbados					
Belgium					
Bermuda	must have a return ticket	must have a return ticket	must have a return ticket	must have a return ticket	must have a return ticket
Bolivia	tourists don't others do	tourists don't others do		■	■
Brazil	need a passport endorsed for Brazil which must not expire within 6 mths from date of arrival, a roundtrip ticket and funds to meet expenses	■	need a passport endorsed for Brazil which must not expire within 6 mths from date of arrival, a roundtrip ticket and funds to meet expenses	■	■
British Virgin Is.					
Burma	■ valid for only 7 days	■ valid for only 7 days	■ valid for only 7 days	■ valid for only 7 days	■ valid for only 7 days
Canada					
Cayman Islands					

Country Travelling To:	UK	USA	Canada	Australia	New Zealand
			VISA REQUIREMENTS AND RESTRICTIONS		
Chile	■				
China		■	■	■	■
Columbia	must have a valid passport and a return or continuation ticket				
Cook Islands	must have a valid passport and return ticket; need visa after 31 days	must have a valid passport and return ticket; need visa after 31 days	must have a valid passport and return ticket; need visa after 31 days	must have a valid passport and return ticket; need visa after 31 days	must have a valid passport and return ticket; need visa after 31 days
Costa Rica			need visa after 30 days		■
Denmark	need visa if stay over 3 mths	need visa if stay over 3 mths	need visa if stay over 3 mths	need visa if stay over 3 mths	need visa if stay over 3 mths
Eastern Caribbean					
Ecuador	need visa if stay over 3 mths	need visa if stay over 3 mths	need visa if stay over 3 mths	need visa if stay over 3 mths	need visa if stay over 3 mths
Egypt	■ must register with Ministry of Interior at al-Mugama within 7 days	■ must register with Ministry of Interior at al-Mugama within 7 days	■ must register with Ministry of Interior at al-Mugama within 7 days	■ must register with Ministry of Interior at al-Mugama within 7 days	■ must register with Ministry of Interior at al-Mugama within 7 days
Fiji					
Finland					
France	up to 3 mths	up to 3 mths	up to 3 mths	up to 3 mths	up to 3 mths
Gambia	up to 3 mths	■	up to 3 mths	up to 3 mths	up to 3 mths
F. Rep. Germany	up to 3 mths	up to 3 mths	up to 3 mths	up to 3 mths	up to 3 mths
Gibraltar					
Greece					
Grenada	up to 3 mths	up to 3 mths	not issuing visas at present – need a return ticket and sufficient funds to stay	up to 3 mths	up to 3 mths
Guyana	■		■	■	■
Haiti		■	■	■	■

VISA REQUIREMENTS AND RESTRICTIONS

Country Travelling To:	UK	USA	Canada	Australia	New Zealand
Hawaii	■			■	■
Hong Kong	up to 6 mths	up to 1 mth	up to 3 mths	up to 3 mths	up to 3 mths
Iceland	need a return ticket	need a return ticket	need a return ticket	need a return ticket	need a return ticket
India	■	■	must have a valid passport	must have a valid passport	must have a valid passport
Indonesia	depends on reason for visit	depends on reason for visit	depends on reason for visit	depends on reason for visit	depends on reason for visit
Ireland (Rep.)					
Israel					
Italy					
Ivory Coast	■ valid for 3 mths	■ valid for 3 mths	■ valid for 3 mths	■ valid for 3 mths	■ valid for 3 mths
Jamaica	up to 3 mths	need proof of citizenship and return ticket for visit not exceeding 6 mths	need proof of citizenship and return ticket for visit not exceeding 6 mths	up to 3 mths	up to 3 mths
Japan	up to 3 mths	■	up to 90 days	■	up to 30 days
Jordan	■	■	■	■	■
Kenya		■		■	
Korea	up to 60 days	up to 15 days	up to 15 days	up to 15 days	up to 15 days
Kuwait	■	■	■	■	■
Luxembourg	up to 3 mths	up to 3 mths	up to 3 mths	up to 3 mths	up to 3 mths
Macao					
Malawi	up to 6 mths	up to 6 mths	up to 6 mths	up to 6 mths	up to 6 mths
Malaysia		up to 3 mths			
Mali	■	■	■	■	■
Malta					
Mauritius					
Mexico	need to get free tourist card	need to get free tourist card	need to get free tourist card	need to get free tourist card	need to get free tourist card
Morocco					

Country Travelling To:	VISA REQUIREMENTS AND RESTRICTIONS				
	UK	USA	Canada	Australia	New Zealand
Nepal	■ valid for 3 mths	■ valid for 3 mths	■ valid for 3 mths	■ valid for 3 mths	■ valid for 3 mths
Netherlands	up to 3 mths	up to 3 mths	up to 3 mths	up to 3 mths	up to 3 mths
New Zealand	up to 6 mths; need an onward ticket and sufficient funds	up to 3 mths; need an onward ticket and sufficient funds	up to 6 mths; need an onward ticket and sufficient funds		
Nigeria	need an entry permit	■	need an entry permit	need an entry permit	need an entry permit
Norway					
Oman	not issuing visas; need a sponsor in Oman to apply for a 'No Objection Certificate'	not issuing visas; need a sponsor in Oman to apply for a 'No Objection Certificate'	not issuing visas; need a sponsor in Oman to apply for a 'No Objection Certificate'	not issuing visas; need a sponsor in Oman to apply for a 'No Objection Certificate'	not issuing visas; need a sponsor in Oman to apply for a 'No Objection Certificate'
Pakistan	up to 3 mths	up to 1 mth	up to 3 mths	up to 3 mths	up to 3 mths
Panama	■	■	■	■	■
Paraguay			passport needs to be fully endorsed for all countries	passport needs to be fully endorsed for all countries	passport needs to be fully endorsed for all countries
Peru	■	■	■	■	■
Philippines	up to 21 days if have an onward ticket	up to 21 days if have an onward ticket	up to 21 days if have an onward ticket	up to 21 days if have an onward ticket	up to 21 days if have an onward ticket
Portugal	up to 2 mths	need visa for Azores	need visa for Azores	up to 3 mths	■
Qatar	■	■	■	■	■
Saudi Arabia	none need if passport issued before 1/1/83 and p.5 reads 'Holder has right of abode in UK' or if issued after 1/1/83 and stamped on p.1 'British Citizen'				
Senegal	■ plus return ticket	■ plus return ticket	■ plus return ticket	■ plus return ticket	■ plus return ticket
Sierra Leone	■	■	■	■	■
Seychelles					
Singapore					
Solomon Is.					

VISA REQUIREMENTS AND RESTRICTIONS

Country Travelling To:	UK	USA	Canada	Australia	New Zealand
South Africa	■	■	■	■	■
Soviet Union	■	■	■	■	■
Spain	up to 90 days	up to 90 days	up to 90 days		
Sri Lanka	up to 6 mths	up to 6 mths	up to 6 mths	up to 6 mths	up to 6 mths
Sweden					
Switzerland					
Tahiti	up to 3 mths	up to 1 mth	up to 1 mth	up to 3 mths	up to 3 mths
Thailand	up to 15 days; if leave by rail, need visa	up to 15 days; if leave by rail, need visa	up to 15 days; if leave by rail, need visa	up to 15 days; if leave by rail, need visa	up to 15 days; if leave by rail, need visa
Togo	■	■	■		■
Tonga		■			
Trinidad & Tobago					
Tunisia				■ delivered on arrival	■
Turkey	up to 3 mths	up to 3 mths	up to 3 mths	up to 3 mths	up to 3 mths
Turks & Caicos Is.					
Uganda	■	■	■	■	■
United Arab Emirates	none need if passport issued before 1/1/83 and p.5 reads 'Holder has right of abode in UK' or if issued after 1/1/83 and stamped on p.1 'British Citizen'	■	■		■
United Kingdom					
US Virgin Is.	■ plus evidence you will be leaving country			■ plus evidence you will be leaving country	■ plus evidence you will be leaving country
United States	■ plus evidence you will be leaving country			■ plus evidence you will be leaving country	■ plus evidence you will be leaving country
Venezuela	■	■	■	■	■
Zambia		■			■
Zimbabwe					■